Randall J. Stump, Minister

The Ministers Manual for 1984

By the same editor

Learning to Speak Effectively
Minister's Worship Manual (co-editor with Ernest A. Payne and Stephen F. Winward)
God's Inescapable Nearness (co-author with Eduard Schweizer)
A Guide to Biblical Preaching
The Twentieth Century Pulpit, Volumes I and II
Surprised by God

FIFTY-NINTH ANNUAL ISSUE

MINISTERS
MANUAL

(Doran's)

1984 EDITION

Edited by
JAMES W. COX

1817

HARPER & ROW, PUBLISHERS, SAN FRANCISCO

Cambridge, Hagerstown, New York, Philadelphia
London, Mexico City, São Paulo, Sydney

Editors of THE MINISTERS MANUAL

G.B.F. Hallock, D.D., 1926–1958
M.K.W. Heicher, Ph.D., 1943–1968
Charles L. Wallis, M.A., M.Div., 1969–1983
James W. Cox, M.Div., Ph.D., 1984–

Acknowledgments are on page 326.

THE MINISTERS MANUAL FOR 1984
Copyright © 1983 by James W. Cox. All rights reserved.
Printed in the United States of America. For information
address Harper & Row, Publishers, Inc., 10 East 53rd Street,
New York, NY 10022. Published simultaneously in Canada
by Fitzhenry & Whiteside Limited, Toronto.

FIRST EDITION

The Library of Congress has cataloged the first printing of
this serial as follows:

The ministers manual: a study and pulpit guide. 1926– . New
York, Harper.

V. 21–23 cm. annual.
Title varies: 1926–46, Doran's ministers manual (cover
title, 1947: The Doran's ministers manual)
Editor: 1926– G. B. F. Hallock (with M. K. W. Heicher,
1942–)

1. Sermons—Outlines. 2. Homiletical illustrations. I. Hallock, Gerard Benjamin Fleet, 1856– , ed.
BV4223.M5   251.058   25–21658 rev*
                   [r48n2]

ISBN 0–06–061598–2

83 84 85 86 87 10 9 8 7 6 5 4 3 2 1

PREFACE

The enormity of the task Charles L. Wallis and his predecessors performed each year in preparing *The Ministers Manual* is now clear to me. Selecting the most appropriate sermons and prayers, the choicest illustrations, and the most potentially helpful materials of other kinds requires examining mountains of material and soliciting the help of many persons.

Ministers of numerous denominations have cheerfully given their permission to quote or digest their sermons for this volume. Publishers of books and journals have likewise extended many courtesies. I am especially pleased that a number of my former students are among the contributors.

Throughout the past fifty-eight years, *The Ministers Manual* has performed a valuable service to the Church. Pastors, Sunday school teachers, group leaders, chaplains, missionaries, and laypeople have used this volume for sermon suggestions, illustrations, church programs, and devotional enrichment.

A primary aim of the *Manual's* editors is to set forth the historic Christian faith in a timely statement and application. Witnesses to this faith, coming as they do from varied backgrounds, vastly enrich perceptions of the Christian message and the way it is expressed.

While several sections of the *Manual* were written by persons whose names appear with their work, this volume represents the competent services of a number of other individuals: Lee McGlone, a pastor and Ph.D. candidate; Alicia Gardner, Office Services Supervisor at the Southern Baptist Theological Seminary; Sheila Voelker, Terri Mathews, Pattie McCollum, and Margo Chaney, who typed and proofread the manuscript. Several persons at Harper & Row San Francisco have also been directly involved in the process from first to last: John Shopp, Editor; Kathy Reigstad, Production Editor; Shelley Thacher, Editorial Assistant; and Tom Dorsaneo, Production Manager. To all these people I am deeply grateful.

Considerable effort has gone into obtaining permission to use materials published in the *Manual,* and it is hoped that the rights and wishes of no one have been overlooked.

James W. Cox
Southern Baptist Theological Seminary
2825 Lexington Road
Louisville, Kentucky 40280

CONTENTS

CONTENTS

SECTION I. General Aids and Resources

Civil Year Calendars

1984

	JANUARY		FEBRUARY		MARCH		APRIL

JANUARY
```
S  M  T  W  T  F  S
1  2  3  4  5  6  7
8  9 10 11 12 13 14
15 16 17 18 19 20 21
22 23 24 25 26 27 28
29 30 31
```

FEBRUARY
```
S  M  T  W  T  F  S
            1  2  3  4
5  6  7  8  9 10 11
12 13 14 15 16 17 18
19 20 21 22 23 24 25
26 27 28 29
```

MARCH
```
S  M  T  W  T  F  S
                1  2  3
4  5  6  7  8  9 10
11 12 13 14 15 16 17
18 19 20 21 22 23 24
25 26 27 28 29 30 31
```

APRIL
```
S  M  T  W  T  F  S
1  2  3  4  5  6  7
8  9 10 11 12 13 14
15 16 17 18 19 20 21
22 23 24 25 26 27 28
29 30
```

MAY
```
S  M  T  W  T  F  S
      1  2  3  4  5
6  7  8  9 10 11 12
13 14 15 16 17 18 19
20 21 22 23 24 25 26
27 28 29 30 31
```

JUNE
```
S  M  T  W  T  F  S
                  1  2
3  4  5  6  7  8  9
10 11 12 13 14 15 16
17 18 19 20 21 22 23
24 25 26 27 28 29 30
```

JULY
```
S  M  T  W  T  F  S
1  2  3  4  5  6  7
8  9 10 11 12 13 14
15 16 17 18 19 20 21
22 23 24 25 26 27 28
29 30 31
```

AUGUST
```
S  M  T  W  T  F  S
         1  2  3  4
5  6  7  8  9 10 11
12 13 14 15 16 17 18
19 20 21 22 23 24 25
26 27 28 29 30 31
```

SEPTEMBER
```
S  M  T  W  T  F  S
                     1
2  3  4  5  6  7  8
9 10 11 12 13 14 15
16 17 18 19 20 21 22
23 24 25 26 27 28 29
30
```

OCTOBER
```
S  M  T  W  T  F  S
   1  2  3  4  5  6
7  8  9 10 11 12 13
14 15 16 17 18 19 20
21 22 23 24 25 26 27
28 29 30 31
```

NOVEMBER
```
S  M  T  W  T  F  S
            1  2  3
4  5  6  7  8  9 10
11 12 13 14 15 16 17
18 19 20 21 22 23 24
25 26 27 28 29 30
```

DECEMBER
```
S  M  T  W  T  F  S
                     1
2  3  4  5  6  7  8
9 10 11 12 13 14 15
16 17 18 19 20 21 22
23 24 25 26 27 28 29
30 31
```

1985

JANUARY
```
S  M  T  W  T  F  S
      1  2  3  4  5
6  7  8  9 10 11 12
13 14 15 16 17 18 19
20 21 22 23 24 25 26
27 28 29 30 31
```

FEBRUARY
```
S  M  T  W  T  F  S
                  1  2
3  4  5  6  7  8  9
10 11 12 13 14 15 16
17 18 19 20 21 22 23
24 25 26 27 28
```

MARCH
```
S  M  T  W  T  F  S
                  1  2
3  4  5  6  7  8  9
10 11 12 13 14 15 16
17 18 19 20 21 22 23
24 25 26 27 28 29 30
31
```

APRIL
```
S  M  T  W  T  F  S
      1  2  3  4  5  6
7  8  9 10 11 12 13
14 15 16 17 18 19 20
21 22 23 24 25 26 27
28 29 30
```

MAY
```
S  M  T  W  T  F  S
         1  2  3  4
5  6  7  8  9 10 11
12 13 14 15 16 17 18
19 20 21 22 23 24 25
26 27 28 29 30 31
```

JUNE
```
S  M  T  W  T  F  S
                     1
2  3  4  5  6  7  8
9 10 11 12 13 14 15
16 17 18 19 20 21 22
23 24 25 26 27 28 29
30
```

JULY
```
S  M  T  W  T  F  S
   1  2  3  4  5  6
7  8  9 10 11 12 13
14 15 16 17 18 19 20
21 22 23 24 25 26 27
28 29 30 31
```

AUGUST
```
S  M  T  W  T  F  S
            1  2  3
4  5  6  7  8  9 10
11 12 13 14 15 16 17
18 19 20 21 22 23 24
25 26 27 28 29 30 31
```

SEPTEMBER
```
S  M  T  W  T  F  S
1  2  3  4  5  6  7
8  9 10 11 12 13 14
15 16 17 18 19 20 21
22 23 24 25 26 27 28
29 30
```

OCTOBER
```
S  M  T  W  T  F  S
      1  2  3  4  5
6  7  8  9 10 11 12
13 14 15 16 17 18 19
20 21 22 23 24 25 26
27 28 29 30 31
```

NOVEMBER
```
S  M  T  W  T  F  S
                  1  2
3  4  5  6  7  8  9
10 11 12 13 14 15 16
17 18 19 20 21 22 23
24 25 26 27 28 29 30
```

DECEMBER
```
S  M  T  W  T  F  S
1  2  3  4  5  6  7
8  9 10 11 12 13 14
15 16 17 18 19 20 21
22 23 24 25 26 27 28
29 30 31
```

Church and Civic Calendar for 1984

JANUARY

1 New Year's Day
    The Name of Jesus
    Day of Prayer
5 Twelfth Night
6 Epiphany
15 Martin Luther King, Jr.'s Birthday
18 Confession of St. Peter
19 Robert E. Lee's Birthday
25 Conversion of St. Paul

FEBRUARY

1 National Freedom Day
2 Presentation of Jesus in the Temple
    Groundhog Day
3 Four Chaplains Memorial Day
5 Boy Scout Sunday
12 Lincoln's Birthday
    Race Relations Sunday
14 St. Valentine's Day
15 Susan B. Anthony Day
20 Washington's Birthday Observed
22 Washington's Birthday

MARCH

6 Shrove Tuesday
7 Ash Wednesday
11 First Sunday in Lent
17 St. Patrick's Day
18 Second Sunday in Lent
18 Purim
25 Third Sunday in Lent

APRIL

1 Fourth Sunday in Lent
8 Fifth Sunday in Lent
14 Pan American Day
15 Palm Sunday
    Passion Sunday (alternate)
15–21 Holy Week
17 Passover Begins
19 Maundy Thursday
20 Good Friday
22 Easter
25 St. Mark, Evangelist

MAY

1 Loyalty Day
3 St. Philip and St. James, Apostles
6 Shavuot
7–13 National Family Week
13 Festival of the Christian Home
    Mother's Day
19 Armed Forces Day
21 Victoria Day (Canada)
27 Memorial Sunday
28 Memorial Day Observed
30 Memorial Day
31 Ascension Day

JUNE

10 Pentecost
    Children's Day
11 St. Barnabas, Apostle
14 Flag Day
17 Trinity Sunday
    Father's Day
29 St. Peter and St. Paul, Apostles

JULY

2 Dominion Day (Canada)
4 Independence Day
25 St. James, Apostle

AUGUST

6 The Transfiguration
15 Mary, the Mother of Jesus
24 St. Bartholomew, Apostle

SEPTEMBER

2 Labor Day Sunday
3 Labor Day
21 St. Matthew, Apostle and Evangelist
27 First day of Rosh Hashanah
28 Frances Willard Day
29 St. Michael and All Angels
30 Rally Day
    Christian Education Sunday

OCTOBER

4 Francis of Assisi
6 Yom Kipper (Day of Atonement)

7 World Communion Sunday
8 Columbus Day Observed
   Thanksgiving Day (Canada)
11 Sukkoth
12 Columbus Day
14 Laity Day
18 Shemini Atzeret
   St. Luke, Evangelist
19 Simhat Day
24 United Nations Day
28 Reformation Sunday
   St. Simon and St. Jude, Apostles
31 Reformation Sunday
   Halloween

NOVEMBER

1 All Saints' Day
2 All Souls' Day
6 Election Day
11 Stewardship Day
   Armistice Day
   Veterans Day

17 Sadie Hawkins Day
18 Thanksgiving Sunday
22 Thanksgiving Day
25 Christ the King
30 St. Andrew, Apostle

DECEMBER

2 First Sunday in Advent
9 Second Sunday in Advent
15 Bill of Rights Day
16 Third Sunday in Advent
19 First day of Hanukkah
21 St. Thomas, Apostle
   Forefathers' Day
23 Fourth Sunday in Advent
25 Christmas
26 Boxing Day (Canada)
   St. Stephen, Deacon and Martyr
27 St. John, Apostle and Evangelist
28 The Holy Innocents, Martyrs
31 New Year's Eve
   Watch Night

Lectionary for 1984

The following Scripture lessons, with occasional alterations according to denominational preferences, are commended for use in public worship by various Protestant churches and the Roman Catholic Church and include first, second, and gospel readings according to Cycle A from January 1 to November 25 and according to Cycle B from December 2 to December 30

CHRISTMAS SEASON

January 1: Eccles. 3:1–9, 14–17; Col. 3:12–21; Matt. 2:13–15, 19–23

EPIPHANY SEASON

January 6 (Epiphany): Isa. 60:1–6; Eph. 3:1–12; Matt. 2:1–12
January 8: Isa. 42:1–7; Acts 10:34–38; Matt. 3:13–17
January 15: Isa. 49:1–7; 1 Cor. 1:1–9; John 1:29–34
January 22: Isa. 9:1–4; 1 Cor. 1:10–17; Matt. 4:12–23
January 29: Zeph. 2:3, 3:11–13; 1 Cor. 1:26–31; Matt. 5:1–12

February 5: Isa. 58:5–12; 1 Cor. 2:1–5; Matt. 5:13–16
February 12: Deut. 30:15–20; 1 Cor. 2:6–13; Matt. 5:17–37
February 19: Lev. 19:1–2, 15–18; 1 Cor. 3:10–11, 16–23; Matt. 5:38–48
February 26: Isa. 49:8–18; 1 Cor. 4:1–5; Matt. 6:24–34
March 4: Exod. 24:12, 15–18; 1 Cor. 12:31–13:13; Matt. 17:1–9

LENT

March 7 (Ash Wednesday): Joel 2:12–19; 2 Cor. 5:20b–6:10; Matt. 6:1–6, 16–21
March 11: Gen. 2:7–9, 15–17, 3:1–7a; Rom. 5:12–19; Matt. 4:1–11
March 18: Gen. 12:1–8; Rom. 4:1–5, 13–17; John 4:5–26
March 25: Exod. 17:3–7; Rom. 8:1–5; John 4:27–42
April 1: 1 Sam. 16:1b, 6–7, 10–13a; Eph. 5:8–14; John 9:1–41
April 8: Ezek. 37:1–3, 11–14; Rom. 8:6–11; John 11:1–45

HOLY WEEK

April 15 (Palm Sunday): Isa. 50:4–9a; Phil. 2:5–11; Matt. 26:14–27:66

April 16 (Monday): Isa. 42:1–9; Heb. 9:11–15; John 12:1–11

April 17 (Tuesday): Isa. 49:1–9a; 1 Cor. 1:18–31; John 12:37–50

April 18 (Wednesday): Isa. 50:4–9; Rom. 5:6–11; Matt. 26:14–25

April 19 (Maundy Thursday): Exod. 12:1–14; 1 Cor. 11:23–26; John 13:1–15

April 20 (Good Friday): Isa. 52:13–53:12; Heb. 4:14–16, 5:7–9; John 18:1–19:42

SEASON OF EASTER

April 22: Acts 10:34–43; Col. 3:1–11; John 20:1–9

April 29: Acts 2:42–47; 1 Pet. 1:3–9; John 20:19–31

May 6: Acts 2:22–32; 1 Pet. 1:17–23; Luke 24:13–35

May 13: Acts 2:14a, 36–41; 1 Pet. 2:19–25; John 10:1–10

May 20: Acts 6:1–7; 1 Pet. 2:1–10; John 14:1–14

May 27: Acts 8:4–8, 14–17; 1 Pet. 3:8–18; John 14:15–21

May 31 (Ascension Day): Acts 1:1–11; Eph. 1:16–23; Matt. 28:16–20

June 3: Acts 1:12–14; 1 Pet. 4:12–19; John 17:1–11

SEASON OF PENTECOST

June 10 (Pentecost): Acts 2:1–21; 1 Cor. 12:4–13; John 20:19–23

June 17 (Trinity Sunday): Exod. 34:4–6, 8–9; 2 Cor. 13:5–13; Matt. 28:16–20

June 24: Deut. 11:18–21, 26–28; Rom. 3:21–28; Matt. 7:21–29

July 1: Hos. 6:1–6; Rom. 4:18–25; Matt. 9:9–13

July 8: Exod. 19:2–6a; Rom. 5:6–11; Matt. 9:35–10:8

July 15: Jer. 20:7–13; Rom. 5:12–15; Matt. 10:26–33

July 22: 2 Kings 4:8–16; Rom. 6:1–11; Matt. 10:32–42

July 29: Zech. 9:9–13; Rom. 7:21–8:6; Matt. 11:25–30

August 5: Isa. 55:10–13; Rom. 8:18–25; Matt. 13:1–23

August 12: 2 Sam. 7:18–22; Rom. 8:26–27; Matt. 13:24–43

August 19: 1 Kings 3:5–12; Rom. 8:28–30; Matt. 13:44–52

August 26: Neh. 9:16–20; Rom. 8:35–39; Matt. 14:13–21

September 2: 1 Kings 19:9–18; Rom. 9:1–5; Matt. 14:22–33

September 9: Isa. 56:1, 6–8; Rom. 11:13–16, 29–32; Matt. 15:21–28

September 16: Isa. 22:15–16, 19–23; Rom. 11:33–36; Matt. 16:13–20

September 23: Jer. 15:15–21; Rom. 12:1–8; Matt. 16:21–28

September 30: Ezek. 33:7–11; Rom 12:9–18; Matt. 18:15–20

October 7: Gen. 4:13–16; Rom. 14:5–9; Matt. 18:21–35; (World Communion Sunday) Isa. 49:18–23; Rev. 3:17–22; John 10:11–18

October 14: Isa. 55:6–11; Phil. 1:21–27; Matt. 20:1–16

October 21: Ezek. 18:25–32; Phil. 2:1–11; Matt. 21:28–32

October 28: Isa. 5:1–7; Phil. 4:4–9; Matt. 21:33–43; (Reformation Sunday) Heb. 2:1–4; Rom. 3:21–28; John 8:31–36

November 4: Isa. 25:6–10a; Phil. 4:12–20; Matt. 22:1–14

November 11: Isa. 45:1–7; 1 Thess 1:1–5; Matt. 22:15–22

November 18: Exod. 22:21–27; 1 Thess. 1:2–10; Matt. 22:34–46

November 22 (Thanksgiving Day): Isa. 61:10–11; 1 Tim. 2:1–8; Luke 12:22–31

November 25: Mal. 1:14b–2:2b, 8–10; 1 Thess. 2:7–13; Matt. 23:1–12

ADVENT

December 2: Isa. 63:16–64:8; 1 Cor. 1:3–9; Mark 13:32–37

December 9: Isa. 40:1–11; 2 Pet. 3:8–14; Mark 1:1–8

December 16: Isa. 61:1–4, 8–11; 1 Thess. 5:16–24; John 1:6–8, 19–28

December 23: 2 Sam. 7:1–5, 7–16; Rom. 16:25–27; Luke 1:26–38

CHRISTMAS SEASON

December 25: Isa. 62:6–12; Titus 3:4–7; Luke 2:15–20

December 30: Jer. 31:10–13; Heb. 2:10–18; Luke 2:22–40.

Four-Year Church Calendar

	1984	1985	1986	1987
Ash Wednesday	March 7	February 20	February 12	March 4
Palm Sunday	April 15	March 31	March 23	April 12
Good Friday	April 20	April 5	March 28	April 17
Easter	April 22	April 7	March 30	April 19
Ascension Day	May 31	May 16	May 8	May 28
Pentecost	June 10	May 26	May 18	June 7
Trinity Sunday	June 17	June 2	May 25	June 14
Thanksgiving	November 22	November 28	November 27	November 26
Advent Sunday	December 2	December 1	November 30	November 29

Forty-Year Easter Calendar

1984 April 22	1994 April 3	2004 April 11	2014 20
1985 April 7	1995 April 16	2005 March 27	2015 5
1986 March 30	1996 April 7	2006 April 16	2016 27
1987 April 19	1997 March 30	2007 April 8	2017 6
1988 April 3	1998 April 12	2008 March 23	2018
1989 March 26	1999 April 4	2009 April 12	2019
1990 April 15	2000 April 23	2010 April 4	2020
1991 March 31	2001 April 14	2011 April 24	2021 Apr.
1992 April 19	2002 March 31	2012 April 8	2022 April
1993 April 11	2003 April 20	2013 March 31	2023 April 9

Traditional Wedding Anniversary Identifications

1 Paper	7 Wool	13 Lace	35 Coral
2 Cotton	8 Bronze	14 Ivory	40 Ruby
3 Leather	9 Pottery	15 Crystal	45 Sapphire
4 Linen	10 Tin	20 China	50 Gold
5 Wood	11 Steel	25 Silver	55 Emerald
6 Iron	12 Silk	30 Pearl	60 Diamond

Colors Appropriate for Days and Seasons

White. Symbolizes purity, perfection, and joy and identifies festivals marking events, except Good Friday, in the life of Jesus: Christmas, Easter, Eastertide, Ascension Day, Trinity Sunday, All Saints' Day, weddings, funerals.

Red. Symbolizes the Holy Spirit, martyrdom, and the love of God: Pentecost and Sundays following.

Violet. Symbolizes penitence: Advent, Lent.

Green. Symbolizes mission to the world, hope, regeneration, nurture, and growth: Epiphany season, Kingdomtide, Rural Life Sunday, Labor Sunday, Thanksgiving Sunday.

Black. Symbolizes mourning: Good Friday.

Flowers in Season Appropriate for Church Use

January. Carnation or snowdrop.
February. Violet or primrose.
March. Jonquil or daffodil.
April. Lily, sweet pea, or daisy.
May. Lily of the valley or hawthorn.
June. Rose or honeysuckle.
July. Larkspur or water lily.

August. Gladiolus or poppy.
September. Aster or morning glory.
October. Calendula or cosmos.
November. Chrysanthemum.
December. Narcissus, holly, or poinsettia.

Historical, Cultural, and Religious Anniversaries in 1984
Compiled by Kenneth M. Cox

10 years (1974). *February 4*: Patricia Hearst is kidnapped in Berkeley, California, by a group called the "Symbionese Liberation Army." *February 13*: The Soviet Union deports Alexander I. Solzhenitsyn, author of *Gulag Archipelago*, a commentary on the Russian penal system. *August 9*: President Richard M. Nixon resigns his office; Gerald R. Ford enters the White House. *September 16*: President Ford announces an earned amnesty plan for Vietnam War draft evaders and deserters. *March 28*: Dwight D. Eisenhower, thirty-fourth President of the United States, dies. *May 4*: James Foreman disrupts communion services at Riverside Church, demanding reparation for blacks.

15 years (1969). *July 21*: Astronaut Neil Armstrong becomes the first man to set foot on the moon. *July 31*: Pope Paul VI flies to Africa for a conference of African bishops and becomes the first pope to visit that continent. *August 15–17*: The Woodstock Music and Art Fair in New York draws more than four hundred thousand people, most of them between the ages of sixteen and thirty. *October 6*: Harry Emerson Fosdick, founding pastor of the Riverside Church in New York City, dies.

20 years (1964). Roman Catholic liturgy is changed to include English in some prayers. The federal government activates a foodstamp program designed to help the needy.

25 years (1959). Fidel Castro assumes power in Cuba. Pope John XXIII calls the Second Vatican Council to promote church unity. The United Nations General Assembly condemns apartheid and any other forms of racial discrimination.

30 years (1954). Korean evangelist Sun Myung Moon founds the Unification Church.

40 years (1944). *June 6*: Allied troops invade France at Normandy on D-Day. The kidney machine is invented.

50 years (1934). Adolf Hitler consolidates the offices of president and chancellor of Germany, becomes Fuehrer. The Worldwide Church is founded by Herbert W. Armstrong. Two synods of German reformed peoples merge to become The Evangelical and Reformed Church. Karl Barth answers No! to Emil Brunner on Natural Theology.

75 years (1909). Admiral Robert Peary reaches the North Pole.

100 years (1884). A financial panic sweeps the New York stock market in May. Charles T. Russell founds the Watch Tower Bible and Tract society (Jehovah's Witnesses) to publish his apocalyptic writings.

150 years (1834). The Spanish Inquisition, which had begun in the thirteenth century, is abolished. French educator Louis Braille's system of raised point writing gains worldwide acceptance.

200 years (1784). John Wesley charters Wesleyan Methodism. The first successful daily newspaper, the *Pennsylvania Packet and General Advertiser*, is published.

250 years (1734). *November 2*: American pioneer Daniel Boone is born.

350 years (1634). Maryland is settled, as protestants and Roman Catholics alike are welcomed.

450 years (1534). French-born religious reformer John Calvin publishes the enormously influential *Institutes of the Christian Religion*. Henry VIII's Act of Supremacy abrogates papal authority and establishes the king as head of the Church of England. The Society of Jesus (Jesuit order) is founded by Basque ecclesiastic Ignatius Loyola.

500 years (1484). *January 1*: Protestant reformer Ulrich Zwingli is born.

600 years (1384). *December 31*: John Wycliffe, translator of the Vulgate Bible into English vernacular and Oxford forerunner of the Reformation, dies.

1450 years (534). Benedict, Italian monk, draws up his Rule, setting forth the main ideas of Benedictine monasticism.

Anniversaries of Hymns, Hymn Writers, and Composers in 1984
Compiled by Hugh T. McElrath

50 years (1934). Birth of Dale Wood, composer of hymn tunes LAUREL ("Now the daylight fills the sky"), EDEN CHURCH ("Christ is made the sure foundation"), and other contemporary tunes. Death of Theodore Baker (b. 1851), translator of "We gather together to ask the Lord's blessing"; Carrie E. Breck (b. 1855), author of "Face to face with Christ my Savior"; Edward Elgar (b. 1857), composer of DRAKE'S BROUGHTON ("Hear thy children, gentle Jesus," "Long ago the lilies faded"); Gustav Holst (b. 1874), composer of CRANHAM ("In the bleak midwinter"); Milton S. Littlefield (b. 1864), author of "O Son of Man, Thou madest known"; and Adelaide A. Pollard (b. 1862), author of "Have Thine own way, Lord."

75 years (1909). Birth of Leslie H. Moore, author of "Jesus, we love to meet" and "Far in the West the sunset's golden splendor." Death of Francis Pott (b. 1832), author of "Angel voices, ever singing"; and Ebenezer Prout (b. 1835), composer of RALEIGH ("Father, who art alone," "Author of life divine") and CAIRNBROOK ("Holy Father in Thy mercy," "Praise, O praise the Lord of harvest").

100 years (1884). Death of Silas J. Vail, composer of CLOSE TO THEE. Birth of Luther B. Bridgers (d. 1948), author and composer of "He keeps me singing"; Everett Titcomb (d. 1968), composer of CARLSON ("Jesus! name of wondrous love").

125 years (1859). Death of James W. Alexander (b. 1804), translator of "O sacred head, now wounded"; and George Washington Doane (b. 1799), author of "Softly now the light of day," "Thou art the way: to Thee alone," and "Fling out the banner! let it float." Birth of Katharine Lee Bates (d. 1929), author of "O beautiful for spacious skies"; Henry F. Benson (d. 1933), composer of AURORA ("The Lord is rich and merciful"); Carl Boberg (d. 1940), author of "How great Thou art"; J. Wilbur Chapman (d. 1918), author of "One day when heaven was filled with

His praises" and "Jesus! what a friend for sinners"; Carey Bonner (d. 1938), composer of TILAK ("Prayer to a heart of lowly love"); Joseph S. Cook (d. 1933), author of "Gentle Mary laid her child"; Basil Harwood (d. 1949), composer of OLDOWN ("O Thou whose love has brought us here"), LUCKINGTON ("Let all the world in every corner sing"), and THORNBURY ("Thy hand, O God, has guided," "O Jesus, I have promised"); Maria Penstone (d. 1910), author of "God has given us a book full of stories"; F. R. Pyper (d. 1915), author of "O God of nations, hear"; Cecil Spring Rice (d. 1918), author of "I vow to thee, my country, all earthly things"; and William Wright (d. 1924), author of "March on, my soul, with strength."

150 years (1834). Death of Samuel Taylor Coleridge (b. 1722), author of "Ere on my bed my limbs I lay"; Francis Scott Key (b. 1779), author of "The Star-Spangled Banner"; and Charles Wesley (the Younger) (b. 1757), composer of EPWORTH ("Thou art the way, to Thee alone") and BERKSHIRE ("High in the heavens eternal God"). Birth of Sabine Baring-Gould (d. 1924), author of "Onward, Christian soldiers" and "Now the day is over"; S. Trevor Francis (d. 1925), author of "O the deep, deep love of Jesus"; John Henry Gilmore (d. 1918), author of "He leadeth me, O blessed thought"; Arabella Katherine Hankey (d. 1889), author of "I love to tell the story" and "Tell me the old, old story"; Marianne Hearn (d. 1909), author of "Just as I am, Thine own to be"; Herbert S. Irons (d. 1905), composer of SOUTHWELL ("There is a book, who runs may read," "Father of mercies, in Thy word") and ST. COLUMBA ("The sun is sinking fast"); Arthur Messiter (d. 1916), composer of MARION ("Rejoice, ye pure in heart"); Charles Haddon Spurgeon (d. 1892), author of "Sweetly the holy hymn"; Mary Ann Thomson (d. 1923), author of "O Zion haste, Thy mission high fulfilling"; and Edward Henry Thorne (d. 1916), composer of ST. ANDREW ("Jesus calls us, o'er

the tumult"). Publication of *The Invalid's Hymn Book* (by Charlotte Elliott), source of "Just as I am, without one plea" and "My God, my Father, while I stray"; and *Spirit of the Psalms* (by James Montgomery), source of "Praise, my soul, the King of heaven" and "God of mercy, God of grace."

175 years (1809). Death of Franz Joseph Haydn (b. 1832), composer of AUSTRIA ("Glorious things of thee are spoken"), CREATION ("The spacious firmament on high"), HAYDN ("Come, my soul, thou must be waking"), and ST. ANTHONY'S CHORALE ("We, thy people, praise Thee"). Birth of Jane Crewdson (d. 1863), author of "O Savior, I have nought to plead" and "O for the peace that floweth like a river"; Oliver Wendell Holmes (d. 1894), author of "Lord of all being, throned afar" and "O Love divine that stooped to share"; Alfred Lord Tennyson (d. 1892), author of "Strong Son of God, immortal love," "Ring out the old, ring in the new," and "Sunset and evening star"; and Robert A. West (d. 1865), author of "Come, let us tune our loftiest song."

200 years (1784). Birth of Bernard Barton (d. 1849), author of "Walk in the light, so shalt thou find"; Carl G. Gläser (d. 1929), composer of AZMON ("O for a thousand tongues to sing"); Thomas Hastings (d. 1872), composer of TOPLADY ("Rock of Ages, cleft for me"), RETREAT ("From every story wind that blows"), and ORTONVILLE ("Majestic sweetness sits enthroned," "O God, we pray for all mankind"), as well as author of "Hail to the brightness of Zion's glad morning"; Joseph Jowett (d. 1856), composer of THANET ("Rise my soul, adore thy maker," "Ere I sleep, forever favor"); and Louis Spohr (d. 1859), composer of GERALD ("I heard the voice of Jesus say," "I want a principle within"). Publication of *Gesangbuch der Herzogliche Hofkapelle*, source of ELLACOMBE ("Hosanna, loud hosanna").

225 years (1759). Death of George F. Handel (b. 1685), composer of ANTIOCH ("Joy to the world! the Lord is come"), CHRISTMAS ("While shepherds watched their flocks by night"), GOPSAL ("Rejoice! the Lord is King"), HALIFAX ("And have

the bright immensities"), MACCABAEUS ("Thine be the glory, risen, conquering Son"), SAMSON ("Glory to God, whose spirit draws"), and SOLOMON ("I sing the almighty power of God"); and Robert Seagrave (b. 1693), author of "Rise, my soul, and stretch thy wings." Birth of William Shrubsole (d. 1829), composer of MILES LANE ("All hail the power of Jesus' name").

250 years (1734). Birth of Thomas Haweis (d. 1820), composer of RICHMOND ("Fill Thou my life, O Lord my God," "What shall I do my God to love"); and Georg Peter Weimar (d. 1800), composer of ALLGUTIGER, MEIN PREISGESANG ("O love divine, how sweet thou art"). Publication of *Morgen- und Abend-segen*, source of "With the Lord begin your task," and William Tans'ur's *Compleat Melody*, source of BANGOR ("Alone, Thou goest forth to die").

300 years (1684). Publication of Part II of *Pilgrim's Progress* (by John Bunyan), from which comes "He who would valiant be." Death of Samuel Crossman (b. 1624), author of "My song is love unknown"; Tobias Clausnitzer (b. 1619), author of "We believe in one true God"; and Johannes Olearius (b. 1611), author of "Comfort, comfort ye my people."

400 years (1584). Birth of Johann M. Altenburg (d. 1630), author of "Do not despair, O little flock"; and Melchoir Teschner (d. 1635), composer of ST. THEODULPH ("All glory, laud and honor").

550 years (1434). Death of Bianco da Siena, author of "Come down, O Love divine."

1350 years (634). Birth of St. Germanus (d. 734), author of "A great and mighty wonder today on earth is done."

1500 years (484). Founding of the Monastery of Mar Saba, from which came "Christian, dost thou see them" (by Andrew of Crete in the seventh century), "Art thou weary, art thou languid?" (by Stephen the Sabaite [?] in the seventh century), and "The day of resurrection" and "Come ye faithful, raise the strain" (by John of Damascus in the eighth century).

Quotable Quotations

1. Gentleness and cheerfulness, these come before all morality; they are the perfect duties.—Robert Louis Stevenson.

2. Prayer is not so much asking for the self as it is realizing the possibilities of the self. It is the art of learning to give, accept, and adjust rather than to get, reject, and dominate.—Edgar N. Jackson.

3. Love is the most universal experience of grace among human beings.—Rollo May.

4. The way to *yes* leads through *no* to *in spite of*.—Fritz Kunkel.

5. Life begins where books end.—W. Béran Wolfe.

6. You will make a lousy anybody else, but are the best "you" in existence.—Zig Ziglar.

7. When a butcher tells you that *his heart bleeds for his country*, he has, in fact, no uneasy feeling.—Samuel Johnson.

8. There is far more opportunity than there is ability.—Thomas Alva Edison.

9. When we want to be something other than the thing God wants us to be, we must be wanting what, in fact, will not make us happy.—C. S. Lewis.

10. Only the hand that erases can write the true thing.—Meister Eckhart.

11. There is a non-Christian in every Christian.—Paul Tillich.

12. The nation had the lion's heart. I had the luck to give the roar.—Winston Churchill.

13. Keep thou from the opportunity, and God will keep thee from the sin.—Benjamin Franklin.

14. If there is no God, nothing matters; if there is a God, nothing else matters.—H. G. Wells.

15. Intercession must never become a substitute for action. Yet sometimes the only—and often the largest—service we can render is to establish spiritual bonds and to work with God for the release of spiritual resources through prayer.—Georgia Harkness.

16. No preacher can bring anyone to the light without having entered the darkness of the cross himself.—Henri J. M. Nouwen.

17. You have not converted a man because you have silenced him.—John Viscount Morley.

18. Courage and good-humor are the vitamins of the good life.—W. Béran Wolfe.

19. If we do not seek out the rejected, the morally homeless of this world, and if we do not see them as individual souls made for God, then we may discover that even in our "churchiness" we are working for ourselves, not for Jesus Christ.—James W. Cox.

20. The oppressed almost inevitably shape themselves in the image of the hated oppressors.—Eric Hoffer.

21. I go to church to join with others in a response none of us would have made by himself, a shared response to a shared Word.—H. Grady Davis.

22. The church is not a stronghold within which the redeemed can take their ease and sun themselves in the salvation of their souls; it is an army on the march against an objective which its commander has already subdued.—Theodore Bovet.

23. In the last analysis a Christian does not live by practicing any ethic or moulding himself on any ideal, but by a faith in God which finally ascribes all good to him.—D. M. Baillie.

24. When you are tempted to give up, turn the key in the lock and go across the tracks and help somebody.—Karl Menninger.

25. Whatever fate befalls you, do not give way to rejoicing, or great lamentation. All things are full of change, and your fortunes may turn at any moment.—Arthur Schopenhauer.

26. The greatest adventure anyone can have with the Bible is when the Spirit of God makes a verse, a passage, or a whole book come alive, and we are confronted with the claims of the living God and nourished by the deepest truths of the gospel.—David H. C. Read.

27. You do not become a friend by writing or reading a book but by coming into a relation with someone else.—Martin E. Marty.

28. He who claims never to have doubted does not know what faith is, for

faith is forged through doubt.—Paul Tournier.

29. Our mistakes keep humility and right thinking alive.—Goethe.

30. Let us not look in the Bible for logic, but for life; for logic is powerless to grasp and to express life.—Paul Tournier.

31. When God gives us eternal life, he gives us not just eternal existence, he gives us *meaningful* eternal existence in himself. —James W. Cox.

32. The mother's heart is the child's school room.—Henry Ward Beecher.

33. By diligence and patience, the mouse bit in two the cable.—Benjamin Franklin.

34. The world is round and the place which may seem like the end may also be only the beginning.—Ivy Baker Priest.

35. None knows the weight of another's burden.—George Herbert.

36. Our main business is not to see clearly what lies dimly at a distance, but to do what lies clearly at hand.—Thomas Carlyle.

37. You need not fear old age if you have invested sufficiently in the social graces and avocations.—W. Béran Wolfe.

38. Moral progress is impossible apart from the habitual vision of greatness.—Alfred North Whitehead.

39. There is no beautifier of complexion, or form, or behavior, like the wish to scatter joy and not pain around us.—Ralph Waldo Emerson.

40. The worst sin toward our fellow creatures is not to hate them, but to be indifferent to them; that's the essence of inhumanity.—George Bernard Shaw.

41. Do not pray for tasks equal to your powers. Pray for powers equal to your tasks. Then the doing of your work shall be no miracle, but you shall be the miracle. —Phillips Brooks.

42. Rare is the person who can weigh the faults of others without putting his thumb on the scales.—Laurence J. Peter.

43. Those who would transform a nation or the world . . . must know how to kindle and fan an extravagant hope.—Eric Hoffer.

44. If a thing is wrong for us, we should not dwell upon the thought of it; or we shall soon dwell upon it with inverted pleasure.—Robert Louis Stevenson.

45. Go often to the house of thy friend, for weeds choke the unused path.—Ralph Waldo Emerson.

46. The statements "God is" and "God loves" are synonymous. They explain and confirm one another.—Karl Barth.

47. We cannot revolt against God without revolting against ourselves.—E. Stanley Jones.

48. To live is Christ, to die is more Christ. We pass into a genial native land. —P. T. Forsyth.

49. Him who destroys one human life, the Scripture regards as if he had destroyed the whole world.—The Talmud.

50. It is not well for man to pray, cream; and live, skim milk.—Henry Ward Beecher.

51. In his will is our peace.—Dante Alighieri.

52. Men are not creatures of circumstances. Circumstances are creatures of men.—Benjamin Disraeli.

53. It is safe to tell the pure in heart that they shall see God, for only the pure in heart want to.—C. S. Lewis.

54. The cry "Jesus is Victor" (J. C. Blumhardt) is more than the applause of spectators. It is the cry of those who are his followers and triumph with him.—Karl Barth.

55. Only he really seeks God, for whom all other doors are bolted.—Emil Brunner.

56. Most of the bitterness of unanswered prayer comes from the assumption that God will juggle his universe to give us what we plead for if we plead long enough. —Georgia Harkness.

57. A religion that has no effect whatever on a person's political views, moral decisions, or philosophy of life is certainly not the religion of the Bible.—David H. C. Read.

58. The capacity for change is beyond the measure of any statistician or pollster. —Studs Terkel.

59. Criticism, however unpleasant, can provide valuable information about ways to improve.—Ari Kiev.

60. Sin is not hurtful because it is forbidden, but it is forbidden because it's hurtful.—Benjamin Franklin.

61. Any man's doubt is faith's opportunity.—James W. Cox.

62. Ask yourself whether you are happy, and you cease to be so.—John Stuart Mill.

63. A moment's insight is sometimes worth a life's experience.—Oliver Wendell Holmes.

64. If we are sinners forgiven, we ought to behave as forgiven, welcomed home, crowned with wonderful love in Christ, and so cheer and encourage all about us.—Father Congreve.

65. To hold fast upon God with one hand, and to open wide the other to your neighbor—that is religion.—George MacDonald.

66. If we take man as he is, we make him worse; if we take him as he ought to be, we help him to become it.—Viktor E. Frankl.

67. God has landed on this enemy-occupied world in human form.—C. S. Lewis.

68. If your morals make you dreary, depend upon it they are wrong. I do not say "give them up," for they may be all you have; but conceal them like a vice, lest they should spoil the lives of better and simpler people.—Robert Louis Stevenson.

69. It is a reproach to religion and government to suffer so much poverty and excess.—William Penn.

70. A home is always a place where a man thinks more of the happy privileges of giving than of the expectation of receiving.—Lynn Harold Hough.

71. A recovery of the old sense of sin is essential to Christianity.—C. S. Lewis.

72. Others can stop you temporarily—you are the only one who can do it permanently.—Zig Ziglar.

73. You grow up the day you have your first real laugh at yourself.—Ethel Barrymore.

74. Smiles are as catchin' as the measles and a whole lot more pleasant.—H. Hamlyn.

75. How seldom we weigh our neighbor in the same balance with ourselves.—Thomas à Kempis.

76. Success is full of promise till men get it; and then it is a last year's nest, from which the bird has flown.—Henry Ward Beecher.

77. This would be a fine world if all men showed as much patience all the time as they do when they are waiting for fish to bite.—Vaughn Monroe.

78. I am neither a pessimist nor an optimist—I am a hoper. And I believe in grace.—Edmund Fuller.

79. Self-righteousness is a loud din raised to drown the voice of guilt within us.—Eric Hoffer.

80. Christ is already here and now the friend and ally of all men, even of those who do not know him, or who deny him and fight against him.—Theodore Bovet.

81. Love begins when a person feels another person's need to be as important as his own.—Harry Stack Sullivan.

82. As the cross retires from religion, it becomes a religion more and more emptied of repentence.—P. T. Forsyth.

83. No recording angel could be more accurate in cataloging the wrong things that we have done than our own subconscious mind.—James W. Cox.

84. Laying down your arms, surrendering, saying you're sorry, realizing that you've been on the wrong track and getting ready to start life over again from the ground floor—that's the only way out of our "hole." This process of surrender—this movement full speed astern—is what Christians call repentence.—C. S. Lewis.

85. Faith is real when we can accept God's answer to our prayers any way he chooses to give it.—James W. Cox.

86. Anyone can carry his burden, however hard, until nightfall. Anyone can do his work, however hard, for one day.—Robert Louis Stevenson.

87. Many a dangerous temptation comes to us in gay, fine colors, that are but skin-deep.—Matthew Henry.

88. The oneness of the church is like the oneness of a family. It depends on something more basic than the way its members feel or act toward one another.—H. Grady Davis.

89. What a pin is when the diamond has dropped from its setting, that is the Bible when its emotive truths have been taken away.—Henry Ward Beecher.

90. I, for one, do not believe in "prayer." I believe in a wise and loving Father to whom I pray.—H. Grady Davis.

91. We must pray wisely if we would pray well.—Georgia Harkness.

92. Behold the turtle: he makes progress only when he sticks his neck out.—James Bryant Conant.

93. All creativeness in the realm of the spirit as well as every psychic advance of man arises from a state of mental suffering, and it is spiritual stagnation, psychic sterility, which causes this state.—C. G. Jung.

94. Perhaps there is no more sublime object in all creation than a man at prayer.—Edgar N. Jackson.

95. In this world, it is not what we *take* up, but what we *give* up, that makes us rich.—Henry Ward Beecher.

96. We are not damned for doing wrong, but for not doing right; Christ would never hear of negative morality; *thou shalt* was ever his word, with which he superseded *thou shalt not*.—Robert Louis Stevenson.

97. A man with God is always in the majority.—John Knox.

98. The first duty of love is to listen.—Paul Tillich.

99. People often ask when the next step in evolution—the step to something beyond man—will happen. Well, on the Christian view, it has happened already. In Christ, a new kind of man appeared: and the new kind of life which began in him is to be put into us.—C. S. Lewis.

100. All who take the name of Jesus seriously and who associate themselves with his work, will, and church are saints by calling, and we all are imperfect until all is made perfect in God.—Peter J. Gomes.

Questions of Life and Religion

These questions may be useful to prime homiletic pumps, as discussion starters, or for study and youth groups.

1. How does the Golden Rule apply in life today?

2. In what ways can we support our new resolutions?

3. Are there any practical strategies for overcoming worry and anxiety?

4. Is there any guarantee that we can avoid suffering?

5. What is the difference between sin and sins?

6. What is the Christian's obligation toward the needy?

7. Can we call sin "stupidity"?

8. Does it help to know that God knows all about us?

9. How can our words tear down rather than build up?

10. What are the values of waiting for God to act?

11. Is it possible to be "saintly" and yet be liked as a human being?

12. When are we justified in turning inward and away from the needs of others?

13. Is suffering ever a blessing?

14. Is contentment ever right?

15. Does spiritual attainment affect our "body language"?

16. What can we know after we have decided for God that we could not know before?

17. How does duty done help us face the future with courage?

18. When is it right to go against custom?

19. How may we increase our knowledge of God?

20. What are the evidences of the presence of God in our lives?

21. What are the signs that God is at work in our lives?

22. Does God provide for our physical needs?

23. How does God care for the oppressed?

24. Is it really possible to eliminate God from our lives?

25. How does God guide us?

26. Is agreement among true Christians always possible?

27. When is it our duty to inconvenience ourselves for the sake of others?

28. What are the values of self-examination?

29. Are we ever justified in speaking ill of other people?

30. Would a good, moral life be worthwhile even if there were no life beyond death?

31. What are the lessons to be learned in difficult times?

32. How does obedience help us to know God better?

33. What good can arise from the quiet times?

34. Is risk of failure a part of obedience to God's will?

35. How does prayer help in times of trouble?

36. How can we be relaxed before God about things necessarily left undone?

37. How do we explain God's seeming indifference at times to human pain?

38. Can we ever honestly say, "Thy will be done," without any self-regard?

39. Why should we trust God?

40. In practical terms, what does it mean to love one's neighbor as oneself?

41. How can we tell right from wrong?

42. How do "trials" contribute to our spiritual growth?

43. Can we enjoy doing God's will?

44. What is the meaning of "Judge not, that ye be not judged"?

45. Can we ask for *anything* in prayer?

46. What is the role of thanksgiving in prayer?

47. What is the relation of world peace to personal peace?

48. Does God care for us as individuals?

49. How does Christian love differ?

50. What is the meaning of hope as the Bible uses the word?

51. Is Christian unity possible?

52. How can we find a sense of meaning in our lives?

53. Is courtesy a Christian virtue?

54. What is the importance of public worship for daily living?

55. Is perfection possible?

56. What is the meaning of the doctrine of angels?

57. Has God always been like the God Jesus revealed?

58. Can we call our bodies our own to do with as we please?

59. How responsible are we for the right use of our money?

60. How can we handle anger?

61. Is it the responsibility of the church to feed the poor?

62. Does God want us to be happy?

63. What are the ingredients of happiness?

64. Why are our prayers unanswered?

65. Is war inevitable?

66. What are the moral limits of sex?

67. What can lonely people do to help their situation?

68. Is it wrong to get angry?

69. How can parents and chidren stay on good terms with each other?

70. In what ways might we "believers in one God" be idolators?

71. What can families do about the drug problem?

72. Is being overweight a religious problem?

73. Does TV violence influence the behavior of children?

74. What are the values of regular times of silence and meditation?

75. Has the New Testament made the Old Testament obsolete?

76. In what ways do we experience the Holy Spirit?

77. How can we keep up our guard against temptation?

78. What are the dangers of power?

79. What are the perils of riches?

80. In what ways can we use the earth's resources more responsibly?

81. How reliable is the Bible?

82. Are there any moral absolutes?

83. What is the meaning of the incarnation?

84. Does the Sermon on the Mount apply to us today?

85. How did God create all things?

86. What responsiblity do we have toward believers of non-Christian faiths?

87. What does taking part in Communion accomplish?

88. Is meekness a virtue?

89. What does it mean when we are asked to take up our cross and follow Jesus?

90. Can we justify violence as a means to achieving a good end?

91. Do radio and TV preachers hinder or help the churches?

92. How is God different from us?

94. Will good works save us?

95. What is the importance of good works in the Christian life?

96. Will we know our loved ones in heaven?

97. What is the meaning of stewardship in the Christian life?

98. Is it right to aim for success in life?

99. Are our acts predetermined by God?

100. What kind of help do we need for important decisions?

Biblical Benedictions and Blessings

The Lord watch between me and thee, when we are absent one from another.—Gen. 31:49.

The Lord bless thee, and keep thee; the Lord make his face shine upon thee, and be gracious unto thee; the Lord lift up his countenance upon thee, and give thee peace.—Num. 6:24–26.

The Lord our God be with us, as he was with our fathers: let him not leave us, nor forsake us: that he may incline our hearts unto him, to walk in all his ways, and to keep his commandments, and his statutes, and his judgments, which he commanded our fathers.—I Kings 8:57–58.

Let the words of my mouth, and the meditation of my heart, be acceptable in thy sight, O Lord, my strength, and my redeemer.—Ps. 19:14.

Now the God of patience and consolation grant you to be likeminded one toward another according to Christ Jesus: that ye may with one mind and one mouth glorify God, even the Father of our Lord Jesus Christ. Now the God of hope fill you with all joy and peace in believing, that ye may abound in hope, through the power of the Holy Ghost. Now the God of peace be with you all.—Rom. 15:5–6, 13, 33.

Now to him that is of power to establish you according to my gospel, and the preaching of Jesus Christ, according to the revelation of the mystery, which was kept secret since the world began, but now is manifest, and by the scriptures of the prophets, according to the commandment of the everlasting God, made known to all nations for the obedience of faith: to God only wise, be glory through Jesus Christ for ever.—Rom. 16:25–27.

Grace be unto you, and peace, from God our Father, and from the Lord Jesus Christ.—1 Cor. 1:3.

The grace of the Lord Jesus Christ and the love of God, and the communion of the Holy Ghost, be with you all.—2 Cor. 13:14.

Peace be to the brethren, and love with faith, from God the Father and the Lord Jesus Christ. Grace be with all them that love our Lord Jesus Christ in sincerity.—Eph. 6:23–24.

And the peace of God, which passeth all understanding, shall keep your hearts and minds through Christ Jesus. Finally, brethren, whatsoever things are true, whatsoever things are honest, whatsoever things are just, whatsoever things are pure, whatsoever things are lovely, whatsoever things are of good report; if there be any virtue, and if there be any praise, think on these things. Those things, which ye have both learned, and received, and heard, and seen in me, do: and the God of peace shall be with you.—Phil. 4:7–9.

Wherefore also we pray always for you, that our God would count you worthy of this calling, and fulfill all the good pleasure of his goodness, and the work of faith with power: that the name of our Lord Jesus Christ may be glorified in you, and ye in him, according to the grace of our God and the Lord Jesus Christ.—2 Thess. 1:11–12.

Now the Lord of peace himself give you peace always by all means. The Lord be with you all. The grace of our Lord Jesus Christ be with you all.—2 Thess. 3: 16, 18.

Grace, mercy, and peace, from God our Father and Jesus Christ our Lord.—1 Tim. 1:2.

Now the God of peace, that brought again from the dead our Lord Jesus, that great shepherd of the sheep, through the blood of the everlasting covenant, make you perfect in every good work to do his will, working in you that which is well-pleasing in his sight, through Jesus Christ, to whom be glory for ever and ever.—Heb. 13:20-21.

The God of all grace, who hath called us unto his eternal glory by Christ Jesus, after that ye have suffered a while, make you perfect, establish, strengthen, settle you. To him be glory and dominion for ever and ever. Greet ye one another with a kiss of charity. Peace be with you all that are in Christ Jesus.—1 Pet. 5:10-11, 14.

Grace be with you, mercy, and peace, from God the Father, and from the Lord Jesus Christ, the Son of the Father, in truth and love.—2 John 3.

Now unto him that is able to keep you from falling, and to present you faultless before the presence of his glory with exceeding joy, to the only wise God our Savior, be glory and majesty, dominion and power, both now and ever.—Jude 2:24-25.

Grace be unto you, and peace, from him which was, and which is to come; and from the seven Spirits which are before his throne; and from Jesus Christ, who is the faithful witness, and the first begotten of the dead, and the prince of the kings of the earth. Unto him that loved us, and washed us from our sins in his own blood, and hath made us kings and priests unto God and his Father; to him be glory and dominion for ever and ever.—Rev. 1:4-6.

SECTION II. *Vital Themes for Vital Preaching*

January 1. Justice: A Stone's Throw Away

TEXT: John 8:1–11.

A group of men are milling around a courthouse square. One passes his verdict on the state of the world: "Ain't no justice anymore."

I. It's obvious why justice has disappeared: our punishments fail to fit the crimes. (vv. 4–5). It's no wonder people are making a mockery out of our legal codes. Things will get no better until our punishments fit the crimes.

II. So what does Jesus say about the matter of justice? "Whoever among you is without sin, let that person first cast a stone" (v. 7). Jesus isn't impressed with our judicial arrogance. He exposes us to be like little kids who bombard one another with rocks when they feel hurt.

III. But, where does that kind of statement leave us *standing*? What have we got left to build our lives on? (v. 5). We in the church can break out our wide Cheshire-cat grins because we have God's Law. We believe in Law so much that we may want it hung in our children's classrooms.

IV. Yet look at what the Law does: God's Law illumines our own injustices (v. 9). Like a stage spotlight that's gone haywire, God's Law exposes our sins when we wanted it to pick on someone else's. As Camus has said, we are "judge-penitents"; at one point judges by the Law, we are now the judged.

V. So the time has come for our moment of truth. We approach the bench to hear our fate, and there's only one person to pronounce it (vv. 9–11). This man is the only one found worthy to pass judgment. He may not be paying good attention, but he does let us off. A hung jury, you say? No, our jury isn't hung—it's crucified. The old man was right: there "ain't no justice anymore." But there's grace—and aren't we glad?

VI. We leave now from this place with a new lease on life (v. 11). Victor Hugo's character, Jean Valjean, speaks to us: "Forgive others as you have been forgiven." Throw away the calculators. We are a fellowship of the forgiven. So why are we still sitting here? The verdict's been pronounced. Not guilty. So go . . . and from this moment on, sin no longer. Instead, forgive one another as God in Christ has forgiven us.—J. Douglas Dortch

January 8. Jesus Revealed as the True Savior.

TEXT: Matt. 3:13–17.

I. When John baptized him in Jordan. Not as a sinner. But as our sinless Brother, come to assume our burden of sin for us. And as our great Representative, omitting nothing that belongs to his holy office and work.

II. When the Father in heaven anointed him with the Holy Spirit. Inaugurating him into his office; him, the Son; in whom he delighted; to whom he gave the divine approval; and all this in a wondrous way. Making him the Christ indeed: giving him all the power of the Spirit; enduing him with all that his great office and work made necessary; assuring his absolute success; and all this again in the most wonderful way.—R. C. H. Lenski

January 15. Believing in God

Text: Mark 9:23.

Jesus and three of his disciples went up on the mountain and there had a marvelous experience. Before the eyes of the disciples, Jesus' raiment became shining. He was transfigured before them. Then Elijah and Moses suddenly appeared and they talked together. It was so wonderful that Peter suggested they stay on the mountain.

But Jesus knew there was work to be done in the valley below. God never gives his power to those who will not use it in service. At the foot of the mountain was a father who had brought his epileptic son. Since childhood the boy had been afflicted. The father had asked the disciples to heal the boy, but they could not. Now he asked Jesus. Jesus said, "If thou canst believe, all things are possible to him that believeth."

I. The belief in God which matters is not a belief based on what others say nor a belief based on our own intellectual reasoning. Rather, it is the belief based on our own experience of God, the one that gives us power. Jesus said to the father who brought his son to be healed, "All things are possible to him that believeth." The father replied, "Lord, I believe; help thou mine unbelief."

(a) He frankly admits to some unbelief, and certainly his belief was not full and complete. Perhaps one reason for his unbelief was that he had been disappointed so many times. No doubt he had bought every new medicine that had come to the market, but nothing had helped. He had carried the boy to the church to be prayed for, but with no results. Now he had even brought him to Jesus' own disciples, and they had failed. Naturally, the father had some disbelief.

(b) It is easy to believe when everything is going well. But when it seems our lives are blocked at every turn, then belief is much more difficult. I have talked with many people who have genuine doubts about the existence of God. Yet, each of these people was someone with whom life had dealt harshly. And when life becomes harsh, it is normal and natural to begin doubting not only the existence of God, but the existence of anything good.

(c) I have had people come to me to talk about God, but I would make them talk about themselves instead. Jesus did that with this father whose son was sick. He asked the father, "How long is it ago since this came unto him?" That is, "I am interested in your problem. Tell me about it." The very fact that the father found Jesus a sympathetic listener helped to lift his burden.

(d) We cannot prove God by argument, but we can make our own lives an argument for God. Discouragement is often the beginning of doubt and unbelief. Encouragement is usually the doorway to God's presence.

II. No doubt another reason for the father's unbelief was the condition of his son. This father had been told that God made us and that God was good. But if that be true, then why would a good God make a child so afflicted? Why would God allow such a child to suffer all of his life, when he had done nothing to deserve it?

(a) Here we have an even greater problem. For now not only do we become concerned about belief in God, but also in the *character* of God. Better to have no God, if he is a bad God. But if we claim a creator God who is good, then how do we explain all the evil in the world?

(b) And yet, if, because of evil, we decide not to believe in God, then we have before us an even greater problem. For how are we to explain the goodness in the world?

(c) When we concentrate on the crosses of our own lives, it makes for unbelief. Storms, earthquakes, and disease produce more despair than faith. But, on the other hand, how do we explain sunsets and music, mothers and laughter, flowers and victories, if we leave out the existence of a good God? Let us never forget that good can and does overcome evil. Faith in God gives us that daring confidence.—Charles L. Allen.

January 22. Our Gracious Guide

Text: Exod. 33:14.

A number of things which the presence of God is said to do for his own people: (1)

it is a saving presence (Isa. 63:9); (2) it is a protecting presence (Exod. 14); (3) it is a separating presence (Exod. 33:16); (4) it is a unifying presence (John 17:21); (5) it is an energizing presence (Phil. 4:13); (6) it is a sanctifying presence (Rom. 8:10); (7) it is a satisfying presence (Ps. 16:11).—W. W. Weeks.

January 29. The Bread of Life

TEXT: John 6:24–35.

I. The bread of life is eternal, not perishing.

(a) This contrast between an inferior and a superior option is typical Johannine dualism.

(b) John shows that Christ wants men to commit their loyalties to eternally significant realities.

II. The bread of life is uniquely Jesus Christ.

(a) The crowd questions the uniqueness of Jesus' earlier sign by suggesting that he has done no more than Moses who gave bread (manna) from heaven.

(b) Jesus points out that the true bread comes from God, not Moses.

(c) The "I AM" sayings of Jesus in John identify the oneness of Jesus with God, the "I AM" who called Moses.

III. The bread of life is for anyone who will believe on him whom God has sent.

(a) In contrast to the desire of the crowd to do the works of God, Jesus says that there is only one work of God: to believe on him whom God has sent.

(b) In John, to "believe" means to come to Jesus with acceptance of and commitment to him in discipleship.—Phillip A. Cooley.

February 5. From Gloom to Glory

SCRIPTURE: Isa. 6:1–7.

How do we explain a life of surpassing usefulness to God and man? We have to go to the wellsprings of the man's loves and hates. To what does he give his highest devotion? What does he reject and condemn?

Why do we have the prophecies of Isaiah, with their sonorous sentences, their searching judgments, and their abounding grace? The basic reason is found in his conversion experience.

I. (a) Isaiah was shaken by catastrophe. His familiar world had collapsed. The underpinning of this world was King Uzziah. Here was a clear case of hero worship that had suffused every earthly object with a radiance of peace and joy. Isaiah sat in silence in the debris of daring dreams; he looked out upon a world whose beauty had been blotted out by a thick cloud of grief. In such a time, only one thing remained, and even that could be doubted: the house of God, the divine presence, the divine purpose. He had to go to the Temple. There was no other place to go.

(b) When catastrophe strikes us or when some great crisis arrives, we may find ourselves right where Isaiah was. Our fancied securities are inadequate. We tremble. We weep. We sometimes strike back through hot, blinding tears. We exhaust ourselves trying to convince ourselves that it isn't so. But at last we see that the bad news is true. The question then arises: where do I go from here? And the only satisfying answer is: to God.

II. (a) Isaiah was further shaken when he met God face to face. "I saw also the Lord sitting upon a throne, high and lifted up, and his train filled the Temple." Thus his experience had a deeper dimension than the accident of a king's demise and the anguish of a soul in travail. Every aspect of what happened served to heighten his awareness of God and his consciousness of sin. When Isaiah went to the Temple, he thought, no doubt, that he had gone to seek God. But God had visited him. Now the seeker Isaiah was face to face with a seeking God.

(b) Many of us live behind an invisible shield, thinking that we know God. But we have effectively sealed him out. Then trouble comes, and God enters through a shattered door or a riven wall. Thus we stand trembling and embarrassed, like children meeting an awesome stranger for the first time. We could flee, for a glimpse of the holy God would send us running if there were any sure hiding place. For we are sinners. But we stay, though shaken by our sins. The mighty One who "plants his footprints in the sea and rides upon the storm" comes not to destroy, but to redeem.

III. (a) The sight of God led Isaiah to confess his sinfulness. He acknowledged the sin for which he was personally responsible and for which, as a member of the community, he shared responsibility: "I am a man of unclean lips. . . . I dwell in the midst of a people of unclean lips." The voices chanting, "Holy, holy, holy," reminded him only too well of the unworthiness of his own lips to speak a word on behalf of God. But in a dramatic, symbolic gesture, the confessing sinner was assured of his forgiveness and cleansing.

(b) The man who does not confess his sins has never really met God. The same is true of the person who gratuitously spends much time confessing the sins of other people. If we get one good glimpse of God, we will acknowledge the sins that we cleverly conceal from our fellow men and that we try to justify to our consciences. Happily, the judgment of God is blended with mercy, so that we scarcely know where one leaves off and the other begins. God judges in order to redeem; he redeems in order to make righteous. When God enters our lives, it is with a dual purpose: "to forgive us our sins, and to cleanse us from all unrighteousness" (1 John 1:9).

(c) When Isaiah met God, he stood on the threshold of a new career, a high service to humanity, and a glorious destiny in God. When any man or woman today meets God in a radical experience of spiritual renewal, a new creation emerges, with new goals, with an intimate understanding of God, and with a genuine compassion for his or her fellow human beings.—James W. Cox.

February 12. A Call for Volunteers
TEXT: Isa. 6:8.

Are you doing with your life exactly what the Lord God would have you do? Have you, as far as you know, made yourself available for the highest uses to which God may put your life?

I. *The divine call.* (a) The call of God comes to those with spiritual qualifications. The call came to Isaiah after he had experienced a dramatic cleansing from sin. Otherwise, his service to God would have been greatly limited. God may use an unconverted man to serve the high purposes of divine justice. But it is an exception.

(b) One who speaks for God may be very conscious of personal shortcomings and unworthiness; yet God, not the individual, is the judge of usefulness.

(c) However, the call of God cannot be fulfilled by merely belonging to a profession formally related to the religious community or to the church. The determination to become a prophet or a preacher, a religious teacher or a missionary does not necessarily answer the divine call. The basis of our Christian witness is, first of all, that we be committed and obedient servants of Jesus Christ. The call is not to privilege and honor; it is a call to service and sacrifice.

(d) The call of God ordinarily comes in a quiet manner. The call of Isaiah was no exception. When he was cleansed from sin, the Temple echoed with the chants of heavenly creatures and the young man's eyes were dazzled by the glory of the Lord. But there was an astonishing stillness when God spoke. Isaiah was not addressed by name. No force was used upon him. The voice of God went forth— who would hear and answer? The voice said, "Whom shall I send, and who will go for us?"

(e) Some of us might argue that God has not called us to special service since he has given no signal evidence of it. We may be inclined to regard the call of God as utterly remote from an ordinary Christian's experience. Yet, the truth is just the opposite. The call is very close to the conversion experience and to the practical business of everyday Christian living. A young preacher indicated that entering the ministry seemed to him the next logical step to take after his Christian compassion had led him to a deep concern for the spiritual needs of the world about him. God spoke to him through the needs of others. So he waited for no light or voice from heaven. He dedicated himself to the task and began making preparations to speak for God.

II. *The human response.* The response of Isaiah to God's call to service suggests several important aspects of our own response. Isaiah said, "Here am I; send me." As far as the record goes, this is all that he said.

(a) When God's call to us is sure, we ought to ask God no questions. However, we will probably ask questions of someone: How dangerous is this mission? What kind of financial security may I expect? Will this thing alienate me from the people whose approval I value?

(b) When God's call is sure, our response should be immediate. Nothing is to be gained by postponement. William James, the noted philosopher and psychologist, said that when one has a good impulse, one should act on it immediately. For the force and thrust of the emotion, which could launch a person on a successful course if acted on immediately, will not have the power and appeal when put off. This is not to say that service for God needs no preparation or training. But the decision that calls for the preparation and training ought to be made when one faces conclusive evidence for it. There is no future for the lukewarm heart that forever ponders and deliberates. The Kingdom of God is held in abeyance when God's servants hedge and wait. When Saul of Tarsus came face to face with Jesus Christ and his call to the apostleship, he immediately committed himself to the call, though he went for a time into Arabia, presumably to prepare himself spiritually and intellectually for the monstrous task to which God had called him.

(c) When God's call is sure, the opportunity of special service should be considered a privilege. We can appreciate the insight of James: "Let not many of you become teachers, ... for you know that we who teach shall be judged with greater strictness" (James 3:1 [RSV]). However, the rewards of answering God's call have always seemed greater than the hazards. To be significantly linked with the eternal purpose of God gives one's life radiant meaning. To have the respect and love of those who have also committed themselves to God imparts a unique richness to our human relationships. To have one's best challenged by the best enables one to achieve the highest potential.—James W. Cox.

February 19. A Strange Kind of Success
SCRIPTURE: Isa. 6:9–13.

A number of years ago, E. Stanley Jones set out on a venture of faith which he felt would make a significant contribution to the peace of the world. But the ideas he proposed were not accepted and used by those through whom they would have had strategic influence. This could have been a crushing disappointment for Dr. Jones. But he called it "an adventure in failure."

The church has conceived its task in terms of a message which offers mankind the hope of salvation here and hereafter. However, for all the books written, for all the sermons preached, and for all the church buildings erected, the saving message receives scant attention. Not only the world, but also the church is often the scene of bitterness and strife. The mission of the church, too, can be frequently characterized as "an adventure in failure."

After the prophet Isaiah had labored for many grinding years, he saw clearly what he had but dimly perceived at the outset of his ministry. His venture of faith and love was "an adventure in failure." The same forces may be at work in each of our lives.

I. When we begin to work for God, we set out with high hopes. After all, it is God who has called us, and who can prevail against God? No doubt Isaiah, when he first heard God say, "Whom shall I send, and who will go for us?" could visualize himself in the vanguard of a mighty conquering army of God. Sometimes we expect that everyone about us will be as happy with our decision as we are, that all problems will be removed so that we shall have smooth sailing all the way ahead, that we are assured of immediate and complete success in the work we undertake in the name of God. We are thrilled with the triumphant words in the Book of Revelation: "The kingdom of the world has become the Kingdom of our Lord and of his Christ, and he shall reign for ever and ever" (Rev. 11:15 [RSV]).

II. However, even the word of God may not achieve what we anticipate. The Lord said to Isaiah, "Go, and say to this people: 'Hear and hear, but do not understand see and see, but do not perceive'" (Isa. 6:9 [RSV]).

(a) Such has been the experience of the prophets of God throughout the ages. The prophet presents the truth. Men hear it. They reject the message. Sometimes they kill the messenger.

(b) But why should the prophet's message from God be refused by the people? There are several reasons. Men are free beings, and they sometimes exercise their freedom by rejecting the God who made them free. Men are so blinded by sin that they see all issues in the light of human reason alone; only what is "practical" seems right. Therefore, though God himself sends us forth, we must not be shocked because the world does not welcome us with open arms. On the other hand, it would be wrong for us to assume that if a man is successful, he is not faithful to God, or that if he is persecuted, he is assuredly doing God's will.

(c) The degree of our apparent failure may be appalling. We may see people become worse, rather than better. We may witness a turning from God, instead of repentance. Trusted friends may desert us. We may suffer economic and physical distress. We may see the work of a lifetime go up in smoke. Isaiah was "sawn asunder," we are told. Jesus was crucified. Shall we expect to go scot-free?

III. Nevertheless, we are sustained by the knowledge that through us, in spite of failure, the purpose of God is being worked out.

(a) It was the faith of Isaiah that God would preserve a faithful remnant. This minority would, again and again, rise apparently out of nowhere to witness to the name and truth of God. Wave after wave of judgment would pass over the land, but out of a standing stump, new life would flourish. "The holy seed is its stump" (Isa. 6:13 [RSV]).

(b) Thus, there is no ultimate failure for God's purpose or for those who, in obedience to God's call, serve and suffer for his name's sake (see Isa. 55:11). The servant of God may be scorned, but even the wrath of men shall praise the Lord. The success man seeks is not always the success God seeks.

(c) This can be explained by the cross and the resurrection. By all human meas-urements, the cross of Christ was a token of failure. But the resurrection indicated the opposite. The resurrection proved that the apparent foolishness of God was indeed the wisdom of God and that the apparent weakness of God was, in truth, the power of God. The victorious power of the resurrection is everywhere applicable to those who "fail" for God. Thus, there is no failure—only success—God's success (see Heb. 6:10).—James W. Cox.

February 26. A Prayer for Times of Crisis

SCRIPTURE: John 17.

For many of us, life could be described as a series of crises with brief interludes of relative calm. In our busy, competitive, and complex world, it seems that every decision we face is crucial, every action we take causes conflict, and every interpersonal relationship requires high-level negotiation. It is as if we carry on global strategy on a personal level, and so often we feel inadequate to handle the crises that come our way.

Jesus faced many crises in his life, but none was more crucial than the conflict that led to his crucifixion. As in all of the critical times in his life, he turned then to his Father in prayer, and in so doing, he provided us with a splendid model for our own praying in times of crisis.

I. We should pray for ourselves (vv. 1–5).

(a) Jesus prayed first of all for himself, not only because he was facing the trial, but also because he needed to be a strong example and leader.

(b) We should pray for ourselves so that we may be of help to those around us.

(c) Presence of mind and serenity are best attained by praying to the Father for his guidance.

II. We should pray for those close to us (vv. 6–19).

(a) Even at this time when Jesus was facing so much personal difficulty, he prayed for his disciples.

(b) When we are facing personal difficulty, it is easy to forget about the needs of those around us.

III. We should pray for all Christians (vv. 20–26).

(a) Jesus looked beyond the small band of believers that was gathered about him and envisioned the countless masses who would follow, and he was concerned about them, too.

(b) Not only are we to be concerned about ourselves and those close to us, but we should pray for all who face trials because of their experience with Christ.—James M. King.

March 4. What Happens When People Get Desperate

SCRIPTURE: Luke 18:10–14.

There comes a time in the lives of many individuals when, for any number of reasons, they are faced with an awful awareness that their lives are a complete mess. They are so fraught with sin and inadequacies and misgivings that they are no longer able to deal effectively with life. Such an awareness usually fills one with a deep sense of despair, a feeling of complete helplessness. People in desperate circumstances do desperate things, but the acting out of desperation may take many forms. What are some of the ways that people in these circumstances react to their desperation?

I. Some may react violently.

(a) Desperation may lead us to lash out irrationally because this seems our only recourse.

(b) In desperate circumstances, even normally peaceful people may react with violence.

(c) Violent reaction may result in self-destruction.

II. Others may react with resignation.

(a) When defeat seems inevitable, we may accept it because we do not know what else to do.

(b) Not to react at all is really to react negatively.

(c) Resignation eventually leads to utter hopelessness.

III. The penitent sinner reacts by trusting in God's mercy.

(a) If we are truly sorry for the type of lives we have lived, it is not enough to resolve to do better.

(b) We must throw ourselves into the arms of the waiting Father.

(c) Our desperation may be the only thing that makes us receptive to God's grace.

Conclusion: The tragedy of the pharisee was that his condition was just as bad as that of the tax collector, but because he did not feel desperate, he did not do anything constructive about his situation. Sometimes, amid the shambles of our lives, God may be speaking to us and showing us that when all else fails, when desperation seems to be all we have left, he is there to impart joy and hope and justification.—James M. King.

March 11. On Baring Our Souls and Bending Our Knees

SCRIPTURE: Ps. 51:3–12; 2 Cor. 5:17–21.

How do you think you'd feel if a church required something of you before you were allowed through the doors?

I. Do you know that the psalmist believes there are prerequisites to worship? He believes that what God demands of his people are sincerity and truth (v. 6). God longs for honesty and not excuses among his people. All of this has something to say about our worship.

II. If we're honest with ourselves, we know where we stand. All of us should be well aware of our status as sinful people (v. 3–4). It is the condition of the human race to turn against God.

III. So since we're sinful people, we do deserve our fate. We deserve every bit of punishment that God decides to dish out (v. 4b). We've knocked the chip off God's shoulder; we must pay the price. We deserve the darkness of the grave, expulsion from God's presence.

IV. But listen to what the psalmist says. He cries from the depths of his soul for a new opportunity (v. 10–12). The psalmist is not satisfied with the fate of Sheol. He petitions God with a list of impressive requests. Give him a second chance and the psalmist will never again prove unfaithful!

V. However, the ticket to another opportunity doesn't come easy. It too involves a price. For the ticket to new creation comes only through sin's forgiveness (v. 7–9). God has taken on most of the burden. What he seeks of us is our confession. The result is clear. We are cleansed from our sins.

And that's why we've come to worship. To bare our souls, to bend our knees, to confess to the Father in the hope of his forgiveness. Because we need it. Every passing day brings us closer to the judgment. But, by the grace of God, we all can receive a second chance.—J. Douglas Dortch.

March 18. The Conquest of Guilt

TEXT: Isa. 1:18.

I. Guilt is the experience of everyone. Not every guilty individual recognizes personal guilt. Some see their guilt, but try to explain it away. Other persons carry their recognized guilt as a daily burden that constantly increases. Still others find a satisfactory resolution of their guilt problem through profound religious experience.

II. Many serious attempts to conquer guilt by means of good deeds fail. These efforts too often are conceived in pride and shaped in selfishness. A man may be preoccupied with saving himself from the consequences of his guilt and may be at the same time practically unconcerned about the honor of the God he has offended. Thus the man bends his efforts to a self-engineered program of salvation by good works. He may become a prig, a prude, or a pharisee, but he hardly becomes a truly religious man. He may know great struggle and even nerve-shattering attempts to be perfect, but he only knows as a mocking silence the peace that passes understanding.

III. But there is a happy way by which the problem of guilt may be solved. God has declared that we cannot make ourselves guiltless, but that divine grace can make the guilty acceptable. God rejects the homemade means we provide for ourselves for our salvation, but God himself provides the means by which one who is lost may be saved. The guilty soul stands justified when standing on divine mercy revealed in Jesus Christ and made available through him. We may find that good news too astonishing to believe. We may find that even if we hopefully believe it, we may not at once abandon ourselves to the sheer joy of our newfound freedom. Or we may. For the victory is won, regardless of the response by the beneficiaries to the tidings of the victory. To expect to have removed every trace of tension between what one is and what one ought to be is to expect too much. However, the tension can become a creative incentive rather than a destructive anxiety.

Also, the finding of spiritual peace through divine grace serves another high purpose. It relieves us of the compulsive need to judge and condemn other people. When we can believe that the mercy of God is for us, we can tear off our masks of pretended piety and dare look at ourselves as we are. Then we can see our own faults with such clarity and objectivity that we regard the guilt of others with compassion and concern, not with disparagement and rejection.—James W. Cox.

March 25. How God Enters Our Lives (Lent)

TEXT: Isa. 45:15; Gen. 28:16.

I. The very despair and dissatisfaction that oppress people when they try to live without God are themselves an experience of God.

II. Conscience, also, is an experience of God. The inner compulsion to do right and the shame we feel when we are aware of having done wrong are an experience of God.

III. If we have eyes to see, we can identify God in beauty, in the beauty of nature and in the beauty that his Spirit inspires man to create.

IV. In many ways, we may identify his presence in our personal relationships. We may find him in our friendships and in our service when we are lifted out of ourselves into real self-giving.

V. Many have found him most unexpectedly in suffering.

VI. It is an experience of when, in a service or in the quietness of our own homes, Christ seems to step out of the pages of the New Testament, and he speaks straight to our need and to our failure, and he calls to the best that is in us, so that aspirations and powers we had never dreamed of seem ready to spring into life. There may be nothing of the mystic about us, but God is very near us then.—Leslie J. Tizard, *Facing Life and Death*.

April 1. Stages in Spiritual Progress (Lent)

TEXT: John 9.

I. The man born blind regarded Jesus first as a "man" (v. 11).

II. Then he believed him to be a "prophet" (v. 17).

III. Later, he was confident that he was one "from God" (v. 33).

IV. Finally, he knew that he was the "Son of man" (v. 35) and called him "Lord" (v. 38).—Adapted from William Hull, *Broadman Commentary*.

April 8. Doubt and Faith

TEXT: Ps. 77:7–9, 14.

I am going to doubt doubt before I doubt faith. I have come to that conclusion for four reasons:

I. My doubts and skepticisms about God tend to grow in frequency and force when my personal life, for one reason or another, has dropped to what can only be called a lower level.

II. As people live in the light of belief in God, so many of those very things in life which help to create and nourish doubt and unbelief tend either to disappear or to lose their power to defeat and overwhelm the soul.

III. A truly personal relationship must have an element of adventurous confidence in it, without a continuous clamoring for full explanations and written guarantees.

IV. I look at Jesus and see a being of tremendous intellectual power, of the keenest aesthetic sensitivity, of the most intense moral purity and strength. Even as he is greater than I in every way, so he is more certain than I am of God.—Herbert H. Farmer.

April 15. The Loneliness of Christ

TEXT: John 16:31–32.

There are two kinds of solitude:

(1) insulation in space.

(2) isolation of the spirit—loneliness of the soul.

There are two kinds of men who feel the latter:

(1) men of self-reliance

(2) men who live in sympathy. This latter will help us understand the text.

I. The loneliness of Christ.

(a) There is a second-rate greatness the world can comprehend—for example, John the Baptist.

(b) There is a greatness that is divinely complex.

Christ felt this loneliness at the age of twelve in the Temple.

Christ felt this solitude in trial: in the desert, in Pilate's judgment hall, in the garden, in dying.

II. The spirit or temper of that solitude.

(a) Its grandeur: "I am alone, yet not alone."

(b) Its self-reliance: "Ye shall leave me alone."

(c) Its humility: " . . . because the Father is with me."

III. Conclusion:

(a) Let your life be a life of faith.

(b) Let his strength be yours. Be independent.—F. W. Robertson.

April 22. The Facts of Life—and Death

I. *Fact one*. The Bible recognizes the reality and finality of death.

II. *Fact two*. The Bible does not try to "prove" eternal life. Belief in eternal life is a consequence of belief in God.

II. *Fact three*. Eternal life is a gift. Fellowship with God is not something of which we are "worthy."

IV. *Fact four*. Eternal life can be described as rebirth. This lies behind Paul's image of the grain of wheat. We must die to the life of self-concern, and begin a "new" life centered in God-concern (John 3:3). To talk of the "resurrection of the body" is a way of saying that all that happens on earth concerns God, and that he will pick up, fulfill, and complete all our partial, incomplete human efforts.

V. *Fact five*. Eternal life is not understood in the Bible simply as something that begins at the moment we die. Eternal life is a possibility here and now.—Robert McAfee Brown.

April 29. Realities We Do Not See

TEXT: Heb. 11:1.

How oddly that compares with the creeping prudentialism of the modern mind as it clings to its maxim, "What can't be proved, can't be believed." Christians cannot pretend to offer proof, but the world would be poorer without their mighty belief.

I. Proof is not all of one sort. The scientist can prove a scientific proposition; he cannot in the same sense prove that truth is *worth* the costly toil he devotes to its service. In his major commitment, he acts by faith.

II. Sometimes this faith impels such forthright witness; but it calls again for the reverent silence before a fellow-human without which there is no real understanding. Dietrich Bonhoeffer called us to "fight for a revival of a wholesome reserve between man and man"—the preservation of an area of privacy and mystery which we refuse to invade, entering only on invitation.

III. If faith powers the witness that opens the way to some realities and hushes us into silence that discovers others, it also commands a modesty about our explanations of things, which is essential to true knowledge. Watching an able physicist, Kierkegaard remarked on how this "gifted man is able to explain nature, but does not understand his own self." Faith has long known that secret; for, beyond proof, it "makes us certain of realities we do not see" (NEB), and without which we cannot live.—Merrill R. Abbey, *Preaching to the Contemporary Mind*.

May 6. The Inner Journey
SCRIPTURE: Ps. 23.

I. Introduction to the inner journey (vv. 1–4).

(a) Because the Lord is my shepherd, I have all that I need (v. 1).

(b) Because the Lord is my shepherd, I shall travel confidently in good times and in bad times (vv. 2–4).

II. The end of the inner journey (v. 5).

(a) Because the Lord is my host, I shall be nourished before my enemies (v. 5a).

(b) Because the Lord is my host, I shall be refreshed before my enemies (v. 5b).

III. The impact of the inner journey (v. 6).

(a) Because the Lord is my shepherd and host, I shall live as if having goodness and mercy as traveling companions all my life (v. 6a).

(b) Because the Lord is my shepherd and host, I shall live as if dwelling in the home of the Lord all my life (v. 6b).—Kyle Johnson.

May 13. Parental Anguish
TEXT: 2 Samuel 18:33.

King David's anguish as a parent after the rebellion and the report of the death of his young son is one of the most moving passages in all literature. Parental anguish is with us. It is neither new nor obsolete. When it occurs, like the psalmist of old, we are bound to cry out: "My God, why?" What are we to do when suddenly we no longer understand our children, when suddenly they grossly disappoint us and turn against all the values we tried to teach them? What do we do when suddenly they become totally irreligious?

I. *High hopes*. Most marriages begin with high hopes. After a long period of dreaming and preparation for marriage, a couple stands before the altar of God. The minister, with divine authority, speaks those seemingly magical words: "Therefore, by the ordinance of God and in the presence of these friends, I pronounce that you are husband and wife." Suddenly, all of their dreams have come to fruition. For each of them for a time, it is as though there is no other person on the earth except the beloved.

Then with the passing of time, in most instances, the fruit of their love issues in the birth of another person. "And baby makes three." No one can witness the miracle of birth without some sense of awe, without a call to worship the Creator of life. Heaven knows we want to be good parents! We work at it so hard.

It's wonderful to be in love, and it's wonderful to be a parent. On Mother's Day or the Sunday before Thanksgiving, we come back to the church. We bring that newborn babe and we stand in the very place where we stood to pledge our vows in marriage.

It's a wonderful time when our children grow up and make their own decision for the Lord Christ. With a child's tears and a child's faith, they come to trust the Lord for themselves. Then it is as though they are doubly ours.

II. *Moral myopia*. I've tried to describe something of the joys of parenthood. But there is a childhood disease far worse than the now-defeated scourge of polio. It might be labeled "moral myopia"— spiritual nearsightedness. What happens when our children go wrong? What happens when they sin against us and their heavenly Father? What happens when they break our hearts?

(a) In the first place, let me say that all this is one of the prices we pay for our freedom as human beings. You see, God has created men and women with a free will. That means we have the privilege and the ability to choose for ourselves. God created us with a free will, and that means we are not robots. He does not manipulate us to insure that we always do what is right. No, we are created free and can make wrong choices, as well as right ones.

Parents are responsible for influencing their children and teaching them correct values. But parents are not totally responsible for how those children shake out. The children themselves are responsible. Children have minds of their own. This means they must answer to God just as we adults do. While parents have a responsibility toward their children, they do not have an ultimate responsibility.

When tragedy occurs and children make wrong choices, parents must be careful not to lay an unfair guilt-trip on themselves. Yes, we may have some responsibility, and we will assume that responsibility fully. But remember that not even God enforces his will on us. Neither can parents enforce their will. Parents are parents, and while they are responsible, the ultimate responsibility for the choices their children make rests with the children themselves.

Nor does the pain of parenthood necessarily end once children graduate from school, marry, and to out on their own. Many parents, even in later years, experience the anguish of tragedy in the life of a child, when, for example, the child's marriage fails. The possibility for anguish is always there.

(b) What do we do as parents when our children disappoint us?

1. One of the things we do is *go for help*. Our pride can get in the way. We are embarrassed, hurt, shamed. Don't be ashamed to go for help—to a friend, to a trusted family member, to a counselor, or to a minister.

2. And when a child fails, we *love the child*, regardless. We love our children with a healthy, agape love. To say we love them does not mean that we are indulgent with them. It does not mean that we excuse them. To love them means we want the very best for them. We will their highest good.

3. We *hold on to the promises of our faith*. There's a marvelous verse in the book of Proverbs which ought to be a great comfort and encouragement to us. It says: "Train up a child in the way it should go, and when it is old, it will not depart from it." That verse didn't say that as a teenager he or she will not depart from the way of our faith. It says that when the child is old, mature, he or she will remember and, hopefully, come back again, come home.

So, we hold on to our faith and to the promises of God for ourselves and for our children. The parents' model is to be found in Luke 15 in the story of "The Waiting Father." Note the father's patience and restraint. He loved that boy, even when he was in the far country, and he welcomed him home, restoring him to sonship.

4. And we *pray*. We pray not just out of a sense of our own desperation, but with a sense that the Father knows of our anguish and that his heart is as broken as ours. Sin is always against love.

We pray because through prayer we lay hold of the power of God. Not that the Father is going to walk in and overrule the child's will to make him or her do what is right. But God can give a clearer understanding. When we pray, we hold on to God, and he holds on to us. —Alton H. McEachern.

May 20. A Christian Sexual Ethic

SCRIPTURE: Phil. 1:9–10 (RSV).

These are fundamental elements of a Christian sexual ethic:

I. To be aware of the many uses of sex in our culture.

II. To recognize the necessity for adequate information about sexuality.

III. To develop a comprehensive understanding of love.

IV. To emphasize the importance of self-discipline in character growth.

V. To believe in the possibility of forgiveness for failure (John 8:11 [RSV]).—John C. Howell, *Training Adults*.

May 27. Here Comes the Judge

SCRIPTURE: Matt. 7:1–5.

The temptation to judge those around us is common to us all. This is a fact of human nature, and it caused Jesus to speak out on one occasion concerning the judgment of others. His words were pointed and plain. And the words he spoke then require our hearing and our heeding today.

I. Jesus wants us to see the comedy of our attempt to judge our brother.

(a) The proportions of the two objects are absurd.

(b) The concern of the nearly blinded person is laughable.

II. Jesus wants us to understand that our attempts to judge our brother will bring judgment on ourselves.

(a) Others will in turn judge us.

(b) We will unwittingly judge ourselves.

(c) We will find it difficult to escape the judgment of God.

III. Jesus wants us to relate to our brother.

(a) We are to help him.

(b) But only when we keep in mind our own faults can we help.

(c) In helping him, we help ourselves.

(d) Judgment then is replaced with love. —Gary M. Greer.

June 3. The Living Lord

SCRIPTURE: Col. 3:1–4.

I. Where is God? Is there no justice any longer? Can one still believe in an almighty God of love? What does God want that he allows so many terrible things to happen?

Our text gives us the answer: set your mind on things that are above! The consequence of this process of radical this-worldliness is what we are experiencing today. "Whatever a man sows, that he will also reap." A humanity that sows what is below must also reap what comes from below. That is one side of the matter. Humanity reaps today what it has sown in past decades and past centuries.

II. But along with the fact that God allows all this to come upon us, he wills something with us. He wills to awake us with it, to jolt us awake from this devastating illusion about life. For mankind, it is necessary that once again all worldly securities be taken from it so that it may learn to turn to God.

III. We cannot say with Paul: I should like to depart and be with Christ. Most of us are just as anxious about death as the others who do not believe.

IV. "Those who belong to Christ," so it says in the letter to the Galatians, "have crucified the flesh with its passions and desires." The flesh, however, is nothing else than our attachment to the world. To be crucified—to be dead in that way—does not mean to have no more interests in the world and in what goes on in the world. Rather, it means to have no longer a will of one's own, but to receive everything from God and to see, will, and do everything from God's standpoint.

V. He who experiences through Jesus Christ the forgiveness of sins and reconciliation with God encounters in this way the resurrected, living, present Lord. Many have asked for years as I myself have, "What does that mean—to experience the living Christ?" We experience the living Christ when we encounter him beneath the cross as the one who reconciles us with God, through whom we receive peace with God. For this reason, Jesus Christ has come into the world so that we, united with him and through him with God, "live henceforth not to ourselves but to him who died for us and is raised."

VI. Either we live wrongly or we live rightly. To live wrongly is to live by oneself and for oneself; to live rightly is to live by God and for God, but also for our neighbor.

VII. So we must understand this remarkable word of the apostle: you have died and your life is hid with Christ in God. It is through the death of the sovereign "I" that God becomes the true sovereign in us. And God's lordship in us is the true life, the life in which we are created, the life in and with God.

VIII. He who is united with Christ, to him it matters that God's and not his own will is done, that God and not he himself is honored, that God and not he himself is Lord.

IX. We must hand over to Christ all our life's functions—our thinking, feeling, and willing, our imagination as well as our activity and inactivity, our sleeping and waking—so that he may forgive us and purify us, as it were one piece after another just, indeed, as one climbs into the bath as a whole man but then, however, washes and cleans one member after another.

X. With all this, however, we always want to keep, and should keep, before our eyes the goal of all this: God's eternal goal, the glory in eternity. The more we receive the air of eternity into our soul, the more the anxiety of the world and our attachment to the world disappear.—Emil Brunner.

June 10. The Upper Room Experience
SCRIPTURE: Acts 2:4.

Several disciples plagued Jesus with questions about Israel's future—*this*, despite the fact that the now-risen Christ stood among them. The question had pressed them, and they were being true to their hopes for their people, but the question was about politics, which is usually parochial and ordinary: "Lord, will you at this time restore the kingdom to Israel?" (1:6). Jesus wisely directed their attention to the deeper human need: "You shall be my witnesses." And he turned them to the wider scenes of life: "Samaria and the end of the earth." This filling experience took place in "the upper room, where they were staying" (1:3) after they had witnessed the ascension. Ordinariness would no longer claim them; thus the tradition that gathered around the story of the Upper Room. Epiphanius, an early church leader, reported that when Emperor Hadrian visited Jerusalem in A.D. 135, he found the building in which the Upper Room was still standing. That room was later made part of a Christian church building. But I am not concerned here with the building —rather, I am concerned with the experience that happened there.

I. The Upper Room experience reported in Acts 2 shows the power of spiritual experience to give vitality to one's life. We all expect this from religion, and we all can bear witness that this is a universal need.

(a) He knew and was observing all the stated legal rules of the national religion. "All these I have observed," he told Jesus, then lamented, "What do I still lack?" (See Matt. 19:20.) Jesus told him that he lacked a full openness to God without which he had no personal tie with God.

(b) We see that openness in the disciples after they were "filled with the Holy Spirit" while in the Upper Room. We afterward see them move forth into history with a sense of purpose, radiating a contagious spiritual concern, and eager to share with others the story of what had fully claimed and deeply affected them. The Upper Room experience addresses our need for a vital religious life.

II. The Upper Room experience also illustrates the extent to which vital religion transforms personality.

(a) He saw deeply into one and all. "He knew all men and needed no one to bear witness of man; for he himself knew what was in man," one gospel writer comments (see John 2:25).

(b) Perhaps he cringed for a moment when Peter impetuously spoke up, "Lo, we have left everything and followed you" (see Mark 10:28). Jesus knew that there was more to follow, and he set himself to hear what anxiety prodded Peter and the others to ask about the rewards of discipleship.

(c) That openness would allow *his* Spirit to influence their development and keep them free from the misdirected ambitions of a self or society intent upon gain, advancement, and reward.

(d) This is surely seen as we watch the later lives of the disciples as Acts reports their work and ways. Vital religion had transformed their personalities. It still transforms personality. The Upper Room experience reminds us of this.

III. The Holy Spirit was not sent only to bless us inwardly and focus us personally. The Holy Spirit came to use us practically.

Mary McLeod Bethune was one of the great black leaders in America as I was growing to manhood. I shall not soon forget my impressions of her and my feelings upon hearing and seeing her address an audience. Fifteenth child among seventeen born to her parents, and a pioneer in education and social equality, Mrs. Bethune knew and testified often about the importance of an understood personal tie with God as she lived and did her work. There was a radiance that flowed from her words, "I have precious contentment in my realization of God as my spiritual father." And when she related how her mother and grandmother taught her to be open to God and his word, long before she could read, it was clear to all who heard her tell about it that her parents had wanted Mary to be prepared to deal with the yearnings sure to rise in her heart. They wanted her to "hold the idea until I was mature enough to do something about it."

Jesus had talked much with the disciples about "the promise of the Father," by which he meant the Spirit of God who would be sent to indwell and fulfill them. He knew that life would stir deep yearnings within them, and he sought to prepare them for those times. He taught much that those followers did not readily understand, but he knew that they would hold the ideas until they were at the point of needing to do something about them. The Book of Acts reports when this time arrived and what those disciples did then.

Behind it all lies an open secret—the Upper Room experience. Like the disciples, you too can move beyond the idea about it all and have the experience itself.
—James Earl Massey.

June 17. What Does It Take to Be a Good Father?

SCRIPTURE: Eph. 6:1–4.

Some people say that any man can be a father, that it's a job that takes little talent. Yet the rate for failure in fatherhood is actually higher than in any other occupation. Fathers have a colossal full-time job that most people underestimate. It's the most important task a man can tackle. A father should be the dominant figure in a family. His role is vital. The Bible implies that a family's greatest affliction is to be without a husband and without a father.

God himself pities the fatherless. Hosea says, "In thee the fatherless findeth mercy" (Hos. 14:3). The psalmist wrote, "He relieveth the fatherless and widow" (Ps. 146:9).

Even worse than a home without a father is a home where the father fails to fulfill his God-given role. Looking at Scripture, I see three main fatherly duties.

I. *Provision for the family.* The first, and probably most obvious, need of every family is its material need. A father must *provide for his family.*

(a) Not many fathers fail here. We may not give everything, but we take pride in giving what we can. The Bible says that's the way it should be. 1 Timothy 5:8 reads, "But if any provide not for his own, and especially for those of his own house, he hath denied the faith, and is worse than an infidel."

(b) Perhaps a greater danger lies in providing *beyond* the family's real needs. A father can set his family's material standards too high, overemphasizing money's importance and leading his children to want and to expect more than they actually need. A wise father does not infect his family with the love of money, which Paul says brings many sorrows (1 Tim. 6:8–10).

(c) A father should be a godly leader. In 1 Timothy and Titus, Paul gives qualifications for elders and deacons—those men with spiritual authority over the church. At the top of each list, he requires men to be strong spiritual leaders first *in their own homes.* This responsibility cannot be overstated. A father's relationship to his family symbolizes Christ's position with his people. We represent God to our families. Having given life to our children, we now must give them what they need for spiritual growth.

(d) Fathers, do you love your children? Do you spend time with them? You may think you have good reasons for making business a higher priority, but God sees through that. And so do your children.

They need your time more than they need your money. Work is never more important than family, no matter what your title.

II. *Protection for the family*. A father must protect his family. God protects and nurtures his own children, and every father has the same responsibility.

(a) Most fathers provide physical protection. I don't know of any man who, were someone to enter his house and try to harm his children, would not give his life fighting for them. This sense of duty seems engraved into our nature.

(b) But physical dangers are not the only threats to our families. Families must also be protected from the spiritual dangers that confront our modern homes. Fathers, do you seek to provide spiritual protection for your family? If Satan gets a foothold in your life, he will have a foothold in your family. You need to set an example of spiritual strength and stability. Don't expose your children to dangerous teaching. Be sure the church you attend teaches and believes God's Word. Notice what comes into your home through television, and train your children in the truth.

III. *Prayer for the family*. Finally, every father has a responsibility to *pray for his family*.

(a) Job was a praying father. Chapter one, verse five tells us that Job prayed regularly for each son and daughter. "And it was so, when the days of their fasting were gone about, that Job sent and sanctified them, and rose up early in the morning, and offered burnt offerings according to the number of them all: for Job said, 'It may be that my sons have sinned, and cursed God in their hearts.' Thus did Job continually." The apostle Paul wrote his spiritual children, "For God is my witness, whom I serve with my spirit in the gospel of his Son, that without ceasing I make mention of you always in my prayers" (Rom. 1:9).

(b) One of the biggest sins a man can commit against his children is to have a weak prayer life. As a commitment to God, we need to uphold our children before him.

Fathers, do you provide for your children? Are you giving them all they need? Do you protect them? Are you praying

consistently for them? God wants to help you be a full-time father.—George Sweeting.

June 24. As Possessed People to Possessed Persons

TEXT: Mark 5:1–20.

Suppose Jesus decided to drop in on our church? Who would be the first to greet him? Look at our text and at the madman who greeted Jesus in the country of the Gadarenes.

I. It's really not a mystery why no one else was around to greet Jesus. Everybody was scared stiff of the madman. And don't you believe that you wouldn't feel the same way (vv. 2–6). Look at Mark's sickening description of the man. It's not a pretty sight, but then who's to say that evil is nice to look at? You know of people who have yielded themselves to the bondage of evil.

II. But while we're scared to death of evil, Jesus has come to confront it (vv. 7–10). We're like children who find ourselves engaged in a struggle we can't win. Though we are prone to fall in our powerlessness, in Christ we have hope. For Calvary asserts the ultimate end of evil.

III. So why is there evil still around us? How do we deal with daily demoniacs? The answer is firm (vv. 11–13). In the presence of Christ, evil has the tendency to self-destruct. The powers of darkness run from Christ until there is no place left for them to go.

IV. All of this sounds like good news. Yet the victory of Christ is not gospel to everyone who hears it (vv. 14–17). You would expect the citizens to have been lined up for miles to thank Jesus. Instead, they were outraged because their economic system was damaged. The world can't be redeemed without some significant structures being changed.

V. But for those of us who have accepted the message, it is a message from which we never want to be separated (vv. 18–20). A new start on everything is offered the demoniac. Most of the time we're secure likewise to "cuddle with Jesus." We prefer the security of the Savior, but Christ bids us go to where people are possessed.—J. Douglas Dortch.

July 1. A Declaration of Interdependence

TEXT: Lev. 19:33–34.

Few Americans have had such a worldwide reputation as Thomas Alva Edison. No question about it, Thomas Edison transformed the world we live in. But note: it was Edison and *those who worked with him*. Every step of the way, he was aided by others, and those others in turn utilized the experiences and skills of their predecessors—confirming the observation that "Edison" is a collective noun, a name that signifies the work of many persons.

I. How much all of us owe to the help of others! How very dependent all of us are upon a vast network of others. We scarcely realize this until some part of our social system breaks down. And then most of us are impatient until a remedy is found. Each person in the world is, in reality, a collective noun, encompassing the labor, interests, and involvement of a host of others. No one is an island, no one stands alone. We speak of independence—and it is a great word! On the Fourth of July, the word *independence* carries overtones of our national heritage, encouraging pride and patriotism. But a greater word is *interdependence*. A declaration of worldwide interdependence is as appropriate to this day and hour as the American Declaration of Independence was appropriate to 1776.

II. Interdependence deserves to be the watchword of this hour—an interdependence that comes from God and is of God.

(a) Our world has reached a point in its history suggestive of that tense moment in the life and adventures of Robinson Crusoe when he discovered on his island the footprint of another man. If humanity is to enter the twenty-first century with any degree of well-being whatsoever, we must discover the footprints, not of one person, but of a world of persons. Nothing less than sincere recognition of our interrelationships with people, both near and far, will insure the perpetuation of the race and the viability of civilization.

(b) Our Christian conviction is that it is only through God and in God that there can be the fullest flowering of respect and regard, each person for the other. Universal brotherhood is a commitment of life, a goal worthy of our utmost striving.

(c) Appreciation of one another, as Carl Rogers suggests, is a key feature of our declaration of interdependence. And notice how he says it: "I like myself best when I express appreciation for others."

III. One of the high points of ancient Hebrew wisdom and understanding was a lesson learned early by of these people. After their deliverance from cruel slavery in Egypt, after they had been subjected to wandering and privation, the Word of God came to them saying, "When a stranger sojourns with you in your land, you shall not do him wrong. The stranger who sojourns with you shall be to you as the native among you, and you shall love him as yourself; for you were strangers in the land of Egypt: I am the Lord your God." The stranger shall be treated as though he were one of your own "and you shall love him as yourself"—that was the divine directive in Moses' day, and it has enduring meaning for our modern day. A big order? Indeed, it is. An impossible dream? Not with God's help, not impossible when our Lord himself is in it.—John H. Townsend.

July 8. The Exclusiveness of Christianity

TEXT: Acts 4:12.

One aspect of Christianity that is perhaps the hardest for a great many intelligent men and women to accept is its exclusiveness.

I. There are at least two good reasons why people are afraid of this particular kind of exclusiveness:

(a) They know more about the religions of the world than perhaps their parents or their grandparents knew.

(b) They have seen the havoc caused by people who think that they have a monopoly on the truth.

II. There are two things, however, that I think they are likely to overlook:

(a) At the center of every life of great achievement, you will find some sort of exclusive loyalty. Take Albert Schweitzer, the great medical doctor of Equatorial Africa. What was it, do you suppose, that was the dynamic of Schweitzer's life? Wasn't it his exclusive loyalty to the principle that he described as "reverence for life"? By that he meant *all* life, not just human life.

And what was it that kept Lincoln going all through the dark days of the Civil War? It was his conviction that all men are created equal—not equal in their ability or talent, but equal in the right to be treated as human beings.

Peter, James, and John are examples of the early Christians. What do you suppose gave them the endurance to face the opposition and all the discouragements of those early days when Christianity had to fight opposition from every side? Their endurance came from their belief that there was no other key to the ultimate mysteries of life save that found in Jesus— and that there was no other name, no other character under heaven by which men might be saved. This is what gave them their incentive.

Every life you look at that amounts to anything has some such exclusive loyalty. We can put it down as a fact that men who are loyal to everything in general are likely to be loyal to nothing in particular.

(b) The other thing that many people are likely to overlook is that these very exclusive loyalties can also be inclusive loyalties. In other words, these loyalties that seem to be so separatist and to exclude a man from a great many other realms of life can be the very loyalties that lead to the lesser loyalties.

For example, the man with an exclusive loyalty to one woman who is his wife, I think, is more likely to respect all women than the man who professes no exclusive loyalty to any woman in particular but a general interest in all women. And isn't it true that a man with one exclusive loyalty to one country for which he is willing to give his life is more likely to respect the rights and privileges of another country and to appreciate its contributions than a man who doesn't care anything about any country? Moreover, isn't it also true that a man who has one supreme, exclusive loyalty to one God, one Lord and Master, is more likely to appreciate, understand, and acknowledge the reflections of that God in other places and other religious cultures than the man who doesn't care anything about any god?

III. There are two things that a Christian can reasonably say about this exclusive claim:

(a) There is something unique about Jesus. Sometimes, I think, we have made claims that were not justified. However, in Jesus, for reasons that we do not pretend to understand, the energies of God were so drawn together and concentrated and focused in one personality that through him God has released powers available to human beings that he has not released in other places or through other people.

(b) Also, we can say that the character of Christ is the ultimate test of all character.

IV. Finally, there the two things that Christians ought to remember:

(a) The first is to leave the future of other people in God's hands.

(b) The second is to avoid trying to impose Christianity upon anybody. We believe that, in Christ Jesus, God opened the doors into life and into possibilities hitherto undreamed of, and we believe that we have every right and responsibility to expose every person on the earth to those riches and wonders. However, we have no right to impose them upon anybody.— Theodore P. Ferris in *Pulpit Preaching*.

July 15. Our Divine Radar

SCRIPTURE: Prov. 16:1–9.

I. Many Christians are increasingly troubled by the seeming irrelevance of God in our modern technological society. Everywhere we turn, human life appears to be organized and manipulated by impersonal regulations and institutions. There seems to be very little in modern society that has not been empirically studied and analyzed. Even the "phenomenon" of God has become an object of empirical scientific study in the departments of religion in modern universities. "God" is thus "reduced" to a set of concepts that can be objectively studied by "neutral" or uncommitted scholars. The direct consequence of all of these developments is that the "relevance" of God to many of the most educated and informed persons of our society is severely undermined.

II. (a) The seeming "irrelevance" of God for many persons in modern society is considerably heightened by their failure to understand the manner in which God interacts with human beings. The explanation of the interaction of God with mankind which many people are taught is naive and simplistic. Many sincere religious people honestly believe, unfortunately, that God interacts with mankind in an arbitrary and observable fashion. The model for such an interaction is often an Exodus account of manna in the desert in which food was miraculously provided. Such a literalistic and miraculous interpretation of God's interaction with mankind, a view that violates all the principles of empirical science, simply renders the very thought of God "irrelevant" to many people.

(b) A more "relevant" and biblical understanding of the interaction of God and mankind can be discovered through an examination of the word *providence*. The English word *providence*, is derived directly from the Latin word *provideo*, which means "to supply," "to furnish," and "to make available." Although there are no words in the biblical text that correspond exactly to *provideo*, the Greek and Hebrew equivalents of this word mean "to see before" or "to see ahead."

These definitions of *provideo* and its equivalents tell us much about the authentic biblical understanding of the action of God in human life. God is thought to interact with mankind in three basic ways. First, God is perceived as possessing the ability to look ahead of human beings and to recognize their impending needs as they themselves cannot do. Second, God is understood to possess the ability to supply the needs that human beings cannot supply for themselves. Finally, God is understood to possess the ability to help human beings to distinguish between those things that they truly need and those things that are merely their selfish and egotistical desires.

III. (a) God can thus be thought to interact in human life like radar and a beacon. God functions like radar because he looks ahead to warn us of the dangerous obstacles that we may encounter during the course of our lives. Second, God functions like a beacon when he guides us toward a

fulfilling and satisfying personal destination amid all of the fruitless and destructive diversions and pastimes that can claim us. In short, the "providence" of God is his continual loving and nurturing interaction with his people.

(b) The "providence" of God, therefore, is not necessarily an observable, empirical phenomenon, but is rather an encounter which usually occurs deep in the human heart and which assures us that God is with us and for us. Thus, in order to be aware of the "providence" of God operating in our lives, we must be willing and able to respond to his presence with trust and openness. We must trust that God guides and informs our lives in our best interests and because of his great love for us. Allowing God into our lives gives each of us of a new life marked by a new direction and a new purpose.—Rodney K. Miller.

July 22. God's People through Christ

TEXT: Deut. 7:7–8.

I. The dangers of the "chosen people" concept are manifest. It adds a dimension of the demonic to the evils of racism.

II. God's people are called to no privileged position. To belong to his people is to be judged by a more rigorous standard. God chose his people for mission.

III. Those who see in the concept of the people of God grounds for lording it over others, or for complacency within themselves, have not even begun to catch the meaning of this concept within the biblical record.

IV. His (Christ's) church becomes the people of God through its corporate identification with him.

V. In Christ, the requirements of God's law are fully met; and because he forgives us, we have a new and joyful freedom to be truly ourselves by giving ourselves up to him who made us, loves us, and can fulfill us.—Merrill R. Abbey, *The Word Interprets Us.*

July 29. God Does Make a Difference in Our Lives

SCRIPTURE: Gen. 39:1–23; Rom. 8:35–39.

The people of the world want to know

exactly what difference God can make in their lives.

I. Our Old Testament text states that God indeed makes a difference. It sees favor coming to those who realize he is with them (v. 1–6). The Bible is a prejudiced book. It presents the belief that those who are yoked to God are better off than those who are not. Some of you may be arguing that what separates folks is pure luck. Maybe some folks aren't lucky —just blessed; not privileged—just trustworthy; not charmed—just committed.

II. But sooner or later something happens, whether or not we are ready. Temptations arise when we least expect them (v. 7). Nothing good lasts forever, and all winning streaks must end. This may not be good news, but it is reality. We live in a therapeutic world, but there's no vaccination against temptation. You may mind your own business, but that still is no guarantee of security.

III. However, the righteous never panic over temptation. They stand firm in following the commands of their God (v. 8–10). Faith enables Christians to see the consequences of their sins. Folks who know a book's conclusion have no further need to read it. Joseph wasn't ignorant. He knew where sin would leave him. Yet his most compelling motive was his duty to obey God.

IV. But even in the presence of such persistence, injustice sometimes still prevails (v. 11–20). Temptation is like a pesky salesman. Let it get a foot in the door and you won't be able to get rid of it without paying a price: This is no equitable world. Who would have thought Jesus could have been treated as he was?

V. Still, what we must realize is that right there in those injustices God is forever in our midst (v. 21–23). Joseph's time in prison is not what we'd expect. But then, nothing ever separates us from the love of God. Now, to realize this isn't easy. It takes faith. And lots of it. But then, that's the way faith works. Put faith to the test and it will grow before your eyes. Not because of anything we do. But because of God. Just knowing his presence is in our midst can make the difference in our lives. —J. Douglas Dortch.

August 5. Live a Day at a Time
Text: Matt. 6:34.

Just for today, let us live as "the better angels of our nature" tell us to live, and as we know we ought to live—aye, as in our hearts we really want to live—and see how it works. One can do anything for one day.

I. Just for today, let us be unafraid of life, unafraid of death, unafraid to be happy, unafraid to enjoy the beautiful.

II. Just for today, let us live this one day only—forgetting yesterday and tomorrow —and not try to solve the whole problem of life at once.

III. Just for today, let us adjust ourselves to what is—our family, our business, our luck—and not try to make the world over to suit us.

IV. Just for today, let us be agreeable, responsive, cheerful, charitable, be our best, dress our best, walk softly, praise people for what they do, not criticize them for what they cannot do, and if we find fault, forgive it and forget it.

V. Just for today, let us not hurry or worry, or fly into a flurry, or hem and haw about a decision, but snap it out, cut the knot, and have done with it.

VI. Just for today, let us get people off our nerves, not get on their nerves, and let us appreciate the noble and gracious things they do.

VII. Just for today, let us ditch all the grudges we have against life because it did not give us what we think we ought to have.

VIII. Just for today, let us study something useful which requires attention, concentration, and let us do a bit of real thinking. Also, let us do a good turn for someone on the sly.

IX. Just for today—every day—let us do at least two things we do not want to do, for exercise, to show that we are still boss. Let us not show anyone that our feelings are hurt—if they are hurt, let us hide it with a smile.

X. Just for today, let us find or make a little time for quiet, to relax, to realize what life is and can be, and to resolve to make more of it. Let us take time to think about God and to get things straight on the inside, untangled and clean.—Joseph Fort Newton.

August 12. Christians in a Non-Christian Society

TEXT: Rom. 12:1–2.

I. (a) The nub of the problem which confronts us as Christians is just this: for all the centuries of the Christian faith, we still have to live our lives, as those who come after us till the stroke of doom will have to do, in a world that is anything *but* Christian. There seemed to be no other chance in the world as Paul knew it.

(b) The least we can do is to begin with the fact he faced. It's familiar enough. Nobody will very seriously dispute the assumption that our society isn't Christian. One of our choicest understatements is that in Christianity we have an ideal religion forever trying to find some footing for itself in an un-ideal situation.

(c) If there is anybody who isn't aware of that difficulty, let him read again the Sermon on the Mount. Why do you suppose we go on talking day in and day out about what we call its lack of realism? Because its text gives us the most exact measure we have of that distance which has yawned between the kingdoms we have built and the Kingdom God wants to build. The moment we catch sight of it, we throw up our hands and exclaim: "But that isn't the way things are!" There was never a truer statement. How can we stomach living among them—just *because they aren't that way?*

(d) In that struggle, we who do the struggling find *ourselves pitted against ourselves!* And that's *every* man's language. It was Paul's. "The good that I would I do not, but the evil that I would not, that I do." He was still talking every man's language when he added: "Who will deliver me from the body of this death?" If there is no answer to that, there is no answer to anything in our distraught world!

II. (a) We've got to understand, as Paul understood, that you can neither run away from a non-Christian society nor lose yourself in it and get anywhere. If you don't try to change things, they foul *themselves* up, and they do it a good deal more promptly than you can! Just like the farm that the atheist left in his will to the devil. The court decided that what the atheist had meant was that the farm be left alone! It would go to the devil by itself! You can't handle life by quarantine methods.

(b) The *easiest* way to get along is not to pull out, but to merge into the background. To be different is to invite trouble. The circle in which you move has its own standards. Everybody else is in line, so why not you? Some wave of emotion sweeps over the community, and the parade forms. Out in front they strike up a tune and we're off! We begin to draw the line almost insensibly further and further back from God, and nearer and nearer the place we want it!

(c) Humanity, to keep human, has to be in revolt somewhere against itself: it can neither let things go nor go with them. I beg you, writes Paul passionately, never allow life to get its hands on you and shape you!

III. What, then, is the answer?

(a) We are set here as men and women to live our lives in trust, and for the very simple reason that we have to live them, whether or not we like it, in a world which isn't ours but God's!

(b) The only real religious question in the world is whether or not God has in you somebody he can use. Putting ourselves at his disposal is what the apostle calls our "reasonable service." Which is to say that no other sort of worship has any significance at all. The creative power of Almighty God can begin to move in again on his world because you are standing there, trying to look a little taller, reach a little farther, and get under some burden that's a little heavier, until you are out of the old pattern at last.

(c) After that, you head yonder for the world, to prove for yourself what is that good, and acceptable, and perfect will of God. It's a will which Paul puts into a single word, over and over again in the last part of this chapter and through the chapters that follow. It's the only really ultimate word and will there is: the love of God. Not ours for him, but his for us. And we are here to give it currency.—Paul E. Scherer in *Pulpit Digest*.

August 19. Whose Slave Are You?

TEXT: Phil. 1:1.

For us, slavery is an ugly word. Yet it is a reality in everyone's life.

I. All people are slaves, but to different masters.

(a) Some are slaves to success.

(b) Others are slaves to pleasure.

(c) Still others are slaves to their own egos.

(d) Paul declares that he is a slave of Jesus Christ.

II. The word Paul uses for *slave* means more than just a servant.

(a) A slave gives absolute obedience to his master.

(b) A slave surrenders his will to the will of his master.

(c) A slave is the absolute possession of his master.

III. Paradoxically, to become a slave of Christ means freedom.

(a) Christ brings freedom from self.

(b) He brings freedom from sin.

(c) He brings freedom from fear.— Mitchell G. Reddish.

August 26. Alcohol: The Enemy of the Family

SCRIPTURE: Prov. 23:29–35.

What is wrong with drinking? Why is it the enemy of the family? And what does the Bible really say about it?

I. *The compulsion.* Consider, first of all, the compulsion for drinking. Why do people drink?

(a) Some people drink because of *social reasons.* In a recent Gallup Poll, drinkers were asked why they drink. Over 50 percent of them said they drank in order to be sociable. Peer pressure and the desire to go along with the crowd—that is a major motivation for drinking.

Some people drink because of *sensual reasons* (v. 31). That is, their motivation is to please their senses, to do what makes them feel good.

II. *The consequences.* Let's take the subject a step further and consider the consequences of drinking. No passage of Scripture more accurately describes the consequences of drinking than our text.

(a) First, the Bible says that drinking causes *impairment.* The one who lingers long over wine is one who has "wounds without cause" and "redness of eyes" (v. 29).

(b) Second, the Bible says that drinking causes *incompetence* (v. 33).

(c) Third, the Bible says that drinking causes *irresponsibility* (v. 34).

(d) Fourth, the Bible says that drinking causes *insensitivity* (v. 35).

(e) Fifth, the Bible says that drinking causes *irritability* (v. 29).

(f) Finally, the Bible says that drinking causes *impoverishment* (v. 32).

III. *The conclusions.* What conclusions can we reach, then, concerning the problem of drinking? What steps should we take in dealing with the matter?

(a) The first step is *consideration.* Before you make the decision to drink or not to drink, carefully consider the matter. To those who belligerently ask, "Why can't I drink?" let me suggest another question, "Why should you drink?"

(b) The second step is *commitment.* Having determined that drinking is not something you need to be involved in, make it a matter of commitment. As a Christian, make the commitment to exclude drinking from your life.

Granted, the Bible does not in any place say, "Thou shalt not drink." But the Bible says that the body is the temple of God and that we are to take care of it. And the Bible says that because of our love for other people, we are not to do anything to cause them harm. And the Bible says that, as Christians, we are not to be controlled by anything other than Jesus Christ himself. Drinking strikes out on all three of those biblical principles—the principle of stewardship, the principle of love, and the principle of control.

Not a strict prohibition, but the desire for physical health, Christian influence, and spiritual sensitivity should be the basis for our commitment at this point.

(c) The third step is *courage.* Having carefully considered the destructiveness of drinking, and having committed ourselves on this matter, be courageous enough in any given situation to act on that commitment, rather than on the basis of our peers, passions, or pressures.— Brian L. Harbour.

September 2. Things Worth Remembering

TEXT: Deut. 2:7 (NIV).

Deuteronomy is a book about "remembering." Moses is "calling to mind" some of the basic ingredients in Israel's walk with God.

I. Moses reminds the children of Israel that they always had God . . . or, his *presence* (*presence* in Hebrew; "face").

(a) They had God even when they thought God was gone from them (Exod. 33:14).

(b) They had God even when they thought they were unworthy (Deut. 4:37; Rom. 5).

II. Moses reminds the children of Israel that they always had God's hand . . . or, his *providence*.

(a) They had food to eat and water to drink.

(b) Throughout Israel's journey, the active hand of God was weaving a story of provision and care (Exod. 15:6).

III. Moses reminds the children of Israel that they always had the ways of God . . . or, his *purpose*. We cannot take the way of God but that it leads to purpose and meaning.

Conclusion: If you will take the presence of God, and the hand of God, and the ways of God, and, then, do the will of God, you will not miss the way home!—C. Neil Strait.

September 9. Our Ministry Together—Things to Get Excited About

Text: Acts 2:1–4, 17ff.

I. *Acts 1:1*. The believers were together for prayer and worship. This is our first step—to meet together to pray and to seek God's corporate will for the Body.

II. *Acts 1:4*. They were *all* filled with the Holy Spirit and miracles began to happen. The community took notice—they were "intoxicated" by the Spirit. This is the magnetic power of the Spirit—things begin to happen!

III. *Acts 2:16ff*. When the Spirit comes, our youth will witness boldly (v. 17). When the Spirit comes, our old people will dream new dreams (v. 17). When the Spirit comes, the poor will feel his presence (v. 18). When the Spirit comes, souls will be saved (v. 21).

We are excited about what God is about to do in our Fall programs. We are ready to go—we have worked hard to be ready—but our programs need to be filled with the Spirit. I challenge you to allow him to infill you. We can float on the surface—or we can plunge deep into the water. I chal-

lenge you to drink deeply from the well that never runs dry.—Charles Worthy.

September 16. On Growing Old Gracefully

Text: John 3:4.

With increased longevity, the process of aging has become a greater concern. It is quite evident that we are going to grow old—the important thing is *to grow old gracefully*.

I. To grow old gracefully, we need, first of all, to accept our age. This is not always easy to do. There are all kinds of formulas for staying young: "You will always stay young if you live honestly, eat slowly, sleep sufficiently, work industriously, worship faithfully, and lie about your age." To make a fetish of youth is not to solve the problem of aging—but to ignore it. In our modern, youth-oriented society, many people make the mistake of thinking you have to be young to enjoy life. Each person needs to develop his or her *own* maturity and enjoy it. Accept your age, whatever it is. Your today can be fun and exciting if you don't spend the time wishing for *another* day.

II. To grow old gracefully, you need to accept your age, but not consider yourself a has-been because of the mounting years. To some people, you need to put the question, "How can you be a has-been when you have never been?" We need to accept our age that we may enjoy every day to its fullest, but we must not give in too easily to some of the physical infirmities that come to us in later years. The body may become infirm and twisted, but the mind and spirit can remain perennially young.

When you get to thinking that you are "over the hill," remember some of the great achievements that other people have made in their later years.

You can grow old gracefully when you realize that life can be lived with zest, fervor, excitement, and productivity at any age.

III. To grow old gracefully, you need to cultivate an interest in life—in all of life. You all know persons who are most interesting because they are just interested in everything.

Do you find yourself yawning at life?

Boredom has little to do with your chronological age; you can be bored at any age if you do not cultivate your curiosity, your interest, your imagination. John Burroughs, the American naturalist, was anything but a bored person. He wrote: "I still find each day too short for all the thoughts I want to think, all the walks I want to take, all the books I want to read, and all the friends I want to see. The longer I live, the more my mind dwells upon the beauty and wonder of the world."

If you stay interested in everything around you, in new ways of life, in new people, in new places and ideas, you'll stay young, no matter what your age.

To grow old gracefully, we need, throughout our years, the curiosity and openness that Nicodemus had in coming to Jesus. "How can a man be born when he is old?" he asked.

Not, how can a man be born when he is old, but, how can a man be born at any age? This is the better question. Jesus answered: "It is of the power of God. The wind blows where it wills; you do not know from whence it comes, or where it goes. So is the renewing Spirit of the living God."

Life is to be a continuing adventure with God. "You are as young as your faith, as old as your doubts; as young as your self-confidence, as old as your fear; as young as your hope, as old as your despair."—John Thompson.

September 23. Church, Home, and School: Partners with God and Each Other (Teacher Appreciation Day)

TEXT: Deut. 11:18ff.

The three great institutions and their responsibilities:

I. *The home.* Every home is a "mini" school, and every home is a "mini" church. Every father is a schoolmaster and a pastor (rabbi) or priest to their children. As James Dobson has said, "If America is to survive, husbands and fathers must take leadership in their homes." The average father spends only 37.7 seconds per day with each child (so says Dr. Dobson).

II. *The school.* The primary job of the school is to teach reading, writing, and arithmetic—not religion. However, the school should teach values—and empathy.

Values such as love, justice, honor, human rights, equality, marriage and family, and property rights.

III. *The church.* The church is to teach religion and spiritual values. We must not depend on the school to teach religion. However, because of this, we must double our efforts to reach young people with the gospel. The church needs to cooperate with the home and the school so that these three together can mould youth into the kind of human beings our world needs.—Charles Worthy.

September 30. God and the Individual

TEXT: Matt. 18:12.

I. God cares for each of us. Christ gave his life to make us sure of it. Every one of us has a place in the heart of God. He drew a picture about which there can be no mistake. A shepherd loses one sheep. He cannot bear the loss and goes out on the search for that one. "Even so," Christ said, "it is not the will of your Father that one of these little ones should perish." And behind his will is his love.

We should remember, however, that love is a personal thing. It binds two persons together. We cannot love a crowd or the human race. We can only love the individuals in it.

II. We need to hold on to this faith today. A good many things threaten to take it from us. When we look up into the heavens, like the psalmist, and see the moon and stars, then say we, "What is man that Thou shouldst be mindful of him?" We feel very small.

(a) It is difficult, when we become a cog in a wheel, to feel that we count for anything vital. The sense of our value is lost.

(b) It is a dangerous thing to lose our sense of being worthwhile to God. The door then opens to all kinds of temptations. Why not let go and do what we please? What does it matter how we live? The spice goes out of life. It becomes just a mean struggle in the dark. If we let go of our sense of individual value, it cuts the very nerve of service and sympathy.

(c) It is a comfort to know that Jesus held fast this sense of individual value. His whole message was dyed with it. Regard for individual value is one of the foundationstones of his teaching, and to remove it would be to destroy the building.

III. Wherever humanity has made progress, it has come by the deepening belief in the value of individuals.

(a) But logic will not convince us. Only love will do that. Only love can give people the feeling that they count.

(b) And the assurance of our personal worth to God does not come through logic. It comes because Christ awakens it. He makes us feel it. There is a strange power in Christ for singling us out. As we listen to his teaching, we know that his message is for us.

(c) Most of all, we feel in the cross the love that came to seek us, the love that reaches out to us. "He loved me and gave himself for me," Paul dared to say. He did not mean that Christ was especially thinking of him when he went to Calvary. But one thing he knew: that love included all. There is a place in that great heart for each.—James Reid in *Making Friends with Life.*

October 7. Taken by Surprise (World Communion Sunday)

TEXT: Mark 14:17–31.

Long familiarity with the celebration of the Holy Communion obscures from us the element of surprise.

I. As they were at the table, eating, Jesus said, "Truly, I say to you, one of you will betray me; one who is eating with me." Mark tells us that, for the moment at least, the security of all of the disciples was shaken. One after another, they began to ask Jesus, "Is it I? Is it I?" In that awkward interval of silence after Jesus had spoken, their self-confidence collapsed. Paul solemnly warns, "Let a man examine himself, and so eat of the bread and drink of the cup; for anyone who eats and drinks without discernment, without recognition of the magnitude of Christ's sacrifice, eats and drinks judgment unto himself."

III. The second occasion for surprise for Jesus' disciples was when he passed them bread and the cup. It is not clear after intensive research whether this loaf and this wine held any religious significance. Uncertainty must remain as to the meaning of Jesus' action for the disciples, but of this

we may be sure: his words took them by surprise. "Take, this is my body"—or again, "This is my blood of the Covenant, which is poured out for many." By the time of the Last Supper, they had hardly begun to understand it. And their reaction on the following day makes this quite clear: not for them was that day *Good* Friday. They knew the kind of spiritual leadership they wanted, the kinds of things they wished the Christ to bring them. They looked to Jesus to fulfill their dreams, to satisfy their personal expectations. And as a result, they were deaf to what he offered them, to what he taught *must* be done for their salvation. They were not willing to hear what he must demand of them for their own good, and as a consequence, they were inadequate for their discipleship. How easy it is for us to hide from ourselves that we often look to Christ to further our personal plans, to bring to pass our dreams. And as a result, how unprepared we are for the unexpected, how unready to accept what he has to offer us.

III. Still another surprise was in store for the disciples. It didn't dawn upon them all at once, but when it overtook them, it was the greatest surprise of their lives. Jesus said to them, "You will all fall away." And sad indeed are the words which are recorded in the Passion narrative: "And they all forsook him and fled." Yet withal, the disciples were held fast in their relationship with the Lord. He came to them, in pity, but more in love than in pity. It was for such persons as themselves that he had died. This is what he had meant when he said, "Take; this is my body, broken for you," knowing all the while that they would desert him and flee. This was the Good News that Jesus had proclaimed all during his life, and at the time of his death: God loves the undeserving. Jesus had died, the truly righteous man, for unrighteous men, that he might bring them to God. But this surprise was not for the disciples alone. The Church of Christ, in its first proclamation, offered forgiveness to those who had killed Jesus Christ, and a share of life in the New Israel to those who had rejected him. God continued to be the great doer of the unexpected.—James L. Price, Jr.

October 14. A New Responsibility

TEXT: 2 Cor. 5:17–19.

I. The "new creation" overcomes our old nature.

(a) Christ living in us results in a new perspective (Gal. 2:20).

(b) We are now seen as being in need of God's saving grace (2 Cor. 5:16).

II. This "new creation" is a gift from God.

(a) God's purpose in Christ is one of reconciliation (2 Cor. 5:19).

(b) Acceptance of God's work results in our forgiveness.

III. The "new creation" leaves us with a specific responsibility.

(a) We are to share in "the ministry of reconciliation."

(b) This means personal witnessing.

IV. Each of us must make a decision.—Alan G. Trent.

October 21. "What, Me Worry?"

TEXT: Matt. 6:25–34.

Modern life is full of worry, but Jesus tells us that we should not worry but trust God to provide for our needs.

I. There are many things that worry cannot do.

(a) Worrying cannot provide us with material possessions.

(b) Worrying cannot lengthen our lives.

(c) Worrying cannot change our situation for the better.

II. There are many things that worrying can do.

(a) Worrying can cause us to place too much value and emphasis on material possessions.

(b) Worrying can affect our health and even shorten our lives.

(c) Worrying can make our situation worse.

III. Instead of worrying, there are several things we should do.

(a) Instead of worrying about material possessions, we should trust God to provide for our needs.

(b) Instead of worrying, we should give our problems to God and therefore relieve ourselves of the pressure.

(c) Instead of worrying, we should pray to God that he might change our situation.—Steven Slusher.

October 28. If We Would Win the Battle

TEXT: Ps. 24.

There is a battle raging in the world today. It is not in the Middle East, as you might expect, or in Southeast Asia, or in some remote part of Africa. This battle is not restricted to any single geographical area, but is being fought throughtout the world. It is a battle for the hearts and lives and allegiances of men and women everywhere. Banded together on one side are the forces of secularism, or indifference, and of evil; on the other side are the forces of the Lord. If we who are on the Lord's side are to win the battle, what must we do?

I. We must acknowledge our leader's authority (vv. 1–2).

(a) All the world is the Lord's dominion, both the earth and all its people.

(b) Any failure to acknowledge this is an act of rebellion.

(c) We must fight within our own hearts and in the world at large for an acknowledgement of God's dominion.

II. We must be fit for the battle (vv. 3–6).

(a) We must be morally upright.

(b) We must search for the truth.

(c) We must avoid falsehood.

(d) We must seek the Lord.

III. We must attack the ancient stronghold (vv. 7–10).

(a) The hearts of men are barred against the Lord's power.

(b) We must begin by opening our own hearts to him.

(c) We must entreat others to let down their defenses and follow him.—James M. King.

November 4. Make the Most of Your Church

SCRIPTURE: Acts 20:18–28.

Let's try to understand more about the church by borrowing the terminology of the airlines. Maybe it will help us to understand what the church might mean in our life.

I. First, let's think of the church in terms of a maintenance base. That's what it should be for us. As I understand it, an airline's maintenance base is the place where machines and tools are available to restore and repair and renew the planes to keep them flying. They also tell me—and I do hope it's the truth—that regularly, after so many hours of flying, a plane is brought in for renewal. They don't wait until something is obviously wrong, or until the plane develops troubles and crashes. Well, the church ought to be such a maintenance base for our soul and spirit.

II. Let's also think of the church as an operations base. For an airline, the operations base is the nerve center for its lines across the state or the nation or around the world. In the operations base, you can see the real purpose of the airline's business at work as it seeks to serve the transportation needs in all the far-flung places. And so the church ought to be such a center through which we serve the Kingdom of Christ and in which we find a reason or a justification for being alive today.

III. If we're to make the most of our church, we should let it be a maintenance base, an operations base, but also an emergency base. For the emergency base is where the airlines take care of the disastrous things that happen and the failure of a plane in a critical time. The words *emergency base* call forth a picture that needs no further explanation. It would be wrong to let the church be only an emergency base, but we must never forget that it can be this for us. There's no need of human life, no problem of the soul, no desperate hour for us which can't be handled better with the church. The church is God's way of reaching and helping us when we need it most of all. It can determine whether or not our faith will be shattered or strengthened by the experience of life.

For almost anyone who has anything to do with the church, it is the place where the sacred ceremonies of life are performed, and it is the place of worship and learning and fellowship. But if this is all the church means, then we're missing so much of the glory and wonder which God intended and for which he paid so high a price. In a sense, we're merely making the best of it, when we should go on to make the most of it. For the church can be for each of us a maintenance base, an operations base, and an emergency base. Perhaps it would help if over the entryway to every church we were to place a sign that read, "This is the church of God, which he hath purchased with his own blood!" —Robert E. Goodrich, Jr., in *Pulpit Preaching*.

November 11. The Secret of Power

SCRIPTURE: Mark 10:35–45.

I. *The request* (Mark 10:35–37). Striving for self-exaltation, and ambitious to obtain prominent places in Christ's Kingdom, James and John asked Christ to pledge himself in advance to give them whatever they might desire, but Christ never issues blank checks. They requested places of preeminence for themselves. They wanted their thrones to rank next to Christ's throne. Their self-seeking led them to bold and impudent self-assertion.

II. *The reply* (Mark 10:38). In his reply to their selfish and ill-advised request, Christ did not expatiate upon their folly and censure them. Realizing that they did not know the significance of the thing for which they were asking, Christ replied: "Ye know not what ye ask." They did not understand the cost of the places of honor they had requested, the suffering that must precede the glory.

III. *The response* (Mark 10:39–40). To Christ's inquiry, "Can ye drink of the cup that I drink of? and be baptized with the baptism that I am baptized with?" James and John quickly responded, "We can," even forgetting to add "by thy help." They revealed their ignorance of themselves when they declared their ability to drink "the cup" of his inward suffering imposed upon him by others. Nevertheless, James became the first martyr of the apostolic group, and John was the last one of them to lay down his life for Christ.

IV. *The resentment* (Mark 10:41). We do not wonder that the other apostles resented the fact that James and John had tried to steal a march on them by asking for the chief places in the Kingdom. Church troubles usually arise from members having a desire to be honored, to rule, or to be pleased instead of a desire to serve and to help.

V. *The reminder* (Mark 10:42–45). Christ was grieved by the jealousy and quarreling of the disciples, so he determined he would nip in the bud their bickering. He reminded them that ambition for power over men belongs to the world. Christ reminded them that greatness comes through dedicated service to others in his name and through his power.—H. C. Chiles.

November 18. You Can't Take It with You (Thanksgiving Sunday)

TEXT: 1 Tim. 6:7.

Jesus said more about money and its related items than he did about anything else, at least in terms of the gospel record. So, what did he say?

I. Jesus did not say that money is evil. Jesus was a man of his time, and he understood the necessity for economics. As a carpenter, he knew the need for payment for his services so he, in turn, could buy food and the necessities for the Nazareth family. While there was little money in the circle of disciples, there was enough so that Judas was appointed the treasurer of the group. And Paul, in quoting the spirit of Jesus, pointed out that money itself is not the root of all evil (as he is often misquoted as saying), but *the love of money* is the root of all evil. Jesus did not deplore the material as such. Jesus knew the limitations of money and taught us to learn them for ourselves. He was aware that one cannot purchase life's important values with dollars alone.

II. (a) Jesus deplored the life that magnifies money and neglects God. Jesus was clear that you cannot magnify money and serve God at the same time. You cannot serve two masters, he said. If you magnify money, then you can figure you will be neglecting God. Yet, how easy we have made it in our society to see money-getting as our main concern! Jesus pointed out the ultimate emptiness of such a life in his parable of the rich fool.

(b) Moreover, Jesus implied more than once that money madness plays into the hands of the personal vices that are the opposite of the gifts of God's Spirit.

(1) Those who magnify money and are successful in its accumulation can hardly avoid a sense of *pride* in their achievements.

(2) Money madness is prompted by *greed* and leads to more greed.

(3) *Selfishness* and *snobbery* are cultivated by money madness. The accumulative instinct is sharpened as people get more and more—however moderate or rich their economic circumstances. Someone likens it to sea water, which is, of course, salty. The more sea water you drink, the thirstier you become!

(4) Jesus said that those for whom money becomes a god find their *vision of God Almighty impaired*.

(c) When we neglect God, we are deprived of personal relationships. We cut ourselves off from moral guidance in the Christian sense. We sacrifice the spiritual support of a religious faith.

III. Jesus concentrated on the treasures of the Spirit. If the secret of happiness lies in personal relationships rather than economic security, then the greatest of all personal relationships has to be our relationship to God. Jesus called these the treasures of heaven which are available to us here on earth in this life and can be taken with us when we go beyond this world. This reflected two things: deeds of kindness and character. For you take only your real self with you when you die. The body and the material wealth you have accumulated remain behind. So, the finer the self, the greater the treasure you are laying up for yourself in heaven. Moths, rust, inflation, depression, and so on—these cannot affect your heavenly treasure as they can your treasure on earth.—Hoover Rupert.

November 25. God's Tools or His Partners?

TEXT: Isa. 45:5.

"I girded thee, though thou hast not known me." This was God's word about Cyrus, king of Persia, by the lips of Isaiah the prophet. Cyrus had just done a remarkable thing. When he captured Babylon, he found the Jewish exiles there, and he set them free to return to Jerusalem and rebuild it. He was the means of their deliverance. No doubt he had ends of his own to serve. He did not in the least understand that in this action he was the instrument of God's purpose for Israel and the world. In serving his own designs, he was really fulfilling God's plan. "I girded thee, though thou hast not known me." This trivial act of his was the one thing that gave his life distinction. The things that really count in our lives may be some little unconsidered acts which we did by the way.

I. The only thing worth living for is to be used by God.

(a) This opens up a very important question: are we to be God's tools or His partners?

(b) It is a very encouraging truth. Even those who seem to be working against the Kingdom can be used by God.

II. But God does not want to use us merely as tools.

(a) God wants us to be his partners. He wants us to cooperate with him, to understand his will, and to use all our minds and our strength in working along with him.

(b) The choice meets us day by day in life. It meets us in our daily work. We can be merely tools there. Or we can see God's purpose to use our labor to get things made and done for his children. We can make work a partnership with God. It is the same with other things. Our life can be the plaything of various currents and desires. But God has a great purpose in the world, and he wants us to share it. That is the message of Christ. He came to call us into a life partnership with God.— James Reid in *The Temple in the Heart*.

December 2. God Incognito

SCRIPTURE: Isa. 53:1–6.

I. God often works incognito. We survey all the signs of human greatness and say to him, "Can you top this?" And he does. But not in the way we expect.

II. He appears in the suffering servant— in weakness and with the disfigurements of a thousand failures. Israel had no power and was the butt of a thousand jokes. Yet God's blessing and use of Israel was out of all proportion to its size and worthiness. Jeremiah and others personified the suffering and style of success of God's servant. Of Jesus Christ it was said, "He came to his own home, and his own people re-

ceived him not." Such, also, is the way of the church, which completes "what is lacking in Christ's afflictions."

III. The world does not know what is good for it and rejects it. Yet God wins through: "with his God's suffering servant's stripes we are healed."—James W. Cox.

December 9. Joyous Assurance

TEXT: Luke 2:10.

How can we celebrate the Advent of God into human life with joyous assurance when we live in a gangsters' world?

Christ comes to free us from the spiritual gangsters who hold us hostage from hope. He restores our sense of human significance. He offers us salvation from our sin. He provides for us fulfillment as persons.

I. The problem of happiness is in the pursuit. How often we hear quoted, or we quote for ourselves, the words about our constitutional right to "life, liberty and the pursuit of happiness." And Christians believe happiness is a gift of God. Why is the joy of happiness so elusive for us?

(a) For one thing, we *look for joy and happiness in the wrong places*. Some there are for whom life is a constant straining for happiness.

(b) Another group of us *identify happiness and joy with the cushioned life*.

(c) Moreover, for some of us happiness is elusive because we *are purely selfish in our search for joy*.

(d) Again, among those who look for happiness in the wrong places are the persons who *bog down in the sad, melancholy gaity of the sensualist*.

(e) Life's greatest tragedy is a joyless life. Yet, the person who makes life a constant mission of seeking joy will seldom find happiness. Happiness is always a by-product of something else.

II. The answer is in Christ.

(a) If the problem of experiencing joy in life is found in our efforts to pursue happiness, the answer to the problem comes to us with the joyous assurance which Advent brings—there is Good News of great joy. It is God's gift to all who will receive it.

(b) Note further that the emphasis of the

New Testament itself is on joy, not sorrow. Consider the Day of Pentecost. Here were Christians who had been confused and sorrowing over the loss of their leader. Then they were behaving in such a fashion in their worship that they were accused of being drunk on new wine! The tragedy of the crucifixion had turned into the triumph of the resurrection. These were happy people who spread their joyous assurance all over the world. They had basis for this in the experience they had with Jesus. He did not take lightly the shadow of the cross. But the joy in his heart was deeper than a superficial pleasant feeling. It was in his final discourse with the disciples that Jesus said, "These things have I spoken to you, that my joy may be in you, and that your joy may be full."

(c) If the answer to our joyous assurance is in Christ, what does he provide for us out of which joy and happiness come?

(1) For one thing, there is *the inner stability of a dynamic faith*. Jesus offers us no outer security against the storms of life.

(2) A second provision God brings us in Christ is *the wholeness of life-giving hope*. Happiness is always a by-product of holiness. Another word for holiness is wholeness. God in Christ provides for us the fulfillment of total self. In no other way can we be fully alive, totally aware, and completely fulfilled.

(3) Finally, God brings us in and through Christ *the redemptive usefulness of vital love*. Jesus lived and taught the fact that the highest form of human happiness is found in self-forgetful devotion to something beyond self. We don't live very long before we discover that self-seeking is self-defeating and never really leads us to joy. What a joy to see stars dance in your child's eyes on Christmas morning. What a thrill to have provided a catch-in-the-voice response of a loved one at her response to the beauty and love of your modest gift! I call that the redemptive usefulness of a vital love. It moves on from the seeker after gifts to the one who becomes the giver of gifts. It saves us from self-seeking and leads us into that happy realm of self-forgetful devotion to someone or something beyond self.—Hoover Rupert.

December 16. Your Move!

TEXT: Isa. 55:6–12.

I once saw a poster upon which was written these words: "If you don't feel as close to God as you used to, guess who moved?" Life today is characterized by separation, alienation, and estrangement. Mankind continually builds walls instead of bridges. But God builds no walls between himself and humanity. Even now he is near and promises to be responsive to our call. We should seek immediately to mend our relationship with him.

I. We should seek the Lord while he is near, because the time is coming when it will be too late (v. 6).

II. We should seek the Lord because he will respond with compassionate understanding (v. 7).

III. We should seek the Lord because his ways are higher and better than ours (vv. 8–9).

IV. We should seek the Lord because his word will accomplish its purpose and bring about reconciliation (vv. 10–11).

The lives of those who have been reconciled to God will be characterized by joy and peace. Their lives will know the joy of a fulfilling relationship, rather than alienation. It is an occasion for all of creation to rejoice (v. 12). God has already done his part. He opened the door through the cross and the empty tomb. Now it is up to us to respond. Don't delay, but "seek the Lord while he may be found."—David Haley.

December 23. Jesus and the Holy Spirit (Advent)

TEXT: Matt. 1:20.

I. Jesus' humanity was due to the Holy Spirit.

II. His whole life was controlled by the Holy Spirit (Matt. 4:1, 12:28, John 3:34; Heb. 9:14).

III. His mission was vindicated and commended by the Holy Spirit (1 Tim. 3:16; John 16:8–11).

IV. His work is continued by the Holy Spirit (John 14:16, 16:13; Acts 16:7; "the Spirit of Christ," Rom. 8:9).—John A. Broadus.

December 30. Assurance of the Journey (Watch Night)

TEXT: Ps. 139:5.

I. *Behind*: All my yesterdays are covered. He saves me from my soiled past.

II. *Before*: All my tomorrows are anticipated. He is undertaking for my future.

III. *Just here*: In this present, he lays his hand upon me.—W. E. Sangster.

SECTION III. Resources for Communion Services

SERMON SUGGESTIONS

Topic: Reflections on Psalm 100

This psalm calls for all people of all lands to praise the Lord God. The image of people coming to God's house for worship plays on our mind in this call to worship. The following are some reflections on the four sections of this psalm.

I. *"Serve the Lord with gladness"* (vv. 1–2). In calling for all people to worship the Lord, we want to emphasize the joy in doing so. Many Christians, unfortunately, have the notion that serving the Lord means dullness or, to use the modern slang, "cramps our style." We should want to serve and praise him, and that with gladness.

II. *"We are his people"* (v. 3). True worship of God involves our recognizing him as Creator and Sustainer of all life. We need to remember that we are not our own and self-sufficient. Rather, we are the "sheep of his pasture." As we affirm ourselves as his, we "know that the Lord is God!"

III. *"Give thanks to him, bless his name!"* (v. 4). We have so much that it is often difficult for us to be thankful as we ought to be. As we come into God's presence in worship, whether privately, with family, or in church, we need to do so with thankful hearts. A very important part of worship is thanking our Lord for all his many benefits and blessings.

IV. *"His steadfast love endures for ever"* (v. 5). God is good, and his goodness is unchangeable. To think of the magnitude of God's love overwhelms me. Even though we fail so often to live up to the standard of Jesus Christ, we encounter again and again a God whose love is "steadfast." Though our faithfulness may slacken, his faithfulness endures "to all generations." The Lord is good!—C. Kenny Cooper.

Topic: A New Commandment

TEXT: John 13:33–35.

These three verses are very suitable for a sermon in Passiontide. They are, of course, closely linked to what goes before them.

I. Verse 30 marks the last and final phase of the Passion of the Son of man. At that moment, in that night, the incarnation of God is accomplished: one last and supreme glorifying is assured him in his very humiliation (v. 31). At the same time, he is glorified in his approaching elevation. The step which Jesus is about to take toward the profoundest depths of suffering already proclaims his transfiguration, his passing into glory.

II. At verse 33, a new element is introduced: "Little children, . . . I say to you . . . ." These words are addressed in the first place to the little group of disciples who are present, but this group already embraces the whole believing world: the entire community of believers exists in these few apostles. Jesus communicates to them and to all his last thoughts. They have to learn and understand that they cannot follow Christ along this path. Neither the world nor the church will be able to imitate what has been given to Christ alone to do. He alone is able to tread the road marked out for

46

him by the Father, and he will follow it for the sake of the world.

III. But at verse 34 there appears, surprisingly, a new commandment. This command does not enjoin imitation: it requires mutual love. Obedience responds to a direct order: "Love one another," for love has become a new nature of those who have seen Jesus. But the world has come to hear the words of Jesus through the mediation of the church and its members, and this will be carried out only "if you have love for one another." We are not told that the whole world will be won by these words of Jesus, but that the behavior of the disciples will show whether they are with Jesus. This behavior is the characteristic mark of the church in the world.—Karl Barth.

Topic: The Meaning of Communion

SCRIPTURE: 1 Cor. 11:24–25; Matt. 26:26.

What do the bread and cup mean? What do these simple and eloquent elements say to the human heart?

I. First, they say to us: remember and take hope. We have heard the words many times. "This do in remembrance of Me." But why do we remember Christ? In order that we may look back to something that happened once? Deeper, it is that by looking back we may look forward again with new understanding. As someone has said, it is looking upon the past as a guiding post rather than a hitching post. We do need to remember Christ so that the words of the hymn can be fulfilled: "Mine eyes have seen the glory of the coming of the Lord." Once we have seen it, we look forward with new hope and with new confidence. Remember and take hope.

II. There is a second word that comes to us at the Lord's Table. Here the word comes: believe and so receive. "And he took bread and blessed it and gave it to his disciples." Here is a time when we are not asked to give, but only to receive.

In some ways to believe in order that we may receive is one of the most difficult things asked of us in the modern world. We are so constantly invited to do this or urged to do that, that we almost instinctively ask what the catch is. But somehow for a few moments we must set aside the modern mood of skepticism, for it will close the doors to receiving the free gift of God.

His giving is more like that of a parent who brings a gift to a child not for some selfish motive, but because of the joy he finds in giving it. That is the remarkable news of the gospel. You do not need to persuade God to bring his greatest gifts into your life. You only need to ask him to help you believe in order that you may receive.

III. Finally, there is the invitation: come and be one. For here we are one people in Christ. Here we must make our peace with each other.

Sometimes people will speak about this, feeling themselves troubled by the invitation which we use here at the Lord's Supper. They are the words of John Hunter, "Ye who do earnestly repent of your sins and are in love and charity with your neighbor." Hearing this, some are troubled. They have tried to be in love and charity with their neighbor and found it exceedingly difficult. Yet, I believe deeply that those who are trying to the fullest extent of their abilities ought to come. "As far as in you lies," said Paul, "be at peace with all men." This is the requirement—to come to this table that we may restore our relationships with our neighbors in one of the deepest of its meanings.—Gene E. Bartlett in *Pulpit Preaching*.

Topic: Newness of Christ

I. *The new message*: John 13:31–35.

The new message that Jesus gave to his disciples now seems old; it has lost the quality of newness. Something of the way in which it appeared to them may be restored for us if we notice what commandments it displaced. Earlier messages had enjoined them to worship God, sacrifice to him, and keep a ritual cleanliness in his sight. Toward their fellowmen they were to observe justice, peace, and the moral codes of their day. Now Jesus came bringing a new message: that they should love one another. It was basic, underlying all other divine messages they had received. Moreover, it was the power to achieve them.

Actually this message of Jesus' is still new, in the sense that it is almost untried by any considerable group, even his disciples. If his message were to be followed today, the world would declare, "This is a new way of life. We have not seen it before." The earliest comment upon the followers of Jesus to be made by their non-Christian neighbors was, "Behold, how they love one another!" That is still our new message—and our most effective one.

II. *The new life*: John 3:1–8.

How often we have heard folks speak of "The Land of Beginning Again." It comes in many wistful variations. Christians know what it means, from their own experience. Indeed, unless we have this experience, we lack the most vital meaning of Christianity. Paul uses this same figure when he says, "If any man be in Christ, he is a new creature" (2 Cor. 5:17). They themselves have been born again and know the joy of a new life. In the new life, they see everything as new; the whole world is viewed in a different light. The writer of Revelation puts it, "Behold, I make all things new" (21:5).

III. *The new character*: Matt. 5:1–16. The Beatitudes have been variously considered: as the laws of life, as the promises of Jesus to those who fulfil their conditions. But they are also a description of the lives and characters of his followers. The description continues as we read through the remaining verses of this section of the Sermon on the Mount. In the new character of their lives, Christians find that happiness in an inward resource. It comes from what they really are, and not from anything that they have. Their meekness is of the quality that inherits the earth; their purity of heart sees God, and their mourning is comforted. It is for them a new character—the character of Christ himself. Such disciples are the salt of the earth and the light of the world. This new character is the result of the new message and the new life. Together they make a new world—the Kingdom of God.—Robert E. Kreighton.

Topic: Reflections on the Lord's Supper
SCRIPTURE: 1 Cor. 11:23–29.

It was not until I put the Lord's Supper into the context of the long tradition of the church's worship and ceased to deal with it as a separate entity that its full efficacy and indispensability broke in upon me. It brought, then, a completeness without which the story of the church's worship would have been for me something defective, truncated, and wanting.

I. When we see the Lord's Supper within the context of the church's worship, we realize that *something complete is given to us*.

We know only too well that preaching by itself falls short because of the very nature of the human words we proclaim. The Word—that is, God's Word—consists not merely of lettered syllables and vocal sounds. God's Word is also action. And we see that action in its fullest expression in a life broken for the sin of man. Therefore, the Word is not completely declared until it is seen in an action. And the nearest to that action we can have on this earth is when we re-present what Jesus did in the Upper Room as he took, offered thanks, broke, and gave, in anticipation of his death.

Here in the sacrament of the Lord's Supper, we see God doing for us what we could not do for ourselves. And the impelling power within it is his love. And this is how it works. It identifies itself with us in Christ, so that by faith we may identify ourselves with him. And in this great transaction, the work of love is most complete. As you and I break the bread and lift the cup, there is indicated fully in this great act the eternal fact that "God so loved the world that he *gave* . . ."

II. When we see the Lord's Supper within the context of the church's worship, we learn that *something complete is given by us*.

In the Lord's Supper, all emphases of Christian worship are present: confession, thanksgiving, proclamation, consecration, and self-dedication.

What is most significant is that all our human faculties are involved as in no other religious act. We hear with our ears the Word declared; we see with our eyes the action; we take into our hands the elements; we taste with our mouths the bread and wine; we assimilate into our bodies the symbols of a broken body and shed blood. Our memory plays upon the words, "we do this"; our imagination recalls the garden, the cross, and the tomb; our conscience examines us by asking, "Have you the right to be here?" Our affections rise in eucharistic praise for what God has done, and our will resolves to live in this faith "till he comes again."

III. When we see the Lord's Supper within the context of the church's worship, *something complete is given through us*. Here and now, if our faith is real, something happens *through* us: God's grace claims us one by one and makes us into his great family—the church—around his table. And he who does this is there as the risen Lord who speaks to the needs of those who come believing.

This table is spread for sinners, but only for those sinful folk who yearn to be made whole. To stay away is to be judged, but to come believing in God's redemptive love is to find peace and joy in the Holy Ghost.
—Donald Macleod in *Pulpit Digest*.

Meditation: An Ever-Lengthening Table (World Communion Sunday)

The day begins in a Christian church in the Fiji Islands, an echo or two west of the International Date Line, and continues for twenty-four hours until all lands and people are embraced in a light and love that is not of this world.

In affirmation and in experience, the day is unlike any other in the calendar year. As the sun rises in each succeeding time zone, the table is lengthened until at last the table encircles the globe.

There is no table of equal length and no table fellowship of equal joy as the table of the Lord to which Christians are invited on World Communion Sunday.

Disciples of Christ sit together to affirm in prayer and praise and thanksgiving that which most matters in worldwide Christendom—a common devotion and loyalty to Jesus Christ.

At his table, all of those things that seemed to matter most now seem to matter least. For at his table of unity, barriers fall and obstacles are obliterated. There is one tongue that speaks only words of love, one loaf that satiates our common spiritual hunger, one cup that assuages a thirst all human beings experience, and "one Lord, one faith, one baptism" (Eph. 4:5).

At his table, race matters little, if at all. God "hath made of one blood all nations of men for to dwell on all the face of the earth" (Acts 17:26). Creeds matter little, if at all. One article of faith suffices: "I believe that Jesus Christ is the Son of God" (Acts 8:37). This is the mighty stream to which all tributaries add their waters. And heritage and denominational history mellow, if only for one day, as we remember that "by one Spirit we are all baptized into one body" (1 Cor. 12:13).

All of which is not to suggest that individual races may not contribute wholesomely and uniquely to the fellowship of nations, or that creeds are not essential to the clarification and preservation of the faith, or that the various churches do not contribute to the necessities and anticipations of individual peoples. But rather to suggest that transcending our differences, like the sun spanning the heavens, is the Son of God to whom we offer supreme devotion. He is the glue, as someone has said, that gives cohesiveness to world Christianity despite or in spite of our insipid or salubrious divergencies.

And World Communion Sunday once each year reminds Christians of their essential unity in Christ. One billion Christians worldwide sitting at one table as equals and as brothers and sisters. It's a mind-boggling idea, as the kids say, and should be profoundly soul-stirring. Here is a fellowship of compassion and sacrifice that could once again turn the world upside down. If we would.

Holy Communion has had a universal orientation since that hallowed night on the eve of his crucifixion when Jesus in that Upper Room broke bread for his disciples and instructed them to do for others what he had done for them. Ad infinitum!

And they did. The earliest gatherings of Christians were for the breaking of bread. By the close of the New Testament period, bread was broken in Christ's name at every crossroads of the Mediterranean world. Chairs were being added continually to the ever-lengthening table of the Lord.

Back in the mid-thirties, when the world was engulfed in the Great Depression, and hearts and minds were clouded with despondency and a sense of hopelessness, a small group of American church leaders initiated the idea of a day when Christians might symbolically express their common concern and commitment at the Lord's table, which always had been the central expression of Christian faith and action.

By 1940, the National Council of Churches called upon all constituent bodies to celebrate world communion on the first Sunday in October. Soon thereafter the World Council of Churches joined in the table invitation. Today, forty years after its inception, the day is universally observed.

In a generation when technology makes us more aware of what is going on at trouble spots half a world away than down the road a stretch from our own homes and when our inventive genius has given us the wherewithal to destroy all human life, it is well to be reminded that great and powerful forces are struggling in behalf of peace and harmony, love and goodwill.

World communion invites us, in the words of the prayer book, "to draw near in faith" and assures us a place at this long table not because of our worthiness, but because we have been accepted by Christ and our fellow Christians.—Charles L. Wallis in *Pulpit Digest*.

A COMMUNION SERVICE

This simple and most moving memorial of our Lord transports us in a moment across nineteen centuries and places us in the Upper Room where the Master with his disciples observed the Passover Feast of his nation and transformed it into the everlasting memorial of his love for his people and for mankind. This is what it signifies. This bread and this wine are symbols to us of the presence with us now, in the world's soul, of the glorious Soul of our Lord, revealer of our God, judge of the world, both as educator and divine friend, and we are holding this feast today at the Judgment Seat of Christ. Will you think of it as the happiest place in the world?

THE BREAD.   Our Lord took the bread, set it apart, and blessed it. Let us ask for his blessing upon this bread. Infinite Father, the blessing we ask, one brief prayer, is that thou wilt make us aware, through sense and circumstances and history, that our souls are in communion with thy Soul, and that our Lord is still the prophet, the judge, and friend of the world, and that we are sitting at that calm, benign, and divinely beautiful tribunal. And we offer our prayer in his name. Amen.

THE CUP.   Our Lord took the cup and blessed it. Let us ask for his blessing while we give our thanks now.

Infinite Father, accept our thanksgiving and our praise, that we may know thee and love thee and so live in thy love and compassion as to have perfect peace as to the meaning of our life and the destiny of our world. Let nothing come between us and thee, O thou Perfect Father and Lover of men, let nothing come between us and thee. May these and all other symbols bring to us, when we deserve it, thy approval, that we may go on and do better; and when they bring thy rebuke, help us to remember that it is that we may cease to do wrong, cease to blunder, cease to injure our life, that we may build again and build better and enter into thy joy. And may thy loving approval and thy loving rebuke be the wings that shall carry us all the way to the end of our flight through time and shall bring us home at last to the courts of our God. And we offer our prayer in our Lord's name. Amen.— George A. Gordon.

ILLUSTRATIONS

FATHER FORGIVE THEM.   G. A. Johnston Ross told of an incident that occurred years ago during the celebration of the Lord's Supper in a little mission church in New Zealand. A line of worshippers had just knelt at the altar rail when suddenly from among them, a young native arose and returned to his pew. Some minutes later, however, he returned to his place at the rail. Afterward, a friend inquired why he had done this. He replied: "When I went forward and knelt, I found myself side by side with a man who some years ago had slain my father and whom I had vowed to kill. I felt I could not partake with him, so I returned to my pew. But as I sat there, my mind went back to a picture of the Upper Room, with its table set, and I heard a voice saying, 'By this shall all men know that ye are my disciples, if ye have love one to another.' And then I saw a cross with a man nailed upon it and heard the same voice saying, 'Father, forgive them for they know not what they do.' It was then I arose and returned to the altar rail."—Donald Macleod in *Pulpit Digest*.

THE SECOND ADVENT.   It is impossible to preach the First Advent and its consequences without reference to the Second Advent. In fact, the First Advent insists upon a Second Advent because clearly God has not yet finished the job. Without the Second Advent, we have to ask ourselves why Jesus bothered coming the first time. If he is not coming again, he has only set us up for a false hope, which is more cruel than no hope at all. But Jesus' Second Advent is God's victory over the death of the universe, just as the resurrection of Jesus is God's victory over our personal death.—Robert M. Herhold.

LIKE JESUS ON THE CROSS.   The cup had been poured for Communion. I stood behind the Lord's table with my arms outstretched to pray the Prayer of Thanksgiving. "Look, Mommie," one of our younger members exclaimed, "He's trying to look like Jesus on the cross."

It's not a bad thing to say about a Christian.—William H. Willimon.

GOD'S NEARNESS.   "Christ nailed to the cross" represents for Christians a universe of meaning in which God is at the side of the weak and the suffering. He experiences aloneness and isolation. He is present not "out there" beyond planets and clouds, but in the need of the beggar or brother, in the attempt to make sense of random experiences, in the reaching hand of love, and in "Christ nailed to the cross."—Martin E. Marty.

RESOURCES.   For long, scientists could not understand how it is that even in the longest droughts of tropical lands, when all the green things are burned up and the watercourses are dry and dusty, the ants manage to keep their huge heaps always moist with that wet steamy heat they love. And only lately was it discovered, in one heap carefully investigated, that they had sunk a cunningly constructed shaft, no less than sixty-five feet long, down to a perennial spring that no drought ever touches and that at night the whole busy little population was detailed to hurry down and up again, time after time, bearing the precious water to keep alive their little fields of fungus crops and to spread abroad the wetness which they need for health.—Arthur John Gossip.

WHO IS WORTHY?   When a man unites with the church, he should not come saying, "I am so holy that I think I must go in among the saints," but "O brethren, I find I am so weak and wicked that I cannot stand alone; so, if you can help me, open the door and let me enter."—Henry Ward Beecher.

CROSS AND RESURRECTION.   We must never forget this fact, that there is no instance in these New Testament records of Jesus referring to his cross, but that at the same time he also referred to his resurrection. The Son of man must go up to Jerusalem, and suffer, and be killed, and the third day rise again. That is not the language of a man who says: I am beaten by circumstances; but I must be loyal to a principle; I must go on, though I die. No! It was the calm, strong, amazing language of one who saw death interpreted by resurrection; of one who must suffer and die and be raised again. In the mystic language of our Lord, even though as yet we have not come to the full realization of it, we begin to hear the thunder of his power, and find the Kingdom coming in power.— G. Campbell Morgan.

COMMUNION.   A girl fled Armenia, ahead of the advancing Turkish army, never to return to her homeland again. Yet, until her death, she kept the key to that house in her pocket as a kind of symbol of home and family.

Communion is something like that. A constant reminder of our home, a home we have never seen and cannot see till life is over. But the Lord's Supper is a visible token, ever present as a symbol and reminder.—C. Neil Strait.

ONENESS IN CHRIST. In a part of China invaded in the 1940s, a Chinese pastor placed a sign upon his humble hamlet church, "Jesus' House." From the Japanese forces came several soldiers and officers to pray with him, to express, despite barriers of language partly bridged by a common alphabet, their oneness with him in Christ, and to do their utmost to protect him and his little congregation from the ravages of war. It was a small, a pathetically small, symbol of that new community which Christ builds.—Henry Sloane Coffin.

CHRIST'S PRESENCE AND OUR SIN. The story is told concerning those wild days of the French Revolution, that once, when the maddened crowd burst into one of the great picture galleries of Paris, intent upon devilry, destruction, and death, they paused irresolute on the threshold. Those behind pushed the leaders on, but first one and then another tugged the cap from off his head, and the wild cries died away to silence as they gazed. There upon the wall was a great painting of Christ. Looking down upon them were the quiet, majestic, pleading eyes of the Saviour. To their knees they went, one after another. Then slowly, uncertainly, some went forward, unhooked the picture from its place, and carefully carried it from the room. The spell was over. The silence was broken. The murmur began, increasing to a roar as the harsh, shrill cries for death and destruction broke forth once more, and the crowd again surged on to their work of devilry, unhindered now by the silent reproach of eyes they could not bear to face. —John Trevor Davies.

STEADFAST LOVE. When I was growing up, I was quite certain that the hymn the disciples and Jesus sang on the night when he instituted the Lord's Supper and then went out to Gethsemane had to be, "Blest be the Tie." Of course, we know that's not accurate, because it's a modern hymn by comparison to what they sang that night. The scholars tell us what Jesus and his disciples sang that night. Psalm 136 is called the great Hallel. The leader, rabbi —Jesus—would have sung or chanted the first half of each verse, and then the disciples gathered at the Passover observances would have recited the second half. You may wonder how they memorized all that much. The second half was the same for all thirty-six verses. It was: "*For his steadfast love endures forever.*"—Alton H. McEachern.

SECTION IV. Resources for Funeral Services

SERMON SUGGESTIONS

Topic: The Life to Come
SCRIPTURE: 1 Cor. 13:9–13.

I. Heaven is homecoming. To be absent from the body is to be at home with the Lord! It is, in the language of the Old Testament, "to be gathered to the fathers." Originally, this meant to be buried in the cave with the ancestors. But with the developing revelation of the Old Testament, and, especially, in the light of the resurrection of Christ, it meant to be at home with the Lord.

Will we know each other on that glad morning? Our text says, "Now I know in part; but then shall I know even as also I am known." Our knowledge will be *more* complete, not *less* complete. We shall know as we are known. We won't have to go around like people at a convention with name tags on our lapels. It will be a glorious meeting with those we have known and loved, and with those we have only known by name.

But in the deepest sense, it will be a homecoming to the One whom having not seen I love. I visualize a corridor to the throne room where, coming, I will cast myself at his feet and say, "Thank you, Lord Jesus, for saving my soul—for giving to me, thy great salvation—so full and free." To see him, face to face, is heaven indeed!

II. Heaven is fulfillment. Every high and holy spiritual goal in this life is pointing toward heaven. All spiritual values will be brought to completion there. We were created for fellowship with God—but we do not yet know what fellowship really is, until it is fulfilled in his presence.

And heaven is much more: it is described in the Bible again and again as RENEWAL, as the NEW CREATION. Have you become aware of the tragic toll that the years take, upon your life and vitality? The treasures here will fade away; the life here is dying; achievements here are always partial—this world is not our home; we are pilgrims passing through! But heaven is the home for which we were made—it is the new creation. This old, broken, and dying body will be exchanged for a glorious resurrection body, like unto the body of our Lord! These tears of sorrow will be wiped away! Behold, he makes *all things new!* Earth has no sorrow that heaven cannot heal.

But lurking in the minds of some is that nagging question: how can it be heaven, if there is someone *missing?* How can there be joy, if there is the "vacant chair"? We will see it as Jesus sees it: he has done all that the love of God can do to reach the last sinner—but he will not force one soul to come into his family.

III. Who will be there? This is the most important question of all. The Bible teaches that only those whose names are written in the Lamb's book of life will be there—only those who have washed their robes and made them white in the blood of the Lamb. What does this mean? It means that those who have been given the new life in Christ, who have been born again by the Holy Spirit's power, will be there. Heaven is not composed of all the churchmembers, or all the so-called Christian nations, or a certain favored race—heaven is the fellowship of those who have been redeemed by faith in Christ and obedience to his saving word. He will gather his elect from the four corners of the earth, and the mark which distinguishes them is the banner of the great apostle: "I am crucified with Christ; nevertheless I live; yet, not I, but Christ liveth in me" (Gal. 2:20).—Wayne E. Ward.

Topic: When Death Comes

SCRIPTURE: 2 Cor. 4:16–5:10 (RSV).

Death is an inevitable experience in life, and you cannot escape it. As life on this earth has a beginning, so it has an ending. "Birth and death are the parentheses that bracket the experience of every person."

Death is not, of course, a topic we like to discuss. On the other hand, we must not ignore death, for it is an experience that will come to each of us. And we all have had those moments in our lives when we have asked ourselves the question, "What happens when death comes?" Paul gives us some answers to that question in our text.

I. First, when death comes, we will be given a reward. This is the truth Paul proclaims in 2 Cor. 4:17–18.

Paul refers to this reward in verse 17 as "an eternal weight of glory far beyond our comprehension." In other passages, the reward is spoken of in other terms (see Rom. 8:18; James 1:12; 2 Tim. 4:3).

What will this reward be like? Whether it is something God gives to us, or simply the experience of heaven itself, Paul says that we will receive this reward after death, and that the reward God has prepared for us will be something so much greater than anything we have ever experienced here on this earth that there is no comparison.

II. Second, when death comes, there will be release. This is the truth he proclaims in 2 Cor. 5:1–4. Paul uses two images to express this truth.

In verse 1, he uses the imagery of a heavenly building. As a tentmaker, Paul's comparison of his body to a tent or a tabernacle was a natural one. When the tent of our physical body is taken down, Paul says, God has a far superior building already prepared for us. The superiority of this future building is evident in the contrast.

In verse 2, Paul speaks of a heavenly garment. At death, we are stripped of the rudiments of this life like stripping off dirty clothes to step into the shower. Then, we are given a new garment to put on.

What is Paul saying? Does he despise the human body? He knew that, at death, the heavenly body prepared for him would have no such limitations.

When death comes, we will be given a new body which will be unlimited, free of pain, and void of suffering.

III. Third, when death comes, there will be relationship. That is the truth Paul proclaims in 2 Cor. 5:5–8.

"While we are at home in the body we are absent from the Lord," while "to be absent from the body" is "to be at home with the Lord."

Have you ever wondered what makes hell, hell? And what makes heaven, heaven?

A prospect of eternal isolation is more fearful than a thousand burning hells. What makes hell, hell, is that it is a place where we will be eternally separated from the One by whom and for whom we were made. What makes hell, hell, is that it is a place where we will eternally be strangers, pilgrims in a foreign land.

What makes heaven, heaven, is that it is a place where we will enjoy eternal fellowship with our heavenly Father. What makes heaven, heaven, is that it is a place where we will eternally be at home.—Brian L. Harbour.

Meditation: The Dead and the Living

The dead and the living are not names of two classes which exclude each other. Much rather, there are none who are dead. The dead are the living who have died. Whilst they were dying, they lived, and after they were dead, they lived more fully. All live unto God. God is not the God of the dead, but of the living. Oh, how solemnly sometimes that thought comes up before us, that all those past generations which have stormed across this earth of ours, and then have fallen into still forgetfulness, live yet. Somewhere, at this very instant, they now verily are. We say they were—they have been. There are no have-been's. Life is life forever. To be is eternal being. Every man that has died is at this instant in the full possession of his facul-ties, in the most intense exercise of all his capacities, standing somewhere in God's great universe, ringed with the sense of God's presence, and feeling in every fiber of his being that life which comes after death is not less real but more real, not less great but more great, not less full and intense, but more full and intense than the mingled life which, lived here on earth, was a center of life surrounded with a crust and circumference of mortality. The dead are the living. They lived whilst they died, and after they die, they live on forever.—Alexander MacLaren.

Meditation: The Witness of a Life

What we do in life is not so important as what we are. However, the things that we do are quite often a clue to what we are.

Actually, what we are may preach a greater sermon than the most eloquent message we might compose. What we are may result in the accomplishment of more magnificent miracles than the ingenuity of our minds and the skill of our hands could devise.

The witness our life bears to certain fun-damental truths is most important.

I. Our life may be a witness to the divine resources. As we observe the life and strenuous activities of the apostle Paul, we marvel that one man could do so much under such adverse circumstances. He took no credit to himself. Rather he boasted in another. He declared: "I am what I am by the grace of God." When Paul was imprisoned—hounded by ene-mies and beyond the help of friends—he wrote joyously to a little church in Phi-lippi: "I can do all things through Christ who strengtheneth me. I have power to meet any emergency in life through him who gives me power."

Some of us have passed through serious illnesses, have survived the perils of battle, and have escaped virtually unharmed from many accidents. We can only attribute our survival to the mysterious workings of the providence of God. Nevertheless, all of us

know devout souls who pray and yet die of their illnesses, who read the Bible and be-lieve its promises and yet fall on the batt-lefield, who trust themselves into the hands of God and yet die in accidents. What shall we say then? Has God de-serted? No, "living or dying, God saves his own child."

II. Our lives also bear witness to human possibilities through faith. We can look at our lives pessimistically and swear that there is little that we can do: the times are not right; we do not have certain skills; our bodies are not strong enough for heavy responsibilities; we do not have enough prestige or pull; and on and on we might go. But when faith comes into play and we begin to see ourselves as God sees us and as God can make us to be, the picture changes. The time is always right for someone who is inspired by God. God can develop in us skills that we scarcely dreamed we had. God makes our strength adequate to the responsibility, and God tells us it is not by might or by power, but by his Spirit.

Lives of great men all remind us
  We can make our lives sublime,
And, departing, leave behind us
  Footprints on the sands of time.
Footprints, that perhaps another,
  Sailing o'er life's solemn main,
A forlorn and shipwrecked brother,
  Seeing, shall take heart again.
—Longfellow

III. Moreover, our lives may bear wit-ness to the goodness of life itself. The idea of some people that this life has no real value and that all real value is to be found in the life to come is not the biblical under-standing of life. According to both the Old and New Testaments, this life itself, though nature is "red in tooth and claw," has many sublime values, and, if lived in the purpose and will of God, is essentially good. William Lyon Phelps, the renowned professor of English literature at Yale Uni-versity, lived enthusiastically. During his lifetime, he knew great sorrows and at times felt the black cloud of depression settle upon him. Yet he said, "I live every day as if it were the first day I had ever seen and the last day I would ever see."

God gives us at best a few years on this earth. They are days in which we have the privilege of coming to know him in a personal relationship, so that we may explore what life was intended to be on his earth and live it to its highest usefulness and distill from the gift of each day its sweetness and satisfactions in our homes, at work, and among our friends. If we understand life in that way, we may discover life abundant—not only a satisfaction to ourselves, but as well a benediction to those about us.—James W. Cox.

Meditation: Basic Living

It is not given to many to achieve immortality through newspaper headlines or through dramatic chapters in the history books. But to many is given the opportunity to know life in its basic dimensions. Their lives are unspectacular, yet they are solid. Their deeds are not flamboyant, yet they are real. Their words are not scintillating, nevertheless they are true.

Actually, most of the best work in the world gets done almost unheralded. Some people live quietly but deeply. They love humanity profoundly, and then love finds its expression in love for individuals.

Too often we measure life by the unusual and extraordinary. Life's truest dimensions ought to be measured by what we can see every day, what is open to every one of us every moment.

I. One of the elements of basic living is the significance of the commonplace.

Frequently the comment is made by a visitor in a village or in the open country: "What do you do around here for fun?" How prosaic seems the making of beds, the cooking of meals, the sweeping of floors, the plowing of fields, and the making of gardens. That is getting close to real living, and yet millions of people miss it.

Dr. James S. Stewart, the noted minister of the Church of Scotland and Chaplain to the Queen, said that once when he was in a home in Scotland, he walked back to the kitchen and over the kitchen sink, printed on a card, he saw these words: "Divine worship will be held here three times daily."

Brother Lawrence, a member of the Carmelite religious order several centuries ago, showed us how it is possible to do everything for the love of God, even to the picking up of a straw from the floor.

When one sees the significance of the commonplace, this humdrum world can be made a veritable garden of God.

II. Another element of basic living is the importance of parenthood.

"A good wife, who can find?" is the question asked in the Book of Proverbs. "She is far more precious than jewels" (31:10 [RSV]).

Again: "She looketh well to the ways of her household, and eateth not the bread of idleness. Her children arise up and call her blessed; her husband also, and he praiseth her" (31:27–28).

The human race began with a home. Our Savior appeared on earth in a home. The home is the first church many noble Christians have known.

The home may be as simple as the primeval beauty of the Garden of Eden, as humble as the stable in which the Christ was born, and as unsophisticated as a dedicated hearth where the Bible is read and prayers are made. Nonetheless, it is the ark of salvation, the cradle of civilization, and the seminary of righteousness.

Especially one is important who has reared children in the nurture and admonition of the Lord.

Likewise, those are also important who, whether by choice or necessity have no home of their own, yet love little children and seek to guide and strengthen their walk in the ways of God and righteousness.

III. A third element of basic living is the sacrament of friendship.

As students of Christian history, we know something of the power of the spoken word. The strident tones of the voice of John the Baptist will linger in his prophetic words for centuries to come. The incisive message of Jesus and his apostles will linger in their kerygmatic words, though heaven and earth should pass away. The golden words of Chrysostom, the thunderous words of Savonarola, the courageous words of Luther, the holy words of Wesley, and the convicting words of Spurgeon have led people by the hundreds and tens of thousands to love, trust, and serve Jesus Christ.

But there are people who, though they have never preached a sermon, have by the sheer power of their friendship guided people to the Savior of the world.—James W. Cox.

ILLUSTRATIONS

GREEN PASTURES.   A chaplain in World War II related a telling incident that occurred on Iwo Jima. When one of the first waves hit the beaches, a lad was hit and fatally hurt. Under a withering fire, the chaplain elbowed his way along the sand to the side of the injured boy. "Son," he asked, "is there anything I can do?" And the boy in agony gasped, "Say green pastures, say green pastures." And then it came to the chaplain what the boy wanted, and he began, "The Lord is my shepherd: I shall not want. He maketh me to lie down in green pastures: he leadeth me beside the still waters. He restoreth my soul." And the boy's agony gave way to peace and his end was quiet.—Gene E. Bartlett.

PARSON'S HEAVEN.   There is no need to be worried by facetious people who try to make the Christian hope of "Heaven" ridiculous by saying they don't want "to spend eternity playing harps." The answer to such people is that if they cannot understand books written for grown-ups, they should not talk about them. All the scriptural imagery—of harps, crowns, gold, and so forth—is, of course, merely a symbolical attempt to express the inexpressible. Musical instruments are mentioned because for many people (though not all) music is the thing known in the present life which most strongly suggests ecstasy and infinity. Crowns are mentioned to suggest the fact that those who are united with God in eternity share his splendor and power and joy. Gold is mentioned to suggest the timelessness of heaven (since gold does not rust) and the preciousness of it. People who take these symbols literally might as well think that when Christ told us to be like doves, he meant that we were to lay eggs!—C. S. Lewis.

THE MANY ROOMS.   Before I was old enough to go to school, I delighted in visiting the elderly couple in the big old house across the road. Downstairs were large spacious rooms that were fun to explore. I do not remember the furnishings of these rooms, but I still recall the graciousness of the small gray-haired lady whose cookie jar seemed to be always full.

Sometimes I was allowed to go up the broad stairs, through a large bedroom, and into a world of mystery and beauty— the studio of the artist daughter. The many sizes of brushes, the tubes of paint, and what the artist did with them were endlessly fascinating.

I recapture that long-ago feeling with happiness and expectancy as I consider the many rooms that Jesus told us are in his Father's house.—Mary Louise Williams, *Sorrow Speaks*.

GOD SEES.   The sum of it is from a story told in the terrible days of the blitz in London. It is said that a father, holding his small son by the hand, ran from a building which had been struck by a bomb. In the yard was a shell hole, and seeking shelter, the father jumped in, then held up his arms for his son to follow. But the small boy, hearing his father's urging him to jump, replied, "I can't see you." The father, however, could see his son outlined against the night sky, standing hesitant and anxious, and replied, "But I can see you. Jump!" So the faith that enables us to confront death with dignity is not that we can see, but that we are seen; not what we know, but that we are known; not that death denies life, nor life denies death, but that both are part of God's gift. Neither can separate us from his love. And that faith *does* give dimension and dignity to life.—Gene E. Bartlett.

WHO IS AFRAID?   Not many years ago, a sixteen-year-old girl lay dying in a Phoenix hospital. A dear friend was a Carmelite priest. The last time he saw her, he must have looked dreadfully upset. As he tells it, "She looked up into my worried and harried face and said: 'Don't be afraid.' " Such, at its most profound, is the Christian theology of death: "Don't be afraid." It is most profound when a child can say to an adult, a girl to a priest, when it is the dying who can say to the living: "Don't be afraid."—Walter J. Burghardt.

SECTION V Resources for Lenten and Easter Preaching

SERMON SUGGESTIONS

Topic: Can This Be the Christ?
SCRIPTURE: John 4.

"Can this be the Christ?" So asks a Samaritan woman after confronting a stranger in the heat of the day at Jacob's well. "Can this be the Christ?" she asks as she reviews an intense and transforming experience with one who at the beginning of their conversation she addresses as antagonist and then progressively as teacher, then as prophet, then, finally, as Messiah, the one exposing the meaning and destiny of her life. For John, that woman's question, and her experience, coincides with our own. He illuminates in this confrontation the ultimate unity of humankind resting in one whom we may finally call Christ.

I. Can this be the Christ? Whom do we see at the well? We see, first of all, the Galilean and the Samaritan. From John's point of view, they represent not simply individuals, but ethnic siblings—Semites, both of them—for whom turf, tradition, and culture overlap, but for whom familiarity over years has bred a virulent mutual contempt. And what happens in this meeting? We see our Galilean operate as if no breach exists. We see our Galilean, Jesus, whom John understands to represent "embracing community." We see the Galilean treat the Samaritan neither with contempt nor with condescension, but with full recognition of deep and full humanity. "May I have a drink?" he asks, with neither hostility nor superior bearing—ethnic and national lines treated as irrelevant!

Can you imagine what difference we might see if the uniting reality we see at Jacob's well were operative in our churches, in our cities? We live still with our equivalent of the Galilean-Samaritan division; we see it in struggles over our schools, we witness it in housing patterns, in our club memberships. At the Well of Jacob, we see Christ, evident as dynamic love embracing differing nations, drawing us into solidarity and communion.

II. But we see more. We see a Galilean *man* and a Samaritan *woman*. Watch carefully, for here again John interprets the Christ as the source of inclusive community. Remember? The disciples come to the well, they discover Jesus talking to a woman, they marvel at this exchange, and challenge neither the woman with the question, "What do you wish?" nor Jesus with their curiosity and surprise: "What do you want with her?" Do you see what John is doing? Here, again, he dissolves contempt and inferiority. A woman in the surrounding culture counts for nothing. But John and the community from which he writes confess: man and woman in the domain of the inclusive Christ exist in their full humanity with and for one another. Traditions, cultures, social structures, ideologies providing deference to anyone because of gender collapse where the inclusiveness we call Christ permeates the life of the community.

III. And yes, can this be the Christ who, in John's ancient imagery, takes the religious tradition of the Jew, whose religious home lies in Jerusalem, and the Samaritan, whose religious home sits on the side of Mount Gerazim? Can this be the Christ who points beyond the parochialism, the orthodoxy of both Mount Gerazim and Jerusalem, toward a new loyalty described as worship in "spirit and truth"?

Here our evangelist abolishes religion. He takes our *isms*, our religious rites, our institutions, our sacred terminology, our theologies and pious words, and he walks right through them. And he exempts none of us. John sees, in the literal commitment of Jews to Jerusalem and of Samaritans to Mount Gerazim, the figurative commitments all of us make to certain places or special buildings that separate us from one another. John sees our routine religious practice as diversion from the investment the loving Christ invites us to make in a suffering, divided, splintered humanity. We're free at last, announces the evangelist from those sectarian, parochial, and orthodox identities we seek in our insecurity—liberated finally to be instruments of justice, peace, and joy bound to recreative, inclusive love we call Christ.
—James W. Crawford.

Topic: When You Look at the Cross
TEXT: Luke 23:25.

Today we celebrate Palm Sunday when Jesus entered Jerusalem amid the hosannas and the palm branches. Yet, the instant of triumph (for it was to be only an instant) he enjoyed this day proved to be a false dawn and was rapidly swallowed up by an even blacker night. On Palm Sunday, we sing our hosannas, but we need also be aware of that shadow of the cross which falls athwart Jesus' way.

So many of us are like the people at Calvary that day. Luke says simply of them, "The people stood looking on." They were spectators at the cross. And most of them failed to look long enough at the cross to see how central it was to become in God's plan for the redemption of humankind.

I. *Humanity's inhumanity.* How easy it is to assume a criminal nature among the persons who sent Christ to the cross! And how simple to conclude that the crucifixion came once and for all long ago on Calvary. Yet, is it not true that Christ is on the cross whenever good persons join in the less-than-good attitudes and activities which put him there in the first place?

(a) When you look at the cross, you see there *the blindness of religious leaders* who cannot or will not see a larger truth. The religious opponents of Jesus were the leaders of his religious faith. And what of our blindness today? Does it not assume we have cornered the truth when we assume that war is an option for those who would make peace, that beliefs are relatively unimportant so long as we are sincere, that morals are relative and need to be adapted to our needs and interests?

(b) *The selfishness of the business community* who cared more for profit than for truth and purity in religion helped put Christ on the cross. His dramatic confrontation with the money-changers in the temple courtyard aroused the enmity of the temple business leaders. He is interfering with the Lord's work," they said. What they meant was that he was threatening their own incomes (cf. Mark 11:15–18). Are there not many among us for whom profits in dollars is the bottom line in every consideration?

(c) What of *the disloyalty of Judas?* However you may explain his actions in betraying Jesus, there is always the feeling that Judas was concerned about his own future. What future could he have as an identified follower of a crucified criminal? Put Jesus on the spot and he will deliver!

(d) And, what about the disciples? Jesus, on the cross, was *deserted by those who were his closest followers.* Their fear of what would happen to them personally was greater than their faith. How many times have you pussy-footed when the chips were down, when you had to stand up and be counted or slink away in an effort to escape?

(e) Humanity's inhumanity that sent Christ to the cross is seen in *the fickle emotionalism of the crowd.* Greet him with hosannas today—it's Palm Sunday! But how about Thursday night? Will we be there, swayed by the emotion of a crowd become a mob? Will we join our voices to the call for crucifying Jesus?

(f) Perhaps, though, you have not yet seen yourself in these portraits. Could it be that you are among the mass of people who were just *indifferent to the cross*? Crucifixions were so common in Jerusalem that people hardly noticed them.

II. *God's self-disclosure*.

(a) If you can look beyond this dark side of human nature as reflected in the cross, you will discover the joyous word that here *in the cross God entered our human life and history*. Here, because of the cross, we hear God speaking from within the human situation to human beings such as ourselves. The cross can change us from separated children of God, stifling in our sin and wretched in our human loneliness, to those who have been united with God in Christ the crucified (cf. Rom. 5:8, 10).

(b) The cross becomes *a symbol of God's unconditional love* for all of us. He has been where we have been, or where we are! Here is a divine love for your human experience which is yours simply through the grace of God! And he disclosed that love on the cross.

(c) When you look at the cross, you see there *the symbol of God's supreme power to transform evil into good*. It seems a paradox that the cross as a symbol of the death of a dream could become at once the symbol of God's victory over death!

(d) Thus God's self-disclosure in the cross becomes *a perfect and final revelation of God's divine love for us*. W. E. Sangster, in pointing out how the cross shows us how loving our God is, said, "The cross shows the supreme power of God to transform evil into good."

(e) Nevertheless, one cannot look at the cross and fail to see that in the obedience of Jesus, we have *the climactic act of devotion*. It was costly. It brought suffering at its most intense degree. No wonder Jesus prayed in Gethsemane for guidance as to some other way or means of fulfilling his mission! Here in the cross, we see God's unconditional love, but we see also Jesus' unconditional surrender to the demands of that love.

III. *Assurance and challenge*.

(a) You and I must see in the cross not only the assurance of Christian hope, but the challenge to obedient Christian discipleship. And the "people who stand looking on," then and now, never quite make it this far. For those who do, there is the assurance that God's redemptive power is the ultimate power in the world, and that his divine love is at the very heart of his created universe.

(b) In the cross, there is a promise of light and hope in the darkness of our chaotic world. The Scripture records that when Jesus died, there was darkness at noon. In a sense, that darkness lasted until sunrise on Easter morning. But rise the sun did, and with it arose our Lord Jesus, victor over death.

(c) We are called to accept God's assurance of ultimate power and love. We are called to an obedient discipleship which embraces sacrificial love in the pattern of the man on the cross. The cross is without power to redeem your life unless and until you yourself accept God's gift of life and love through Christ. With the acceptance comes not only the gift of God's love and power, but the challenge to be God's person in our times. It means actively to follow Jesus in the pattern of our daily lives, seeking to make his spirit alive in us and those around us.—Hoover Rupert.

Topic: God's Love and Our Sins
Text: Isa. 53:6.

Earth has seen nothing more beautiful or compelling than that of self-denying, vicarious suffering, a love that takes the burdens and pain that belong to another and bears them for its healing. The fifty-third chapter of Isaiah belongs to the "servant passages" scattered through the latter part of the book. These passages set forth the role of Israel among the nations. But more significantly, they foretell the meaning of the sufferings of Christ. Indeed, Christ understood his mission in terms of these passages (Matt. 3:17; Isa. 42:1).

One verse tells the need and gives the remedy (Isa. 53:6).

I. *We have sinned*. "We . . . have gone astray." What happens to us is like what happens to sheep.

(a) *We are tempted as sheep are tempted*. Sheep that have food enough and to spare may go beyond their prescribed limits. They are tempted to eat where eating is forbidden. There is nothing essentially wrong with the food, but it is the wrong food. However, the forbidden food looks so much like the food permitted that the sheep may easily be led astray.

God gave human beings their basic hungers and desires. Such hungers and desires are not sinful. Nor is the feeling of these hungers or the fulfillment of these desires sinful. But we can be led astray by the temptation to nibble our way past the commandments of God and the rules of society.

(b) *We sin as sheep go astray.* Sometimes sheep go astray individually. Jesus told the parable in which one sheep out of the flock went astray.

However, sheep more often go astray by groups. It is easy for us to be swept along with the current trends in clothes, hair style, automobiles, houses, and entertainment. Is it any wonder, then, that we listen to confident voices that subtly lure us to evil?

Sheep go astray because they ignore the shepherd. Whatever the immediate reason, the basic reason for sheep going astray is that they lose the shepherd's voice. In the name of freedom, we go astray with urges or with leaders that enslave us.

(c) *We suffer the consequences of disobedience as sheep suffer.* We become lost. We are spiritually dislocated and not of use to our Lord. We are spiritually exposed to our enemies. We are increasingly in danger of spiritual disaster. Therefore, the promise of freedom that came with the first temptation was an illusion (Prov. 16:25).

II. *God has made possible our salvation.* "The Lord hath laid on him the iniquity of us all."

(a) *Jesus Christ suffered for us.* This was love in action from first to last. It was God himself at work in Christ (John 10:18).

It was love that surrendered itself to the worst that sin could do. He who knew no sin was made sin for us (cf. 2 Cor. 5:21). Calvin said, "He endured in his soul the dreadful torments of a condemned and lost man." Remember, this was the sinless Son of God (Isa. 53:9).

(b) *By his sufferings, Jesus Christ made possible our deliverance from the sin that nailed him to the cross* (Rom. 3:25). In the light of the cross, we can see clearly the perils of temptation, the heinousness of sin, and the catastrophe of being lost. Our proper response is: "Love so amazing, so divine, demands my soul, my life, my all."—James W. Cox.

Topic: Christ: The Man in the Middle
TEXT: John 19:18.

Anyone in any generation who seeks to respond to the call of God, rather than to conform to the expectations of man, will find himself a man in the middle. How vividly this fact is demonstrated in the life-and-death struggle of Jesus that we commonly call Holy Week. This position indicated that he was considered the chief criminal on this occasion. It symbolizes for us what he always was throughout his life and ministry—a "man in the middle."

I. In the first place, Jesus was a man in the middle because he was caught between the old and the new. Frequently he taught: "It has been said to you of old, but I say to you." "I have come not to destroy," he said of the old, "but to fulfill." On another occasion, he counseled: "Do not put new wine into old wineskins, lest both be wasted."

II. Jesus was a man in the middle, too, because he tried to keep the church socially sensitive and responsibly involved. How often he took a position between the exploited and the exploiter. When there were those who put institutions before people, he declared a principle of universal application: "The Sabbath was made for man, and not man for the Sabbath." Although it was the pattern of his life to stand between the oppressed and the oppressor, it was probably this invasion of the holy ground of religion that got up the ire of the high priest and his collaborators to devise some way to get rid of this troublesome fellow. Do *we* hide out some place in the institutional life of the church rather than live out on the frontiers of life in response to the Master's invitation, "Follow me"?

III. Christ was the man in the middle, too, because he was caught between the parochial and the universal. You may recall that the cleansing of the Temple actually took place in the court of the gentiles.

This court was the only place in the Temple gentiles were permitted. It was the gentile, the foreigner, who was being deprived of a place to worship by this noisy merchandising. Note in the one-line sermon which Jesus preached on the occasion that he lifts up the universality of the church: "My house shall be called a house of prayer for *all* peoples." When we can talk about Catholics being our brothers and sisters, when we can talk about Jews being our brothers and sisters, when we can talk about blacks being our brothers and sisters, when we can talk about communists being our brothers and sisters, when we can talk about our employers being our brothers and sisters, when we can talk abut our employees being our brothers and sisters, and so conduct ourselves, the Kingdom of God will be here. For that day to come, it is going to take a lot of middle men, bridge builders as the Master was.

IV. (a) Only a man in the middle can be the Savior of men. At the cross, there were those who spat upon Jesus and ridiculed him. One of the jibes that the Jewish mob shouted at him was, "He saved others, himself he cannot save." One can still hear the sneer of their cry. They did not know it, of course, but they were declaring the gospel truth. If *you* are going to save yourself, you cannot save anyone else. The only love that ever redeems is the love that pours itself out in behalf of others. It takes a man in the middle to be a conciliator of the affairs of men.

(b) Christ did not allow anything that others could do to him to alienate him from them. This amazing quality of spirit did not go without notice, for the apostle Peter has recorded of him in one of his epistles: "Who, when he was reviled, reviled not again; when he suffered, he threatened not; but committed himself to him who judges righteously."

(c) The word from the cross, from the man in the middle—"Father, forgive them; for they know not what they do"— is a plea for those whose sin has caused his own agony. It is this love of man, even in his sin, which maintains the bond between Jesus and ourselves. He shared our common lot in this world as it is, not as it might ideally be conceived; and this sharing is the supreme identification that God in his love has made with us. "For God so loved the world that he gave his only Son."— John Thompson.

Topic: The Intrusion of the Cross
TEXT: Gal. 6:14.

There is a certain majesty to the cross when we gaze at it from the world, and it is so easy to romanticize it. But what a difference when we take a new perspective on the world *from the height of the cross*! The world and the cross come together—my world, your world—and that central timber intrudes, confronts, and shatters all we crave for and grab and grasp. All that we so fiercely cherish is thrown into discard and the price is spelled out in the words of Isaac Watts: "My richest gain I count but loss, and pour contempt on all my pride."

Now, what will be your spiritual advantage and mine when we take our perspective from the height of the cross?

I. Looking from the summit of the cross, *we are able to perceive the inner dynamic of the Christian religion.*

Many of us can be misled by the slogan, "God Is Love," which permits us to cling perfunctorily to Jesus without noticing he is nailed to a cross. But from the summit of the cross, we see the world through Calvary and the real dynamic of our faith emerges in the words of St. John: "God so loved the world that he gave his only begotten Son, that whosoever believeth in him should not perish but have everlasting life." Notice the verb in "he *gave*." Like his Word, God's love is always God's act. "God Is Love" is not merely a dead slogan; it is something dynamic. And John's declaration indicates that God's way of reaching the heart of his world was through an action at a place called Calvary. This is the heart of the Christian religion, and it is most real when we see its dynamic in action in the work and witness of an Albert Schweitzer, or a Thomas Dooley, or a Dietrich Bonhoeffer, or a Mother Teresa.

II. Looking from the summit of the cross, *we recover the revolutionary character of the Christian religion*.

Look at it again and in this way: on the

level of our daily existence, it is so easy to be negative about human life and destiny. The ancient philosophers compared this state of things to a serpent swallowing its own tail.

But then came Paul to declare that only by means of the cross of Christ could he be liberated from the endless cycle of failures and be radically transformed into what God wanted him to be.

This was the intrusion of the cross. It declared that God's concern for us was greater than any we could have for ourselves, and hence we had a new standing. Life is no longer symbolized by a circle, but is stamped with the image of a cross. Our whole bundle of values is shattered and shamed, and we are challenged to take our stand in Jesus' way of life—for he said, "Whosoever will save their life will lose it; but whosoever will lose their life for my sake will find it." Here is portrayed a greater risk and a more revolutionary change than any other religion or philosophy has called for in human history, and Christianity attaches to its basic requirements an enormous price tag—namely, Calvary.

III. Looking from the summit of the cross, *we see how salvation works in the Christian religion*.

Jesus gave himself as our representative, interceding for us and assuring us forever of that forgiveness without which none of us can ever be free. Judgment and mercy met at the cross and emerged in freedom and forgiveness for us, endorsed by a lonely cry, "Father, forgive them for they know not what they do." This is how salvation works in the Christian religion. This is what gives Christianity the integrity which no worldly force or tyranny has been able to destroy.—Donald Macleod.

Topic: He Rose Again

TEXT: Acts 1:3.

Let's think together today about the resurrection of Jesus from the dead. Two things will concern us: first, whether it really happened, and second, what difference it makes if he *did* rise again.

I. There are many ways of stating the evidence of the resurrection of Jesus. Consider three phenomena:

(a) First, *the disappearance of the body*. I can't imagine any disciple in or near Jerusalem *failing* to visit the sepulcher to see these things for himself. They all saw the same astonishing sight—namely, that the tomb was open and empty. What happened to the body? There is no satisfactory explanation for its disappearance except that he had risen from the dead. All the alternative explanations which have been proposed create greater problems than those they are thought to solve.

(b) The second evidence is *the reappearance of the Lord*. It is claimed not only that the body of Jesus disappeared from the tomb, but that it reappeared, although changed into a new and glorious form, clothing the now-risen and living Lord. Far from being victims of wishful thinking, the disciples needed to be persuaded, and Thomas's stubborn unbelief is well known. Again, they were normal and balanced people. True, Mary Magdalene may have been an excitable woman, but Peter and John were rough fishermen who were not given to dreaming dreams and seeing visions. When we remember that they were neither neurotic people nor gullible, and that they needed clear evidence before they were themselves convinced, it is just not possible to dismiss the resurrection appearances as hallucinations.

(c) The third evidence for the resurrection is *the emergence of the Church*. On Good Friday night, the apostles were plunged in unrelieved gloom. But within thirty-six hours, the whole picture was altered, as they became convinced that Jesus had been raised from the dead. Within a few weeks, they began to turn the world upside down. Coming out of hiding, they calmly defied the very Jewish Council which had condemned Jesus to death. They proclaimed the gospel with such *boldness* that they were arrested, scourged, imprisoned, and in some cases, killed. And they preached it with such *power* that thousands were converted and began to follow the despised Nazarene. This change of outlook which came over the early Christians, this upsurge of power, this bursting forth of the blossom of Christianity from the bud of Judaism, these things are inexplicable without the resurrection of Jesus from the dead.

II. We've considered the *fact* of the resurrection. Now, what is its meaning, its significance?

(a) The resurrection looks *back* to the past, to both the life and death of Jesus which preceded it. His divine person and his saving death were both vindicated by the resurrection. Jesus, wrote St. Paul, has been publicly and powerfully "designated Son of God . . .by his resurrection from the dead." So the resurrection, seen as God's seal upon both the life and the death of Jesus, can bring us unspeakable comfort and assurance. It tells us that Jesus of Nazareth is, in truth, the Son of God and can be the Savior of men, *our* Savior.

(b) We turn now from the past to *the future*. The resurrection of Jesus throws floods of light upon the future, especially the life beyond death. As Peter put it, "we have been born again to a living hope through the resurrection of Jesus Christ from the dead." Death is a shining gateway to newness and fullness of life. Moreover, the Christian expectation of life after death is not merely of survival, but, in the end, of resurrection. The New Testament tells us that our souls are going to be clothed one day with a glorious body like the resurrection body of Jesus and that the whole creation is going to be glorified (Rom. 8:18–25).

(c) What about *the present*? I want to assure you that the resurrection of Jesus is no mere dry theological doctrine; it has a tremendous message for us today. It tells us that we may live our lives every day in the power of Christ's resurrection. The resurrection and exaltation of Jesus are regarded as the supreme exhibition of the power of God. And we are told that the same divine power which raised Jesus from the dead can operate "in us who believe."

No temptation is too strong to conquer by this resurrection power. No task is too difficult to accomplish by this same power if God has called us to it. Are you defeated? Burdened? Overwhelmed with worries or fears or responsibilities? Then think of the resurrection of Jesus. Ask God to open your eyes to know the immeasurable greatness of his power which raised Jesus from the dead, and then as you look to Him in quiet, steady confidence, you'll find the same power made available for you.—John R. W. Stott.

ILLUSTRATIONS

DOES GOD CARE?   An elderly man spoke to the preacher at the church door after morning worship. Deeply concerned, he said, "We believe that God is a God of love, don't we?" The preacher nodded in agreement. "And that he cares for little children?" Yes was the obvious answer. "Then, how can he let little children get burned up and blown away?" As the preacher started to say something, the man interrupted, "Tell me—I'm a man seventy-nine years old, and I want to know. Tell me!"

There are no easy answers. We have to look for something better than an explanation, something more satisfying than an idea, something more challenging and creative than a piece of logic. What we need is a firm faith. But that will not come because we can unravel the mystery of suffering and evil. It will come because we have been sought, called, and taken captive by a love that gives no final answers but its own self.—James W. Cox.

COMFORT.   Harry Lauder, the famous Scottish comedian, was grief-stricken at the loss of his son. But he found the Shepherd. Later he was giving a concert in Chicago before an overflow crowd. He responded to repeated encores, and finally he quieted the audience and said very quietly, "Don't thank me. Thank the good God who put the songs in my heart."—Charles L. Allen.

SALVATION.   I have known moments—like everybody else—when discouragement crept into my heart and I felt utterly stricken. My work in Stuttgart seemed to have gone to pieces, my listeners were scattered to the four winds, the churches lay in rubble and ashes. On one occasion when I was absorbed in these gloomy thoughts, I was looking down into the concrete pit of a cellar which had been shattered by a bomb and in which more than fifty young persons had been killed. A woman came up to me and asked whether I was So-and-So, since she was not sure who I was in the clothes I wore. Then she said, "My husband died down there. His place was right under the hole. The clean-up squad was unable to find a trace of him; all that was left was his cap. We were there the last time you preached in the cathedral church. And here before this pit, I want to thank you for preparing him for eternity."—Helmut Thielicke.

THE LIVING GOD.   For five days, Purvis Short, Golden State Warriors basketball player, held the hand of a fourteen-year-old victim of an automobile accident. Steve, near death, showed flickers of response on the monitoring machines and occasionally would squeeze Short's hand. Short had been Steve's hero, and his "responsibility and faith and love and hope" helped to work a miracle of healing. Short said, "I was wondering if people in comas or who are vegetables have souls. I used to believe in God, but it was in the past tense. Now it's in the present tense."—Martin E. Marty.

CONVERSION.   How would you, then, define conversion? Do you need to define it? Won't describing it do? The converted man is facing the way his Master faces; he is following in the same direction; he is watching more and more closely what interests his Master; he is getting to be quicker to understand the wishes of his Master and to carry them out; he grows more and more conscious of the tie of common interests, and then of stronger ties that bind heart to heart, and life to life, and then of the meaning of each of them to the other; he knows "who loved me and gave himself for me."—T. R. Glover.

WHERE IS GOD?   Elie Wiesel, incarcerated in a concentration camp during World War II, tells of having watched a young boy of his own age (about ten) being hanged by the Nazi soldiers. As the boy writhed in agony, refusing to give in to the rope, one of the witnesses asked another, "Where is God?" The response was silence. The boy continued to struggle, and the man asked again, "Where is God?" Still, silence. Finally, as the boy succumbed, the man asked again, "Where is God?" And his fellow prisoner replied, "God is there. Hanging on the gallows."—Carter Heyward.

SECTION VI. Resources for Advent and Christmas Preaching

SERMON SUGGESTIONS

Topic: Ready or Not, I Am Coming
SCRIPTURE: Mark 13:33–37.

When I was a boy in Virginia on a warm summer evening, we used to play hide-and-go seek. There was a ritual we always followed. Whoever was "it" closed his eyes and began to count. Everyone else ran to hide. When the one who was counting reached one hundred, he opened his eyes and shouted, "Ready or not, I am coming." He then went to find us.

So my theme on this first Sunday in Advent is the Lord who comes whether we are ready or not.

I. Let us first recall the past, that first silent and holy night when the angels sang and Mary wrapped the babe in swaddling clothes and laid him in a manger. In that special place, in that child Jesus, God himself made his appearance in this world.

(a) Not everyone in the world was ready for him to come. There was no room for him in the inn. Herod the king was not ready. Neither were the scribes and the Pharisees nor the rich and powerful ready for him.

(b) But there were a very few who were ready and who opened their hearts and their souls to him. The publicans, sinners, and harlots needed mercy. The crippled and the blind, the lepers and the paralyzed were ready.

(c) So today, as we look forward to Christmas, we remember the past and that first Christmas when Jesus came to a world that was part ready and part not ready at all.

(d) Before we turn to the present time, note one thing more. The first Christmas is not a story of men and women who finally found God. It is a story of a God who confronted men and women, who took them by surprise, who found them out. My problem and your problem is that, ready or not, God has found us, and we can no longer equivocate. We must say yes or no.

II. This leads me from the past tense to the present tense.

(a) In Advent, we open our eyes to the Lord who is even now breaking into this world and who at this very moment is active in the history of this globe. We believe in a living Lord who even now, ready or not, is coming into life and intruding into this world.

(b) This Lord who comes is only visible to eyes of faith. We see the Lord everywhere. Can't you recall those days when you were alone, separated from love, stuck with your old self, its guilt and shame, its weakness and pain? And then something happened. Forgiveness overcame your shame. Love broke through your loneliness. You knew you were not alone. You were loved. The Lord was breaking in to bring you from death to life.

(c) There are also those moments when the Lord appears and is rejected. If we are in touch with reality, we heard the voice of God and we shut our ears and turned our eyes away and tried to hide from that presence. "He came unto his own, and his own received him not." We live in a world which for a long time now has been sys-

66

tematically rejecting the Lord. Slowly but surely, our age has convinced itself that God is superfluous. And what is the price we are paying for our arrogance and pride? You know all too well.

III. This is not the last word. Thank God for that.

(a) The future of all things is in God's hands. At the end, the victory will not go to death and the devil; it will not go to sorrow and tears, and it will not go to injustice and oppression. We live in joyful expectation, for God is God. God will come again, and he will prevail.

(b) We are in the middle of the game now, but we know how it will end. The one who was born in Bethlehem and the one who comes to us today will come again to bring heaven down to earth. Then we will be safe, we can come out of hiding, and we can come home free at last.—Thom W. Blair, *Pulpit Digest.*

Topic: "Christ Our Catalyst"
SCRIPTURE: Titus 2:11–3:7.

I. (a) A catalyst is a chemical that, when introduced into a mixture of other chemicals, facilitates a chemical reaction. The most amazing property of a catalyst is, however, that throughout the chemical reaction that it facilitates, the chemical structure of the catalyst remains unchanged. This is in sharp contrast to the structure of the other chemicals in the reaction, which are often profoundly altered. A catalyst, therefore, is essentially an unchanging agent of change. The essential properties of the catalyst are especially relevant during this season of Advent when we pause to reflect on the coming of the Christ into our lives and our world. Titus understands the significance of the coming of Christ to have been the appearance of the grace of God which works through the transformation of human life. This transformation of our human lives, however, is not an automatic phenomenon. It is the result of the *training* that we receive through the presence of Jesus Christ in our lives.

(b) Our training through the presence of Christ achieves in our lives a two-fold result: 1) we are *redeemed* from iniquity and 2) we are *separated* from the world as a people who belong to Christ. These two results of the presence of Christ in our lives reflect the two basic realities of the Christian life—the salvation and the in-gathering of the community of faith.

II. (a) "Being redeemed from iniquity," sounds quaint and archaic to most sophisticated minds of the twentieth century. Yet, if we understand the word "iniquity" to mean the power both within and without us that is responsible for selfish and destructive forces and impulses, we can easily understand how the presence of Christ in our lives can cleanse and save us. We can easily understand that the transforming presence of Christ in our lives can give us the strength and courage not to participate in actions that cause ourselves and others pain and discomfort. Christ the catalyst makes us aware of our true relationship with our fellow human beings and with God by transforming the contents of our hearts and minds from indifference to love and from selfishness to compassion.

(b)"Being separated from the world as a people of God" is the direct result of "being redeemed from iniquity." This "separation" of which Titus speaks is not, however, a separation which cuts us off from the world. We need not become desert hermits such as St. Anthony of Egypt or dour Puritans who fear the expression of human pleasure. In short, being separated from the world does not mean that we reject or despise the world. Separation from the world does mean that we distinguish ourselves from our fellow human beings in that we establish ourselves as a convenanted people of God. This "distinguishing" of ourselves from the world is not in any way a judgment upon others. It is simply the result of our relationship with God through our Lord Jesus Christ. We recognize that Christ has entered our lives and has changed and transformed us. We are thus new creatures who have been "redeemed from iniquity" and "separated from the world as a people of God."

III. We cannot exhibit the character of our transformed lives through spectacular deeds or pious behavior. We can only manifest our transformed lives through adherence to a simple formula of "presenting ourselves blameless before the world." This means that a life that has truly been transformed through the presence of Christ is that life which is marked by control and concern. We must obey the justly enacted statutes of our community, be prudent of speech, engage in honest and productive labor, and display gentleness and courtesy in human relations. All of these personal attributes, none of which is showy, indicate an abiding love and care for our fellow human beings—a love and care wrought in us through the presence of Jesus Christ.

IV. The truly amazing fact about our transformation is that Christ remains unchanged. Christ remains the same Lord and Savior for all generations of men and women. Christ remains the same to challenge the selfishness, indifference, idolatry, and pride which cause us to ignore our God and our fellow human beings. Christ remains the same Christ who loves and nurtures us and who desires to grant us life abundant and life eternal.

This unchanging Christ, catalyst of our transformation into sons and daughters of God, cannot be altered or reshaped by our selfish wishes and desires. He cannot be transformed into a private idol, a heretical cult deity, or a pleasant grandfather figure. Christ the catalyst enters our lives on his own terms. He triumphantly and confidently confronts us as the bearer of the promises of God, as the bearer of the demand of God, and as the embodiment of the life of God. As obedient and expectant people of God, we open our lives to the Christ who is able to truly transform us into creatures who are more faithful believers of his promise and more truly heirs of his Kingdom.—Rodney K. Miller.

Topic: The Absurdity of Christmas

TEXT: Luke 2:10–11.

I. (a) Absurdity—surely a strange word to use about Christmas. But Christmas is absurd if you take it seriously. So long as Christmas is a pretty, pretty tale, nobody really takes it seriously.

(b) But, when the miracle of Christmas first took place, it was a deadly serious business. That group of shepherds watching their flocks were practical men, no doubt talking business.

(c) And, then the miracle! The night was filled with light. And, the voice of an angel spoke (see Luke 2:10–11). For centuries, generations of Jewry had waited for precisely this word from God. Suppose there came through your radio or television a voice telling you that the world's problems had finally been solved. Would you not thrill to such a news bulletin?

(d) Men, wiser than we are, went to the place where they expected to find this messenger of peace—Herod's palace. But, those shepherds were led to a little town set on a hill, a town called Bethlehem, to a khan, a caravansary, to a cave on the hillside. When they arrived, it was to behold the sleeping child of a peasant woman, and they were asked to believe that this was the Miracle of the Ages. Look again at this story. And, this Christmas, take it with deadly seriousness.

II. This Child brought three basic facts to earth that the world sorely needs.

(a) The Child of Bethlehem brings new life to an aging world. When the first baby comes, the life of the family is geared to a new life, as if the family were beginning all over again. Religion had lost caste with the people. Moral decay was setting it. The people were tired and wearied of the darkness, and longed for the light of the spring. The high resolves of this festive season, the sudden glow of goodwill that people feel toward their neighbors, the incoherent desire to be worthier citizens and better neighbors, more faithful and loving husbands and wives and parents—all this is the magic of this Child's birth touching our hearts again and making us new. The Gift of God is the perennial gift of a new and loving heart to all mankind.

(b) This Child of Mary brings change, even revolution, as does every child in every home. One's whole outlook is completely transformed and adapted to suit the dominating influence of this little one around whose cot your universe now revolves. And, since Jesus was born in Bethlehem, the world has never been the same again. This Child cleft time into the age before his birth and in the years afterward. And, if we give gifts at this hallowed time, it is because Wise Men brought their gifts to him. If our hearts go out in love and help to homeless bairns at this time, it is because he was homeless on the night of his birth.

(c) This Child, he brought hope, as every child does. Children are tomorrow. Life is worth living; if not for ourselves, it's worthy living for them.

(d) At Christmas time, pilgrims are already singing the age-old carols in every civilized tongue. Despite life's injustice and trouble and care, they march onward and upward in reverent pilgrimage of hope.—George M. Docherty.

Topic: God's Personal Word

Text: John 1:1–14.

Our God is a God who speaks and a God who, just as truly, demands an answer.

I. (a) The life of God has been manifested as light shining in darkness. The light appeared in the remotest ages of man's history. The light appeared to Abraham, to Moses, to Hosea and Amos, to Isaiah and Jeremiah.

(b) The light appeared to all mankind (Rom. 1:20).

(c) The light shines today. It has penetrated the darkness far more deeply than ever before. Christian missions gird the globe.

II. The light came especially in Jesus Christ, for he was "the true Light" (John 1:9). Besides being called the true Light, Jesus Christ is also designated as "the Word" (John 1:14), because he is the expression of the power and activity of God. A responsible person speaks purposefully and wisely, and things happen. God speaks, and a world is created, a prophet is inspired, history is guided, or man is visited by God in the person of his Son.

III. (a) Human history is one long story of the rejection of light and life. Into the darkness, light has come. But men have tried to extinguish the light. When Jesus Christ, the true Light, came, men rejected him. But not the Jews only! The message of Jesus was not welcome in many a gentile city.

(b) Wherever sin has been entrenched and loved in personal life, in society, in business, and in government, men have been less than glad to receive Jesus Christ. Light reveals filth, injustice, dishonesty, and greed. Therefore, when the deeds of men are evil, they love darkness (John 3:19).

IV. The story does not end with the rejection and crucifixion of Jesus. There were many who welcomed him, loved him, walked with him, and died for him. "To all who received him, who believed in his name, he gave power to become children of God" (John 1:12 [RSV]).

The story of our Christian experience begins with a conversion experience. At first, there may be little emotional evidence that anything remarkable took place when Christ was received. But an intimate friendship with Christ will, sooner or later, make many definite differences. We receive "grace upon grace" (John 1:16 [RSV]).—James W. Cox.

Topic: A Time to Be Generous

Scripture: Matt. 2:1–11.

Christmas is a time of giving. At no other time in the year are we so kind, thoughtful, and generous.

What we need more than most things are laughing hearts, and there is a greater possibility of having them at Christmas than at any other time of the year. Generosity is one of their basic sources.

We have such fine examples of generosity at Christmas, and there are the generous impulses of our own hearts that lie so close to the surface at this wonderful season.

I. (a) Giving helped celebrate the first Christmas. Matthew tells of the wise men's search for the Christ child. "They presented unto him gifts: gold, frankincense, and myrrh." They were appropriate gifts. Gold was a gift for a king. Frankincense was used as incense and therefore was a gift for a priest. Myrrh, used in one of the most ancient of arts, that of embalming, was a gift for one who must die.

(b) They were looking for a king, and Jesus was a king, but radically different from what the wise men expected. Frankincense would rise as sweet incense from an altar presided over by a priest. A priest is one who represents men to God. It was Jesus who spanned the great chasm of sin and alienation that keeps men from God. No other priest could do that. The myrrh was an appropriate gift to Jesus for he was a person who must die. He would accomplish more in his death than the wise men could ever understand.

II. It was God's gift, not the gifts of the wise men, that gave us Christmas. The wise men only celebrated God's wonderful gift (John 3:16; Gal. 4:4–5).

(a) Time was full and ripe.

(b) God gave with unsparing love, and he gave unconditionally.

(c) Christmas tells us the meaning of grace. God has made a gift beyond our worthiness to merit or our ability to achieve. So real life begins when we come to God in our shattered pride, confessing that all our goodness is like filthy rags.

III. We learn essentially from God and, in some lesser way, from the wise men and the many generous people we have known that giving is one of the secrets of life. It is a basic clue to life's meaning.

(a) Giving is built into the structure of the universe, into the warp and woof of life. In holding on to life, we lose it. In giving it away, we keep it.

(b) On the other hand, it is the selfish, grasping spirit that afflicts life, often destroying it.

(c) It is so important that we know the art of giving. We learn to be generous very much the same way we learn to love. We cannot learn to love unless somebody loves us first. We have been the recipients of grace and gifts, especially at Christmas. Therefore, we can give.

(d) Like the wise men, we can do no better thing than bring gifts to Christ. He bids us bring to him what we have, be it big or small, and he accepts, blesses, and multiplies it. Jesus told how shocked people will be, who had given to others with no obvious connection with Jesus, when he will say to them: "Truly, I say to you, as you did it to one of the least of these my brethren, you did it to me" (Matt. 25:40 [RSV]).—Chevis F. Horne, *Pulpit Digest*.

Illustrations

GOD'S QUIET ARRIVAL.   F. W. Boreham, author of numerous inspirational books, wrote one when he was past eighty years of age. He called it *I Forget to Say*, and the preface explains that it was filled with random thoughts which he had quite neglected to mention before. As it turned out, it is one of the most gracious and stimulating books from his pen. It represents the overtones of his life, and in them, one meets God. When did God so beautifully take up residence in his soul? He would not, because he could not, say. He simply looked back at a late hour upon his life to discover that it had long been within the boundaries of the Kingdom. All along the line, growing old, he had been growing wise. He was content. Somewhere, somehow—unobtrusively—Christ had quietly entered and found a home. In retrospect, he was not surprised. But it was good, and he was grateful.—Hughes Wagner.

ONCE-FOR-ALL.   What happened in Jesus Christ flows from eternity, belongs to eternity and leads to eternity. For this reason, in contradistinction to everything, even the greatest and most significant of earthly events, it is *unique, once-for-all in character*. No doubt we are tempted to say: yes, but that, too, happened once, long ago. . . . Indeed, two thousand years ago, it took place, and thus lies far away in the dim past, almost as distant as the history of Julius Caesar and of Alexander the Great, almost as shadowy as the times of the Egyptian pharaohs. All that belongs to the dead past; of what concern can it be to us in the living present? But the Word of God makes answer: what then happened has significance for today. That event is just as alive and decisive for every man and woman of today as it was for the disciples who walked with Jesus over the plains and hills of Galilee. Why so? Because in that event, eternity, the eternal world of God, disclosed itself as the world to which we, too, we of today, belong through Jesus Christ. Then, in what happened in Bethlehem, in Nazareth, in Jerusalem, your eternal destiny was decided. For in the life of God is that joy and peace of which the angels sang, and you, too, in the present hour, are called to share that plenitude of life and joy and peace which is in God.—Emil Brunner

GOD'S STRANGE ENTRY.   "She gave birth to her firstborn son and laid him in a manger, because there was no place for them in the inn." We are on firmer ground when we approach the subject by asking what Jesus' being born in a stable tells us about God and his ways with men. We may assume that if ever providence operated anywhere, it operated in the arrangements that surrounded Jesus' birth. Details of time and place and manner were not left to chance. Why then the stable and not the inn?

Because God has a way of coming into history from the outside—from outside our theological systems, our social and religious institutions, our ingrown patterns and ways of doing. Let the inn, therefore, represent the Establishment, and let us learn from that first Christmas that God, more likely than not, will come to us without benefit of the Establishment's succor or support. Paul understood this. In his first letter to the Christians at Corinth, he noted that, "to shame the wise, God . . . has chosen things low and contemptible, mere nothings, to overthrow the existing order" (1 Cor. 1:27, 28 [NEB]).—Ernest T. Campbell.

PREVAILING LOVE.   Oh, the grandness of Christ's salvation! Every facet of a man's life is touched. The vistas of life continually expand. Christ stands on the horizon, beckoning us to follow him. When his love prevails, life is not a squirrel cage, but an exciting adventure, ever growing, ever expanding, full of zest and purpose and significance. When his love prevails in our lives, we are freed of our fears, our prejudices, and our anxieties. Kindness is expressed toward all men regardless of their rank or color or condition. And Jesus Christ becomes the Alpha and Omega of our lives—the source of our inspiration and the goal of our striving. When his love prevails in us, we are people who respond to the good spontaneously because we have his life within us.— J. Herbert Gilmore, Jr.

SOMETHING NEW.   When angels draw near, as they do, the earth begins to shake beneath our feet as it began to shake beneath Mary's feet, which was why she was greatly troubled. Instead of everything standing still and sure, suddenly nothing is standing still, and everything is unsure. Something new and shattering is breaking through into something old. Something is trying to be born. And if the new thing is going to be born, then the old thing is going to have to give way, and there is agony in the process as well as joy, just as there is agony in the womb as it labors and contracts to bring forth the new life.— Frederick Buechner.

DESIRE FOR GOD.   Some years ago, a novel named *The Greatest Desire*, told of a young writer coming from New England to New York City to gather material for a novel by that same title. In his quest, he plied people with one question: "What do you want?" He would not let any man take refuge in proximate answers. If the man answered, "I want to be an engineer," the writer would pursue him with, "But why do you want to be an engineer? What do you really want?" Thus he tracked down the "great desire." Perhaps Rudyard Kipling could have given him the answer, for when he stirred restlessly in a serious sickness and the nurse asked him, "Do you want anything?" he murmured, "I want God."—George A. Buttrick.

SECTION VII. *Evangelism and World Missions*

SERMON SUGGESTIONS

Topic: The Power of the Gospel

SCRIPTURE: Rom. 1:16; 1 Cor. 15:1–4.

If someone caught you today and said, "Please, tell me what the gospel is"—could you do it? The gospel is the reason we build our churches; it is the reason we call our pastors, educators, and musicians; it is the only hope of this lost world. But can you really say what it is?

The Greek word for gospel means "good news." From it we get our words *evangel* and *evangelist*. The gospel is literally the best news this sinful world ever heard. And if we have heard it a thousand times, it is ever new.

I. The gospel is Good News about what God has done! Most of our news in the newspapers is about man—and most of it is *bad*. But in the gospel, man stands back, for *God* is at work! The gospel really begins in the eternal heart of God, and it is expressed in his boundless love which broke forth in the creation of man, for fellowship with God.

For the gospel is the overwhelming news that in the Judean village of Bethlehem, God came bodily into the human race through the Virgin of Galilee! What incredible news!

The very heart of the gospel hinges on this fact: *God was in Christ*; the divine Word became flesh and dwelt among us. The incarnation is the very foundation of the *gospel* message.

II. But what does this mean for you? (a) These are just words—unless they mean something to *you*. Here is what they mean:

they mean that you are not *alone* in your struggle in this world. We do not worship a God who is far away. Our God has *come to us*. Only Christianity makes the audacious claim that the living God entered into our human flesh, shared our human lot, and died our human death—and triumphed over it. If man was ever to be saved, it had to be this way. Man could not lift himself up by his own bootstraps: he had to wait upon God! He became flesh and dwelt among us. *Immanuel*—God with us—this is the Christian gospel. If it is true, as we believe, then it is the point from which everything else takes its meaning; if it is *not* true, then Christianity is *nothing at all*. About this, every individual must make his or her own decision. Have you made yours?

(b) But the gospel is more: it is the Good News that God was in Christ on Calvary's cross, offering up his incarnate life for sinners like you and like me. The living Lord of this universe entered into this human vale of sin and suffering and bore my guilt and stain on that bloody cross. How could he love me so? He *died for all*; and yet he did it just for me!

(c) But every Christian knows that the gospel does not end on Calvary. Some people exalt the crucifix—and this cross is rightly central. But the climax is *this*: on that third morning, in Joseph's garden, there was an empty tomb! He arose! Death could not hold its prey; the grave could not defeat his love. Redeeming love triumphed over all! Ten thousand times ten thousand little men have tried to bury this One and his followers. But he *lives*, and one day he shall reign from shore to shore and sea to sea.—Wayne E. Ward.

Topic: Saved by Grace

SCRIPTURE: Luke 18:9–14.

The world religions, created by men, are basically the *same* at the root. All religions, including much of Christianity, are a form of "works salvation"—the attempt of humanity to save itself by religious rituals.

Jesus stands against all such misunderstandings of the true nature of religion.

I. When we hear the word *pharisee*, most of us say, "Those hypocrites. None of them were sincere." Now, it is true that many Pharisees were hypocrites. And Jesus condemns them soundly.

(a) However, in this parable, Jesus is describing a truly *good* man. This Pharisee was one of the most deeply religious and moral men you could ever hope to see. Measure him by the law of Moses, or by the standards of religious piety in which he lived, he would pass up most of us by a thousand moral miles! Do you doubt that he was a *good* man? "The Pharisee stood and prayed thus with himself, God, I thank thee that I am not as other men are. . . ."

But this man could back it up! He really was a better man morally than anyone you are likely to meet today—and his religious devotion surpassed all bounds. Listen:

(1) "*I am no extortioner.*" In plain words that means he never took advantage of anyone in a business deal. His word was his bond.

(2) But there is more. "*I am not unjust.*" Turn it around—*I am just.* This Pharisee was actually claiming—and remember that Jesus is telling the story and making the point—that he lived his life straight in line with the will of God as expressed in the moral law.

(3) And this Pharisee could say more. "*I am no adulterer.*" His marriage vows had been kept pure and inviolate.

(4) This man was the most devoted worshipper and churchman you ever saw! "*I fast twice in a week.*" Do you know what *that* means? Some of our best Bible scholars have discovered that it was often the practice of these devout Pharisees to arise before sunup, make their way to the Temple, and cast themselves upon their faces on the altar of the Lord. They might remain there in prayer and fasting from sunup to sundown—because they loved the Lord and wanted to serve him.

(5) This Pharisee is about to meddle. "*I give tithes of all that I possess!*" Tithes—*plural*! Bible scholars have found that these devout men often gave tithes of tithes, and offerings on top of that—until many of them gave up to half of their total income to the service of the Lord and his Temple.

(b) But now comes the *shocker*—if Jesus had not said it, we could hardly believe it: This man—this good, moral, deeply religious man—went down to his house *lost*. He was lost in his religion—and the number of his brethren is legion today!

II. (a) But look back in the corner of the Temple . . . someone else is there. He had no trumpet blowing before him to announce that he was coming to church. He had no bells to call attention to his piety. In fact, he was almost hiding. He was ashamed even to look up to God—but smote upon his breast, a sign of contrition and remorse over his sins—and cried out, "God, be merciful to me a sinner!" Like all the other publicans or tax collectors of his day, he sold himself as a traitor to the hated Romans—to exhort tribute money from his own people. They got everything the law allowed and put the rest in their pockets. They were *hated*. Jesus was trying to pick the most outstanding example of a confirmed sinner that his listeners could visualize—the despised publican!

(b) But what does he say about *him*? *This man went down to his house justified*—made right with God—rather than the other! How can this be?

III. Neither one of these men was *really good*. Both of these men were sinners. But the difference is dramatic—one of them proudly protested his goodness and basked in his religious pride, while the other humbly confessed his sinfulness and cast himself upon the grace of God. The way of the publican in confessing his sins and throwing himself upon the mercy of God is the way to heaven; the way of the Pharisee in trusting his own righteousness and his religious piety is the way to everlasting destruction. "For by grace are ye saved, through faith, and that not of yourselves; it is the gift of God, not of works, lest any man should boast" (Eph. 2:8).—Wayne E. Ward.

Topic: The Life of Prayer and the World of Action

SCRIPTURE: Isa. 60:1–3.

It is no wonder that praying has had a bad press in the world of action. Words are cheap. Praying is a habit. Sometimes we don't really mean what we say. We want God to do it all without any cost to us. We forget what praying cost our Lord.

I. The biblical view of prayer is that it leads directly to action. It may be communion of "the alone with the Alone," but it does not remain alone for very long. The idea that praying is for escapists, for people who want to avoid contact with the hard, cruel facts of life, is simply mistaken. Jesus began his ministry by going into the wilderness to pray. He was alone, quiet, away from the world. But he ended his ministry by entering the turbulent city to face the evil men who were corrupting the simple faith of the people.

Again and again, the Master confirmed a singular rhythm in his life-style; from his hours of aloneness, when he worshiped the Father and sought the Father's will in his life, he returned invariably to a hectic ministry among the sick, the degenerate, and the victimized inhabitants of what was still, despite our romanticized view of it, a dark and barbaric land.

It was to be the same for his disciples, once they were put in charge. They were all at prayer, the book of Acts tells us, when the Holy Spirit broke over them like a tidal wave of fire, baptizing them with courage and the urgency of bearing witness to all they had seen and heard during those extraordinary years with Jesus. Later, Peter was at prayer when he had a remarkable vision confirming God's acceptance of the gentiles; it was the strength of this vision that swept him up in the ministry to the gentiles in which he eventually lost his life at Rome. Paul was similarly at his prayers when he felt compelled to go to Rome, even as a prisoner,

in order to share his experience of the gospel with those in the imperial city. We may safely assume that the same thing happened to Thomas, who, legend tells us, carried the banners of Christ into India and to whomever it was that carried them into Northern Africa, and Spain, and Gaul, and the lands of the long shadows beyond the Alps.

Prayer was no retreat from the world of action. If anything, it plunged them into the very heart of that world. Instead of shielding them from trouble, it invited trouble, it courted trouble, it guaranteed trouble.

The reason is simple: prayer was the means by which they learned the pattern of God's new world. Yielding themselves to the Uncreated, they began to see and understand his design for creation. And from that point forward, they had to obey what St. Paul called "the heavenly vision." There are some who insist that religion's business is not with the real world.

II. Prayer and action belong together. Each serves the other. Prayer without action misses the point of prayer and never arrives at its fullness, the surrender of the self to God as an act of love. Action without prayer, on the other hand, is always imprudent, unimaginative, and lacking in the power of the Holy Spirit, so that it becomes lost in a welter of confusion and misdirection. Prayer leads us into creative action in behalf of the needy world around us.

Think of the enormous needs today. There is the need for food. Millions of people in the world go to bed at night with hunger pains. We may complain about the rise in energy prices, but we have the energy. We forget the people who don't. Then there is the need for *love*. Our world is teeming with people who feel cut off, alone, rootless in an alien society. Multiply that by billions of times, by all the orphans and refugees and transient families in the world, and you have some idea of the enormity of the problem in our time.

What is the answer to all of these tremendous needs? We know God's answer: "Arise, shine; for your light has come, and the glory of the Lord has risen upon you" (Isa. 60:1 and vv. 2–3).

The early Christians, who were people of prayer and devotion, heard this word and responded. Their lives were transformed by it. They rose above the greedy, dark culture of their time to become guiding lights of morality, courage, and unselfishness. And now it is ours to do something.

III. Prayer is the way we can turn the unlimited resources of God into saving the world around us. When we truly pray, when we open ourselves to God without reservation, it is like turning a valve in the largest dam in the world, so that the tremendous power embraced behind the dam is suddenly released through the aperture the valve was controlling, and goes shooting forth with incredible energy into the valley below. We are not the power. We do not have to be powerful in ourselves. All we have to do is be an opening, and let God do the rest.

I have a friend who became an opening. In his praying, he kept seeing all those little villages in India where people were poor and starving because there was no water for irrigation or raising cattle. When he really prayed, so that he became an opening, he saw what he could do. He went around to churches and business people, and to whomever he could tell his story, and asked for money to dig wells all over India. "For every thousand dollars," he said, "I can sink a new well. One well, in a small village, will bring new life and hope to all the people. They can water their gardens. They can have cows. The children will not starve any longer. They will have a chance for the future."

Soon my friend had collected thousands of dollars and went to India. Everywhere he went, he brought in the government agricultural service to help with the planning, and then he paid for a new well. Now, in dozens of places all over India, there are villages where people no longer have to walk miles with pails to get water for their cooking and drinking. They can raise grain and vegetables and cattle. There is milk for the babies. All because my friend prayed and became an opening for God.

Do you see? It is what we must do for the world. Hundreds of us, thousands of us must become openings for God.

In the end, it all has to do with love. God's love for the world. Our love for the world. Our opening ourselves to God, so that his love can reach the world through us. This is what it means to become Christians, for it is what Christ did. By praying constantly, he became the perfect opening. God came into the world through him. We call that the Good News. But it is only part of the Good News. The other part is, God comes into the world through us too!—John Killinger, *The Cup and the Waterfall* (Paulist Press).

ILLUSTRATIONS

INTERCESSORY PRAYER.   Joan Winmill, English actress and movie star, in her autobiography titled *No Longer Alone*, writes of her years in the theatre. Success brought no inner happiness and, finally, after a nervous breakdown and becoming dependent on prescription drugs, she was on the verge of suicide, when a friend included her in a party going to Harringay Arena, where Billy Graham was in his first London Crusade. Billy's message went straight to her heart. A kindly lady (Ruth Graham) met and talked with her and led her to Christ. She writes:

"Among my memorabilia is a letter that has meant a great deal to me. It is dated September 25, 1957, and was written by Mrs. J. Edwin Orr, Port Shepstone, South Africa, to Mrs. Ruth Graham. Here is an excerpt from it:

'You know when Edwin was in a very remote part of New South Wales, more than five hundred miles from Sydney, a man approached him. He told Edwin an amazing story and I knew you'd be interested.

'He said he'd been looking at an Australian picture magazine more than four years before and his eye was attracted to a photo of an actress. Having nothing to do with the movies, he was not impressed, but a strange conviction from the Spirit burdened him to pray for her conversion. He personally felt it was a waste of time, nevertheless, he kept praying for the girl. In 1954, the burden lifted, as if the Lord said, "You need not carry this burden any longer." He had no idea whether the girl died or was truly converted . . . .but he remembered her name—Joan Winmill—and when Edwin checked dates with him he found that the burden had lifted during the Harringay Crusade, when you were actually helping Joan!' "—Clara McCartt.

MISSION SUPPORT.   In 1792, at the home of Widow Wallis, a group of Christians gathered to discuss the challenge of Christ to go into the world with the gospel. Fresh in their mind was the sermon William Carey preached at the Nottinghamshire Baptist Association when he said, "Attempt great things for God and expect great things from God." In the home of Widow Wallis, the first society for the work of foreign missions was formed, and the modern mission movement was begun. William Carey offered himself as a missionary. "I will go down into the well," he said, "if you will hold the ropes."—Brian L. Harbour.

MORAL EQUIVALENT OF WAR.   Sir Wilfred Grenfell, the famous doctor to the Eskimos on the Labrador Coast, used to travel around college campuses saying to the young men who attended the chapel services, "Boys, each one of us must decide whether life is an arena which we enter to do conflict with others, to win things for ourselves, or whether life is a field of honor in which to engage in conflict with that which is evil in order to accomplish that which is good." Those who have any real concept of God as revealed in Christ Jesus have found life not to be an arena but a field of honor.—Clifford E. Barbour.

LOVE FINDS A WAY.   Jesus says the central thing is *a commitment of your life in love* to me. If that love is there, wonderful things can happen, in spite of opportunity, talent, equipment, training, etc.

I saw this so well demonstrated some years ago when we were in Kenya on a safari hard against the Somali border in the semidesert area of the Tana River. We came to eat one day at a little settlement operated by a Catholic brother by the name of Mario. He had 2,000 acres, irrigated and under cultivation, raising cantaloupes—sending them by truck to Nairobi, by air to England to be sold—thus financing his whole mission project. He had a boys' orphanage—about fifty boys in little mud huts. He was winning these Somali people through the abandoned children he picked up. He had a water purification plant—taking the muddy water from the river and purifying it—ridding it of the germs that afflicted the people. When the Somali women lined up at the faucet to get free water, he had a chance to preach to them.

Brother Mario told me about himself: "I was a nightclub operator in Denver, Colorado—over forty years old, when I felt the Lord speaking to me to be a missionary. But, you know, my church did not have any place for me. They laughed at me. I applied to nineteen different orders for admisison and they would not let me in. I was too old—I was not trained—I was not equipped. I needed to go to Seminary. Finally, I was admitted to an order in Switzerland. I stayed there two winters and just about froze to death. I said, 'Lord, I'll go anywhere—maybe even down there, if I can get warm.' " I could see a twinkle in Brother Mario's eye.

An opportunity did open up—they needed a missionary to go to Garissa, in the northern frontier area of Kenya. They did not have a thing up here—not a convert, a station, or even a contact. And Brother Mario volunteered. He continued: "I did not know a thing about farming—or water purification—or irrigation—I did not know any of this. I just came up here and took hold of things." And, with this kind of entrepreneur attitude, he has done a great work. You can look all over the world and see people who just say, I love the Lord—I love you, Lord. The Lord says, Feed my sheep. And they just go out and start doing it.—Wayne Dehoney.

SECTION VIII. Resources for Preaching Christian Doctrine

BY ERIC C. RUST

Topic: The Mystery of the Incarnation— The Historicity of God

SCRIPTURE: John 1:14.

The central affirmation of our faith is that Jesus of Nazareth is the Son of God incarnate. Here is the greatest miracle of all time, the central act of God in human history. He who spoke aforetime through the prophets has in these latter days spoken in a new way, in his Son (Heb. 1:1, 2). His Word was borne on human lips and mediated through human personalities, with all their frailty and weakness. But now the Word has personally identified himself with human flesh and blood. The Eternal Son has become flesh and pitched his tent among us (John 1:14).

Here is mystery beyond our understanding! The Son who was in the bosom of the Father has become a historical person living in the world which was created through him (John 1:3; Col. 1:16). He who is the principle of world order and the source of all meaning has become a part of that order. He who dwells in eternity has subjected himself to our creaturely time with all its transience and dissolution. He who is the source of all life has submitted himself to this realm of death and decay. What we celebrate at the manger bed every Christmas is the abiding reality of our Christian life.

I. *The glory of the pre-existent Son.*

(a) First of all, let us remind ourselves that Jesus of Nazareth is the act of God. His birth of Mary was a divine act. God played a part in initiating this human coming in a way that he does not with every other birth. All that Mary could do was to accept the gracious approach of God. "Be it unto thine handmaid according to thy word" (Luke 1:38). So the Spirit of God hovered over the womb of Mary as he hovered over the beginning of the whole creative process. Our faith affirms the divine presence at the coming of Jesus as the beginning of a new creation. Here was God taking up into his own life, in the womb of Mary, a human life and making it mysteriously his own.

(b) He who was born of Mary was the God-man. At the level of outward being —man. But, in the depths of his personal being—God, very God of very God. Furthermore, this was no case of man growing to such perfection that he became God. The scriptural testimony is quite clear that we are not to understand any idea of adoption here. From the beginning of his earthly life—nay, from his conception in the womb—Jesus of Nazareth was God as well as man. Hence, the apostolic witnesses are careful to affirm that as Son of God, Jesus of Nazareth was eternal. When you and I are conceived and issue from the womb, this is our beginning. Before this, we are not. But John preserves the testimony: "Before Abraham was I am" (John 8:58), reminding us that the human birth was only the origination in our human history of One who from all eternity was the Son of God. He who is God and who eternally dwells in the triune bliss of the Godhead, he who is the agent of creation and the light that lightens every individual coming into the world, has united himself with a human life, taken up into his being a human personality, and lived our life among human beings.

(c) Here was a descent from sublimity to the commonplace. We are increasingly aware of the immensity, maybe infinitude, of our universe, with its myriads of galaxies, its blackholes and quasars and novas. We know that our earth is a little speck of dust whirling around a second-rate star on the outer fringe of our own galaxy. Yet, in faith, we dare to affirm that God's Word, who is the agent of creation, the ordering presence of the universe, the divine utterance which brings cosmos out of chaos, has yet stooped to our common dust and deigned to share the common life of his creatures on this little speck of dust. The infinite has poured himself into the life of the finite!

(d) This is the mystery of the incarnation. No wonder that Paul can describe it as the self-emptying of the Son (Phil. 2:5ff). The cross on Calvary's hill is the culmination of the self-giving begun in the inner being of God when the Father gave up his beloved Son. This issued in the acceptance of a human mode of existence, with all its limitation and creatureliness, its suffering and its sorrow. He took the form of a servant and walked the way of the cross. That is what we mean by the grace of God that comes to us in the Lord Jesus.

In *Green Pastures*, Connelly makes the Archangel Gabriel ask Father God for permission to blow the trumpet and bring everything to an end. The world is in such a pass that he sees nothing else to do. But God stands on the rim of heaven and, gazing at the world he has made, refuses to give the word. Love must stand in with those who have rejected it, and suffer, and bring them in. He must go down among his creatures. And so the play finishes with a crowd in the front of the stage and, in the background, a lonely figure carrying a cross up a hill. "Look!" someone cries "Dey going to make him carry dat Cross up dat high hill. Oh, dat's a terrible burden for one man to carry!" But it is not his burden. It is our burden, and God carries it in his Son!

II. *The manifestation of true humanity.*

(a) We are not as God intended us to be. We are estranged from God and alienated from our fellows. God created us to be in his image (Gen. 1:26), and this clearly means that he intended us to live in responsible fellowship with himself and in loving responsible relationship to our fellows. He planned to make humanity into a blessed society of love in which his own love would be reflected back to him, like the image in a mirror. But we have rebelled against him and gone our own paths. This is the deep meaning of sin. We live in a rebellious and estranged world.

In his novel *The Castle*, Franz Kafka tells us in a symbolic way of this alienation from God. A Mr. K. is employed by a group that lives in a castle to act as its land agent. He comes to the village beneath the castle and endeavors to make his way to it in order to meet his employer. But as he approaches it, the castle recedes before him, and he can never reach it. At last, he gives it up and settles in the village. But there, too, he finds himself in trouble. He cannot enter into close relationship even with the villagers. He is separated from the castle and separated from them. In being alienated from God and the true meaning for his life (the castle), he is alienated from his fellows as well.

(b) Humanity is not as it ought to be. Human beings are sinners. Human history is the story of rebellion and estrangement. It has gone wrong. But into our human story there has come one man who is also God. In him, the divine image has been restored, and we see ourselves as we ought to be. Here is man, real man. Let us make no mistake about that! Flesh of our flesh and bone of our bone! So much so that they could utter of him the blessed blasphemy that he was a gluttonous man and a winebibber. A blasphemy, and yet it reminds us that he was man! He knew what it was to be deserted by his friend, to face a homeless existence in which the foxes might have their holes and the birds of the air their nests but he had nowhere to lay his head, to bear the agony of suffering, and to stare death in the face. He, too, was tempted like as we are, yet without sin (Heb. 4:15). It behooved him to be made in all points like unto his brethren (Heb. 1:17).

(c) Yet what a man! For here was man walking in utter obedience to the Father, giving himself in total self-giving for his fellows, performing God's will to the point of death. Here was love unlimited, the outpouring of personal being that knew no bounds, a compassion as wide as the ocean, a goodness as transparent as crystal, a righteousness as undeviating as a beam of light, a faithfulness as steady as the rock. Here we see ourselves as God intended us. Here actualized in our human history is a life that is the pattern of all human life. So Paul could call him the second Adam, the new man.

III. *The unveiling of inclusive love.*

(a) Yet it is not sufficient for sinful man to show himself as he ought to be. Here is not simply man, but inclusive man—man drawing others into his own being, man re-creating his fellows, because he is more than man. In Jesus, the love of God takes human form. Through his human life, humanity is reconciled to God and drawn into the Father's love. The early church fathers sought to describe this when they said that the humanity of Jesus was a universal humanity, that he was representative man. In these days, we describe it better in terms of human relationships. We are all persons in relationship. We are created in relationship to others. We are made for fellowship, but in our sin, we refuse to relate ourselves positively to God and so turn our backs upon our fellows. We reject the way of love. But here came One who was God in man. In him, the love of God shone through a human life that was totally open to his fellows. Here was an inclusive love that drew others in, and that ever since, down the story of time, has continued to draw others into loving relationship with himself. God was in Christ reconciling the world to himself (2 Cor. 5:19). Paul was describing the love of Christ in that wonderful hymn of love in 1 Corinthians 13.

(b) We should remind ourselves that this inclusive love embraces the whole creation. If there is intelligent and responsible life alien to ours on other planets in this vast universe, then this redeeming love includes them, and the Word who became flesh on this earth of ours will find a way of redemptive revelation wherever that life is.

Furthermore, man is himself a microcosm of the cosmos. In his bodiliness are included the chemistry and physics of the universe. His genetic structures are derived from the primitive replicating molecules at the beginning of the process. Structurally, man belongs to the mammalian order. In becoming man, the Son of God has perfected the whole created order. Nature and the universe are embraced in his redeeming love—their contribution is also included in the new heaven and the new earth of the Christian hope. The historicity of God is also concerned with ecology.

(c) The love that redeems sinners is that love that so identifies itself with them that it loves them unto death and beyond. This is the love of God in Jesus. "Do you know what Christ would say to you, my girl?" asked Robert Falconer of a lost soul in the slums of Glasgow. "He would say: Thy sins be forgiven thee." "Would he though? Would he?" she cried, starting up. "Then take me to him, take me to him." And so to this sinful weary world, we offer the redeeming love of God revealed to us in the Man of Nazareth.

Topic: The Message of the Cross

SCRIPTURE: 1 Cor. 2:2.

The cross is the heart of our gospel. Cried the apostle Paul: "I determined not to know anything among you, save Jesus Christ, and him crucified" (1 Cor. 2:2). The Johannine testimony affirms that only by the lifting up of the Son of man will the true redemptive purpose of God in Jesus be disclosed (John 8:28; 12:32). Our Lord steadfastly set his face like a flint to go to Jerusalem (Luke 9:51). And in Gethsemane, with bloody sweat and tears, he accepted the bitter cup of the cross as the Father's will for him (Mark 14:32–36). To his disciples, he declared that he, the Son of man, came to give his life a ransom for the many (Mark 10:45), and at the Last Supper, the cup of wine became the sign and symbol of his own blood whereby a new covenant would be established between God and men (1 Cor. 11:25).

I. *Man's sinful bondage.*

(a) We do not understand the significance of the incarnation and the cross unless we face the estranged state of humanity. We emphasized this estrangement in the preceding study, but now we need to probe it more deeply. Man is estranged from God, and this carries with it estrangement from his fellows. At its deepest level, the biblical testimony views sin as rebellion and as rebellion that brings man into a demonic bondage from which he cannot escape by his own efforts. At its roots, sin springs out of a creaturely pride in which man sets himself up against God. This is the revelatory insight of the story of the fall in Genesis. Man is led to believe that he can be like God. He is not big enough to conceive this himself. It has to come from beyond him. The serpent whispers, an indication of a demonic presence bigger than man which tempts man to his own destruction. Furthermore, fallen man finds himself outside in the wilderness, unable to return to fellowship with God. The barred gate and the angel with flaming sword stand as reminders that man cannot save himself. In his pride and rebellion, he is in a demonic bondage from which he cannot escape.

(b) Even his human righteousness will not save him, for his morality is shot through by his pride (cf. Rom. 2). He cannot obey the divine law without being proud of it. And, when he repents of being proud, he soon becomes proud of having repented. So historical man finds himself caught up in a treadmill of pride from which he cannot escape. "O wretched man that I am! Who shall deliver me from this body of death? I thank God through Jesus Christ our Lord" (Rom. 7:24, 25). Here is man's tragic state. He is sold under sin as a slave (cf. Rom. 6, 7). He is in thralldom to the demonic. His disobedience has brought him under the dominion of sin and death, and his dilemma is that even his righteousness, his good works, his respectability, will not save him. His obedience is so bound up with pride that the demonic holds him prisoner.

(c) We need to emphasize this demonic influence and understand it. Our selfishness and sin grow until they dominate our lives and hold us in thrall. They become a demonic power. Still more is this true in our social relationships and corporate life. Our sinful state is reinforced by the attitudes of our fellows. Our sin and theirs constitute a demonic pattern which can dominate a group, reduce its moral perception, and rob men of their conscience. We descend several rungs of the ladder of civilization and moral concern when mob consciousness and corporate solidarity rob us of personal responsibility.

(d) You will remember our Lord's parable of the Pharisee and the publican, in which the Pharisee's pride vitiates even his repentance (Luke 18:9–14). The story is told of a Sunday school teacher who was teaching this parable and warned her children about the Pharisee's arrogant thanksgiving that he was not like the publican. Then she said: "Now children, let us thank God that we are not like that Pharisee!" Here is the terrible reality: not only our obedience, but even our penitence can be vitiated by the demonic grip of our pride.

(e) If we are to get right with God, we must obey with humility and repent in a clear-sighted vision of what our pride and sin mean to our Creator. Yet this we cannot do. Only so can our demonic bondage be broken and man be set free to become the child of God. Now this is what God has done in the incarnation. Christ has broken our bondage and set us free. He has offered the perfect sacrifice that covers our disobedience and brings us home.

II. *The triumph of the cross.*

(a) Our Lord clearly regarded his Messianic task as involving deliverance from the power of Satan. He cast out demons and claimed to do so because the Kingdom of God was present in his person (Luke 11:20). When the Seventy returned from their successful mission, he rejoiced because he saw Satan fall like lightning out of heaven (Luke 10:18). The Johannine testimony affirms that our Lord, on the eve of his passion, recognized that this meant the casting out of the prince of the world (John 12:31). Paul declares that on the cross, our Lord triumphed over principalities and powers, making a show of them openly (Col. 2:15). The tyrants which hold men in thrall were decisively defeated. Indeed, if the princes of this world (and Paul means here the demonic forces which hold men in thrall) had known what they were doing, they would not have crucified the Lord of glory (1 Cor. 2:8). The demonic overreached itself when it brought Jesus to the cross. Its seeming victory was really its defeat. He rose from the dead and decisively broke its power over men. Here the cross and the resurrection are inseparable. They constitute God's victory over sin and evil, a victory which sets men free.

(b) The New Testament men believed that the work of our Lord's life was brought to a focus in his death. Here the kingly power of God was brought to decisive issue with the powers of darkness, and the triumph won on Calvary determined the future course of human history. The grace of God had now appeared bringing salvation (Titus 2:11). Man's thralldom to sin and evil was broken, and freedom was his if only he committed himself to the Christ. In the World War II, the successful landing on the Normandy beaches presaged the end of the whole conflict. Because D-Day was won, V-Day was certain. So it was with the cross. Here the decisive battle had been fought and won. The Kingdom of God had been manifested with power, and the ultimate outcome of history was sure.

God has set men free. Once for all, the triumph has been won, and we are living in the aftermath of Calvary. Evil still lifts its head, but the demonic is defeated, and the powers of this world are passing away. We can lift up our heads and rejoice, for now is the day of salvation. When Jacques Cartier met the Red Indians for the first time on the banks of the St. Lawrence River, he did not tell them of the might of Rome and the glory that was Greece, of the greatness of European civilization. He lifted up a cross and told them about Jesus. So into this weary and sin-bound world we go with the triumph of God on Calvary's tree.

III. *The sacrifice of Calvary*.

(a) Christ set men free because he did for men what they could not do for them-selves. Because in their pride and rebellion, they had sold themselves under bondage, they could be delivered only by humble obedience and a contrite spirit. They could be reconciled to God only if God himself broke their bondage and performed for them what they could not do themselves. To live with him, they must walk humbly, love mercy, and do justly (Mic. 6:8). Yet this they could not do. In reconciling them to himself, he would also break their bondage. And so God becomes man, walking for them the road of selfless obedience and utter humility, entering under their bondage and bearing their judgment. Grace is God doing for men what they cannot do for themselves. Grace is God meeting his own demands himself.

(b) The sacrificial system of the Old Testament Temple found its fulfillment in the sacrifice of Christ. The offering of an animal life but imperfectly covered men's sin, but now their sin was covered by the perfect sacrifice of a human life offered in total obedience to the Father's will. "Lo, I am come to do thy will, O God" (Heb. 10:7). In this statement, the author of Hebrews finds the central meaning of the cross. Our Lord so identified himself with us sinners that he walked our path in all its judgment and darkness, and yet walked it without sin. In utter obedience to the Father's will, he gave himself for us to the point of death, undoing our disobedience by his obedience, covering our sin by his own outpoured life. He tested all the consequences of sin, entered under our judgment, faced our death, until he stood on our side of the abyss and knew the separation from God that sin brings. "My God, my God! Why hast thou forsaken me?" And he knew it as only the Son can know it! He who knew the bliss of God experienced the state of sinful man, confessed for us that this is our just desert, cried out our guilt, and carried us back across the abyss of sin and death to the Father's love. As in faith we commit ourselves to him, his perfect sacrifice of obedience covers our sin and his confession of God's holiness brings our penitent hearts near to God. In him, the great high priest, and his sacrifical death, we may draw near.

(c) During World War I in 1916, there was a stretch of front-line trench on the Vimy Ridge in sad disrepair. No Man's Land was at most only one hundred yards wide, and sentries had to be on the alert at night. One night, a sentry, already tired out with labor in the trench, stood on the firestep. He fell asleep, his rifle held in his nerveless hand, and the officer of the watch came along, the most rigid disciplinarian in the company. Yet this man with this reputation did not wake the sentry and reprimand him. He took the rifle and stood sentry in his place. He did not lose his reputation for discipline. Rather, it was enhanced. He won the loyalty and the regard of all his company. So God demands, and wins us back by his love. This is the grace of God manifested in Jesus Christ our Lord.

Topic: The Miracle of the Resurrection.
SCRIPTURE: 1 Cor. 15.

The Christian faith is grounded in the historical fact of the resurrection of Christ. Deny this and the whole is shattered. If Christ has not been raised, our faith is in vain. Furthermore, we are still in bondage to sin (1 Cor. 15:17). Paul, with clear insight, sees that the cross without the resurrection is not victory, but defeat. Like an erratic boulder in the movement of human history, there stands that moment when the God-man returned from the dead, when the stone was rolled away and the Incarnate Lord came forth in his post-resurrection splendor. This is the miracle that makes all other miracles credible, and it is the miracle which creates faith. We have to do, not with a dead, but with a living Lord. Napoleon and Washington, Lincoln and Cromwell may moulder in the dust of the past, but the Risen Christ is a living presence down the story of time, present to men of every age as other big figures of history cannot be. In this world, where time runs its inexorable course and where the shadow of death and dissolution covers all historical existence, one man has stayed the inexorable movement and caused a saving light to shine in the darkness that covers the peoples. But he has done so because he is God as well as man.

When we describe the resurrection as a miracle, we are affirming that it was no accident, no contingency of history, no inexplicable exception to the normal processes of human existence, but the act of God. Immanuel—God with us—rose from the dead. Here the mystery of the historicity of God reached its consummation. The divine purpose in human history was actualized in one life and made redeemingly possible for all men by faith. Here the Christ was declared to be Son of God with power. That which was hidden beneath the flesh and blood of his humanity was disclosed in his risen splendor. The God in the man shone forth and his disciples could behold his glory. To deny the resurrection is to deny the essential meaning of the Christian revelation and to suggest that our God is not the Lord of history. Here is the final *skandalon*, stumbling block, to which as Christians we commit ourselves. Foolishness to men, it is the crowning manifestation of God's power to those who believe.

I. *The historical actuality of the resurrection*.

(a) In our time, the historical actuality of the resurrection has been challenged frequently. The last challenge has its roots in the past decades among the followers of the late German scholars, Bultmann and Tillich. They contend that the resurrection as historical actuality is incompatible with the findings of modern science and that it must be treated as an attempt on the part of the church to preserve the truth that the Christ was still a living reality. We shall later deal with the scientific issue, but let us at once dismiss the suggestion that faith in Christ creates the resurrection. The latter becomes thereby an imaginative way of expressing inner experience rather than a historical event. The truth is surely that the resurrection created faith. The gospel records, the narrative of Acts, and the epistles of Paul testify clearly that until the resurrection morn, the disciples were a despondent and defeated group. It was the miracle of Easter that created faith and brought to birth in their hearts the conviction that Jesus of Nazareth was indeed the Son of God with power.

(b) The resurrection has two aspects— a public and a private. The public aspect is the empty tomb and the rolling away of the stone. In their diversity, the gospel testimonies all point to this. Their difference in detail serves to affirm the authenticity of their testimony, for it reminds us that here we have to do with the memory of many eyewitnesses, a memory curiously unanimous unless grounded in fact. Furthermore, it is clear that this fact of the empty tomb was sufficiently wellknown for Jews and others to endeavor to explain it away. Hence the suggestion that the disciples had stolen the body (Matt. 28:13ff), which continued in circulation down to the time when Matthew's gospel was written.

(c) The private aspect was the appearance of the Risen Lord to his disciples. He appeared only to his disciples. Here attempts to explain such appearances as subjective visions or to employ explanations from spiritualistic phenomena will not suffice. Our Lord rose in bodily form and thus confronted his disciples. The very bodily resurrection made recognition possible. It implied a continuity between the historical life and the risen mode of existence. It assured them that the personality and experience of Jesus of Nazareth was a reality beyond death. If scientific skeptics raise their eyebrows, the answer is that we do not know enough about the physical energy of which the human body is composed to be so dogmatic. We know what energy does and what form it takes, but we do not know its essential nature. We have no right to affirm that the Creator could not transform it within the empty tomb to take on a glorified form. Glorified it was, for our Lord could both take on his physical aspect and yet pass through closed doors. Thomas could put his hands in the wounds, and the Risen Lord could share a meal with his disciples, yet he could be in Galilee and Jerusalem at almost the same time. This glorified body transcended our distinctions of space and time. Wedded to the eternal Word by whom all things were ordered and created, it was so under his control that it could be physically recognizable, taking its earthly form, and yet pass into another dimension which transcends our creaturely existence in space and time (cf. 1 Cor. 15). So our Lord could make himself visibly and bodily present to faith.

II. *The conquest of death and sin.*

(a) The disciples were quite clear that this resurrection meant that sin and death were defeated. Our Lord was the first fruits of them that sleep (1 Cor. 15:20). He had shown himself to be the resurrection and the life (John 11:25). He had brought life and immortality to light.

(b) The biblical testimony clearly binds up the ultimate meaning of death with sin. The tree of life is in the Garden. Historical man in the wilderness, alienated from God and barred from the Garden, cannot eat of the tree of life. Sin spells death (cf. 1 Cor. 15:56). Death is the ultimate separation of the sinner, the final judgment of historical existence upon his sin. To be delivered from sin is to be delivered from death. Our Lord rose from the dead to open the Kingdom of heaven to all believers. The most terrible thing about death is its demonic grip over our human existence. All our lives we live in fear of death, not knowing.

(c) But Christ has conquered death. In reconciling us to God, he has removed the fear of death. In his book of eastern travel, *Eothen*, A. W. Kinglake tells of a night on the desert when they pitched their tents in the sand with no sign of inhabited land. But that night an Arab stalked out of the camp across the sands. He returned in the morning with a fresh green blade of rice. He had been to the realm of life and brought back its first fruits! So our Lord was raised from the dead by the Father to be the first fruits of the realm of life. In the midst of the shadow of death, new hope comes to birth. Christ has conquered death and brought life and immortality to light through his gospel (2 Tim. 1:10). In his reconciling sacrifice, he overcame sin, and, in his resurrection, he conquered death. The cross and empty tomb constitute two facets of one great triumphal act. Beyond death is Christ, and to die with him is gain.

III. *The unveiling of eternal life.* Paul is clear that because Christ has been raised from the dead, the believer may come to share in the life of the same victorious quality. By faith, the believer, too, has died with the Lord and already been raised with him (Rom. 6:4, 5; 8:11). In the husks of the old man, a new man is already being brought to birth. Though the outward man perish, yet the inward man is being renewed daily (2 Cor. 4:16). The Johannine testimony makes it clear that, in Christ, believers *have* eternal life as a present possession. This is the life of the future age, the life of the eternal Kingdom, a life free of the limitations of space and time, a life from which the shackles of sin and death have been struck off. Believers have it. They, too, are dead in Christ. Death as a physical phenomenon awaits them. But they are already with the Lord (Rom. 6:11). The fear of death and its separation have gone for them. They are already living with Christ, and they know the freedom of the children of God.

In *Crime and Punishment*, Dostoevski tells the story of a wasted life redeemed by human trust. He tells of Sonia, driven to become a prostitute by poverty, and of Raskolnikoff, whose thwarted ambition leads him to commit a revolting murder. When the two meet, Sonia has still her New Testament, and she opens it at the story of the raising of Lazarus. She reads this story because she dare not tell her own. Her womanhood, stricken by death, waits in eager longing for the voice that wakes the dead. As she reads, "I am the Resurrection and the Life," her voice trembles. But she goes on firmly and boldly to read the confession of Martha and make it her own: "Yea, Lord, I believe that Thou art the Christ, the Son of God, which should come into the world." So we make our confession, for we, too, are Lazarus, and behold, in Christ, we live!

Topic: Meaning of the Ascension

SCRIPTURE: Luke 24:50–51; Acts 1:9, 10.

The ascension of our Lord is rarely a subject for preaching these days, and yet it is a very important aspect of the mighty act of God in the Christ. Without the ascension, the resurrection remains a matter of the conquest of death. With the exaltation to the right hand of the Father, we have the affirmation that the Christ is Lord of history. His redeeming sacrifice becomes contemporaneous with all historical time and his glorified humanity is lifted eternally into the divine life.

The New Testament witnesses are unanimous in affirming the heavenly ascension of our Lord at the right hand of the Father. The human testimony in both the gospels and Acts preserves the memory of the passage of the glorified and risen Lord from the historical mode of existence to the eternal mode. After all, this is what we mean by the ascension. Our Lord passed from the particularity of space and time to that eternal order and dimension to which all our spaces and times are open. He was set free from the bounds of our creaturely existence to become universally available to all men of all ages and in all places. No longer was he held by the particularity of Palestine in the first century of our Christian era. What he had achieved on the cross and in the empty tomb had become an event in eternity as well as in time.

I. *The lordship over history.*

(a) Our Lord is seated at the right hand of power. He has ascended on high, leading captivity and giving gifts to men (Eph. 1:18; cf. Ps. 68:18). Indeed, he is exalted to the throne above all heavens, whence he had come to deliver humanity. Now he fills all things, for his presence is universalized and his victory brings all things under his subjection (Eph. 1:10; cf. Heb. 1:5–10). On the cross and in the empty tomb, Christ triumphed over sin and every evil power. He won the decisive victory which sets mankind free from its demonic bondage, and history can never be the same again. His triumph has made him Lord of all historical existence, the Judge who decides the destiny of men, the Savior whose intervention has determined the course of our human story. He is seated on the throne and all powers have been subjected to him (1 Pet. 3:22). His ascension is the divine affirmation that God has reclaimed his world and dealt decisively with the powers of darkness. They are in the process of passing away. Amid the darkness of our world, evil may seem in the ascendant, but Christ is Lord.

(b) That Lordship may be hidden, but the Christ is moving on his triumphant way in judgment and in mercy. To him every knee in the end must bow, and the whole created order must acknowledge his kingly power (Phil. 2:9–11). He is enthroned in eternity, and so he accompanies all historical times. He is now our eternal contemporary, confronting us in his exalted God-manhood at every moment of our historical existence, laying his kingly claim on us and offering us his grace. At every point of history, mankind and nations confront him, his atoning work, and resurrection-triumph. The forces of history hide another dimension—that of eternity. We cannot escape him. He is Lord.

You may remember how in Ibsen's play, *Emperor and Galilean*, the apostate Roman Emperor Julian, having tried to destroy the church and eliminate Christ from his world, cries out in desperation: "Thou canst not comprehend it, thou who hast never been under the power of the God-man. It is more than teaching that he spreads over the earth: it is witchcraft that takes the mind captive. They who have been under him, I believe, can never get free."

(c) Christ is in his world because he is above his world. He is seated at the right hand of power, the focal point from whence the world is sustained and by which its course is determined. The destiny of all men is in his hand. He won this right on Calvary's hill. Secular history is subject to his judgment. He is Lord in spite of its sin. The church acknowledges him as Lord. Here is a King by the willing consent of his subjects. All history has to do with him.

II. *The universality of the atoning sacrifice*.

(a) The ascension was the entrance into glory. The atoning sacrifice had been offered once for all, and Christ had taken his finished work back to the heavenly session. We celebrate the finished work of Christ! We need no reenactment of his sacrifice to bring us near to God. Our sacrifice has been offered once for all in human history. The biblical testimony is quite clear about that (cf. Heb. 9:23–26).

(b) But the ascension means, too, that this atoning sacrifice has been lifted into its eternal dimension. It has been lifted above time and thus becomes available to all times, to individuals of every age and clime. This is what we mean when we affirm that our Lord took his glorified humanity to the right hand of the Father. It was the God-man who ascended in all the glory and triumph of his sacrificial life. Henceforth he stands in heaven, the great and perfect High Priest who is himself also the sacrifice. The historical event of the cross in time is also an event in eternity, in the heart of God. Evermore, before the Father, stands One on the palms of whose hands we, like Jerusalem, have been graven (Isa. 49:16). Hence, the author of Hebrews declares it possible for all men to draw near to divine presence in Christ, the great High Priest, who has taken his sacrifice with him to the heavenly places (Heb. 4:14–16 and other passages). The apostle Paul sees the Christ at the right hand of God, making intercession for us (Rom. 8:34). With all our imperfection and sin, he covers us with his sacrifice and eternally reconciles us to God. The mystery is, of course, that this is God acting, God in man bringing us back home and making it possible for us to approach his holy presence.

(c) We have spoken already of the contemporaneity of the ascended Lord. One aspect of this is that the gospel of the atoning sacrifice is a reality for all of us. Every time the gospel is preached in word or in the Lord's Supper, the sacrifice of Christ becomes contemporaneous with our lives and his grace becomes effective in our hearts. This is the meaning of the Holy Spirit, for it is he who takes the things of Christ and makes them plain to us. The work of Christ is effective in our hearts because the historical sacrifice has been lifted into the heavenlies and made available through the Spirit. In the Spirit, the ascended Lord confronts all men and reigns in their hearts.

(d) Indeed, we may regard the historical life and the death on Calvary as the historical climax of the eternal atonement in the heart of God. For, from the moment of creation, with the presence of contingency and its attendant evil and the emergence of human freedom, there was a cross in the heart of God. In all his dealings with his creatures, God was a gracious creative presence, bearing their rebellion and the evil in his world and wooing them with his love. That cross in the divine heart was brought to a focus in the historicity of God and the ultimate triumph of Calvary. There God's redemptive identification with his creatures reached its climax. The divine and eternal atonement became manifest and historically effective in our human story.

III. *The inclusiveness of the new humanity.*

(a) We have seen in a previous study that our Lord's humanity was an inclusive humanity. In his love, he draws all human beings into himself and makes them new, a new creation. They, by faith, may die with him and be raised to his newness of life. Already, though in the flesh, they may participate in the life of the Age-to-Come, share in his glorified and redeemed humanity. He is the Second Adam, and it is as the Second Adam that he has ascended to the heavenly mode of existence. So we, too, are quickened together with Christ. We are raised with him and made to sit in heavenly places in Christ Jesus (Eph. 2:5, 6). We, who have been raised with him, are to seek the things that are above, where Christ is seated at the right hand of God (Col. 1:1–3). Our lives are hid with Christ in God.

(b) Hence, the New Testament can describe the Christian as living, at the same time, in two environments, in two modes of existence. He is in the flesh, but he is also in the Spirit. He has the life of this world, but he also has eternal life. He is in Colossae, but he is also in Christ. This is the mystery of the Christian life, and it is also the mystery of the church. The new humanity of the Lord moves down in the Spirit into human history and draws mankind into itself. We are embraced within Christ and become his body, his hands and feet. From his heavenly session, he moves out into historical existence. From our earthly life, we move into that other dimension and share in the new humanity that Christ makes possible.

In the days of the early church, a Christian was brought before Pliny, the persecutor and governor of Bithynia. Said Pliny: "I will take away your treasure." The Christian replied: "You cannot, for my treasure is in heaven." "All right," said Pliny, "I will take away your friends and you will not have one left." "You cannot," answered the Christian, "for I have a friend, Jesus, from whom you cannot separate me." Cried Pliny, "I will take away your life. I will kill you." "You cannot," came the answer, "for my life is hid with Christ in God."

SECTION IX. *Resources from Jeremiah*

BY DWIGHT E. STEVENSON

Topic: The Legacy of Jeremiah: A "Book Sermon"

I. Jeremiah, a young man in his mid-thirties, was dictating to his scribe, Baruch, in their winter lodgings somewhere in Jerusalem (ch. 36). The year was 605 B.C.

(a) Baruch was writing down his master's words on a papyrus scroll with a quill pen. They kept at it for several hours.

(b) Then, at Jeremiah's direction, Baruch took the scroll to the Temple, which was thronging with worshippers at a festival time, and there he read it aloud. Among those who listened with alarm was Micaiah, son of the Temple secretary, Gemariah. Filled with alarm, he hurried down to the secretary's chamber in the palace, where he found a number of nobles sitting. He poured out his report to them.

(c) Quickly they dispatched a messenger to go fetch Baruch. When he came bearing the scroll, they said to him, "Sit down and read it." As they heard the words, they turned to one another in fear. "Tell us," they said, "how did you write all these words? Was it at his dictation?" "He dictated," Baruch answered, "and I wrote them in ink in a scroll." Then the princes said to Baruch, "Go and hide, you and Jeremiah, and let no one know where you are."

(d) Leaving the scroll in the secretary's room, the nobles went to the winter house, where King Jehoiakim was sitting before a glowing brazier. When the king heard their report, he dispatched Jehudi

to get the scroll and ordered him to read it to him. As Jehudi read three or four columns, the king took his penknife and cut them off and threw them into the fire until the entire scroll was consumed.

(e) When Jeremiah learned what had happened, the word of the Lord came to him a second time: "Take another scroll and write on it all the former words that were in the first scroll, which Jehoiakim the king of Judah burned." This they did, and Jeremiah added "many similar words," so that the second scroll was longer than the first.

II. At this point, you will probably want to raise two questions: Why did Jeremiah dictate the scroll rather than go to the Temple and deliver it as a speech? And what was in the scroll?

(a) The answer to the first question is that Jeremiah was barred from the Temple. After a famous sermon of his in the Temple (chs. 7 and 26), Jeremiah had been beaten and thrown into the stocks by Pahhur, the chief security officer of the Temple (20:1–2). Several of the priests would have dealt with him still more severely—they wanted him killed.

(b) As for what was in the scroll, we can surmise that it contained a number of the oracles which now make up a large part of the first twenty-five chapters.

(1) To begin with, it surely contained the call of Jeremiah in chapter one. He had protested that call. But God had said, "Do not say, 'I am only a youth'; for to whom I send you you shall go, and whatever I command you you shall speak." "Behold,

I have put my words in your mouth. See, I have set you this day over nations and over kingdoms, to pluck up and to break down, to destroy and to overthrow, to build and to plant." "And I, behold, I make you this day a fortified city, an iron pillar, and bronze walls, against the whole land, against the kings of Judah, its princes, its priests, and the people of the land. They will fight against you; but they shall not prevail against you, for I am with you, says the Lord, to deliver you."

(2) One by one, groups of people turned against Jeremiah, even his former friends. What hurt most was ridicule. "I have become a laughingstock all the day; every one mocks me," he complained in his prayers (20:7). Finally he was forced to conclude that no one, or hardly anyone, was serious about doing God's will.

An appalling and horrible thing
    has happened in the land:
the prophets prophesy falsely,
    and the priests rule at their
        direction;
my people love to have it so,
    but what will you do when
        the end comes? (5:30–31)

(3) He even thought of renouncing his message altogether, for the word had become "a reproach and a derision all day long." But he could not:

If I say, "I will not mention him,
    or speak any more in his name,"
there is in my heart as it were a burning
    fire shut up in my bones,
and I am weary with holding it in,
    and I cannot. (20:9)

(4) There were moments so miserable that he even wished he had never been born:

Cursed be be the day on which I was
    born!
The day when my mother bore me,
    let it not be blessed! (20:14)

III. Jeremiah lived in the twilight years of the kingdom of Judah, just before the exile. Three empires threatened her fate: Assyria, whose star was falling; Egypt, who enticingly beckoned to Judah; and Babylon, whose victorious armies were marching westward. The nobles hoped to save Judah through foreign alliances. The priests hoped for rescue through the mystical power of the Temple. Jeremiah found no hope either in military might or in superstitious fetishes—only in covenant faithfulness to God:

"For if you truly amend your ways and your doing," he proclaimed, "if you truly execute justice one with another; if you do not oppress the alien, the fatherless or the widow, or shed innocent blood in this place, and if you do not go after other gods to your own hurt, then I will let you dwell in this place, in the land that I gave you of old . . ." (7:5–7).

But it was not to be. Judah toyed with Egypt, then rebelled, toyed with Babylon, then rebelled. And Nebuchadnezzar came marching with his crushing armies. By Jeremiah's own count, in 597 B.C., Nebuchadnezzar carried away 3,023 captives to Babylon, the cream of the land. He placed Judah under a puppet king, Zedekiah, who also rebelled.

IV. By 588 B.C., Jerusalem was under siege again, as Jeremiah had warned. Jeremiah chose a lull in the fighting to slip out of Jerusalem to purchase a field to keep it in the family—thus voting his own firm hope for his nation's return from exile. His motives misconstrued, he was arrested, charged with treason, and thrown into prison (37:11–15).

Nevertheless, the king Zedekiah knew that there was no one he could trust, save Jeremiah. So he summoned him under cover of darkness to hear if there was any word from the Lord. "There is," Jeremiah said. "You shall be delivered into the hand of the king of Babylon." His message was unchanged: if not covenant loyalty, then dire destiny. This time Jerusalem fell, the city was sacked, the Temple burned, and 832 more of Judah's leaders were carried into captivity.

Given his freedom by the victors, Jeremiah chose to remain with the leaderless people in Judah, and he did so until they, too, rebelled and brought down the armies of Nebuchadnezzar a third time. So, in 582 B.C., 745 more of Judah's citizens were carried into exile. Jeremiah and Baruch were kidnapped by a band of Jews who fled into Egypt.

Jeremiah's legacy is a call for a new covenant, an inward covenant, in which God's word is written not on tablets of stone, but on the tablets of the heart: "I will put my Law within them, and I will write it upon their hearts; and I will be their God and they shall be my people" (31:33). From that was derived the name of the New Testament.

Topic: Putting God Out of Our Thoughts

TEXT: Jer. 10:8–9.

I. God for Jeremiah was not a comforting idea. Rather, he was a disturbing force. There were times when Jeremiah even wished that God would leave him alone.

II. But he could not stop thinking or speaking of God and become a happy pagan, for the fires of transcendence burned within him, as within us. We are made for self-transcendence. If not upward transcendence toward God, then sideward transcendence into idolatrous culture, or downward transcendence into drugs, alcohol, obscenity, and sex without love. We are restless until we rest in God.

Topic: Hiding from God in His Temple

SCRIPTURE: Jer. 7:8–15.

Just as there is a brand of patriotism that is "the last refuge of a scoundrel," there is a kind of piety that is the refuge of the unjust. Jeremiah accused some of his contemporaries of using the Temple as "a robber's hideout." Idolaters, murderers, adulterers, perjurers, they sought shelter from God in God's own house. Clever! And fatal.

The Temple is a holy place, not a refuge from justice. Judgment begins at the house of God. The password for entry is repentance, genuine repentance from the heart.

Topic: Looking for a Man

TEXT: Jer. 5:1.

Like Diogenes of Greece at a later date, scouring the streets of Athens in broad daylight with a lantern in his hand, looking for an honest man, Jeremiah ran through the streets of Jerusalem looking for a man who did justice and sought truth. He found many who were enemies of both justice and truth, but his search was not fruitless:

I. There was Ahikam, the man who stuck his neck out to save Jeremiah's life after the Temple sermon (Jer. 26:24). Uriah, who had preached a like message, had been killed for it.

II. There was Baruch, the faithful scribe (chs. 36, 35).

III. There was Ebedmelech, "the Good Samaritan of the Old Testament" (Jer. 38:7–13; 39:15–18).

Topic: Buying a Share in the Future

SCRIPTURE: Jer. 32:1–44; 37:11–15.

I. Jerusalem in 587 B.C. had no foreseeable future. The city lay under siege by the armies of Babylon. In a previous siege, the cream of Judah's leadership had been taken into exile. This time the city was about to fall, the kingdom of Judah was teetering on the brink.

II. Jeremiah was never to see the resurrection of Israel or the return of the exiles. He himself died in a foreign land, a victim of collapse.

III. Nevertheless, he bought the field of Hanamel, his cousin, to keep it in the family, risking life to do it. Like a man planting a tree under whose shade he could never hope to sit, he was providing for future generations. He had little to say about hope for the future, but his example spoke volumes.

Topic: Singing the Lord's Song in a Foreign Land

SCRIPTURE: Jer. 29:13; Pss. 42, 137.

I. Jeremiah wrote to exiles in Babylon shut off from God's Temple, the holy land, and all the familiar symbols of their religion. Not only had they lost their fatherland; it seemed to them that they had even lost God.

II. Jeremiah assured them that they would find God even in that foreign land and would learn how to sing God's song there, but they would need to seek with all their hearts and minds.

III. Our familiar fatherland can become foreign through cultural change. Although we may not be hauled away into exile, the landscape can change right under our feet.

IV. When this happens, the situation will require a lot of hard thinking and praying. We must learn to sing the Lord's song in a strange land. And we can, if we will seek God with all our hearts.

Topic: The Wake-tree

Scripture: Jer. 1:4–12.

I. The call of Jeremiah comes to a climax in the blossoming of an almond tree.

(a) In the original Hebrew, the meaning turns on a pun, which becomes clear in Moffatt's translation: "This word from the Eternal came to me: 'Jeremiah, what do you see?' I said, 'The shoot of a wake-tree.' The Eternal said to me, 'You have seen right; for I am wakeful over my word, to carry it out.' " Arabs to this day call the almond "the wake-tree." It represents the waking up of nature after the long sleep of winter.

(b) Highly valued in themselves for their beauty and their nuts, almond trees came quite early to play a symbolic role in Old Testament religion. The cups of the seven-branched candlestick, or menorah, were carved in the shape of almond blossoms. Aaron's rod was an almond branch. Hence it was a symbol of priesthood.

II. The revelation that came to Jeremiah through the almond blossoms was evidently twofold.

(a) It confirmed his private vocation in a toppling world.

(1) Judah was entering a long twilight. Jeremiah's nation was on the verge of a calamity that would wipe out the monarchy, topple Jerusalem into a heap of ruins, reduce the Temple of Solomon to rubble, and carry the leaders into exile. The Judean world was falling.

(2) All that Judah could salvage from the wreckage was something invisible, a faith which could become the seed of the future. To that work, Jeremiah gave himself wholly.

(b) It also confirmed the living reality of God's work in the midst of Judah's troubles.

(1) On the surface, it appeared that God was sleeping.

(2) Jeremiah saw beneath that surface. History did not, and does not, stumble along as a rumbling landslide of political and military accidents, burying its victims in rubble. It moves as a dialogue between mankind and Maker.

III. The Word of the Lord that Jeremiah had to speak was not a comfortable word.

(a) Jeremiah shrank from uttering it; but it was a necessary word, and it was a word from the living God.

(b) God, like a wrecking contractor moving into the asphalt jungle of rotting tenements and ugly, superannuated hovels and festering slums, comes into these apocalyptic times as a destroyer: "to pluck up and to break down, to destroy and to overthrow." This, evidently, is his present work. The giant steel ball at the end of the cable on the tall crane swings with thunderous might against the decaying walls, and down they come with billowing clouds of dust. "Make way," says the wrecker, "make way for a new and fairer city."

Topic: The Potter at His Wheel

Scripture: Jer. 18:1–12.

Nothing deserves to be a symbol of history more than pottery. Today archaeologists digging in the *tells* of buried cities "read" their history in the broken pottery which litters their slopes. Likewise, Jeremiah went down to the potter's house about 2,500 years ago to read the meaning of the current history of Israel at the potter's wheel.

I. *A symbol of history.* God is the potter. Nations are his clay. He works with that clay at his wheel, shaping it to his intention. But the vessel in his hands can frustrate his intention by its poor quality. If that happens, God as potter will change his intention and shape it otherwise—not as the clay dictates—but as seems best to him.

(The potter's wheel was actually two stone wheels on an upright axle. The potter turned the axle by spinning the lower wheel with his feet. The clay he shaped on the upper wheel with his hands and fingers.)

II. The clay by its poor quality can frustrate the potter's intention and cause him to change it (v. 4). God's will for Israel could be frustrated by Israel, forcing God to change his intention for her.

III. As the clay, Israel had two options:

(a) To change God's intention to judge Israel as resistant clay by repenting (vv. 7–8).

(b) To continue unrepentant, thus changing God's intention to make her into a beautiful vessel and causing God to reshape them in judgment (vs. 9–10).

IV. God's present intention was to judge Israel for her sins, but Israel could save herself by repenting (v. 11).

V. This, it appears, Israel refused to do (v. 12). Nevertheless, Jeremiah issued his summons to rescue: "Return, everyone from his evil way, and amend your ways and your doings."

Topic: Crisis Religion

SCRIPTURE: Jer. 34:8–16; 37:6–10; 2:27–28.

The year was 588 B.C., early in the reign of King Zedekiah, puppet of Babylon. He had rebelled and Nebuchadnezzar was laying siege to Jerusalem. Suddenly many of the wealthy citizens "got religion." In an apparent attack of conscience, they emancipated their Hebrew slaves. Actually, they were obligated by Mosaic law to do so, crisis or no crisis: see Exodus 21:2 and Deuteronomy 15:⹂, which provided that a Hebrew slave could not be held by a fellow Hebrew more than six years. This law they had continually broken. And now they were hoping to receive special merit for observing it, in hopes of influencing the fate of Judah to a favorable end.

Then, just as suddenly, Pharaoh Hophra came marching toward Jerusalem. Many Jews had hoped for just such help from Egypt. The Babylonian army lifted the siege of Jerusalem and withdrew to confront the Egyptians. Interpreting the withdrawal as a deliverance that would last, the wealthy citizens promptly reimpressed their former slaves. This outraged

Jeremiah's sense of justice, and he denounced their actions vehemently.

I. It is in commonplace times that we store up our religious resources, which get us through both ordinary and extraordinary times.

II. A crisis will bring out the neglected religiousness of some people, but it is seldom genuine. It is really an attempt to manipulate God.

III. Such "a sudden run on the bank" finds all accounts overdrawn.

> But where are your gods
>   that you made for yourself?
> Let them arise, if they can save you
>   in your time of trouble . . .
>   (Jer. 2:28).

IV. Likewise, a crisis will bring out the genuine religion which has been built up day by day in ordinary surroundings and customary ways. In such times, people find unsuspecting strength from a secret store.

Topic: For a Time between the Times

SCRIPTURE: Jer. 29:1–32.

I. The exiles in Babylon after 597 B.C. were suffering a grief reaction over the loss of their homeland.

(a) They were refusing to face the facts and to take up their life again in their new situation.

(b) In this, they were being encouraged by certain false prophets, who told them that the exile would soon be over so that they could return to their own land and to their former way of life (Jer. 29:8–9, 15, 21, 29).

II. Jeremiah wrote a letter from Jerusalem and sent it by two friends going as Zedekiah's couriers to Nebuchadnezzar. In that letter, he gave three pieces of advice:

(a) Continue vigorous family life (29:5–6).

(b) Be good citizens of Babylon (29:7).

(c) Work to grow into a mature faith in God (29:12–13).

SECTION X. *Children's Stories and Sermons*

January 1. Brother Lawrence

About three hundred years ago, there lived a great man called Brother Lawrence. He lived in a monastery where he worked as a cook for the others who lived there. He discovered that all the time he was cooking and working in the monastery, he could think about God. He thought about God's being with him, and he told God all the things he was thinking. He called this "practicing the presence of God." He believed that we can get to know God better when we think about God's being with us wherever we are.

Lots of times, when we think about prayer, we think about the prayers that we say. We say the Lord's Prayer, or we say a prayer to thank God for our food before we eat, or we say a prayer before we go to bed at night. Sometimes we stop what we are doing and say a prayer about something special.

But Brother Lawrence taught us that there are other ways to pray, too. He taught that all through the day, we can know that God is with us, and we can be praying all the time. That may sound strange, but we are praying when we say "thank you" silently when God helps us get through a hard test. Or we can silently say, "Please help me, God," when we are afraid. Without anyone else hearing, we can say, "I love you, God," when we think of the wonderful world God has given us. We don't even have to say silent words.

If we are aware that God is with us, that is praying, too. On the school playground, or at the park, or while playing with a friend—anytime at all—you can know that

God is with you. It is part of our adventure of getting to know God!—*Pockets*.

January 8. The Legend of the Rider

You probably all know the legend of the rider who crossed the frozen Lake of Constance by night without knowing it. When he reached the opposite shore and was told whence he came, he broke down, horrified. This is the human situation when the sky opens and the earth is bright, when we may hear: *By grace you have been saved!*

In such a moment, we are like that terrified rider. When we hear that word, we involuntarily look back—do we not?—asking ourselves: Where have I been? Over an abyss, in mortal danger! What did I do? The most foolish thing I ever attempted! What happened? I was doomed and miraculously escaped, and now I am safe! You ask: "Do we really live in such danger?" Yes, we live on the brink of death. But we have been saved. Look at our Savior and at our salvation! Look at Jesus Christ on the cross, accused, sentenced, and punished instead of us! Do you know for whose sake he is hanging there? For *our* sake.—Karl Barth.

January 15. Sealed Orders

The Fiji Islands used to be called the Cannibal Islands. Fierce and treacherous tribes once lived there. Their main object was to kill and eat their enemies. John Hunt, a young Methodist missionary, went there many years ago. As a young man in England, he was studying for the ministry and had just agreed to go to Africa as a missionary. He was engaged to a young

92

woman who was willing to go with him, and, what was more difficult, he had gotten her mother to agree that she could go. Then, one day, the missionary society called him and told him that they wanted him to go to Fiji instead. John Hunt was willing, but he wondered what Hannah would say. So he wrote her a letter and told her about the change of plans, then waited for her answer. His friend saw how nervous and upset he was. Finally, John told him that he was unsure of Hannah. Then her letter came, and with a shout, John burst into his friend's room with the news. "It's all right," he said. "She says she will go with me anywhere."

Something like this happens to people who commit themselves to Jesus Christ and his Kingdom. Perhaps the most wonderful part of it all is knowing in your heart that from that moment on, Christ will go with us wherever he wants us to go.—Adapted from Gerald Kennedy.

January 22. God Saves His Own Child

Four men I knew, a father and three sons, sailed upon a summer's evening to an island port in the Hebrides. Suddenly the sky turned blacker than a raven's wing. A north wind churned the sea into a thing of fury. The storm leapt upon them with gleaming jaws. Their boat, in a moment, became less than a child's toy—the brown sail, a rag. Four men fighting death for life. A desperate, unequal conflict. Yet, now and then, clear and high above the hurricane, the father's voice rang forth. "Living or dying," he cried in a kind of calm passion, "God saves his own child." And so it was. With almost miraculous abruptness, the gale fell. The water slept. At twilight, when the western rim flamed with gold, four silent men came to harbor. In their hearts was the hush of great awe. Today I see that the story of everybody's life is the romance of God's deliverance.—Alistair MacLean, *High Country*.

January 29. Without Wax

Do you ever wonder how words came to be? There are some words that are no older than you are—words that have to do with television, atomic energy, new medicine, and various new discoveries. There are other words so old that scholars are not sure how they grew.

Take the common word *sincere* for instance. You all know what that word means—frank, honest, true. When you sign a letter "sincerely yours," you are saying that you have written a frank and honest letter. When you say of a friend, "I like him because he is always sincere," you mean that you feel safe with him because you can trust him always to be himself and to say what he really believes.

All the dictionaries agree that the word *sincere* comes from the Latin word *sincerus*. It is when they start to explain how the Latin word *sincerus* grew that the dictionaries disagree. The most interesting theory is that it comes from the Latin words *sine cera*, which mean "without wax." And there is a story behind those words.

In ancient Rome, people needed furniture just as they do today. There were no great furniture factories, but there were many small shops where carpenters made furniture. They made benches, tables, stools, chests, and chairs. Sometimes the furnituremakers could find boards large enough to make a tabletop or a chair seat or the cover of a chest all in one piece without any patching. Sometimes the craftsmen could fit two pieces of wood together with such skill that they were proud of their handiwork and did not try to cover it up. Sometimes, however, their piecing of woods was not so cleverly done. Perhaps they were working with odds and ends of wood, or perhaps the job was done by a carpenter who was just learning the trade. There would be cracks or tiny niches where the boards were joined. Then the carpenter would use wax to fill the cracks. He would rub and polish the surface until the poor fitting was hidden.

The early Romans, just like anyone today, did not like to be fooled when they bought their furniture. A man who bought a table or a bench that looked very fine in the carpenter's shop—smooth and polished—was angry when it had worn a while and the wax had begun to dry and chip away. People who had bought such furniture made so much fuss about it that the Roman rulers heard their complaints and passed a law.

And this is what the law said: A piece of furniture made of honest wood by honest workmanship, with no wax rubbed in to make it look better than it really was, had a special right. It could be labeled *sine cera*, the Latin for "without waxing." There was no law against covering the cracks with wax, but woe to the furniture maker who labeled such work *sine cera*!

So we today, if we are honest and frank without cheating or any pretending to be something we are not, have the honor to be called *sine cera*, shortened to our own word *sincere*.—Alice Geer Kelsey in *Pulpit Digest*.

February 5. Sour Grapes

It is not easy to be honest with ourselves and other people. When we do not measure up to what we really think we ought to be or to do, we may find a "good" excuse for it. Aesop pictured this for us in one of his fables. A fox tried its best to reach some grapes that hung from a vine trained on a tree. But they were too high for the fox. Try as it might, it could not reach them. So the fox went on its way, comforting itself with the thought, "They weren't ripe anyhow." From this story, we get the expression "sour grapes."

If we fail to get something we try for, why can't we admit our disappointment and at the same time think of what we can do? Perhaps we can do better later, or we can do something else better, or we can honestly see how blessed we are right now with what we already have.

February 12. A Love Letter

The preferred model for looking at the Bible is the model of a letter from a loved one. Letters from people we know and love are prized. Receiving mail is exciting. We are disappointed when we receive only junk mail. Junk mail is commercial advertisements or "come-on's" which promise us many things. The sender does not know us. He only wants our business. But letters from friends and loved ones are addressed to us by someone who knows us and cares for us. They include things we need and want to know. They have all kinds of news and instructions. They reassure us that we are known and cared for by the sender, and they help us to make plans for the future.—William L. Hendricks.

February 19. Money Isn't Everything

A great and revered teacher quotes from Ruskin the tale of a man who was shipwrecked. Before leaving the sinking vessel, he bound about his person a belt that contained two hundred sovereigns in gold pieces. Then he adjusted his life preserver and went into the water. But, unhappily, the weight of the gold more than offset the buoyancy of the life belt, and so he sank slowly to the bottom, where he miserably perished. "Now," says Ruskin, with sardonic humor, "as he was thus sinking, did he have the gold or did it have him?" That man kept his world and lost his self, his soul.—Albert Parker Fitch.

February 26. Who Is the Enemy?

Did you know that being afraid can make people enemies, when they might be friends? A bunch of little kids are out playing. They have a leader called Ron who always decides what they're going to do ... ride bikes, build forts, or go swimming. He's kind of a natural leader, and all the kids respect him. Anyway, a new kid moves onto the block. He's bigger than Ron. "Uh-oh," says Ron, "we're in big trouble. This new kid's going to push us around and tell us what to do. He's going to bully us and beat us up!" So all the kids get together and start piling up stones, just in case. When the new boy finally comes out of the house and looks around and sees the neighborhood crowd with all their stones, he goes behind his own house and starts collecting stones. So the story ends: "This was it for the rest of the summer. No more bike rides or playing in the tree house. No more building forts or swimming. All through July and August—fifteen kids on one curb staring at one kid on the opposite curb and two big piles of stones."—Adapted from Leslie Merlin.

March 4. Helpful Strangers

On a visit in northeastern Luzon in the Philippines, my wife and I were caught in a tropical rainstorm. Soon the rivers began to rise. We came to one river crossing where there was no bridge, and vehicles had to go through when the water was shallow.

Since there was no other way to get to the next town, we decided to take a chance by driving through. However, before we could get to the other side, the engine of our station wagon stalled. We were in real trouble because the water was rising quickly. I was about to get out to ask some truck drivers on the bank for help, when a rope was suddenly tossed to us with instructions to tie it to the bumper of our car.

In a short time, we were pulled out of the river by a truck. But before we could thank the ones who helped us, they had driven off. We never found out who those "good Samaritans" were, but their assistance was our salvation.

How willing are we to be good Samaritans? How willing are we to be good Samaritans without recognition?—Paul L. A. Granadosin in *The Upper Room*.

March 11. Angel of the Grass

The legend is told of God's assigning an angel to bless and guard every living thing he created. Everything—from human beings and birds to even the grass had its own angel. The angel assigned to the grass was not pleased with his responsibility. He became jealous that God had given other angels beautiful flowers, tall trees, and powerful birds over which to watch. The frustrated angel decided the plain old grass could grow by itself, and he no longer cared for it. Within a season, the trees and flowers died because the grass had withered and held no dew. The animals of the field died with nothing to eat. In rather short order, one angel after another went to God to ask for help. Finally even the people prayed that God would let them die because their beautiful world had died and they had nothing to eat and nothing to enjoy. God then turned to the angel of the common grass and asked whether or not his assignment was important. With humiliation and shame, the angel asked God's forgiveness and requested that he again be assigned to his vital task of watching over the grass.

An imaginary story, but it holds an important truth for each of you. Regardless of your age, your size, your grade in school—there is something important you can do. Your love for God and the people of his world and your own offering for home missions are very important. Enjoy doing what you alone can do as you show your love for God and for others.—Robert W. Bailey.

March 18. Riding a Wooden Horse

Sometimes we don't have the slightest idea of what is going on inside another person's mind and heart. People may feel ashamed, guilty, embarrassed, mixed-up, or afraid, and we may not understand at all. We may be like the stupid peasant that the Danish philosopher, Kierkegaard, told about. He said that in olden times, the army used a very cruel punishment. They made a man ride a wooden horse that had a very sharp back. The man was held down by weights. One time when this was being done to a man, and the man was groaning with pain, a peasant looked down on the drillground where the punishment was taking place. The man on the wooden horse was in such pain and so irritated by the sight of such a blockhead that he shouted at him: "What are you staring at?" The peasant answered, "If you can't stand to have anybody look at you, then you can ride around by another street."—Adapted from Søren Kierkegaard.

March 25. When Dreams Come True

Over eighty years ago, a young woman in Georgia got together a small group of boys and started the Berry Schools. She was Martha Berry. Martha had grown up in a wealthy, aristocratic Georgia family. She had made many trips into the hills with her father and had seen the hardships of the mountain people. A deep desire came into her heart to help those people. When her father died, she inherited the plantation and opened a school in the little log cabin that her father had built for her as a child, where she had studied with a teacher.

Her friends and family members tried to discourage her. They felt she was throwing her life away and that what she was doing was not what a Southern lady should do. A beloved black woman who had worked in the home thought the same thing and told her that she ought to be getting herself a home. But Martha shook her head and replied, "No, auntie, I have said good-bye forever to a home of my own. I have just married an *idea*. I'll have to be faithful to it, lonely as it is."

So Martha Berry built a school, and thousands of boys and girls came through to prepare themselves for life. When she was very, very old, she said, "Not one of my dreams has failed yet. They say I have too much enthusiasm for a woman of my age. Well, I hope I never lose it."— Adapted from Robert M. Bartlett.

April 1. The Boy and the Turtle

Roald Dahl tells a beautiful story about "The Boy Who Talked with Animals." Some fishermen in Jamaica had caught a huge sea turtle and had brought it to shore. The turtle measured about five feet long and four feet across and was dangerous. One man in the crowd that had gathered poked at the turtle with a stick of driftwood, and the turtle bit a piece out of it. Just as several men were about to drag the turtle up to the hotel, where it was to be used for steaks in the dining room, everyone heard a boy's screams: "No-o-o-o! No! No! No! No! No!" The boy begged the men to let it go. His father offered to buy the turtle, but the men would not sell it to him. In spite of warnings that the turtle would bite him to pieces, the boy ran straight to the turtle's head, flung his arms around its wrinkled neck, and hugged the turtle to his chest. He whispered soft words that nobody else could hear. The turtle became still. At last, the hotel manager who had bought the turtle decided to sell it to the boy's father, who let it go back to the sea. And away it went, far, far out of sight. There is more to the story, but just this much teaches us a lesson: Boys and girls sometimes understand how much God's creatures are worth in more important ways than money, for they may, in some strange manner, speak their language.

April 8. The Light of Life

There was once a printer's son who was not as bright as any of the other boys and girls in the neighborhood. Hans learned very slowly, but none of them loved God and his neighbors more than he. One day he sat moaning over a dying rose tree in the corner of a little backyard behind his father's house: "What more could have been done for it than I have done?

Because he loved flowers, a goodnatured nursery gardener who knew his father had given him a real rose tree. He told Hans how to plant it, water it, and fertilize it. Hans dug a hole and did everything his friend told him. He did even more. He took some planks and made a shelter around and over the rose tree. At first, he was very happy, expecting to see flowers as big as hats and as bright as cherries before the summer was over. But the buds began to shrivel, and the leaves began to turn brown.

The nursery gardener happened to pass by, and Hans took down the planks to show him his poor, dead rose tree. The nursery gardener saw at once what was wrong. Hans had shut off all the light from the rose tree, and no matter how much he did to water it and fertilize it, it could not live without light. "Hans," the nursery gardener said, "it's been my fault, not yours. And you shall have another rose tree, or we'll save this one yet, for if there's a bit of life left in it, God's light may bring it 'round."

Because Hans loved bright flowers and because he learned how to care for them, the nursery gardener soon after turned one side of Hans's backyard into a flower garden. Later on, he gave Hans a job in his own place of business.

Flowers and people need light. Jesus said, "I am the light of the world."— Adapted from "Mrs. Gatty."

April 15. The Red Badge of Mercy (Passion Sunday)

Crowds lined the usually barren, dusty road. There was a strange sense of expectancy among the people as they stretched their necks and strained their eyes.

Startled by a sudden noise from the crowd, a little bird, nesting in a nearby tree, looked down to see what had caused the crowd to gasp.

Struggling up the road was a man, bent

under the weight of a huge cross. A crown of thorns encircled his head and sent tiny red rivulets down his cheeks.

A woman ran from the crowd and knelt in the dirt. With a cloth, she wiped the man's face. His eyes said a silent thank-you to her before he continued on his painful way.

Moved by the suffering of the man, the bird followed, flitting back and forth. Suddenly it swooped low and, with its beak, pulled one of the thorns from the man's forehead. Again the eyes said thank-you, and again he moved on.

As the bird flew away, a drop of blood fell from the thorn, staining the bird's breast scarlet.

And for the almost two thousand years since, so the legend goes, this red badge of mercy has glorified the humble robin redbreast.—*Guideposts.*

April 22. What Is Hope?

The word *hope* is a slippery word. We use it to mean different things. We say, "I hope I can take an exciting trip next weekend." Or, "My dog got hit by a car, but the doctor said we can hope he will be completely well soon." Then, there is another meaning. In the Tate Gallery in London, there is a picture by Frederic Watts. Underneath it is the title: *Hope.* A beautiful girl is seated on a globe. She is blindfolded. She is holding a musical instrument—a lute—in her hand. All of the strings on the lute but one are broken. She is touching that one string with her hand, and her head is bent toward the string. She is waiting to hear the note of that one string. She has hope—she believes in the best in the worst of times. Because we have hope, because we believe God can bring the best out of the worst, our hearts are comforted when something bad happens to ourselves or to someone we love. —Adapted from Clarence E. Macartney.

April 29. God's Goodness

Suppose you were playing the game Twenty Questions and had to guess the "mystery object." This is your clue: "The earth is full of it," or "It covers the whole earth." What would you guess?" Violence? Wickedness? Suffering? The psalmist wrote, "The earth is full of the goodness of the Lord."

One day while traveling northward through Scotland, I caught a glimpse of a bright yellow patch on a distant hillside. None of us could think what the yellow area could be. Out of curiosity, we turned off to locate the hill. Soon we came to it and stopped to marvel at the sight of daffodils—a field of them.

Over against all the works of darkness, we must set the goodness of the Lord which covers the earth. God's goodness—God's good plans for the world and for us —is the basis of our hope.—William Nicholl in *The Upper Room.*

May 6. The Hand of God

A young pastor and his family on vacation were traveling through the southern part of Kentucky. As night came on, a storm was gathering, so they sought the shelter of a motel room. Just as they were settled in their room, the storm descended in all its fury. The lightning flashed and the thunder roared. Finally, with one loud crash of thunder, the lights went out and the room was left darker than the blackest midnight. The quiet that followed was broken only by the whimper of their three-year-old son.

'I can't feel anything," he cried. Then his hand touched his father's outstretched hand, and he added with assurance, "Except you, Daddy."—Charles Treadway.

May 13. It's Better to Be Safe

I remember crossing the Atlantic on one of the old Queen ships, and one evening while exploring the passages, I found myself going down a very long corridor that joined one section of the ship to the other. Suddenly, without any person being near, a door began to close before my eyes as if by magic. I started to pull a little bit and to push a little bit at the door, but it wouldn't budge a fraction of an inch!

An old British sailor appeared as from nowhere. "It's like this, mate," he said, "it's like this. It's no use trying to get through that door. You can push as much as you like, you won't get through it. See, the skipper 'as given the order that this section must be closed. If the old ship cracks with a storm, this section, mate, will float. Don't forget it! And the skipper's more worried about you floating than he is about getting you through them doors!"

That's the kind of God we have. He has closed the door of his forgiveness on the past, and he has sealed off tomorrow with the door of his providential care and protection because he wants this section—Today—to be able to float, and for you and me to be upheld in it, not to live our own way, but to live his way. The Skipper is much more concerned about you and me "floating today" than he is about getting us through the doors of yesterday and tomorrow.—Elam Davies.

May 20. Real Determination

Calbraith Perry Rodgers wanted like mad to win the Hearst $50,000 prize offered to the first person to make a transcontinental flight. He finally made it from Long Island to Los Angeles in 1911, but only after eighty-four days and fifteen washout crashes. He followed the railroads. If he took the wrong switch, he'd end up in the wrong place. He didn't win the prize because he took too much time . . . but he did make it.

He left Long Island and flew right over New York City, without a seatbelt or even an instrument—all he had was a waving piece of string. If it was waving at you, you knew you were on course. If it was going the other way, you had to correct for the wind or something. If it flew up or down, you knew you were climbing or falling—a good instrument. . . .

Rodgers crashed in a chicken yard on one leg of the trip. It took three days to repair the plane. By the time he got to Oklahoma, he'd used up all the time allotted for the prize, but he decided to keep on going. He went down into Texas, Arizona, and California: got to Pasadena, but wanted to get to Long Beach. But he crashed before he got there, broke up the plane, and badly smashed and broke several of his own bones. But when he got out of the hospital in a wheelchair and on crutches, he helped to rebuild the plane and flew on to Long Beach. There's a real flier.
—Paul Garber in *The Changing Challenge*.

May 27. Charlie the Chemist

I want to introduce Charlie the chemist. He wasn't the kind of chemist who deals in pills and bottles of medicine. He was what might now be called an "industrial chemist." It was his business to try and find out what to do with waste products from the gasworks. Everybody already knew that coal gas was good for lighting dark rooms and heating cold ones. But what was to be done with all the waste things that were let in the gasworks?

At this point, Charlie the chemist came on the scene. One dull day when it looked as if it would rain, he got a good idea. Coal naphtha and india rubber, it seemed to him, might very well join together to make a water proof substance. They might even make a water proof coat. (You've got a waterproof coat for wet days, haven't you?)

Charlie's experiment was a success. Nobody had worked out such an idea before. The next thing to do was to patent it and start making coats for the people to buy in the shops. Charlie's kind of coat was Patent No. 4804. Now it was only a matter of finding it a name—and it wasn't necessary to hunt far. Charlie's other name was "Macintosh."

So now, when you put on your "mac" to go out to school and come home dry, think of Charlie the chemist. For he was one of God's good helpers—saving boys and girls and big people from getting wet. Charlie's birthplace was the great Scottish city of Glasgow—and the city honors his name to this very day. And any one of us with a "mac" ought not to forget him.

In this great world, God has a great many helpers—people whom he can trust with good ideas. Some are famous as the world 'round—like Charlie. Some are hardly known at all. But all who are God's true helpers can say, together with St. Paul and his friends of long ago, "We work together in God's service." You and I can join that glorious company!—Rita F. Snowden.

June 3. How to Swallow a Camel

Jesus had different ways of teaching people important lessons. One of them was to exaggerate something so much that the people who heard him could see how silly or stupid or wrong it is to do some things. We can make a big fuss over some little, unimportant thing and overlook something else that is very, very important. Jesus said that some of the people who lived in his day strained out gnats and swallowed camels. What a funny picture he painted! Think of the long hairy neck of a camel sliding down a man's throat—the hump—two humps—both of them sliding down—and the man never noticing—and the legs—all of them—with the whole outfit of knees and big padded feet. The man swallows a camel and never notices it! —Adapted from T. R. Glover.

June 10. On Flag Day

Long ago—so legend tells us—a man named Orpheus played such beautiful music on his lyre that rivers stood still to listen and trees and rocks moved nearer. Dogs stopped barking, men ceased their quarreling, and the whole world was at peace. When Orpheus died, the gods could not bear to bury his wonderful lyre, so they carried it up to heaven and made it a new constellation: Lyra, sing of harmony. . . .

In 1777, a little group of men sat around a table trying to reach a decision. The thirteen American colonies were fighting to win their freedom and the new nation needed a flag.

But the flag committee was having trouble. Each of the thirteen new states had its own flag; each thought its own the best. They could not agree on one flag that would symbolize the nation as a whole.

The one that came closest was a flag that some of the American soldiers were carrying. It had thirteen red and white stripes—and, in the upper left-hand corner, the Union Jack. But the Union Jack was the flag of England, the very country they were fighting. What should they put in its place?

And then one of the committee members remembered the legend of Lyra, the constellation of harmony, and made a sketch of some white stars against a deep blue background.

On June 14, 1777, the Congress of the United States, meeting in Philadelphia, resolved: That the flag of the United States be thirteen stripes, alternating red and white; that the union be thirteen stars, white in a blue field, representing a new constellation rising in the West.—*Guideposts*.

June 17. Apostle to Garbage City

In a suburb of Cairo, Egypt, lives a man named Boulas Goda, a poor man, but a very happy one. He had been rich. He was a shopkeeper and made much extra money selling drugs, not the helpful kind that a doctor prescribes to make us well, but the terrible kind that make people feel good for a while and then destory them.

A little over twenty-five years ago, Boulas came to know Jesus Christ as his Lord and Savior, and his life was completely changed. He threw away the drugs, left his old crowd, and went out into the streets and coffeehouses to witness boldly about what had happened to him. People called him crazy and quit buying from him. His business failed, and within three months he was a poor man.

Boulas has become a rug weaver and now uses every opportunity to tell others about Jesus Christ. He goes among the garbage collectors with the Good News of his Savior. And they believe in him. Some accept Jesus.

His pastor says, "The only way to get away from him is either to run away or to accept Jesus Christ. Otherwise there is no way to avoid him." What Boulas tells the people is backed up by the good life he now lives.

His name, Boulas, is the Egyptian name for Paul. Don't you think the great apostle who met Jesus on the Damascus road and became a new person, and went everywhere sharing Christ, would be proud of the man who was named after him?—Adapted from *World Vision*.

June 24. Help in Bad Times

Betty Malz told a story of her family during the days of what was called the Great Depression, a time when many, many people had no jobs and families were hungry. When things were at their worst, some church people had given them 23¢ as a love offering. But there was just not enough for their needs.

That night they knelt beside the bed and thanked God for the 23¢. While they were kneeling, they heard a scratching sound at the front door. They were afraid someone looking for food was breaking in. After the noise had stopped, Betty's father cautiously opened the door to the porch. There he stumbled onto a large cardboard box. In it were a ham, milk, orange juice, bread, and butter.

Betty Malz recalled a song of that era that summed up those years, as sung by Ray Stevens: "Everybody needs a Mama and a Papa that will take enough time to play, take enough time to pray."—Adapted from *Super Natural Living*.

July 1. Honeysuckle

I spent several hours pulling and cutting out honeysuckle that had grown into the holly and other shrubbery outside. The task left me weary.

I remembered when the first honeysuckle vine had appeared, clinging to the back fence. How fragrant and pretty it was! I had welcomed it (and allowed it to stay). Now, two years later, the honeysuckle had taken over. It had sent shoots out in all directions and firmly entwined itself with holly and other shrubs. It was sapping their strength and life. The vine was difficult to remove; now I must watch lest unseen roots take over again and destroy the shrubbery.

As I tugged away at the honeysuckle, the thought came to me: How like this honeysuckle are the forces of evil that take hold of our lives! At first they look inviting, and we happily welcome them into our lives. But once allowed entrance, how quickly they take over and how hard they are to uproot.

It would have been easier for me if I had not allowed the honeysuckle to get a start on the fence!—Olive I. Clark in *The Upper Room*.

July 8. The Cigar and the Circus

I can remember a scene that occurred during my boyhood which illustrates one of the problems we all face in trying to make prayer an effective experience. One summer day, when I was youngster growing up in a small Ohio town, I walked into a drug store and bought a large and very black cigar.

Out on the street, I took off the band and lit the cigar. I found a quiet side street where no one would see me and puffed my way along. The cigar tasted awful, but I was feeling so bold I didn't mind. Until I saw my father half a block away.

Quickly I pulled the cigar from my lips and hid it behind my back.

"Hello," I said, trying be casual as I walked up to him.

"Hello, Norman."

I looked up, and I looked down, and I looked around: anywhere but toward my father's eyes. I searched desperately for something to say. And then I saw a bright poster, pasted on the side of a building: "Circus." I remembered how badly I'd been wanting to go to that circus.

"Can I go, *please*? Can I go to the circus, Dad?"

My father's voice wasn't harsh when he answered; it was simply firm. "Norman," he said. "One of the first lessons you should learn is this: never make a petition and at the same time try to hide a smoldering disobedience behind your back."—Norman Vincent Peale in *Guideposts*.

July 15. Praying for Others

Sometimes God helps others by letting us know how we can help them. When we are quiet and listen to God, God can help us know better what to do. When someone is sick, God sometimes heals that person with a wonderful miracle. God sometimes heals people by helping the doctors think of the best ways to treat them.

But sometimes we pray for someone who is sick, and that person doesn't get well. Those are the times when it is hardest to understand. Grown-ups don't always understand, either. Sometimes we can understand better if we talk with someone about what has happened. Do you have someone you can talk with? Your parents can help, and so can your minister or Sunday school teacher.

There are many things about prayer that we cannot know, but we do know that God loves us and wants to listen to us and help us. And we know that God wants us to listen, too. If we don't always understand, that's okay. After all, there are lots of things about God that we don't understand. But we always know that God loves us.—*Pockets*.

July 22. Salary

What is it that your father brings home at the end of every week, boys and girls—a nice fat envelope with a little window in it? It is his wage, his pay, as it is called in some places. If he waits a little longer for it until the end of the month, it is an even fatter envelope and gets a longer name. It is called his salary. That's an odd word. I wonder if you know what it meant at first? You know what your father receives for all the work he does. It would be very funny and not a bit convenient if he were paid in eggs or bread or bananas!

Once upon a time, people were not paid in money, they were paid in things. Indeed, they were sometimes paid in something you ate this morning. You would put it in your porridge, if you are a Scot, and in your boiled egg whether you are a Scot or not. Yes, you have guessed it—salt. We don't pay much for salt nowadays, but once upon a time it was very expensive. It was so precious, indeed, that people used it instead of money, and so, when they had done their work they got their salt or their "salary." When we say that man is "not worth his salt," we simply mean that he is not worth the pay he receives.

In Christ's time, salt was very precious. That is why he once said to those who loved him, "Ye are the salt of the earth." By that he meant that they were very precious, very useful, and very much needed. And if you are Christ's, boys and girls, you too, are the salt of the earth.—John R. Gray.

July 29. The Golden Rule for You

Here are just a few of the things you will do if you take the Golden Rule as your safety rule:

You will never leave marbles or any small or sharp objects lying around where a baby can find them and put them in its mouth.

You will never jump off your end of the seesaw while your playmate on the other end is high in the air.

You will never leave your baseball glove, your books, your dolls, or anything else on the stairs where someone might trip over them.

You will not ride your bicycle as though you owned the street or the sidewalk.

You will help smaller children when they have to cross the street.

You will remember that anyone who uses darts or arrows or toy pistols must be very careful to see that nobody is within range.

You will remove from the sidewalk anything that might cause someone to stumble or slip.

You will take care of broken glass, boards with nails sticking out, jagged tin, or anything that might cause cuts or bruises.

You will not, by being a show-off, dare other boys and girls to climb trees that are too high, or swim in water that is too deep, or jump from roofs that are too high to be safe.

You will, as soon as you are old enough, study first aid and lifesaving to be prepared to help persons who are in danger.

These are just a few of the things you will do, if you take the Golden Rule as your own rule of safety. You can think of others right now, and you will think of more as you go on living the Rule.

How safe our world would be if everyone—children and grown-ups alike—would follow Jesus' Golden Rule: "All things whatsoever ye would that men should do to you, do ye even so to them." —Alice Geer Kelsey in *Pulpit Digest*.

August 5. Honesty the Best Policy

I stole a geranium which was exhibited in front of a grocery store. I saw these geraniums advertised for ten cents a plant. I knew that my mother kept geraniums in tomato cans outside on the window sill, and assuming that I would do her a favor, I picked up one of the flowers, brought it home to my mother at noon and said: "Here, Mother, is a geranium for you." "Did you buy it?" "No, Mother." "Did you steal it?" "Yes, Mother." She then sent me to my piggy bank and made me shake out of it fifty cents. I objected that the plant cost only ten cents and one single flower was not worth fifty cents. But she insisted that I make that kind of restitution. My act of dishonesty thus punished by restitution taught me for life that honesty is the best policy. In any case, when I took money to Mr. Madden, he gave me two pots of geraniums.—Fulton J. Sheen in *Treasure in Clay*.

August 12. The Courage to Be Different

One of the basic purposes of religion, indeed perhaps its *only* purpose, is to make people different and to give them the courage to be different.

E. Stanley Jones, the well-known missionary, told how this courage was given to him. When he was at college, it was the fashion among most of the undergraduates to scoff at anything connected with religion. Some chapel attendance was required, however, and on one occasion, the speaker challenged any student who was interested in a religious life to stay and talk to him afterward.

As the other students rose to go, Jones hesitated. A fraternity brother jeered, "Hey, Stan, going up to see Jesus?" The rest laughed, and for a moment Jones almost weakened. Then, he says, something shot fire within him. "Yes," he said, "I am." Later, he told his friends that this was one of the most important moments in his life, the moment when he lost his fear of the crowd.

It takes courage to be different, but there is also an art to it. The truth is, you can do almost anything you like and get away with it, so long as you don't give your neighbor the impression that you consider him beneath you because he doesn't do it, too.—Arthur Gordon in *Guideposts*.

August 19. Prayers God Doesn't Answer

The other day I heard a story about a little girl who was being very naughty. It seems that the people who live next door to her very often take her with them on a picnic. On this particular day, however, she hadn't been asked. As soon as she saw the preparations for the picnic being made, she started to cry, and she cried solidly all through breakfast. After a while, the kind neighbors actually heard her. Taking pity, they came in and said she might come. As soon as she heard that, she cried all the louder. At this, her mother quite lost patience with her. "You cried when you weren't going on the picnic," she said, "and now you cry because you are. What *is* the matter with you?" To which, through her tears, the little girl replied, "It's too late for them to ask me now. I've prayed for rain." Well, of course, fortunately for her, God wouldn't hear that prayer or, rather, wouldn't answer it. He never does answer us when we ask for bad things for people. Indeed, he only gives us the sort of things which we can ask for in the name of Christ, the sort of things which Christ himself loves to give. That's why Christ said, "Whatsoever ye shall ask *in my name*, that will I do."—John R. Gray in *Expository Times*.

August 26. The Best Part of Church

I asked during the chidren's sermon, "What do you like about church?"

One little boy replied honestly, "Leaving."

Though I hadn't expected the response, the boy started me thinking. In a way, leaving really could be the highlight of each worship service. At the end of the service, the church is sent into the world, to serve, to love, to minister. What if we opened the church doors and a bunch of ready-and-willing-to-serve, chomping-at-the-bit Christians rushed out joyfully to proclaim the gospel and to love those around them to Christ?

Leaving really is the best part of the worship service—not leaving to go home and watch television and lie around, but leaving to go out and to enlighten, enliven, involve, include, and love.—Grady Roe in *The Upper Room*.

September 2. Look for the Blessing

A postcard which a friend sent from Hawaii showed fields on fire. In Hawaii they set fire to the sugar cane fields to burn away the dead leaves.

No one seems to know how long this fire method has been used. A Hawaiian legend tells that it started when a man got angry with his neighbor and set fire to his fields. The angry man thought he would destroy everything, but the sugar cane was not hurt. In fact, the neighbor was helped, because when the dead leaves were burned away, it was no longer necessary to cut them back.

Similar things happen in our lives. Sometimes things happen to us that seem unfair—a door closes, a relationship ends, a possession is lost. It seems like the end, but it turns out to be the beginning of something better.

God has a way of turning disappointment into blessing. Do we have the faith to wait and realize that blessing?—Astrid Sirles in *The Upper Room*.

September 9. Gathering Feathers

There is an old Jewish story about a woman who came to her rabbi and told him that she had been telling things about her neighbors that were not true—lies! She wanted the rabbi to help her make everything right.

He told her to go and pluck a chicken and scatter the feathers all the way from her home to his, then to gather them up again and bring them to him. He promised her that if she did this he would give her his answer. She agreed and left. The next day she came back and told the rabbi that she had done as she was instructed. She had plucked the chicken and scattered the feathers. But, she said, she could not bring the feathers to him, for the wind had scattered them everywhere. Then the rabbi said, "Lies are like feathers. Once you have scattered them, it is impossible to pick them all up again. You cannot undo the damage or completely change it. So, from now on, make up your mind to speak only the truth."—Adapted from William Silverman.

September 16. God's Flashlight

Have you ever walked into a cave? Maybe you have visited Inner Space, or Wonder Cave, or Carlsbad Caverns. Once I was in a cavern, deep under the ground. Our guide led us along a rocky path. Suddenly, all the lights went out. It was dark —so dark you couldn't see anything. I stumbled over a rock and almost fell.

The guide said, "Don't anyone move! You could fall and hurt yourself. I have a flashlight." Then he turned on his flashlight (display lighted flashlight) and we could see again. With the aid of the flashlight we walked along the rocky ledge without tripping or falling. The light helped us get out of the cave safely.

Did you know that God has a flashlight? Psalm 119:105 says that the Bible is "a flashlight to light the path ahead of me, and keep me from stumbling"(TLB).

This means that the Bible helps us. When we might do something that would hurt us, the Bible says, "Watch out, there is a rock that will trip you." When we are headed in the wrong direction, the Bible says, "Look out, there is a deep pit over there you can fall into and get hurt."

So the Bible is like a flashlight. Just as you carry a flashlight in your hand, you can carry the Bible in your heart. The more you read it, hear it, and live it, the happier you will be. The Bible will keep you from stumbling. It is God's flashlight. It will guide you through the darkest night.—Joe E. Trull.

September 23. Harmony Lost and Found

Two famous Scandinavians, Ole Bull, the marvelous violinist, and John Ericsson, the clever inventor who revolutionized ocean travel by introducing the screw into steam navigation, were great friends in their youth. Eventually they drifted apart and did not meet again until they had both become famous. It was during one of Ole Bull's American tours that the two friends met again.

Bull tried several times to persuade his friend to attend one of his concerts and hear him play the violin, but Ericsson declined. He was too busy; he had no time to waste on music. After several invitations, Bull finally said to him, "If you won't come, I'll bring my violin down here to your shop and play."

The engineer laughed heartily. "If you do, I'll smash the thing to pieces."

The famous musician, knowing the strange power that his instrument had over the human heart, was eager to see what effect it would have on the engineer. To realize his ambition, he decided to use a bit of diplomacy.

One day he arrived at Ericsson's workshop with the violin under his arm. Taking the instrument to pieces, he pointed out certain defects. He asked the engineer several questions about the scientific and acoustic principles involved. Ericsson's interest was aroused. They discussed the varying effect of the different grain of certain woods, and then the sound waves. Finally, to illustrate his meaning, Ole Bull replaced the parts, and drawing the bow across the strings, played a few bars of marvelously sweet music.

Ericsson's soul was stirred to the depths as he listened. Tears glistened in his eyes, and when Ole Bull paused, he said softly: "Play on! Don't stop. Play on! I never knew before what it was that was lacking in my life."—William L. Stidger.

September 30. The Importance of Numbers

Did you know that numbers are very important in our religion? *One* stands for God, for there is only one God. *Two* stands for the two natures of Jesus Christ, for he was both human and divine. *Three* stands for the Holy Trinity, for we know the one God as Father, Son, and Holy Spirit. There were *four* evangelists—Matthew, Mark, Luke, and John. Jesus had *five* wounds when he was crucified. The Book of Revelation tells about *seven* churches. Jesus Christ was raised from the dead on the *eighth* day that is, Sunday. *Ten* stands for the tithe, which was the tenth part of a person's earnings. Also, there were *ten* commandments. There were *twelve* tribes of Israel, and there were *twelve* apostles of Jesus.

There are other important numbers in the Bible. But the Bible tells us about a great crowd of people, *too large to number*. They were the people who would be saved and live with God and Jesus forever. This is the way the Bible pictures it: "After this I looked, and there was an enormous crowd—no one could count all the people! They were from every race, tribe, nation, and language, and they stood in front of the throne and of the Lamb, dressed in white robes and holding palm branches in their hands. They called out in a loud voice: 'Salvation comes from our God who sits on the throne, and from the Lamb!' " (Rev. 7:9–10 [TEV]).

October 7. Tagged!

A not-too-nice trick of boys and girls is to tape signs or notes on the backs of their friends. This creates an embarrassing situation in which the victims walk about with something added that they do not know about and that make them seem different from the usual smiling faces one sees in the front. Humanity has such a tag on the back, and it reads: *sin*. It is an added sign that we were not intended to have. Unfortunately, it is no laughing matter. One can scarcely smile at others or judge them because on the back of each of us is the same tag written in our own shape and illustrated in our own particular ways.

Have you ever looked in the mirror and found on your back an unexpected sign on your clothes or some bruise or blemish which was causing pain and irritation? The first instinctive question is: where did I get that? In reality, that is not the important question. The important question is: how do I heal that? or, what do I do to get rid of it?—William L. Hendricks.

October 14. Revolution

Dr. T. R. Glover liked to quote a little boy who said that the Bible began with Genesis and ended in Revolutions! He meant "Revelation," of course, but I think it was a very good mistake to make. The Bible does end in revolutions!

What is a revolution? The word means a "turning around." The older ones among you will have heard of the French Revolution. The dates (I've just looked them up!) are 1789 to 1795. The poorer classes in France were being ill-treated by the noblemen and clergy, and there was a grim uprising. The end of it all was a turnabout in the government of France.

In this country, we had our Industrial Revolution in the last century. Up to a hundred and fifty years ago, the people of Britain worked on the land. Some were farmers and shepherds, and others worked at crafts which were associated with that kind of life. Then machinery came. Steam had been discovered, and later what we call the internal cumbustion engine was invented. And that kind of thing completely changed our way of living. It brought great prosperity to our country and a good deal of ugliness, too. It was a turnaround. And that is why we call it the Industrial Revolution.

What revolution, then, does the Bible give rise to? Let me tell you of one. In the north of India, there is a district known as the Lushai Hills. When Christian missionaries first went there some seventy years ago, the people were headhunters. A few years ago, a choir from Lushai toured America giving remarkable performances of Handel's *Messiah*!

I could give further examples. There is no doubt at all that the Bible can make wicked people good and wild people God-fearing. The little boy was right when he said it ends in revolutions!—J. Ithel Jones.

October 21. More Valuable Than Much Fine Gold

The ancient Talmud tells the story of a king who had a dream. And in his dream, he saw a huge pair of scales held in the hand of Justice. The scales seemed to reach from earth to sky. In one side of the scales was a pile of gold, jewels, lumber, houses, lands—all symbols of earthly, material power. In the other side of the scales was a nest of straw. The gold, jewels, houses, and lands had tipped the scales down until the nest of straw was high in the air, and the gold-laden side of the scales touched the earth.

Then some guardian angel robed in white came along with a child in her arms and put that little child in the nest of straw. The king in his dream saw the scales immediately begin to move until the child outweighed the side laden with gold, jewels, houses, and lands. Yes, the side with the child touched the earth, and the material side tipped to the sky.

"That means," said the king to himself, "that the most valuable thing on this earth is a little child. The child outweighs them all in value."—William L. Stidger.

October 28. All Saints' Day

Do you know how Halloween came to be? The word is a shortened form of "All Hallows' Eve." *Hallow* is another word for *holy*, and the holy ones are the saints. November 1 is All Saints' Day, a day when we celebrate all the great Christian saints.

Halloween is the "eve" (or evening) before All Saints' Day.

Costumes on Halloween began when church members dressed up like the saints as part of their celebration of All Saints' Day. The tricks come from the belief of some people that ghosts roamed around the countryside making mischief.

Our "Jack o' Lanterns" come from Ireland, where they used to be made from turnips instead of pumpkins. The legend is about a man named Jack who was unable to enter heaven because he was so stingy. He had to walk the earth forever, carrying his lantern. And so he was called "Jack o' Lantern."

There are many customs that have grown up around Halloween. Most of them are fun and harmless. But sometimes these pranks can become harmful. If we are really celebrating the lives of the saints, then we ought to be doing helpful and fun things. Let's think of some different things to do this Halloween. Perhaps we can plan some special celebration.—*Pockets*.

November 4. God Is Our Father, Too

Let me tell a story which seems to me to be a kind of parable of the lives of us all. It is almost too awful to tell. A boy of twelve or thirteen, in a fit of crazy anger and depression, got hold of a gun somewhere and fired it at his father, who died not right away but soon afterward. When the authorities asked the boy why he had done it, he said that it was because he could not stand his father, because his father demanded too much of him, because he was always after him, because he hated his father. And then later on, after he had been placed in a house of detention somewhere, a guard was walking down the corridor late one night when he heard sounds from the boy's room, and he stopped to listen. The words that he heard the boy sobbing out in the dark were, "I want my father, I want my father."—Frederick Buechner.

November 11. Good Advice (Stewardship Day)

There is an oft-told story of the unknown deacon who saw a young boy on the road to New York. He was setting out on a journey of more than a hundred miles. The deacon looked at the poor lad, who had all his possessions tied up in a little bundle that he carried over his shoulder, and asked him what he expected to do in New York. The boy said that the only thing he knew anything about was soapmaking. The old man answered, "My son, someday there is going to be in New York the greatest soapmaker in the world. Be that soapmaker." The boy replied, "I will try." Then the old man knelt with him by the roadside and prayed for his success. Arising from his knees, he said, "My boy, give your heart to the Lord Jesus, give your best service to your employer, and give one-tenth of all you earn to God." The boy obeyed the three precepts and became a success in business and gave millions to the cause of God. His name? William Colgate.—Adapted from W. W. Weeks.

November 18. The Right Kind of Operation

There are boys and girls who haven't fathers and mothers to look after them, and the church to which I belong—and other churches, too—have homes for them where good people try to bring them up in the right way. I know one of these homes well, and I know the children there so well that all twenty-two of them call me "Uncle."

Among them is a boy, Alec, and Alec is a "wee mischief." You can see it in one look at his bright black eyes. He is never out of trouble for long and never done making trouble for those who have charge of him. Well, one day, he was just out of one spot of mischief into another, and the matron was at the end, or nearly, of her patience with him. "Oh, Alec," she said, "is there nothing we can do to make you a good boy?" At once Alec answered, "You might try getting my tonsils out."

I'm afraid that would not help. Getting the tonsils out will sometimes make ill boys into well boys, but never bad boys into good ones. But I don't think really that Alec needs to have anything taken out. It would be a great pity if he were to stop being a lively and high-spirited boy. God, who made him, I am certain does not want him changed from a naughty boy into a nobody.

What Alec needs is not anything taken out, but something put in—and that something is thoughtfulness. If he could only get into the way of thinking of other people and the effect on them of what he does, then he would still give them surprises—but pleasant surprises. He would not exasperate those who look after him, but he would often make them laugh. That's the change Jesus would like to make in Alec, and could make and may yet make—and in you, too, if you are like Alec.—James Wright.

November 25. Faith in the Future

In 1838, a man resigned from the United States Patent Office because, as he said in his letter of resignation, which is still on file in the hall or archives at Washington, "there is no future in the Patent Office; all the great inventions have been accomplished."

Since that foolish man, who had little faith in the future, resigned, we have discovered the steam engine, the Diesel engine, the jet propulsion engine, the telephone, motion pictures, radio, radar, submarines, airships, insulin, sulpha drugs, penicillin, and atomic power.

In 1886, a government official in Washington announced that all the canals and railroads had been built and that there would be no further progress in transportation in the United States. At the time that statement was made, Thomas Edison was thirty-nine years of age, Henry Ford was twenty-three, Steinmetz was twenty-one, Orville Wright was fifteen, Marconi was twelve, and Einstein was seven.

In 1899, a great newspaper came out with an article stating that it had had its research workers go carefully into the matter of the "horseless carriage," and while it might be a "toy for the wealthy to play with," it would never come into common use and certainly would never approximate the popularity and usefulness of the bicycle.—William L. Stidger.

December 2. A Special Wonder

Do you know the Seven Wonders of the World? We have heard of them, but most of us could not name them. The first wonder is a group of three pyramids in Egypt, outside the city of Cairo. They were built almost five thousand years ago. They alone of all the Seven Wonders still stand. Then there were the Hanging Gardens of Babylon with terraces that were said to rise from 75 to 300 feet. They were probably built more than twenty-five hundred years ago by King Nebuchadnezzar to please his wife. There was also the statue of Zeus or Jupiter, one of the Greek gods, at Olympia; there was the Temple of Artemis or Diana, a Greek goddess, at Ephesus; there was the Mausoleum at Halicarnassus, a monument which a queen erected in memory of her husband; there was the Colossus at Rhodes, a bronze statue of Apollo, about 105 feet high; and there was the Pharos of Alexandria, a lighthouse on an island off the coast of Egypt.

But the greatest wonder of all was not one of those seven. It was and is the love of God in Jesus Christ, who brought us his wonderful salvation—forgiveness and eternal life—through his cross and resurrection. John Jacob Niles expressed it well in a beautiful folk song. He said that he wondered as he wandered how Jesus the Savior could love poor lost sinners like you and me.

December 9. Windshields

When he was a boy, Joseph Egan climbed a bluff near LaCrosse, Wisconsin, and there carved his initials on a rock. Years later, in the summer of 1978, when he was fifty-one, Joseph Egan climbed that same bluff to revisit his initials.

Losing his footing, he slipped and fell thirty feet to his death. Egan, a hospital chaplain, had with him some altar boys. It is believed he was attempting to show them this souvenir from his own boyhood.

There's nothing wrong in carving one's initials or revisiting the scenes of one's childhood. This was a freak accident from which we dare not try to draw a "lesson."

However, it suggests a basic principle in life, which is the danger of being so preoccupied with yesterday that we live in the past.

All cars and trucks have a big windshield, plus one or more rearview mirrors. This is a parable of life. Most of our attention should be focused on today's traffic, on what's happening right now.

Yet a safe driver frequently checks his rearview mirror so he knows what's coming up on him. Likewise, we study the past, we review the past, we profit from the past, because it continually has a bearing on today.

But we don't dwell on the past, lest, like a driver who focuses constantly on the mirror, we drive blindly into tomorrow, as if windshields had never been invented.—Robert J. Hastings.

December 16. Feast of Lights

At this time of year, our Jewish friends celebrate a very special thing that happened many, many years ago. It happened before Jesus was born. The Syrians had captured Jerusalem and the Temple where the Jews worshipped. But a great Jewish hero, Judas Maccabeus, and his army defeated the Syrians. Then they went into Jerusalem and found that the Syrians had done terrible things to the city, especially the Temple. After that, work began to clean up and purify everything and make it a fit place to worship God once more. One hundred and sixty-five years before Christ, the Temple was dedicated again. Every year since that time our Jewish friends have celebrated that great happening. They call their celebration Hanukkah. It is the Feast of Dedication, the Feast of Lights. Eight candles are lighted. On the first night, two wax candles are lighted—one to serve as a torch and the other to show that it is the first day of the feast. On the second night after sundown, a second candle is lighted, and so on until by the eighth night there are eight candles, besides the torch. It is not correct to call Hanukkah "the Jewish Christmas," for Christmas celebrates the birth of Christ and that has a very different meaning.

December 23. After the Quarrel

Two neighbors have quarreled and parted company for some reason or other. Then it occurs to one of them that this situation is just not right. He writes a letter to his former friend suggesting that they make peace. He receives no reply. Come now, he thinks, I must try again. "Let us make peace and get along once more."

Still no reply. Then the man decides one evening—it is a bitterly cold winter's night with howling wind and snow—to undertake the long journey to the other man's house on foot. He arrives panting, snowed up, and petrified with cold. He repeats by word of mouth his invitation. And now it begins to dawn on his neighbor that he has before him a real human being, frozen, drenched with snow, and panting. Now his heart melts, and he takes the invitation seriously. Now he says Yes.

This neighbor is God. He has written to us many a letter, and we have not answered. Finally he himself has come to us. —Adapted from Emil Brunner.

December 30. The Doll Lady

Five-year-old Susie was very weak. So weak that her doctor at the Children's Home didn't think she would live until Christmas. So Susie was given her doll early. Quietly she lay in her crib, cuddling the doll tightly against her cheek.

"She seemed to get better as soon as she got the doll," the doctor later told the Doll Lady. "Susie kept looking at the doll and murmuring, 'My doll, my doll.' I think it must have been the first thing of her own she'd ever had. Evidently, having the doll gave her the will to live."

For fifteen years, the Doll Lady has been sending dolls to hospitals and schools for the crippled, sick, and handicapped. Each doll is beautifully dressed with handsewn clothes; every garment is different.

Every January, the Doll Lady begins to dress the dolls for the following Christmas —a dozen a month for nine months a year. It takes about twelve hours to complete one doll, since many have crocheted or knit hats, collars, or edgings. And then, too, there are the bonus dolls.

"After I finish my quota of a dozen each month, I dress a larger doll for a wheelchair child. That's an extra bonus of pleasure for myself every month."

"Why don't you sell me one?" a friend once asked, thinking that the money from the sale would help the children.

"The dolls are just for the sick children. I could give money, too, but working and sewing on the clothes means I'm giving a part of myself," the Doll Lady explained. —*Guideposts*.

SECTION XI. Sermon Outlines and Homiletic and Worship Aids for Fifty-three Weeks

SUNDAY: JANUARY FIRST

MORNING SERVICE

Topic: The Head and the Heart in the Christian Faith (New Year)

SCRIPTURE: Mark 12:28–34.

A student posed a perceptive question: is Christianity subject to reason, or must I just accept it all on faith? The question is perceptive because it points to an age-old problem which every generation must answer for itself: is Christianity a matter of the head or the heart?

I. (a) There are many who practice what I would call "head faith." That is to say, they believe only what can be proven scientifically. This purely rational approach to life has been brought to a culmination in our century. Building on the philosophies of men like Nietzsche and Feuerbach, who claimed that religion was merely a crutch for those who lacked faith in pure reason, we have fallen down before the gods of science and technology. This is not to say that science and technology have not been of great benefit to us all. Many of us would not be here today were it not for medical technology. Science has opened fascinating new worlds for us, and we are in great debt to committed and honest people in these fields.

(b) Yet there is something wrong, even something unhealthy, with head faith which excludes heart faith. Maybe some of us can live by reason alone, but not all of us. Even Arnold Toynbee, the British historian noted for his skepticism about religion, said that "science and technology cannot survive as substitutes for religion."

II. (a) So we come to what may be called "heart faith." There are many who react to the opposite extreme and are convinced that the Christian faith leaves no room for the use of reason and intelligence. Yet heart faith is very appealing. The gospel cannot help but stir emotions. Just as a man cannot propose to a girl scientifically, we cannot gaze on the cross scientifically. The fact is, Christ can and does enter our lives and can change us in ways that defy all reason. We pray, not because it is reasonable, but because strange things happen when we pray. God does not fit into a test tube; if he did, he would not be God.

(b) Still, there are problems with heart faith when it excludes all reason. For example, in the understanding of Scripture, pure heart faith ignores the work of devout scholars who have committed their lives to the study of Scripture. Pure heart faith claims that anybody's idea of the meaning of Scripture should carry equal weight. Such an approach leads to all kinds of sub-Christian cults built on faulty interpretation of Scripture. There are more problems. Pure heart faith ignores the fact that feelings are deceptive. What feels right may not be right. If our faith is based solely on feelings, we are apt to accept anything, no matter how outlandish, which stirs the emotions (especially if it is wrapped in religious language). Heart faith alone is the easy way out. It is just as easy for us to be deceived by our heart as by our head. So where do we go from here?

III. (a) We take a hard look at Jesus, the author of our faith. We need to be reminded that he did not lead a pastoral life in a simple culture. He spoke Aramaic and knew at last some koinï Greek. In school, he learned Hebrew. From Roman garrisons, he probably picked up some Latin. Although his hometown of Nazareth was small, it was located on an international trade route. Many times as a boy, Jesus must have run down the hill behind the city to watch caravans from the east and west. He was cosmopolitan. Neither was he ignorant of the Old Testament. The fact that a scribe would ask Jesus which law is greatest is an indication that Jesus had earned intellectual respect among the elite of Jerusalem.

(b) And what did he consider the greatest commandment? "Hear, O Israel: The Lord our God, the Lord is one, and you shall love the Lord your God with all your heart, and with all your soul, and with all your mind, and with all your strength." This is not a lesson in Jewish psychology, but simply a way of saying that we are to love God with every aspect of our lives. This is, without doubt, heart faith; but we cannot ignore the fact that we are to love God with our minds! That is head faith! Christianity is not only for the intellectually elite; but neither is it only a set of pious platitudes for mindless morons. "Faith," as Hans Küng has said, "must not be blind, but responsible." To be responsible to God is to offer him our heads as well as our hearts.

(c) Jesus did not stop with the first commandment. He lifted an obscure commandment from the book of Leviticus and set it alongside the love of God. "You shall love your neighbor as yourself." In its original context, it meant that a good Jew was to love his fellow Jews as he loved himself. He was allowed to hate non-Jews. But Jesus took an old law and gave it new

meaning. He did not mean "love" in the sense of a sentimental affection. He meant "love" in the sense of working for a person's good even if you can hardly stand the sight of him. Think of what this will mean! Loving our neighbors with all our minds will take us much further than personal evangelism. It will involve an intelligent approach to the problems of prison reform, hunger, health, armaments, pollution. It will even mean a thoughtful consideration of how our own life-styles affect our neighbors. This is Christian faith in action. This is head and heart faith attempting to do the will of God in a complex world.—Thomas R. McKibbens, Jr.

Illustrations

THE OLD AND THE NEW.   Strolling recently through Cumberland National Forest, I was struck afresh by the large number of fallen trees. A forest is not only a land of the living, it is a cemetery of once-living forms which now rot and return to the earth whence they came. A forest is also living trees whose arrowlike trunks pierce the shadowy darkness, straight to the sunlight overhead. That is not all—a forest is fresh every spring, every leaf a chlorophyll factory, a pulsing engine of new life. But most of all, a forest is a silent, growing, mighty surge of new life creating new forms, enlarging old forms. If, while walking down a forest trail, you stop and hold your breath, you might think that you ought to hear the mighty roar of such an upward Niagara of growing. But the growing is too powerful to be noisy. Even death is not static here; it is the rotting of dead forms which in their dying and rotting create a rich loam, nourishing the living forms at whose roots they lie. A culture is not unlike a forest. It has its living forms, its discarded past, its growing edge, and its pulsing interior life.—Dwight E. Stevenson.

FEARLESS AND FEARFUL FATIH.   There is a story in the annals of the British Navy which tells that on one occasion a destroyer was lying in a harbor of the West Indies, where five other ships of various nationalities were anchored. Suddenly a furious storm descended, with a wild, terrifying wind, and great waves sweeping right into the harbor. What did the British captain do? He weighed anchor and steamed straight out to sea in the very teeth of the storm. Two days later he returned, battered but safe—and there were the other five ships lying piled up, wrecked upon the foreshore. It was their very refusal to face the seas and the storm, their clinging to security, which had been their undoing. Only the ship that ventured everything came through.—James S. Stewart.

Sermon Suggestions

LOOKING FORWARD. We can look forward to this new year: (1) If we dedicate ourselves to a new life at deeper levels of prayer. (2) If we dedicate ourselves to a life of greater loyalty to Christ and his church. (3) If we dedicate ourselves to a life of increased service to the church and our neighbors. (4) If we dedicate ourselves to a life of more purposeful evangelism to win others to Christ. (5) If we dedicate ourselves to a life of more responsible stewardship of our resources.—Thomas F. Hudson, *Pulpit Digest*.

FOLLOWING JESUS INTO THE FUTURE. Scripture: Matt. 8:19–20. The scribe: (1) willing—to accept the teachings of Jesus, to share his fortunes; (2) warned—to count the cost of following him (cf. Luke 14:28–33); (3) went on—notwithstanding. So let us suppose he did, and so let us do. —John A. Broadus.

Worship Aids

CALL TO WORSHIP. "The Lord is in his Holy Temple: let all the earth keep silence before him" (Hab. 2:20).

INVOCATION. O Lord, our God, we remember thy promise that wheresoever two or three are gathered together in thy name, there thou art in the midst of them. We claim that promise this morning and pray that each one of us may be aware of thy presence, for thou knowest our needs and how inadequate we feel ourselves to be in the presence of world problems and the challenges of this hour. If thou wilt help us, O Lord, then shall we be better than we are, wiser than we know, and stronger than we dream.—Peter Marshall.

OFFERTORY SENTENCE. "This is the thing which the Lord commanded, saying, 'Take ye from among you an offering unto the Lord: whosoever is of a willing heart, let him bring it, an offering of the Lord' " (Exod. 35:4–5).

OFFERTORY PRAYER. Lord, let this first offering of the new year reflect our gratitude for the year just past, our hope for the future, and our determination to serve thee in the present with Christ-centered stewardship.—E. Lee Phillips.

PRAYER. O God, thou art the First and the Last, the Beginning and the End, the Alpha and the Omega—the Eternal One; but thou art our Father, also. We are awed by thy majesty, yet we are comforted by thy love. We take refuge in the tenderness of thy strength.

We bring to this beginning of a new year all the weight of sin not confessed, duties not completed, plans not fulfilled, and hopes disappointed. We bring them into thy presence with the confidence that thou wilt enter into our need and do something redemptive: forgive our sins, help us to carry forward tasks unfinished, give us wisdom to re-evaluate all that we have proposed, and grant us the courage to accept realities that cannot be altered. But may we not too soon give up on our duties, plans, and hopes, assured as we are that thou wilt supply the strength to do whatever is right and needed.

We pray for patience as we experience the slow unfolding of thy will for us. We pray for tolerance and charity when family, friends, or neighbors forget thy commands. We pray for a spirit of sharing, so that both those who give and those who receive may know the fullness of the blessings of the gospel of Christ.

EVENING SERVICE

Topic: A Fresh Vision of God
SCRIPTURE: Isa. 55:6–9.

The deepest need of your life is a fresh vision of God. Your attitude toward God determines the quality of your life.

It makes a decided difference whether you believe that you can flee from God's presence, or believe, with the psalmist, that "if you take the wings of the morning and dwell in the uttermost parts of the sea, even there shall God's hand lead you"; whether you believe that you can fall or drift from God's care, or affirm, with the apostle Paul, that "nothing in all this world can separate us from the love of God."

I can never erase from my mind the statement of a dynamic Christian who had spent months in a concentration camp: "It is only when everything in life is gone . . . save God . . . that one discovers that God alone is enough."

I. *You can have a fresh vision of the supernatural God.*

(a) "As the heavens are higher than the earth, so are my ways higher than your ways." This statement is not an exaggeration and emphasizes the wonder and grace of your God. God, in his majesty and love, has said, "My thoughts of you . . ." (put your name right into that statement) ". . . my thoughts of you are more exalted than the greater distance existing between the heavens and the heart."

(b) Men are selfish and exclusive, bent on securing revenge. Men like to disguise their guilt, pretend they are innocent, and insist they are worthy of heaven. Unbelieving men try to save themselves by their noble intentions, their contributions, and through mere church membership. They have failed to discover the Savior's forgiving and strengthening power.

Christ requires the crushed and contrite heart, the humble and penitent soul, and the believing and trusting mind. To these, Jesus gives his marvelous conversion, the provision of an all-wise, ever-present, all-powerful eternal God, and unquestionably an evidence of his greatness, his deity, and his compassion for you and me.

II. *A fresh vision of God makes him personal.*

(a) When you think in terms of millions of people, it is difficult to believe that each soul stands out distinctly before God. You tend to think of yourself as an insignificant cog in the great machinery of our civilization. You perhaps wonder at times whether it makes any difference if you live or die. You do count with God. Jesus said, "You are of more value than the entire world," and he supported that statement by laying down his own life for you.

(b) Faith in God carries with it an assertion that God knows you most intimately. In fact, there can be no region of life from which God is absent. It is impossible to say that anything is beyond or inaccessible to God. Believe me, there is no soul neglected or abandoned by God. You can say, "Thou God seest me . . . as no man on earth can see me." There is no more important or emphatic statement that can be made than "God loves you."

III. *A fresh vision of God magnifies Jesus Christ.*

(a) It is indeed an ill sign in our day that Jesus Christ is so lightly considered. It is sheer tragedy that people lose him so easily and still more amazing that we accept him so coolly.

(b) However, when Peter saw Christ's glory, he cried out, "Depart from me." John the Baptist shrank almost cowardly, saying, "I am not worthy to unloose his shoes." For nearly two thousand years, it has been the sight of the cross of Christ that has moved men to repentance and has lifted the burden of sin from our shoulders. At the cross, you find rest from sorrow, life by his death. In the agony of Christ, you see what sin cost God, and in the marvelous spirit of Jesus in the presence of his enemies, as the blows of evil were inflicted, you see the power of God.

(c) Jesus said, "Have I been so long with you and you still do not know me? He that hath seen me, hath seen God." And again, our Lord said, "No man cometh unto God but by me." In Christ, you see God loving, forgiving, saving.— Harold W. Seever.

SUNDAY: JANUARY EIGHTH

MORNING SERVICE

Topic: The Relevance of Christ
SCRIPTURE: Mark 1:24.

This question was thrown at Jesus as he preached in the synagogue one Sabbath. In varying forms, and with increasing scepticism, people are throwing it at his church today. Is Christ really relevant to the modern situation? Isn't Christianity out of date for man come of age? After all, his world and ours are centuries apart. Ancient Palestine would seem to have little in common with modern Toronto, New York, London. This is the age of jet propulsion, television, the computer, space exploration. This is the age of affluence in which Western man, at least, is distracted by, and preoccupied with, the sophisticated pleasures and comforts of a complex civilization.

Have we an answer? Assuredly, we have. Jesus Christ is supremely relevant to modern man. His day is not over: it has hardly begun. We have everything to do with him, whoever we are, and for two main reasons.

One is to be found in the uniqueness of Christ as the Son of God. Because of who he is, of his divine personality, Jesus Christ will not, and cannot be, casually dismissed. In him, we confront ultimate reality.

The other reason is to be found in the indispensability of Christ to the life of man. We may be happy, active, apparently self-sufficient and secure in our materialism, but there exist in the depths of human nature basic needs which only Christ can satisfy. These needs are constant from age to age. What are they?

I. *There is the need for personal identity.*

(a) In Arthur Miller's famous play *Death of a Salesman*, Willie Loman is a pathetic figure, swaggering his way through a shabby life of second-rate illusions about everything, especially himself. At the end, with Loman in his grave, one of his sons sums up the tragedy of his existence in this illuminating sentence: "He never knew who he was."

It would not be a gross exaggeration to say that this is modern man's predicament. He may have plenty to live *with*—gadgets galore, money to spend, an inexhaustible supply of things to spend it on, a place in the sun. But what has he to live for?

(b) The absence of any sense of personal significance, of any clue to the meaning of his existence, is obvious enough in the behavior of contemporary man. Take his experiments with drugs and his suicide rates. Take the best selling novels and long-running plays he reads and watches —they are packed with distorted, groping, lost characters who lie, cheat, steal, drink, kill, and fornicate their way through their nasty lives. This should not surprise us. A world without meaning is a tragic world, and life is "a tale told by an idiot, full of sound and fury, signifying nothing."

(c) Thank God for Christ! His relevance is that in him man finds himself and his purpose in life. From him, you learn that you belong to a God who made you for himself, who loves you with an unwearying love, who suffers and forgives, who purposes to train you by the free probation of life on earth for a high calling that defies adequate description. You are called here and now to serve his Kingdom, to be his steward on earth, and to grow a character —such a character that one day the angels of heaven will look at you and whisper excitedly, "How like Christ he is!"

II. *There is the need for moral victory.*

(a) Modern man has mastered the atom, but he has not mastered himself. Our age has been described as one of intellectual giants and moral dwarfs. There is evidence in plenty to support this. Look around the world we live in. The failures of man have been monstrous. Who can forget the gas chambers of Nazi Germany, where one of the most civilized countries on earth murdered six million Jews? Who can forget the agonizing destruction of Hiroshima and Nagasaki? Who can forget that scandal of our time, the accusing army of the hungry, the homeless, the hopeless? Look, too, within—at the selves we live with. The most decent of men are conscious of a civil war raging inside them. We are victims of clashing loyalties and competing impulses. Sins of commission, and omission—that nightmare of every good man—haunt and harass us, flooding us with feelings of shame, regret, and guilt. Paul gave classical expression to this problem of the divided self, and the need for moral victory: "For the good that I would I do not: but the evil that I would not, that I do. O wretched man that I am! Who shall deliver me from the body of death?"

(b) Who shall deliver us? (1) Legislation, reply some. And we would not belittle the power of legislation. It is an effective weapon in the fight against evil. But the purest, most high-minded legislator is himself tainted with the curse of sin and self; he is part of the problem, not the answer to it.

(2) Who shall deliver us? Education, reply others. This is a belief as old as Plato. The Greeks equated sin with ignorance and passionately proclaimed education as the only solution. To be sure, it is our duty to educate the mind. Realism, however, compels us to recognize that the best education in the world is as powerless as legislation to give peace to a guilty conscience or to lift a single, defeated soul to moral victory. Indeed, it can actually complicate our human predicament, enabling sin to take on a high polish, to speak grammatically, and to live in the suburbs.

(3) Who shall deliver us? Christ, we reply. Where all else dismally fails, he dynamically succeeds. When we call him "Savior," we call him by his name. This is the thrilling, triumphant assertion of the Christian gospel. "He is able to save to the uttermost." "Neither is there salvation in any other, for there is none other name under heaven given among men whereby we must be saved." Let Tolstoy speak to us. This literary genius was a slave to his lower nature, a defeated husk of a man—until he discovered that Christ had everything to do with him. "Five years ago I came to believe in Christ's teaching," he wrote, "and my life suddenly became changed. I ceased desiring what I had wished for before. The direction of my life, my desires, became different. What was good and bad changed places." "This is the victory that overcomes the world," cries John lyrically, "our faith."

III. *There is the need for final security.*

(a) Today we tend to place an inordinate emphasis on material security. Every effort is made to protect men from the contingent and accidental. A measure of security is a legitimate demand for all responsible people to make.

(b) Yet here is a curious paradox: the age which clamors so stridently, and schemes so expertly, for security is also the most nervous and neurotic on record. We have lost the sense of final security, of being, before the cradle and beyond the grave, in the everlasting arms of God, the Father of our Lord Jesus Christ, and our Father!

(c) We must come to terms with the inevitable death awaiting us. It is frivolous, and, indeed, a delusion, to adopt a devil-may-care attitude toward death. It remains the grim specter that it is—the enemy of reason, of achievement, and of love. Death is the final contradiction, the shadow over our sunlit hours—and no man can live with joy and abandon and self-sacrificing endeavor until he has discovered a security that transcends it and enables him to laugh in its face. So we need Jesus Christ today as desperately as our fathers needed him. Our final security is in the God who has declared himself in Christ to be the lord of life and the conqueror of death. Christ is risen. He has abolished death. He has led captivity captive. As in Adam all die, even so in Christ shall all be made alive." "For to me to live is Christ," declared the apostle, "and to die is gain." That is real security.—John N. Gladstone.

Illustrations

PORTALS OF TRANSCENDENCE. If a Christian takes the position that ugliness, inhumanity, and artificiality are wrong in the place of worship, they are also wrong elsewhere. The burden Christians must undertake is to make not only church buildings into metaphors of the holy, but all architecture for which they have responsibility. If it is true that secular buildings can be vehicles of grace, then they ought to be. Anything less is a denial of the faith. In addition to our church buildings, our factories and stores and workplaces, our cities in general ought to be portals of transcendence.—E. A. Sövik.

TRIED AND TRUE. Halley, the astronomer, was denouncing Christianity. Sir Isaac Newton said, "Halley, when you speak of astronomy and mathematics I will listen to you, but not when you talk of Christianity, for you have never tried it. But I have tried it and know it to be true." —John MacNeill.

Sermon Suggestions

WHAT DO YOU SEE IN JESUS. Text: John 1:43–51. (1) Only a dim vision—Jesus of Nazareth the son of Joseph? (2) Or the fuller glory—the Son of God, the King of Israel? (3) Or complete revelation—the Son of man in the opened heaven?—R. C. H. Lenski.

THE LIGHT FOR ALL PEOPLE. Text: John 1:9. (1) His coming dissipated the shadows of *doubt*. (2) His coming dissipated the shadows of *despair*. (3) His coming dissipated the darkness of *death*.—William Barclay.

Worship Aids

CALL TO WORSHIP. "From the rising of the sun to its setting my name is great among the nations" (Mal. 1:11 [RSV]).

INVOCATION. O almighty God, who pourest out, on all who desire it, the Spirit of grace and of supplication: deliver us, when we draw nigh to thee, from coldness of heart and wanderings of mind, that with steadfast thoughts and kindled affections, we may worship thee in spirit and in truth. —Book of Common Prayer.

OFFERTORY SENTENCE. "Give unto the Lord the glory due unto his name: bring an offering, and come before him: worship the Lord in the beauty of holiness" (1 Chron. 16:29).

OFFERTORY PRAYER. Most gracious and benevolent heavenly Father, accept these our gifts as our humble effort to return unto thee a portion of thy bounty entrusted to our care. Grant unto us, O Lord, the wisdom and compassion to use these gifts offered unto thee for the care of all thy children throughout the world; in the name of our Lord and Savior, Jesus Christ.—Rodney K. Miller.

PRAYER. To thee, O God, we pray, who hast comprehended our whole life in the gospel of thy Son, Jesus Christ, who hath not left us alone with Christmas, with all its beauty and fair tradition and its sweet story; because we have to live our life with the heights above us and on the level plain. We make our roadway down through the abysses and across the gorges. And there is another side to live beside the greatness of heroism: the richness of thine own Spirit in the children of man, and we thank thee that he who came to us the incarnate Christmas, bringing to us the Christ-mass, bringing to us the very solution of the problem of life with its humiliation and its meagerness and its straitness—we thank thee that he bore our griefs and carried our sorrows; that it was not alone the visit of the Wise Men, but the visit of the fools, also; that it was not alone the song of angels, but the cry of the disgraced and the sorrowful and the pained. We thank thee that he heard not only the voice of the Infinite above him, but that he heard the cry of the dying thief.

Surely he hath borne our grief and carried our sorrows and knows our pathway between these experiences. We ask thee to help us to look upon it seriously, with the utmost friendship, in the atmosphere one for another, not boasting, but humble. We ask in the name of the Captain of our salvation, even Jesus.—Frank W. Gunsaulus.

EVENING SERVICE

Topic: God's Revelation of Heaven
SCRIPTURE: 1 Cor. 2:9, 10.

The preaching of the apostle Paul was rejected by numbers in the cultivated town of Corinth. It was not wise enough nor eloquent enough—nor was it sustained by miracles. To all which the apostle was content to reply that his judges were incompetent to try the question. For every kind of truth, a special capacity or preparation is indispensable.

Therefore, the apostle's whole defense resolved itself into this: the natural man receiveth not the things which are of the Spirit of God.

I. By the natural man is meant the lower faculties of man; and it is said of these that they can not discover spiritual truth.

(a) Eternal truth is not perceived through sensation. "Eye hath not seen the things which God hath prepared for them that love him."

(1) There is a life of mere sensation. The highest pleasure of sensation comes through the eye. Let us not depreciate what God has given. There is a rapture in gazing on this wondrous world. It is a pure delight *to see*.

(2) But all this is bounded. The eye can only reach the finite beautiful. It does not scan "the king in his beauty, nor the land that is very far off."

(3) Again, it is perishable beauty—a sight to sadden rather than delight. Even while you gaze and feel how fair it is, joy mingles with melancholy, from a consciousness that it all is fading. It is the transient—not the Eternal Loveliness, for which our spirits pant. Therefore, when he, who was the Truth and the Life, came into this world in the body which God had prepared for him, he came not in the glory of form: he was "a root out of a dry ground: he had no form nor comeliness." When they saw him, "there was no beauty that they should desire him." The eye did not behold, even in Christ, the things which God had prepared.

(4) Now observe, this is an eternal truth, true at all times—true now and forever: The world of which he speaks is not a future, but a present revelation. God *hath* revealed it. He speaks not of something already shown, only not to eye nor ear. The distinction lies between a kingdom which is appreciable by the senses and another whose facts and truths are seen and heard only by the spirit.

(5) Again—no scientific analysis can discover the truths of God. Science can not give a Revelation. Science proceeds upon observation. It submits everything to the experience of the senses.

Men have supposed they discovered the law of deity written on the anatomical phenomena of disease. But if a man, startled by all this, gives up this sin, has he from this selfish prudence learned the law of Duty? The penalties of wrongdoing, doubtless—but not the sanction of Right and Wrong written on the conscience, of which penalties are only the enforcements.

No, it is in vain that we ransack the world for probable evidences of God and hypotheses of his existence. It is idle to look into the materialism of man for the Revelation of his immortality, or to examine the morbid anatomy of the body to find the rule of Right. Eye hath not seen the truths which are clear enough to Love and to the Spirit.

(b) Eternal truth is not reached by hearsay. "Ear hath not heard the things which God hath prepared for them that love him."

(1) No revelation can be adequately given by the address of man to man, whether by writing or orally, even if he be put in possession of the Truth itself. For all such revelation must be made through words; and words are but counters—the coins of intellectual exchange. There is as little resemblance between the silver coin and the bread it purchases, as between the word and the thing it stands for. Looking at the coin, the form of the loaf does not suggest itself. Listening to the word, you do not perceive the idea for which it stands, unless you are already in possession of it. Each man in this congregation has a God before him at this moment, who is, according to his own attainment in goodness, more or less limited and imperfect. The sensual man hears of God and understands one thing. The pure man hears and conceives another thing. The conceptions conveyed by the same word are essentially different, according to the soul which receives them. A verbal revelation is only a revelation to the ear.

(2) Now see what a hearsay religion is. There are men who believe on authority. Their minister believes all this Christianity

true—therefore so do they. He calls this doctrine essential—they echo it. The Corinthian philosophers heard Paul; the Pharisees heard Christ. How much did the ear convey? To thousands, exactly nothing. He alone has a religion whose soul knows by experience that to serve God and know him is the richest treasure. And unless Truth comes to you, not in word only, but in power besides—authoritative because true, not true because authoritative—there has been no real revelation made to you from God.

(c) Truth is not discoverable by the heart—"neither have entered into the heart of man the things which God hath prepared for them that love him." The heart—two things we refer to this source: the power of imagining, and the power of loving.

(1) Imagination is distinct from the mere dry faculty of reasoning. Imagination is creative—it is an immediate intuition, not a logical analysis—we call it popularly a kind of inspiration. Now imagination is a power of the heart. Great thoughts originate from a large heart: a man must have a heart or he never could create.

But all this is nothing more than what the material man can achieve.

(2) There is more in the heart of man—it has the power of affection. The highest moment known on earth by the merely natural is that in which the mysterious union of heart with heart is felt. Call it friendship—love—what you will. This is the purest, serenest ecstasy of the merely human—more blessed than any sight that can be presented to the eye or any sound that can be given to the ear, more sublime than the sublimest dream ever conceived by genius in its most gifted hour, when the freest way was given to the shaping spirit of imagination.

This has entered into the heart of man, yet human love is but the faint type of that surpassing blessedness which belongs to those who love God.

II. We pass, therefore, to the nature and law of Revelation.

(a) First, Revelation is made by the Spirit to a spirit—"God hath revealed them to us by his Spirit." Christ is the voice of God *without* the man—the Spirit is the voice of God *within* the man. The highest revelation is not made by Christ, but comes directly from the Universal Mind to our minds. Therefore, Christ said himself, "He, the Spirit, shall take of mine and shall show it unto you." And therefore it is written here: "The *Spirit* searches all things, yea, the deep things of God."

Now the Spirit of God lies touching, as it were, the soul of man—ever around and near. All men are not spiritual men, but all have spiritual sensibilities which might awake. All that is wanted is to become conscious of the nearness of God. Our souls float in the immeasurable ocean of Spirit. God lies around us: at any moment we might be conscious of the contact.

(b) The *condition* upon which this self-revelation of the Spirit is made to man is love. These things are "prepared for them that love him" or, which is the same thing, revealed to those who have the mind of Christ.

(1) Let us look into this word *love*. Love to man may mean several things. It may meant love to his person, which is very different from himself, or it may mean simply pity. Love to God can only mean one thing: God is a character. To love God is to love his character.

(2) This love is manifested in obedience; love is the life of which obedience is the form. "He that hath my commandments and keepeth them, he it is that loveth me . . . He that loveth me not keepth not my sayings."

(3) To this love, adoring and obedient, God reveals his truth for such as love it is prepared—or rather, by the well-known Hebrew inversion, such are prepared for it. Love is the condition without which Revelation does not take place.

In the same way, there are conditions in the world of Spirit, by compliance with which God's Spirit comes into the soul with all its revelations—reverence, love, meekness, contrition, obedience—these conditions having taken place, God enters into the soul, whispers his secret, becomes visible, imparts knowledge and conviction.

Therefore, the apostle preached the Cross to those who felt, and to those who felt not, the Revelation contained in it. The cross is humbleness, love, self-surrender—these the apostle preached. To conquer the world by loving it, to be blest by ceasing the pursuit of happiness and sacrificing life instead of finding it, to make a hard lot easy by submitting to it—this was his divine philosophy of life. It was God's own wisdom, felt by those who had the mind of Christ.

The application of all this is very easy:

Love God, and he will dwell with you. Obey God, and he will reveal the truths of his deepest teaching to your soul. Not *perhaps*—for as surely as the laws of the spiritual world are irreversible, so are these things prepared for obedient love. An inspiration as true, as real, and as certain as that which every prophet or apostle reached, is yours, if you will have it so.—Frederick W. Robertson.

SUNDAY: JANUARY FIFTEENTH

MORNING SERVICE

Topic: The Importance of Jesus
TEXT: Mark 8:27–30.

The scene was the district of Caesarea Philippi, near the city which perpetuated the name of the caesar. Jesus had retreated with his disciples for a time of fellowship and instruction. By way of introduction, Jesus asked, "What do people think of me? What is their opinion?"

This was, however, only an opener to prepare for a more basic question which was directed at the disciples themselves. Jesus turned to those who were his closest followers, these who had committed their lives in service to him, and he asked, "What do you think of me? Disciples of mine, what think ye of Christ?"

The most important question that every person here this morning will ever face, the question that will determine whether or not you are a Christian, the question that will determine the quality of your life on this earth, the question that will decide your eternal destiny, is the same question that Jesus asked his disciples at Caesarea Philippi: "What think ye of Jesus Christ?" Who is this one called Jesus?

I. The first certainty about Jesus is that he is *history's inescapable fact*. The entire story of the life and death of Jesus is considered by some to be "the superstitious expedient of the unintelligent" or "a necessary encumbrance of the emotional." Some say that it simply could not have happened.

(a) Remember again how Christianity had its start.

(1) The Bible tells us that Jesus was born in a stable adjoining a roadside inn. For the greatest part of his life, he worked as a carpenter and lived in an obscure provincial village called Nazareth. The applause of the listening senate was never his to command.

(2) When he left home and began to preach, his family thought he was mad. He died a criminal's death, hanging between two thieves, and was buried in a borrowed grave.

(3) But then a strange thing happened. The tomb where he had been buried was found to be empty. Soon after that, quite suddenly, and with amazing boldness, his disciples appeared on the streets of Jerusalem, proclaiming that Jesus had risen and that he had appeared to them. Through his resurrection from the dead, he had been declared to be the Lord of life.

(b) How the world scoffed at that message.

(1) But the extraordinary thing was this: neither with laughter, nor with force, nor with sophisticated arguments, nor with the might of her thundering legions could Rome stop Jesus.

Tacitus, a Roman historian who wrote thirty-five years after Calvary, said this about Christianity: "though checked for the time being, [it] broke out afresh, not only in Judea, where the mischief started, but also at Rome, where all manner of horrible and loathsome things pour in and become fashionable."

(2) Rome tried to stop Jesus, but what actually happened was that Jesus stopped

Rome, and on the dust and ashes of her broken splendor, set the foundations of the Kingdom of God. He has been the master force behind the onward march of mankind. Every person, sooner or later, will have to come to grips with him.

II. We can take it a step further this morning and say that not only was Jesus history's inescapable fact, but he is also *the church's sole foundation*.

(a) The church is under attack today, and some of the criticism is justifiable.

(1) Some say that the need is to restate our faith in intelligible terms. Others say that the most urgent need is for the church to recognize the social dynamic of the teachings of Christ. Both of these needs are urgent. I believe, however, that the greatest challenge facing the church today is to re-establish the foundation of the church on the person of Jesus Christ. He is the church's sole foundation, and we will rediscover the power of the church when we return to the source of that power, Jesus Christ.

(2) The Pauline expansion of Christianity, as the faith was transformed from a local sect into a worldwide religion, was motivated from beginning to end with the proclamation, "I am determined to preach nothing but Christ and him crucified."

(3) The church of the Catacombs was the same.

(4) It was also true of the church of the Reformation when, under the leadership of Luther and Calvin, the church regained the power of its early days, and hearts were once more warmed with the gospel.

(b) In every age, the church's power was derived from its personal relationship with the Living Lord. And it is still true today. In our day, when the church lacks power and we try to combat this situation by appointing committees, completing surveys, and changing organizational form, how we need to hear again the words of the Master: "And I, if I be lifted up, will draw all men unto myself."

III. We must take it a step further in answering the question, "What think ye of Christ?" by stating that Jesus was not only history's inescapable fact and the church's sole foundation, but he is also *the sinners' only savior*.

(a) What is wrong at the heart of man? The Bible says man is a sinner. What can we do about this problem? Take a man to a psychiatrist, and he will become an adjusted sinner. Take a man to a physician, and he will become a healthy sinner. Give a man a million dollar,s and he will become an affluent sinner. Get a man to turn over a new leaf, and he will become a reformed sinner. But he will still be a sinner.

(b) Let a man, any man, go in sincere repentance and faith to the foot of the cross and what will he become? A new creature in Christ Jesus, forgiven, reconciled to God, with meaning and purpose in life, on the way to marvelous fulfillment in God's will. Only Jesus can make a man over into a new creature.—Brian L. Harbour.

Illustrations

MESSAGE OF THE GOSPELS. It is on these four little books that all our study of the life and teaching of Jesus must be based. And let us remember that they give us three things. They give us history. For here we have a solid bedrock of historic fact, fixed and impregnable. But they give us something more than history—they give us revelation. For, as we turn the pages, it is God's voice that we hear, God's face that we see. But they give us more than history and revelation: they give us a Challenge. Every page renews the challenge, every line drives it home. The challenge is: "What *think* ye of Christ?" That first, then: "What shall I *do* with Christ?" And the challenge haunts us till we answer.—James S. Stewart.

THE APPEAL OF JESUS. Havelock Ellis says of Napoleon that there must have been in him "the answer to some lyric cry of the human heart." One should perhaps apologize for mentioning Napoleon and Jesus in the same breath, but the remark applies to Jesus in a sense and measure in which it does not begin to apply to Napoleon. The experience of every generation since his own age demonstrates that there is in Jesus an appeal stronger than that of any warrior, statesman, artist, or thinker, of antiquity or of modern times. Although the Kingdom of heaven which he preached may sometimes seem as far from realization as when the caesars ruled the world, he remains the most epic figure to ever appear upon the scene of man's life. And for hundreds of millions, the most radiant day of all the bright and dark days in the story of mankind is that which saw his birth—no wonder an earlier and more imaginative age made it a day of weird unearthly beauty, when a strange star hung low above the city of David and a multitude of angels broke with sudden glory the silence of the dawn.—John Knox, *Jesus: Lord and Christ*.

Sermon Suggestions

WHEN FAITH FALTERS.   Text: Heb. 11:1. (1) The Christian faith opens my eyes that I might see. (2) An adequate faith changes the heart. (3) An adequate faith sets us to work.—Gaston Foote.

OUR GOD IS ABLE.   Text: Jude 24. (1) God is able to sustain the vast scope of the physical universe. (2) God is able to subdue all the powers of evil. (3) God is able to give us interior resources to confront the trials and difficulties of life.—Martin Luther King, Jr., *Strength to Love*.

Worship Aids

CALL TO WORSHIP.   "I was glad when they said unto me, Let us go into the house of the Lord" (Ps. 122:1).

INVOCATION.   God, who spared not thy Son for our salvation, let us not withhold our devotion to thee as we worship thee. Encourage bright praise, spark true contrition, honor sincere prayer, bless deep surrender, and reveal to us the Christ.—E. Lee Phillips.

OFFERTORY SENTENCE.   "And he said to them all, If any man will come after me, let him deny himself, and take up his cross daily, and follow me" (Luke 9:23).

OFFERTORY PRAYER.   Grant, O Lord, such a view of our neighbor that even

needs at the ends of the earth will call forth our compassion, our prayers, and our gifts of love. Through him who loved us.

PRAYER.   O God, we beseech thee to save us this day from the distractions of vanity and the false lure of inordinate desires. Grant us the grace of a quiet and humble mind, and may we learn of Jesus to be meek and lowly of heart. May we not join the throng of those who seek after things that never satisfy and who draw others after them in the fever of covetousness. Save us from adding our influence to the drag of temptation. If the fierce tide of greed beats against the breakwaters of our soul, may we rest at peace in thy higher contentment. In the press of life may we pass from duty to duty in tranquillity of heart and spread thy quietness to all who come near.—Walter Rauschenbusch.

EVENING SERVICE

Topic: Andrew: The Man of Decision
TEXT: John 1:40.

We find here an apostle who was known chiefly as the relative of a great man. "You know Andrew, Simon Peter's brother," men would say. "One of the two, who followed him, was Andrew, Simon Peter's brother."

It is not an unmixed advantage to shine with a reflected light. The moon has never ranked with the sun or the stars. "Let every man bear his own burden, then he shall have rejoicing in himself and not in another." Andrew, Simon Peter's brother, had best not make too much of that relationship!

As a matter of fact, he never did. He was a quiet man, but he earned his right to sit down with the twelve apostles at the table of the Lord by the sheer strength of his own inner worth. He was preëminently a man of decision.

He stood one day where the great forerunner, John the Baptist, was speaking. When the man of Galilee approached, John pointed to him and said, "Behold, the Lamb of God, that taketh away the sin of the world." He followed this Galilean.

"We have found the Messiah!" he said—and that experience molded his entire future.

I. He did three things which were distinctive. First, he brought a man in every way abler than himself to Christ. "He first found his own brother Simon and brought him to Jesus." He was the first "home missionary"—his first sense of responsibility was for his own brother.

(a) It is easier oftentimes to talk to a man in China about the claims of Christian life than it is to talk to one's own brother or sister or child.

(b) How much is implied in "bringing a man to Christ'!

(1) It is no perfunctory act, like persuading him to submit to certain forms or to pronounce certain theological shibboleths or to assume certain ecclesiastical relations.

(2) The whole promise of a character, a service, a destiny that will enable that person to outlast and outshine the stars, is contained in that transaction when he is brought into personal fellowship with Christ. How evil tendencies are overcome, how waywardness is corrected, how the impulses which are fine and true are confirmed when we begin to live daily and hourly with him!

(c) "He brought him to Jesus"—it was the way the whole Christian movement began! One person feels sure that, in becoming a Christian, he or she has found the secret of worthy, joyous, useful living. Then that person persuades another to enter upon the same mode of life. No ecclesiastical machinery in the modern evangelism, which proceeds often by wholesale methods, will compare for one moment in value with that sense of personal touch. In the Day of Judgment, it will be remembered to his honor that Andrew brought a man much abler than himself to Christ.

II. In the second place, Andrew discovered the hidden resources of a boy. There came a day when Jesus saw a great company of people in a desert place. They were hungry and they were without food. He said to his disciples, "Whence shall we buy bread that these may eat?"

(a) Andrew, the man of decision, came to the front. He reported the presence of a boy with five loaves and two small fishes. Andrew himself was not quite sure as to what could be done with such modest resources. But that was all the food there was in sight, and he brought the boy with his lunch basket to Christ.

(b) It turned out that the boy held the key to the whole situation. When his meager food supply was placed unreservedly in the hands of Christ, the Master did wonders with it. He fed the whole crowd—and Andrew was the man who had brought the boy to Christ.

(1) "There is a boy here," the father says, as he glances around the living room of his own home. The very sight of that unfolding life, making itself even now a small copy of the father's life, causes him to feel that he ought to be a better man.

(2) "There is a boy here," the Sunday school teacher says to herself, in preparing her lesson or in kneeling down to pray for Tom or Dick or Harry. When the boy is in Sunday school, he may be restless, thoughtless, mischievous. He often gets that way. Nevertheless, he may be a real Christian leader in the making.

(3) "There is a boy here," the minister says to himself many times when he stands in his pulpit. The boy may be wriggling around in his pew like some unhappy eel. Well and good! If the Lord had not intended that healthy boys should wriggle around, in church and everywhere else, he would have made them different in the first place. We are all glad that the boy is there. This man Andrew was too level-headed to overlook the hidden possibilities in any boy's life.

III. In the third place, Andrew introduced a group of strangers to Christ. "There were certain Greeks who came up to Jerusalem to worship at the feast." They had heard about this man of Galilee and they wanted to meet him. They came to Philip, whose name was Greek, and said to him, "Sir, we would see Jesus."

(a) Philip was not sure at that time that the Hebrew Messiah was sent to all creation. Those Greeks were foreigners, and Philip did not want his church to be too promiscuous. He did not give the Greeks any encouragement, but he told Andrew about it. "There are some foreigners out there," he said. Andrew was a man of decision—he saw the promise of a worldwide movement in the coming of that bunch of Greeks. He knew that God is no respecter of persons, but that in every nation, those who hunger after righteousness will be filled. He was ready even then for the Day of Pentecost. He brought those Greeks to Christ at once. When Jesus saw them, he was overjoyed. "I, if I be lifted up from the earth," he said, "will draw all men to me."

(b) "Sir, we would see Jesus." That is what all the strangers say when they come to church—they say it by their presence in the place of worship.

(1) When these strangers come, the first person they meet is Andrew, the usher. He is there near the door to introduce them to the service.

(2) In every church, "the order of St. Andrew" is a great deal larger than the body of ushers. All the men and women who belong to that church regard themselves as the hosts and hostesses of those strangers who come as the church's guests. The atmosphere of quiet, thoughtful friendliness which they create and maintain becomes a part of that welcome which is extended to all who come.

(3) Andrew brought those Greeks to Christ, and Jesus said, "The hour is come that the Son of man should be glorified." The modern members of this Order of St. Andrew are following the same path. They are scattered abroad throughout the whole earth, engaged in bringing foreigners to Christ. They are all candidates for that high reward suggested in the words of the Savior: "Come ye blessed of my Father, inherit the Kingdom prepared for you, for I was a stranger and ye took me in."—Charles Reynolds Brown.

SUNDAY: JANUARY TWENTY-SECOND

MORNING SERVICE

Topic: Slave of Christ

TEXT: Rom. 1:1.

The word is not *servant*—it is "slave." The world of that day knew what the word meant. There were menial slaves, "hewers of wood and drawers of water," and there were cultured slaves—secretaries, stewards, and even poets. But whatever a slave's gifts or work, he was bought or sold by his master, controlled and commanded by his master, and thrashed or killed at his master's whim.

Paul, beginning a letter and wishing to identify himself, writes: "Paul, a slave of Jesus Christ, called to be an apostle, separated to the gospel of God." The description recurs in the New Testament. It was common and accepted in the early church. A Christian was then, and is now, the "slave of Christ."

You see that such a commitment is at violent odds with our modern world, for our motto is "Freedom." The modern man is committed to freedom without knowing what the word means, while the Christian freely chooses to be "the slave of Christ."

Freedom is not freedom to do as we like, for that is slavery to our likes and makes a thousand civil wars. Freedom is not even freedom to do as we ought, for that word, however noble, would spell coercion. No, rather, freedom is that consent in us, together with the opportunity and the power, to fulfill our true nature. That is the claim of Christ: "If the Son shall make you free, you shall be free indeed"—in very truth.

In those days, on occasion, a slave who had been offered his liberty would say to his master, "But I never wish to leave you"; and the master would thereupon, at the slave's desire, brand him with his owner's mark. Paul says, "Let no man trouble me" (let no other master enter a claim) "for I bear branded on my body the marks of the Lord Jesus." Wonderful Lord who can kindle that kind of love!

I. He had bought Paul out of degrading secret slavery.

(a) Paul had a conscience, like the rest of us; and Paul tried to keep the law. But he failed, like the rest of us. There was always something that he had not done, like the rest of us, like a recurring decimal—three into ten goes three times, and there is one left over; add a nought, three into ten goes three times, and there is always something left over. Then Paul began to flog himself inwardly, and then he began to flog his fellowmen outwardly (it is a natural sequence): he began to persecute the Christians because he knew they had the secret he lacked. Meanwhile, failure was in his memory, and the more he flogged himself, the more he felt the pain of failure.

(b) Then Christ found him, by the cross, through followers who were "the slaves of Christ." Paul looked on the cross and said: "The heart of this world is not law, but love—the very love that sent him into human history thus to live and thus to die." Then Paul said: "I do not need to strive or agonize over failure. The strife and the agony are caught up into his love, and I need only trust him and let him live through me." Then Paul began to sign himself "slave of Christ."

II. He had bought Paul and therefore controlled him.

(a) Ransomed from "the law of sin and death" is Paul's phrase, who therefore added, "The love of Christ constraineth us" (controls us).

(b) Paul could not resist the high enchantment of the cross, and passed beneath the archway, and was bound by the vows. Amusements? Yes, of course—life's necessary respite, but only such as can bear his eyes. Daily work? Yes, a man must carry his share of the world's labor, but only in such a way and of such a kind as Christ approves.

(c) So Paul went his way, amid such persecutions as stop the mind even in the reading of them, but with a greater joy. "Love so amazing, so divine, demands my life, my soul, my all!'

III. He never asked what Christ did not share.

(a) A Russian emperor said to his followers: "I cannot spare you the battle, but I can eat your black bread, and lie with you on the hard ground." Christ himself was "Servant of Jehovah"—Slave of Heaven— because in him, God was slave to the needs of men; so Paul was slave to a slave. Ever Christ said to him from some desperate encounter: "The slave is not above his lord," so Paul was well content. Besides, power flowed into him, for his Lord had risen from the dead.

(b) Paul still failed, but his Lord had taught him to pray: "Give us this day our daily bread, and forgive us our debts." God gave daily pardon with as lavish a hand as he gave harvests. Therefore, being committed to Christ, he was free from the thralldom of mammon, lust, and every other secret foe. And, being inwardly free, he had power to withstand every outward tyranny.

It is worth remembering: only those who are inwardly free, because they are inwardly bound to God in Christ, can cope with any dark threat. We had better begin to gather real armaments! So Paul signed himself "slave of Christ" and, as one of the covenanters, in prison for his faith in Christ, put his address at the top of the letters he wrote from captivity: "The King's Palace, Aberdeen."

IV. (a) Some here call themselves Christians, with whatever sense of unworthiness, and do not let unworthiness keep them from membership in the church, for the church, properly understood, is a home for failures—the fellowship of forgiven sinners. Some here have, as yet, made no life commitment. Both groups should know what Christian faith requires.

(b) The Christian is "the slave of Christ." He is not his own, because he is owned.

(c) Christianity is not a success story, not the account of One who rose from poverty to a throne, but of a Love which for our sakes came from a throne into our poverty; and the slave is not above his Lord.—George A. Buttrick, *Pulpit Digest*.

Illustrations

SLAVES WITH ABILITY.   There are three reasons, at least, why the word *slave* did not upset Paul. First, he did not think of "slave" as we do, in terms of a hewer of wood or a drawer of water, or of *Uncle*

Tom's Cabin and "My old Kentucky home far away." Many slaves in the Roman Empire held positions of responsibility. Here is John Buchan's listing of them in his *Augustus*: "Slaves were secretaries, copyists, and accountants; carpenters, metalworkers, jewellers, weavers, and plumbers; cooks, bakers, and coiffeurs; managers of country estates as well as rural laborers; painters, artists, and builders; physicians, surgeons, and oculists." Some of us here have the equipment to be acceptable slaves in Roman society. Such men and women were prisoners of war— Greeks, Egyptians, and the like. We need but think of the peoples enslaved by Nazi and communist rule to realize that many Roman prisoners could have been persons of ability. Therefore, when Paul used the designation *slave*, he did not mean that a Christian was a person of no native or trained ability. He was what he was—able, skilled, intelligent—in the service of another.—James T. Cleland.

THE POWER OF A NAME.   How much depends upon what you call a man! Many years ago, Mary A. Livermore undertook one night to give an address on women's suffrage on Boston Common. The idea was most unpopular at that time, and she was speedily surrounded by a mob of rough men who had come to break up her meeting. Her friends were alarmed as to her personal safety, and they urged her to withdraw. But her heart was in her cause, and she did not intend to be driven off. Her friends insisted that she was in danger. They said: "There are no police in sight! Who will protect you from this mob?" "This gentleman," she replied, pointing to the roughest man in sight, the ringleader of the mob! "This gentleman will protect me and see that I have a chance to be heard." And the "gentleman" did—he was as good as her word. He proceeded to put the other men in their places, and the woman made her speech under the chivalrous protection of that man who, a moment before, had been yelling with the mob. When Jesus called Peter "a rock," it helped the man to move ahead at a rapid pace toward that moral stability which the new name denoted.— Charles R. Brown.

Sermon Suggestions

FISHERS OF MEN.   Text: Matt. 4:19. (1) Humble workers, but a lofty work. (2) It requires tact, perseverance, patient endurance of frequent failure. (3) He who calls us to it promises that we shall not labor in vain.—John A. Broadus.

THE GOSPEL IN ACTION.   Text: Acts 10:37–38. (1) It is inspired and empowered by the Holy Spirit. (2) It is manifested in doing good for one and all. (3) It is evidenced by constructive healing and help. (4) It culminates in a worldwide mission of grace.—Chalmer E. Faw.

Worship Aids

CALL TO WORSHIP.   "Let the words of my mouth, and the meditation of my heart, be acceptable in thy sight, O Lord, my strength and my redeemer" (Ps. 19: 14).

INVOCATION.   O Lord, help us to make the prayer of the Psalmist our very own, to the end that we may offer acceptable worship this day and acceptable service in the days ahead.

OFFERTORY SENTENCE.   "And he said unto them, Take heed what ye hear: with what measure ye mete, it shall be measured to you: and unto you that hear shall more be given" (Mark 4:24).

OFFERTORY PRAYER.   Our Father in heaven, you did not spare your own Son, but gave him up for us all. In him, you have blessed us in every way. As we have freely received, may we freely give.

PRAYER.   We thank you, O Lord, that you have revealed your Son to us. Through his light, we are no longer captives of darkness. Through his life, we are no longer captives of death. Help us to walk in the path of his light and life all the days of our lives, and allow faith to grow steadily stronger in our hearts, and inspire us to spread the Good News of his coming to all persons. We pray that the coming forth of your Son will touch those in pain and need. Heal of affliction those whose lives have been marred by adversity, and give compassion and courage to those who heal in your name. Remember also those whose lives take them to distant places, unusual life-styles, and into lonely isolation. Grant them all of the things that they need for joyful and satisfying life.—Rodney K. Miller.

EVENING SERVICE

Topic: Peter: The Man of Impulse

Text: Matt. 4:12–23.

Divine grace is not a steamroller which irons all the wrinkles and individuality out of people. Divine grace brings out in a finer way the personal traits in every life.

Peter was a man whose name stands first in every list of the apostles! He was no modest, shrinking petunia, blossoming in the backyard or wasting his fragrance on the desert air. He was out on the front porch talking, acting, taking the lead. He was heard as well as seen.

He was a man of impulse, a rushing, impetuous type of man, like a mountain stream hurrying over the rocks on its way to the valley below. Let me notice the strength of such a nature, and then its weakness, and then what the Lord can make of that sort of man!

I. First, the strength of it. The man who can make up his mind and act promptly in business, in politics, in the presence of danger, while other men are still thinking it over and talking about it, has a certain advantage. He strikes always while the iron is hot.

(a) Jesus saw this man with a net in his hands, fishing. He said to him, "Follow me, and I will make you a fisher of men." Peter decided then and there that he would do it. He forsook his net, leaving it there in the water, and followed Christ.

(b) Peter was fishing on another occasion, without success. He had fished all night and had caught nothing. Just at daybreak, Jesus stood on the shore, calling out to the seven men in the boat: "Have you caught anything? Have you any meat?" Peter did not wait to make any remarks. He girt his fisher's coat about him, jumped overboard, and swam ashore to be the first to greet his Lord.

(c) When Jesus was at Caesarea Philippi, he wondered how men were regarding his ministry. "Whom do men say that I am?" he asked his disciples. The disciples answered that there was a wide difference of opinion on that point. "But *ye*, whom say *ye* that I am?" Well, they had not quite decided yet, all of them. But Peter burst out, "Thou art the Christ, the Son of the living God." He was ready then and there to stake his all upon the claim that Jesus was the Savior of the world.

(d) There came a day when the Master was speaking about forgiveness. Then Peter burst out: "Lord, how often? How oft shall my brother sin against me and I forgive him? Until seven times?" Jesus, however, suggested a still higher standard of forgiveness. "Until seventy times seven!" Peter accepted it, apparently. He did pray for mercy, and that same prayer taught him the need of showing mercy.

II. In the second place, notice the weakness of the man. When one is carrying a pan of water and it slops over on one side, his hasty action in changing the level usually causes it to slop over on the other side. So is the man of impulse!

(a) When Jesus celebrated the Last Supper with his disciples, he took a towel and a basin of water and washed their feet. When he came to Peter, the man drew back. "Never!" Peter said. "Thou shalt never wash my feet." Then at a word from Christ, he melted down into a desire for a still closer intimacy. "Lord, not my feet only, but my hands and my head!"

(b) That same night, there was a tragic scene in the life of this impulsive man. Peter felt very sure of himself. "Though all men should forsake thee, I never will." But what a sorry showing the man made before the cock crew! Then there came an ugly oath and the third denial of his Lord. Jesus heard the oath "and turned and looked at Peter." This impulsive man broke down and cried like a child—"he went out and wept bitterly." What a strange combination of courage and cowardice, of rugged strength and instability! It goes with the impulsive temperament. Such men are always striking twelve, either in some high noon of glorious action or in some midnight of dismal failure. It is never nine o'clock in the morning or three o'clock in the afternoon with them—they are at one extreme or the other.

(c) Here is another instance of Peter's fickleness! When he went forth to preach the gospel, he had a vision. He saw a lot of four-footed beasts and fowls and creeping things. He heard a voice saying, "Rise, Peter, kill and eat." He answered, "No! I never have! I never have eaten anything common or unclean." Then the voice came again, "What God hath cleaned, call not thou common." And when Peter came to think upon his vision, he realized that this wiping out of artificial distinctions between the various animals, whose flesh is good for food, would apply also to men. Jews or gentiles, barbarians or Scythians, bond or free, no man was to be called common or unclean on the ground of race difference. This was a big, long step ahead to be taken by a man who had been brought up in a narrow creed.

(1) Peter took that step. When the Holy Spirit came upon those who heard his words, he baptized them as Christians. At Antioch also, Peter ate with gentile Christians and gave them the right hand of fellowship. But when some of the stricter party came down from Jerusalem, they told Peter that he was letting down the bars altogether too fast. Then he drew back. He would not associate with gentile Christians any more.

(2) Paul, the apostle of Christian liberty, at once rebuked him. "I withstood him to his face," he said. That was the weakness of this impulsive man, sometimes right, sometimes wrong, but always eager and intense.

III. In the third place, what use did the Lord make of such a man? He did not make light of his limitations—he knew what was in man. But he did not refuse to enroll him as an apostle because he was fickle.

(a) He gave him a new name to live up to. His name had been Simon, but Jesus said to him, "Thou shalt be called Peter" —*petros*, "a rock," the same root of our word *petrify*. Every time Jesus spoke to him after that, he called him "my rock."

(b) When Jesus gave Simon that new name, he was walking by faith and not by sight. He was looking to the future rather than to the past. "Forgetting the things that are behind and reaching for the things which are ahead," he pushed Simon along toward the mark of the high calling of God in steadfastness of life. He was thinking not of what the man had been, but of what he could become. "Simon," he would say, "you are a rock." It was a steady challenge to this fickle soul to do its best. It put stamina and backbone into him. "Thou art Peter," *petros*, a rock, "and on this rock I will build my church." There is a rock of strength in any fickle, impulsive nature—send for the Savior that he may bring it out.

(c) We are not to blink at the faults of this impulsive man. He ran away like a moral coward when Jesus was arrested and had to face the cross. He was laughed out of his Christian faith by a servant girl when he stood that night by the fire warming himself. He denied the Lord who loved him, three times over, with an angry oath. What sort of man was he, one might ask, to be placed at the head of the list of the twelve apostles?

(d) But read on! Read on—we have not come to the end of the chapter yet! "Now when the Day of Pentecost was fully come, Peter standing with the eleven said, 'Ye men of Judea, Jesus of Nazareth was approved of God by the signs which he did. You took him with wicked hands and slew him.' And when the people saw the *boldness* of Peter and John, they took knowledge of them that they had been with Jesus." And when the Jewish officials urged them not to speak any further in the name of Christ, Peter flatly refused to be bound by their command. "We ought to obey God rather than men." He was carrying on—he was showing himself indeed "Peter, a rock."— Charles Reynolds Brown.

SUNDAY: JANUARY TWENTY-NINTH

MORNING SERVICE

Topic: When Christ Comes
TEXT: 2 Cor. 3:1–18.

The organization of the church was at a very primitive stage in Paul's day. Each church had a local spiritual leader. In addition, itinerant ministers known as "prophets" often came to the churches. These "prophets" claimed to speak God's word and asserted authority in the churches. The problem was that many of these traveling ministers were not genuine in their commitment. How could a church determine their genuineness? The only evidence the church had was letters of commendation which these prophets would carry with them.

Evidently, Paul's critics categorized him with these religious peddlers. The fact that Paul did not carry letters of reference to commend him proved to his critics that he was an imposter. But notice in verses 2 and 3 how Paul answered this charge. Their conversion, the evidence of God's work in their lives, the change which they experienced were all the commendation Paul needed. When Christ came, he brought about a difference in their lives.

I want to use this passage from Paul and this example of the Corinthians to understand what happens in the life of a person, any person, when Christ comes.

I. *Power*. First, when Christ comes, there is power.

(a) Paul said that the Christian life is a life of confidence. Then he explains why. We can be confident as we face life, Paul said, not because we are "adequate in ourselves," but he says "our adequacy is from God" (Matt. 8:8). The original root from which the word *power* comes can mean "to be able to reach something with your hand" or "to attain a goal for which you strive." Paul said that when Christ comes into our lives, we who are unworthy, incapable, and unqualified are made to be worthy, able, and qualified.

(b) How do we receive this power? The process is something like this. When Christ comes, the desire to pray is stirred up within us. Prayer leads to closeness with God, which leads to receptivity with God, which leads to spiritual power. When Christ comes, there is power.

II. *Purpose*. Second, when Christ comes, there is purpose (v. 6). God's power comes for a purpose, and the purpose is that we might become "adequate as servants of a new covenant."

(a) The word *covenant* means an agreement between two parties, between a greater and lesser power. This is the covenant agreement made between God and man. Paul calls it a *new* covenant.

(b) Now notice what Paul says. He says that when Christ comes, we become able servants or ministers of this new covenant. A minister is one who serves God in response to his call. And, Paul says, all of us are called to be ministers.

III. *Permanence*. Third, when Christ comes, we have permanence (vv. 7–8).

(a) The key word is the word *glory*. It referred to the glory of God which throughout the Old Testament was manifest as a bright light, an explosion of brilliance. Referring to Exodus 34:29–35, he admitted that when Moses received the Ten Commandments from God, he encountered the glorious brightness of God's presence. Coming down from the mountain, Moses' face reflected the brilliance of God's glory. So bright was his face that Moses had to cover it with a veil. Yet, Paul explained, the glow on Moses' face was temporary.

(b) Paul said that when Christ comes the indwelling spirit of God vitalizes the believer with new life which provides a permanent glow in his life. What Christ offers is not temporary and fleeting. Instead, it is permanent.

IV. *Perception*. Fourth, when Christ comes, we have perception (vv. 14–16).

(a) Paul wrote to the Ephesians this word of consolation (1:18–19). I did not truly understand that passage until I read something recently that had been written by Ralph Sockman, an outstanding preacher of a recent generation. He said that we have three ways of seeing: the eyes of the body, the eyes of the mind, and the eyes of the heart. The eyes of the body ask the "what" questions of a given experience. The eyes of the mind go deeper and ask the "how" questions of the experience. The eyes of the heart go deepest of all and deal with the "why" dimension of our experience.

(b) Only when we go beyond the "what" questions and the "how" questions to the "why" questions do we have a true perception of life. How do we have such perception? How can we see with the eyes of our heart? Go back to the passage in Ephesians 1, and Paul answers. He says that when we see with the eyes of our heart, it is "in accordance with the working of the strength of . . . [God's] might which he brought about in Christ . . ." (1:19–20).

V. *Progression*. Finally, when Christ comes, he gives us progression.

One of the finest verses in all of the New Testament is the final verse in chapter 3 of our text. When Jesus comes, and we behold his glory, we will be "transformed into the same image from glory to glory" (v. 18). Someone asked a black pastor who was the minister of a growing and dynamic church how he accomplished it. He replied, "I hold a crown a few inches above my people's heads and watch them grow into it." If that could happen to us, then we, too, like the Corinthians to whom Paul wrote, could be living testimonials to the sufficiency and supremacy of Christ.— Brian L. Harbour.

Illustrations

CARING. In the early summer of 1947, the North American Inter-Seminary Conference met in Oxford, Ohio. This study conference was a students' prelude to the World Council of Churches, which would meet the following year in Amsterdam to consider "Man's Disorder and God's Design." Of particular interest were the disorder of society and the international disorder.

In one study group, the question of psychological "normality" came up, and Seward Hiltner said that being normal was not a goal to strive for. Normal people, he said, are not concerned enough about the world to go to the trouble to attend such a meeting as the one we were attending.— James W. Cox.

RELIGION: INDIVIDUAL AND SOCIAL. The Philosopher Alfred North Whitehead said, "Religion is what the individual does with his solitariness." Quite different from the advice given to John Wesley in his search for faith: "The Bible knows nothing of solitary religion." H. Wheeler Robinson comments: "Both are true, or rather both are half-truths. The reality of religion is never possessed until it is a firsthand experience of God, unfettered by the conventions of the crowd, unique as is every voluntary product of personality. But the reality of religion is not known until it is socially tested and developed; we do not know how we are reacting to God until we know how we are reacting to man."—H. Wheeler Robinson.

Sermon Suggestions

THE STRATEGY THAT WINS. Text: Rom. 12:21. (1) The text is a call to conquest. It strikes a responsive chord in every human heart. (2) We must face the disappointing truth that it has not become an actuality in many of our lives. (3) Much of our failure is born of a wrong technique. We have an almost irresistible tendency to focus our attention upon the evil that is to be destroyed rather than upon the good that is to take its place. (4) There is no way to conquer evil except by the might of the good.—Clovis G. Chappell.

LIFE'S GREATEST ISSUE. Text: Matt. 27:22. The ways men attempt to deal with the issue of Jesus: (1) Some would avoid the issue. (2) Some are indecisive about the issue. (3) Some would postpone the issue. (4) Some would attempt to compromise the issue. (5) Some decide the issue now. —Withrow T. Holland.

Worship Aids

CALL TO WORSHIP.   "For thus saith the high and lofty One that inhabiteth eternity, whose name is Holy; I dwell in the high and holy place, with him also that is of a contrite and humble spirit, to revive the spirit of the humble, and to revive the heart of the contrite ones" (Isa. 57:15).

INVOCATION.   O God of peace, who hast taught us that in returning and rest we shall be saved, in quietness and in confidence shall be our strength; By the might of thy Spirit lift us, we pray thee, to thy presence, where we may be still and know that thou art God.—*Book of Common Prayer*.

OFFERTORY SENTENCE.   "Therefore, my beloved brethren, be ye steadfast, unmoveable, always abounding in the work of the Lord, forasmuch as ye know that your labor is not in vain in the Lord" (1 Cor. 15:58).

OFFERTORY PRAYER.   Almighty God, whose loving hand hath given us all that we possess, grant us grace that we may honor thee with our substance, and remembering the account which we must one day give, may be faithful stewards of thy bounty.

PRAYER.   Almighty Father of us all, we thank thee for these associations and rejoicings and psalms of praise, and for this place of prayer. We rejoice that we are all understood here by One whose eye never faileth, whose pity is everlasting, and whose sympathy is as large as all the universe dominated by the throne of our great Father, our God.

We are here this morning with so many needs, such intricate ways, such complex and serious problems that only the divine hand may touch our wound in safety; only the divine kindness that moves amidst many sicknesses with stillness; only a love that remembers our griefs and would not make them more agonizing; only the power to redeem that may save the lowliest—only this we ask for, the presence of

thyself, O God, in Christ Jesus, our Lord. —Frank W. Gunsaulus.

EVENING SERVICE

Topic: Be a Christ
TEXT: Gal. 4:19.

We assume, of course, those great and sublime truths about the person of Christ, his deity, his mediatorship, and his kingship. We confess, too, that after we have done our best to follow in his steps, we are but unprofitable servants and need, and must have, the redeeming work of our Lord and Savior. Christ is alone and unapproachable in the glory of his person and in the majesty of his work upon the cross.

All this we reverently believe and take for granted. But at the same time, there is this other and important side of Christian life and doctrine. It is strikingly set forth in that phrase which an English journalist heard on Christmas day in the organ loft of a prison chapel, "Be a Christ." When you think of it, the same thing is spoken by the Holy Spirit in the Scriptures. Perhaps the most arresting instance of that is what Paul says here to the Christian disciples at Galatia. He was in great distress of mind and heart because of a threatened decline from the faith among these people, lest they be tempted and seduced to believe on "another Christ," which is not another and has no power to save. He resorts to every weapon of the speaker and the writer—righteous anger, irony, pathos, and apostrophe. Here, with great affection and earnestness, he says, "My little children, of whom I travail in birth again until Christ be formed in you."

I. Here we have the high and lofty Christian thought of man.

(a) Christianity teaches the irrefragable truth of original sin and of the fall of man. This is a truth affirmed by common sense and logic and reinforced by the indisputable facts of mankind's life and history. To this fact, the woes and wars and sorrow of our world bear sad and powerful witness. Long ago, Christ told us about the heart of man, that it is desperately wicked and deceitful above all else.

(b) Yet it was Christ, who knew what was

in man, who at the same time had such a sublime conception of man's nature that he said to men, "Be perfect," and again, "The Kingdom of God is within you." It was Christ who took upon him man's nature and who on the cross offered up his life for man's salvation. The incarnation of the Son of God in human nature was, of course, unique and peculiar. Yet that incarnation of God in man set the seal on the sacredness of man's nature.

(c) How beautiful the thought that Christ saw possible incarnation, a forming of himself, even in publicans, in thieves, and in harlots. When we say then, "Be a Christ," we are not talking to an educated or developed beast. I cannot conceive of either Christ or Paul speaking to such a creature and telling it to have Christ formed within; but I can conceive of the incarnation for the sake of a man created in the image of God, though now through sin fallen from it. And I can conceive of St. Paul writing to these disciples on the windswept plains of Galatia, saying to them, "Until Christ be formed in you."

II. (a) When we ask ourselves just what this means to have Christ formed in us, the simple and natural answer is that it means to be Christlike. Christ told men, "Follow me," and Paul said, "Follow me even as I follow Christ." To have Christ formed within us is to follow Christ and to do his will. How severely, too, Christ spoke of those whose views of his Lordship were correct and who said to him, "Lord, Lord," but were anything but Christlike in their lives and who failed to do his will! Not those who said, "Lord, Lord," but those who followed him and did his will should enter the Kingdom of heaven. There may be times when the path of Christian duty is not clear. But suppose that you could get all the members of all our churches and all our statesmen and rulers to do every day in their personal relationships and in the discharge of their respective offices what they gather, from the New Testament, Jesus would have done under similar circumstances? What a transformed world we would have!

(b) When we think of the Christlike life and the spirit of Christ, we think of purity, and patience, and kindness, and pity, and comfort and sympathy, of helping and giving to others. It must ever be remembered that it was not what men said or claimed, but what they had done to him in the person of the sick, the prisoner, the hungry, and the naked. That was the test.

(c) But this passive, or perhaps benevolent, side of the Christian life is not all, nor indeed the most difficult. Christ, on one occasion, looked around him in anger. He was capable of righteous indignation. He denounced hypocrisy, denounced wickedness in high places, denounced men who made long prayers and robbed widows and orphans, denounced unfilial children, who by a technicality of religious ritual, excused themselves from their duty to their parents. He denounced evil thoughts as well as evil deeds, and he pronounced the judgment of God upon those who defiled the purity of marriage. This side of the Christian life is more difficult than the other. When you follow Christ there, when that kind of a Christ is formed within you, it will bring adversaries and opposition, and sometimes persecution. Remember, it was not his words of sympathy, nor his miracles of kindness and compassion which brought Christ to the Cross, but his opposition to evil. Who can follow Christ there?

III. A being who is capable of having Christ formed within him was not made for the grave. "Dust to dust" has no application to him. That was what Paul thought about the matter when he said in his splendid way, "Christ in you the hope of glory." Christ in you the hope of glory, the hope of immortal life, of rising to stand by the side of the saints of God, of living as long as God himself shall live, with God and with Christ. "O Death, where is thy sting! O Grave, where is thy victory!"—Clarence Edward Macartney, *Pulpit Preaching.*

SUNDAY: FEBRUARY FIFTH

MORNING SERVICE

Topic: The Hope of the World in Its Minorities

TEXT: Matt. 13:33.

One of the most arresting statements made by a public man was made by Mr. Einstein when he said that if 2 percent of our population should take a personal, resolute stand against the sanction and support of another war, that would end war.

I. The creative ideas destined to remake society have always taken the possession of the minority. History has depended, not on the 98 percent, but on the 2 percent. Far from being a matter of sociological and political interest alone, this principle gave Christianity its start. When the Master in Palestine began calling out his first disciples from the mass of their countrymen, he was interested not in quantity but in quality—in seed, though but a few kernels, which, if carefully sown, might multiply itself. He was thinking not primarily of the 98 percent, but of a germinal 2 percent. To use his own figure in the thirteenth chapter of Matthew's gospel: "The Kingdom of heaven is like unto leaven, which a woman took, and hid in three measures of meal, till it was all leavened." Quantitatively small, vitally active leaven—that is a true simile of the method of Christianity's transformation of the world.

(a) We do not answer to that description. Too frequently forgetting the mission that the Master left us and the way of working he committed to us, we have become a majority movement standing for the status quo.

(1) For one thing, we live in a democracy, where the only way of carrying on public business is to accept the voice of the majority. In consequence, the notion naturally prevails that the majority in the end probably is right and that, anyway, the majority rules. But neither of those ideas is true. The majority is almost certain to be wrong on any matter of fine taste or sound judgment, and, whether or not the major-ity is right, it certainly does not rule. The dominant influence in every situation is a militant minority. The decision of public policy in this country now is largely determined by resolute, militant, compact, closely organized minorities that want something and get it. Even in a democracy, the minority rules.

(2) Again, this truth of Jesus is deflected from many modern minds because of our worship of bigness. One of my friends calls it "Jumboism." Especially in this country, many people are impressed by nothing that is not big—big cities, big buildings, big corporations. We all are tempted to worship size. But size is an utterly fallacious standard when we are trying to estimate power. Could anyone, at the height of Rome's colossal power, have thought of anything much smaller than Paul in a Roman prison writing his few letters? But the result!

(b) Looked at from one angle, this truth is encouraging. When one thinks of the causes that are on our hearts today, we would welcome the good news that we do not have to wait for the majority. Wherever a true idea is born and a creative minority rallies around it, there is the beginning of victory. That is encouraging and it is true. It is not, however, a truth to go to sleep on. We Christians were intended to be that minority. We were to be the salt of the earth, said Jesus. We were to be the light of the world. We were to be the leaven in the lump of the race. When a man becomes a real Christian, he is supposed to move over into that small, creative, sacrificial minority seized upon by visions of a better world and standing for them until they shall permeate mankind with their truth. That does make being a Christian serious business! That is joining the real church in the original Greek meaning of the word *church*—ecclesia or "called out"—a minority selected from the majority to be leaven.

(c) Only as we succeed in getting more Christians like that will power return to the Christian movement. There was a time, however, when Christianity was very powerful. Little groups of men and women were scattered through the Roman Empire —"not many mighty," said Paul, "not many noble." They were far less than 2 percent and the heel of persecution was often on them, but they flamed with a conviction that they represented truths to which the future belonged. Do you remember what Paul called them in his letter to the Philippians? "We are a colony of heaven," he said. The Philippian Christians would understand that figure, for their city of Philippi was a Roman colony. When Rome wanted to Romanize a new province, it took Roman people and planted them as a colony in the midst of it. There, as a powerful minority, they stood for Roman law, Roman justice, Roman faith, and Roman custom, leaven in the lump of the province, until the whole province was leavened. Rome understood the art of government. When, therefore, Paul said to that little group of Philippian Christians, "We are a colony of heaven," they understood. Then Christianity was very powerful. It was a minority movement with nothing to lose, with everything to gain, joining which a man pledged his very life as a forfeit. At last, it became so powerful that it captured the empire, entrenched itself in wealth and worldly prestige, stopped challenging the world, began compromising with the world, went on to defend the status quo of the world, and never again, I fear, on so vast a scale has exhibited such creative, superhuman power.

II. Let us, therefore, for our own sakes and for the sakes of our generation, see if we can recover even a little the meaning of that saying of Jesus, "The Kingdom of heaven is like unto leaven, which a woman took, and hid in three measures of meal, till it was all leavened."

(a) In the first place, this clearly applies to our churches themselves. Not infrequently one is asked in these days whether or not one believes in the church. Just what is meant by "the church" in this question? My faith is in the church within the churches, the 2 percent, the spiritual leaven, the inner group of men and women who have been genuinely kindled by Christ's spirit and are today living and

thinking above the average and ahead of the time. Always the real church has been not the dough of the masses but the leaven of the few. Church of Christ in America, with all your wealth and all your prestige, beware! Could Paul say of you, "Ye are a colony of heaven"? Vital experience of God, for example, as a living force in daily life, has always been the possession of a minority.

So, too, a living faith in Christ, which enables one in some deep sense to say, "I live; yet not I, but Christ liveth in me," has always belonged to a minority. The majority have worshiped Christ—indeed, have recited resounding creeds about him and made obeisance at his altars. But to live Christ in private quality, in social life, in sacrificial devotion—has that belonged even to the 2 percent? How much we do need both minorities that pioneer and minorities that keep the high values of the faith amid a time that popularly surrenders them!

(b) Our truth applies also to social problems. Men today, making their characteristic reactions to the social, economic, and international difficulties which beset us, fall into three classes: (1) those below the average—lawless, criminal, antisocial; (2) those on the average, who play the game according to the rules with a fine sense of honor for observing them; and (3) those above the average, who question the rules. Are the rules themselves fair? Is the game itself equitable? Does it not minister to the advantage of the few against the many, and cannot the rules be altered so that the game itself will be more just? The hope of the world depends upon that third class.

(c) Of course, the fact that an individual happens to be a member of a minority is no guarantee that he or she is right. There are all sorts of minorities—good, bad, and indifferent— and not simply every saving idea, but every foolish fad can be a minority. That fact, however, argues not against but for our plea. Just because today there are so many uninformed, irresponsible, even violent minorities, let the forward-looking and responsible citizens the more assume their obligations! As for being Christian, I suppose that, reduced to simplest terms, it means answering Christ's two-word appeal, "Follow me." Where do we think it takes us when we do follow him? Never into a majority. I wonder where you and I are this morning—three measures of meal or leaven?—Harry Emerson Fosdick.

Illustrations

KNOWING CHRIST THROUGH EXPERIENCE. He comes to us as One unknown, without a name, as of old, by the lakeside, he came to those men who knew him not. He speaks to us the same word: "Follow thou me!" and sets us to the tasks which he has to fulfill for our time. He commands. And to those who obey him, whether they be wise or simple, he will reveal himself in the toils, the conflicts, the sufferings which they shall pass through in his fellowship, and, as an ineffable mystery, they shall learn in their own experience who he is.—Albert Schweitzer.

COSTLY COURAGE. Among the men whose stories are told by John F. Kennedy in his *Profiles of Courage* is Edmund G. Ross. He is known as "the man who saved a president." Andrew Johnson was determined to carry out the policies of reconciliation initiated by Abraham Lincoln for the healing of the nation after the Civil War. However, radical leaders in Congress were determined to follow a policy of punishment for the defeated South. These congressmen saw President Johnson as the obstacle to their success. Therefore, they attempted to get rid of the president by impeachment and dismissal from office. As the congressmen solidified their position, it eventually became clear that impeachment hung on the vote of one man—Edmund G. Ross. Later, he commented, "I almost literally looked down into my open grave. Friendships, position, fortune, everything that make life desirable to an ambitious man were about to be swept away by the breath of my mouth, perhaps forever." His answer was, "Not guilty." Shortly after the trial, he said to his wife, "Millions of men cursing me today will bless me tomorrow for having saved the country from the greatest peril through which it has ever passed, though none but God can ever know the struggle it has cost me."—*Profiles of Courage.*

Sermon Suggestions

WHY GO TO CHURCH? Text: Luke 4:16. Why is it so important to follow Jesus in this respect? (1) Churchgoing is a remarkable means of Christian witness. It is a silent testimony to the values we hold precious. (2) Churchgoing is a remarkable means of confession. We are making bold confession that worship is much more than an aesthetic experience, infinitely greater than an individualistic mystical rapture. (3) Churchgoing is a remarkable performance of Christian work. Those who come to church and know what it is about are not observers—they are workers engaged in the service of God.—Elam Davies, *This Side of Eden.*

LOOKING UNTO JESUS. Heb. 12:1–2. What does a steady Christward look involve? (1) Looking outward, and not inward. (2) Looking upward, and not downward. (3) Looking forward, and not backward.—James S. Stewart.

Worship Aids

CALL TO WORSHIP. "O send out thy light and thy truth: let them lead me; let them bring me unto thy holy hill, and to thy tabernacles" (Ps. 43:3).

INVOCATION. O God, by whom the meek are guided in judgment, and light riseth up in darkness for the godly, grant us, in all our doubts and uncertainties, the grace to ask what thou wouldst have us to do, that the Spirit of Wisdom may save us from all false choices, and that in thy light we may see light, and in thy straight path may not stumble.—*Book of Common Prayer.*

OFFERTORY SENTENCE. "So then every one of us shall give account of himself to God" (Rom. 14:12).

OFFERTORY PRAYER. Accept, O Lord of Life, these gifts that we offer in the name of our living Savior, thy Son Jesus Christ. May we be empowered through our faith in thy mighty act of resurrection to use these resources placed before thee for the proclamation of thy truth and for the healing of thy people.—Rodney K. Miller.

PRAYER. O Lord, we take into our prayer this morning all conditions, all achievements, all frustrations of hope, all blighted buds that shall never fully bloom, all the grief and all the tears, that we may take into the little cup which we offer to thee; and we recognize that on the outside there are millions untouched by our comprehension. Thou knowest all; thou knowest everybody's need. We commend unto thee the child Humanity, the blundering, faithless, mistaken, rising, hoping, believing child Humanity—in the name of our Lord and Savior, Jesus Christ.—Frank W. Gunsaulus.

EVENING SERVICE

Topic: The Haughty and the Humble
SCRIPTURE: Luke 18:9–14.

Often the way we see things is not the way they really are; we get our priorities wrong. This parable of the Pharisee and the tax collector serves as an "example story" for us. Let us look at them to see what they have to show us about themselves and God.

I. How did others view them?

(a) The Pharisee was noted for his strict obedience to the law, and he was usually respected by others.

(b) The tax collector was employed by the Roman government, and he was despised by both the Jews and the Romans.

II. How did they view themselves?

(a) The Pharisee saw himself as righteous, and therefore he thought he was better than others.

(b) The tax collector did not deem himself worthy to approach the Holy Temple of God, and he called himself *the* sinner.

III. How did they view one another?

(a) The Pharisee knew that the other man was a tax collector, and he said he was glad he was not like him.

(b) The tax collector was so burdened down with his own sin that he did not look for the sin of others.

IV. How did they view God?

(a) The Pharisee viewed God as one who owed him something for his self-righteous living.

(b) The tax collector viewed God as holy and himself as unworthy even to ask God for mercy.

V. How did Jesus view them?

(a) Jesus regarded the Pharisee as condemned because of his sin, but not his goodness that he told God about.

(b) Jesus regarded the tax collector as being justified, not because of his sin, but because of his response to God.

Conclusion: Regardless of how we look at things, we are all sinners, just like the Pharisee and the tax collector. We all need forgiveness and therefore we are all equal in the sight of God. The difference comes when we humble ourselves, confess our sin, and ask God for his mercy and forgiveness. However, if we continue in our pride, as did the Pharisee, to consider ourselves self-righteous, we will die unjustified in the sight of God.—J. Milton Knox.

SUNDAY: FEBRUARY TWELFTH

MORNING SERVICE

Topic: Love Your Enemies
SCRIPTURE: Matt. 5:43–45.

I. (a) For one thing, Jesus was certainly not referring to an act which, performed with literal exactness, would automatically win for a man the approval of God. For it must have been as obvious to him as to us that the act of turning the other cheek or walking the second mile need not be synonymous with the kind of life he had in mind, and that a man might obey these specific commands without knowing the quality of heart and soul which gave the commands their meaning and power. He might turn the other cheek and be bitter about it. He might walk the second mile and hate the one who made him do it.

(b) Nor did Jesus mean that we are to love just our enemies or that we are to love our enemies more than our friends.

(c) Still further, Jesus did not mean that we must like the enemies who he commands us to love. When a boy and a girl decide to be married, they have liked each other before they have loved each other. But in the treatment of our enemies, it is usually necessary that we love them before we like them, and each of us will have many occasions to love people whom we never will like.

(d) Nor does loving our enemies prevent us from disapproving of their opinions or conduct.

(e) And hence it needs to be understood that loving the enemy does not necessarily mean submitting to the enemy. Turning the other cheek and going the second mile do not mean resigning ourselves to the triumph of evil, throwing up our hands in easy defeat, and feeling that in surrender to what God abhors we have done what God wants.

II. Let us think next about some of the steps which loving the enemy entail.

(a) First, then, when we love our enemies, we utterly repudiate hatred and malice in our thoughts about them. It would be futile to claim that even this phase of loving our enemies is simple or easy. The ability to love our enemies is acquired like any other skill. We learn to love by loving.

(b) Second, when we love our enemies, we recognize who our enemies actually are.

(c) Third, loving our enemies requires understanding our enemies. And we shall not love the people whom we do not like until we understand them—know the origins from which they came, recognize the pressures which have bent and twisted them, discern the secret burdens which have sapped away their strength and objectivity, appreciate the fear and guilt and hope which make them what they are.

(d) And then, fourth, it is a part of loving our enemies that we actively seek their welfare.

III. But what motive do we have for a life of that kind? There are at least three sound motives for loving our enemies.

(a) The first of them is simple decency. It is highly probable that there are those who find us as unattractive as we have found our enemies, and if our enemies have fallen short of the glory of God, could not the same be said of us?

(b) The second is more important: Jesus commands that we love them. "Love your enemies," he said.

(c) The third motive for loving our enemies grows out of the second: there is no other way of doing what needs to be done. There is no other way of establishing justice, building peace, and making earth the fair and goodly land which God intended it to be. If God is not mocked himself, neither does he make fools of his creatures, and he never imposes upon anyone a commandment which is impossible, unnecessary, unwise, or absurd. If we do not love them because we want to, we shall love them at last because we have to. There is no other answer to evil. There is no other alternative to chaos.—Roy Pearson.

Illustrations

HAVING OR BEING.   Mark Hopkins, the famous president of Williams College, is said to have once given it this picturesque illustration. "How many of you," he said to his senior class, "would accept from me a million dollars at the price of your hearing? Probably a good many of you. How many of you would be willing to be both deaf and dumb for the sake of a million dollars? Perhaps there are some here who would be willing. But if I said to you, how many of you here, for the sake of a million dollars, would be willing to sacrifice both sight and speech and hearing, you would pause, for the time would then have come when you would have to decide whether you would rather have something or be somebody!"—Albert Parker Fitch.

WHAT MEN SEEK.   It is good that men want, not evil. It is truth they want, not lies. It is beauty they want, not ashes. It is life they want, not death. The poor fellow who drinks his fifth whiskey and soda is not seeking a drunkard's grave. The poor girl who accepts the cheap and awful substitute for a good man's love is not seeking the ashes of a burnt-out heart. The conscienceless profiteer who grows fat on the misery of his fellows is not seeking the hell of loneliness that will inevitably be his. People who let themselves hate other people are not seeking the bitterness that hate involves. And it is, I suppose, only right to assume that people who by their economic or political policies bring on wars are not seeking to destroy their fellows. Certainly they are not seeking to destroy their own sons. It is life we want, "more life and fuller." But we need to have someone tell us how to get it—someone who really knows.—Ernest Freemont Tittle.

Sermon Suggestions

THE OPEN SECRET OF A GREAT LIFE. Text: Gal. 2:20. (1) It was a life lived under the usual human conditions: "the life which I now live in the flesh." (2) It was a life redeemed from the ordinary by the outworking of a great principle: "I live by the faith of the Son of God." (3) It was a life glorified in its response to the highest sentiment: "who loved me and gave himself for me."—Edwin C. Dargan.

HOW JESUS TAUGHT. Scripture: Matt. 7:28f.; John 15:15; 7:17; Luke 10:29ff.; Mark 12:30; Matt. 11:15; 2 Cor. 3:6. (1) It was authoritative teaching. (2) It was never, in any overbearing sense, didactic or dogmatic or forcing assent. (3) Closely related was his determination to make men think for themselves. (4) What he taught, he lived. (5) The last great principle of Jesus' teaching to which we shall point is this—his intimacy with and love for those he taught.—James S. Stewart.

Worship Aids

CALL TO WORSHIP. "He that dwelleth in the secret place of the most High shall abide under the shadow of the Almighty. I will say of the Lord, he is my refuge and my fortress: my God, in him will I trust" (Ps. 91:1–2).

INVOCATION. O God, you have shown us how we should behave toward one another. Today, show us that pattern again. May the grace of our Lord Jesus Christ truly change our hearts.

OFERTORY SENTENCE. "The earth is the Lord's, and the fullness thereof; the world, and they that dwell therein" (Ps. 24:1).

OFFERTORY PRAYER. Gracious Lord, we acknowledge your ownership of all the earth and everything and everyone in it. What we confess with our lips may we prove with our deeds. Through him who gave his all for our salvation.

PRAYER. We thank thee, Almighty God, for the rich heritage of this good land; for the evidences of thy favor in the past; and for the Hand that hath made and preserved us a nation. We thank thee for the men and women who, by blood and sweat, by toil and tears, forged on the anvil of their own sacrifice all that we hold dear. May we never lightly esteem what they obtained at a great price. Grateful for rights and privileges, may we be conscious of duties and obligations.

On this day, we thank thee for the inspiration that breathes in the memory of Abraham Lincoln, and we pray that something of the spirit that was his may be ours today. Like him, may we be more concerned that we are on thy side, than that thou art on ours. In our hearts may there be, as there was in his, malice toward none and charity for all; that we may, together, with thy blessing and help, "bind up the nation's wounds, and do all which may achieve and cherish a just and lasting peace among ourselves and with all nations."—Peter Marshall.

EVENING SERVICE

Topic: The Traitor Who Sold Jesus
TEXT: Luke 6:16.

I. Judas is the supreme enigma of the New Testament because it is so hard to see how anyone who was so close to Jesus could ever come to betray him into the hands of his enemies.

(a) We must remember when reading the New Testament that anything the evangelists say about Judas was set down long after the betrayal—a dark deed which would influence their estimate of his character. This explains his place at the bottom of the list of the disciples: "Judas Iscariot, who also betrayed him."

(b) Judas was patriotic, religious, and eager for the coming of the King and the Kingdom. There is no reason to doubt that Jesus called him into the circle of the twelve because he saw in him the makings of a true disciple. The other disciples must have trusted him or they would never have made him their treasurer. Dr. Barclay says that it is not impossible that Judas was the chief one of the apostles.

II. But we can see that a process of degeneration soon set in. St. Luke, with his fine sense of the value of words, says, "Judas Iscariot who *became* a traitor."

(a) Judas felt his superiority to the other disciples. His aloofness caused him some loneliness, which he attributed to the clannishness of these Galileans who did not want him. This loss of the sense of fellowship may account for the story of Judas' dishonesty. His zeal in regard to the box of ointment which Mary broke in honor of Jesus and which Judas decried as a waste was, St. John thinks, a cover for his sin. Dr. Eric Waterhouse says, "Judas began with pride and went on to lose the sense of fellowship, to thieve and then to cover his theft with hypocrisy. The result was a perished conscience. Peter, at a look from the Lord, went out broken-hearted. Judas, as Jesus looked at him, went out to betray him."

(b) It is a mistake to attribute the crime of Judas to any one particular passion, whether that of avarice or jealousy or ambition.

(1) We come nearer to the truth when we discover all three at work in the heart of the disciple, driving him on, step by step, to his final deed of shame. Judas had the power of choice right to the end, and he chose the night.

(2) It does not appear that the other disciples suspected Judas of disloyalty. They thought he had gone out to buy something. When Jesus intimated that one of them would betray him, they all said, "Lord, is it I?" But Jesus from an early period noticed the process, first of alienation and then of enmity, developing in the heart of Judas.

(3) After the desertion of the crowd, Jesus turned to the disciples and said, "Will you also go away?" Peter replied, "Lord, to whom shall we go? You have the words of eternal life." Then follows the startling and apparently irrelevant statement of Jesus. "Did I not choose you, the twelve, and one of you is a devil."

The soul had been arrested in its progress. Only one noticed the change. It was not obvious to the other eleven, probably not to Judas, but Jesus knew. He saw beneath the surface. Not yet will the Master give up the conflict for the soul of the apostle, but he spoke the word of warning in the hearing of all so that each might examine himself and especially Judas.

(c) The warning was meant to awaken and arrest Judas on his downward course, but it was in vain. Perhaps he was tortured by doubt as to how much Jesus knew or suspected of him. The knowledge that Jesus knew what manner of man he was brought about a feeling of resentment and a desire for revenge.

III. Judas had enlisted under the banner of Christ with hope and enthusiasm. He had been prepared to join in a holy crusade against their Roman masters, to play his part in establishing the Kingdom. Now after two years of discipleship, nothing had come of it, save a counsel of resignation and a willingness to meet death.

(a) So Judas, convinced that he had been deceived, sought to betray his Master. It was not greed but the spirit of hatred and revenge that moved Judas, and he may have felt a measure of gratification that he had sold his Master for the price of a slave.

(b) Judas was present in the Upper Room when Jesus washed the disciples' feet and said, "You are clean but not all of you." Nobody but Judas could understand the meaning of those words. Later Jesus said, "One of you will betray me," and he gave Judas another warning by saying, "Woe to that man by whom the Son of man is betrayed. Good were it for that man if he had never been born." At the supper, Jesus gave Judas the sop of honor, the mark of highest distinction, but he remained unmoved, for Satan had entered into him. Our Lord tried to touch and win him in every loving way, but at the end when tenderness had done its work there was only one thing left to say, "What you are going to do, do quickly. If your heart is set on this I cannot stop you." God cannot save a man who will not be saved.

Dr. Rendel Harris suggests that the words spoken by Jesus to Judas in the Garden of Gethsemane, when he came at the head of that motley crowd of Jewish priests and Roman soldiers and kissed his master—"Friend, why are you here?"—were intended to remind him of the cup of which he had drunk in the Upper Room.

(c) He followed the crowd to the mock trial of Jesus first before Annas and then before the Sanhedrin under Caiaphas. As they emerged, they were confronted by a strange figure holding in his right hand a bag with thirty pieces of silver. Kneeling before the high priest, Judas cried out in the bitterness of his heart, "I have sinned in that I have betrayed innocent blood." He got cold comfort. "What is that to us? See to it yourself." For the first time, the full enormity of his deed came home to him. Then he hurried away to put an end to his miserable life. His suicide was an act of sheer despair.

(d) The priests gathered up the silver pieces, but as they were blood money, they could not put them in the Temple treasury. Not far away was a disused potter's field. The thirty pieces would suffice to buy it to be kept as a burial place for strangers. The people called it "the Field of Blood"—the only monument to the memory of Judas, and his own body was the first to be buried there. Thus ended the life of the man who was called to be an apostle. He was not an incarnation of the devil, but a man of like passions to ourselves. The temptation is still with us on the spiritual side.

(e) It is easy to cast stones at Judas, but it will better become us to turn the eye inward upon ourselves- better still to turn our thoughts to our Savior and every day and every hour to put the question of the disciples, "Lord, is it I?"—John Bishop.

SUNDAY: FEBRUARY NINETEENTH

MORNING SERVICE

Topic: Born to Eternal Life
TEXT: John 17:3.

Jesus could accept the fact of death because he had assurance of God's gift of life eternal. He brought that assurance to others (see John 3:16).

Later he was prayerfully talking with God about eternal life. He made the consummate definition when he said, "And this is eternal life, that they may know you, the only true God, and Jesus Christ whom you have sent." St. Francis picked this up and made it the climactic word in his beloved prayer.

O Lord, make me an instrument of thy peace. Where there is hatred, let me sow love . . . where there is despair, hope. . . . For . . . it is in dying that we are born to eternal life.

How do we learn to pray such a prayer?

I. *Accept the reality of death.* "Accept the reality of death!" you say. "Who doesn't? The death rate is still 100 percent. Everybody dies sooner or later." Yet, am I far wrong that death is avoided in conversation, camouflaged in our culture, and pushed constantly to the back of our minds?

(a) It would seem that one could report some progress or growth in our understanding the need to face death as reality. Something has happened to spark an interest in reading books on death and dying. We have a near plethora of such books coming out from every publisher, it seems. I rejoice in this because it denotes growth in our willingness to face the reality of death.

(b) Yet, I dare not be too optimistic at this point, because there is still very much a conspiracy to deny death among us. Some of us cannot face up to the reality of death because we don't want to think about our own death. We regard as morbid any reference to the fact that one day, sooner or later, *we* will die. Yet, is it not true that each of us is more concerned about the possible death of someone else? Death does not haunt me when I think about myself. It is my wife and children and grandchildren whose death would shake me up!

(c) Perhaps I am victimized by our culture's obsession with survival. Survival in this instance means continuation of our physical and earthly life. Because of this obsession, we are prone to push death back from our conscious thought. As Blaise Pascal said, "Since men could find no cure for death, they simply chose not to reflect on it at all." We get the idea that if we just put death out of mind, it will somehow go away.

(d) When we are willing openly to accept the reality of death, we can be most helpful to other persons, particularly the young. Nowhere is the conspiracy of silence more complete than in dealing with children about death. Too long we wait to talk about it. Too often we have left them without any preparation whatsoever. Death comes to a family member or friend, and they are forced to face its reality in the grip of unruly emotions.

(e) We can never accept the reality of death without understanding that the most tragic death is the death of meaning. How many people have died to meaning even though they still move around and have their physical being! But does life have to be a miserable repeat of our unhappy and meaningless yesterdays? The Christian faith says it does not have to be this way.

(f) A final way to accept the reality of death is to find a satisfactory assurance that death does not end it all. To accept death as the end is most tragic, for it casts a shadow of purposelessness on this life here. But does one have to go further than Mother Nature to find assurance that life goes on beyond death? The seed falls into the ground and dies only to live again as a plant or tree, but Christ and the Christian faith shout above the noisy clamor of such absurdity as annihilation, "Death does *not* end all!" The Christian faith has produced the idea that life does not end in the grave, though the body may return to the dust from whence it came. We are assured that there is more beyond because of God's gift of eternal life.

II. *Accept God's gift of eternal life.*

(a) As one writer states it succinctly: "God had set eternity in the heart." You and I have it there, whether or not we have recognized it, whether or not we have appropriated it for our conscious thinking.

To be sure, the history of civilization reports that all peoples have believed in some kind of afterlife. The concepts of immortality have varied, and the Christian faith comes to add resurrection to our concept. Immortality holds the belief that the spiritual part of the human person survives death. Resurrection, in the Christian context, means the hope for the survival of the person himself or herself.

(b) Jesus said the pure in heart see God. He said the lowly of spirit, the humble persons, can be certain of the presence of God here and in the hereafter. He proclaimed that those who love God as he is revealed in Jesus walk with Christ in an eternal experience that begins here and now. The fact that God has put eternity in your heart means that "your spiritual equipment proclaims you are made for everlasting life." Have you not found that belief stronger and more compelling when you have faced the fact of a loved one's death?

(c) Eternal refers to a quality of life, not to a quantity of years. And we can live in such a quality of life here and now as well as after death—at least, that's what Jesus taught. We need to get the assurance that eternal life is not some future destination but a present possession, if we are fully to understand and fully to enjoy this gift of God.

(d) For the Christian, belief in eternal life is basically something that grows out of our acceptance of the fact that Jesus rose from the dead. The resurrection gave a dimension and meaning to his life which no human life had before had. The apostles went out to preach that resurrection faith: "He is risen from the dead." And that makes all the difference in the world—in this world and the next, for the Christian. For, "this is eternal life, that they may know you, the only true God, and Jesus Christ whom you have sent."—Hoover Rupert.

Illustrations

CHRIST IN YOU. A new pastor had come to the village and called at a certain cottage. When the husband came home from his work, the wife said, "The new pastor called today." "What did he say?" asked the man. "Oh," she answered, "he asked,

'Does Christ live here?' and I didn't know what to say." The man's face flushed. "Why didn't you tell him that we were respectable people?" he asked. "Well," she answered, "I might have said that, only that isn't what he asked me." "Then why," pursued her husband, "didn't you tell him that we said our prayers and read our Bible?" The wife replied, "But he didn't ask me that." The man grew more vexed. "Why," he continued, "didn't you say that we were always at church?" The poor woman broke down and said, "He didn't ask that either. He asked only, 'Does Christ live here?'" This man and woman pondered for many days what the grave pastor had meant by his question. Little by little, their lives were changed. Little by little, they grew to expect Christ—not dead, but gloriously alive. And in some way, they knew not how, through great love and through a willingness to be surprised by the mystery of his radiance, they knew him. He did indeed live there.—Charles Lewis Slattery.

BIRTH OF A GUARDIAN ANGEL. An ethical book written by a Jewish mystic of the eighteenth century tells a naïve and charming folktale. There lived somewhere a lonely and pious Jew, poor and forgotten of men, whose entire possession in life was one single tract of the Talmud. He had no other books. The pious man spent all his days reading and re-reading this one sacred tract. It filled his entire life; it became his world. He guarded it, he loved it, he treasured it. When he died, so runs the tale, this precious tome of sacred lore was transformed into a radiant maiden of surpassing loveliness, who led this faithful devotee to the Gates of Paradise. Quaint, is it not? But how profoundly true! In similarwise did Beatrice lead Dante along the terraces of heaven. For every high devotion, for every transfiguring wish, or hope, or prayer, an angel is born unto us to be our ministrant and guardian.—Abba Hillel Silver.

Sermon Suggestions

THE MINISTRY OF INTERCESSION. Text: 2. Cor. 1:11. The ministry of intercession always produces three results: (1) It deep-

ens and enriches the lives of those who pray for others. (2) The ministry of intercession always brings blessing, whatever its results, to those who know they are being prayed for. (3) The ministry of intercession, whether or not God seems to grant the prayer, always unlocks extra possibilities in the situation. When we truly pray for others, it is as if we put into the hand of God an added instrument for the working out of his saving purpose.—R. Leonard Small.

HOW TO BEHAVE IN PRISON. Text: Phil. 1:12. Paul learned three things from his Master, Christ Jesus: (1) Paul forgot his imprisonment. (2) He transfigured his imprisonment. (3) He used his imprisonment.—W. Russell Maltby.

Worship Aids

CALL TO WORSHIP. "Oh that men would praise the Lord for his goodness, and for his wonderful works to the children of men! For he satisfieth the longing soul, and filleth the hungry soul with goodness" (Ps. 107:8–9 [KJV]).

INVOCATION. Today, O Lord, give us such keen vision that we can see what thou dost mean to us and all thy chldren every day of our lives. Then help us to render to thee fitting praise in psalms and hymns and spiritual songs; in the reading and preaching of thy word; and in the offering of our very selves to thee.

OFFERTORY SENTENCE. "For every beast of the forest is mine, and the cattle upon a thousand hills" (Ps. 50:10).

OFFERTORY PRAYER. We are thine, O God. Thou has created us. Thou hast redeemed us. Thou hast given us the power to gain the fruits of our labors. And now we bring as offerings of gratitude and love only what is already truly thine.

PRAYER. Eternal God, before whom sinners cannot stand, we come humbly into thy presence. Out of the turbulence of the world, our hearts disquieted by its confusion, our lives contaminated by its sin, we come to thee. Give us an hour of insight and cleansing; grant us grace to be honest with ourselves, sensitive toward our neighbors, reverent toward thee.

We dare not come to worship thee without bringing our brother with us. Father of all men, who hast said that we cannot love thee unless we love our brother also, we would come bringing him with us in our hearts' compassion and goodwill. Before we seek forgiveness, help us to be forgiving; before we ask for mercy, help us to be merciful. Take from our hearts the hidden grudge, the secret vindictiveness, the lurking hate. Give us an inclusive spirit of sympathy and understanding. From all bigotry and prejudice of race and class, deliver us. Teach us what it means to care even for those who despitefully use us, and so abiding in love may we abide in thee.

Though we come with our brother in our sympathy, nonetheless thou seest how alone we are. We come from the world, where men look on the outward appearance, to thee who dost look upon the heart. We ourselves hardly know the secret motives or our own lives; we are so busy in the world that we seldom meet ourselves face to face. O God, seek us out now in the inward, untrodden recesses of our souls. When we confront our severest troubles, our profoundest temptations, we are solitary, and when death comes, we die alone. Companion of the companionless, inner source of strength, comfort, and fortitude, deep well from which the living waters rise, be with us today.—Harry Emerson Fosdick.

EVENING SERVICE

Topic: The New Life

SCRIPTURE: 2 Cor. 5:17; Gal. 2:20.

I. When I speak about Christ, I am speaking of a New Life that pursues you, and which you either accept or reject.

II. The only way to see what this New Life is like is to look at Jesus, for the New Life came into the world in him.

(a) He was an undivided, undisturbed person. There were no splits in his personality, as there are in yours and mine.

(b) This negative fact about him is the fruit of a positive fact: he and God were at one. His will was to do the Father's will.

(c) He was *the* New Life. The old life was a self-preserving life. The New Life was a self-giving life, rooted so completely in confidence and trust that it had no need to fear.

(d) This undivided and undisturbed New Life gave Jesus enormous power.

(1) He had power to heal people.

(2) He had, above all, that enormous power to bring men and women together with God. In him, God was reconciling the world unto himself.

(e) Now this is the New Life that began to take hold of people like Paul. It made Paul a new man. It did not make him a more moral man; Paul was already so moral that it was hard both for himself and for society to bear. But it made him a more creative man. He not only told about the Reconciling Life of Jesus; he himself was a source of reconciliation.

III. This is the New Life that can be in you, and in which you can be incorporated. How can I do it?

(a) First, say now that you want it. You may have to say it again and again, but say it now.

(b) Keep close to other people who want it. You have to have the support and enthusiasm of other people who sincerely want it.

(c) Make your supreme aim in life, no matter what you happen to do by way of a career, the communication of the New Life to other people. I know it is easier to say it than to do it, but start doing it!—Theodore Parker Ferris, *The New Life*.

SUNDAY: FEBRUARY TWENTY-SIXTH

MORNING SERVICE

Topic: The Paradox of Anxiety
Text: Phil. 4:6.

What we need to grasp is that anxiety is not simply a problem to be solved: it is also a paradox to be accepted. Take these two statements of Paul. "There is the daily pressure upon me of my anxiety for all the churches." Now turn the pages of the New Testament, and you will find this very same man writing: "Have no anxiety about anything. . . ." Was he a blatant humbug? Was he guilty of preaching but not practicing? No! This is the paradox of anxiety. We must understand that it is never possible to overcome it entirely this side of eternity. It is a mark of our creatureliness, a symbol of our finitude. And there is a very real sense in which Christianity adds to, rather than subtracts from, our anxiety. It places burdens on us that we may well wish to escape. The point is—there is anxiety and anxiety. Some is wrong and some is right. The same Christ who promised, "Peace I leave with you, my peace I give unto you. Let not your hearts be troubled," also said, "I came not to send peace on earth, but a sword."

Let us look closely at this paradox of anxiety, and work out some of its implications.

I. On the one hand, *anxiety is a sign of maturity*. In a world like this, only the immature and shallow are without care. The mature know lifelong anxiety, and it is right that it should be so. Think of some areas of deep concern we cannot, and would not, avoid.

(a) Take the commands of God. Anxiously we must ask: are we obeying them? Men and women who break these commands with impunity, who talk of God only with a sophisticated sneer, who never lie awake at night and fret over their sins, are wise indeed—if there is no God. But if there *is* a God—then that's another story! Believing all that will make us anxious—anxious to obey, to repent, to receive his grace and pardon. Such anxiety is a prelude to peace of mind!

(b) Take the responsibilities of citizenship. Anxiously we must ask: are we accepting them? The more we love our country, the more concerned we should be about its direction, moral tone, government, laws. Public apathy over the crucial issues of our contemporary world—inflation, poverty, drug addiction, the highway slaughter, easy abortion—is a disgraceful dereliction of plain duty. These matters should worry us to active participation, to making our voices heard and our votes count.

(c) Take the duties of churchmanship. Anxiously we must ask: are we fulfilling them? To join a church is to accept the duties of membership. It is to be concerned about the welfare of Christ's body, to be personally responsible for its worship, work and witness, its spiritual impact and financial stability. To be sure, the church is finally in the hands of God. His care never falters. Nevertheless, he calls us into partnership.

(d) Take the needs of people. Anxiously, we must ask: are we serving them? First, we must feel them, assume them as our own burdens. A parent must be anxious about the welfare of growing children. Children must be anxious about aging parents. The affluent must be anxious about the poor, the hungry, the hopeless. The healthy must be anxious about the sick.

II. Turn now to the other side of the paradox of anxiety. It is this: *anxiety is a sin of unbelief*. I know that sounds severe. We are more inclined to speak of our worrying nature as an amiable weakness. The severity, however, carries the authority of Jesus. In that section of the Sermon on the Mount which deals with anxiety, he made it clear that worry is really practical atheism. It is sheer faithlessness, an absolute distrust of God. If you trust, you do not worry. If you worry, you do not trust. Paul was echoing His Master's words when he wrote: "Have no anxiety about anything. . . ." Anxiety is a sin, a sin of unbelief.

(a) Why is it a sin, and why do we succumb to it?

(1) Sinful anxiety is rooted in self-interest, self-pity, self-centeredness. So many chronic worriers are wrapped up in themselves, are fretful and fearful about themselves, are living in a narrow world bounded north, south, east and west by themselves.

(2) The answer to such self-centeredness is a revolution that makes us God-centered, turns our thoughts toward others, and enables us to realize that we are members of a family.

(b) Consider carefully what Jesus had to say about anxiety as a sin, and what Paul had to say, and you will find a practical strategy for overcoming it. It can be summed up in four words.

(1) The first word is: *bury*. Conduct a joyful funeral service, as a friend of mine puts it, and bury a lot of the past that haunts and harasses us. Bury your past sins, if they have been repented of and forgiven. They are over and should be forgotten. Bury your past resentments—the smouldering anger we feel toward others who have injured or insulted us. Bury your past sorrows—not, of course, the genuine sorrow rooted in the love we have for those who have died and whose presence we sorely miss, but the morbid, introspective self-pity that makes us a burden to ourselves and a trial to others (see Phil. 3:13).

(2) The second word is: *simplify*. This was Thoreau's famous exhortation—'Simplify! Simplify!" He was echoing Socrates, who said: "How many things I can do without!" Much of our modern anxiety springs from our passion to acquire *things* —material things, money, possessions. This is a point Jesus made forcefully in his teaching. It is useless trying to insulate ourselves against imaginary hardships and calamities in the future by piling up things. Such worry never robs tomorrow of its sorrow; it merely saps today of its strength and joy. If we simplified our lives, we might well enrich them beyond measure (see Matt. 6:25, 33).

(3) The third word is: pray. "But in everything by prayer and supplication, with thanksgiving, let your requests be made known to God. . . ."

Pray in detail—for our God is a father who takes a father's interest in the details of his children's lives. If anything is big enough to worry about, it is big enough to pray about. Pray with thanksgiving—for gratitude, which is an awareness of our blessings and assets, simply cannot exist side by side with anxiety. Pray and work— do anything within your power to correct the situation that worries you, and by action seek to achieve the answer to your own prayers.

(4) The fourth word is: *trust*. The positive alternative to anxiety is faith. That is why anxiety is a sin of unbelief. "Why are you anxious?" Jesus asked. "O men of little faith." Our basic need is security. And real security cannot be found in ourselves or in any facet of a world which is passing away. It can be found only in the God who has been made known to us in Jesus Christ, and whose everlasting arms are always underneath us. Why don't we trust him?—John N. Gladstone.

Illustrations

FREE FROM FEAR.   Our Bible is only sixty-six verses old when Fear appears as the villain on the stage of Eden. Fear waves his devil's wand over the mind of Adam and makes him say to God, "I heard thy voice in the garden, and I was afraid." And this villain Fear haunts the scenes of the biblical drama until, at the end, the writer of Revelation catches a vision of the Eternal City, whose gates "shall not be shut at all by day: for there shall be no night there." An unguarded city, a nightless day—what more perfect symbols of a people freed from fear!—Ralph W. Sockman.

GOD WHO FEEDS AND CLOTHES.   Isn't it true that everything depends upon *who* it is that says these words about the birds and the lilies? A person who sees, as Jesus Christ did, the human and the nonhuman domain of the cosmos pervaded with fissures, menaces, and rebellions against God and throws himself and his whole existence into it, who sees not only the flaming signs of his own downfall, but those of the whole world flickering on the horizon, who already knows the hour when the mountains shall cover us and the sun and moon will be darkened—well, I should say that, coming from him, these words about the birds and the lilies and their marvelous freedom from care mean something different from what they would if they were spoken by some romantic nature lover and dreamer.—Helmut Thielicke.

Sermon Suggestions

FORGET IT! Text: Phil. 3:13. (1) Past triumphs are past. (2) Past failures are past. (3) Past sins are past. (4) Past hurts are past. (5) Forget—and press on.—John Dunford.

A SOUL-WINNING CHURCH. Text: Acts 1:8. The program of a church that wins souls includes: (1) The *person—you.* (2) The *place*—starting right where you are. (3) The *power—the* power of the Holy Spirit.—Walter L. Lingle.

Worship Aids

CALL TO WORSHIP. "Jesus answered and said unto him, If a man love me, he will keep my words: and my Father will love him, and we will come unto him, and make our abode with him" (John 14:23).

INVOCATION. Today, our Father, increase our love for thee, that we may know more of thy infilling presence and in turn share in a greater way with the world the Good News of thy salvation.

OFFERTORY SENTENCE. "The silver is mine, and the gold is mine, saith the Lord of hosts" (Hag. 2:8).

OFFERTORY PRAYER. What we bring to thy treasury, O God, we bring with an awareness of our stewardship. Help us to reflect on every aspect of our living, working, and saving, to the end that we shall make our lives richer toward thee.

PRAYER. O Lord, amid all threats to our security we look to thee to protect us.

We would not dictate the terms of thy providence. Thou knowest what is best. If our loyalty to thee means that we shall be misunderstood, disliked, or even persecuted, then give us the grace to bear patiently and creatively this burden of our obedience. But grant that we shall never, through lack of love or lack of courtesy or lack of tact, bring on ourselves needless burdens and call them thy will.

As we look back across the years of our lives, we can see how, again and again, we have been spared through thy mercy. Thou hast, again and again, set our feet upon a rock and put a song on our lips. Give us the faith to feel that solid foothold and sing that song even before the deliverance comes. For it befits us who believe in thee to stand firmly and sing joyfully even before the fruition of our salvation. So renew our hearts in praise and gratitude.

EVENING SERVICE

Topic: Faith—Creative Insecurity
SCRIPTURE: Mark 10:17–22.
I. *Religion as a security system.* One of the biggest mistakes church people make is to think that they can turn what God has made the greatest adventure there is, into a security system. But life is for living and not for the practice of religion. The New Testament church preserved the encounter of the rich young man with Jesus for a good reason. We discover here the heart of the gospel—the thrust of what it meant to be a Christian in that first century, and what it means today. When the young man comes asking the question, "What must I do to be saved?" he is prompted by selfish motivation. He practices religion as a way to play it safe. For him, it is a security system. Of all of man's idolatries, Jesus discerns religion as the most insidious. Instead of leading persons to God, it becomes a hideout from God. Instead of awakening persons to life and its possibilities, it is stultifying, thwarting, stupifying —even puts us to sleep as a tranquilizer.
II. *Faith—not destination but direction.* As Jesus challenged this young man, we need to get beyond the practice of religion to participate in faith. Faith is not the destination, but the direction of life. Jesus was saying here what he says elsewhere: he

who is intent on saving himself will lose himself, but he who is willing to give himself for my sake and for the sake of others, will discover himself. In contrast to the attitude of this young man, I am suggesting that those who have entered into eternal life are not even conscious of the fact; at least, they are not parading it. If it is your own salvation, your own security that you are seeking, then you don't want Christ. This young man was in love with religion—he was in love with himself in the church—as some of us are in love with ourselves in the church.

III. *Christianity: An adventure of the spirit.* You see, Christianity is not at all what many of us think it is. It is not a security system but an adventure of the spirit. In the history of Israel, there is an illustration of a people choosing death rather than life which should be a warning to us. When the children of Israel came to the borders of Canaan, the Promised Land, Moses sent out twelve men as scouts. Ten of them came back with very negative reports that the inhabitants were like giants and they would never be able to take the land. But Joshua and Caleb came back with a positive report: it is going to be difficult, but we *can* move forward and possess the land. The people listened to the doubters, and they literally chose death rather than life. It is not safe to believe in the God of the Bible. It was not safe for Abraham, or for Moses, or for Amos, or for Jeremiah, or for Jesus, or for Paul, or for Peter, or for Martin Luther, or for Martin Luther King, or for Mother Teresa. When the young man turned away disappointed in Jesus (or was it in himself?) the apostle Peter turned to the Master and said: "We have left all to follow, what are we going to get?" Part of Jesus' answer was given in that strange paradoxical statement of reversals: "The first shall be last and the last shall be first."

IV. *Only insecurity is creative.* It isn't safe to believe in the God of the Bible. In fact, it isn't safe to live. Security is little more than sterility. Only insecurity is ever-creative.

(a) Christianity is not a salvation, but a call to adventurous living. Eternal life is not the perpetuity of the status quo, but it is becoming alive at such depths that nothing can ever kill you. It is life to participate in the eternal Spirit. As Jesus informed the young man in our Scripture lesson, it is not found in playing it safe, but in risking all. The way of faith—of creative insecurity —is the way of growth, of maturing, of becoming.

(b) The church as the community of faith is to create faith, provoke faith, nurture faith. But what the church resists more than anything else—because this is what we resist as persons—is to live by faith in the living God. Faith is not something to rest on, to take one's ease on—but it beckons one to the growing edges of the self, to the frontiers of life. God calls us to missions, to get beyond ourselves, to participate in his great love purpose for all peoples. Love is always on the frontier— bringing light to darkness, forgiveness to guilt, hope to despair.

V. *Looking unto Jesus: pioneer and validator of our faith.* This is what conversion is: accepting the freedom with which Christ makes us free. The apostle Paul, as the man Saul of Tarsus, had known the security of religion, but he never experienced life until he encountered Christ on the Damascus Road. Christ freed him from religion that he might live to God. "For me to live is Christ," he exclaimed. Christ is the faith-man in each of us who frees us to be fully ourselves in the experience of God's love in our creation and in our re-creation. Who among us, looking into the eyes of Jesus, cannot see the person he or she was intended to be?—John Thompson.

SUNDAY: MARCH FOURTH

MORNING SERVICE

Topic: Approaching Lent

TEXT: Luke 17:7–10 (Phillips trans.).

This coming Wednesday is "Ash Wednesday," the first day of the long Lenten fast. The three days before Ash Wednesday are known in England as "Shrovetide." *Shrove* is derived from the Anglo-Saxon *scrifan*, which means "to shrive," to make confession, or to hear confession and to grant absolution.

I. *Keeping Lent.* Lent is the name given to the forty days, *excluding Sundays*, between Ash Wednesday and Easter eve. It may be derived from *lencten*, the Anglo-Saxon word for "spring," or from a Teutonic word meaning "long," since the hours of daylight are longer at this time of year than in the winter months. Ecclesiastically, it is the long, spring season marked, as was said, by penitence, prayer, and fasting, and symbolized by some disciplined act of supererogation. I suppose some of us are going to give up one or more of our happy habits during Lent. There are three things that should be said to those who plan to discipline themselves in some self-denying fashion to the greater glory of God, during the forty days beginning on Wednesday.

(a) First, we do not give up sins as Lenten discipline. That does not count. Sins are never valid acts for the Christian. There is no open season for conscious transgression, for willing nonconformity to the will of God. We give up what is good, as a personal, intentional, lively sacrifice. We give up the good for a temporary better. What is the "temporary better"? It is the proving to ourselves that, under God and with God, we are in control of our desires and appetites and legitimate pleasures, and that they are not in control of us.

(b) Second, Sundays don't count. There are six Sundays *in* Lent. Note well the preposition *in*. The Sundays are not liturgically known as the six Sundays *of* Lent, but the six Sundays *in* Lent. Why? Because Sunday is never a day of fasting. Sunday is always a festival. Why? Because Sunday is always the celebration of the day on which Jesus Christ was raised from the dead. It is a "Hallelujah" day. Every Sunday is a little Easter. That is why Sunday is properly named "The Lord's Day." What we give up is not sinful; it is good. And Sunday is a good day, a joyous day, a little Easter, always a festival, never a fast. Therefore, if you are planning to "keep" Lent, remember: never on Sunday.

(c) Third, let those of us who do discipline ourselves beware of the sin of pride, the sin of having a good conceit of ourselves, the sin of pharisaism, the sin of thinking we are better than others who do not discipline themselves, the sin of justification by works. Isn't that what Jesus was trying to show his listeners in that terrible parable of the Bond Servant?

That is rough talk. That is the severe Jesus. It is, thank God, not the whole gospel. But it is an emphasis which should not be forgotten, particularly by those of us who "keep" Lent. Here is Jesus' antidote for the conceit of merit, for the absurd belief that one can put God under an obligation by interested obedience. No man can make God his debtor. We cannot acquire a right to thanks. So when we come to Easter even and look back on our Lenten sacrifice, let us say: "We are not much good as servants, for we have only done what we ought to do."

II. *Using Lent.* There is another way of observing Lent, to my mind a better way, though you may disagree. Instead of cutting something off, let us add something. Let us consciously devote a period of time, maybe daily, maybe weekly—forty times or six times—to a conscious effort to broaden or deepen our understanding of the Christian faith, to cultivate the things of the spirit, the religious undergirding of our day-to-day living. How? Here are a few suggestions.

(a) Buy a copy of *The Gospel According to Peanuts*, by Robert L. Short. Persuade some others to do likewise, and spend some hours together during Lent discovering some of the central ideas in Christianity as enlivened by the art of the cartoon strip. For Charles M. Schulz, the creator of *Peanuts*, on his own confession, admits that he is preaching. Lucy is original sin incarnate; Charlie Brown is the despairing common man; Linus is a psychiatric case, full of "pantophobia": fear of everything, utterly dependent on the portable security of his blanket; Snoopy is a hound of heaven. The interpreter of the strips calls on Tillich and Barth and Kierkegaard and Shakespeare and T. S. Eliot and Graham Greene to shed light on this "Good Grief" collection of junior varsity adults. *The Gospel According to Peanuts* is a good textbook for a discussion group during Lent.

(b) If you are more sophisticated, then read what has almost become a Christian classic, *The Screwtape Letters*, by C. S. Lewis. Here are thirty-one letters from an old devil, Screwtape, one of his Satanic Majesty's "Lowerarchy," to his nephew, Wormwood, a junior devil who has been given the job of keeping a person from becoming a Christian. The book sparkles with wit and with unexpected twists. Jesus is the Enemy; Satan is "Our Father Below." All you talk about is here: sex, pacifism, pleasure, prayer, time, spiritual fatigue. This little volume must have caused considerable annoyance in hell. It will give you, by yourself or in the company of others, food for thought and chuckles of delight and insight into the faith.

(c) Yet, there maybe is a more excellent way. Read slowly and carefully through one of the gospels. Come to know Jesus: the author and finisher of our faith. Let us look *at* him and *unto* him during Lent, as we have never looked before. Let us walk with him through Galilee, listening to what he is saying, watching those to whom he is talking. Let us walk with him to Jerusalem into that last week, which began so successfully on Palm Sunday, ended so despairingly on Good Friday, and was transformed so wondrously on Easter Sunday.—James T. Cleland

Illustrations

BEYOND CONVERSION.   The little church of my boyhood was visited by traveling evangelists. The burden of the message in their revival meetings was: "Come to Jesus. Give your heart to God." Quite a lot was said about what would happen to us if we did not give our hearts to God. But not much light was thrown on what we should do after we surrendered our wills to God. Thoughtful persons are not content merely to come to Jesus. They want to know where they are to go with Jesus, and what they can do for and with God when they have given their hearts to him.— Ralph W. Sockman.

VICARIOUS SACRIFICE.   A nun saw one of the girls she had helped to train throwing herself away in an illicit love affair. All efforts to dissuade the girl failed. Then the nun began flogging herself daily. Every day, as that girl continued her loose living, she knew that her friend, the nun, was alone in her cell, flogging herself. That girl had to give in, for she found herself facing, until she no longer could endure it, the most tremendous moral force in the world. I can say as well as you that what that nun did is not literally reproducible in our lives, but I cannot escape the towering fact that being a Christian involves essentially that spirit—caring enough for persons and causes to sink our lives in them. —Harry Emerson Fosdick.

Sermon Suggestions

WHEN FOUNDATIONS FALL.   Scripture: Heb. 12:26–27. (1) God shakes the world because he is the judge of the world; he is a God of judgment. (2) God shakes the world because he is a God of purpose. He has a plan, a goal, a chart of progress. (3) God shakes the world because he is a God of eternity. God's goal is an unshakable world.—Gaston Foote.

THE FLAT PLACES OF LIFE.   Text: Ps. 84:6 (ASV). What are the flat places of life? Sickness, monotonous work, life itself. How can we handle them? (1) Remember that we are passing *through*. (2) Remember that there is something in the flat places of life (see Moffatt trans.). (3) Remember that under the flat places of life, there are riches.—Jack Finegan.

Worship Aids

CALL TO WORSHIP.   "The hour cometh, and now is, when the true worshippers shall worship the Father in spirit and in truth: for the Father seeketh such to worship him" (John 4:23).

INVOCATION.   Almighty God: you love all your children, and do not hate them for their sins. Help us to face up to ourselves, admit we are in the wrong, and reach with confidence for your mercy.—*The Worshipbook*.

OFFERTORY SENTENCE.   "Seek ye first the Kingdom of God and his righteousness, and all these things shall be added unto you" (Matt. 6:33).

OFFERTORY PRAYER.   Our Father, we have trouble establishing our priorities in life. Help us to know what really counts in the end, so that we may give our hearts to matters of first importance. Let no earthly love stand between us and our doing what life is all about. In the name of him who loved us, lived for us, and died for us.

PRAYER.   Almighty God, sovereign creator and ruler of all things, help us to prepare our hearts and spirits in this coming season of Lent in which we remember the sacrifice of thy Son on a cross for our sins. We ask that as we humble ourselves before thy divine majesty that thou wouldst empower us to be more faithful servants of thine in the days to come. Enable us to render willingly unto thee that greater measure of devotion that signifies our increased discipline of thought and action and our increased stewardship of resources and talent. Allow us to learn, O Lord, that the most lasting joy and meaning of life arise from a deeper understanding and experience of thy Son's life, death, and resurrection.—Rodney K. Miller.

EVENING SERVICE

Topic: John: The Man of Temper

SCRIPTURE: Luke 9:51–56; 1 John 3:2.

It is not the general belief of scholars today that a single man, whose name was John, was the "beloved disciple" and the author of the fourth gospel, the writer of the three letters ascribed to "John," and the author of the book of Revelation which stands last in our Bible. It is commonly believed that there were at least three different Johns who took part in all that. I would go one step farther—I would say that there were at least three different Johns in this one man whose character and conduct I wish to study with you here.

I. First, there is the John of legend and of art, who has been portrayed as a mystic, quiet and modest, gentle and tender. And this whole portrayal, in my judgment, goes wide of the mark. It shows us an apostle who might have been, but who never was.

II. In the second place, there is the real John of the four gospels. Here is another type of man altogether! Their associates called him and his brother "Boanerges, the sons of Thunder." There was something powerful, electric, startling about him. He was a child of the storm. There were times when he was hot and terrible in his outbursts of feeling.

(a) Jesus and his disciples were once on their way to Jerusalem. It came to pass that they entered just at nightfall into a village of Samaritans. These Samaritans refused him entertainment overnight "because his face was as though he would go to Jerusalem." He was a Jew, and the Jews had no dealings with Samaritans. The Samaritans would not allow him to sleep in their town overnight because he was a Jew. When James and John saw this bit of rudeness, they said: "Shall we call down fire? Shall we call down fire from heaven and burn them up, as Elijah did?" They had Scripture for it—"as Elijah did." There was the Old Testament precedent for such action. This man of temper was ready to burn up a whole town because it offered an affront to his Master in refusing him entertainment overnight.

Jesus rebuked him: "Ye know not what spirit ye are of!"

(b) His quick, hot temper and his fierce loyalty to his Master sometimes made John narrow and intolerant. There came a day when he saw a man going about doing good. The man was casting out devils. He was casting them out in the name and by the power of Christ. He was making men better by the message he brought and by the wholesome influence of his own spirit. But John rebuked him. "Stop it," he said. And he was rather pleased with himself over that performance. Then Jesus rebuked John. "Forbid him not—he that is not against us is for us."

(c) This man John was not conspicuous in his early life for modesty and humility. It was just the other way around. It was commonly believed by all the disciples, in the early part of Christ's ministry, that he would speedily set up a visible kingdom at Jerusalem, that he would organize a revolt against the Roman Empire and throw off the hated yoke. Therefore, two of the disciples—James and John, the sons of Zebedee—came to him and said, "Grant that we may sit one on thy right hand, the other on thy left in thy kingdom." When Jesus raised the question as to their fitness for such high honor, there was no doubt in their minds on that score. They replied promptly, "We can"—we are fit. John was one of those two men. Here he was, a man of temper, liable to quick and hot resentment, capable of being intolerant and vindictive! He was a man of swift and high ambition.

III. But there was a third John, the John of later years, when divine grace had done its work. Here we have another sort of man altogether, one who shows the results of consecration, devotion, and intimate fellowship with Christ.

(a) "Now are we the sons of God," we are told in the first letter which is ascribed to him. "It doth not yet appear what we shall be." We are facing a future of undeclared possibilities.

(b) In the first year of his Christian life, he made bold to ask for place and position for himself—he wanted to sit at the right hand of power. As time went on, his boldness found its consecration to higher ends. When Jesus was betrayed into the hands of his enemies and brought before Pilate and before the high priest, John followed him, not afar off.

(c) When that lame man was healed at the gate of the Temple called Beautiful, Peter and John were arrested and brought before the high priest. They were arrested because they had been speaking to the people about the power of Christ to heal and to save. The rulers strongly urged them not to speak again in the name of Christ, but they showed the same splendid courage and went right on with the deliverance of their message.

(d) How full of promise are those strong, warm, intense natures when they are brought under the power of Christ by willing surrender and glad consecration! They have in them such a wealth of potential goodness waiting for the divine call!— Charles Reynolds Brown.

SUNDAY: MARCH ELEVENTH

MORNING SERVICE

Topic: It Is Necessary

SCRIPTURE: Matt. 16:21–23.

"From that time, Jesus began to show his disciples that he must go to Jerusalem and suffer many things from the elders and chief priests and scribes and be killed. And on the third day be raised."

I. With these words, Matthew introduces the subject which is at the center of Christian reflection, the death of Jesus.

(a) For some, such as Paul, it was the subject not simply for meditation during Holy Week, but it was the consuming subject of his life. Christ crucified: to the Greeks, foolishness; to the Jews, a stumbling block. This Paul understood to be the offense that lies at the heart of the gospel. In fact, in the Western world and Western Christianity, the central symbol is the cross.

(b) For the gospel writers, this was the area of greatest demand upon their faith, upon their theology, upon their understanding of Scripture. They had to face the death of Jesus, make some sense of it, and set it in the context of God's searching grace. After all, the early church had to embrace the execution of its leader, and shape its understanding into a proclamation.

(c) In the four gospels, more than 35 percent of the narratives is devoted to the death and suffering of Jesus. All of the gospel writers introduce these into their stories quite early. Mark has hardly begun the story of Jesus when he says as early as chapter 2, "The days will come when the bridegroom will be taken away." Here in Matthew, eleven chapters before the event itself, the long shadow of the cross falls across the page. Near Mt. Hermon in the north, Jesus turned his disciples toward the south and showed them Golgotha. Matthew is certainly not seeking to create an early emotional effect, not squeezing pathos from the reader. A novelist might introduce into the story of the hero or the heroine some dreaded childhood disease as a fatal flaw, a shadow that appears and reappears to haunt every page of a brief but beautiful life. But Matthew is no novelist, and there is more at stake than sustaining the interest of an easily bored reader.

II. The way the subject of the death of Jesus is introduced here by Matthew is most attractive and yet most disturbing.

(a) He says that Jesus must go to Jerusalem and suffer and be killed. There is here no whining, no whimpering, no sighing and beating the breast. There is here the clear-eyed embrace of that horrible future. Sentimental biographers wrote of him as brave, bold, heroic. Psychiatric studies of Jesus upset us with phrases like "death wish" and "martyr complex." But even more disturbing is Matthew's way of putting it: Jesus *must* go; he must go to Jerusalem and suffer and be killed.

(b) How are we to handle that word *must*? He *must* go? What is the source of that "must," that sense of necessity? Is it excerpted from the eternal will and purpose of God, unavoidable and inevitable? Harsh as that may sound, there is a way of reflecting upon the death of Christ that properly describes it in precisely those terms. After the resurrection, the disciples of Jesus were quickened and enlightened to see the meaning of the events surrounding and including Jesus' death, and they saw them as the gracious hand of God. They re-read the Old Testament and re-thought the tragedy until light dawned and the cross was no more a tragedy.

III. In biblical thought, strange as this may seem to you or to me, once an event is over, the result of that event is viewed as having been the purpose of it from the beginning. Even after a tragedy, biblical writers are able to say that from the beginning it was to be so. Recall a few painful passages.

(a) Jesus chose as one of his friends and helpers a man named Judas Iscariot. He shared with Jesus the joys and pains known only to the inner circle. He was trusted as treasurer for the group. In the critical and tense days in Jerusalem, Judas betrayed Jesus and delivered him to the enemy for thirty silver coins. When it was all over, the tellers of the story said briefly, "He was a devil from the beginning." The end was seen as the beginning.

(b) Isaiah of Jerusalem was called to prophesy, the net result of which was deaf ears, hard hearts, turned backs. Later Isaiah reflected upon that result and understood it as the purpose of his call.

(c) Paul was converted and called to be a missionary in his mature years. He wrote of it later as a necessity laid upon him, having been set apart from his mother's womb. Result was interpreted as purpose. Strange, you say? Yes, to us.

(d) The result of Jesus' ministry was crucifixion, and so they were able to write "the purpose was crucifixion." It could have been no other way, they said. This was how they understood it. This was for us and our salvation. He was delivered up according to the plan of God. With Joseph in Egypt, in that beautiful moment of reconciliation with his brothers who had sold him into slavery years before, one could say here, too, "You intended it for evil, but God intended it for good." He is able to make even the wrath of man to praise him."

IV. But is it really this unusual perspective on events that bothers us about the "must" of Jesus going to Jerusalem? Is the statement that he "must go to Jerusalem and suffer and be killed" really a theological problem?

(a) Sure, we join battle on the issue because it poses a threat to that most prized possession, our freedom to choose our paths and our destinies. But does not our real problem lie in our having no place in our lives for the word *must*? You must do this, I must do that. We hardly know how to pronounce it. It's too heavy, it's too burdensome, it's too confining. Many of us and our children have been reared on the principles of self-expression, self-assertion, self-fulfillment. Some of us, as young parents, were so afraid we would damage the fragile psyches of our children that we dared not intrude into their lives a crippling "must," even if they were setting fire to the living room or sawing the family dog in half. There simply is no room for "must," and especially in religion. Certainly not in religion! All right, so we admit sometimes that we say we *must* go to work, or we *must* go to school, but who is going to say, I *must* go to worship? Surely, no one. In religion, the guiding principle is wanting to do it, enjoying it. Have you not said, or heard it said, "If you don't enjoy it, you won't get any good out of it?" If you don't really want to, it has no value. All religion is to flow from a free and willing heart; otherwise it's just sheer hypocrisy. Right?

(b) And so when we meet those who speak of their religion and faith with "must" or "have to," we say they need therapy. Do they? Maybe. But it also may be that this common resistance to "must" and "have to" is really a massive cop-out, a rejection of responsibility on our part. When this country was faced with the ugly truth about the treatment of blacks, many church people said, "Well, you can't compel morals, you can't legislate morals. Now when all of us feel right in our hearts, then we'll not have this problem." For how many hundreds of years can one say that? How long will this subjective captivity of the church last?

V. Just how does one get to feeling right in order to act as a Christian? Is it not true that feeling right most often comes *after* and not before doing right?

(a) Suppose that the matters of getting out of bed, facing freeway traffic, cleaning the carpet, preparing for exams, shoveling snow, or grading papers all had to wait upon our having hearts aflutter and leaping up with love of the task. The world would grind to a halt. "Our organist is not playing today because his heart was not in the prelude and he certainly did not want to be a hypocrite." "The pulpit is empty today because the minister's heart is down, and we all know one cannot preach up when one is down." Ridiculous! And yet the church sits in our world before a green light, with traffic backed up to Alaska while she tinkers with her soul to bring it to a fine tune. Maybe our resistance to "must" and "have to" really accounts for the poor record that some of us individually, and some of our churches, have in terms of effectiveness in making a difference in the life of the world.

(b) For so many of us, everything has to remain optional. No assignments, please. We don't want to box ourselves in with obligations or burdens. But look for a moment at the major contributors to our lives.

(1) For instance, Madame Curie, pioneer in the field of science, who isolated radium and, with that breakthrough, opened many new avenues in the field of medicine. You remember how it was with her, with frostbitten toes out there in the shed, with inadequate food, no financial support, working night and day through tons of rock to isolate this one element. Step out there in the shed and ask her about it. "Are you having a good time, Madame Curie? Isn't science wonderful?"

(2) Stop the apostle Paul, if you can, for a brief interview. Converted as an adult, sick much of his life, imprisoned often, stoned, beaten, rejected, shipwrecked, exiled, chased in the country, and trapped in the city, and yet here was one who was able to say in his later years, "I have labored more abundantly than all of them." Stop him and ask him, "Isn't missionary work really just a piece of cake? I wager you are having a ball, and all that travel! I love to visit exotic places, don't you?" And hear him say, "If I preach the gospel, I have nothing to boast about, for necessity is laid upon me."

(3) Or talk with Jesus. "Jesus, some of us have been thinking about having a picnic in the Garden of Gethsemene. We understand that it's nice there—do you recommend it?" And he says, "I have not come

to do as I please, but I have come to do the will of him who sent me."

(4) They did what they *had* to do. And that is the key to achievement. You never know what you can do until you have to. Ask the man who lies in a hospital bed, his body wrapped like a mummy, cooked and rotting away with severe burns, "How do you stand the pain?" He will tell you, "You never know what you can do until you have to." Ask the widow on her pitifully meager pension, "How are you able to feed, clothe, and school those three chldren?" She will tell you, "You never know what you can do until you have to." And until we have to, as long as everything is optional, as long as we spend our energies protecting all our alternatives, keeping them alive and well, we will achieve very little.

(c) Do you recall meeting now and then a really significant person, someone who impressed you as really making a difference? Then I am sure you noticed one thing about such people: they possess a sense of having something they have to do. To others, they may look burdened, perhaps obsessed. But to themselves, their joy is in knowing that their work is more important than how they happen to feel about it on any given day. The really burdened person is the one who gets up in the morning, goes to bed in the evening, struggles with great issues such as what shall we eat? what shall we drink? what shall we wear?—gets up in the morning, goes to bed in the evening, grows old and dies, without a burden.

VI. Here's the way the story of our redemption begins: "From that time Jesus began to show his disciples that he *must* go to Jerusalem, and suffer and be killed."—Fred B. Craddock.

Illustrations

WORK AND PLAY. One day when I was ten, I was playing baseball in an open lot near our home in Peoria. My mother called me to go to the grocery store to buy something she urgently needed for dinner. I complained: "Why can't I finish the game? There are only two more innings to play." Her answer was: "You are out there for exercise. What difference does it make if you are running the bases or running to the grocery store?" Years later, when I fell into the wisdom of Thomas Aquinas, I received the answer to her question. This learned philosopher asks: "What is the difference between work and play?" And he answers: "Work has a purpose, play has none, but there must be time in life for purposeless things, even foolishness."—Fulton J. Sheen in *Treasure in Clay*.

REPENTANCE. We can make the past remain nothing but *past*. The act in which we do this has been called repentance. Genuine repentance is not the feeling of sorrow about wrong actions, but it is the act of the whole person in which he separates himself from elements of his being, discarding them into the past as something that no longer has any power over the present.—Paul Tillich.

Sermon Suggestions

THE TEMPTATION OF JESUS. Text: Matt. 4:1. (1) The occasion of our Lord's temptation: temptation came to Jesus along the path of his vocation. (2) The forms of our Lord's temptation: to pander to the people's materialistic expectations and desires; to put God to the test, trying to force his hand; to achieve world-dominion by force. (3) The way in which our Lord overcame His temptation: the secret of His victory lies in His unswerving obedience to the revealed will of his father. The *forms* which Jesus' temptation took are not those which it takes for us, insasmuch as his unique vocation is not ours. But the way of victory over temptation is the same for us as it was for him.—Owen E. Evans.

"I AM SURE." Text: Phil. 1:6. Paul could say, "I am sure," because: (1) he had witnessed God's mighty acts in history; (2) he had personal insight into the meaning of God's mighty deeds; (3) he had himself experienced Christ; (4) the Holy Spirit witnessed with his spirit that God can finish that which he has begun, and this witness was the inspired experience of going from light to light.—Nels F. S. Ferré.

Worship Aids

CALL TO WORSHIP. "Rend your heart, and not your garments, and turn unto the Lord your God: for he is gracious and merciful, slow to anger, and of great kindness, and repenteth him of the evil" (Joel 2:13).

INVOCATION. Father of our Lord Jesus Christ, we beseech thee to engender in us during these holy days of Lent such spiritual understanding that we may remember the life and labor of our Lord, not vainly as a thing long gone, but fruitfully, seeing in our own days the same eternal Spirit which in him revealed the glory of thy great love to men, bearing the cross for our sakes.—Samuel H. Miller.

OFFERTORY SENTENCE. "Unto whomsoever much is given, of him shall be much required: and to whom men have committed much, of him they will ask the more" (Luke 12:48).

OFFERTORY PRAYER. O God, some of us have been given much, yet we are afraid some calamity will overtake us. Our anxiety has made us untrusting and poor stewards of thy bounty. Increase our faith, allay our fears, and open the wellsprings of generosity in our hearts, so that our giving may not be decided by our worries, but by thy expectations.

PRAYER. O God, we turn to thee in the faith that thou dost understand and art very merciful. Some of us are not sure concerning thee, not sure what thou art, not sure that thou art at all. Yet there is something at work behind our minds. In times of stillness, we hear it, like a distant song; there is something in the sky at evening time, something in the face of man. We feel that 'round our incompleteness flows thy greatness, 'round our restlessness, thy rest. Yet this is not enough.

We want a heart to speak to, a heart that understands, a friend to whom we can turn, a breast on which we may lean. O that we could find thee. Yet could we ever think these things unless thou hadst inspired us? Could we ever want these things unless thou thyself wert very near? Some of us know full well, but we are sore afraid. We dare not yield ourselves to thee, for we fear what that might mean. Our foolish freedom, our feeble pleasures, our fatal self-indulgence suffice to hold us back from thee, though thou art our very life, and we so sick and needing thee. Our freedom has proved false, our pleasures have long since lost their zest, our sins—oh, how we hate them.

Come and deliver us, for we have lost all hope in ourselves.—W. E. Orchard.

EVENING SERVICE

Topic: The Sin of Getting By

SCRIPTURE: Matt. 24:45–25:30.

The evil servant who feigns loyalty and praise of his master thought that in his master's absence, he could get by with his cruelty and debauchery, but the day came when his unreality was discovered. In the two parables that follow are genuine similarities. The foolish virgins, careless of the necessities of the wedding feast, thought in the moment of crisis that others would supply their need. But it was not so. They could not get by with their carelessness. The selfish and slothful servant in the Parable of the Talents tried to justify himself by a specious argument and a show of fear. But he failed. Judas thought to get by undetected in his theft from the money bag and in the treachery of his kiss. But his own shame and despair became his executioners.

No, there is no such thing as getting by. Sooner or later, a man reaps the harvest of his own sowing. If he sows unreality, he will reap emptiness; if he sows carelessness, he will reap unpreparedness; if he sows self-saving idleness, he will reap self-destroying poverty; if he sows treachery, he will reap despair.

Even if one could successfully sidestep the difficult and exacting adventurous demands of life, certainly there ought to be in a group such as this not one man to come to so cheap and chiseling a way of life.

I. Here we face life in the meaning and perspective of Christ as a stewardship under God to be cherished and fulfilled at any cost to one's self.

The spirit of "getting by" sees life under discipline as something to be avoided, tasks as lions in the way. Its superficial vision fails to see the hard task of today as vitally linked with one's strength tomorrow. It fails to see that time marches on to crisis, yielding life to drift when every wind that blows is a challenge to drive. It builds its house on the sand with foolish unconcern for the inevitable storms of time.

II. Here we hold to love as the central motivation of life—love to God and love of men for whose reconciliation to God we have committed our lives.

The spirit of getting by is essentially selfish. It regards neither God nor man. It has no sense of belonging to great movements—great fellowships in which every man carries his own load and helps his neighbor. It refuses the second mile. Its kindness is an exchange where one's own profit is the motive. It specializes in minimum responses.

III. Here we set ourselves for moral development—seeking to be full-grown men in Christ.

The spirit of "getting by" moves always in the direction of moral breakdown. Beginning it may be in a triviality, it moves toward tragedy. That which was marginal moves toward the center of life. Ask Judas. Ask Demas. Ask Ananias and Sapphira. "Getting by" is the road to moral suicide. The futility of it! "Our lamps are going out," said the foolish virgins. And as they scurried away to find light for their darkness, the door was shut. You can get by in the spring, leaving your fields unplanted and untended, but you cannot get by in the harvest time.

But finally, notice this in the parables: there was a faithful and wise servant who did, day by day, what he was commissioned to do; there were wise virgins who were ready with their light and song; there were diligent and adventurous stewards who did their best. Get on!—Jesse B. Weatherspoon.

SUNDAY: MARCH EIGHTEENTH

MORNING SERVICE

Topic: What to Do with Your Sins

Text: Prov. 28:13.

One of the conditions to being converted is the demand to be honest and open with God about the sins we have committed. Scripture makes it quite clear that no one can be forgiven who tries to cover up sins committed against God and others. That is the point of the text.

Confession of sin means to admit having failed God. It in turn leads to further action, allowing us to identify with God's position and God's will.

We see this meaning at work in the call made by John the Baptizer for the people who were honest about seeking the Kingdom to confess their sins publicly (Matt. 3:6; Mark 1:5). Their baptism at his hands meant that they were parting from the sins they were confessing.

The decision to break with sin is made when we feel the claim of God upon our souls. Biblical truth is always specific about our sinful condition and our human need for an inward change. Biblical truth has been given to help us have a needed change of life before God. The Bible is always clear and forthright about what constitutes sin.

I. In the Christian faith, conviction begins with an inner upheaval, an upheaval so real and so disturbing at the deepest level of life that individual guilt makes us want to decide against following the former path any longer.

(a) The will to confess is stirred in the soul by the strong grip of conviction. It results from the awareness before God that we are guilty, yes, and that we have responsibility for that guilt. We realize that we have violated the will of God, that we have offended him, and that we willingly did our deeds. Conviction follows when we realize that we used our freedom wrongly, and so we feel anxious, troubled, guilty, distressed, under judgment, unacceptable to God, and even unacceptable to our own selves.

(b) Psalm 32 (vv. 3–4) describes this whole experience most vividly. There David talks about how remembered sins made him feel isolated, insulted, and sick. His whole self sickened—until he decided to open up to God. God is still ultimate, and never is his ultimacy more clearly realized than when we dare to ball our fists and raise them defiantly against his will. Never are we humans more creaturely than when we confront the Creator and there realize that we cannot win, that we are lost, undone, unclean, unworthy, under judgment, sick, and in need of inward healing.

(c) But yet another thought was lurking in the background of David's mind: God can be found. David knew that his life did not have to be that way (v. 5).

(d) God's truth about us has a way of gaining the upper hand, but it never forces us to do what we refuse to do. The living God does not force us, but he does prod us. Those who respond to God's loving call will discover that heavy guilt feelings are only preludes to the mercy and grace needed to set their lives on a straight path out of sin into righteousness.

II. The text promises that those who confess and forsake their sins will obtain mercy. Confessing sin, then, is not enough. We must forsake sin as well.

(a) According to the Bible, we must confess our sins to God and forsake sin through obedience to God. All sin is an affront to God because every transgression is a departure from his will. Thus, only God can forgive sin.

Remember how Psalm 32 opens. The psalmist begins with a conclusion, then moves into those lines of flashback to show why that conclusion is so important to him and his readers: "Blessed is he whose transgression is forgiven, whose sin is covered. Blessed is the man to whom the Lord imputes no iniquity, and in whose spirit there is no deceit" (vv. 1–2). The psalmist had confessed his sins to the Lord and now knew the joy of forgiveness.

(b) But at times confession must also be made to another person or group as well as to God. Confession must be made to another person when he or she has been wronged by our sins; it has to be made to anyone to whom we must make restitution.

(c) At other times, *public* confession is proper, but we need counsel in order to know how far to carry a public statement about what we have done or failed to do. Certain *unhealthy* forms of confession are to be avoided, as every wise pastor knows. And mature Christians who hear confessions must be a forgiving community whose ears are open to hear and to help, but whose mouths are forever sealed thereafter.—James Earl Massey.

Illustrations

MEANINGFUL DETOURS.   Apparently, the very successful Moses had been carefully programmed in the rituals and education of Egyptian royalty. His true being and identity began emerging. No one around him heard the cries of his destiny. Chaotic behavior changed the course of his prepackaged and preplanned life. The creative God moved into the chaos and brought a new direction to his life. For all who observed, and probably for Moses himself, this new direction *looked* like a detour. From God's point of view, though, the wrath of man was being made to praise God the Creator. God does not give up on men and women so easily or so quickly as we give up on ourselves and each other.— Wayne E. Oates.

IDENTITY.   Arthur Miller's play *Death of a Salesman* owed no small part of its phenomenal public reception to the fact that most of us could see something of ourselves reflected in its winsome, tragic central figure, Willy Loman. It is significant that the final interpretation of Willy Loman's character is given, just before the final curtain, by his son Biff, who says of him: "He never knew who he was." Earlier in the play, Willy Loman had said much the same thing about his own bewilderment with life: "I still feel—kind of temporary about myself."—Merrill Abbey.

Sermon Suggestions

MYSTICISM AND USEFULNESS.   Text: Matt. 17:2, 18. (1) What our world needs is not more machines, nor more money, but more *mystics*—men and women who are genuinely in touch with God through prayer and dedication. (2) You and I need to develop far more completely our faculties of mysticism. (3) It is time we gathered in companies to pray and to plan. Every Christian ought to be in some kind of small spiritual "cell."—Samuel Shoemaker in *Pulpit Digest*.

GOD ON THE DOORSTEP.　　Text: Rev. 3: 20. (1) Human life for the vast majority of people has been transformed in the brief space of a hundred years or so. (2) Is it any wonder that man worships the things he manufactures? (3) Side by side with material affluence is deep spiritual hunger. (4) It is in this troubled sphere of personal and social relationships that God is needed, and because he is needed, he is to be found. (5) Yet if modern man admits such a God into his sinful, self-seeking society, he must be ready for all that his coming will involve.—Norman C. Parsons.

Worship Aids

CALL TO WORSHIP.　　"The sacrifices of God are a broken spirit: a broken and a contrite heart, O God, thou wilt not despise" (Ps. 51:17).

INVOCATION.　　O thou God of all pardon, of all comfort, thou who dost repair the waste places, thou who dost come to us as the dew in all the tenderness of thy love when we have been wounded by the scythe, thou who descendest as rain upon mown grass, thou who speakest in the cloud, in the thunder and lightning, speak to us as thou wilt, but speak to us, dear Lord, this morning in the name of our Lord and Savior, Jesus Christ.—Frank W. Gunsaulus.

OFFERTORY SENTENCE.　　"It is required in stewards, that a man be found faithful" (1 Cor. 4:2).

OFFERTORY PRAYER.　　Most gracious heavenly Father, we often lay our offering before thee with reservation in our hearts and murmuring in our lips. Our gifts to thee are often given grudgingly, and we often consider them to be a burden. Help us to remember thy gift to us, O Lord, in the form of thy only Son, Jesus Christ our Lord. Our reluctance to offer our lives and means in thy service must thus perish when we remember thy loving sacrifice for our salvation.—Rodney K. Miller.

PRAYER.　　O God, who hast formed all hearts to love thee, made all ways to lead to thy face, created all desire to be unsatisfied save in thee—with great compassion look upon us gathered here. Our presence is our prayer, our need the only plea we dare to claim, thy purposes the one assurance we possess.

Some of us are very confused; we do not know why we were ever born, for what end we should live, which way we should take. But we are willing to be guided. Take our trembling hands in thine and lead us on.

Some of us are sore within. We long for love and friendship, but we care for no one and we feel that no one cares for us. We are misunderstood, we are lonely, we have been disappointed, we have lost faith in man and our faith in life. Wilt thou not let us love thee who first loved us?

Some of us are vexed with passions that affright us; to yield to them would mean disaster, to restrain them is beyond our power, and nothing that earth contains exhausts their vehemence or satisfies their fierce desire.

And so because there is no answer, no end or satisfaction in ourselves, and because we are what we are and yet long to be so different, we believe that thou art and that thou dost understand us. By faith, we feel after thee, through love we find the way, in hope we bring ourselves to thee.— W. E. Orchard, *The Temple*.

EVENING SERVICE

Topic: Such As I Have

SCRIPTURE: Acts 3:1–10.

The postresurrection Simon Peter was totally willing to give. The midnight of his life had passed, and the new day that had dawned brought light and new life. He was now the "Man of Rock" that our Lord intended when he called him, "Petros"— Peter. He was again alive, filled with purpose, saturated with mission, ready to go, eager to lead, determined to be the Master's man.

Now just what did Peter *have* that was the backlog from which came the response, "Money I do not have, but such as I have, I give to you. In the name of Jesus Christ of Nazareth, you are healed"? Everything that Peter had he had received, developed, experienced in his faith and love relationship with his resurrected Lord. There were at least three things that made up his "such as I have."

I. *A promised power.* The object of our faith is the only possible thing which can validate that faith. The same principle holds true in the matter of the power which the disciples had been promised.

(a) Jesus could give that power to others because he possessed it, it was his, it had been given him by his Father (see Matt. 28:18; John 17:2; John 10:18).

(b) And just as the power which Jesus had was the fulfillment of a promise from his Father, even so was the power which Peter had the fulfillment of the promise of the Christ himself (Luke 24:49; Acts 1:8). When Jesus, in his prayer for the church, said, "Father, as you have sent me into the world, even so have I also sent them into the world" (John 17:18), he was keying on the promised power to overcome, power to create, power to establish, power to build, power to grow, power to forgive, power to declare, power to encourage, power to love, power to share, power to be —that was the promised power that Peter had.

What else did Peter have?

II. *A personal presence.* Nothing in the world is as strong as a personal presence which can transcend both time and space to be right where we are at all times in all places. And love is the only explanation that can even begin to point us toward knowing, understanding, and experiencing just what real personal presence is all about.

(a) What was it that enabled the believers to snap back from the chasm of disillusionment to the challenge of discipleship? How can we explain their ability to make the transition from that training period of revelation to the real world of responsibility? What was their secret for getting from principle to practice, from doctrine to doing? There can only be one answer: Christ is alive, and he is personally present with us. He is alive! He is alive!

(b) Look back with Peter in his own mind as this man who had denied his master three times saw the resurrected Lord walking on the Galilean beach. Peter was so caught up in the moment, which was filled with the personal presence of the One whom he loved more than life itself, that he jumped overboard and swam in, hoping to salvage every possible precious moment that he could be with his Lord. There was so much that he wanted to say, feelings that he had to explain, questions that cried out for answers, guilt that had to be relieved, forgiveness that had to be won.

(c) More than at any other time in his life, Simon Peter needed the personal presence of the Lord Christ. And now it was his from that day forward, life for Peter was never based on theology, doctrine, dogma, or creed. All that he was, ever hoped to be, and all that he would ever *have* could be traced back to that personal presence in his life. Nothing in life can take the place of the risen Christ when he is personally present as Lord and Savior.

And there was a third thing that Peter had.

III. *The courage to commit.*

(a) The courage to commit to a cause has been the very heart of every movement that has changed the world for better or for worse. And this certainly has been the case in the arena of faith.

(b) But look at the other side of the coin. The major threat to the cause of Christ has always been (and, I am convinced, shall always be) the willingness of his friends to remain silent. We know of a certainty that this is true today, and we can state case and point to confirm that belief. So could Simon Peter.

Zechariah 13:6 records, "And one shall say unto him, What are these wounds in your hands?" Then he shall answer, "Those with which I was wounded in the house of my friends." The wound of silence, the silence of his friends, is the only thing in the world that can stop the cause of Christ. When Simon Peter found the courage to commit, he was then ready to be the Master's man.

(c) Now I want to ask this question: "What do we have that we can give or use or introduce into the life of another that would enable God to reclaim, restore, or reactivate that life?"

(1) I keep hearing, over and over in my mind, the question that God asked Moses:

"What is that in your hand?" He's asking us the same thing right now.

(2) What do you have that our Lord can use? Your wealth or your means? Yes, but wherein lies true wealth? That which is lasting is that which we become while we are building, growing, accumulating, amassing.

(3) What do you have that our Lord can use? Let me cover it all. The thing he needs is our selves. And we can become the selves that he needs, only as we live life in and through him.—James D. Moebes.

SUNDAY: MARCH TWENTY-FIFTH

MORNING SERVICE

Topic: A Love You Can Trust

TEXT: I John 4:15–21.

Our text speaks to us about love. It is always a timely subject. Through thirteen years of pastoral ministry, I observed that most of the problems of my parishioners could be traced back to the issue of love—too little or too much of the wrong kind. I invite you to join me in discovering what is meant by the Perfect Love of God, and exploring how such love may be experienced.

Love defined primarily in terms of feelings will fluctuate day by day. That kind of love will change with the seasons, or the new moon or the full moon will bring a different reality. Even what we eat or the outward circumstances of our day-to-day existence may change that kind of love. You can't afford to trust love as good feeling too much. Even the best of that kind of love turns out to be inadequate.

Our human love in general—how imperfect it is even at its best! And therefore, how wise it is sometimes to avoid it, or at least not to trust it. We cannot afford to put all our weight down on our own love for ourselves—the love of mother, father, sister, brother, husband, wife. You just can't trust that human love.

I. That at least provides a backdrop, then, for consideration of a Perfect Love—the Perfect Love of God, of which our text speaks. Our text tells us of a love we can truly trust. It tells of a lover who is with us

and for us forever. One who loves beyond consideration of our virtues or our vices, whose love does not seek to cancel our freedom to be who we are, but a love which gives of itself to enable us to be and to become all we were ever meant to be. Such is the love of God. Such is the love God revealed in Jesus Christ. Such is the love that explains why we can trust God as the context in which we can live and move and have our being. And in loving us in this way, God does not go out of the way, for it is God's nature to love. For our text says, God is love. God didn't have to do it, but out of God's own nature, love came to all of us who are part of the created order. In God, we find fulfillment. In God, our destiny is achieved.

II. I am prepared to trust that kind of love.

(a) I am prepared to trust the love of God because it casts out fear. In the presence of God, we find the power, we find the ability to affirm ourselves. For if the One who made us is so interested in our well-being, if the One who has started us on the journey of life is so committed to our continuation in a fulfillment beyond our imagination, then we can afford to relax, to put down the defenses, and to keep on living. It is in the glory of that loving presence of our God that fear just seems to be out of place. Thank God for that kind of love.

(b) The love of God not only casts out fear, but it enables us to respond to God's love for us. So that the text says, we love

God because God first loved us. Something about the nature of God's total acceptance of us, in spite of our virtues, in spite of our vices, gives us something of a natural response. God informs us that we are the apple of his eye, and if we are the apple of the eye of God, then something of that love seems to call forth its own natural response. Therefore, we can trust the love that God gives, for it enables us to respond to God himself.

(c) But beyond that, the love of God helps us to love others. It helps us, when we have experienced God's love, to join in the prospect of loving all humankind—so that having been recipients of that love, we then turn to become agents of God's love. That love found in God frees us to go forth in a ministry of love. It gives us the courage to risk being rebuffed. It gives us the kind of audacity to be open to those who have sought to love us but have failed in the process. It enables us to forgive. It enables us to try again. It enables us to go beyond the barriers that we have erected to protect ourselves in order that we might know the power of life in communion.

(d) I'll tell you my story. My story is that in God, revealed through Jesus Christ, I have experienced that my shortcomings do not cancel the policy of God's love for me. I have come to understand that God's care for me is based on an unlimited supply of power by which the possibilities of my becoming will be eternally funded. And, therefore, it is a natural thing when I'm faithful to that love, when I'm mindful of it, that I should seek to love those who love me and those who do not love me, that I should seek to be an agent of forgiveness, that I should seek to be an agent of enrichment for others.—James A. Forbes, Jr.

Illustrations

FATHERHOOD. The first child of James Martineau and his wife died in infancy and was laid away in a little French cemetery near the city of Dublin. And years passed, many years, until there were only two people in the world who remembered that little child—its father and its mother. More years passed and the mother died, and there was then but one person who recollected that once a life, like a lovely flower, had blessed their home. More years passed and at length, at the age of eighty-seven, James Martineau returned to Dublin to attend the tercentenary of the university. And one day, the famous old man left a brilliant function and slipped out to a little French cemetery on the outskirts of Dublin, and baring his head, he knelt beside the grave of the little child buried there over sixty years before.

Surely Fatherhood means this: that back of all the flux of circumstances, there is Someone who loves, who values, who cares, who can never forget, who can never forget even the downmost man!—William Scarlett.

GOD QUESTIONS. I have gone through a number of stages in my own thoughts on God. I shared in my childhood the usual picture of divinity—a daguerreotype, as it were, of my grandfather—a heavenly replica of an old, bearded, patriarchal figure. Later, as a theological student, I lived through anguished years when nothing in the external world could stifle the question, "Where is God? What is his nature?" I realize now that my adolescent sufferings were a disguise for a deeper distrust of life, a sense of personal uncertainty. Yet I know that those adolescent years of searching for God were invaluable for my own spiritual maturation. No religious teacher who has not himself tasted of the bitter cup of rejection, agnosticism, and fear can be of help to other men and women.—Joshua Loth Liebman.

Sermon Suggestions

THE THREE LEASHES WHICH JESUS PUT ON FEAR. Matt. 10:26, 28, 31. (1) The assurance that the truth will win. (2) The assurance that character is more sacred than life. (3) The assurance of a fatherly providence.—Arthur A. Cowan.

WHY BE A CHRISTIAN? Text: 1 Pet. 3:15. I am a Christian: (1) Because Christianity makes sense for me of the riddle of existence. (2) Because Jesus Christ is for me "the Lord of all good life." (3) Because

Christianity holds out the blessed hope of everlasting life.—A. M. Hunter.

Worship Aids

CALL TO WORSHIP. "I acknowledge my transgressions: and my sin is ever before me" (Ps. 51:3).

INVOCATION. We come to thee, our Father, confessing our sins. We could not hide our misdeeds from thee if we would. Yet we come with the confident expectation of thy forgiveness and cleansing. May we listen for the word or hold ourselves in readiness for some movement of thy Spirit which will purge us of those transgressions that have hindered our fruitful fellowship with thee.

OFFERTORY SENTENCE. "Each one, as a good manager of God's different gifts, must use for the good of others the special gift he has received from God" (1 Pet. 4:10 [TEV]).

OFFERTORY PRAYER. Gracious God, we have nothing but that which we have received. Take what we offer to thee that others may receive and in turn become benefactors of yet others.

PRAYER. Almighty God, our heavenly Father, who art the creator and preserver of all life, lift from our shoulders the many burdens and cares that grieve and frustrate us. Help us, O Lord, to turn more readily to you with our needs and more honestly open our lives to your healing grace. Enter into our lives that, through your presence, our hearts may be cleansed and our spirits renewed. Cast from us the bonds of pain, despair, and loneliness, that we may be transformed into men and women who conform more closely to the image of your Son, our Lord Jesus Christ.

We pray especially, gracious Father, that we may more truly share your love with our fellow creatures. Help us to be so concerned with the needs and concerns of others that we willingly bear, with others, their burdens of pain, despair, and loneliness. Make us more willing to love and forgive, and less ready to judge and con-

demn. Be with those to whom we minister in your name, and be their guiding strength, comfort, and hope. Enter into the lives of all people, O Lord, both in our church and community, and in church communities around the world, who have special need. Bless and heal them according to your divine will and purpose, through Jesus Christ our Lord.—Rodney K. Miller.

EVENING SERVICE

Topic: The Science of True Prayer
TEXT: Luke 11:11.

Dr. Leslie D. Weatherhead, minister of the City Temple, London, recalls that, as a boy of fifteen, he experienced a grave disappointment in prayer. He very much wanted to pass a matriculation examination. Having read in the Bible that whatever we ask in Jesus' name we shall receive, and thinking that this means anything we may desire, he prayed fervently for success in his examination. When the results were announced, he found that he had failed. His faith in prayer was sadly shattered.

Do you recall the case of little Kathy Fiscus of California, who, while playing in a field, fell into a narrow open well? Frantically, relays of workers dug into the earth to release her. The story was front-page news. Millions of people prayed for her safety. When at last the rescuers reached her, she was dead. Indeed, she had been dead for some hours already while prayers were being offered for her safety. All across the nation, multitudes of people wondered about prayer because of their disappointment that these petitions were not answerd.

Now does this mean that it is vain to expect an answer to prayer—that God will not or cannot hear our supplications?

(a) Let us begin by noting some of the things that true prayer is not.

(1) It is not a blank check on which God's signature appears, guaranteeing us anything on which we may set our hearts.

(2) Prayer is not a rabbit's foot or other charm, warranted to preserve us from misfortune.

(3) It is not a "parachute project," to be

reserved for us in some extreme emergency.

(4) Prayer is not a child's letter to Santa Claus. It is not just an appeal devoted to securing "things." This type of prayer is often given a central place in our thinking. While the saints and seers and mystics, who are experts in prayer, regard petition for material things as legitimate, they unfailingly relegate it to a secondary place.

(5) True prayer is never an attempt to change God's mind, or to bring him around to our way of thinking. It is not directed to overcoming divine reluctance.

(b) That is enough of negatives. Let us now look at the positive side of the problem. Is there a science of true prayer? *No true prayer ever goes unanswered.* But isn't this a contradiction of human experience?

It is quite true that a particular request that has been made in prayer may be denied, but true prayer itself never goes unheeded. Unfailingly it brings a response from God. That divine response belongs to the very essence of prayer.

What are the general truths at which we arrive after formulating our knowledge of prayer?

I. First, no true prayer can ever go unanswered, because in true prayer we confront God and have fellowship with him. There is no gift of which the human imagination can conceive or that we can ask of God greater than this, that in prayer we meet him and have converse with him.

That encounter with a holy God can cleanse and strengthen us, can exalt and redeem us, so that the problem no longer matters. Augustine was at the heart of the issue when he prayed, "Give me thine own self, without which, though thou shouldest give me all that ever thou hadst made, yet could not my desire be satisfied." So shall we know that high above the strutting tyrants of our time is a sovereign God, and that those who live in fellowship with him are undefeatable.

II. The Christian revelation declares that, living on this little island in the sky that we call our world, we are not confronted by a universe unfriendly, meaningless, implacable, that will finally grind us back into dusty death, but that at the very heart of creation is One who upholds all things by the Word of his power and who is patient, loving, just, holy, who knows his human children one by one and loves them all with an everlasting love.

(a) On one occasion, when our Lord was discussing prayer with his disciples, he suggested that if they wished to understand God's relation to many, they should think of a kindly and just human father. "If a son shall ask bread of any of you that is a father, will he give him a stone? or if he ask fish, will he for a fish give him a serpent? or if he shall ask an egg, will he offer him a scorpion?"

In each case, the thing asked for looks like the substitute mentioned by Jesus.

But what if the son had asked his father for a stone in place of bread? Would he have given it to him? One fault of modern praying is that we are continually asking God for stones instead of bread, and we think our prayers are unanswered because he insists on giving us bread rather than a stone.

(b) Here, then, we are at the heart of prayer. The God whom you meet is your heavenly Father.

(1) Wherefore, as his child, bring all your problems, all your desires, all your longings to him and ask him to decide what is your deepest need. In his infinite wisdom, he will give you that which will be a blessing, not an evil, to you.

(2) Keep alive in your heart an awareness of the divine presence. There is no stimulus half as great as the assurance that God is with you and that the spiritual forces of the universe are on your side. But this conviction can be yours only as you have sought and found the will of God. Then you will be able to say with the psalmist: "I called upon the Lord in distress: the Lord answered me, and set me free. The Lord is on my side; I will not fear: what can man do unto me?"—John Sutherland Bonnell.

SUNDAY: APRIL FIRST

MORNING SERVICE

Topic: A Question of Values
SCRIPTURE: Matt. 6:19–34.

Our Lord is concerned with our daily routine, our commerce, our times, our choices, and investments. He asks us, "When it comes to value, just where do you put the accent?"

I. Jesus insists that the real treasures in life are those things money cannot buy. To say that is a clichï. But we cannot say it, reflect on it, and forge it into our value systems enough.

(a) Surely we need take an inventory of our real treasures on occasion. Our families, for instance. Where are our treasures there? In the things money can buy? Money can provide glue and freedom for families, yet who is not aware of those homes where financial assets are the least of problems, where relationships are in shambles? To be sure, things of the marketplace can be important, but in the long run the qualities which make for secure and loving family life cannot be purchased there.

(b) Indeed, when Jesus talks about laying up for ourselves treasures in heaven, he points toward nourishing the qualities which make our lives a heaven—not tomorrow, not next year, not after we die, but right now. The cynic finds every hope an illusion, every dream a fantasy.

(c) What a contrast to those whose life has not lost zest, whose hope is full, whose courage and joy are alive. One may pass along a difficult journey, but life is sympathetic, radiant, encouraging.

(d) Our family, ourselves, our churches —how important that we church people get our treasures straight. Although we know our treasure lies in the gospel of Christ, his compassion, his redemptive and healing presence in this city, Christians and churches often misplace their real treasure. We are no less skillful in cloaking greed with platitudes, squandering resources on ourselves, clinging to money, or antiques or architecture than any other human institution or person.

We have a full arsenal of rationales to justify our ways. Opportunity for ministry in the name of Christ can be a taste of heaven. We need to gauge the treasure of our calling against the treasure of our possessions and make some significant and perhaps even liberating choices.

II. (a) Our Lord knows that we not only confuse the real treasure in life; He knows our priorities are unfocused and scattered. Why else, he asks, are we anxious about so much? What *are* we anxious about? Food, clothing, shelter? Of course we are, and Christ does not suggest we *forget* them. But he says that we often give them too high a place in our lives. Jesus knows our anxiety about inflation and taxes, rent and fuel is not frivolous, but our Lord knows that anxiety over necessities may deflect us from keeping other values. "Are you anxious about the morrow? Seek ye first the Kingdom of heaven and all the rest shall be added unto you." The point Jesus is making is that when we get ourselves off our own hands and into God's, the things which worry us now will fall into their proper places. If we aspire to transform the human race into a human family, our other ambitions for status or money might pale.

(b) Jesus is telling us to throw ourselves onto the scales in his behalf. We may still spend some sleepless nights, but our anxiety will be over his will for our lives, not our own needs, frustrations, and disappointments.

III. Can you live a Christian life? Can I? The answer is not a simple yea or nay. But clues can be found in our choices, our priorities, our values. And in what are they grounded? Mary Byrne tells us in her translation of that old Gaelic lyric: "High King of heaven, my treasure thou art."— James W. Crawford.

Illustrations

PERSISTENCE OF EVIL.   The things that make world community possible are the things that threaten world community. The airplane makes us all neighbors, but it also makes it easier for us to kill our neighbors. Worldwide communication binds us closer together, but as a propaganda medium, it can drive us apart. Atomic power can make poverty unnecessary, but it can also make us extinct.—Robert McAfee Brown.

SHAME. Whether or not a sense of guilt will make us a better people, the loss of shame threatens our survival as a civilized society. . . . The Greeks made of shame a goddess—Aidos. She was the source of dignity, decency, and good manners. An offense committed against Aidos was avenged by the goddess Nemesis. Long live shame.—Eric Hoffer.

Sermon Suggestions

THE EVILS WITHIN OURSELVES. Eph. 6: 13. Let us explore the evils in our own minds which are the fruitful sources of all the outward evils in the world. (1) A feeling of personal satisfaction. (2) Caution or prudence. (3) Allowing one's attitude toward difficult problems to be dictated by one's emotions rather than by clear thinking. (4) The indulgence of high sentiment and the failure to follow the sentiment with action.—Frederick Keller Stamm.

THE TONIC OF A GREAT TASK. John 1:42. The tonic for the greatest of all tasks—soul-winning—must contain four essential ingredients. (1) A deep and heartfelt conviction that souls out of Christ are lost. (2) A tender solicitude for souls. (3) A most intense activity to win the lost. (4) A conviction that Jesus Christ is sufficient for lost souls.—R. C. Campbell.

Worship Aids

CALL TO WORSHIP. "To the Lord our God belong mercies and forgivenesses, though we have rebelled against him; neither have we obeyed the voice of the Lord our God, to walk in his laws, which he set before us by his servants the prophets" (Dan. 9:9–10).

INVOCATION. God of love, God of judgment, we are reminded again of our rebellion and disobedience. Show us thy mercy and thy forgiveness today, so that our lives and our words may truly praise thee.

OFFERTORY SENTENCE. "And the children of Israel brought a willing sacrifice unto the Lord, every man and woman, whose heart made them willing to bring for all manner of work, which the Lord had commanded to be made by the hand of Moses" (Exod. 35:29).

OFFERTORY PRAYER. Gracious Father, thou has set before us many ways to do thy work in the world. Though not all of us can preach or teach, most of us can bring an offering from the fruits of our daily work. As we present to thee our gifts, open new channels of blessing to others through what we bring.

PRAYER. O heavenly Father, whose unveiled face the angels of little children do always behold, look with love and pity, we beseech thee, upon the children of the streets. Where men, in their busy and careless lives, have made a highway, these children of thine have made a home and a school, and are learning the bad lessons of our selfishness and our folly. Save them, and save us, O Lord. Save them from ignorance and brutality, from the shamelessness of lust, the hardness of greed, and the besotting of drink; and save us from the great guilt of those that offend thy little ones, and from the hypocrisy of those that say they see and see not, whose sin remaineth.

Make clear to those of older years the inalienable right of childhood to play, and give to those who govern our cities the will and ability to provide the places for play; make clear to those who minister to the appetite for recreation the guilt of them that lead astray thy children; and make clear to us all that the great school of life is not encompassed by walls and that its teachers are all who influence their younger brethren by companionship and example, whether for good or evil, and that in that school all we are teachers and as we teach are judged. For all false teaching, for all hindering of thy children, pardon us, O Lord, and suffer the little children to come unto thee, for Jesus' sake.—Mornay Williams.

EVENING SERVICE

Topic: When You Can't Understand Yourself

SCRIPTURE: Rom. 7:15 (Phillips trans.); Mark 7:15 (NEB).

I. A cartoon that I saw in a magazine shows a doctor looking in anxious solemnity at a patient and saying to him, "This is a very serious case; I am afraid that you are *allergic to yourself*." The apostle Paul confessed that he was at times allergic to himself. His testimony is given in the seventh chapter of his letter to the Romans.

(a) But does he not describe an experience that we, in some way, have all had? If you have never at times felt impelled to cry, "My own behavior baffles me," you probably are deceiving yourself about yourself.

(b) Paul is discussing not only past experience, but also experience potentially always present.

(c) These inner conflicts must be distinguished from conflicts of a person with other persons—although the two kinds of conflicts are closely related and often become entwined in one another.

(d) You do at times—do you not?—find yourself not doing what you really want to do and doing things you loathe when you dare to think about them.

(e) We sometimes talk a morality appreciably higher than the one we actually live by. We all, at times, fall short of our own avowed ideals of character and conduct.

(f) Our will for good is not always able to control our impulses to evil. Paul is describing inner realities that are in no way unusual or abnormal.

II. What, then, can you and I do about our inner conflicts? How can we deal with the moral confusions and contradictions of our lives?

(a) We cannot resolve inner conflict by giving impulse a free gallop. Even the people who tell us that it is unnatural, even unhealthy, to suppress one's impulses recognize that the reins must be held quite tightly on most impulses if a tolerable sort of life is to be lived.

(b) Most of us, as we mature, are able to work out moral compromises for ourselves, compromises established in our experience. Maturity and the wisdom that can come with experience do help us a little in our handling of our inner conflicts—but we do not come in that way to the final resolution of those conflicts.

III. (a) But Paul doesn't stop here. He continues his exercise in self-examination. Then he cries, "Who can set me free from the clutches of my own sinful nature?" He recognizes the futility of relying on his own resources. But after sounding this note of despair, he quickly sounds a stronger note of hope: "I thank God there is a way out through Jesus Christ our Lord."

(b) Dr. C. Leslie Mitton, the English scholar, uses a helpful analogy to explain what Paul is saying. He compares our inner confusion and conflict to the disease of diabetes. "Man," he says, "is a moral diabetic. Left to himself, he is in spirit terribly diseased and morally ill."

The physical diabetic, through the regular use of insulin, can become what is called "a controlled diabetic," and live a normal life. The ordinary moral diabetic, if I may use the expression—that is, you and I and those other people—can be established in a similar "control" through receiving reinforcements of strength from God. A physical diabetic neglecting to take insulin regularly endangers his or her life. A moral diabetic neglecting to avail himself or herself of the grace and guidance of God can become a victim of tormenting inner conflict that tears the heart and shatters peace of mind.

(c) This way of faith, this way *in* faith, is open to all of us. The grace of God—that is, the "energy" of God working in our hearts and minds—comes to us as we engage in the disciplines of faith: in worship and prayer and meditation, in embracing biblical insights, in service of witness and compassion. Faith will work for you if you work at faith, work hard at it, work regularly at it. And our great hope is in being able to say "Amen" to Paul's assurance: "I thank God there is a way out through Jesus Christ our Lord."—J. A. Davidson.

SUNDAY: APRIL EIGHTH

MORNING SERVICE

Topic: A Different Kind of Jesus (Passion Sunday)

SCRIPTURE: Rev. 1:9–20.

A friend of mine told me an amusing story about his child. The little fellow came up to him one day, held up a tiny fist, and said, "What's in my hand?" My friend couldn't guess what it was, so the child opened an empty hand and explained, "God is there, for nobody can see God."

That exactly is our problem. No one can see God, yet we may have him in our hand. He is so strange, so very different, that we cannot really gaze upon him so long as we are men of this earth. Yet our very existence depends on the fact that he is with us and we are with him, in the closest possible relationship.

I. John tells us how he gazed upon the risen Christ and how God himself took hold of his life through that experience and met him face to face.

(a) But what an incredibly strange Jesus it is—this Jesus who is about to meet us in the Scripture that records what happened to John! It is a Jesus quite different from the one we are accustomed to.

(b) From the mouth of this Jesus issues a two-edged sword. His word can inflict pain. John knows that. In fact, the Risen One has sent him forth as his witness. Certainly some men did listen to him and liked what they heard. But others wanted to hear nothing from this witness and drove him away. It isn't easy to give up a house, a job, and a little bit of security and flee into an uncertain existence (v. 9). What Jesus wants of us often cuts as a two-edged sword through all our wishes, plans, and comforts.

(c) But that is not all a two-edged sword can do. It can not only inflict pain; it can kill (v. 17a). John knows that it can really kill. Later he describes those who were put to death because they stood up for this Jesus. But he himself experiences this dying. When God becomes real, men experience it as death. What distinguished

John from the Old Testament prophets is this: God encounters him in the form of Jesus. He is permitted to know that God is no longer some indefinite God who is differently conceived of by every nation. God is the one who comes to us in the man Jesus of Nazareth: God is the one who has given himself to us.

(d) This Jesus can be so incredibly strange that we almost die when he actually comes into our life. A Jesus who says, "He who loves father or mother, son or daughter, more than me is not worthy of me," is incredibly strange. A Jesus who leads his disciples into prisons and to the executioner's block, rather than from victory to victory for God's Kingdom, is incredibly strange. If we can be untroubled and comfortable Christians, then it may be that this Jesus has never yet become a reality in our lives. You and I are not prophets, so we cannot expect him to come to us in the same way he came to John. But what if those many things in our lives that ought to die do not die? What if, instead, they grow and proliferate? If that is the case, we should ask ourselves whether he is actually with us or if perchance up to now we have passed him by?

II. All that is only the prelude (vv. 17b-18).

(a) "I am the first and the last" is an age-old word of God to be found already in Second Isaiah. However, the Son of man adds to it the words: ". . . and the living one." So it is not true that God simply sits enthroned in heavenly glory, aloof from us, and threatens from there to destroy us. His concern for us was so incredibly great that he completely entered into this one man Jesus and so completely identified himself with him that he—the God of heaven and earth—blazed the trail for us. But precisely at the point where God moved into solidarity with us, Easter took place. Jesus did not remain dead.

(b) What we know for sure about our present life is this: death will strike it down. But here—in Jesus, who encountered his disciples after Easter—real life was present. It was God's life, life without end, life no longer threatened by death. Death is now locked up, and Jesus Christ holds the key.

III. But how can a man come to believe that? Just as John learned how to do it!

(a) We begin to live with the Word of God and with the testimony for Jesus. One thing and then another has to die, and we will feel the touch of the sharpened sword. Habits to which we are very attached, plans that were very important to us, conveniences that we imagined we could not do without—these are taken from us. And Jesus will even many times become very strange to us; perhaps the more we try to live with him, the stranger he will become. We discover that he is alive and does not let us go. Perhaps we could not put into words what we believe or do not believe. But he lives with us; he is not merely dead and gone. And slowly, perhaps without our noticing how it happens, something is changed.

(b) Have you observed that in the case of John (v. 9a)? He no longer lives just his own private life. He lives as the brother and partner of many others who find life hard. And in everything, Jesus is no longer merely his Lord. He is the Son of man who walks among the seven candlesticks—which is to say, among his churches.

(c) What happens when one learns from Jesus even a tiny bit of this dying? At that point, he liberates us from incessant preoccupation with our own happiness. In other words, he makes us open to other persons with whom we share our life. Then we often see that it can help another man unbelievably if we for once do not come out ahead.

(d) Wherever Jesus becomes so alive to us in such ways, there we learn to look into the future with joy. No longer do we spend our time looking back, like tired old men who still dream of the exciting experiences of their youth, which have been glorified in retrospect. Rather, we look forward, full of excitement about what our Master has in prospect for us yet. Anyone who, for the first time, begins to live seriously with Jesus, as John did, knows what it is for God to become real to him. He knows and can say, "Not even death can destroy the reality of God and his care for me." Therefore, we do not fear the end; we know that the full, complete life lies before us, not behind us. Then, my dear brothers and sisters, we shall see God as he is.—Eduard Schweizer.

Illustrations

THE LIMITS OF KINDNESS.   If kindness alone were enough, there would have been no cross. Jesus would have formed a sensitivity group and urged us to share our feelings, or a support group where we could affirm each other. Knowing full well the limits of humanity, the seriousness of our sin, and the depths of evil, he formed the church and charted a different way.—William H. Willimon.

BODY OF CHRIST.   A distinguished American theologian, on being reminded that we are the body of Christ, remarked sarcastically, "Poor Christ; to have such as we are as his body!" And it is true that we Christians cut a sorry figure. And yet this is precisely what the New Testament does assert. If the ministry of Christ is to continue at all, it can continue only in and through Christians.—W. D. Davies.

Sermon Suggestions

THE TASTE OF DEATH AND THE LIFE OF GRACE.   Heb. 2:9. (1) Jesus Christ not only died, but he tasted death as incredible bitterness and penury of soul. I would dwell on the psychology even more than on the theology of it. (2) He did so because he died for every one of us. He experienced in a divine life the universal death. (3) Yet this desertation and agony of death was a gift and grace of God, not only to us, but to him. And he knew it was so. And that faith was his victory and our redemption.—P. T. Forsyth.

GOD REVEALS HIMSELF.   (1) In historical events. (2) Through persons. (3) Supremely through one person—Jesus Christ. (4) Through the life of a community. (5) Through a book.—Robert McAfee Brown.

Worship Aids

CALL TO WORSHIP.   "Is it nothing to you, all ye that pass by? Behold, and see if there be any sorrow like unto my sorrow, which is done unto me, wherewith the Lord hath afflicted me in the day of his fierce anger" (Lam. 1:12).

INVOCATION.   O God, the sufferings of our Lord Jesus Christ overwhelm us, as we survey the wondrous cross. Help us this day to see in the depths of his sacrifice the depths of thy love.

OFFERTORY SENTENCE.   "Every man shall give as he is able, according to the blessing of the Lord thy God which he hath given thee" (Deut. 16:17).

OFFERTORY PRAYER.   God of grace, we know that you are able to do exceeding abundantly above all that we ask or think. Though we also know that we cannot outgive you, help us to know if we are giving as we are able and grant us the faith and willingness to give as we ought.

PRAYER.   Almighty and most gracious heavenly Father, we cry out to you from the very midst of our need and imperfection. We are perishing, O Lord; rescue us from our unbelief. We are hungry, O Lord; feed us by the milk of your Word. We are sinful, O Lord; cleanse us of our iniquities. We are often too weak to control our tendency to sin, and our pride and selfishness seize control of our lives. We then lose sight of the path that you would have us follow. We most humbly ask, O Lord, that your Spirit will enter our lives anew to guide us, to heal us, and to sustain us. We pray that your presence will dwell continually in us and that your grace will abound ever more strongly in us. Make us whole, O Lord, that we may completely conform to the image of your Son, Jesus Christ. Enter this day into the lives of those of our number whose lives have been complicated and disrupted by the stress of illness and loss. Grant unto those persons and their families the courage and resources that they may creatively cope with the difficulties that beset them.—Rodney K. Miller.

EVENING SERVICE

Topic: The Hardest Thing to Take
TEXT: Isa. 53:3.

"He is despised and rejected of men, a man of sorrows, and acquainted with grief." The most cutting word in that familiar sentence is the word *rejected*. It means to be turned down, dropped out, unaccepted; it implies that one is unfit, unusable.

We do not know who the writer was who described this man in such unforgettable words.

"Despised . . . rejected . . . acquainted with grief." Jesus himself is largely responsible for the fact that we instinctively think of him, for in many ways he fits the picture. Not in every way, but in many ways he fits the picture.

I. Whoever the man was, whenever and wherever he lived, the experience of rejection is something that we *do* know about. Different people know it in different ways.

(a) A parent who does everything that he or she knows how to do for a child is rejected by the child. And a child is sometimes rejected by parents—more often than some of us are likely to think.

(b) A man in public life is often rejected by the people he has served— not because he hasn't done the best he knew how, but because he does not appeal to the people, or because another man undercuts him.

(c) A person in any position of leadership—in business, education, church, or state—is sometimes rejected by the people he has done most for.

(d) Sometimes people have the feeling of being rejected when they really are not. There are people who, for reasons which are too deeply buried for us to understand, begin to say to themselves,

"Nobody likes me, no one wants me. I am not much good, I am a reject." And people are rejected not only by other people, but by life itself. There is a young man who lives as good a life as any young man can be expected to live, and in a flash, he is crippled, rejected by life, as far as anyone can see at the moment, unusable, for any further activity. Or, less spectacularly, he simply does not get anywhere. Or, he becomes too old to be any further use in the world.

(e) It is safe to say, I think, that the experience of rejection is as universal as the experience of sorrow and grief, and that on a large scale or on a small one, in a real sense or in an imaginary sense, everyone at some time in his or her life has the terrible experience of being rejected.

II. The important thing, therefore, is not that you feel rejected. The important thing is what it does to you and what you do with it.

(a) You are tempted to say at a time when you feel rejected, "What's the use?"

(b) Was there, do you suppose, a moment when that question flashed even through the mind of our Lord and Master, Jesus Christ? May this be what he meant when he said, "My God, why hast thou forsaken me?" Did he, just for an instant, ask himself, "If, after all I have done and said, it comes to nothing but this, what's the use?"

(c) Yet, even though this kind of a thought may have flashed through his mind, he would be the first to tell you that rejection is part of the suffering woven into the fabric of life. We do not know why. Some are embittered by it, and some are enlarged by it.

(d) It is true to say that, in a figurative sense, every nail driven into the body of Jesus deepened his compassion, made him more understanding of humanity, more forgiving, more all-inclusive in his love, more perfect in his being here and now what the Father is always.

III. What is the secret of this? Why is it that some are shrunken by rejection while others are stretched by it? I think the difference lies somewhere in this area. It is to be found in that area in which a man or a woman comes to the point where he or she can say, "No matter how often others reject me, or how cruelly life rejects me, God never rejects me."

(a) When you are tempted to say, "What's the use of going on, say?"—say instead, "God can use my rejection as a means of showing other people his acceptance."

(b) When and if you are ever tempted to say, "What's the use of going on trying to be good when everything seems to be against me?"—say instead to yourself, "The very moment when I feel most useless may be the time when I am needed most." What other people think of you, or do to you, is not the decisive thing. The decisive thing is what *you* do.

If you can accept rejection, unfair though it be, as part of life's strange, mysterious, creative way, you will be enlarged. Gradually, your feeling of rejection will be crowded out by the conviction that God can use you, as you are—young or old, successful or failing, sick or well.

(c) And remember how Jesus, most cruelly rejected, reminded the people of words that they had heard before, written by the psalmist: "The stone which the builders rejected is become the head of the corner." The marble block that Michelangelo finally used for the Pieta was one that was quarried out of the highest mountains of Carrara, the purest, whitest marble that could be found. It had been ordered by someone else, but never paid for, and so it was sent to Rome to be sold to anyone who could use it. This was the stone out of which he made that incredible figure of the young mother holding her dead Son.—Theodore P. Ferris.

SUNDAY: APRIL FIFTEENTH

MORNING SERVICE

Topic: Triumph and Tears (Palm Sunday)

SCRIPTURE: Luke 19:28–44.

Today marks the opening of Holy Week, the season which calls to remembrance the defeat and death of Jesus the Christ. The first Holy Week began so well: his triumphal entry into the city of Jerusalem. The first Holy Week ended so badly: his corpse, in a borrowed tomb, behind a sealed, stone door.

Today, Palm Sunday, we remember and celebrate a very human triumph. It is not entirely without reason that one New Testament scholar has asserted that Palm Sunday was the happiest single day in Jesus' life. Jerusalem, the headquarters of the Jewish religion, seemed ready to capitulate. Matthew describes the entry in these words: "When he entered Jerusalem, the whole city went wild with excitement" (21:10 [NEB]). The author of the fourth gospel jotted down what the Pharisees were captiously mumbling to one another: "You see? There's nothing we can do! The whole world is running after him" (12:19 [Phillips trans.]).

I. (a) Jesus and his followers are coming to the holy city along the Jerusalem-Jericho road. The time of year is that of the Passover, and the thoroughfare is busy with people. It *is* a mob. Joseph and Mary, his parents, once thought they had lost Jesus in a crowd like that, at the same time of year, on the same road (Luke 2:41–45). Jesus was twelve years old then. This first Palm Sunday is twenty years after.

(b) Twenty years after, and Jesus has decided to do something dramatic. Thus far, he has not claimed in public, in so many words, to be the Messiah, the Christ, the Anointed One of God. He is going to do it now—not in words, but in an act. He is not going to say it,—he is going to pantomime it (see Zech. 9:9). Jesus acts that out. Jesus, the unofficial prophet of Galilee, is claiming to be the Messiah, the inaugurator of the Kingdom of God.

(c) Now, the question is: will those who see the charade understand the intent of it? Will they remember the prophecy of Zechariah and really believe that it is being fulfilled before their eyes? Jesus' followers, mostly Galileans, seem to catch something of its purpose, enough to transform a caravan into a procession. As a sign of allegiance to their rabbi, they strew the road with garments and palm branches. The Messiah has come to Jerusalem! It is "the happiest single day in Jesus' life."

(d) But is it? Is it? Look at his face. There are the marks of tears on it. He has been crying. Well, maybe they are tears of joy. He is being recognized for what he is, in the very headquarters of the Jewish faith! Yet that isn't what he seems to believe (see Luke 19:41–44).

II. What is wrong? Why did Jesus weep when he saw the city? We are not told, but here are two hints at an answer.

(a) First, he may have had a premonition that Jerusalem would not listen to his gospel. It is almost too much to expect a capital city to behave like that. Yet, if Jerusalem will not behave like that, then destruction and doom await it. That actually happened to Jerusalem forty years later, as Jesus may have seen it happen to another town twenty-five years before this first Palm Sunday. Four miles from Nazareth, where Jesus grew up, was the town of Sepphoris, which Rome took stone from stone in A.D. 6 because it harbored proud, religious revolutionists who were not in any way interested in the humility of love. Yet do arrogant people listen to gentle counsels, however sensible? Would Jerusalem listen? He knew the likely answer: it would not. And Jesus wept.

(b) There may be a second reason for his weeping: he may have been too well aware that people did not understand what *he* meant by Messiah. His own disciples hadn't. Peter had given him that title, but when Jesus linked it with possible suffering and death, Peter had ejaculated: "God forbid! This shall not be!" (Matt. 16:21–23). And what about James and John? Jesus had nicknamed them "Sons of Thunder" (Mark 3:17). They had once suggested that they call down fire from heaven and burn up a Samaritan village which had refused to receive Jesus and his disciples (Luke 8:52–56).

(c) We should not be too quick to criticize Peter and James and John. Jesus' view of the Messiah was hardly a popular, contemporary interpretation. But, if the *disciples* did not grasp the purport of his message or the quality of his person, then would those shouting "Hosanna" understand him and his claim any better? They understood him—in *their* fashion. And Jesus knew their interpretation was hardly one which pertained to peace. So, after we have studied the Lucan account carefully, we are not so sure that the scholar was right who said that Palm Sunday was the happiest single day in Jesus' life.

III. Well, here we are on another Palm Sunday, worshipping, remembering a procession, cheering the Messiah. And, as our acclamations rise, one wonders if Jesus is weeping again, weeping over this modern Jerusalem. Is he saying again, even now, through his tears: "Would that you, too, knew, even today, on what your peace depends. But no, it is hidden from you. And all because you would not understand when God was visiting you."

(a) Do we really know *him* for whom we sing "Hosanna"? Do we know what *he* stands for? If we did, would we live with such angry tension and frustrated fatigue? Are we, intentionally or unintentionally, misunderstanding him? Are we moulding the Christ to fit *our* patterns, even as we gather to honor him? Has he anything to say about our behavior in corporate life: international, national, civic, campus?

(b) What am I getting at? I am suggesting that, in all areas of our corporate life, we hesitate before we give *our* definite answers in *his* name. If we are sure of anything about Jesus, it is that his ways are like God's ways. And the Bible reminds us that God's ways are not naturally our ways. It may be that our desire is not really to be on *his* side, but to have him on *our* side. We dare not forget that the first Palm Sunday was followed in five days by a cross on a hill outside of a wall surrounding a city called Jerusalem. Jesus carried a cross after others carried palms. "Hosanna" is drowned out by the crys, "Crucify him!" The phrase which should be on our lips this week, as we head toward the real triumph of Easter, is: "Lord, I believe; help thou my misbelief. Help thou the misbelief that is *in* my very belief." Yes, let us walk tentatively, very tentatively into Holy Week, as we remember that while *many* men cried "Hosanna," *one* man wept for their enthusiastic mis-understanding.—James T. Cleland.

Illustrations

FACING DEATH.   We ought, I am sure, neither to face death nor to wish for it. We ought to feel that death simply does not count: that it does not matter whether a life lasts thirty, or sixty, or ninety years. All that matters is that life should be well lived up to the time of its close, for we are not creatures of the day, but immortal spirits. Therefore, what can it matter whether we spend a few years, more or less, in this scene of our probation? There have been men of very great achievements in history, men who have died very prematurely. Our blessed Lord ended his earthly life at thirty-three. Alexander the Great died at the same age. Mozart and Raphael died at thirty-six; Keats at twenty-six; Shelley at thirty; Shakespeare and Napoleon at fifty-two.—W. R. Inge.

THE POWER OF INCARNATION.   The power of his incarnation has become so weak among men, for one reason, because its explanation has been sought at the wrong end of his life. The wonder has been transferred from Good Friday to Christmas, from the festival of the second birth to the festival of the first, from redemption to nativity, from the fellowship of his death to the sentiment of his babyhood.—P. T. Forsyth.

Sermon Suggestions

THE ACTED PARABLES OF CHRIST.   Scripture: Mark 9:36; John 13:4; Mark 14:22. (1) "He took a child." (2) "He took a towel." (3) "He took a loaf."—A. M. Hunter.

THE RIGHT TO BELIEVE.   1 John 5:4. Man is so made that faith is the natural or normal expression of his nature. Certain deep instincts in him cannot be evaded. They impel us to believe in God. (1) The instinct of thought. (2) The instinct of conscience. (3) The instinct of prayer. (4) The instinct of suffering, which looks to God for relief. (5) The instinct of courage. (6) The instinct of hope.—Edgar Young Mullins.

Worship Aids

CALL TO WORSHIP.   "Let us praise God for his glorious grace, for the free gift he gave us in his dear Son! For by the death of Christ we are set free, that is, our sins are forgiven. How great is the grace of God, which he gave to us in such large measure" (Eph. 1:7–8a [TEV]).

INVOCATION. All things belong to thee, O God. Our very lives are thine, for thou hast created us and thou hast redeemed us. Open our eyes today that we may behold the riches of thy grace and rejoice in the many blessings that have come from thee and that continue to flow into our lives.

OFFERTORY SENTENCE. "Will a man rob God? Yet ye have robbed me. But ye say, Wherein have we robbed thee? In tithes and offerings" (Mal. 3:8).

OFFERTORY PRAYER. Thanks be to thee, our Lord Jesus Christ, for all the benefits which thou hast given us, for all the pains and insults which thou hast borne for us. O merciful Redeemer, Friend, and Brother, may we know thee more clearly, love thee more dearly, and follow thee more nearly.—St. Richard of Chichester.

PRAYER. Almighty and most holy God, we come gratefully into thy presence. We thank thee for gathering us together here in thy house on this sabbath day. Help us to be still and know that thou art God. Visit us with thy salvation and restore our souls. Fill us with the beauty of thy holiness. Quicken us with a sense of what is good and right in thy sight. Grant us the firm assurance that no matter what may befall us, nothing shall separate us from thy love as we have come to know it in Christ Jesus.

Grant us the wisdom, the strength, the kindness, and the patience to be good neighbors to those about us who are in need. Help us to love others as we would be loved. Help us to hear the prayers of others and move to offer ourselves to thee to be used by thee in the answering of their prayers.

O God, in these difficult times make us people of vision and not prophets of doom. Make us pioneers of faith and not prisoners of despair. Let our words and deeds show that we are marching with all the saints in an endless line of splendor toward the new Jerusalem.

Hear our prayers for loved ones who are far from us. May they be in thy constant care and keeping, and may they be comforted by our continued concern for them and for their well-being.

Most gracious God, thou knowest our several necessities. Comfort those who are bereaved. Heal those who are sick. Strengthen those who are weak. Enlighten those who are perplexed. Lift up those who are cast down. Be especially present to those who are lonely.

We earnestly beseech thee to prosper the efforts of those who are seeking the way to world disarmament. Give thine aid to those who are striving to negotiate a just and lasting peace. For the sake of the widowed, the orphaned, the maimed, and the refugees, give us peace in our time, O Lord.—Harold A. Brack.

EVENING SERVICE

Topic: The Hands of Jesus

TEXT: Luke 24:39.

There is no authentic portrait of Jesus, but only artists' conceptions of him. References in Scripture to his body serve to remind us that he was human as well as divine and that "the Word became flesh."

Hands are revealing. Palm reading is an old and distrusted cult, but it does take note of the hands. A musician's hands are long, tender, sensitive; those of a laboring man are callused and strong; those of an invalid are weak and nervous. Hands folded suggest resignation or cowardice, while hands clenched into fists indicate determination or pugnacity.

I. The hands of Jesus were accustomed to labor. In the carpenter's shop, he learned the trade by which he was later to support his widowed mother as well as his brothers and sisters. Through work, he gained understanding of the toils and burdens of men. Surely manual labor is not to be regarded as a penalty for sin, nor is it a less worthy kind. Work with the hands has dignity and may be dedicated to God. The greater one's skill, the more valuable the work performed, as is seen in the surgeon, the musician, or the painter. There is great satisfaction for one who comes to the end of the day or the life that has been well spent.

II. His were also healing hands, always restoring. Many a diseased body felt the firm, healing hand of Jesus. He touched a leper saying, "Be thou clean." With his hand, he anointed blind eyes and sight was restored. In an unforgettable parable, Jesus portrays the good neighbor in the Samaritan who drew near to the wayside sufferer and, with his hands, administered first aid, put him on his beast, gave money for his keep. All around us are those who need a lift—a hand of encouragement, of confidence, of friendship.

III. And his were saving hands. The cross was very real, indescribably cruel. Jesus took it, laid it on his shoulder, and bore it to the place of a skull where they drove spikes through his hands and his feet, and waited for him to die there. Mocking voices shouted, "Come down from the cross . . . save yourself and us!" "He saved others, but he cannot save himself!" they cried. But he could not come down, and I think it was not the nails that held him there. He could not come down, for if he did, they and the world would have no Savior. It was love that held him there, "love divine, all love excelling." Those hands and that cross have become symbols of hope and salvation for all sinners. Those hands are now extended in invitation and are knocking for entrance to our hearts.

IV. The word *hands* is sometimes used figuratively. For example, hands suggest security. Of his trusting disciples, Jesus said: "No one shall snatch them out of my hands." In almost the same breath, he said: "No one is able to snatch them out of the Father's hands." His ability, not ours, is here indicated. He will not let us go; he is able to keep us. He will keep us if we commit ourselves to him.

V. Hands also suggest guidance. Often in restrospect, we can see that his hand was guiding us, even when we least suspected it. This was true in Paul's case, I think, when he was forbidden to go into Asia, not permitted to enter Bithynia, and not allowed to work at Troas. Doors were successively closed on what he doubtless thought were fruitful fields, for God was leading him into Macedonia. God sometimes guides us by closing doors as well as opening them. Ours must always be a walk by faith and not by sight. One has well said that it is better to walk with God in the dark than to follow a known way.

VI. And too, hands suggest fulfillment. "Our times are in his hands." He never leads us into the wilderness to perish along some dead-end road, nor does he leave us in the mountain "thunder riven." Instead, he leads us to achieve, to attain the "high calling of God in Christ Jesus." It is only under the mastery of Christ that human life comes to its best.—Owen F. Herring.

SUNDAY: APRIL TWENTY-SECOND

MORNING SERVICE

Topic: Christ's Mighty Victory (Easter)
SCRIPTURE: Phil. 2:5–11.

Behind the deed forever stands the creed! As Christians, we act because God has already acted! To quote James Stewart, "The dynamic for our unaccomplished task is the accomplished deed of God"—or, put in the words of my theme, *Christ's mighty victory*.

Here are three imperishable acts of God that constitute the core of our Lord's mighty victory.

I. *The incarnation*. "God was in Christ" (2 Cor. 5:19a). (a) How incongruous this assertion has seemed in recent years! Radical theology says simply, but not freshly, "God is dead." Hegel, William Blake and Nietzsche said it in earlier days. This illusion of illusions is based upon mankind's arrogant metaphysical and actual independence of God. It rests upon the assumption that modern man can get along very well without God.

(b) What an illusion! (1) A man prays and knows an answer. A great congregation sings with enthusiasm, "A mighty fortress is our God," and the atmosphere of worship is charged with living power. A man who has just learned that he has an inoperable cancer receives Holy Communion and rises with quiet courage to take up his tasks for the time that remains. God absent from his creation? What an illusion!

(2) Or, ask yourself—you who don't always believe in him, who think you operate your life with reasonable efficiency and effectiveness without him. Can you be honest enough to recall a moment when some alluring temptation to dishonor brought your soul to the edge of the precipice—and *something* held you back? God absent from His creation? What an illusion! Do you remember how Isaiah pictures God saying to Cyrus the Persian, King of Babylon: "I girdeth thee, though thou hast not known me."

(c) The incarnation, foundational doctrine of the Christian religion, reminds us again and afresh that God has betrothed himself forever to humanity! He is not only not absent from his creation; he is forever identified with it. That the God of creation—infinite, holy, omnipotent—should care enough to identify himself with his creatures, putting on for a while the garments of flesh in order that he might understand us and we might know him—this is history's supreme fact, and its message of nearly incredible hope and joy is a light for life's dark valleys and a song in its long nights. The God who made us has come to save us!

(d) If some of the early Christians came dangerously close to forgetting his humanity, then some of us in nearer days have come dangerously close to ignoring his deity. If we believe that God walked the dusty paths of this planet in the garb of flesh, we have no right to preach a disembodied gospel which scorns human needs, earthly problems, and all mundane concerns.

II. *The crucifixion*. (a) The cross, for me at least, is not ultimately subject to minute theological analysis. Men have seen many ideas in it—sacrifice, atonement, expiation, ransom, substitution, and propitiation- each with at least a modicum of truth to contribute to the whole. The cross is vastly bigger than the ideas men have had about it.

(b) The rugged, rigid disciplines of Christianity, by which the saints have been made, issue from an understanding of the cross. Willingness to bear scorn coura-

geously, to make sacrifice daily, to endure hardship, and to face danger—these are the attributes of those who have taken a long look at Calvary. Here, again, is Christ's mighty victory!

III. *The resurrection*. (a) Albert Payson Terhune, in the little book interrupted by his death, said, "God always finishes his sentences." If the identity of Jesus Christ is our authority for the Christian enterprise and the redemption of the cross our message, then the resurrection is our hope and the earnest of our triumph. The resurrection is God's ringing pledge of victory for his gospel's cause and for those who labor in it.

(b) Today's headlines and telecasts have little of a hopeful nature to suggest about the coming of the Kingdom! But in the midst of all of this and in spite of all of it—perhaps because of it—the perceptive Christian senses a strange and wonderful *wistfulness* about our tragic moment in history. He begins to wonder with tremulous hope if the long tide is turning.

(c) As someone has said, "We cannot be children of the resurrection and not see all the world bathed in resurrection light." The resurrection was the divine fiat that validated the facts and the philosophies of the incarnation and the cross. Here is Christ's mighty victory brought to tremendous and triumphant climax.—Earl G. Hunt, Jr.

Illustrations

CRUCIFIXION DEMANDS RESURRECTION. The Son of man *must* rise again. For at the core of all reality is the loving heart of God. God cannot abandon his Christ to oblivion and be the God he is. To say that God is love and to say that the Son of man must suffer and be killed, and after three days rise again, is to say one and the same thing.—Ronald Goetz.

EXPERIENCE OF GOD. Our experience of God as a present factor in our lives, inspiring us to fight evil while it is still preventable, and transforming it into his messenger when it is inevitable, is the ground of our confidence that he will continue to reveal himself to us during our life here and that, when this life is over, he will provide opportunity for further fellowship in a life to come. From this vantage ground of assured conviction we may contemplate with quiet minds the uncertainties that still remain, confident that God, who has given us enough light for today, will supply the necessary guidance for tomorrow.—William Adams Brown.

Sermon Suggestions

THE LIVING CHRIST.   Text: Rev. 1:17–18. Faith in Christ is: (1) Faith in a historical Christ. (2) Faith in a living Christ. (3) Faith in a Christ personal to each of us.—P. T. Forsyth.

CHRIST AND THE GOLDEN CANDLESTICKS. Text: Rev. 3:7–13. (1) We have the same spiritual resources and defenses which made the church in ancient Philadelphia invincible. (2) We have the confirmation of nearly two thousand years of Christian history to validate our faith. (3) We have the same divine Overseer who encouraged the faithful Philadelphians.—Charles W. Koller.

Worship Aids

CALL TO WORSHIP.   "Ye seek Jesus of Nazareth, which was crucified; he is risen." "The Lord is risen indeed." (Mark 16:6; Luke 24:34).

INVOCATION.   Thou hast conquered, O living Christ, and thou hast brought life and light into our dark world and into the dark places of our personal lives. Continue to shine upon us today, and banish the lingering shadows of guilt and fear and unbelief that may still haunt our hearts.

OFFERTORY SENTENCE.   "Jesus sat over against the treasury, and beheld how the people cast money into the treasury" (Mark 12:41).

OFFERTORY PRAYER.   Lord of creation, thou hast made the desert rejoice and blossom as the rose; the thirsty land has brought forth springs of water. Bless our poverty-stricken lives with new life, new gifts, and new generosity. May we find, in the little that we think we have, the true riches of possibility. Amplify like the loaves and fishes what we now bring to thee.

PRAYER.   Almighty God, thou hast brought again from the dead our Lord Jesus Christ, and we believe that mighty works can be done in our lives today. Raise us from our despair by a boundless hope. Raise us from our guilt by an unfaltering trust in thy forgiving mercy. Raise us from our fears by a new measure of courage. Raise us from our lethargy and inactivity by a growing love and concern for others. Help us to see that no circumstance in life is beyond improving, that no duty is beyond our doing, and that no impossibility is beyond thy power or will to change either the situation or us.

EVENING SERVICE

Topic: Faith and the Resurrection
SCRIPTURE: 1 Cor. 15:1–28

Easter came as a surprise to the early disciples. They could never get through talking about it. And because they believed it and went everywhere talking about it, telling the good news that their crucified Lord had arisen from the dead, the church sprang to life like some young giant born full grown.

I cannot explain the resurrection. Yet, I can believe it; I can experience its power; I can affirm and proclaim it.

I. (a) Because God raised Jesus from the dead, we can believe that our sins are forgiven. I speak of whatever it is that separates you from God, that makes you feel at a distance from him and estranged from him, or that makes you feel guilty.

(b) No personality in the Bible presents our situation as well as Simon Peter. In our human weaknesses and failures, all of us can identify with him. We are so much like him. We yield to pressure; we sin; we deny our Lord. We can scarcely believe that we belong to him. Like Simon Peter, we may go out and weep bitterly. But it is when we have sinned that our Lord comes to us. Actually, he has been present all along, though we have not recognized his presence. But how obvious his presence when we have sinned! In that moment, we want both to run from him and to cry out to him. And he comes to us, for that's his business: he is the Savior. He says, "You have done wrong. You know it. But you do belong to me. I knew what you were when I called you to follow me. You have failed me, but you still belong to me. I have carried the burden of your sin, and I will carry it again." What pain such words of love can inflict! It makes us see that our cowardly silence and our indolent neglect, as well as our feverish acts of disobedience, are a betrayal and crucifixion of him, new denials and new wounds compounded of the same evils that did him to death two thousand years ago.

(c) He does not come to avenge the wrongs we have done him, but to save. He forgives us freely and fully, saying, "Go, and sin no more." He is determined that love shall at last win the victory over all our sins.

II. Not only can we believe that our sins are forgiven because God raised Jesus Christ from the dead, we can believe also in a future life in Christ.

(a) Those who walk with Jesus Christ, who enter into the struggles and triumphs of fellowship with him, realize that this new life and relationship is the beginning of something that has no end (2 Cor. 5:17 [RSV]). Because of Christ, life has a new quality, a new dimension (John 17:3). That is why the apostle Paul said, "For to me to live is Christ, and to die is gain" (Phil. 1:21).

(b) How could Paul have felt this way if Christ had not been raised? How could you and I have radiant certitude and hope about the future if Christ had not been raised? Our belief about the future life is based on the risen Christ. It is inextricably tied up with him. He is the firstfruits, the first harvest, of those who have died. And he says to us as we shudder at the thought of our own death, "Because I live, you shall live also" (John 14:19).

(c) We can be certain of this: God will handle your death and mine in a way best suited to his purposes and to our needs. I do not quarrel with my Creator about this life that he has given me, nor do I question his wisdom and love with respect to the next world. I was born into a world compatible with my physical needs; I received a Savior adequate to my spiritual needs. Surely I can trust God to meet whatever the next world requires. The Bible talks in terms of the reconstitution of the redeemed personality. We shall be total persons, not just disembodied spirits floating aimlessly in space. So the term *resurrection*, rather than *immortality*, is the biblical term, the rich word that describes the future life of those who belong to Jesus Christ (1 Cor. 15:38 [RSV]). "Beloved," wrote John, "we are God's children now; it does not yet appear what we shall be, but we know that when he appears we shall be like him, for we shall see him as he is" (1 John 3:2 [RSV]).

III. Because God raised Jesus Christ from the dead, we can believe in the ultimate victory of God. The resurrection of Christ is the decisive clue to the meaning of the universe and the final purpose of God. The truth of the resurrection is of cosmic proportions.

(a) All creation shares in his redemption. Borrowing a figure from the process of natural childbirth, Paul described the whole creation as groaning and travailing in pain together, awaiting God's final act of redemption. The God revealed in Jesus Christ, who brought him again from the dead, is infinitely resourceful and redemptive. Nothing can stop him from achieving his purpose (2 Pet. 3:13 [RSV]).

(b) Again and again, the momentary victories of evil—crime, sickness, death, floods, and tornadoes—confront us with the cross and its tragedy. Circumstances sometimes force us to live out many of our days in the noonday darkness of Good Friday. But Easter says to us, "God is alive. God has won the victory over sin and death. The power of the enemy is broken."—James W. Cox.

SUNDAY: APRIL TWENTY-NINTH

MORNING SERVICE

Topic: To Whom Shall We Go?
TEXT: John 6:66–68.

What else can we turn to but the gospel of Christ? That is what Simon Peter's question amounts to.

I. *What would life be without some high purpose?* What would life be without some high, serious purpose, some gleam to follow, some dream, some endeavor, to lift it above the mere struggle for existence and give it a meaning?

(a) In recent years, there have been vast numbers of young men and women in the world who have been driven desperately to ask the question whether life has any meaning at all. Perhaps they gave their hearts to some big movement which captivated their youthful idealism, and then it failed them. They saw through it and were disillusioned, and now they are looking for something, wondering what there is to live for.

(b) In such a world, you can't accept all your privileges complacently and set out to have a good time for yourselves. You can't take life like that. If you do, it goes bad, it goes rotten in your hands for want of a high purpose in such a tragic world.

II. *What would an ideal be without religion?* That is to say: *without God.* What would life's dreams be if they were only human dreams, with no God behind them?

(a) You will perhaps wish impatiently to remind me that many an honest skeptic has had high moral ideals, and that, God or no God, our moral convictions stand fast. Many who do not profess to believe in God have a greater social concern, a finer devotion to the cause of reform among their fellow men, than many Christians. But I wonder how long that kind of thing can last—high ideals and noble service without any faith. For one generation, perhaps, and then mainly by living unconsciously on the religious capital of the last generation. But the more sincere they are, the more tragic they are, because it is in the end a tragic business to try to have morality without religion, to cherish an ideal without God.

(b) You get hold of an ideal of character for yourself, and you strive to mould your character upon it. That is something to live for. And then presently you discover that, with all your concentration on cultivating an ideal character, you have only succeeded in making yourself more self-centered than ever. Then perhaps, in disgust of yourself, you turn outwards to the dream of an ideal of humanity, to the service of mankind and the crusade of making the world a better place with a nobler, happier breed of human beings. But very soon you begin to discover that the world is a much bigger problem than you had imagined. Is it possible that you want God? Can you go forward to what we call religion?

(c) Suppose it should be true that the ultimate reality of this universe is not humanity, but God. Suppose it should be true that all you call your ideals come from him. Suppose that, underneath all the chaos of human history, there is an unseen and eternal Kingdom of God, which he is continually carrying forward, and that God himself has redeemed and is redeeming the world. Suppose that when you have lost and betrayed all that you call your ideals, you find that God has not given you up, but forgives you and accepts you and even uses you and sends you out again—not to realize an ideal or to redeem the world (for you can't do these things), but to do his will and serve his Kingdom.

That changes everything, your personal life and all your service of mankind. It is all transformed, because of God. That is what you want. And that is religion.

III. *What would religion be without Christ?* That is the climax. I have not until now spoken of Christ in my argument, but of course it has all been pointing to him.

When it comes to the vital issues for you and me, standing where we are, what other religion is there to be seriously considered except the gospel of Christ?

All those things I have just been hypothetically describing as the things that we desperately need—all that pattern of belief and life is not simply *any* religion or *every* religion: it is the religion of Christ, the gospel of Christ.

And to crown it all: if the gospel is true, then not only is the ideal an eternal reality in heaven, not only is the dream an invincible purpose of God, but also, the Word became flesh and dwelt among us on earth —God himself was incarnate in Jesus Christ and bore the sin of the world for our salvation.—D. M. Baillie.

Illustrations

PATH TO CERTAINTY.   It is through what we do, even more than through what we think, that our certainty of God must be won. Thought may help to remove the obstacles which make faith difficult, but in the last analysis, it is the will that must speak the deciding word.—William Adams Brown.

A CHRISTIAN IDENTIFIED.   A Christian is a person who confesses that, amidst the manifold and confusing voices heard in the world, there is one Voice which supremely wins his full assent, uniting all his powers, intellectual and emotional, into a single pattern of self-giving. That Voice is Jesus Christ. A Christian not only believes *that* he was; he believes *in him* with all his heart and strength and mind. Christ appears to the Christian as the one stable point or fulcrum in all the relativities of history. Once the Christian has made this primary commitment, he still has perplexities, but he begins to know that joy of being used for a mighty purpose by which his little life is dignified.—Elton Trueblood.

Sermon Suggestions

WHAT JESUS CHRIST WANTS MEN TO THINK OF HIM.   Matt. 22:42. (1) Jesus Christ wanted men to accept him as the supreme teacher. (2) To think of him as the revealer of God the Father. (3) To think of him as the object of our faith. (4) To think of him as the conqueror of sin and death. (5) To think of him as one who could demon-

strate practically in the lives of his people his own claims to be Lord and Savior.— Edgar Young Mullins.

SAINTS IN STRANGE PLACES.   Phil. 4:22. (1) The saints of caesar's household teach us that the Christian life can be lived and a high order of Christian character developed in the midst of unfavorable surroundings. (2) They remind us that loyalty to Christ can be maintained in the face of persecution. (3) They proclaim the reality of Christian communion.—W. A. Cameron.

Worship Aids

CALL TO WORSHIP.   "This is the day which the Lord hath made; we will rejoice and be glad in it" (Ps. 118:24).

INVOCATION.   Though many high and holy experiences fade soon from our hearts and leave a lingering sadness, grant, O God, that we may know this day the exultation of those who have risen with Christ and are seeking the things that are above, where Christ is, seated at thy right hand.

OFFERTORY   SENTENCE.   "Whoever shares with others should do it generously" (Rom. 12:8 [TEV]).

OFFERTORY PRAYER.   Gracious Father, we have opened our mouths and thou hast filled them with good things. Now open our hearts to others, we pray, that we may help bring fulfillment to their hopes and prayers. Bless these offerings and direct their use, so that nothing be wasted.

PRAYER.   Eternal Father, because our Lord lives today, we live. But some of us have not felt the lifting power of that truth. We go about as those who know that our Lord was crucified, but hardly knowing that he was raised from the dead. We have been told that thou hast caused us to sit together in heavenly places with him, yet the sights and sounds and smells of earth are still too much with us. May we hear in thy word the trumpet blast of victory and rise with confidence, wide awake to what we are and what we should be doing. Help us to live on this earth as those whose citizenship is in heaven, but as those who are eager to bring the life of heaven to this earth. Grant strength to those sorely tempted every day to live as if this world were all. Grant concern and tact to those who see others tempted and wish to help. And give us all a knowledge of thy comradeship with us in our pilgrimage.

EVENING SERVICE

Topic: Thomas: The Man Who Found Faith Through Doubt

SCRIPTURE: John 20:19–31.

I. (a) John's gospel is appreciably different in purpose and in form from the other three. He was not primarily concerned to present bare facts: his concern was to present meanings and hints of understanding that go beyond simple fact and yet which are grounded in fact. John so mingled his knowledge of Jesus the man with his awareness of Jesus the risen Christ that we cannot always in his gospel distinguish between the two. Keep this in mind, then, as we examine the passage from John's gospel, the twentieth chapter, verses 19 through 31. In the first part of the passage, the first scene of a little drama, we are shown Jesus meeting, behind locked doors, with his disciples in a room in Jerusalem on the evening of Easter.

(b) The disciples are bewildered and demoralized by recent events—the arrest of their Master, the hasty trials, the crucifixion. Suddenly, and despite the locked doors, Jesus is standing among them. They are filled with joy and assurance. Here among them is the risen, living Jesus, giving them his blessing and his peace and his Spirit, and granting them authority to carry on his mission.

II. (a) But only ten of the disciples are there. Judas disappeared after he had betrayed Jesus to the authorities. Thomas was not there either, as we learn when we read the second scene in the drama (see vv. 24–25).

(b) We do not know why Thomas was not there. He is a strange fellow, this Thomas. We know very little about him.

He is a vague, shadowy figure, but we can discern certain of his qualities of personality and character.

(c) There is a touch of slander in the nickname he has carried through the centuries, "Doubting Thomas." He did have a quizzical, questioning tendency, but he certainly did not specialize in doubt. After all, he did respond to Jesus' call to discipleship, and he served his Master faithfully. Thomas was a man of insight and courage. In John's eleventh chapter, we see him in action when Jesus hears about the illness and death of his friend, Lazarus, in Bethany, a village near Jerusalem. Jesus decides to go to Bethany. Some of his disciples think this unwise because of the jeopardy Jesus might get himself into by going so near to Jerusalem. But Thomas rallies his fellow disciples by saying to them, "Let us also go that we may die with him." Thomas had insight into Jesus' intentions and awareness of his probable fate—and he had the courage to take his own chances with his Master.

(d) Thomas was not in the room with the other disciples on the evening of Easter, and when they tell him that they have seen the Lord, he shows that he is the kind of man who demands direct evidence, treating what they tell him with some skepticism. He says, "Unless I see the mark of the nails on his hands, unless I put my fingers into the place where the nails were, and my hand into his side, I will not believe it."

III. (a) The third scene of this little drama takes place one week later, on the Sunday following Easter (see vv. 26–29a). It took Thomas longer to work his way through skepticism and doubt, but it is important to note that he did not separate himself from the fellowship and came to awareness of the risen Jesus within the fellowship.

(b) This extended passage, this little drama in three scenes, is John's way of declaring that the disciples had an intense experience of the risen Jesus, the living Lord. Their reports of this experience, after being passed by word of mouth through the early Christian community, inspired John to write, in his characteristically dramatic way, his meditation on it.

Then John added his epilogue (see vv. 30 –31).

IV. (a) Thomas came through doubt to his final faith in the risen Jesus Christ, his living Lord. By temperament, he was inclined to be skeptical; no easy answers would satisfy him. He was a compulsive questioner, but he seemed to have confidence that answers could eventually be found for his questions.

(b) Thomas had an open mind; he kept in touch with his fellow disciples, and he was always ready for any new light that might come to him. And his story shows that certainty in faith—enough certainty, anyway, for the living of faith—is most likely to come to a person who, despite doubts and misgivings, keeps close to a community of faith, a fellowship of believers.—J. A. Davidson.

SUNDAY: MAY SIXTH

MORNING SERVICE

Topic: He Did Not Quit!
TEXT: 2 Tim. 4:7.

As we grow older, we come to see how important it is to hold on. What Paul is saying here is simply that he did not quit. Such a sentiment is hardly ever spectacular or dramatic. We are much more impressed with sudden brilliance or isolated acts of genius. But finally, most things come down to fighting the fight, finishing the race, and keeping the faith. The Bible puts a very high estimate on people who do not quit.

I. *Life is the long pull.* Paul was using the figures of the arena and the race. Many a man is good at running dashes, but straining forward toward the goal when he is exhausted is another matter.

(a) Civilization is not attained by a single decisive battle or a brief sudden effort. Civilization is a matter of the long pull and of millions of unknown, faithful people consolidating the gains that have been made and preserving them. Something in men has driven them on and persisted in spite of all the setbacks of war and disease. Always there are those people who, in their own way and in their own place, are strengthening the good and fighting the evil. Nations have their roots in the patience of many men and women of whom it can be said, "They did not quit."

(b) Any good cause will have an appeal to many persons who certainly prefer goodness to evil. If the engagement is going to be a short one, any number of people will enlist. But great causes are never easily attained, and the short-term-ers are of very little value when it comes to the final victory. The world is full of dramatic starters, but so often they are disappointments. Every pastor knows the laymen who are good for a quick shot in the arm for any Christian enterprise. But if the church is engaged in any long enterprise, do not depend upon these brethren for leadership.

(c) So it is that usually less gifted men who have finishing power are the ones who do the work. This does not mean that the able man is doomed automatically to short-term adventures, but it is a familiar pattern. This is what makes St. Paul's example so rare and makes us believe that God put his hand upon him in a wonderful way. With the kind of mind that comes along only once a century, he still was the faithful missionary who seems never to have lost his enthusiasm nor his will to finish the course.

II. *One of our continuing temptations is to quit.* Life is so constructed that we are constantly under this pressure. For very seldom do things move so swiftly and satisfactorily that we do not feel ourselves betrayed.

(a) We start out with great enthusiasm, which is one of the signs of youth. Certainly a burden older people have to bear is listening to young people define the issues and describe how easily they can be solved. To youth, the whole mess of the world is due simply to older people who grew weary, lost their first enthusiasm, and finally became corrupt. Yet the time comes when we begin to see that not all of this talk was due to weariness tinged with cynicism. The whole affair was more complicated than we realized, and vitality which is not undergirded with stubbornness is not much good. We will not go very far without enthusiasm, but neither will we go very far if that is all we have.

(b) No one who has lived very long finds it in his heart to blame people who quit. There are always many reasons why it happened, and they are usually good ones. We have all had promises made to us which were denied. Sometimes life itself seems to dangle a great hope before us, only to dash it to the ground when we reach out to grasp it. Somebody told us how marvelous it would be, and we have found it quite otherwise. Perhaps the whole thing is a sham and nothing we have been told can be believed. In the darkness of such a moment, we quit.

(c) We might have the courage to continue if we could be sure of the ultimate success. Ah, there is the rub! We cannot be sure this continued sacrifice will mean victory. We only know that we grope in the darkness for hopes which seem to grow dimmer as we approach them. Enthusiasm ebbs away and doubts have their way with us. The cost has a way of rising to frightening heights, and the reward fades away on the horizon.

III. *We need help*. When a man believes he can define the issues by himself and come to his own conclusion, he is in real danger. We need Someone to make us aware of duty which, as the poet said, is the stern voice of God.

(a) Let us realize that we are all having a hard time. I do not know anyone who finds life easy, for with all the comfort and affluence of our modern civilization, personal life does not get any easier. We are in great need of a strength not our own to persevere in the daily difficulties and disappointments of living.

(b) Here we discover one of the great responsibilities of the church. We need a fellowship to encourage us, and we need to be reminded constantly of our moral and spiritual obligations. The church, when it is truly the redeeming fellowship that it ought to be, keeps us close to the source of our power and makes us aware of the distant goals.

(c) We have a tendency to get too proud and too unsympathetic with our brethren. Character is primarily staying power, and if we are not careful, we shall despise those who yield to their weakness. Every now and again, I face things that are too much for me, as if God were reminding me that with all my advantages, I am in constant danger. When this happens, I have a new appreciation for the foibles of my brethren and the weakness of my friends. For there is more excuse for them than there is for me, and how many times I find myself at the edge of despair.

(d) Most of us have experienced this truth, and we have lived enough to know that there is not much hope for us in our own strength. We must have help beyond ourselves.

IV. *Our hope is in the gospel*. What Paul found, we can find, and sometimes the only thing that saves us is a willingness to wait a little longer for God to act.

(a) We must learn to live one day at a time. This is Jesus' teaching which becomes more realistic with every new experience that comes to us. If we look too far ahead, we shall then be tempted to seek some way out. But if we can get through today, there will be fresh strength for tomorrow.

(b) It is amazing how many of the troubles which loom so large as we look far ahead, never materialize. God is always visiting us with divine surprises and miraculously eliminating some of the obstacles in our way. If I can finish the day, tomorrow will have some fresh light which will illuminate the dark picture.

(c) It is Good News indeed that he who walks with Christ is kept faithful to the end of the fight. We do not walk alone, and in that desperate moment when we begin to define a hundred reasons why we should desert, we can hold out a little longer if we can see again the great resources of power he has given us. Christians through the years have testified that they are upheld by Everlasting Arms. While there are very few St. Pauls among us, there are thousands who can testify that the same power which saved Paul, saves them.—Gerald Kennedy.

Illustrations

STRENGTH IN WEAKNESS.   It is a simple matter of history that some of the noblest lives which have been lived on earth have been those of chronic invalids who have made their agonies a triumph and conquered all deadly things with Paul's word of life: "Power is made perfect in weakness."

We cherish the memory of Robert Louis Stevenson. A paragraph from his letter to George Meredith, from Samoa, in 1893: "For fourteen years I have not had a day's real health; I have awakened sick and gone to bed weary; and I have done my work unflinchingly. I have written in bed, and written out of it, written in hemorrhages, written in sickness, written torn by coughing, written when my head swam for weakness; and for so long, it seems to me I have won my wager and recovered my glove. I am better now, have been rightly speaking since first I came to the Pacific; and still, few are the days when I am not in some physical distress. And the battle goes on— ill or well, is a trifle: so as it goes. I was made for a contest, and the Powers have so willed that my battlefield should be this dingy, inglorious one of the bed and the physic bottle. At least I have not failed, but I would have preferred a place of trumpeting and the open air over my head."—C. F. Aked.

THE PRICE OF CHRISTIANITY.   Jesus may or may not be the Savior of the world. It depends on the world. He may or not be the Savior of the individual. It depends on the individual. The condition of Saviorhood lies in this: are we willing to pay the price? What privations men have suffered to get an education! There was Alexander Whyte, lodging with two others in a little room with a bed that could hold only two of them, so that they took turns to sit and work, four hours a shift, all through the night, paying about fifty cents per week for their garret and their food, and yet spending on occasion fifteen dollars for books, gathered from who knows where and by what desperate privations! And if a man wants Christ-likeness like that, he'll get it.

It is a business for adventurous spirits. Let us cease our glib talk about a certain event on Calvary until we are willing to say to men, "You can have Christianity only upon the same condition that you get other things—that you want it badly enough to pay the price."—Frederick K. Stamm.

Sermon Suggestions

THE ABIDING COMPANIONSHIP.   Exod. 33:14. Some of life's lonelinesses which this wonderful companionship will destroy: (1) The loneliness of unshared sorrow. (2) The loneliness of unshared triumph. (3) The loneliness of temptation. (4) The loneliness of death.—J. H. Jowett.

LIFE'S DETOURS.   Scriptures: Rom. 8:18 –28 (RSV); Jas. 1:2 (Phillips trans.). (1) Life's detours: teachable moments. (2) Life's detours: opportunities to re-examine our values. (3) Life's detours: opportunities to trace the rainbow through the rain. (4) Life's detours: put us in touch with the resources of the Eternal Spirit.— John Thompson.

Worship Aids

CALL TO WORSHIP.   "Grace to you, and peace, from God our Father, and from the Lord Jesus Christ" (Phil. 1:2).

INVOCATION.   We thank thee, our Father, for the fellowship of the gospel, for thy gracious work among us present here today, for the promise of the fulfillment of thy purpose through us. Strengthen us in that good work by all that is said and done in this service of worship. For thy name's sake.

OFFERTORY SENTENCE.   "If you are eager to give, God will accept your gift on the basis of what you have to give, not on what you don't have" (2 Cor. 8:12 [TEV]).

OFFERTORY PRAYER.   Gracious Lord, no true offering is ever too small for thy notice or ever too large for our earthly well-being. May we give remembering the widow's mite and Jesus' yielding of his all to thee. So we bring to thee the fruits of our labors and the produce of thy grace. In the name of him who loved us and gave himself for us.

PRAYER. O God, thou hast heard our prayers. Many times thou hast spared our lives and delivered us from temptation. Thy hand is never shortened that thou canst not save. Even when we felt forsaken, we were not alone.

We love thee because thou didst first love us. We have received redemption in thy Son, who loved us and gave himself for us. Through the years, we have been blessed by thy providence. Every moment of our lives, we are upheld by thy grace.

Give to us, we pray, a greater awareness of thy many gracious acts toward us. Then let thanksgiving rise to our lips and gratitude sanctify our lives.

EVENING SERVICE

Topic: Jesus the Door
TEXT: John 10:9.

A door excites our curiosity and challenges our attention. A door shuts us in and provides security and protection. But there are times when to be shut in is to be imprisoned.

Sir George Adam Smith was looking at a sheepfold in Bethlehem. He noticed the hole in the wall around the fold through which the sheep went. But he looked in vain for the piece of wood which might serve as the door. So he turned to the shepherd and said, "Where is the door?" and the shepherd replied in the very words of Christ, "I am the door." A door leads two ways. If I pass in by Jesus, the door, it means that I pass from one state to another.

I. We come to Jesus, the door, from our work in the world, from our task of living.

(a) We are tired and travel-stained. Jesus is the door by which we may enter into rest and find new courage to face the tasks and trials of life. "Come to me, all you working people with your heavy loads. It will rest you to be with me. Take the yoke that I carry on your shoulders and learn from me how to bear it. You see how easy I am to get on with, how ready to make allowances. You, too, shall discover for yourselves the secret of restful living."

(b) Weariness descends on us all at times. Some who are young are weary and lose their enthusiasm for a while. "Even the youths shall faint and be weary and the young men shall utterly fall," says the prophet. People in middle life sometimes become despondent. Life disappoints them. The old are often weary. This or that seems to promise a way out for all to find peace and plenty. Blindly, the crowd surges along only to find a notice, "No Road This Way." Mankind is wearying itself to find the door, and all the time Christ is there, quietly saying, "I am the door. Come to me, all you who labor and are heavy laden and I will give you rest."

II. We come to Jesus, the door, from the world's pleasures unsatisfied.

(a) This is an age of unparalleled freedom, freedom which almost amounts to license.

(1) Off with all restraints, away with all convention—that is the cry. Yet with all this unchartered freedom, are people really happy?

(2) People are groping along the walls that enclose them, searching for an exit into some larger, freer world. Every time I grapple with a problem, every time I indulge in an unlawful thought, every time I seek relief from the monotony of life, I am trying to force a door.

(3) Very often, the doorway which seemed so full of promise turns out to be the entrance to the dungeon of despair. Jesus alone is the door by which we may enter into a happiness that does not cloy.

(b) Many people, when they think of the Christian religion, think of it as something negative which is always saying, "Thou shalt not." They imagine that it fetters the free expression of our personality.

(1) But Christianity is no narrow joyless religion. The followers of Christ have a right to every innocent pleasure, every healthful interest and joy. "And shall go in and out and find pasture."

(2) There is the suggestion of a spacious freedom. To go in and go out is a biblical phrase which always suggests the free ac-

tivity of daily life. All things are ours because we are Christ's, the privileges of the church and the beauties of the world, the means of grace and the joys of living. "I am come that they might have life and that they might have it abundantly."

III. We come to Jesus, the door, from the world's sorrows and cares.

(a) Jesus is the door by which we enter into courage and the hope that makes us not ashamed. "I will give the valley of Achor for a door of hope." The valley of Achor was the scene of Israel's defeat and Achan's shame and sin. It is the old place where one has already failed and fallen that God gives to us as a door of hope.

(b) There is a door of hope even in the valley of trouble, and those who tread that valley in God's company will not fail to find it. On a Good Friday, the disciples must have felt as if the cross was a door slammed in their faces; but on Easter Day, it turned out to be a door opening into new joy and a new power for living. When we look at Calvary, we know that Christ has been afflicted in all our afflictions and that he is the door by which we may pass from our sorrows into peace and hope.

IV. Lastly, we come to Jesus, the door, from the world's temptations.

We have played with foolish things, like children with fire. Some of us have touched pitch and been defiled. About us are the chains of habit, and we are held in subjection by our own follies. Jesus is the door by which we enter into the peace of forgiveness. As the writer to the Hebrews says of Jesus: "He has been tempted in all points like as we are and is able to succor us when we are tempted and to keep us from falling."

The preaching of the gospel is so urgently needed today that people may know where to find the door, the way of escape from death to life. He is the only way. His door is always open, ready to receive us. Dr. Hort, the great New Testament scholar, would never lock his study door, lest his children should not have access to him at any hour. We have freedom of access to the Father anywhere and at any time. He calls us to go in and look upon his face and hear his words. We cannot go to him too often.—John Bishop.

SUNDAY: MAY THIRTEENTH

MORNING WORSHIP

Topic: "When Trouble Comes"
SCRIPTURE: 2 Cor. 1:3–11.

Have you ever faced a difficulty from which no escape seemed to be available? Have you ever been confronted by trouble?

Paul was, but God had delivered him. Paul used this deliverance as the starting point of his second letter to the Corinthian Christians.

In verses 3–7, Paul talked about this trouble in a general way. Then, in verse 8, he moved from the general subject of "tribulations" to a specified experience of "trouble" which he faced in Asia. The significance of the event for Paul is evidenced by the phrase, "for we do not want you to be unaware, brethren." Or as the King James Version puts it, "For we would, brethren, not have you ignorant." Paul used that phrase six times in his letters. In

every case, the phrase introduced a point that Paul wanted to emphasize. It was like ringing a bell or blowing a whistle. "This is something that is important!" Paul was saying, "I want you to know about my trouble."

Actually, we do not know what this trouble was. The text implies only that it was recent and severe. The severity of it is seen in the phrases used in verses 8 and 9.

I. *The resource*. Notice, first of all, our resource when trouble comes. Where can we turn in the midst of trouble? In this letter to the Corinthians, he began with an expression of gratitude to God, for God is the one who delivered him from his trouble.

(a) Paul began in verse 3 by calling God "the Father of mercies"—"Father" in the sense that the mercies came from him, and "mercies" in the sense that God's characteristic way of relating to man was merciful.

(b) Then, in the last part of verse 3, Paul called God a God of all comfort. Comfort is the key word in this passage. In one form or another, this word appears ten times in verses 3–7.

(c) Notice the comprehensive scope of this resource in verses 3–4. God is "the God of all comfort" (v. 3) who brings comfort "in all our tribulation" when we are "in any trouble" (v. 4). There is no trouble you will ever face from which or through which God cannot deliver you. Based on his own resources, Paul knew that he could not win. Based on the resources of God, Paul knew that he could not lose.

II. *The result.* But what is the result? When trouble comes and we find in God our resource for help, what happens? What is the result? Notice several things in our text.

(a) The first result which comes when we turn to God in a time of trouble is *comfort.* Look at verse 4. Paul blessed God because He is a God "who comforts us in all our affliction."

As you go through life, in every experience you face, if you look closely enough and deeply enough, you will see that underneath you and those with whom you share life are the everlasting arms of God who brought deliverance. Sometimes God will deliver you from your trouble as he did for Jesus that day when the crowd wanted to stone him. Sometimes God will deliver you through your trouble as he did for Jesus at Calvary. But when trouble comes, the deliverance of God from your trouble or through your trouble will bring comfort to your soul.

(b) The second result which comes when we turn to God in a time of trouble is a *commission.* Notice how Paul puts it in verse 4.

God's comfort comes to us not to make us comfortable, but to make us comforters, not to make us safe from our troubles, but to make us sensitive to the troubles of others.

(c) The third result which comes when we turn to God in a time of trouble is *confidence.* Confidence radiates from verses 5–7.

Paul assures the Corinthians in verses 5

–6 that God's comfort is abundant. In fact, he says that the greater the problem, the greater the power. This confidence grew out of his experience with God's comfort in his own life. When you know the comfort of God, it gives you confidence to face whatever life has to offer (see 1 Sam. 17: 37; Job 19:25; Jer. 32:15; Acts 3; 2 Tim. 1:12).

(d) The fourth result which comes when we turn to God in trouble is *community.*

This sense of community is beautifully described in verse 11: "For much thanks and praise will go to God from you who see his wonderful answers to your prayers for our safety!" (TLB).—Brian L. Harbour.

Illustrations

INCOMPATIBILITY.   Dr. Orchard, one-time minister of the King's Weigh House in London, was once told by his wife that there was a certain place where divorces were granted to people on the grounds of "incompatibility of temperament." And Orchard remarked to her, "How odd! Because that is the very purpose of marriage —to bring two people who are different together and make them compatible." Compatibility is never merely a gift, it is an achievement; and the home is the sphere in which the world is first to learn the cost and nature of living together.—W. D. Davies.

PREMARITAL SEX.   Before marriage, sexuality is in a state of development and preparation. Any attempt to satisfy it *in isolation*, either alone or with a partner to whom one is not married, means the partial experience of something that can only properly be known in totality, and may be compared to the enjoyment of an unripe fruit. For this reason, such ideas as "sexual freedom before marriage," "the right to live a full life" or "to sow one's wild oats," or the alleged necessity of "gaining sexual experience before marriage" represent a basic misunderstanding both of the divine order and of human nature.—Theodor Bovet.

Sermon Suggestions

GOD'S EYE IS ON YOU.   Scripture: Mark 1: 16–20. (1) God cares for us. (2) God is doing something for us. (3) God is preparing us for some important role.

GOD'S SPECIAL PEACE.   Text: Phil. 4:7. (1) Peace, in one form or another, seems to be a universal desire. (2) Peace is a worthy goal. (3) There is a kind of peace that is different—the peace of God. (4) God gives this peace to those who believe in Jesus Christ. (5) The peace of God is beyond our utmost understanding. (6) If we have this peace, it will keep guard over our hearts and minds.

Worship Aids

CALL TO WORSHIP.   "Behold, I stand at the door, and knock: if any man hear my voice and open the door, I will come in to him, and will sup with him, and he with me" (Rev. 3:20).

INVOCATION.   O Christ, we open our hearts individually to you; we open the heart of our fellowship of believers to you; and we would open the hearts of men and women everywhere to you. Grant that the intimacy of our communion with you may deepen our finest motives to serve you both here and wherever we go in this world.

OFFERTORY SENTENCE.   "Give unto the Lord the glory due unto his name: bring an offering, and come into his courts" (Ps. 96:8).

OFFERTORY PRAYER.   Loving Father, we do not always understand why we have enough and to spare when others have so little. But we do understand that we are stewards of what we have. Grant that our offerings may help supply bread where it is needed, and send forth your word, the bread of life, without which no one can truly live.

PRAYER.   Eternal God, Great Shepherd of the sheep, we look to you for all our needs. You provide our food and drink, the warmth of friendship, our health and strength, and human understanding and forgiveness. And when all these blessings are scarce, you give us courage to go on, patience to wait, and love that will not give up on you or on those who doubt us. In the best of times, we rest in you and find peace that passes all understanding. We thank you, Lord.

Even at this moment, we face testings: we are tempted to renege on the best we know, to take shortcuts to happiness, to allow those who are blind to their own needs and careless of ours to pressure us into foolish ways. May your rod of discipline keep us in right paths.

Because you are with us, we do not have to be afraid, whether of our sinful nature, of adversaries around us, or of the baffling brutalities of the world in which we live.

Bring us ever closer to you and to those who love and serve and praise you, both now and forevermore.

EVENING SERVICE

Topic: Motherhood and the Stages of Life

SCRIPTURE: 2 Tim. 1:5.

The whole mystery of life itself is tied up with the miracle of motherhood. And in the providence of God, there is no time in life when we are not in some way touched by our mothers. That makes the demands and the responsibilities of being a mother at least as commanding as its joys.

As a way of honoring mothers this day, let's examine what the Bible says about them as related to the various stages in our lives. And as we honor mothers, may they be challenged and inspired to allow God to guide them as they serve him in shaping life and loving.

I. Motherhood begins with love . . . love of wife for husband and, equally, of husband for wife. Love is vital. I don't think any of us would question that. But it is very difficult to establish this fact based on the Bible. You may be asking yourself, "Doesn't the Bible support this basic principle of love?" Well, yes, it does, but in a different way than we often realize.

Both the Old Testament and the New Testament were produced in cultures like most ancient cultures in which women were little more than property. It was a man's world by every standard. To tell a man that he had to provide materially for his wife—or wives, in the Old Testament —was expected. But to talk in terms of loving her was unheard of. It was unheard of until an itinerant missionary named Paul happened upon the scene and said, "Husbands, love your wives," as recorded in Colossians 3:19 and other places as well. Paul was talking about more than feelings, though these were and are obviously important. He was talking about the husband acting in the wife's best interests, even though self-sacrifice might be necessary and whether or not he happened to feel like it. The same thing was expected of the wife, but now she, too, was to love her husband, not just to care for him out of a sense of duty. Love is a self-giving relationship in which there is a mutual respect, mutual admiration, open communication, and joy in one another's presence. This is where motherhood begins.

II. Motherhood should become a possibility only when a child is truly wanted— by mother and father. Every child has this right. Even an unplanned child has this right.

(a) Much of the child abuse in our society is the result of unwanted children. When infants and children make demands upon parents who don't even want them, the stage is set for those parents to respond in irrational ways to their offspring. In the middle of an already sleepless night, a baby cries and cries and cries. This is a very difficult problem even for those who absolutely want the child. But for those who don't, it's impossible-beyond tolerance—beyond reason. Psychological abuse can take place when a child is unwanted. One child is singled out from the others. He or she becomes, without any justification, the black sheep of the family. Every time anything goes wrong, the whole family knows whom to blame.

These children grow up to be adults who can never feel good about themselves, who can never quite accept themselves. Many times they become society's scapegoats, too.

(b) Every child has the right to be wanted and loved unconditionally. Parents should be able to say, and act accordingly, "You don't have to do anything to earn our love." Even those strange and wonderful adolescents should feel the same kind of acceptance.

(c) So what does the Bible say about wanting children? It was a very different world then, and the parallel with today's world is tough to draw. Everybody back then wanted children—at least, a son. They could take or leave daughters. In the average family, a daughter only meant extra support by the father all her life, culminating in that big expenditure, at age thirteen or fourteen, when she *finally* was old enough to marry off. What self-respecting man would marry without a suitable dowry?

(d) There are a few exceptions to this treatment in the Old Testament. Some women were able to rise to prominence in spite of their natural "place" in society. Then Jesus came along, and as a matter of living, he interacted with women; some of his closest disciples were women. Gender made no difference to him. And finally Paul—of all people—verbalized what Jesus had acted. In Galatians 3:28, Paul wrote, "There is neither Jew nor Greek, there is neither slave nor free, there is neither male nor female; for you are all one in Christ Jesus."

(e) All children are precious—boys and girls. But no one should bring either into the world without wanting the child. And these days we should also say that children aren't for everyone. A women's worth is not dependent on her decision or her ability to bring chidren into the world. Yes, God did say to the human race, "Be fruitful and multiply and fill the earth" (Gen. 1:28). But we've already done that. On a world scale, we have a population problem, children and adults who have no place to live and not enough to eat. So, wanted children are those for whom we can provide materially, emotionally, and spiritually. And every child has the right to be wanted.

III. Certainly the unique bond between

mother and child is established during pregnancy, long before birth. Mother is providing for baby from conception on. I can't tell you exactly when that developing embryo becomes a human being, but the mother knows for a long time that something is living inside her.

IV. The demands of loving, caring for, and teaching the child are called for from birth, and they continue in a primary way until the child reaches adulthood or gets married.

(a) Just think about what all must go on during those years in which we are directly responsible, legally and morally, for our children. In the very beginning, parents are responsible for meeting all of baby's needs. This is symbolized in no better way than seeing baby at mother's breast.

(b) Perhaps satisfying the baby's physical needs is paramount in those earliest days, but soon—in addition- other needs must be satisfied, too. There are safety needs, love, affection, and belonging needs, esteem needs, and so on. Satisfying the physical needs slows through the years as the child becomes more and more capable of doing this for himself or herself. But personal love and support are always needed, and mothers have a special way of providing this, even when we're grown.

(c) During the growing-up years, there are a great many tasks to accomplish. There are many traumas involved in maturing—from a skinned knee to rejection by a high school peer group—and motherly comfort helps most of all. Perhaps a mother is most like God when she is comforting her children. In Isaiah 66:13, the prophet records the words of God to Israel, "As one whom his mother comforts, so I will comfort you; and you shall be comforted in Jerusalem."

(d) Then, there's the challenge of leading our children to accept Jesus Christ as personal Lord and Savior. Paul paid Timothy's mother and grandmother the highest of compliments when he said to Timothy, "I am reminded of your sincere faith, a faith that dwelt first in your grandmother Lois and your mother Eunice and now I am sure dwells in you" (2 Tim. 1:5). Is there a higher compliment than for a child to be able to look back on his or her life and to say, "I was able to accept Jesus because of the Christian home in which I was reared," or "I was able to know the love of God in Christ because of the way my parents loved God, each other, and me." A high compliment—yes! And a sobering challenge all along.

V. Motherhood doesn't stop when the children are grown. There are new ways to relate to one another, to be sure. But our need for our mother and her need for us continues so long as the Lord graces us both with life.—David Farmer.

SUNDAY: MAY TWENTIETH

MORNING WORSHIP

Topic: Living Like Kings

SCRIPTURE: Rom. 5:17.

(a) One day Frederick the Great of Prussia was walking along a pathway on the outskirts of Berlin, when accidentally he brushed against a very old man who was proceeding in the opposite direction. "Who are you?" asked Frederick, out of idle curiosity. "I am a king," replied the old man laconically. "A king!" laughed Frederick." Over what kingdom do you reign?" "Over myself," was the proud reply.

(b) Samuel Shoemaker says that he believes there are "three levels of life on which men live: the level of instinct, the level of conscience, and the level of grace."

(c) The way of grace has been described epigramatically by P. T. Forsyth when he said that "unless there is within us that which is above us we shall soon yield to that which is around us." Paul was plainly aware of this as he unfolded his great argument in his letter to the Romans. There he rehearsed the age-old problems of law versus grace, moral defeat versus spiritual victory, sin versus salvation.

It is the difference Paul claimed when he said, "By the grace of God I am what I am." For you and me, it is the difference between living as kings and living as slaves, between being on top of life and having life crushingly on top, between reigning in life and running the whole gamut of moral defeat. According to the New Testament, God's grace is his own activity and all we can do is to receive it. No one can earn it. No one can grab it. "They that receive abundance of grace shall reign in life by one, Jesus Christ."

I. We are in the world, but not of the world. We are all in this world. We did not request it, but at any rate, we are here. But there is a broad difference between being in the world and being of it. To be *in* it is our inescapable lot. To be *of* it is our own moral choice. Those of us who are merely of the world are constantly in a state of uncertainty; we are victims of circumstances and are pushed around by forces too big to cope with or put down. But the man who lives by grace, although in the thick of things, is never a part of the mess nor a party to it. His whole destiny is in hands greater than his own, his gains are given to a glory not his own, and his hopes are for a future not his own. A real Christian reigns in life, because the day-to-day trivia do not shake him.

Hear St. Cyprian, writing in the third century, "It is really a bad world. . . . Yet in the midst of it I have found a quiet and holy people. . . . They are despised and persecuted, but they care not. They have overcome the world. These people are the Christians—and I am one of them."

II. We are above the world, but not out of the world. Once the grace of Christ enters the life of any man, he is a new person, but that grace becomes in him, among other things, a loving concern for the needs of others. The real Christian is above the world, but never out of it. And this work of grace makes the big difference between Christianity and the pagan religions. E. Stanley Jones tells how, when an epidemic swept through his district in India, he asked two Brahmin saints to leave their wayside meditations and help him with the diseased and dying. "We are holy men," they said. "We don't help anyone."

Remember how Jesus said on the morning of the resurrection, "I ascend unto my Father and your Father; and to my God and your God." And by this, he meant that all his genuine followers would be co-workers with God because they were co-heirs with himself. "The Christian's life," said Evelyn Underhill, "is lived in the open, not in a pious cubbyhole."

He confronts reality with all its difficulties and reigns in life by the vital energy of God.

III. We are for the world, but not with the world. President Mackey, of Princeton Theological Seminary, wrote, "We become related to Christ singly, but we cannot live in Christ solitarily." Some people we know live by instinct and mere duty; they go along with everything the world suggests and become wholly identified with its passions. They are with the world. And they leave the world a worse place than they found it. But the Christian who lives by God's grace in Jesus Christ is always for the world—enthusiastically in favor of its betterment, enlightenment, and transformation—although he is never with it in the sense of being a party to its lower desires and baser impulses. He's saved by grace, but not solitarily; he wants the world to be saved, too. And with the sure step of a kingly life, he moves purposefully among men, and by the warmth of Christ's burning presence in his soul, he changes the ordinary into something superior, the rough into smooth, and the dark into light.

This is the destiny of all who receive abundance of grace. They live like kings. And it can begin simply by letting Christ do it for them.—Donald Macleod.

Illustrations

FOR THE WORLD.   Imagine that next summer, as you drive toward your vacation haunt, you overtake a loosely slatted truck in which are herded a tightly packed company of poor and unkempt people. Presently it dawns on you that these are migrant workers being carted to dig potatoes on Long Island or pick grapes in Michigan or California. As you make your way to your vacation cottage, your conscience begins to gnaw away at you. Here you are in this comfort while just on the other side of the road are these people forced to live in huts unfit for human habitation and paid a pittance. Your conscience nags you to the point where you wish to do something. You decide initially to do something on a warm and personal basis, so you buy some candy and a few games, go over to the migrant workers' camp, and befriend a child or two.

You might even go into the second stage and decide to avail yourself of some organized benevolence by relating these boys and girls to a local troop of Boy Scouts or Girl Scouts or the nearby Y. But is it not true that if you really cared about the plight of those people, this would not be enough for you? You would also become concerned about sanitation standards, building codes, the minimum wage, education for migrant children, etc. Your sincerity would get you talking with other people about these matters. Eventually, you would be making your way to Albany or Sacramento or Lansing—and to Washington, D.C.! If we wish to do more than put verbal band-aids over people's wounds, we will of necessity involve ourselves in the changing of laws and structures from what they are to what they ought to be. —Ernest T. Campbell.

AN UNSEEN HAND. The late Henry Sloane Coffin tells of a Scottish minister who, while en route through Niagara, decided to see the falls and visit the famous Cave of the Winds. His description: "It is like living amidst the breakup of an old universe or the creation of a new. You are shut off from the whole world of nature and humanity for the time, enwrapt in this wild smother of thunder and foam. Your only link with the entire world of humanity is the presence of the hand of your guide. You cannot see him, you cannot hear him; all that you are conscious of is a hand with a pull in it."—Donald Macleod.

Sermon Suggestions

THE MINISTRY OF REST. Mark 6:31. What will deliberately contrived seasons of spiritual rest do for the stunned and distracted soul? (1) They will help us to realize the reality of the invisible. (2) We shall gain a bird's-eye view of the field of life and duty. (3) We can obtain the restoration of our squandered and exhausted strength.—J. H. Jowett

LEST WE MISS OUR PROPER DESTINY. Scripture: Isa. 55. (1) We must consider how God thinks. (2) We must change our ways. (3) We must accept God's mercy.— James W. Cox

CALL TO WORSHIP. "Holy, holy, holy, is the Lord of hosts: the whole earth is full of his glory" (Isa. 6:3).

INVOCATION. Almighty God, our Father, from east to west extends thy Kingdom, from north to south, thy royal rule. Come now to reign over this little place on earth and over the heart and life of each of us. So may we glorify thee, thrice-holy God, now and forever.

OFFERTORY SENTENCE. "Honor the Lord with thy substance, and with the first fruits of all thine increase" (Prov. 3:9).

OFFERTORY PRAYER. Loving Father, thou dost care for all living things. Not even a falling sparrow escapes thy notice. Help us in the giving of our gifts to become extensions of our love, especially to thy creatures made in thy image. May the gifts we bring minister to their deepest needs.

PRAYER. God of mercy, many of us cry unto thee out of the depths—depths of discouragement, depths of guilt, depths of loneliness, depths of despair. Our ways have taken us through experiences that test our faith to the breaking point. We are comforted when we remember that thy servants of old, whose names adorn the story of thy people, walked through the valley of the shadow of death, passed through menacing floods, and survived the flames of persecution: David with his sin, Job with his suffering, Jeremiah with his doubt, and our Lord Jesus Christ with his betrayal and crucifixion.

We confess that we are not worthy of thy notice. We are sinners all. Yet thou art a

God of forgiveness. Without that forgiveness, none of us could stand; but because of that forgiveness, we bow trustingly and hopefully before thee.

Take away our estrangement from thee, and the worst of our discouragement, guilt, loneliness, and despair will flee from us. So we look to thee. We hope in thee. We believe that thy love is unfailing and that thou hast power to set us free, that the depths of thy mercy will answer the depths of our need.

EVENING SERVICE

Topic: Rebellion Against Ourselves
SCRIPTURE: 1 Cor. 12:12–21, 26–27.

I. (a) During my first four months as a chaplain intern at a major medical center, one of the units on which I served was a cancer unit. I knew relatively little about cancer when I started on that unit, but gradually I learned about the medical aspects of that disease in its many forms. The most striking realization that I made about cancer, however, was not a medical one, but a philosophical one. One of the doctors put the disease of cancer in profound perspective when he said, "Cancer is the body's rebellion against itself." Some of the cells just "decide" not to cooperate with the other cells any more and begin to grow uncontrollably. The result is that the cancer cells kill other normal cells, destroy bodily organs, and eventually produce death. Cancer, moreover, is very often difficult to detect in its early stages and is difficult to treat. In addition, since all of us possess bodies that contain billions of cells, we are all suseptible to cancer.

(b) Yet, cancer is a disease that strikes not only our human bodies, but also the "body of Christ"—the church. The church, like our human bodies, is comprised of many individual parts- persons who work together to promote its health, vitality, and mission. However, when the members of a church cease to work together harmoniously for its health and vitality, the "body of Christ" then becomes sick. Various groups of cells within the body have rebelled against the body—the result is cancer.

II. (a) The apostle Paul was confronted with a very sick church at Corinth. The "body of Christ" was torn by internal factions that were destroying the health and vitality of the church. Each faction had a leader and each demanded his own way. All of these factions, moreover, behaved like cancer in that they refused to cooperate with the rest of the body and sought their own ends. The final result of their activity would inevitably be death to the "body of Christ."

(b) The apostle Paul, however, was a great physician as well as a great missionary, and he prescribed a stiff dose of corrective medicine for the Corinthian church. He sternly reminded them what it means to be the body of Christ—a fellowship of human beings bound together by bonds of love to the Lord Jesus Christ. These bonds of love fall into three categories: faith, acceptance, and care.

III. (a) We are bound together by our common faith. We all worship the same God. We are all redeemed by the same Christ. We are baptized into the same body of Christ through the same Holy Spirit. We can never alter these realities of our relationship with God and our fellow human beings. We are bound to our fellow human beings to form the body of Christ.

(b) We are all equal to one another, as members of the body of Christ, regardless of our stations in life. There must be nobody within the body who claims superiority over other persons. There must be no persons who are devalued, and no gifts and talents that are exalted above others. On the contrary, we must encourage all persons to glorify and serve God through the effective use of their God-given talents, whatever those talents may be.

(c) We must care for each other's needs. We must always be concerned about the feelings and problems of others and be ready to offer comfort and support to them. There must be no "winners" nor "losers." We must not allow "neglect" to exist within the body. We must take the time to care and nurture one another.—Rodney K. Miller.

SUNDAY: MAY TWENTY-SEVENTH

MORNING SERVICE

Topic: Living in the Here and Now
TEXT: Gal. 2:20

Authentic Christianity is not concerned solely with the next life. Nor is it, as some would have us believe, primarily concerned with the end of the world. Authentic Christianity is concerned with what we do with our life here and now and between the now and the then. Paul wrote to the Galatian Christians and said, "The life I now live in the flesh I live by faith in the Son of God who loved me and gave himself for me." What does this say to us today?

I. *Worthy purpose.* We cannot deny that some of those early Christians lived life only for tomorrow's hope of heaven. But I believe in life before death as similarly God's gift to be used with purpose in the here and now. (a) Christian faith holds that no life is created without a God-given purpose. Some people meander through life and never discover that this applies to them. They live life like a swamp rather than a river—spreading out but seldom going anywhere.

(b) Some reject the purpose God has for them and turn back into a life without a worthy purpose. They get through the days, and that's about all. Many of us have heard God call us to a high purpose for our lives, but we turn aside when we discover that any worthy purpose has a price tag attached.

(c) One way to develop the purpose God has in mind for you is to realize how much you can help change the environment for the better. This includes an effort to conserve, to make good stewardship of the gifts of natural resources which God has provided in the earth and the skies.

(d) Even more significant is the fact that every one of us has a number of social environments of which we are a part and for which we are in part responsible: family, work, school, sports, civic and social organizations, the church—these are among the environments which call forth from all of us an acceptance of a divine purpose. The Christian is empowered of God to change these environments for the better. Could one find a better purpose for life here?

II. *Significant meaning.* When people respond to God's call to worthy purpose in life, they find that life has a deep, abiding, and significant meaning. God provides for us those high and holy moments of spiritual reality which keep life going in the midst of trouble, tragedy, and sorrow. What steps are there to assure us that we can find meaning through such high moments?

(a) We need to let these high moments happen. This is one reason for regularly sharing in the corporate worship of the church. We expose ourselves to these symbols, these elements of liturgy, this place of beauty and devotion, that perchance on occasion such a high moment will be ours.

(b) We need to let our high moments command us. I do not mean we should constantly relive the past—that's deadly. But allowing the implications of such a high moment to command our actions in the here and now can be life-giving! We are called to live out the implications of that moment when God was most real to us, his command most imperative, his power most realized.

III. *Redeeming hope.* Such meaning and purpose bring to the Christian a redeeming sense of hopefulness about the future. (a) To live well in the here and now is not to deny in any sense the richness of the life in the hereafter. Suffice it to suggest that life in the hereafter is life lived closely with God through eternity.

(b) I am convinced that life is fuller and richer over there if we have prepared for it by living richly and fully the life we have been given in the here and now. Then life will have the redeeming hope that the future as well belongs to the God of our todays.

(c) Many of us seem to lose hope in the future because of suffering and sorrow in the present. We conclude that life has little to commend it even beyond the grave, since life today is so overwhelming in its tragic dimension. We assume that when life is tough here, it is tough everywhere. Paul suffered a good bit more than most of us. Yet he could write to the Roman Christians these words that reflect the basic confident hopefulness that belongs to the Christian: Rom. 5:2–5.

(d) Faith in Christ can give us faith in the future by assuring us of the significance of life in the present. Does your situation in life seem to promise only a continuation of suffering and sin? It takes faith to believe that God can produce, that he is as good as his word, that he is able to do for us that which he has promised through Jesus Christ. God is your friend, not your enemy. And it is he who has created your life. Your life is not your enemy, but your friend. When you can accept this, then you will have discovered the kind of hope Paul is talking about, a hope that can redeem you from the roughs of life, that can sustain you in the turbulence of stormy seas, and that can bring assurance of hope for the future.—Hoover Rupert.

Illustrations

HEROES AND HEROISM. Wendell Phillips and a young friend had been sitting by the fire for a whole evening. Memory had flushed the cheeks of the veteran abolitionist; the heroic days of long ago came rushing back upon him; his tongue was unloosed and the old man completely lost himself in the thrilling recital. The youth sat enthralled. At last he realized that the evening was gone. As he rose to leave, he took the old man's hand and said, "Mr. Phillips, if I had lived in your time, I think I should have been heroic, too." And the veteran was aroused, and replied: "Young man, you *are* living in my time, and in God's time. And be sure of this: no man could have been heroic then, who is not heroic now. Good night." So it is. We are still living in heroic times. "Others have labored, and we have entered into their labors." —Andrew Mutch.

VALUES TO LIVE BY. A truly religious marriage requires affinity at three levels—physical, mental, and spiritual. G. K. Chesterton says that when interviewing a housekeeper the crucial question is not "Can you cook?" or "Are you a good housekeeper?" but "What is your view of the universe?" It is even more crucial in choosing a life partner. Differences there may and almost certainly will be in taste, in temperament, in opinion, but not in the basic issues of life—not in standards, values, motives, matters of faith. If marriage is to be success, there must be an essential affinity in the things of the spirit—fundamental agreement as to what is right and what wrong, what is true and what false, what is praiseworthy and what contemptible, what is primary and what secondary. —Robert J. McCracken

Sermon Suggestions

THE "FELLOWSHIP OF THE HOLY SPIRIT." Text: 2 Cor. 13:14 (RSV). (1) Properly understood, the church is itself the fellowship of the Holy Spirit. (2) We experience the fellowship of the Holy Spirit in various kinds of smaller companies that are often a kind of "church-within-the-church." (3) We find the fellowship of the Holy Spirit where the word of God is being preached to people within and without the churches.—Samuel Shoemaker.

THE ALL-TIME FAVORITE TEXT. Text: John 3:16. Why do we love it? (1) It appeals to our instinct of self-preservation: we do not want our lives to come to nothing. (2) It appeals to our sense of need for cosmic support: only the love of God can satisfy our deepest hunger for security. (3) It appeals to our sense of what is right and fair: it is for everybody.—James W. Cox

Worship Aids

CALL TO WORSHIP. "He that hath an ear, let him hear what the Spirit saith unto the churches" (Rev. 2:29).

INVOCATION. Speak now to us, O God. Tell us again of thy loving judgment, which ferrets out the wrong in our lives, to make life better and happier for us all. Tell us again of thy judging love, which brings to life again the dying embers of neglected faith, to give new purpose and drive to our futile wanderings. And may we carefully listen as thou dost speak to us.

OFFERTORY SENTENCE.   "Bring ye all the tithes into the storehouse, that there may be meat in mine house, and prove me now herewith, saith the Lord of hosts, if I will not open you the windows of heaven, and pour you out a blessing, that there shall not be room enough to receive it" (Mal. 3:10).

OFFERTORY PRAYER.   Almighty and most benevolent heavenly Father, bless the giving of these gifts as a symbol of our renewed dedication to thy service. Consecrate our resolve to respond more readily to the leading of thy Holy Spirit, that we may live lives of greater devotion and more fruitful service. —Rodney K. Miller

PRAYER.   Almighty God, in whom alone we live, we turn in all our need to thee, the fountain of our life. Thou hast made all things dependent upon thee for their existence, and thou hast made our hearts so that they fail without the inspiration of thy presence. Forgive us if, knowing this, we have been careless about that which should be our chief concern, if we have taken no pains to establish a life of communion with thee, if we have not hungered and thirsted after righteousness. We have been slack in prayer, careless in living, until we have found glory departing from the earth and thy rest from our hearts. We thank thee that thou dost never withdraw thyself from us without our knowing that the Spirit of God has departed. Thou makest us quickly to cry after thee. O visit us early with thy mercy, satisfy us with thyself, for thou art out God. Bind us to thee with the bond of an endless love. Find us in the wilderness, lead us to where fountains of living waters flow, shepherd us where flowers for everbloom. Bring us in sight, most Gracious One, of the Cross, at once life's mystery and life's healing. And may our foolish wandering and false self-worship come to an end this day. Hold us, for thou art stronger than we. Forgive us, for thou art kinder than we dare to be.— W. E. Orchard.

EVENING SERVICE

Topic: The Second Touch
TEXT: Mark 8:24–25

(a) Every new religious fad or fashion attracts many followers. All this is evidence of spiritual hunger. The issue is whether we can convert this hunger into spiritual growth.

(b) Nineteen centuries ago Jesus healed a blind man at Bethsaida. At our Lord's first touch, the man opened his eyes. When asked, "Do you see anything?" he replied, "I see men, but they look like trees walking." His vision was dim and confused. Then Christ laid his hand a second time on the man's eyes. The record is that "he looked intently and was restored and saw all things clearly."

(c) People are hungry for something more than secular living gives. They are waking up to the fact that there is something more. Can this awakening be made into a revival of real religion?

I. First we need the second touch of Christ to transform the seekers into servants of Christ. Jesus drew great multitudes at the beginning of his ministry. Some came to be healed, some came to be fed, some came out of mere curiosity. But Christ did not start his church with the 5,000 whom he fed with the loaves and fishes. He had to develop a core of trained disciples to carry on his work. Likewise today, Christ must count on consecrated disciples rather than on crowds of the curious and self-seeking.

(a) No modern method of gaining spiritual power and peace can be substituted for Christ's original command: "If any man would come after me, let him deny himself and take up his cross and follow me." The good life starts with the will. Jesus said, "Blessed are the pure in heart, for they shall see God." "The pure in heart" are those who are pure in will and motive. They want to know God's will whether it be pleasing to them or not.

(b) We know the general direction of the divine will, for we see it revealed in Jesus Christ. If we are to transform religious awakening into real revival, the first question to answer is this, Do we want to be like Christ? Do we want it enough to surrender our wills to him?

II. We need Christ's second touch to advance us from servants to friends. As he came to the close of his earthly ministry, Jesus said to his disciples: "No longer do I call you servants, for the servant does not know what his master is doing; but I have called you friends, for all that I have heard from my Father I have made known to you." It is not enough to say, "Come to Jesus," or even, "Follow Jesus"; we must learn what it means to follow him. We must study and teach Christ until we enter into understanding friendship with him.

(a) We must gain an understandable and an adequate view of the historic Jesus. The Bible makes this possible if properly taught. Every great religious awakening in the history of Christianity has been preceded and accompanied by a revival of Bible study.

(b) When we let our minds dwell long enough on Christ, he comes to life in our lives as the Eternal Contemporary. He is right beside us. He is ever present.

(c) When we thus become friends of Christ, we not only have an understanding of what Christ means; we also come to like what he liked. Our minds are convinced, and our tastes are converted. One of the weaknesses of traditional evangelism is that it did not go on to a cultivation of the taste. A person is not safely good until he feels good being good. And certainly he is not contagiously good or convincingly Christian until his tastes have been brought into harmony with Christ's. A genuine Christian carries his virtues with an easy grace which makes goodness attractive to others.

(d) We need to convert the will, convince the mind, and cultivate the taste. Viewed in this light, religious education is the task of the whole church to train the whole man for the whole life. Think what the twentieth-century homes and churches, with their modern equipment, could do if they caught the spirit of the early Christians, of whom it was written, "And every day in the temple and at home they did not cease teaching and preaching Jesus as the Christ."

III. We need Christ's second touch to advance us to a third stage, from friend to witness. Luke closes his Gospel by recording the risen Christ as saying, "You are witnesses of these things."

(a) The word *witness* may be used has two obviously different meanings. If you were to go to a courtroom tomorrow where a trial was in progress, you could take your seat in the spectators' section and thereby become a witness of the trial. But up near the judge's bench and the jury box is a seat reserved for those who give testimony. It is called the witness chair. Those who take that seat are not mere witnesses *of* the trial. They are witnesses *at* the trial. The word *witness* as used by the risen Christ means one who testifies. And I believe that is the word our Lord would say to us.

(b) Our world needs witnesses who give testimony for Christ. The trial of Christ is on today, between the spiritual and the worldly. The spectators' gallery is well filled. The counsel table is staffed. But the acute need is for more witnesses to take the chair and testify for their Lord. An ounce of personal testimony is worth a ton of professional propaganda financed by silent spectators.

(c) Our best hope of a great religious revival in America is through the pew rather than the pulpit. The early Christians were just an unprofessional company of the friends of Jesus telling and demonstrating what they knew of their Lord. The contagion of their faith spread like wildfire through the Mediterranean world. What a mighty revival of religion we could have within a year's time if laypeople would start talking about their religious experience in the same straightforward, matter-of-fact manner which they use in discussing their everyday affairs.—Ralph W. Sockman.

SUNDAY: JUNE THIRD

MORNING SERVICE

Topic: Where is the Love of Jesus Now?
TEXT: Eph. 4:9, 10.

I heard one of the senior permanent officers of the United Nations Organization talking about the state of the world and what he sees ahead for the human race. He declared his belief in the possibility of transforming human conduct by a response to the right kind of religion, and ended by confessing that, for him, the star of hope for our world is that invisible and immensely potent power that goes by the name of love.

You expect to hear that from a preacher. It comes with much more force from a diplomat. But it is in tune with what others are perceiving, in this time of confusion and threat.

Yet, there is one question that nags us all. What confidence can we have that, in the world invisible that lies around us, love is really supreme? Does it really look as if our world were ultimately in the control of a God of love? Every one of us here could produce evidence to the contrary.

So many are tempted to think: Sure, the love of Jesus was great while it lasted, but where is the love of Jesus now? After all, didn't they hang him on a cross till he died? And with him was there not buried that brief, bright flicker of what human life is meant to be? In spite of our brave Easter hymns, in spite of our prayers to the Father invoking Jesus' name, doesn't it sometimes look as though this love of Jesus was an episode in the human story, for which we are grateful, but which no longer throbs in the heart of any God we know? Where is the love of Jesus now?

I reached this point in preparing my sermon last Ascension Day. Suddenly I felt drawn to worship. So, I slipped off down the avenue to our neighbors at St. James Episcopal, where there was a Noonday Ascension Service, with Holy Communion. I came back refreshed, and more sure than ever, that there are some things that can only be expressed in worship, in a living communion with Christ himself, rather than in the convolutions of our thinking. But, the words of the Nicene Creed came through loud and clear. I was meeting the Christ who, "for us and for our salvation, came down from heaven," and, after his death and resurrection, "ascended into heaven." These words chimed in with the rather difficult text on which I was working: "He who descended is no other than he who ascended, so that he might fill the universe."

Some find difficulty in this language about descending and ascending, or so preachers are led to believe. I doubt if many are really incapable of understanding a metaphor and have a mental picture of Jesus going down and up in some invisible elevator. So, it's not too hard to understand that the Bible can speak of heaven as *up*, the sphere of all that is good and true and beautiful, from which Christ came "down to earth" and even, as our text says, "to the lowest level which is hell on earth."

In the great cosmic drama of the gospel, Christ brought God's love right down here. He descended into our human nature, he descended into the sufferings and despair of human beings who were being pulled down by evil forces, he descended into that agony of desolation where he seemed abandoned by his God. If that were the entire drama, it would have no consolation for us. Even if we are told that he rose again from the dead, how would we know that now all was well? A resurrection two thousand years ago could mean little to anyone looking for the love of Christ right now, where *we* live. Jesus, we are told, this Jesus whose love we want to know, carried that love back to the heart of God. The love of Jesus is now there, and for ever there (see Eph. 4:16).

What an extraordinary thing to say about one who lived and died so long ago —that he now "fills the universe." Where is the love of Jesus now? In the all-pervading Spirit that is to be found in the world invisible. Human love, as we see it in

Jesus, is now and forever the divine love that nothing can ultimately frustrate.

The New Testament doesn't offer us a story of miraculous levitation. It simply tells us that, after the risen Christ had appeared on various occasions to his disciples, he vanished from their physical sight. In all the four gospels, all that is said about the ascension as an incident, are the laconic words of Luke: "Then he led them out as far as Bethany, and blessed them with uplifted hands; and in the act of blessing he parted from them." That's all. Luke fills out the story a little more in the opening of his Book of the Acts, but almost all that we read about the ascension in the New Testament is in the epistles where all the emphasis is on the triumph of Jesus who now reigns from the heart of God. The love of Jesus now fills the universe. To believe that is to face our daily round, and the alarming news that fills our TV screens, with a new strength and an indomitable hope.

In this epistle, the words of our text, about the Christ who descends to the lowest level and then ascends "far above all heavens, so that he might fill the universe," are a kind of parentheses. The passage is dealing with what are called "spiritual gifts." The apostle lists the various ways in which church members are to reflect the love of Christ (vv. 11–12). Elsewhere, we are told that it was the ascended Christ who poured out these gifts of the Spirit on his people. And Paul tells us in another place that every single one of us has a gift to be offered for the spiritual enrichment of us all. But, in a famous passage, he makes it clear what is the greatest gift of all. "Now I will show you the best way of all," he writes, and then follow the glorious words that end: "the greatest of these is love."

So, we arrive at another answer to our question: "Where is the love of Jesus now?" It is to be found wherever a group of ordinary people, with differing temperaments and gifts reflect that love in their common life and action.

Churches, like all other institutions, are going through agonies of self-appraisal these days. Our goal must be that of which the Scripture speaks (vv. 13, 15–16). That is the one question to ask: "Is all that we do, in worship, in fellowship, in service, and in social action, helping to create a community where the love of Jesus can be found?"—David H. C. Read.

Illustrations

THE SECOND COMING.   Our task, in connection with the second coming, is neither that of denial on the one hand nor precise dating on the other, but simple obedience to witness and to work now, doing the tasks which are within our scope.—Elton Trueblood.

UNDEFEATED HOPE.   On the roof of a church around the corner from where I live is the figure of the angel Gabriel, his horn lifted to his mouth, ready to give out with a mighty blast to announce the second coming of our Lord in glory. Day after day, he stands there at the ready. Warmed by the summer sun, frozen by winter sleet, year after year goes by, but there is no mighty blast. Not even a tentative toot. Below him are the streets of the city, crawling with traffic, edged with apartment houses and slums harboring birth and death and love and conflict and a thousand shattered hopes between dawn and sunset every day. What is this hope but feeble, wishful thinking? . . . Perhaps the future of the angel Gabriel standing high above the streets of New York, his horn raised to his lips, is not so ridiculous or irrelevant after all. For that figure, high above the city below, is the constant reminder, day in and day out, year in and year out, that God's will of love *will* be done.—Edmund Steimle.

Sermon Suggestions

HE MOUNTS IN TRIUMPH.   Text: Acts 1:9. (1) Our Lord was not taken *away* from us (see Matt. 28:20). (2) Our humanity is now in highest heaven. (3) the ascension is the most emphatic sign of victory. (4) On the other side of death is a known and dear Friend.—W. E. Sangster.

CHRIST AT THE DOOR.   Text: Rev. 3:20. I. Christ's position. II. Where Christ stands, there is pressure. III. Where Christ presses, there is promise.—R. E. O. White.

Worship Aids

CALL TO WORSHIP. "Since then we have a great high priest who has passed through the heavens, Jesus, the Son of God, let us hold fast our confession. For we have not a high priest who is unable to sympathize with our weaknesses, but one who in every respect has been tempted as we are, yet without sin. Let us then with confidence draw near to the throne of grace, that we may receive mercy and find grace to help in time of need" (Heb. 4:14 –16 [RSV]).

INVOCATION. O God, we come to thee with boldness this day, not because we are worthy, but because thou hast assured us that we may come, that mercy is available, and that our needs will be met. Give us a fresh vision of our Savior, our great high priest, who sympathizes with all our weaknesses and has power to strengthen us at our most vulnerable points.

OFFERTORY SENTENCE. "Every good gift and every perfect gift is from above, and cometh down from the Father of lights, with whom is no variableness, neither shadow or turning" (Jas. 1:17).

OFFERTORY PRAYER. We thank thee, our Father, for thy many gifts, which have continued to bless us in spite of our unworthiness. Help us to learn from thee how to be faithful, in season and out of season.

PRAYER. Most gracious and benevolent heavenly Father, heal the many pains, doubts, and frustrations that daily assail us. Enter into our lives with thy empowering presence that we may know thy comforting and sustaining Spirit. Help us to be the persons that thou hast created us to be through the putting aside of our pride, egotism, selfishness, indifference, and fear, which drive us from thee. Create in us, O Lord, clean hearts that are capable of loving thee with ever greater constancy and devotion. Grant that our healing, given through thy Spirit, may help us to reach out in a spirit of love and fellowship to those about us. Give unto us, O Lord, the courage and commitment to share of ourselves with those in distress, despair, and need, that we may truly be thy hands in this thy world.—Rodney K. Miller.

EVENING SERVICE

Topic: Christ Will Come Again (Ascension Sunday)

SCRIPTURE: Luke 21:25–28.

In the text, we are confronted with a succession of statements about coming events. First, people faint and fear with foreboding of *what is coming*. Then it is said that they will see *the Son of man coming*. And finally, this is explained by the words, *"Your salvation is drawing near."* So the question, "What?" is answered by the statement, "He!" and the relevance of him is identified with "salvation."

I. Whether we use the Bible for better or worse, whether or not we like, respect, and understand it, this book contains the promise of God that what salvation we need from all distress and perplexity is to come from and in the person of Jesus Christ.

(a) Of course, we all are inclined to greet such a promise with grave doubts or frank disbelief. But God has his own ways to substantiate and to verify his promise against our emotional or scholarly skepticism. When seven hundred years before Jesus Christ's birth—at a time of most confused and confusing military and political constellations—the prophet Isaiah announced that the birth of a baby called Emmanuel, "God with us," would be the sign of redemption from misery, who would have believed that this would ultimately mean nothing less than Christmas, the coming of God himself upon earth in the form of a baby? And yet Christmas came. The Word was incarnate. God himself became our helper. The fulfillment of God's promise has actually transcended the keenest literal or spiritual interpretation of those prophetic words.

(b) And again, after the incarnation had taken place, who would have believed that

God would carry out his association with man to the extent that Jesus Christ would voluntarily choose and follow the way of the cross? Whether or not we like to believe it, he did exactly this. In Christmas and Calvary, and finally in Christ's vindication by the resurrection, God showed man the way in which a divine promise is verified. If worst comes to worst, God himself has to be the man who comes to our rescue.

(c) Can we, do we believe this? We cannot help but believe it. Or else, why do we continue to pray, "Thy Kingdom come"? Why do we celebrate Christmas? Why do we look up to the cross and to the resurrection? "I believe; help my unbelief!" We know that if there is any help left, God alone is left as our helper.

Before he came in fleshly appearance, he gave his word that he would come. When he came, he pointed out that he would come again. It is typical of the evangelist Luke to affirm this again and again. The time and the events of his first advent are also the pattern and model of the time and the events to come. "This Jesus will come in the same way as you saw him go."

II. But do not believe those voices whispering or shouting that Christ, that our faith and our salvation, is exhausted by some past events! By being fulfilled once, God's promise is not simply over. We need hope for a specified future as much as we need knowledge of those specific past events that molded us.

(a) Scientists are looking with ever-increasing skills into the causal connection between the past and the present. There is no conflict between natural sciences and faith in God, if we realize, with Teilhard de Chardin, that God gave man a future and a purpose toward which to move. God does not push us around as do the forces of the past, of the environment, or of our own nature. Rather, through the Bible, he wants to give and to manifest to us a direction and hope which cannot possibly be derived from laws of nature. It is God alone who gives us a future, a destiny, a hope.

(b) Therefore, it is not true that we live in a godless age, a post-Christian era, or— as some would have it—in a god-forsaken mess. Christ came and will come again: these two advents are the grip in which God holds us, as though they were his left hand and his right hand. As the present era started with the man Jesus Christ, it will also be terminated by the same Jesus Christ (Acts 17:31).

III. Why should it be relevant that precisely this man stands at the end of all things—as it is written, "Then they will see the Son of man coming with power and great glory"? Why does Jesus always speak of the "Son of man" when he speaks of the last things and the judgment?

(a) Nobody and nothing else but Jesus Christ himself will appear for judgment. The man Jesus Christ is appointed to come again—he who is the stranger among all nations, races, groups; the Jew bare of beauty and comeliness; the servant who does not recommend himself; the associate of the poor and needy. He and no one else will be judge before whom we are to stand. His standard is the gauge with which we shall be measured.

(b) The final Judge will have the appearance of a man. We are promised that to the Son of man is given the final word and decision. The last judgment will be not only a vindication of God; it will also be the vindication of man. Notwithstanding his divine origin and commission, the Judge will bear the likeness of those he is to judge. He himself will be their advocate, the advocate of humanity!

(c) This is the reason why the same words of Jesus that speak so realistically and movingly of man's tremors in the time of judgment conclude with the ring of encouragement and hope (Luke 25:28). Indeed, Jesus Christ will be judge of all of us —but his judgment is a judgment of grace. His coming is the triumph of humanity.

(d) Here is more than daydreaming and wishful thinking. Here is the only reason not to despair of the cause of man. The promised Parousia of Jesus Christ is a ground to stand upon. He is better than the hope of a final dissolution and lapse into senselessness. He is that future and ending which is worth clinging to and waiting for.—Markus Barth.

SUNDAY: JUNE TENTH

MORNING SERVICE

Topic: Let Religion Be Religious (Pentecost)

SCRIPTURE: 2 Cor. 5:14–17.

It was at Pentecost that the Christian faith finally came into full flame in the life of the followers of Jesus, that their relationship to him became truly faithful, fully religious. Up to that point, they had been wavering and floundering. They had really only been observers before. Now they were true participants.

To get at the meaning of Pentecost, go to a piece of theological reflection found in St. Paul's Second Letter to the Corinthians (5:14–17).

I. "From now on," he says, "the new has come." What is the old, and what is the new, and what is the "now" of transition?

(a) The "old" is obviously the human point of view, the worldly way of looking at things according to the flesh. He indicates that even Christ can be considered from this perspective— that is, simply historically, factually, commonsensically. But it is an "old" perspective.

(b) It is here that a "new" point of view must be found, says Paul: "From now on, we regard no one from a human point of view." What is the new perspective, then? An inward or existential awareness of identification with Christ, a relationship of mutual love and self-giving. It is obviously a "responsive" or an interpretive stance, a commitment to a spiritual view of things. It takes the historical facts about Jesus, even the most drastic fact of all, his cruel death on the cross, and finds them all symbolic of religious meaning. Paul could look the ugly fact straight in the face and say: "He died for me, and such love and sacrifice demands my life, my soul, my all!" From that moment, everything was new. He was now "in Christ," and Christ was "in" him.

II. We do not, in the New Testament, have the kind of straight recordings of historical events which simply describe the actual, objective happenings. Instead, the stories mix together fact and faith, interpreting facts faithfully and expressing faith factually.

(a) In view of this, it is so much the more surprising to find that in none of these stories is there made any attempt whatever at glorifying the picture of the disciples, tidying up the impression of confusion and blundering which they leave on practically every page.

(b) There was one bright moment of understanding and revelation, though. Peter, in response to Jesus' direct question, did manage to utter the key confession, "Thou art the Christ, the Son of the living God." But when Jesus took the lead from it and began to tell them what now lay ahead of him, Peter fell flat on his face again, not understanding why such tragedy could not be avoided. So, just as soon as it had come to him, revelation obviously was gone from him again. And Jesus said: "Peter, you are on the side of men, and not of God." It was this way, it seems, all the time. Never did these disciples really get a hold of what it was all about. So, when Jesus died, they also seemed to be finished. "We had hoped that he was the one to redeem Israel," they said, commiserating about what had happened. Then suddenly, there he was, appearing again in the story in his old role as a frustrated teacher: "O you foolish men," he said, "how slow you are to believe."

(c) How did these people ever find the "new," when they were so solidly stuck in the "old"? Well, there are these pointers that keep recurring. They are actually promises of something more, something dramatic that was to take place, something essential that was to happen to them ("I have yet many things to say to you, but you cannot bear them now. . . . I did not say these things from the beginning, because I was with you. But now I am going . . . . It is to your advantage that I go away, for if I do not go away, the Counselor will not come to you. . . . The Counselor, the Holy Spirit, whom the Father will send in my name, he will teach you all things and bring to your remembrance all that I have said to you. . . . He will glorify me, for he will take what is mine and declare it to you" (John 14, 16). I said these are pointers to something more; they are actually pointers toward Pentecost (see Luke 24: 49; John 14:16, Acts 1:4–5, 1:8).

Those were the promises of the new, and Pentecost was the answer. I am not thinking of the odd phenomenon of "speaking in tongues." Much more significant by far was the dramatic change which occurred in them. Look at Peter, for example, the very same man who had pulled Jesus aside at Caesarea Philippi and told him that suffering and death must at all price be avoided. Now he stood forth and testified openly (Acts 2:23, 33, 36). What had happened was nothing less than a transformation! Now, at this point, Peter at last understood the gospel. Before, he had looked at everything "from a human point of view"; now he was "on the side of God," and "the new" had come.

III. Now, finally, if this understanding of Pentecost points to the true nature of the Christian faith and life, what are the consequences for our life and faith now? What is it to be a Christian now?

(a) The "more" that we are talking about is not simply a matter of quantity. It is quality. It is the result of a transformation of the inner man, not just an extension of our outward reach. It is actually the outcome of a "conversion," a *metanoia*, the transformation of one's mind, one's point of view. It is to have "the mind of Christ," to be "in him," in his love, or as the Pentecost story expresses it, "to be filled with the Holy Spirit."

(b) And I must struggle with it, for I want to understand what it is that makes our religion truly religious. It is an old struggle. And I can see the church is struggling with it also, everyone of us very much the same way. We do not really find spiritual satisfaction in the outward observation of a ritual of worship. We do not in the final analysis find personal fulfillment simply in performing the duties we have, responsibly. Nor do we, when all is told, find ultimate meaning in the theoretical understanding of Christian teachings.

(c) Is it, perhaps, that our religion is still "old," still human—not "new," not "in-

spired"? Is it, perchance, that we have not yet reached the moment when we are "convinced" within, when our worship is worship in spirit and truth, when our ethics are the ethics of free responsibility, and when our theology is a glad confession of faithful reflection? Have we, perhaps, not yet become true lovers of God? On our side of Pentecost, the side of confusion and wavering and floundering, Jesus the Christ still stands before us, and he lifts his hands above us, as with the first of the faithful, and he breathes our way and says: "Receive ye the Holy Spirit."—Thor Hall.

Illustrations

POWER OF THE SPIRIT.   A great biblical scholar, H. Wheeler Robinson had a serious illness, during which it seemed that the truths of the Christian faith which he had preached to others now failed to bring him personal strength. They seemed true to him, but they lacked vitality. They demanded more faith than he had the physical energy to generate. He imagined that the truth of the faith was like a giant balloon, "with ample lifting power—if only one had the strength to grasp the rope that trailed down from it." What brought him out of his despondency and weakness was a fresh understanding of the Holy Spirit, God's real presence in his life. He trusted God to do for him what he could not do for himself.

AN UNSEEN PRESENCE.   Some years ago, a little company of Russian peasants met for worship. While their worship was proceeding, suddenly the door was flung open, and there entered an agent of the secret police, followed by a body of his men. "Take these people's names," he commanded. They were warned to wait their summons, and then the agent turned to go. But one old man in the little group stopped him at the door and said, "There is one name you have not got." The officer looked at him in surprise. "I assure you that you are mistaken. I have them all!" "Believe me," said the old peasant, "there is one name you have not got." "Well, we'll prove it, we'll count again!" And they did—verified every name they had taken and recounted the number. There were thirty. "You see!" cried the official of police. "I have them all, every one. I told you I had!" But still the peasant persisted. "There is one name you have not got." "Who is it, then?" "The Lord Jesus Christ. He is here!" "Ah," sneered the officer, "that is a different matter."—James S. Stewart.

Sermon Suggestions

POWER OF PENTECOST.   Text: Acts 1:11. The essential element in unity and the growing together of the churches lies in its local manifestations. (1) Christianity is a local religion and Pentecost is tested by its local power. (2) Christianity is an amalgam of dialogue and decision. (3) The Christian church today is a foreshadowing of the Great Church to be.—Cecil Northcott.

NEW STRENGTH FOR COMMON TASKS. Luke 4:39. (1) Health is imparted at the touch of the Lord. (2) Health is sustained in the channels of service. (3) Our field of service must first be sought in the need that is most immediate.—J. H. Jowett.

Worship Aids.

CALL TO WORSHIP.   "Ye shall receive power, after that the Holy Ghost is come upon you: and ye shall be witnesses unto me both in Jerusalem, and in all Judaea, and in Samaria, and unto the uttermost part of the earth" (Acts 1:8).

INVOCATION.   Open thy Word to us this hour, O Lord. Increase our acquaintance with Christ. Seal truth in our hearts, and by thy Spirit, bind us in the fellowship of thy love that knows no end.—E. Lee Phillips.

OFFERTORY SENTENCE.   "Offer the right sacrifices to the Lord, and put your trust in him" (Ps. 4:5 [TEV]).

OFFERTORY PRAYER.   Teach us, good Lord, to serve thee as thou deservest: to give and not to count the cost; to fight and not to heed the wounds; to toil and not to seek for rest; to labor and not to ask for any reward, save that of knowing that we do thy will.—St. Ignatius Loyola.

PRAYER.   Holy God, Uncreated Light, near yet far away, within and without the focus of our soul's adoration and our life's delight, we pause to worship thee and ponder the alluring silence of thy Mystery.

We confess our shortcomings and sins: criticizing, when we should have listened; speaking, when quiet should have silenced our hearts; dividing truth to suit our purposes, instead of heeding truth to edify our souls; waiting for opportunities, instead of creating them; hoping for maturity, instead of claiming our gifts and joining in to do our part.

We have harbored guilt overlong so we could wallow in self-pity. We have denied our anger and dumped it on an innocent party. We have courted evil that now, viewed in retrospect, is difficult to forgive or forget. We realize, Father, if we confess our sins, thou art faithful and just to forgive our sins and to cleanse us from all unrighteousness. Orchestrate the music of our souls to sing the joy notes of thy mercy.

We are especially grateful today for a country of religious freedom where the founding fathers left wide open the door to religious diversity and rejected any set form of religious conformity. Grace us with liberty's preciousness, without which freedom's privilege is a mockery.

Hear our prayer for those among us in the throes of pain or grief or rejection. Stabilize them in the storm. Undergird those, who, were it not for Scripture, incarnation, and this fellowship of believers, would long ago have succumbed to temptation. Enfold those whose secret turmoil we do not know, whose private struggle seems more than they can bear, and allow them a special sense of thy presence until they are met by cleared light and can risk again a reach to one another.

We do not always know how to pray as we ought, but we do know, though our prayers be worded awry, thou wilt answer the intent of our hearts. So, just for a while, just for these moments, here in this place, let our hearts beat more of Christ than of self, and rise with golden choruses of praise that surround thy endless throne and at last are met by peace.—E. Lee Phillips.

EVENING SERVICE

Topic: Finding Your Place in the Spirit

SCRIPTURE: 1 Cor. 12:4–11.

There was a time when the baptism of the Holy Spirit seemed to be the special interest and unique emphasis of Pentecostal churches. But today, Christians of all denominations are expressing increased interest in the Spirit-filled life.

This concern which claims our attention today, then, takes us back to the Christian congregation at Corinth. Many unusual developments had taken place there. Charismatic experiences had become the norm for that community; indeed, some say things had gotten out of hand. Certain issues had come to St. Paul's attention which he felt called upon to clarify. His clarification speaks directly to the issues many Christians are raising in our time of charismatic excitement (see vv. 4–7).

The Holy Spirit cannot be limited to one person's experience of him; nor is the Spirit's creativity exhausted in one type of manifestation. Note three meanings of that theme: finding your place in the Spirit.

I. The first meaning is discovering your personal relationship to the Spirit.

(a) It is not enough to talk about the Holy Spirit. Jesus said when the comforter is come, he shall be in you. This points to a personal experience which is closer than breathing, deeper than thought. Perhaps this is what Jesus was talking about when he encountered Nicodemus: "Verily I say unto Nicodemus, it's not enough for you to interview me about the work I'm doing; you must be born again." What is this business, being born again? Whatever else one may answer, it involves coming to the conviction that life in God is real—coming to recognize that life apart from response to God stands in need of repentance. To be born again is to have a spiritual experience. It may or may not be accompanied by any unusual signs or any great wonders, but it signals new life. To be born again is to have a complete new basis for life.

(b) Now beyond this conversation about being born again—or being converted, as some call it—there is an experience which indicates that the believer has so opened himself or herself to the control of the Spirit, that there is within the believer, to a degree not characteristic of nominal Christians, a spiritual presence which brings peace, joy, love, and power. It is my conviction, and I think St. Paul urges us in this direction, that every believer ought to have such an experience that he or she can come to a fundmental conviction that God is really at work in one's life—sustaining, lifting, transforming, and empowering.

II. There is another level, however, of what we mean when we say "finding one's place in the Spirit." That level is discovering the particular gift and manifestation of the Spirit in one's personal life. St. Paul has already said in our text: "There are diversities of gifts, but the same Spirit." There is no one set pattern. St. Paul speaks of a body—hand, foot, eye, ear—all different, located in different places, but all contributing to the wholeness of the body.

(a) There is one Spirit. Quite diverse gifts, but one Spirit. Therefore, a need for us in discovering the particular gifts and manifestations of the Spirit is to overcome the temptation to imitation.

(b) Not only the temptation to imitate somebody else's piety, but a real fear to let the Holy Spirit be free in our lives.

III. Let us look at a third basis of what we mean when we speak of finding one's place in the Spirit. It is discovering one's place in the Spirit's plan. It is good for us to know how we fit into the broader picture. In factories, it has been discovered that if a person making a part has no understanding of how that part fits with the other parts being prepared in that factory, the quality of work will be reduced. So it is in the body of Christ. If we have no sense of how the little part I play on my corner fits into the little part you play in your congregation, we are robbed of the sense of the wholeness of the mission we are about. It's important for each one of us to find out: Where does the Spirit stand in my life? What gifts has the Spirit made available in my life? And in what way does my little task fit into the broader responsibility towards which God moves us in this day?—James Forbes.

SUNDAY: JUNE SEVENTEENTH

MORNING WORSHIP

Topic: How Shall We Think of God?
TEXT: John 14:5–11; 1 Tim. 3:16.

How shall we think of God? I suspect many Christians know God in personal experience but are unsure of how to picture him.

This is the problem at the heart of the doctrine of the Trinity. The creed says that God is Father, Son, and Holy Spirit. Through this formulation, our Christian forefathers intended to convey the reality of God in a way that made him more understandable. It was precisely the special relationship of Jesus to the Father that made the doctrine of the Trinity necessary. His was a relationship of such intimacy and devotion that the early church realized that here was a special manifestation of the eternal God himself. The question, "How shall we think of God?" was answered by the church's memory of Jesus' statement, "He that has seen me has seen the Father." At least three purposes are served by the doctrine to aid our thinking about God.

I. The doctrine of the Trinity serves as a summary of the Christian faith.

(a) Notice that there is no explicit doctrine of the Trinity in the Bible or particularly in the New Testament. There are trinitarian statements which became the basis for later developments leading to the doctrine of the Trinity (Matt. 28:19; 2 Cor. 13:14).

(b) As the early church reflected upon its experience with Jesus, it was necessary to modify the Old Testament picture of God. By presenting God as Father, the church affirmed the God who is creator of us all. He is the God of Israel and the Father of Jesus Christ. However, he is not just the all-powerful God and judge portrayed in the Old Testament. He is to be thought of as intimate and loving—a portrait drawn by the image of the Son. The third element is his all-pervasive presence experienced as the power and immediacy of the Holy Spirit.

(c) Each of these elements affirms what the church has experienced in its relationship to God. As Father, he is eternally God, the originator and sustainer of all creation. God is also to be thought of as Son. In Jesus was "the image of the invisible God" (Col. 1:15). The third element is that God is Spirit, which preserves the fact of God's activity in power in the world. God is literally everywhere in power, love, and mercy, moving toward us that we may know his salvation.

All three elements are necessary to our thinking of God. No one element standing alone is sufficient to convey the fullness of God or the richness of his revelation. Each element helps to fill out the Christian understanding of God who revealed himself to Israel and was made manifest in Jesus and works in power as Spirit.

II. The second purpose or function of the doctrine of the Trinity is to preserve the mystery of God. Having affirmed the variety and power of the revelation of God, there is still a great deal not known about God. Who would pretend to fathom fully the "depths and riches of his being" (1 Tim. 3:16)? Revelation both reveals and conceals. One knows God but knows he does not know all there is to know of God. Each element taken alone is idolatrous, but all taken together remind us of his mysterious greatness (Rom. 11:33–34).

III. The third function of the doctrine of the Trinity is to aid our knowledge of God. Each element is inadequate to convey the full reality of God, but each image is faithful and to be trusted.

(a) The doctrine of the Trinity asserts that those who take refuge in agnosticism are playing games. God can be known, for he has revealed himself to humanity. He continues to reveal himself to people of faith and sincere hearts. The claim that one cannot know God is a refusal to acknowledge that God has made himself known in a variety of ways.

(b) The most concrete and personal portrait we have of God is in Jesus Christ.

The Christian understanding of God begins in what we know of Jesus. W. T. Conner said, "Jesus is the only God that I shall ever know." He was not saying that Jesus was all there is of God, but that the most perfect knowledge of God he had is that seen in Jesus Christ. We are able to know him at our level of understanding as one who lives, walks, and talks among us. Truly he has "dwelt among us" (John 1: 14).

(c) The second move of God toward us was at Pentecost. There God's purpose to dwell in us and among us in power was revealed. He wishes to make residence in us that we might become living incarnations of his word—Paul D. Simmons.

Illustrations

THE HOLY SPIRIT.   This is what divine Spirit means: God present to our spirit. Spirit is not a mysterious substance; it is not a part of God. It is God himself; not God as the creative ground of all things and not God directing history and manifesting himself in its central event, but God as present in communities and personalities, grasping them, inspiring them, and transforming them.—Paul Tillich.

KEEPER OF THE VINEYARDS.   As I come near to the end of my days, the one thing that haunts me more than anything else is that I have been so unsatisfactory a husband and a father. As the Song of Solomon has it: "They made me keeper of the vineyards; but my own vineyard I have not kept."—William Barclay.

Sermon Suggestions

THE MYSTERY OF THE TRINITY.   Text: 1 Tim. 3:16. That is a kind of compressed creed, telling the story of the incarnation, finishing with the ascension, and with a phrase also about the work of the Holy Spirit. So this text may serve to remind us of two great truths symbolized by the doctrine of the Trinity: (1) How mysterious God is! (2) How accessible God is!—Donald M. Baillie.

FOUNDATIONS.   Text: Matt. 7:24–27. (1) All men are building. (2) All builders have a choice of foundations. (3) All foundations will be tried. (4) Only one foundation will stand.—J. Solomon Benn, III.

Worship Aids

CALL TO WORSHIP.   "Out of my distress I called on the Lord; the Lord answered me and set me free" (Ps. 118:5 [RSV]).

INVOCATION.   Today, heavenly Father, teach us, thy disobedient children, that in thy will is our peace. And grant that those of us who are fathers may learn from thee the importance of being an example to our children both in goodness and in love.

OFFERTORY SENTENCE.   "Lay not up for yourselves treasures upon earth, where moth and rust doth corrupt, and where thieves break through and steal: but lay up for yourselves treasures in heaven, where neither moth nor rust doth corrupt, and where thieves do not break through nor steal: for where your treasure is, there will your heart be also" (Matt. 6:19–21).

OFFERTORY PRAYER.   Almighty and most merciful heavenly Father, source of all peace and love, bless the giving of these our gifts as our reconsecration into thy service. Strengthen our resolution to live lives in which we more readily respond to thy Spirit through greater love and more fruitful service.—Rodney K. Miller.

PRAYER.   God, our heavenly Father, who has revealed thyself to us not only as our creator and the provider for our life, but through thy Son showed us that thou dost love us even when we wander far from thee and receive us home with joy when we return, to help us who are parents, especially on this day as we remember fathers, to pattern our care the way thou has cared for us.

We give thanks for the fathers who have shaped our lives, for the guidance that they gave us, or tried to give us, and we either accepted or didn't always receive. For the care that they showed us, for the blessing that they bestowed upon our lives by revealing their pride in us. For all fathers who sought to be the best they could be for us, we give thee thanks.

We gather here this morning with concerns about our world, so we pray for peace. We pray for the peacemakers whom thy Son called blessed, that thy Spirit will use them to bring a new era of peace to a war-torn world, especially in that part of the world we call holy, where all of us have a spiritual home.

As a church on this day, we once again ask thy guidance as we exercise our stewardship over this place and over the heritage that has been given to us. Be with us in our thinking and in our speaking, that what we decide for the days ahead will be according to thy will and receive thy blessing.

Finally, we are concerned about many things in our private lives which we now offer unto thee. We know that there are things we must do, so we simply ask for strength to do them. We know there are things about which we don't know what to do, so we ask for insight and for wisdom. And there are those things about which we can do nothing, so we pray for patience to be still and know that thou art God.—Mark Trotter.

EVENING SERVICE

Topic: The Fellowship of the Holy Spirit
Text: 2 Cor. 13:14.

I. (a) It is a cornerstone of the Christian faith that God expressed himself completely in human terms in the life of Jesus Christ. The human body which he wore was changed after his crucifixion and before his resurrection.

At the ascension, that body was withdrawn from human touch and sight, and his human manifestation in this world was at an end. But his spiritual life in this world was not at an end—it entered a new phase. He promised them, when he was here, that when he was parted from them, he would send the Holy Spirit. The Holy Spirit, being one with the Father and the Son, and—as the Nicene Creed says—"proceeding from the Father and the Son," was to be Jesus' continued presence in his church. The local presence of the human Jesus gave way to the universal presence of the Holy Spirit.

(b) The great realization of the Holy Spirit was at Pentecost. The Holy Spirit had been with the Father and the Son from all time; but he was manifested to the Christian disciples with great power at Pentecost. This goes beyond our ordinary spiritual experience, but the spiritual realization which underlies it does not go beyond our own experience.

(c) It would be a miracle of the same proportions as Pentecost if the Holy Spirit could teach all our people to speak to those outside the faith in words they could understand. When the Spirit is truly with us, he gives us utterance so that we help interpret to others what means so much to us.

(d) The power then given has never been withdrawn. Men let it lapse through their sins and unbelief, but God is faithful and his Spirit is ever there, waiting for men's faith to let him work again in power.

We need to discover "the fellowship of the Holy Spirit" anew.

II. How are we going to do it?

(a) We need a great deal more knowledge about the Holy Spirit and a much deeper faith in him. Begin with some of the things Jesus said and taught about the Holy Spirit in the gospels, especially the fourth gospel. Then study the Acts, perhaps marking and underlining in red all references to the Holy Spirit. Do the same thing for the epistles. You may find you have been missing an important, perhaps the climactic part, of God's revelation. We need to let our spiritual life move up from those levels of mere ethical imitation to those far deeper levels of trust in the Holy Spirit, the expectation of being guided and empowered and used by the Holy Spirit.

(b) We must discover the "fellowship of the Holy Spirit" in a small company. Part of the growing edge of spiritual awakening today is found in the very large number of these small fellowships that spring up where two or more people feel the need of combining spiritual forces and enhancing their own spiritual experience by learning that of others.

(c) We must make the great, organized, institutional church just as much of a "fellowship of the Holy Spirit" as possible. The best way I know to find fellowship in a church is not to look for it, but to create it. If you have really looked on the face of God with reverence during the service, there is no better place to look next than on the face of your neighbour with friendliness when the service is finished.—Samuel M. Shoemaker.

SUNDAY: JUNE TWENTY-FOURTH

MORNING SERVICE

Topic: You Can't Be Two People
SCRIPTURE: Mark 2:1–12.

One of the heaviest burdens of man is the burden of a guilty conscience. One of the chief concerns of the Christian faith is the lifting of the burden of guilt. The assurance of forgiveness and the subsequent removal of the feeling of guilt is indeed the happiest and most power-giving experience which can come to man.

I. One might say that people feel guilty because they sin. But that is not the full answer. There are people who commit the grossest of sins with no feeling of guilt. One of the tasks of the preacher is to produce a feeling of guilt, thereby causing the guilty to seek salvation. There is a normal sense of guilt that is good. It is a sign that we still have spiritual life. It warns us of our danger and it stimulates our will.

II. In all "normal" people there are two natures. Goethe said it is regrettable that nature has made only one man of him when there is material aplenty for both a rogue and a gentleman.

(a) Some people try to bring inner peace by trying to appease both sides of their nature. Man feels the call to the high life. Created in the image of God, he instinctively desires to become like God. But at the same time, man often indulges his animal nature. He plays with his baser appetites until finally those animal appetites get him out of control.

(b) Thus, not being like God and yet not having the power within himself to master his animal nature, man becomes caught between his own inner conflicts. Between the two there is conflict out of which come many of our "nervous breakdowns," our tensions and our guilts.

III. Some feelings of guilt come not from any conscious wrongdoing, but rather from failure to "fight the good fight" (Rom. 3:23). As long as man is what he is, a creature in the image of God, then he can never be satisfied "short of the glory of God."

The answer for those torn inside by higher and lower impulses is not so much repentance and forgiveness as inner unity through consecration. Having no great life-consecration, man becomes disunited and at war with himself. But when he finds something to which he can completely give himself, his inner conflicts are resolved.

St. Paul looked inside himself and cried, "O wretched man that I am" (Rom. 7:24). Then he looked outward and upward and said, "I can do all things through Christ who strengtheneth me" (Phil. 4:13). And finally he triumphantly declared, "I have fought a good fight" (2 Tim. 4:7).— Charles L. Allen, *Pulpit Preaching.*

Illustrations

TRUE TO GOD.   I like that story of one of England's greatest statesmen. He often went into the old family portrait gallery. He stood as if in worship before the portraits, and he could be heard to say again and again: "I will not forget. I will be true." One day he took his eldest son with him, and he said, "My boy, you must hear these people speak." "But, father," said the lad, "what can they say?" Then his father, pointing to each portrait, said, "This one says, Be true to me. That one says, Be true to thyself. That other one says, Be true to your home. And that last one, which is my mother, says, Be true to God. And my son, I go out from them saying I will be true." That is the payment we can all make in the present, for our debt to the past.—Albert Mutch.

INVISIBLE PEOPLE. Looking out a few miles into the darkness, we see the stars which make the radiant company of our world. We number and name these hundreds of constellations which are visible to our gaze. But beyond those constellations lie unmeasured leagues of space which are as invisible to the telescope as to the naked eye. In the same way, again, we are living here in the midst of a little group of human beings. Our family, our friends, the members of our church and club, the citizens of our neighborhood and town, a few of our fellow countrymen from other states—these are all the persons that we ever see or know. All around us, however, in places near and far, are those hundreds of millions of men and women whom we never see, but who have an existence as real, and to themselves as important, as the lives that we are living.—John Haynes Holmes.

Sermon Suggestions

THE NECESSITY OF CHRISTIAN FRUITBEARING. Text: Matt. 21:17–19. (1) For growth. (2) For joy. (3) For maximum usefulness.(4) To be of maximum inspiration. (5) For good stewardship of life.—Chester Swor.

LIFE'S SAVING TENSION. Scripture: John 9:4; 12:27; Matt. 9:36. (1) We need a tension between our actual and our potential world. (2) We must keep the tension between our achieved and our possible self. (3) Keep the tension between the visible and the invisible world.—Halford E. Luccock.

Worship Aids.

CALL TO WORSHIP. "Awake, awake; put on thy strength, O Zion" (Isa. 52:1).

INVOCATION. Eternal God, our heavenly Father, you have given us every reason to rejoice. You have forgiven us of our sins through our Lord Jesus Christ. You have strengthened us in times of temptation. You have led us in marvelous ways all the days of our lives. Help us now to cast aside our fears, confess our unacknowledged sins, look to you for guidance, and praise you with all that is within us. For the sake of your glorious name.

OFFERTORY SENTENCE. "Give, and it shall be given unto you; good measure, pressed down, and shaken together, and running over. . . . For with the same measure that ye mete withal it shall be measured to you again" (Luke 6:38).

OFFERTORY PRAYER. Gracious Lord, give us generous hearts, not holding back through fear or selfishness, but imitating your blessed example in our prodigality of love.

PRAYER. O God, we who are bound together in the tender ties of love, pray thee for a day of unclouded love. May no passing irritation rob us of our joy in one another. Forgive us if we have often been keen to see the human failings, and slow to feel the preciousness of those who are still the dearest comfort of our life. May there be no sharp words that wound and scar, and no rift that may grow into estrangement. Suffer us not to grieve those whom thou hast sent to us as the sweet ministers of love. May our eyes not be so holden by selfishness that we know thine angels only when they spread their wings to return to thee.—Walter Rauschenbusch.

EVENING SERVICE

Topic: What Is the Church?

SCRIPTURE: 1 Pet. 2:1–10.

What is the church?

In answer to this query I should like to make two simple declarative statements of fact about the church.

I. The church is the institution dedicated to the perpetuation of a religious tradition. The Christian church is dedicated to the perpetuation of the Christian tradition. Vital religion always expresses itself in and through some kind of institution.

II. The second fact that goes into the

answer to your question: the church is a religious fellowship, a fellowship of people engaged in doing many different things but, again, with one basic purpose in view.

(a) The church is a sanctuary; it is the place and the people who consciously and deliberately cultivate the practice of the worship of God.

(1) And the God we seek in worship is, and must be, a living God.

(2) The forms we use in service of worship are important, but decidedly secondary to the aim of worship. There is no one final form for the worship of the living God.

(b) The church is a school for young and old alike. We do not start from scratch with our own experiences in religion. We stand before the cornucopia of 3,000 years of human experience and seek to weigh our inheritance.

(1) The Bible itself is a rich record of nearly half of that period of time, and church history and tradition pour the rest at our feet. Therefore, we teach the Bible in our schools here, and we seek to make it live, not only in terms of the day in which it was written, but in terms of our own as well.

(2) Whatever the church teaches must be presented in terms as vital, as relevant, as sensible as anything our students hear elsewhere.

(c) The church is a "nucleus of brotherhood." Historically, the church began in the homes of the faithful. Too few to need and too poor to build a separate building for worship, they gathered in the largest of their homes at the close of day for an evening meal and service of worship. The ministry of brotherhood is an indispensable part of the work of the church. For man is a social being.

(d) The church is a crusade! The church must have a ministry of social conscience if she would be true to her Lord, her Gospel, and her history. The church has no choice but to accept as her own any and every sincere concern and problem of her people. To do less is to admit her irrelevance at precisely those points where she has or ought to have the most to contribute.—Harold A. Bosley.

SUNDAY: JULY FIRST

MORNING SERVICE

Topic: What It Means to Be Saved

SCRIPTURE: Acts 16:30–31; Eph. 2:4–10.

To understand what *saved* means we shall need to come at it through a few very simple and direct questions.

I. First, what are we saved from? Immediately some will answer that it is sin or lostness or punishment in life to come. All of that is profoundly true. Sin is a reality. Life does have eternal consequences. Stated as simply as I know how, I believe we need desperately to be saved from a life that is centered in self. For one aspect of sin is self-centeredness. Our personal astronomy still insists that everything must revolve around us. It is that world-view that sets us on the journey into misery. The astronomy of the soul is wrong. That person who subscribes to it is trying to make something work that is predestined for failure. He is headed for trouble and misery.

Sooner or later those who put themselves at the center of everything cry, with Paul, "Who will deliver me from the body of death?" They are caught in contradictions that can only bring pain and conflict. They try to save themselves when they know that it will take something outside themselves. A man playing tennis with himself is no more of a contradiction than a man trying to live utterly upon self-reliance. It is both his sin and his hell. He would be the first to tell you that the day is coming when he needs to be saved from this futile and anxious game which he has started.

II. There is, of course, the second question, What are we saved to? It seems to me the answer is almost implied by all that we have said: we are saved to a life that is centered in God. A new system of personal astronomy has come to the soul of one who is saved. He finds his own orbit and lets life revolve around God.

III. But there is another equally important question. What are we saved for? If you are really saved, let us see the evidence of it. And what is that evidence? What, indeed, but a life centered in loving service. This is one of the marks of the saved soul. It is turned outward, no longer content to withdraw from the storehouse of life but seeking to make its own contribution.

What wonderful discoveries are waiting for some of us in the remaining years of our lives if we will ask what we are meant to live for! Wherever there is encounter with people, there some kind of spirit is imparted one to the other. It can be the spirit of Jesus Christ. Suppose we want it to happen to us. How do we do it? Do we just make up our minds to it?

Anyone who has earnestly tried it knows this is not the answer. We are left standing before the meaning of Jesus Christ. For in him God has given us the means by which that journey to new life can be made. Christ came and said, "Follow me." That's something everyone can understand. You can do it one step at a time. You don't have to wait until all the theories are made clear. You can still say yes to one who has invited you with the words, "Follow me." And that is the way that leads to life. Believe in Christ and follow him, and that journey from a self-centered to a God-centered life shall come about with all the joy that it brings.—Gene E. Bartlett, *Pulpit Preaching*.

Illustrations

SOUL AND BODY. I wish that I could get the ear of some doctors. It would seem that when they counsel patients who are rundown, the first prescription is to rest up on Sundays and the second to cut down on church work. It would be refreshing to hear of more doctors prescribing as a tonic and morale-builder attendance at church on Sunday. A man has a soul as well as a body, and psychosomatic medicine is demonstrating that a neglected soul may take its revenge in an ailing body. To cut down on commitments and obligations is the tendency, but simplification should be introduced where it is harder—in our addiction to things, in our wants, in our spending.—Robert J. McCracken.

GOD WORKING THROUGH US. Last summer I had my first opportunity to walk through some of the great cathedrals of England. It was an overwhelming experience for me. And I almost wished at the time that this were all there were to the experience of God present here and now in his majesty and love: beauty, spaciousness, awe, and changelessness. But it's not so, is it? For it has pleased him to work out his mighty purpose of love for this mad, mad world not through breathtakingly beautiful monuments to him, priceless as these may be for the lifting of our spirits, but through ordinary lives like yours and mine that are willing to go out into the world with all its grime and tragedy and complexity. It's a staggering thought that he has left it all strictly in your hands and mine. "Working together with him, then, we entreat you not to accept the grace of God in vain."—Edmund Steimle.

Sermon Suggestions

SHADOWS. Text: Acts 5:15. (1) The most potent influence is characterized by silence. (2) It is unconscious. (3) It is conditioned by a man's relationship to Christ. —W. A. Cameron.

SELF-CONTROL. Text: Gal. 5:23. (1) Recognize the problem for what it is. (2) Act on the knowledge you have. (3) Set some goals for your life. (4) Challenge your feelings occasionally. (5) Find someone who has the kind of difficulty you are going through and share your life with him.—Dan Baumann.

Worship Aids

CALL TO WORSHIP. "Lift up your hands in the sanctuary, and bless the Lord. The Lord that made heaven and earth bless thee out of Zion" (Ps. 134:2–3).

INVOCATION. Most gracious heavenly Father, we come into thy presence this day broken and fragmented by the many pressures and demands of life. We often feel overwhelmed by these pressures and demands. We lose our sense of own personal wholeness, and we lose contact with our fellow human beings and with thee, O Lord. We struggle quietly with our fear and inadequacy. Enable us to see, O Lord, that the secret to bearing our burdens is to share with others their burdens. We pray that thou wouldst enable us to share willingly with one another not only the needs and problems but also the strengths and joys that all of us possess. Impart unto us, O Lord God, this new vision of thee and of our fellow creatures that will enable us to form anew the community of faith that Christ envisioned for his church.—Rodney K. Miller.

OFFERTORY SENTENCE. "Unto whomsoever much is given, of him shall be much required: and to whom men have committed much, of him they will ask the more" (Luke 12:48).

OFFERTORY PRAYER. O Lord, we know that you love a cheerful giver, but that you do not excuse a grudging giver. Grant that we may assess our abilities and our opportunities in such a way that by doing our stewardship duty faithfully we may learn at last to do it cheerfully.

LITANY.

Minister: O God, before whose face the empires of the past have risen and fallen away, establish this nation in righteousness; and in personal character and public integrity make her foundations sure.

Response: Lord, hear our prayer and mercifully bless this people.

Minister: From the ravages of crime, the disgrace of political corruption, and all malicious designs of lawless men,

Response: Good Lord, deliver us.

Minister: From prejudice of race and color, making schism in the commonwealth; from all inequity that, causing a few to be rich and many poor, begets ill will and spoils fraternity; from loss of liberties

bequeathed us by our sires and from careless acceptance of our heritage and neglect of its responsibilities,

Response: Good Lord, deliver us.

Minister: From the decline of pure religion, from failure of moral fiber in our citizenship, from all accounting of things material above virtues spiritual; from vulgarity of life, loss of social conscience, and collapse of national character,

Response: Good Lord, deliver us.

Minister: By the deep faiths on which the foundations of our land were laid and by the sacrifices of its pioneers,

Response: We beseech thee to hear us, O Lord.

Minister: By the memory of leaders in the nation, whose wisdom has saved us, whose devotion has chastened us, whose characters have inspired us,

Response: We beseech thee to hear us, O Lord.

Minister: By the undeserved wealth of a great continent committed to us and by our trusteeship of power to work weal or woe on the earth,

Response: We beseech thee to hear us, O Lord.

Minister: Keep us from pride of mind, and from boasting tongues deliver us; save our national loyalty from narrowness and our flag from selfish shame; by our love for our land may we measure the love of others for their lands, honoring their devotion as we honor our own; and acknowledging thee one God, may we see all mankind one family and so govern our national affairs that the whole world may become one brotherhood of peoples.

Response: Lord, hear our prayer and mercifully bless this people.— Harry Emerson Fosdick.

EVENING SERVICE

Topic: Do Not Adjust!

TEXT: Rom. 12:2 (NEB)

Our evangelical great-grandparents used to demand of one another, "Have you been saved?" Today we ask, "Are you well-adjusted?" We must, of course, adjust in various ways to one another. But adjustment is not the only significant dimension of mental and emotional wellbeing. A sentence in Paul's letter to the Romans brings into focus a biblical insight on what we call "adjustment."

I. Look now at the first part of the text, as amended: "Adjust yourselves no longer to the pattern of this present world." Is Paul here commending nonconformity? Perhaps he is, in some way. And here we come to a confusing and controversial issue.

(a) Much human progress has come from nonconformists, from men and women who have refused to adjust to the world's standards and conventions.

(b) But not all who carry banners of nonconformity are to be accepted as creative persons, as men and women who are constructively concerned for fundamental values. One of the great frauds of our time —one of the great bores, too—is the person who cultivates nonconformities, eccentricities, conspicuous maladjustments, mainly to draw attention to himself or herself. Is the antiestablishment, liberated-from-the-rat-race young man who will wear nothing but blue denim less of a conformist, really, than his father, who wears pinstripe three-piece suits?

(c) But even the bogus kind of nonconformity can have some value as a warning against the mind-numbing and heart-corroding pressures of life today. Conformity doesn't cause much trouble—but, then, conformity doesn't cause much of anything.

(d) But we must not misunderstand Paul here. He was not calling Christians to nonconformity simply for its own sake. The Christian is not called to respond affirmatively to any external pattern, to any pervasive ethos or secular "life-style," to any general approach to life.

II. Paul then went on to say, "Let your minds be remade, and your whole being thus transformed." The way for the Christian, then, is neither in being conformed to the world's pattern nor in necessarily refusing to be conformed to it, but in being transformed by the opening of the mind and heart to God's Spirit.

(a) Behind Paul's teaching here, and inspiring it, stands the figure of Jesus. The Gospels show that he did have many of the qualities of personality and character that we would accept as signs of good adjustment. But the Gospels also show that on many occasions he adjusted very badly. If Jesus had been a little better adjusted to the society in which he lived, if he had been just a little more of a conformist, he would not have been crucified.

(b) Paul discerned that Jesus was completely guided by the Spirit of God, that he was adjusted only to the will and purposes of God—and that, said Paul, is what followers of Jesus should strive for. If we wish to be well-adjusted, we should be very careful with the Gospel of Jesus Christ. For Christians the distinctions between adjustment and maladjustment, between conformity and nonconformity, are quite irrelevant—and therein is the key to our personal freedom under God, own liberation from bondage.

III. "Adjust yourselves no longer to the pattern of this present world, but let your minds be remade and your whole nature thus transformed." The Christian tries to sit loosely, as Jesus did, to all the paraphernalia of life in the world. This is the way of what Reinhold Niebuhr called "genuine Christian nonchalance"—a special kind of indifference. But Christian nonchalance is not indifference toward the needs and sufferings of the world. It is one of the practical paradoxes of the Christian faith that through nonchalance toward the world's pattern, a person of faith is enabled to serve God's purposes of justice and mercy and compassion for the world.
—J. A. Davidson

SUNDAY: JULY EIGHTH

MORNING SERVICE

Topic: On Living in Style
TEXT: 1 Cor. 16:23.

The word *grace* towers above all others in Paul's vocabulary, and it is very familiar to us. What really would it mean to us if this prayer happened in our lives? *"The grace of the Lord Jesus be with you."* It would mean living in style, in all circumstances and at all times. For "grace" involves style at its best, a style of living that is never out of date, a style that finds expression on various levels of our existence.

I. Living in style, with the grace of the Lord Jesus, involves living *thankfully*.

(a) We are to live thankfully always. "In everything give thanks," Paul urged the Thessalonian Christians. He calls us not to an act, but to an attitude, to a steady "yes-saying" to life. To be sure, we can't be thankful *for* everything. That would be moronic. But we can be thankful *in* everything. Stylish living maintains a thankful attitude in all circumstances and conditions.

(b) The very word *grace* is a constant reminder to every Christian of our unpayable indebtedness to God in Christ. Grace is the undeserved love of God, taking the initiative in Christ to seek and to save us, to stoop to where we are that we may become as he is. By grace, not merit, we are saved. By grace, we are a free, prosperous people, living in a land of freedom. If the grace of the Lord Jesus is with us always, we shall live in style. We shall live thankfully.

II. Living in style, with the grace of the Lord Jesus, involves living *usefully*.

(a) Whenever Paul speaks of God's grace or love, he doesn't speak of a general disposition or kindness on God's part. He speaks of the active love of God, God in action, proving his love. "He loved me, and gave himself for me."

(b) So it was with Jesus himself. He went about doing good, helping, healing, the servant of the Lord, coming not to be served, but to serve. Living in the style of Jesus is living in the service of Jesus. And he raised a new, revolutionary criterion by which to judge what it means to be somebody, to be great. It means being useful, serving, helping.

(c) Our society tends to measure stylish living and greatness in terms of the services we can command. The gospel measures it in terms of the services we can perform, how useful we are to the lowliest and least, the needy, our city, our country, the church. This is true greatness and a style of living that will survive.

III. Living in style, with the grace of the Lord Jesus, involves living *courteously*. The Greek word for "grace"—*charis*—is the word from which we get our word *charm*.

(a) Such a word clearly belongs to our Lord Jesus Christ. In one glimpse of his childhood, Luke tells us that Jesus "grew in favor" with God and man. In his ministry, Jesus never despised the conventional courtesies of the day. But the real measure of his charm was in his respect for publicans, sinners, harlots, lepers, outcasts of society, all of whom he saw as people to be loved. Real courtesy is not merely a matter of polished manners—a rogue can have those!—but a consistent respect for others, high-or low-born, educated or ignorant, rich or poor.

(b) Our rough, tough world needs a revival of Christian courtesy. It needs stylish living, an attention to apparently trivial things that can transform our relationships and actions.

IV. Living in style, with the grace of the Lord Jesus involves living *magnanimously*.

(a) When Paul spoke of "grace," he did so as one who could never get used to the incredible wonder of his own forgiveness by God in Christ. He had been accepted, made an apostle! It was a thing most wonderful, almost too wonderful to be! It was all of grace, sheer, unmerited favor, groundless, spontaneous. This was the matchless, magnificent magnanimity of the Lord Jesus Christ. "While we were yet sinners, Christ died for us."

(b) If that grace is with us, then we shall live magnanimously, generously forgiving those who injure and insult us. Paul experienced the grace of another Christian right at the start of his new life in Christ. There was a heroic churchman named Ananias, who received instructions to welcome the converted Saul of Tarsus. He recoiled from the task! Saul had a terrible reputation. But Ananias obeyed the instructions and, in a marvelous gesture of forgiving love, went to Saul, laid his hands on him, and said: "Brother Saul." Brother! It was a healing word of acceptance.

That is stylish living at its best. Gracious men and women are forgiving men and women, big enough to follow in the steps of a gracious Lord.—John N. Gladstone.

Illustrations

FRUITS OF GRACE.   I confess to some weariness of spirit when I hear critics of the church say they believe in Christ, but not in the church. Were it not for the church—with all her weaknesses—they would know of no Christ to believe in. The disciples who gathered around him in adoration and love were the first church. Their recollections and teachings provided the materials from which the New Testament was written. The continuing church wrote the New Testament, which contains practically all we know of Jesus Christ. The church treasured and taught the New Testament until it became the spiritual discipline of Christians in all ages. The church has taught this faith, lifted this witness, lived for it, and been willing to die for it. That is why it is available to us today.—Harold A. Bosley.

CYNICISM.   This age has three sneers for everything and three cheers for nothing.—E. Stanley Jones, *The Divine Yes*.

Sermon Suggestions

A JOYFUL HOMECOMING.   Text: Luke 15:20. (1) The prodigal son came to want. (2) He came to himself. (3) He came to his father.—W. W. Melton.

OUR FUTURE WITH JESUS.   Text: John 14:3. Jesus has promised: (1) To return to us. (2) To receive us. (3) To be reunited with us.—Adapted from Alfred E. Garvie.

Worship Aids

CALL TO WORSHIP.   "This is how we know what love is: Christ gave his life for us. We too, then, ought to give our lives for our brothers! If a rich person sees his brother in need, yet closes his heart against his brother, how can he claim that he loves God? My children, our love should be not just words and talk; it must be true love, which shows itself in action" (1 John 3:16–18 [TEV]).

INVOCATION.   O divine love, help us today to rise to the challenge of the needs of the world, and to do it by making new commitments, followed by faithful service to you and to every soul for whom Christ died. Make us strong in your strength.

OFFERTORY SENTENCE.   "They gave according to their means, as I can testify, and beyond their means, of their own free will" (2 Cor. 8:3 [RSV]).

OFFERTORY PRAYER.   God of grace, God of glory, help us understand that we are recipients of thy mercy. What we are, thy grace has made us. What we have, thy providence has given us. And now, do thy gracious work also in others, through the gifts we bring.

PRAYER.   O holy God, our creator and redeemer, we thank thee for the beauty of the earth, the splendor of the heavens, the melodious songs of birds, the delicious food from our gardens, and the cool breezes of evening.

We thank thee for this church: for the way it lifts up our hearts, for the strength it gives to our lives, and for the good friends that we have come to know here.

In the business and stress of our lives, help us to take time to behold the beauty and majesty of thy creation and to appreciate and share our goodly company of Christian friends.

Especially do we thank thee for the friendship of thy son Jesus, who loved us before we knew him and with cords of love has bound us to him and to one another.

Help us, we pray, to fix our minds on those things that are true, honest, lovely, pure, and of good report; and to leave behind those ways that are arrogant, rude, and boastful. Save us from rejoicing in evil, and teach us to rejoice in good. In these times of economic distress, help us to remember that we do not live by bread alone, and enable us to lay up treasures in heaven.

Today we pray for all health-care workers and for nurses and doctors. Bless their efforts to heal the sick, and bless the work of all the homes and hospitals which we in this church support.

We pray for those who mourn and ask that they may be comforted through thy presence and with thy promise of eternal life.

We pray for those of our fellowship who are on vacation. Let this be a time of refreshment and recreation for them, and return them safely to our midst.

For ourselves, O God, we ask strength and courage that we may walk in paths of righteousness and serve thee faithfully all our days, doing what thou wouldst have us do.

For the nations, we ask that thou wilt prosper the work of peacemakers and spare their peoples from the anguish and suffering of war.

All this we ask in the name of Jesus Christ, our Savior, Redeemer, and the very Prince of Peace.—Harold A. Brack.

EVENING SERVICE

Topic: Do You Know Where Your Children Are?

TEXT: Luke 2:52.

We need to re-examine our family life. Do we know where we are as parents? Do we know where we are as children? Do we know where the other members of the family are?

Our thematic question today is not one related to geography, place, or location. It asks: "Do you know where your children are in terms of growth, purpose, and love?"

I. *Not geography—but growth.* You may know where your children are in terms of geography, but do you know where they are in terms of growth and maturity?

(a) What parent is not concerned about the physical health of a child? How is it that many such concerned parents seem not to care where their children are in terms of spiritual growth? They may not even know that their children need soul-growth. They ignore the church as an agency of God's love and wisdom.

(b) Do you know where your children are in terms of their sense of self-identity? The Christian faith says that we have a healthy self-identity—knowing who we are—only when we learn Whose we are. And your children cannot learn that in early life without your help and guidance. Values are caught, not taught, through the routine interaction of family members.

II. *Not place—but purpose.* The big problem is not where your children are in terms of physical place, but where they are in terms of a wholesome life purpose. What kinds of goals are your children accepting for themselves? Are you helping your children develop a sense of responsibility for self? Are they growing in this, or are you wet-nursing them?

(a) The future of our children is being determined in their childhood by the values and purposes to which they are led to give allegiance. If parents don't assist them, they will find help outside the home. So many family tragedies come because such youths look to their peers for creating a value system in life.

(b) We cannot talk about purpose in life for today's children without taking an honest look at the world in which we are forcing them to grow up. What must it mean to a child never to know a day of peace in the world? It is not inappropriate to remind you of the threat of nuclear destruction in your children's world.

(c) Youths respond to a challenge. There is no greater challenge you can give them than to help them develop into makers of peace. Could it be that among your children there is one who will indeed become the person whose leadership provides a just and lasting peace for this world? Someone's child is going to have to be that person.

III. *Not location—but love.* Do you know where your children are in terms of love? Have they learned through their experience of your love and affection what wholesome family love means? Love is indispensable in family life.

(a) There is the kind of love that does not do all the talking. It is love that listens. Children need that kind of love. Parental love must listen to know where children are.

(b) This kind of love is the love that gives. We come by this naturally as parents. Some of us love and give sacrificially as parents. Yet, can children ever learn what love really is without experiencing it in a home where the family circle is united by love? Children cannot learn what love is if they themselves are not loved, do not feel loved, do not believe they are loved.

(c) When there is love in the home, you will know where your children are. And you can count on it: they, with Jesus, will, as they grow up, "advance in wisdom and in favor with God and man."—Brian L. Harbour.

SUNDAY: JULY FIFTEENTH

MORNING SERVICE

Topic: Overcoming Our Heredity
TEXT: Col. 3:1–15.

All of us are engaged in a continuing personal struggle with ourselves. The nature of this personal struggle revolves around the issue of just what the priorities of our lives will be. Most of us, if we but think a moment, recognize that there are many things that could be priorities: commitment to family, employment, recreation, or social clubs. Yet, these tangible things are only the objects that we choose to be the vehicles of our priorities. The real basis for our priorities is, therefore, our attitude toward the world around us. If we thus consider our priorities to be shaped by our attitudes toward the world, there are but two basic attitudes that establish our priorities: (1) we can assume the attitude that life is to be lived primarily for the benefit of self, or (2) we can assume the attitude that life is to be shared with our fellow men and women. In short, we can choose between living lives that are either primarily self-centered or primarily other-centered, between lives of selfishness and lives of sharing.

I. The Bible refers to the struggle to determine our priorities as the struggle between our "old nature" and our "new nature." Our "old nature" is the disposition with which each of us is born. The primary characteristic of our "old nature" is that it is essentially self-centered. When we are under the control of our "old nature," we are concerned only about our own needs and gratification.

(a) A telling example of the exercise of our "old nature" is to be found in the behavior of infants. The primary concerns of an infant are food, sleep, and attention. When these needs are met, the infant is contented. However if mother is late with the bottle, cries of discontent and irritation are soon heard. Indeed, only gradually can a child be taught to delay gratification of needs, consider the needs of others, and share possessions.

(b) Unfortunately, the "old nature" with which we are born remains in control of the lives of many persons. The self-centeredness of the child grows into the selfishness of the adult, and selfish adults clamor through life, hurting and damaging others by their actions. Indeed, the prevalence of such antisocial behavior as crime, corruption, brutality, alcoholism, and warfare would seem to support the contention that there are many who are controlled by their "old nature."

(c) The "old nature" that we all possess is, therefore, a sinful nature. It is sinful because it has been corrupted by pride, lust, selfishness, and envy. All of the tremendous evils that plague the world thus issue forth from the free exercise of our "old nature."

II. The apostle Paul wrote to Christians who were experiencing the struggle between their "old nature" and their "new nature." They were being tempted by the ways of the world and being drawn away from their faith in Christ. In short, the Colossians were in danger of forsaking their "new nature" that they had received through their faith in Christ, for a return to their "old nature."

(a) The "new nature," about which the apostle Paul writes, is the key to resolving the struggle that we have in establishing the priorities of our lives. The "new nature" that Christ gives to us can help us establish our priorities because it is radically different from the "old nature" with which we are born. Our "old nature" is characterized by self-centeredness and selfishness. Our "new nature," on the other hand, is characterized by love.

(b) This love is described by Paul as being compassionate, kind, meek, patient, and forebearing. This love is the power that binds us both to our God and to our fellow creatures in bonds of perfect harmony and peace. Moreover, this "new nature," characterized by love, represents in our lives the image of a living God who is constantly renewing us. We thus are being continually and steadily transformed into more faithful servants of Christ by the indwelling of his "new nature" in our lives.

III. (a) The indwelling of Christ's "new nature" in the lives of faithful men and women across the ages has been a vital witness to the power of Christ in the midst of life. Many men and women, such as Francis of Assisi, Augustine of Hippo, and John Wesley, are outstanding examples of persons whose transformed lives were agents in the transformation of countless other lives. In each case, as well as thousands of others, the "new nature" imparted by Christ resolved the struggles that plagued Francis, Augustine, and Wesley. Yet, in each case, the transformation from the "old nature" to the "new nature" was not easy. The "old nature" of each man—whether it was pride and stubbornness in Wesley, sensuality in Augustine, or wealth in the case of Francis—was strongly entrenched.

(b) The lives of these men reveal that we are unable to acquire our "new nature" through our own efforts. The apostle Paul reminds us that our "new natures" are a possibility only because of the resurrection of Jesus Christ. We, therefore, in order to receive our "new nature" must have faith in Jesus Christ as the source of our salvation from sin and death. We must

allow Christ to dwell in us and assume control of our lives. We must allow love to control our relationships with others. Like John Wesley, we must believe, in the depths of our hearts, in the saving power of Jesus Christ.

(c) Yet, lest we be tempted to believe that simply "putting on" Christ's "new nature" is the solution to all our earthly struggles and temptations, let us remember the example of the Colossians. Let us never believe that "putting on" Christ's "new nature" is easy—it demands commitment and sacrifice. Let us never believe that "putting on" Christ's "new nature" is ever complete—our "sinful old nature" is never completely subdued as we live among the many temptations of human life everyday.

The major difference that we experience when we "put on Christ's new nature" is that we are recipients of God's grace and love, mediated through Jesus Christ. This grace and love empowers and strengthens us to resist the egotistical temptations of the world and to share with others our love and care. Through the exercise of our "new natures" upon our lives and behavior, Christians become part of that great Kingdom of God which Christ established in heaven and which he will one day establish on earth.—Rodney K. Miller.

Illustrations

PERSONAL GROWTH. Karen Horney, a distinguished psychiatrist, after working with many patients with many and difficult problems, concluded: "I believe that man can change and go on changing as long as he lives. And this belief has grown with deeper understanding."

GOD DOES EVERYTHING. In Dostoevsky's great novel *Crime and Punishment*, Raskolnicov, a young murderer, conscience-stricken, makes his way to the room of a young woman in the slums to confess his crime. The woman, saintly Sonia, was heroically supporting her stepbrothers and sisters. Her mother had died of consumption, and her drunkard father had been killed in an accident. Raskolnicov was bewildered by her courage in the face of the unspeakable horrors of her existence. He wondered how she could keep sane, why she didn't throw her life away. In the cynicism of his own despair, he questioned her: "So you pray to God a great deal, Sonia?" After a pause, she whispered: "What should I be without God?" "And what does God do for you?" he demanded, probing her further. Sonia was silent for a long while, as though she could not answer. Emotion gripped her. "He does everything," she whispered quickly, looking down again.—John N. Gladstone.

Sermon Suggestions

A BANQUET IN THE WILDERNESS. Scripture: Matt. 14:15–21. (1) Human limitations. (2) Human consecration. (3) Human organization. (4) Human conservation.—W. W. Melton.

THE SECRET OF SUCCESS IN LIFE. Text: Mark 8:35. (1) Selfishness is always fatal. (2) The way to get the most from life is to throw it away in a great cause.—Ambrose White Vernon.

Worship Aids

CALL TO WORSHIP. "How beautiful upon the mountains are the feet of him that bringeth good tidings, that publisheth peace; that bringeth good tidings of good, that publisheth salvation; that saith unto Zion, thy God reigneth" (Isa. 52:7).

INVOCATION. We thank thee, O God, that thou hast given to all of us the privilege of making known thy goodness and mercies. Give to us today the joy of those who believe the Good News, who experience it, and who share it. May we receive and pass on thy rich gifts in the confidence of those who truly believe that thou hast the whole world in thy hands.

OFFERTORY SENTENCE. "For ye know the grace of our Lord Jesus Christ, that, though he was rich, yet for your sakes he became poor, that ye through his poverty might be rich" (2 Cor. 8:9).

OFFERTORY PRAYER. As we have been amazingly blessed in the salvation of our Lord Jesus Christ, so let us share out of our riches of grace and goods with all those persons and causes that need what we can do and give, to the end that people everywhere may know and love thee.

PRAYER. First of all, let us pray for greater awareness of God's presence with us, to know that God is with us even when we have strayed from him; to know that God is love that will not let us go, even if we do not love him; to know those moments in our life which come to us as his judgment and to use those moments for renewal and new birth; to see that when we are in sickness or in sorrow or in any distress that we are in his hands. O God, our Father, we would pray that we might open our eyes and our minds and our hearts to see thy presence in righteousness and in mercy in our lives.

And we pray for others. Remembering those who are strangers to us, whom we have known all our lives, but cannot understand now. We would remember those who are enemies to us, whom we know but have difficulty loving. And we would remember those who are gone from us, whom we have loved but lost. We would remember those who are near and dear to us, whom we have neglected and taken for granted. O God, grant us grace that overcomes all barriers and breaks down all dividing walls that we may love those for whom we have prayed with the love with which thou hast loved us.

We cannot come to church to hide from the world and its problems, so we pray for the whole wide world. O God, thy world is not what thou wouldst have it be, and yet it is so close. With each generation, we are given a new chance. By thy grace, there are always new possibilities and new opportunities for peace and for thy Kingdom to come. We realize that so much rests on the decisions that we as human beings make, and so we pray for those in authority, that they may have wisdom and compassion in the exercise of the terrible duties that they may perform, that they might hold the image of what this world should be and seek in what they do to move the world toward that dream.

And finally, we lift our special prayers for those for whom we have special concerns and ask thy Spirit's presence to touch all of us, that we may leave here renewed and prepared to become instruments of thy peace.—Mark Trotter.

EVENING SERVICE

Topic: Faithfulness: The Foundation of the Family
TEXT: Heb. 13:4.

What is the proper foundation for the family? Let's study the text and the implications of it in seeking to discover the proper foundation upon which our homes are to be built.

I. *The plan*. In God's plan, what is to be the foundation of the home? The writer of Hebrews says that it is faithfulness, a truth which he expressed in both positive and negative terms.

(a) This is the positive expression of it: "Let marriage be held in honor." Marriage is to be valued above all else. It is to be given the highest priority.

(b) Then, the writer of Hebrews expresses the idea negatively: "The marriage bed is to be undefiled." As pure as a priest is when he goes into the holy of holies, as pure as is the heavenly inheritance which Christ will give to us at his coming, as pure as is the experience of meeting God in worship, even so is marriage to be. We are not to allow anything to stain or color or spot our intimate, exclusive relationship as husband and wife. The marriage bed is to be undefiled.

II. *The perversion*. Let's take it a step further and consider the perversion of God's plan. Unfaithfulness was a problem when the letter of Hebrews was written, for he refers in our text to those who "traffic in the bodies of others and defile the relationship of marriage" (Phillips trans.). Unfaithfulness is no new problem. But it has become more acceptable and more prevalent in our day. Why does it happen?

(a) Sometimes personal motivations are responsible for unfaithfulness. Many become involved in affairs to feed their sagging egos or to gain a sense of being valued.

(b) At times, social motivations are responsible for unfaithfulness. Movies, television, and magazines have suggested to us that fidelity in marriage is old-fashioned, that marriage itself is out of date, and that sexual permissiveness is acceptable.

(c) Physical motivations are sometimes responsible for unfaithfulness. Many turn to affairs because of sexual dissatisfaction at home. Others, because of reduction in sexual capacities, turn to affairs to prove their virility.

(d) Interpersonal motivations are often responsible for affairs. Over-critical mates, the lack of communication between husband and wife, a breakdown in the marital relationship often sets the stage for an attempt to find understanding, communication, and companionship with someone else.

(e) The primary reason for unfaithfulness, however, is spiritual. Even if all of the other factors are present, the only reason husbands or wives could be unfaithful is if they are so far removed from God that they forget the sanctity with which God ordained their marriages and the clear proclamation that nothing is to be done to pervert that sanctity.

III. *The prescription*. What can we do to stem the tide of adultery and re-establish faithfulness as the foundation of the home?

(a) The first step is communication. In a day when the world is communicating the message that unfaithfulness is all right and adultery is acceptable, we need to communicate to our young people and to our members and to the world that it is not okay to pervert God's plan for the home.

(b) The second step is cleansing. There are those within the sound of my voice who have considered unfaithfulness, maybe even been guilty of it. You need to confess that to God and seek the cleansing of his forgiveness.

(c) The third step is companionship. The best way to prevent unfaithfulness is to build such a strong relationship with your mate that unfaithfulness will never even be considered.

(d) The fourth step is commitment. The only way the tide of unfaithfulness will be halted is for Christian people to enter the marriage with this commitment: I will never do anything to call into question the sanctity and the exclusiveness of my commitment to my family.—Brian L. Harbour.

SUNDAY: JULY TWENTY-SECOND

MORNING SERVICE

Topic: Mastering Our Masters
SCRIPTURE: Rom. 6:15–23

I. The word *slave* conjures up an image in our minds of a human being who is owned as property by another person and who is subject to his or her will. The slave is thus a person who possesses no freedom or rights. The television series "Roots" presented a vividly dramatic portrayal of the historical reality of slavery on American soil. Since the ancestors of most of us were not slaves, we have difficulty imagining how it must have felt to be a slave—or do we? "Slavery" is much more than being the legal property of another person. "It is also a way of describing how we can be shaped, influenced, and controlled by our relationship to the people, events, and circumstances that surround us.

II. (a) We cannot escape from the influence that these forces have upon us. Indeed, in order to be fully human, we must constantly interact with our fellow human beings; we must constantly react to human events; and we must constantly act in the circumstances in which we find ourselves. These people, events, and circumstances, moreover, help us to decide just how we are going to live our lives. They determine what we think is important and what goals we strive toward.

(b) This means that in the lives of most people there is usually one or perhaps two things in which a person invests an unduly large amount of energy, time, and money. Perhaps some of the more celebrated cases can be illustrated in the lives of three men. Each of these three men was "enslaved" by a particular object or goal which exacted on inordinate amount of energy, time, and concentration. One man concentrated his life upon the acquisition of money. Another dedicated his life to the pursuit of sensual pleasure. A third, a professional politician, concentrated his life upon the acquisition of political power.

(c) These three men, as well as millions of other persons, became "enslaved" by the very things that they most earnestly and avidly sought. They became "enslaved" because the thing that they sought conferred upon each of them a reason and rationale for living—a rationale upon which they could construct their lives. Understood in this context, "slavery" is not a bad word. It denotes a manner in which a person is deeply involved in some aspect of life and the manner in which he or she has made a deep commitment to some goal.

III. (a) "Slavery" is thus an appropriate word to describe the deep level of commitment and involvement that God demands of us as Christians. God's claim on our lives, which he exercises through Jesus Christ, means that we make him the center of our lives and make the doing of his will the goal of our lives. We must push competing goals and competing masters into the corners of our lives.

(b) Yet "slavery" to God is inherently different from the "slavery" experienced by the three men. "Slavery" to God leads us to a state of sanctification that grants us eternal life. It is thus a constructive bondage to Christ through which we grow in grace and love.

(c) On the other hand, "slavery" to such things as money, sensuality, and power is, in the words of the Apostle Paul, "slavery" to sin. Persons who become enslaved to these and other such things lead lives that end only in death. Such "slavery" is in no way acceptable to God, because it is a "slavery" based upon individual pride, selfishness, and greed, and not on the love of Jesus Christ as Lord and Savior.

(d) In conclusion, the real issue that the Apostle Paul addresses in Romans is one of the source of meaning, value, and direction in our lives. By calling commitment to either God or "sin" by the word "slavery," Paul proclaims the inclusive and total demand of commitment to God through his Son, Jesus Christ. Such commitment can tolerate no competition. We cannot divide our loyalties. Being "enslaved" to Christ, however, is not a fruitless bondage. Our commitment to Jesus Christ is the source of our hope as a people of God—the hope of abundant and eternal life.—Rodney K. Miller.

Illustrations

EARTHBOUND PRAYER.   There is a kind of prayer which is not looking up, but looking down; and there is small help, but rather great injury, in this kind of prayer. It is prayer which is concerned entirely with our own affairs. In a history of Wessex I once read there is recorded a quaint prayer of this kind, uttered by a man named John Ward, who lived in 1727. This was his prayer: "O Lord, I beseech Thee to have an eye of compassion on the County of Hertfordshire, for I have a mortgage in that County. Likewise give, I beseech Thee, a prosperous voyage to the Mermaid sloop, because I have not insured it." Now that is not prayer at all, it is merely an attempt to make God a partner in a commercial transaction.—W. J. Dawson.

PREOCCUPATION WITH SELF.   While lecturing at Melbourne University some years ago, I was given a boomerang as a souvenir. In contemplating this gift I concluded that in a sense it symbolized human existence. One generally assumes that a boomerang returns to the thrower; actually it returns only when the thrower has missed his target. Similarly, man returns to himself, to being concerned with his self, only after he has missed his mission, only after he has failed to find meaning in life.—Paul Tournier.

Sermon Suggestions

THE THINGS THAT STRENGTHEN FAITH. Scripture: Ps. 37:7; John 7:17; 1 John 4:18. (1) Exercising patience. (2) Practicing

obedience. (3) Living by the law of love.— James W. Cox

THE LAST BEQUEST.   Text: John 14:27. Jesus' last bequest—his peace—has three characteristics: (1) It is personal. (2) It is genuine. (3) It is seasonable.—Alfred E. Garvie.

Worship Aids

CALL TO WORSHIP.   "If we say that we have no sin, we deceive ourselves, and the truth is not in us. If we confess our sins, he is faithful and just to forgive us our sins, and to cleanse us from all unrighteousness" (1 John 1:8–9).

INVOCATION.   Today, Our Father, may we learn the meaning of our new standing with you: darkness past, and the true light shining. Help us to live out of that new light where love prevails, and to turn away from the old darkness, where hate festers and prejudice grows. This we ask for the sake of him who loved us and commanded us to love one another.

OFFERTORY SENTENCE.   "It is written, He that had gathered much had nothing over; and he that had gathered little had no lack" (2 Cor. 8:15).

OFFERTORY PRAYER.   O Lord of our lives, as our material blessings multiply, grant that the grace of giving may be increased. May we sustain no spiritual loss because of an abundance of material goods, nor may we fail of thy grace when the fig tree does not blossom, and no fruit shall be in the vines. At all times and in all conditions may we be thy faithful stewards.

PRAYER.   O thou, who didst lay the foundation of the earth amid the singing of the morning stars and the joyful shouts of the sons of God, lift up our little life into thy gladness. Out of thee, as out of an overflowing fountain of love, wells forth eternally a stream of blessing upon every creature thou hast made. If we have thought that thou didst call into being this universe in order to win praise and honour for thyself, rebuke the vain fancies of our foolish minds and show us that thy glory is the joy of giving. We can give thee nothing of our own. All that we have is thine. Oh, then, help us to glorify thee by striving to be like thee. Make us just as pure and good as thou art. May we be partakers of the divine nature, so that all that is truly human in us may be deepened, purified, and strengthened. And so may we be witnesses for thee, lights of the world, reflecting thy light.—Samuel McComb.

EVENING SERVICE

Topic: Sitting Where They Sat

TEXT: Ezek. 3:15.

Ezekiel has his commission to go to the exiles with the message of God. If he is to do his work effectively, he must needs be in touch with men as well as with God. He had intended to utter some sharp words concerning their idolatries. But when he saw the conditions under which they were living, he was over-whelmed. It must have meant everything to the people in captivity to have their religious leader lay aside the pomp and circumstance of his office and for seven days manifest the silent sympathy of a heart that understood. Then and there did Ezekiel understand his mission, receive his message, and begin his ministry. No Christian work will be effective or permanent that is not based on the willingness to "sit where they sat."

I. We have here the secret of harmony in our social relations.

(a) Sympathy is the force which binds free men together in communal life. Without it we are unorganized individuals, pulling against one another. For progress comes in the measure in which a community of men and women can set themselves a common goal and work loyally together to reach it.

(b) This principle of Christian identification with others will alone prove able to bring harmony out of the discords of our industrial world. If only capital would sit where labor sits, and if labor would sit where capital sits, we should have an era of brotherhood and a glad recognition of the fact that what the Lord requires of us all is to act justly and to love mercy and to walk humbly with him.

II. We have here the secret of harmony in our religious relations.

(a) If our own vision becomes narrow we can take only a narrow view of the thoughts and feelings of others. When will the church learn to apply this truth in the realm of religious belief and opinion? When will we learn to rejoice that God raises up men who are no longer content with decaying forms, but who in their thirst for truth go down to the bottom wells again and draw the water straight from the rock?

(b) In all this the spirit of religion is lost in contentions about religion. Men become more interested in the forms of faith than in the propagation of faith. There are many churches, and all are needed as the complements of each other. Let the servants of Christ look less at what divides and more at what unites them.

III. We have here the secret of ennobling friendship.

(a) Ezekiel sat with these hardpressed people during their period of adversity, and from that time on, we may be sure, he was bound to their hearts with hoops of steel. The most lasting friendships are usually formed in mutual sorrow, just as iron is most firmly joined when placed in the fiercest flame.

(b) Dean Inge contends that the duty and happiness of friendship have been made more prominent, have filled altogether a larger place in the scheme of life before Christianity and outside Christianity than in the Christian church. There is nothing the great mass of humanity so much needs as ennobling friendship.

(c) This makes clear to us the relationship we should hold to Jesus. We may all enter that sacred circle of his friendship. He meets all the conditions and demands of friendship. He will stick closer than a brother. We will never discover the glory and beauty of life until we are sheltered with his comradeship.

IV. We have here the secret of the incarnation. "I sat where they sat"—is not that what the incarnation means?

(a) If human goodness shows itself most clearly in a great desire to give itself in service and in sacrifice for those who are in need, all that passion for service, all that desire to sacrifice must be infinitely greater in God. And if looking down human history we cannot see such sacrifice, I do not see how we can vindicate our claim that God is good. The incarnation is the answer. The Word became flesh and dwelt among us. If that is not an answer, none can be found. We who know Christ can testify that that is a true account of what he has done in every circumstance in which we find ourselves, as well as in death. I do not mean that he has been in precisely the same circumstances as ours; but his experiences seem always sufficiently close to ours to give him a fellow feeling. It is impossible to turn to Christ from any experience and not feel that there is a point of contact between you and him.

(b) And if the first incarnation was wonderful, it was not more so than the second. This was the real birthday of Christianity —when the risen Christ sent forth his spirit into the hearts of his people and made them feel that, though unseen, he was still with them, carrying on his work through them. Here is the ultimate fact of our religion. Christ is no longer imbedded in history in a faraway century; he is perpetually creative in the souls of men. You may see him in changed characters, in social transformation, in all the spiritual forces that have made the world perpetually new.—W. A. Cameron.

SUNDAY: JULY TWENTY-NINTH

MORNING SERVICE

Topic: Serving a Limited God

SCRIPTURE: Acts 22:3–4, 6–10.

Have you ever sensed that something was missing in your relationship with God? Have you ever taken that feeling a step farther, deciding that God is actually far away? Even those who sincerely try to serve God often have such feelings. There must be some way for us not to be caught in a rut like this. It's one thing to feel separated from God periodically; it's something else entirely to sense a separation continually.

I believe that a constant haunting feeling that God is absent or that we are suffering from relationship problems with him stems from our trying to serve limited gods, rather than the whole God. There can be many limited gods, but there is only one whole God. A limited god is one we want based on our own needs and/or misunderstandings about God's nature. As we become aware of his many attributes, it is all too easy for us to pick out just one of his characteristics and try to make the whole God fit into this limited mold.

In *Your God Is Too Small*, J. B. Phillips points out some of our limited gods. He talks about the "Resident Policeman God" who is basically an overdone and very punishing conscience; he makes us feel guilty and unhappy before, during, and especially after any wrongdoing. And then there's the "Grand Old Man God," a grandfather type who's as nice as he can be and someone we can brag about, but still—really and truly—just not *with* the modern scene. Notice that both these limited gods—and our infinite number of others—are not false gods, really. They are just not whole and therefore are lacking; they are constructed from only one part of God's personality taken to the extreme.

Besides the fact that God cannot be boxed in by our limitations of him, when we try to limit him, we discover that a limited god must always remain distant. While our own psychological state has something to do with how we feel about God at a given time, much of the distance and difficulty we feel toward him must be attributed to our attempts at serving our limited versions of him. Saul of Tarsus tried to serve a limited god, a god of Absolute Perfection: *no* love, *no* forgiveness, *no* compassion. But he had a dramatic experience one day which changed all that; because of it, his God became whole.

I. *A limited god is created by or for us.* Nobody served his or her God as Saul did! This devout man had everything going for him. He was a champion bloodline Jew, and his natural traits were strongly complimented by all of the religious, social, and academic "right things."

(a) It is a reliable fact of developmental psychology that we human beings are products of all we experience. This was certainly true of Saul. During his growing-up years and throughout his educational experiences, he had worked out a concept of God which he thought was the final word on the subject.

(b) But no whole God could have asked Saul to do what he did: to persecute everyone who practiced religion differently than he did. Even amid his great zeal for his God of Absolute Perfection, something was missing.

(c) The limited god Saul had created, or had created for him, was distant. No wonder! The whole God cannot be meaningfully forced into some narrow mold. That isn't just Saul's problem. We, too, try to serve some limited god created by or for us. If it's not our creation, it has been created for us by our family, by our denomination, by a local church, or by a particular person. When isolation from God persists, we need to let him be whole . . . to open ourselves daily experience *all* he is.

II. *The whole God is revealed in Jesus Christ.* On his way to Damascus, Saul was knocked to the ground by the presence of God. Inside himself, he was being asked the penetrating questions, "Why are you persecuting me? What do you mean trying to limit the boundaries of my love?" As Saul lay sprawled on the ground, he responded, "Who are you, sir?" The answer came: "I am Jesus Christ—the whole revelation of God whom you are persecuting."

(a) When did Saul begin to realize that his God was a limited God? Was it at this bright-light conversion experience? Likely not. The realization had been in process for some time, along with some feeling that God was distant. I think Saul began to suspect that there was something more to God, as a result of his continuous encounters with Christians—especially the ones he had persecuted. They were persons who wouldn't back down from what they believed, even in the face of torture. Stephen bravely faced death rather than deny

his faith in the Lord Jesus. Saul did not go unaffected by these events. These people had something more than Saul could find in his relationship with God; God seemed to be particularly near to them.

His sequence of encounters with Christians formed a backdrop for his actual moment of conversion, at which point Saul began to know the whole God. God was not a one-talent robot, but as revealed in Jesus Christ, he was a loving, challenging, unifying, ever-present Spirit.

(b) I have a fear that many of the people in our world—and maybe even some of us —haven't opened our eyes enough to see the whole God revealed in Jesus Christ. We've become too secure with our limited, though distant, gods, and we're not up to the risk of change.

(c) The whole God is multifaceted and certainly difficult to know fully. Still, we must let God be God, and that means a whole God. If we have only one perception of God, we'll miss him. If we can only see him in one way, he can be with us, and we won't know it. The whole God will be as present as we let him be.—David Farmer.

Illustrations

HUNGER FOR GOD.   We hunger for Love, for companionship, for the happiness and the delight of freely chosen friendships. We yearn for the affection of father, for the tenderness of mother. Over the smile of a baby, our own or anybody's, we go into ecstasy: the chatter of baby lips, the patter of baby feet seem to hold something divine. We cry out for the Eve who still stands in the paradise of our dreams, flowerlike and inviolate, wreathed with fadeless light. We run to and fro to find the friend who, in disinterested communion with ourselves, might call forth the best in us and give us moments of purest bliss in which the blending of two lives would but serve to enhance each. But, much as these things mean to us, much as they fill our days with rich content, they still leave us empty, hungry, and unfulfilled. Our capacity for fellowship is so great that, after we have satisfied the claims of all these earthly loves, we send out the tendrils of our spirit into space to lay hold of the Very God, and to find in loving him—him and not merely his manifestations; him, as a felt presence very near us—the last fulfillment of our being. No earthly love, no matter how pure, can fill this aching want for God. "When my father and mother forsake me," or when we forsake father and mother, too, in our search for infinite companionship, "then the Lord will take me up," for then we take up the Lord.—Joel Blau.

EXPERIENCING TRUTH.   To demand a correct creed as a condition prerequisite to the beginning of life of Christian discipleship, is manifestly to demand an impossible thing. The story out of the life of Horace Bushnell is instructive just here. He had been converted from almost universal skepticism. He had resolved to do God's will, and the knowledge of God had come to him in the way of personal experience. But still there were many things that remained dark. On one occasion, after returning from church, he came into a room and, throwing himself into a seat with an air of abandonment, thrusting both his hands into his black, bushy hair, he cried out: "O men! what shall I do with these arrant doubts I have been nursing for years? When the preacher touches the Trinity and when logic shatters it all to pieces, I am all at the four winds. But I am glad I have a heart as well as a head. My heart wants the Father, my heart wants the Son, my heart wants the Holy Ghost—and one just as much as the other. My heart says the Bible has a Trinity for me, *and I mean to hold by my heart.*" Exactly so! The great truths of religion are primarily truths of the heart.—Edwin D. Mouzon.

Sermon Suggestions

WHO BEARS THE BURDEN.   (1) "Each man shall bear his own burden" (Gal. 6:5). (2) "Bear ye one another's burdens" (Gal. 6:2). (3) "Cast thy burden upon the Lord" (Ps. 55:22).

STEPS IN FOLLOWING CHRIST.   Text: Luke 9:23. (1) Make up your mind. (2)

Give up yourself. (3) Take up your cross. (4) Keep up your cultivation. (5) Gather up your loyalties.—E. Stanley Jones.

Worship Aids

CALL TO WORSHIP.   "Lord, who shall abide in thy tabernacle? who shall dwell in thy holy hill? He that walketh uprightly, and worketh righteousness, and speaketh the truth in his heart" (Ps. 15:1–2).

INVOCATION.   Spirit of holiness and peace! Search all our motives; try the secret places of our souls; set in the light any evil that may lurk within, and lead us in the way everlasting. Take possession of our bodies. Purge them from feebleness and sloth, from all unworthy self-indulgence, that they may not hinder, but help the perfection of our spirits. Take possession of our wills that they may be one with thine, that soul and body may no longer war against each other, but live in perfect harmony, in holiness and health. Wake us as from the sleep of death, and inspire us with new resolves, and keep us blameless in body, soul, and spirit, now and ever. Let thy light fill our hearts more and more, until we shall become in truth the children of light, and perfectly at one with thee.—Samuel McComb.

OFFERTORY   SENTENCE.   "He which soweth sparingly shall reap also sparingly; and he which soweth bountifully shall reap also bountifully" (2 Cor. 9:6).

OFFERTORY PRAYER.   O God, you did not spare your own Son, but gave him up for us all. Your daily mercies are beyond our counting. May our joyous giving reflect something of the prodigality of your giving.

PRAYER.   O thou great Father of us all, we rejoice that at last we know thee. All our soul within us is glad because we need no longer cringe before thee as slaves of holy fear, seeking to appease thine anger by sacrifice and self-inflicted pain, but may come like little children, trustful and happy, to the God of love. Thou art the only true Father, and all the tender beauty of our human loves is the reflected radiance of thy loving kindness, like the moonlight from the sunlight, and testifies to the eternal passion that kindled it.

Grant us growth of spiritual vision, that with the passing years, we may enter into the fullness of this our faith. Since thou art our Father, may we not hide our sins from thee, but overcome them by the stern comfort of thy presence. By this knowledge, uphold us in our sorrows and make us patient even amid the unsolved mysteries of the years. Reveal to us the larger goodness and love that speak through the unbending laws of thy world. Through this faith, make us the willing equals of all thy other children.

As thou art ever pouring out thy life in sacrificial father-love, may we accept the eternal law of the cross and give ourselves to thee and to all men. We praise thee for Jesus Christ, whose life has revealed to us this faith and law, and we rejoice that he has become the firstborn among many brethren. Grant that in us, too, the faith in thy fatherhood may shine through all our life with such persuasive beauty that some who still creep in the dusk of fear may stand erect as free sons of God, and that others who now through unbelief are living as orphans in an empty world may stretch out their hands to the great Father of their spirits and find thee near.—Walter Rauschenbusch.

EVENING SERVICE

Topic: Charisma

Text: Rom. 12:6.

Charisma is a religious word that has been secularized and has somehow caught the public fancy. The religious significance of charisma has been both extended and illicitly narrowed in the word *charismatic*. Paul's intention here is obvious: he is urging Christians to use their special gifts, their particular talents and capabilities, their personal charisma, in service of Jesus Christ.

I. Charisma is not something that is given only to the favored few, but is something available to all. Paul declared that all Christians have special gifts allotted to them by God's grace. And these gifts do not miraculously change natural endowments and talents, but they baptize them, so to speak, for the special service of the purposes of God in Jesus Christ.

Through the centuries, the church has had leadership from men and women possessing charisma—charisma in our now popular sense of the word. And the church owes much to these people. But the church owes even more to the millions of ordinary men and women who have used their gifts, their charisma, their skills and talents—simply and inconspicuous as they often have—in Christian service. And as Paul is careful to point out, "The gifts we possess differ."

II. Charisma, in the Christian sense, is a product of faith and a test of faith. Charisma develops in and through the disciplines of faith; and in your exercise of your special gifts, your charisma, the reality of your faith is shown.

(a) "The gifts we possess differ as they are allotted to us by God's grace." Grace is not a thing, not a sort of heavenly substance or commodity that can be dispensed to us. Grace is simply God's love in action, God's creative Spirit impinging on the minds and hearts of persons. Grace is God in his influence on us, cleansing and forgiving us, enlightening and encouraging us, guiding us, empowering us. The word *grace* represents the active, creative relationship between God and us. But God does not force his grace on us. God does not come into our lives unless we choose to let him in. We are free to receive God's grace, and we are free to reject it.

(b) These gifts of ours are not a matter of our being miraculously granted special skills and talents above and beyond those we naturally have: they are, rather a matter of what we do with our skills and talents, our capabilities and our knowledge, as we respond to God's grace and use them in service of the purposes of God in Jesus Christ.

III. Charisma has its reality in acts of faith and mercy, of justice and compassion. In our exercise of our special gifts, our faith is validated and demonstrated. Charisma, in the New Testament sense, is the source and dynamic of Christian witness in the world and Christian service to the world. Romans 12 is a set of practical guidelines for Christians who would express their gifts of grace, their charisms, in the opportunities and circumstances of their lives.

Notice that Paul says nothing about our gifts differing in importance in the eyes of God. Each of you has his or her special gifts for the service of God's purpose. Use them!—J. A. Davidson.

SUNDAY: AUGUST FIFTH

MORNING SERVICE

Topic: **The Jericho Road Revisited**
Scripture: Luke 10:25–37.

One of the indisputable principles of the Christian life is presented clearly in the parable of the Good Samaritan. It begins with a man who wants to argue with Jesus about theological matters. Jesus refuses to engage in theological speculation and philosophical interrogation. Instead, the Master tells a story.

There are several characters in this little tale. (1) Some of the main characters never appear here—the robbers. We are told little about the traveler except that he was a Jew who was careless and traveled with reckless abandon. (2) The priest was a man who served God by ministering in Jerusalem's Temple. He journeyed along the road to Jerusalem, anticipating his opportunity to serve God and minister to the people of Israel. The rituals and rules of religion dictated that he cross over to the side of the road and ignore the man. (3) The Levite was only a religious functionary. He cleaned the Temple, guarded its doors, and led its choirs. The Levite's fear of risk sent him on his way. (4) The hero of the story, a Samaritan, finally appeared on the road. He was probably not a racial Samaritan because the story indicates that he frequently traveled and traded in the Jerusalem area. He was more likely a Samaritan by way of his religious beliefs. *Samaritan* was a term of contempt for those who were religious renegades. Yet, it was this man who saved the traveler's life and cared for him with compassion and courtesy. He acted out his love where the religious leaders callously kept the rules or guarded their own safety.

Here is a magnificent story about shallow religion and salty love. What shall we make of it today? We are to conclude the same things that Jesus hoped his listeners would have concluded.

I. *The needy need us.* There are many kinds of needy people in our world. The lonely need friendship! The dying desire hope! The loveless search for acceptance! The lost look for a home! The sick long for health! The starved require bread! The helpless seek a champion! The elderly need a worthy task! The young desire affirmation! There are numerous Jericho Roads that pass through our city. There are several individuals on your block who need a neighbor. There are millions in our world who must have our assistance. You and I cannot look the other way. The needy of the world are our neighbors. The cry of the helpless forces us to revisit the Jericho Road. The needy need us.

II. *We need the needy.*

(a) We need all the hungry, helpless souls of our world to allow the love of God, which we have experienced in Christ Jesus, to discover an object of expression. His love wells up in our lives and searches for a rendezvous with the desperate and the despairing of the world. The needy offer us the opportunity to obey Christ's command that we love our neighbor.

(b) We minister to Christ when we minister to them. The parable of the sheep and goat judgment portrayed in Matthew 25:31–46 paints a vivid picture of the servant's rendezvous with his master. Christ is to be found in the cries, the hungers, and the tears of the needy.

III. *We are the needy.* Do not walk proudly to the other side of the Jericho Road and continue on your carefree way. You have traveled this road before. Come closer to this stranger in the ditch who lies there bleeding and perhaps dying. Don't turn away. Look into his face. Do you recognize him? Yes, you are right, it's your face. It is you—ambushed by your sins. It is you—set upon by some personal crisis. It is you—fearful of the future. It is you—in need of help. And, help came. A good Samaritan visited you and ministered to your needs.

(a) Travel back to the time of your conversion. You were dead to the higher, nobler self within you; you were helpless to help yourself. Then, remember when Christ flooded your life with his helpful presence. Recall the miracle of his grace and forgiveness which mended your broken, bleeding soul.

(b) Step now into the pressing needs of today. Your whole world is gray. You wonder: "Is there any help for me and my loved ones?" Then it happens— the Good Samaritan comes. Help is here. His love and power lift you from the road of need. Sometimes a miracle bursts upon the scene and transforms the situation. More often though, Christ's presence strengthens your shoulders so you can manage the load.

(c) Stride forward into tomorrow, with all of its challenges, with the firm faith that the Good Samaritan is already there waiting to walk with you. Say good-bye to fear and anxiety because He who has been with us in the past and lingers with us in the present will journey, arm in arm, with us into tomorrow.—James E. Sorrell.

Illustrations

POWER OF THE HUMAN TOUCH.   I once participated with other medical men in a discussion of the practice in hospitals of what we might call "medicine of the person." Several of the participants declared that the personal relation between physicians and patient plays a most important role in the physician's office, but that a large hospital is too impersonal a machine for such a relation to obtain there. Then Professor Richard Siebeck, head physician at the Ludolf-Krehl-Spital in Heidelberg, one of the largest hospitals in Germany, said: "I think I can say that my hospital is pervaded by a personal spirit, but I believe we owe this almost entirely to a single person—our Sister Superior, who is so profoundly human that everyone whose life she touches feels that he is considered a person, feels himself becoming a person." —Paul Tournier.

SERVING IN SILENCE.   Dr. W. E. Sangster, the British Methodist preacher, was one of my heroes. Sadly, he died at the height of his powers at the age of fifty-nine. After ten months of illness, he wrote a letter of retirement from the active ministry to the Methodist Conference. He explained the situation, that he knew he would not preach again, and then wrote this: "Yet I would like you to know that God has never been nearer to me than now. I have had grace never to murmur. At no period of my life have I had so much time for prayer, and perhaps part of my pain in not being able to preach is the knowledge that I have deeper things to say than ever. Infinite wisdom and infinite love are at work for me, and a man who is sure of that can endure anything."—John N. Gladstone.

Sermon Suggestions

THE CLEMENCIES OF GOD.   Scripture: John 16:32; 2 Tim. 1:12. (1) Ours is a God who never leaves or loses us. (2) He has set purposes before us in the doing of which he translated loss into love. (3) God surrounds life with a realm of spirit that is able to sustain even life's greatest loss and most adverse denial. (4) In Jesus Christ, we find the promise that in and through every denial and lonely crucifixion of love, there is a redeeming power at work.—Robert E. Luccock.

RECIPROCAL INDWELLING.   Text: John 15:4. (1) As to fellowship, John 6:56. (2) As to obedience, 1 John 3:24. (3) As to confession, 1 John 4:15. (5) As to love, 1 John 4:15.—F. B. Meyer.

Worship Aids

CALL TO WORSHIP.   "Delight thyself also in the Lord; and he shall give thee the desires of thine heart. Commit thy way unto the Lord; trust also in him; and he shall bring it to pass" (Ps. 37:4–5).

INVOCATION. O God, humble our hearts before thee, that we may truly know thee; soften our hearts toward thee, that we may gladly obey thee; lift up our hearts in thy joy, that we may exalt thee.

OFFERTORY SENTENCE. "Every man according as he purposeth in his heart, so let him give; not grudgingly, or of necessity: for God loveth a cheerful giver" (2 Cor. 9:7).

OFFERTORY PRAYER. O Lord, may these gifts we bring go forth in quietness and strength to do thy work in the world, in the sanctuary and in the slums; in the healing of body, mind, and spirit; in the proclamation of the gospel at home and abroad.

PRAYER. We praise thee, O God, for our friends, the doctors and nurses, who seek the healing of our bodies. We bless thee for their gentleness and patience, for their knowledge and skill. We remember the hours of our suffering when they brought relief, and the days of our fear and anguish at the bedsides of our dear ones when they came as ministers of God to save the lives thou hadst given. May we reward their fidelity and devotion by our loving gratitude, and do thou uphold them by the satisfaction of work well done.

We rejoice in the tireless daring with which some are now tracking the great slayers of mankind by the white light of science. Grant that under their teaching we may grapple with the sins which have ever dealt death to the race, and that we may so order the life of our communities that none may be doomed to an untimely death for lack of the simple gifts which thou hast given in abundance.—Walter Rauschenbusch.

EVENING SERVICE

Topic: The Tragedy of Not Growing Up
TEXT: 2 Pet. 3:18.

The early Christian writers recognized that while the efforts to copy Christ's perfection would lead to despair, we can grow up toward him. Hence the call to grow up is a recurring motif. And Peter closes his second epistle with the injunction, "Grow in the grace and knowledge of our Lord and Savior Jesus Christ."

I. Consider first how a Christian is called to grow in mind.

(a) This means, for one thing, growing in information. If I leave my mind uninformed on vital issues, it is a sin. Others may not be sufficiently conscious of my ignorance to condemn me for it, and I may not be aware of what I am missing. But even in the eyes of our statute law, ignorance does not excuse our misdeeds or our mistakes.

(b) And in the eyes of Christ, the plea of ignorance does not exonerate. Christ came to "open the eyes of the blind" not only physically but mentally. He came to make us alive to the world around us, its people, its needs, its beauty. And not to be alive to what we should be aware of means loss to ourselves and to those around us. In fact, it is a sin against God.

(c) We must learn that we are to keep growing in our religion as in our secular work. The Ten Commandments have not changed in principle since the days of Moses. But their application must be brought up to date. "Thou shalt not steal!" Of course, we have known that since childhood. But it is one thing to have integrity enough to be honest in the simple man-to-man dealings of a village store; it is quite another to see and observe the implications of honesty in our long-range complex transactions of modern business and international exchange.

We are in danger of drifting into a hell on earth, unless well-meaning but uninformed and short-sighted people awake from their ignorance and lethargy to study what it means to be a follower of Jesus Christ. While we are calling for more scientists to make missiles, let us have more and better workmen of God to make peace.

II. Secondly, we must grow in heart as well as in mind.

(a) When are we going to grow up enough to get on with our fellowmen? Over two thousand years ago, the prophet Zechariah proclaimed the message he heard, "Not by might nor by power, but by my Spirit says the Lord of hosts." Of course, we must not be blindly sentimental. But let us realize that our strength lies in Christian principles even more than in military power.

(b) With the help of Christ, we can grow up out of that littleness of nature which keeps us from being generous in our judgments and magnanimous toward our critics. When we root our minds in Christ's words, we can grow up into that big-heartedness which forgives our enemies and rejoices in the success of our friends. When we can keep in communion with Christ, we can outgrow that vindictiveness which is ever trying to get even and that jealousy which is ever trying to hold others back.— Ralph W. Sockman.

SUNDAY: AUGUST TWELFTH

MORNING SERVICE

Topic: So You Want to Be Great
TEXT: Matt. 20:26.

I. (a) Jesus Christ, of all people who ever walked this earth, knew that men and women everywhere want to be great. The last thing we ever want to be said about us is that we are "nobody."

(b) We can go further and say that not only did Christ know that we want to be great, but he encourages us to want to be great. Listen to his words: "Whoever wants to be great among you must be your servant, and whoever wants to hold the first place among you must be your slave" (Matt. 20:26).

(c) "Whoever wants to be great." Think of these words. If most oriental religious leaders were to complete that sentence, they would say, "Let him realize that his very desire is a sin and let him put it out of his mind." Modern secular thinkers would say, "Whoever wants to be great, let him assert himself; man can do anything he wants to do if he wants to bad enough."

(d) But closer to home is the spirit of our whole structure which places a premium on "keeping up with the Joneses," outstripping our neighbors, becoming famous, and getting rich. We may be dishonest or vulgar or immoral, but we must appear well in the eyes of the public. That is why I maintain that about the only hope for most young people today is a conversion, and usually it means a conversion from the ideals of their own churchgoing respectable parents—to Christ.

II. But what did this Christ say about our desires to be great? Did he condemn this motive as unworthy and ungodly? Not at all. He made us that way.

(a) These disciples of his who spent three years with him did not come out with any self-effacing disposition. He had inspired each of them not only to be somebody, but to want to be great. That is why in the account just preceding this text, we read of James's and John's asking for the chief places of honor in his Kingdom.

(b) But what is wrong and what is right, if anything, with such a request? Jesus explained what was wrong. He said: "You are trying to be great by the standards of the world. I will show you how to be great, and this will permanently satisfy these deep motives which I placed in every human breast." Read it for yourself in Matthew 20:17-28.

(c) My mind stands in gaping wonder at this marvelous answer to these disciples. For I believe that there is no other problem which every human being faces which is quite as deep as this lust for greatness. Notice Jesus' recipe for greatness. He said, "If you want to be great, you must do the hard dirty work of serving your fellow man. And if you want to be really great, outstandingly great, you must serve like a slave."

(d) The trouble with us is that it costs too much to be great. Therefore, we hold on to our worldly standards and to mediocrity. It is easier, because these pagan ideals are down in our bones. They were there before we were mature enough to become Christians.

III. But let us not think that because we see the superficiality of our lives, we will be able to mend our ways. I would like to suggest some definite steps toward greatness.

(a) First, we must remember the tendency of our own nature to be misled. We need to suspect our own hidden thoughts.

(b) We need some new models. As long as we publicly praise servants and privately admire selfish demagogues, there is little chance for improvement. This is why Jesus becomes so important to the true Christian. He is our model.

(c) The only way to learn to serve is to serve. The kind of greatness which Jesus had in mind is trudged out, ached out, worried out, prayed out. To be a slave is to do things which others do not like to do. It means long hours, loss of pleasures, and usually criticism. It means self-sacrifice, but it is God's way.—R. Lofton Hudson.

Illustrations

THE ETERNAL REALITY. When I was in Harvard College, one day William James sent me to his father's house, where the professor was then living—it was before his marriage, so long ago did I know him —to get a book from his library. I was a total stranger to the family. I was met at the door by Henry James, Sr., whose blazing eyes and austere aspect were not unlike one of the Greek Furies. He admitted me, as I thought, with some reluctance, examined and cross-examined me, led me into the library, and finally being satisfied that I was human, fell into a friendly familiar conversation. He told me of a debate between his two sons, William and Henry, when they were boys, upon the church. Henry was nimbler than William in argument; William was more profound and serious. Henry said, "I am willing to confess the reality of God, but as for the church, it is a mere conventionality, made of stone and lime, and I have no respect for it." William replied, "Whoever confesses the reality of God thereby confesses the reality of the church, for ultimately God is the church." So we read in the text, "And I saw no temple therein; for the Lord God the Almighty, and the Lamb, are the Temple thereof." Here we find the boys' debate leading to the heart of the profoundest things in the Christian faith.—George A. Gordon.

PRICE OF GREED. Leo Tolstoy told the story of a man who had grown richer and richer in his land holdings. Selling his thousand acres, he took a journey to a place where there were vast stretches of land at giveaway prices. He was told that for one thousand rubles, he could have all the land he could walk around in a day. If in the course of the day he did not return to the place he had started from, he would forfeit his money. He began measuring his land at sunrise. Toward sundown, because he had taken in too much territory in his greed, he ran frantically, mile after mile, only to fall dead at the top of the hill where he had started. The chief of the land threw a spade to the man's servant and said, "Here, dig!" So the servant dug a grave for the man in all the land he needed: six feet—and no more.

Sermon Suggestions

JESUS THE RESURRECTION. Scripture: John 11:1–44. (1) "Lazarus is ill," say Mary and Martha to Jesus (v. 3). (2) "Lazarus is dead," says Jesus to his disciples (v. 14). (3) "Lazarus, come out," says Jesus to Lazarus (v. 43).—Donald E. Demaray.

CONFIDENCE FOR THE JOURNEY. Text: Isa. 45:2. (1) A warning: there are "crooked places" on our necessary journey. (2) A promise: "I will go before thee." (3) A plan: the promise works out in the life of "a good man" (cf. Prov. 37:23); the promise does not give license for carelessness.—Adapted from Joseph Parker.

Worship Aids

CALL TO WORSHIP. "Whatsoever things are true, whatsoever things are honest, whatsoever things are pure, whatsoever things are lovely, whatsoever things are of good report; if there be any virtue, and if there be any praise, think on these things" (Phil. 4:8).

INVOCATION. O God, as we strive to achieve our place under the sun, grant us the wisdom to trace the steps of our Lord Jesus Christ in his servanthood and grant us the courage to follow him. To that end, give us a new vision of true greatness as we wait before thee.

OFFERTORY SENTENCE. "God is able to give you more than you need, so that you will always have all you need for yourselves and more than enough for every good cause" (2 Cor. 9:8 [TEV]).

OFFERTORY PRAYER. Gracious Lord, thou hast given us all things to enjoy, to share with others, and to make us better and more useful servants of thine. Now deepen our love, open our hands, and help us to know the joy of a cheerful giver.

PRAYER. O Jesus, we thy ministers bow before thee to confess the common sins of our calling. Thou knowest all things; thou knowest that we love thee and that our hearts' desire is to serve thee in faithfulness; and yet, like Peter, we have so often failed thee in the hour of thy need. If ever we have loved our own leadership and power when we sought to lead our people to thee, we pray thee to forgive. If we have been engrossed in narrow duties and little questions, when the vast needs of humanity called aloud for prophetic vision and apostolic sympathy, we pray thee to forgive. If, in our loyalty to the church of the past, we have distrusted thy living voice and have suffered thee to pass from our door unheard, we pray thee to forgive. If ever we have been more concerned for the strong and the rich than for the shepherdless throngs of the people for whom thy soul grieved, we pray thee to forgive.— Walter Rauschenbusch.

EVENING SERVICE

Topic: Greatness in the Church
SCRIPTURE: Acts 2:37–47.

Generally, when we speak of a "great church," we mean that the church has a great set of facilities, or that it has an eloquent preacher, or that it has an exceptional music program, or a finely perfected organizational life. A church, however, can be great without having any of these things. Any church may be a great church if it has the qualities and characteristics which were found in the church described in Acts 2.

Let us direct our attention to some of the qualities of greatness in that first church.

I. *It was great in preaching*.

(a) Consider that Peter was "full of the Holy Spirit of God." The Scripture adds that when he stood up, there stood with him a group of divinely called and divinely ordained men. He stood in the midst of the 120 men and women whose lives had been brought under the control of the living Christ.

(b) This church was great in its preaching because they had a spirit-filled preacher. But they also had a spirit-filled congregation. They had a united, ordained group of men to stand in the church with the preacher. You see the results of such preaching (Acts 2:14–17). The record says, "Now when they heard this, they were pricked to their heart, and said unto Peter and to the rest of the apostles: Men and brethren, what shall we do?" (Acts 2:37).

II. *It was great in teaching*. "And they continued steadfastly in the apostles' doctrine" (Acts 2:42). Here is a characteristic of the early church which should characterize the church in our time. They stayed by the teaching! When it is said that they continued in the apostles' teaching, it means that they wanted to learn more of the eternal truth which the apostles had to share. Today we are ignorant of the things of God. There is a death of spiritual knowledge in the church.

IV. *It was great in its outreaching*. The Christians were continually "praising God, and having favor with all the people. And the Lord added to the church daily such as should be saved" (Acts 2:47). Here is one of the first characteristics of a New Testament church. Beginning in its own area, it reaches out into the whole world.

This first church found favor with all the people. They believed that Jesus lived, that he lived in them, and they lived like him. Until you and I come to that place, I doubt seriously that we have the right to call ourselves a great church.—Carl E. Bates.

SUNDAY: AUGUST NINETEENTH

MORNING SERVICE

Topic: Jesus' Model Prayer
SCRIPTURE: Matt. 6:9–13.

This prayer is truly a model by which we should compare our usual praying and by which we should consciously pattern our future praying. For the Lord Christ said to pray "after this manner." He did not propose that our every prayer should be a reproduction of these exact words, for he was instructing those learners how to pray. As the perfect model, this prayer demonstrates the correct order of our requests and our needs which parallel Jesus' guidance.

I. First, we encounter the invocation, "Our father which art in heaven." Basic in genuine conversation between persons is the factor of relationship.

(a) Our spirits hunger for his presence when we realize that we talk with God, our Father.

(b) Our intimacy with the Father is never to degenerate into disrespect, for he is "our father which is in heaven."

(c) This invocation emphasizes the family relationship of all Christians. The salutation is "our father," not merely "my father."

II. The body of the model prayer consists of six petitions, equally divided, three Godward, three manward.

(a) The first request is, "Hallowed be thy name"—let your name be holy. This request is that God's holiness be recognized everywhere throughout our entire world. This is partially accomplished by his working through you. His reputation is dependent on your living testimony. This petition is a desire of one's soul for which he prays, for which he lives, and for which he works—that God's character be recognized as supremely holy.

(b) A second request which is also Godward is, "Let your Kingdom come." This driving desire is for the rule, the reign of God to be effective in the hearts of the citizens of our world. The person who utters such a far-reaching request assumes obligation to work for its fulfillment in convincing people to accept God's control. The victory note surrounds this prayer when the sacred Scriptures offer the promise, "The kingdom of this world will become the Kingdom of our Lord and his Christ."

(c) A third petition arises from devout disciples, "Let your will be done on earth, as it is in heaven." While sheltered by the repellent coat of decency, some people ask, "Let your will be done on earth in the lives of other people, but I want to do as I please." That God's word be operative, his law obeyed, is the request.

The order of these petitions is instructive as to their importance. God's glory and Kingdom come first, before our wants. As in prayer, so in life: "Seek ye first the Kingdom of God, and his righteousness, and all these things will be added unto you."

III. The other three petitions are manward.

(a) The first of these is, "Give us this day our daily bread." "Give us bread" means everything necessary to sustain life. Jesus the Christ taught us here and elsewhere to trust our loving Father to provide the necessities of our living. This petition underscores our dependence, our continuous dependence, on God for every blessing of life. To mention to God our physical needs is to reveal the fact that we should pray for our livelihood as well as work for it. Be assured that if such cooperation is realized, that which God furnishes is never articles stolen from the needy or gains of ungodly activity.

(b) The second manward request is for forgiveness of sins. F. B. Meyer wrote that this shows we need forgiveness as often as daily bread. While most of us are aware of our need for forgiveness, many fail to know that it is determined by our relationship with other human beings. The spirit which is open to receiving love is of necessity open to show love. Only this petition of all six was given an explanation by Jesus.

(c) Forgiveness of the past is not completely sufficient. We must have guidance and strength for the future: "And lead us not into temptation, but deliver us from the evil." This is one point at which we must put feet to our prayers. We ask God to deliver us from temptations, and we must likewise deliver ourselves from enticements.

IV. The last division of the model prayer is the doxology. For his is the Kingdom, meaning his sovereign control over all things. For his is the power to do all things, including the needs of your soul for cleansing and of your life for development. For his is the honor and the glory which our lives are to magnify when he has granted our requests.—Franklin Atkinson.

Illustrations

PREPARED.   Phillips Brooks uses the analogy of a ship at sea, fighting a gale. The winds howl, and the waves roll. Will the ship hold together? You say it is a terrific struggle. But really, that battle was fought long before, in the forest where the timbers grew, in the shipyards when the nails were pounded in and the planks laid and the seams calked. The battle was fought in the care given to the ship through the years in guarding against dry rot and broken ribs and loose fittings. The storm is merely the test; the battle was fought and either won or lost before.

Quietly, mysteriously, unobtrusively, almost casually, worship feeds the soul, stores up inner reserves. When the storm comes—as it does at last to all—those reserves, such as they are, become our strength.—Hughes Wagner.

THE RIGHT TIME TO PRAY.   George Beasley-Murray said that many years ago, he heard Stephen Winward give a message on prayer and was astonished at the very first thing he said: "If you want to learn to pray, the first thing you need is an alarm clock!"

Sermon Suggestions

MEANING OF SALVATION.   Scripture: Rom. 8:14–39. Not only has God worked the wonder of the resurrection, he is still at work. (1) God has made us his children,

with a twofold consequence: We are set free from fear, and we are able to pray with confidence (vv. 14–17). (2) God opens the future before us (vv. 18–25). (3) God now shares his people's struggles (vv. 28–30). Thus our whole salvation is God's doing. Therefore it cannot fail (vv. 31–39).—Merrill R. Abbey.

LIFE FROM A NEW ANGLE.   Scripture: Matt. 9:10–17. (1) Christ is for those who need him (vv. 10–13). (2) Christ blesses those who are open to him (vv. 14–17).—William E. McCumber.

Worship Aids

CALL TO WORSHIP.   "Know therefore that the Lord thy God, he is God, the faithful God, which keepeth covenant and mercy with them that love him and keep his commandments to a thousand generations" (Deut. 7:9).

INVOCATION.   Lord Christ, teach us again to pray. Help us to see our needs clearly and honestly, and grant us the faith and dedication to think thy thoughts after thee, to follow our understanding with fitting deeds, and to trust thee to make of our obedience building stones of thy Kingdom.

OFFERTORY SENTENCE.   "God, who supplies seed for the sower and bread to eat, will also supply you with all the seed you need and will make it grow and produce a rich harvest from your generosity" (2 Cor. 9:10).

OFFERTORY PRAYER.   We could not be here today, our Father, if thou hadst not given us our daily bread. As thou hast provided for our needs through thy manifold mercies, now make us instruments of that same providence that others' needs may also be met.

PRAYER.   Almighty and most gracious heavenly Father, we pray that we may better learn to love and serve thee in all that we do. Guide us all the days of our lives that we may truly know your will for our lives; allow us to be examples of thy love to others; and grant unto us the love and faith in thee to share our lives with our fellow creatures.

Make us responsible, O Lord, in the difficult task of removing the blight of misery and oppression from your world. Allow us to be strong and compassionate servants of yours in the unending battle against the violence, cruelty, and hatred of the world.

We pray, moreover, that in the midst of realizing your Kingdom in the world, we may forget not the many people who have special needs this day: needs that arise from family and personal problems such as illness, hospitalization, loss, confusion, and grief. We would pray, O Lord, that you would rest your hand of healing upon the life of each person here this day.—Rodney K. Miller

EVENING SERVICE

Topic: When All You Have Is Benign Piety

TEXT: Rom. 12:11 (Moffatt trans.); Jas. 2:14 (Barclay trans.).

Many of us may be suffering from a benign piety. Now piety is the right attitude toward God. Yet, the problem with piety is that it can become benign. Benign piety may mean that we have cultivated all the ingredients of a life of holiness, but fail or refuse to apply those ingredients in the daily pattern of life.

Our Scripture verses suggest the need for both inner piety and outward Christian action. Paul wrote the first word to the Romans and called upon them to "maintain the spiritual glow," to "be alive in the Spirit." James in his epistle suggested you could not stop with just that inner glow. It is important, but of little meaning if it is not linked with action.

I. *Piety can be distorted.*

(a) In our time, we have come to regard the "pious person" as one who is sour-faced, sanctimonious, holier-than-thou, and self-consciously superior in his attitude. This is unfortunately typical of a common misunderstanding of the word *pious*. We need to understand that *piety* is a positive word in the Christian's vocabulary. It expresses the right attitude toward God. Piety is the manner in which we exercise our obedience, loyalty, and devotion to God and to Jesus Christ.

(b) Passive piety distorts a needed element in our Christian lives: the combination of a deep inner sense of the Spirit of God and the active application of that faith in daily living.

(1) Some of us spend our entire religious-time-provision in seeking to develop our own inner spiritual lives. But too often we exclude the second half of the faith-works combination essential to all valid Christian life and living. (2) We need to beware lest such a removal from the workaday world is merely a means of escape from the involvement which must naturally follow if one is to live with and by the right attitude toward God and his demands brought to us in Jesus.

II. *Piety can be productive.*

(a) Paul and James combine to remind us that piety must be linked to productive Christian deeds. One cannot claim faith who does not allow that faith to issue in works of good. We are called to link piety to action, faith to deeds. Only applied piety can be fully productive. Personal piety in devotion and prayer can certainly lead to a sense of closeness with God. But life can never be fully meaningful until we are motivated by that piety to become close to other persons and sensitive to their needs. The Christian is called to a combination of inner reverence and outer devotion, piety, and good works. Faith without works is dead. Works without faith can never stand the test of time.

(b) Would any disagree that today's world requires this combination of the vertical and the horizontal in faith—faith that reaches up in devotion, and prayer and faith that reach out the helping hand in concern and love? True piety, in the biblical sense, makes us identify with God's children everywhere. Notice the development of the Christian faith and concern as Peter describes it in his epistle (1 Pet. 1:3, 5–7). Our faith is either an inner assurance or an inner emptiness. Our faith is either involvement with others or it is completely irrelevant. Without inner assurance (piety) and social involvement (good works) there is no way we can be fully Christian.—Brian L. Harbour.

SUNDAY: AUGUST TWENTY-SIXTH

MORNING SERVICE

Topic: A Little Letter with a Time Bomb in It

SCRIPTURE: Philemon.

I. One of the complaints that is sometimes made about the Bible as a guidebook for men and nations is that it is not explicit enough.

When we think like this, we are, of course, asking for more than we really want. For if our desire is to have a huge rule book in which we can look up the answers to every practical question that confronts us, we are really asking for our humanity to be taken away from us.

According to the Bible, God takes the risk of bringing into being creatures who can choose. Therefore, he will not map out for them every inch of the way they have to go. He shows us his design for mankind, the kind of people he wants us to be, and the kind of society that he plans and makes possible for us, but he leaves us to make our own decisions right along the line.

II. So the Bible is not a colossal book of rules. Yet it does contain sufficient guidance in the form of laws and examples, and supremely the story of the perfect Son and the contagious moral strength that flows from him, to enable those who are willing to listen to find the way to go. Sometimes a biblical insight has dawned on a man or a community like the rising sun, and in a short space of time, there has been a moral revolution. The gospel broke on the pagan world with a stunning new sense of man's infinite value and his immortal destiny as a child of God. At once, the infant church was led to see every kind of human being as one for whom Christ died.

III. But there were some implications of this new gospel that were not immediately perceived. Clearly there is a growth in the possibility of our grasping what God has to say. We can see now very well that Christians in past ages were singularly blind to some clear indications of the Bible message. And we can be sure that future generations will look back and wonder how we, who profess the Christian name today, could have been so unresponsive to some facet of the gospel.

This delayed-action mechanism that seems to be built into the Bible is fascinatingly illustrated by the presence and power of one little book that few people bother to read. It is, in fact, the shortest book in the whole collection. It covers less than a page in most Bibles. This is the little letter with the time bomb in it. For centuries, the implications of this note were not fully understood. When they were, there was an explosion—and what was shattered was nothing less than the institution of human slavery.

IV. Nowhere in the Bible is it stated in so many words that slavery is wrong. The institution itself is neither denounced nor defended. It is just there. But there is latent in the Bible attitude toward human life, in the teachings of Jesus, and in the liberating and dignifying power of the gospel, a moral dynamic that was bound to abolish any system by which one man could own another. It took centuries to happen, but in the end, it was the Bible view of man that exploded in the human conscience and the fight against slavery itself was on. The letter to Philemon is about a slave. Yet nothing whatever is said in it about slavery being wrong. Yet every line of it breathes the spirit of a gospel which was bound in the end to bring this degrading system to an end.

When you consider the temper of the Roman Empire, the fierce laws there were dealing with runaway slaves, and the class barriers that divided society, the whole story is a minor miracle. It is typical of the Bible that such a tale of real life is included rather than a set of maxims of human conduct concerning the treatment of slaves. Though laws are necessary to reform evil institutions and to protect human rights, what makes such laws really effective is the warm response of individuals to the plight of their fellow men.

V. At first, it seems as though the gospel worked on the master-slave situation from the inside, transforming the relationship. But eventually it had to be seen that the very system of owning human beings was an offense, and full-scale assault on slavery took place. It is hardly to the credit of the church that it took about eighteen hundred years for this to happen.

When it is said that the church should not concern itself with questions of justice among men or peace among nations, we must reply that such concern is bound to spring from an understanding that in God's sight every human being is of equal value, that everyone of us is equally a sinner for whom Christ died, and that his will is eternally for peace and goodwill among men.

The Lord, we may be sure, has still many things to say to us. I wonder if we can bear them now? Are we yet ready for a full acceptance of our brethren, or are we to go on giving them labels that make them somewhat less than real people, consciously or unconsciously thinking of them as inferior or less valuable human beings than ourselves?—David H. C. Read.

Illustrations

SPIRITUAL REBIRTH. Each individual must fill in for himself the circumstances that have broken his grip on the old self. Sometimes a terrible upheaval in world events shatters old patterns and compels a new beginning. Sometimes an individual has been so wronged that something must die—either his bitterness or his love, but one or the other. And sometimes, as Alan Paton's novel, *Too Late the Phalarope*, makes clear, disaster may come through strange forces in the self. A man falls into evil so deadly that what he has done either destroys him, or a part of him is washed away so that he rises at last—chastened, broken, but healed.—David E. Roberts.

Sermon Suggestions

STILLING THE STORM IN YOUR LIFE. Mark 4:35–41. (1) Accept the reality of the storm. (2) Go to Jesus for help. (3) Overcome fear with faith.—John R. Brokhoff.

THE NEW COMMANDMENT. Text: John 13:34–35. (1) The nature of the new commandment. (2) The reason of the new commandment. (3) The purpose of the new commandment. (4) The challenge of the new commandment.—Alfred E. Garvie.

Worship Aids

CALL TO WORSHIP. "Ye shall know the truth, and the truth shall make you free" (John 8:32).

INVOCATION. God, this could be the day when some truth may dawn upon us with a brighter and surer light. Open our minds and hearts to be ready to hear the old, old story with its timely message for each of us. Through him who is the Light of the world.

OFFERTORY SENTENCE. "The rendering of this service not only supplies the wants of the saints but also overflows in many thanksgivings to God" (2 Cor. 9:12 [RSV]).

OFFERTORY PRAYER. O God, some of us are able to give much, yet we give little; some of us would give more, but we have little. As thou dost increase the ability of some, increase the ability of others, to the end that no need will go unmet and no one of us will go unblessed.

PRAYER. We come to thee, our Father, that we may more deeply enter into thy joy. Thou turnest darkness into day, and mourning into praise. Thou art our Fortress in temptation, our Shield in remorse, our Covert in calamity, our Star of Hope in every sorrow. O Lord, we would know thy peace, deep, abiding, inexhaustible. When we seek thy peace, our weariness is gone, the sense of our imperfection ceases to discourage us, and our tired souls forget their pain. When, strengthened and refreshed by thy goodness, we return to the task of life, send us forth as servants of Jesus Christ in the service and redemption of the world. Send us to the hearts without love, to men and women burdened with heavy cares, to the miserable, the sad, the broken-hearted. Send us to the children whose heritage has been a curse, to the poor who doubt thy providence, to the sick who crave for healing and cannot find it, to the fallen for whom no man cares. May we be ministers of thy mercy, messengers of thy helpful pity, to all who need thee. By our sympathy, our prayers, our kindness, our gifts, may we make a way for the inflow of thy love into needy and loveless lives. And so may we have that love which alone is the fulfilling of thy law. Hasten the time when all men shall love thee and one another in thee, when all the barriers that divide us shall be broken down, and every heart shall be filled with joy and every tongue with melody.—Samuel McComb.

EVENING SERVICE

Topic: Life—Lost and Found

SCRIPTURE: Mark 10:17–22.

The rich young ruler had everything we think we want. But from him came that surprising question, "What do I still lack?"

This man comes closer to us than many in the New Testament. While our sins are greater than most of us would admit, often they are of the hidden kind. How do we find the fullness of the Christian experience?

I. It is more than probable that most of us still need to make an unreserved decision. This I deeply believe to be the most urgent need of modern Christians. Their faith is good as far as it goes, but it needs to have a new direct relationship with Jesus Christ.

One of the essentials for this transition is to review your decision. Is it without reserve? When is a decision unreserved? The problem with most of us seems not that of saying yes to Christ as much as saying no to something else. Our hearts already go out to Christ. But we have not yet learned the other side of it—how to say no to the other things that he might have priority.

II. Some of us do need an unafraid freedom.

(a) It was no small part of the concern of the Master to set people free, and he did it by saying in all the load of the commandments you carry, there are essentially only two, "Thou shalt love the Lord thy God and thy neighbor as thyself."

(b) When one accepts Jesus Christ as Lord and Savior, it is an act of freedom. It does not mean that he has to accept a great many earlier interpretations or primitive stories that only confuse instead of clarify his faith. Jesus himself came not to destroy, but to fulfill. And that fulfillment is freedom.

III. Deeper than these, I think, is another need, our unashamed dependence.

(a) There is a heresy in our time. It is the heresy of self-sufficiency. No one could calculate how much anxiety has been caused by this false doctrine. Against this stands the Good News of the gospel of Christ. We are increasingly dependent, and God is lovingly dependable.

(b) There is something in the heart of an individual which nothing but God can satisfy. This is the heartbreak of an hour like this, that all too many people try to solve their insecurity by trying to possess more, or to cover up the haunted feeling of being unloved by taking any cheap substitute they can find. The great atheism to which the gospel of Christ must address itself now is that which falsely believes that the spiritual needs of every man's soul can be met without God.—Gene E. Bartlett.

SUNDAY: SEPTEMBER SECOND

MORNING SERVICE

Topic: The Risk of Discipleship
TEXT: Luke 14:27.

Jesus made it pretty clear that there are no disciples without discipline and no saints without sacrifice. He constantly point out that there is no doubt that faithfulness to God is demanding and that Christian discipleship is both risky and costly. He was calling all would-be disciples to calculate the risk, count the cost, and carry the cross.

I. *Calculate the risk.* Jesus warned his prospective disciples that there is risk in discipleship. There is always the risk of alienation from family, vicious threat and condemnation by your peers, poverty, and even death as a criminal.

(a) The disciple is called to calculate the risk of involvement. That can be a far-reaching decision—to become involved. Christian discipleship is not a matter of speculation or scholarship so much as it is a matter of risk. It is an act of commitment in which the whole personality is involved. No Christian can become a disciple without the risk of involvement with others. If you don't want to get involved with people and causes, then you don't want to get involved with following Jesus.

(b) The disciple is called to calculate the risk of loving concern. This rules out the conformity which keeps life comfortable and untroubled. The basis of this concern for the Christian is the love which God has revealed in Jesus Christ. Love itself is a risk. Love always involves the risk of being hurt. Love always runs the risk of being rejected. Jesus, too, experienced this risk. He came as God's man to bring God's love. He was despised, rejected, and killed.

This comes home to us in the turbulence of our world. To take a stand on Christian principles in any phase of human experience and thought is to run the risk of being misunderstood, having our motives questioned, our patriotism impugned, and our character assassinated.

II. *Count the cost.* Jesus said you must count the cost before you enter the arena of Christian discipleship.

(a) Sometimes we gloss over the cost of being Christian. We make it relatively easy for people to become members of the church. We don't talk much about risk and cost and sacrifice as requirements for membership. There is, however, a high cost in following Jesus as a disciple. Jesus said there could be no competitors for the devotion and loyalty of the Christian to God. Ultimate loyalty and primary devotion for the Christian disciple must be given to God, said Jesus.

(b) Much of our problem as seeking Christians is that we trip on the hard parts of discipleship. We listen to the hard sayings of Jesus and then try to dismiss them as not being for us in our day. Some soon learn that the practice of discipleship is a demanding discipline and drift away.

(c) Sometimes we miss completely Jesus' call to discipleship. He established the principle that discipleship means witness and service where God has planted you!

The risk of discipleship may well be that we will miss out on what God has really called us to do because we are looking in a different direction. Discipleship requires the kind of fidelity which gives ultimate priority to the Kingdom of God, ultimate loyalty to God, and a willingness to serve where we are at the moment.

III. *Carry the cross.* Sometimes we make carrying the cross seem easy. We wear a lapel cross, or a cross on a chain around our necks. But is this what Jesus meant? Hardly. He was asking his disciples to be willing to stand up and be counted in a crisis. He was asking them to forget themselves in the service of God. No one can build a Christian life without carrying its high concerns willingly on his own shoulders. He assumes the responsibility. He takes on the cross and thus becomes a follower of Jesus.—Hoover Rupert.

Illustrations

DIGNIFYING LIFE.   God calls us to walk the earth with dignity. Jesus Christ dignified life at every point. He made all of life honorable and worthy by glorifying God in all that he did. Those who walk in the steps of the Master walk the earth with dignity. While my wife and I were on vacation, we drove out of our way to see the place where one such man lived and worked. We drove to Tuskegee, and there on the campus of that great school, we stood before the grave of that humble black who was born a slave, but who dignified life as few men have done. George Washington Carver never lost the sense of the unity of life. To him all things were sacred, and he used all matter for a holy purpose. When asked how he had been able to produce such an amazing number of products from the peanut, he said that he had placed it in his hand and asked the Creator to reveal to him its secrets. He never lost the meaning and purpose of work. He lived for others. There in Tuskegee we saw the beautiful and brilliant colors he had produced from common clay of the fields. He gave all this to the people, because he wanted them to beautify their homes. He found great joy and happiness in his work because he served his fellow men. He never lost the sense of stewardship. Whatever he did was for the glory of God. Because he had the spirit of Christ, he dignified life.—Earle W. Crawford.

FINDING GOD'S WILL.   When I was deciding the question of my life's work I received a letter from a college president saying, "It is the will of the faculty, the will of the student body, the will of the townspeople, and, we believe, the will of God that you should teach in this college." At the same time I received a letter from a trusted friend saying, "I believe it is the will of God that you should go into evangelistic work in America." Then a letter came from the Board of Missions saying, "It is our will to send you to India." Here was a perfect traffic jam of wills! They were all secondhand, and I felt that I had a right to firsthand knowledge in such a crisis. Not that I would despise the opinions of friends in spiritual guidance, for God often guides through them, but obviously here they could not be depended on. So I took the letter from the board, went to my room, spread it out and said, "Now, Father, my life is not my own and I must answer this. Lead me and I'll follow."

Very clearly the Inner Voice said, "It is India."

"All right," I replied, "that settles it—it is India."

I arose from my knees and wrote at once, saying that I was ready. The Inner Voice did not fail me then. It has never failed me since. In many a crisis, too intimate to spread on the pages of a book, I have looked to him to give me a clear lead. He has never failed to give me that lead sooner or later, and when he has given it, it has always turned out to be right. He has never let me down. I have let him down, time and again, but I find him utterly dependable. I am sure that outside of that Will I cannot succeed; inside of that Will I cannot fail.—E. Stanley Jones.

Sermon Suggestions

THE INSECURITY OF WEALTH.   Scripture: Mark 1:17–27. (1) Our ignorance of our true self. (2) The love of Christ for such people. (3) The immense danger of trusting false securities.—Adapted from J. C. Ryle.

OUR OWN HOUSE OF PRAYER.   Text: Matt. 6:6. (1) Room 1: The room in which we affirm the presence of God. (2) Room 2: The room in which we praise, thank, and adore God. (3) Room 3: The room of confession, forgiveness, and unloading. (4) Room 4: The room set aside for affirmation and reception. (5) Room 5: The place for purified desire and sincere petition. (6) Room 6: The room of intercession for others. (7) Room 7: The big room at the top of the house set aside for meditation.—Leslie D. Weatherhead, *A Private House of Prayer*.

Worship Aids

CALL TO WORSHIP. "I will praise thee with my whole heart: before the gods will I sing praise unto thee. I will worship toward thy holy temple, and praise thy name for they lovingkindness and for thy truth: for thou hast magnified thy word above all thy name" (Ps. 138:1–2).

INVOCATION. O Thou who dost neither slumber nor sleep, but keepest a watchful eye over thy creation, sustaining it by thy power and might, grant that we may join thee more heartily today in what thou seekest to do through us. May thy service in the sanctuary continue in our service outside. To that end help us to worship thee in spirit and in truth.

OFFERTORY SENTENCE. "My God shall supply all your need according to his riches in glory by Christ Jesus" (Phil. 4: 19).

OFFERTORY PRAYER. O God, we bring to thee the tokens of our toil. As thou dost sanctify the work of our hands, now receive and use to thy glory what our hands have wrought.

PRAYER. O God, we rejoice that today no burden of work will be upon us and that our body and soul are free to rest. We thank thee that of old this day was hallowed by thee for all who toil, and that from generation to generation the weary sons of men have found it a shelter and a breathing space. We pray for thy peace on all our brothers and sisters who are glad to cease from labor and to enjoy the comfort of their home and the companionship of those whom they love. Forbid that the pressure of covetousness or thoughtless love of pleasure rob any who are worn of their divine right of rest. Grant us wisdom and self-control that our pleasures may not be follies, lest our leisure drain us more than our work. Teach us that in the mystic unity of our nature our body cannot rest unless our soul has repose, that so we may walk this day in thy presence in tranquility of spirit, taking each joy as thy gift, and on the morrow return to our labor refreshed and content.—Walter Rauschenbusch.

EVENING SERVICE

Topic: What God Requires

TEXT: Mic. 6:8.

Micah 6 begins with a summons (vv. 1– 5). God brings suit against his wayward people, Israel. With a poetic flair, he calls on the mountains, hills, and foundations of the earth to bear witness to his charges. God calls attention to this generous provision for Israel.

I. *The Israelites respond* by saying, "How shall we approach God?" They protest, "We are religious! What more does God expect of us?

Israel was religious, all right, just as they claimed. But they had neglected a matter weightier than the law. They were ethically crooked. They were pious and religious, but unethical. That became a stench in the nostrils of the Almighty.

II. *What God requires* (6:8). "You know what is good," wrote Micah. People seldom need to be told what is good or bad, right or wrong. It is one thing to *know* what is right and another to *do* what is right.

(a) *Justice.* To live justly means to live with personal and corporate integrity. Our word is to be our bond. We are to keep our promises and live up to our contractual agreements. Micah is calling for basic honesty in all our dealings.

(b) *Mercy.* To show mercy means to be kind. Some things are true, but repeating them would not be kind. Justice writes a check, but mercy gives oneself. God is merciful and kind to us. And he wants us to be the same toward others.

(c) *Faith.* "Walk humbly with God." Faith is not *punctilio.* Faith is a process.

III. *Real religion is a balanced experience.* It includes both worship and morality, belief and behavior, character and conduct. A mature faith incorporates both an inward piety and outward expressions of social conscience and action. Real religion embraces both theology and ethics.

What a trilogy: justice, mercy, and faith! The first two relate to man, whom we have seen. The third relates to God, whom we have not seen. Religion, biblical religion, is as large as life. It permeates all of life as leaven a loaf, salt the meat, or light the darkness.

Micah 6:8 may sound simple until you try it. But believe me, it is an impossible ethic without the grace of God. It means that God wants you—all of you. Jesus put it simply: "Follow me."—Alton H. McEachern.

SUNDAY: SEPTEMBER NINTH

MORNING SERVICE

Topic: Why Pray?

TEXT: Luke 11:1.

I. *Why many no longer pray.*

(a) They get along so well otherwise. Things are going so wonderfully well. Many, like these friends, do not pray until life flounders or some dire threat hangs over life. A national crisis or some personal catastrophe may produce the climate of prayer, but there seems to be little need of it when things are going so well.

(b) They tried it and it didn't work. The Apostle James seemed to have anticipated this group. "Ye ask and have not, because ye ask amiss, that ye may comsume it upon your lusts" (James. 4:3). Prayer, for many believers, is nothing more than the petted privilege of a spoiled child seeking ideal conditions in which to indulge his spiritual propensities. "Prayer changes things," we say. No denying it. Prayer releases mighty forces which God in his mercy and goodness releases under no other condition. But would it not be nearer the truth to say, "Prayer changes people and people change things"! Prayer, for many Christians, is nothing more than a spoiled child crying for a bottle which, if he continues to get it, will prevent mature spiritual development.

(c) It is beneath their dignity. A visitor to our city tells of two college student who were discussing religion. One said to the other, "You don't pray, do you?" The other confessed, as though caught in a crime, "Once in a while I say, 'Our Father.'" The other promptly nailed him, "So . . . you've sold out to the father-image!" As I listened to the story I remember vaguely the teachings of Sigmund Freud. Even in his greatness this man left partial truths which remain like a virus to infect the minds of the educated. Prayer, to him was an illusion. It suggested a vast image painted in the sky. Only self-seeking cowards unable to face reality and fulfill selfhood resorted to it. The only people who can fulfill selfhood are men and women who have learned how to use Christian prayer. It is not self-seeking cowardice to admit personal inadequacies. On the contrary, we are mortal fools to assume the opposite extreme and turn amateur providence!

II. *Why we ought always to pray.*

(a) We ought to pray because this is the way to get to know God better. Just as little children come to know and understand the principles, the character, the purposes of their own daddy, so must we come to know God. There came a time in my life when I would say to my brother, "It won't do any good to ask daddy; I know he won't let us go." In retrospect I now understand that this actually was a glowing tribute to my dad. He already stood for some things by the time I came along. Had there been time and opportunity, he might have explained the basis upon which the household operated, but I had to learn all of this. And how? By asking!

(b) A Christian is one who has looked. He has seen not only the need of his own heart but the urgent need of the whole world. His vision is of "fields white unto harvest." Multiplied thousands of them are under the convicting work of the outpoured Spirit of God just waiting to be gathered in. Jesus said, "Pray, 'Thy kingdom come.'" He also said, "Pray the father to send forth laborers." In this very passage we find the heart and center of prayer as it relates to the waiting multitudes.

Prayer is the means whereby God pours through us into other lives the blessings he waits to bestow upon them.

(c) We pray because our life depends

upon it. When will we learn that God engineers the circumstances of our lives? When will we learn that the diet for each day is prepared for us by our heavenly Father? We cry for chocolate ice-cream when what we need is spinach. When the spinach comes our first reaction is to pout at God and accuse him of injustice. He gives us what we need. It is not always what we want, but always just exactly what we need. There is no other way for the new nature in us to develop.—Carl E. Bates.

Illustrations

WORDS TO LIVE AND DIE BY.   In Hollywood there is a business firm which challenges its competitors by saying, "Find a better price and we'll beat it." If we can find better words to live by than Moses' admonition, we at once should claim them. For myself, I am skeptical that any improvement can be made. For now as well as all eternity I am willing to relax into that ancient assurance, the last, best words of Moses: "The eternal God is your dwelling place, and underneath are the everlasting arms."—John H. Townsend.

THE TIME TO PRAY.   When a person is uprooted he is profoundly affected. He may become homesick to the core of his being. He may be like the five-year-old son of a friend of mine who moved away from the neighborhood in which he had been living. The little fellow was sad to tears for having to leave his playmates. As they were moving into the new home, he said to his father, "Daddy, we need to have a little room in our house specially for prayer so we will have a place to go in times like these!" Similarly I recall having left home at the age of thirteen to become a page in the United States Senate. I remember the spirit of heaviness, the lump in my throat, the sheer loneliness of the dark room I occupied all by myself, and the way in which I counted the days of my first year there.—Wayne E. Oates.

Sermon Suggestions

THE RIM OF YOUR WORLD.   Text: Mark 1:38. (1) The physical horizon is an artificial one for the soul of man. (2) There is the liability of accepting prematurely an artificial horizon for our own character and personality, of losing the horizon of the possible person we might be. (3) We all face the danger of the too near horizon of personal interest and advantage. We see Jesus facing the farther horizon rather than staying comfortably in one little town.—Halford E. Luccock.

A MIXED RECEPTION OF JESUS.   Scripture: Mark 3:7–35. (1) The common people, vv. 7–12. (2) Disciples, vv. 13–19. (3) "Friends," vv. 19b-21. (4) Enemies, vv 22–30. (5) His family, vv. 31–35.—Ernest Trice Thompson.

Worship Aids

CALL TO WORSHIP.   "Lord, I have loved the habitation of thy house, and the place where thine honour dwelleth" (Ps. 26:8).

INVOCATION.   O God our Father, make this truly a house of prayer today. May we call upon thee in the confidence that thou dost hear us. May we surrender to thee our selfishness and greed so that nothing will hinder our prayers.

OFFERTORY SENTENCE.   "Bear ye one another's burdens, and so fulfil the law of Christ" (Gal. 6:2).

OFFERTORY PRAYER.   Most gracious heavenly Father, we thank you for the many gifts that we have received of your bountiful and benevolent hand. We humbly and lovingly return unto you a portion of that which you have bestowed upon us. Accept these our gifts, O Lord, as a symbol of the consecration of our lives and means for the coming of your Kingdom.—Rodney K. Miller

PRAYER.   O Infinite Source of life and health and joy! the very thought of Thee is so wonderful that in this thought we would rest and be still. Thou art Beauty and Grace and Truth and Power. Thou art the light of every heart that sees Thee, the life of every soul that loves Thee, the strength of every mind that seeks Thee. From our narrow and bounded world we would pass into Thy greater world. From our petty and miserable selves we would escape to Thee, to find in Thee the power and the freedom of a larger life. It is our joy that we can never go beyond Thy reach; that even were we to take the wings of the morning, and fly unto the uttermost parts of the earth, or were we to make our bed in hell, there should we find signs of Thy presence and Thy power. Wherever we may go Thou art with us, for Thou art in us as well as without us. We recognize Thee in all the deeper experiences of the soul. When the conscience utters its warning voice, when the heart is tender and we forgive those who have wronged us in word or deed, when we feel ourselves upborne above time and place, and know ourselves citizens of Thy everlasting Kingdom, we realize, O Lord, that these things, while they are in us, are not of us. They are Thine, the work of Thy Spirit brooding upon our souls.—Samuel McComb.

EVENING SERVICE

Topic: Life's Growing Pains
Text: Heb. 5:8

I. Consider first the growing pains that Jesus must have suffered *in his relations with his family*. (a) The gospels give us one glimpse of Jesus as a growing boy. His parents had taken him to the Temple. Jesus must have suffered in causing anxiety to his parents. But he was growing beyond his family's understanding.

(b) There are times when the tension between parents and children can be termed growing pains. We cannot call it growing pains when a youth thinks he is smarter than his parents and looks condescendingly on those who sacrificed to give him an education.

(c) Parents should remember that they can learn from their children, as well as teach them.

(1) A little child sometimes has the freshness of insight and purity of mind which parents need to get.

(2) We adults should also be aware that the younger generation has to face greater strains and more complex situations than we faced in our youth.

(3) Sometimes a high sense of duty drives a son or daughter to go beyond the family pattern and thus cause growing pains.

II. Let us go on to consider the growing pains Jesus suffered *in relation to his community*.

(a) As was his custom, Jesus went into the synagogue on the Sabbath. They asked him to read. He opened the scripture to the words of the prophet Isaiah. Those words astounded his neighbors. Jesus was asserting that he was the anointed one of God. Not only were people doubtful of Jesus' divinity because of his commonplace circumstances, but they were also resentful because he was not doing the amazing cures in Nazareth which he was reported to have done in Capernaum. He had to break through the narrowness and provincialism of his community. He wanted people to realize that God can reveal himself through the humble and commonplace. They were looking for divine deliverance through spectacular means, but God was with them in a carpenter's garb.

(b) Like those Nazarene neighbors of Jesus, our communities with all our conventional church-going keep our narrow interests, calling for God to do things for us but unwilling to be used of him for the helping and healing of others.

III. (a) Let us consider the growing pains which Jesus experienced *in relation to his disciples*. Observe him at Caesarea Philippi. Jesus was at the peak of his popularity. Matthew records, "From that time Jesus began to show his disciples that he must go to Jerusalem and suffer many things," even death itself. Peter began to rebuke Jesus. But the Master turned to Peter and said: "Get behind me, Satan! You are a hindrance to me, for you are not on the side of God but of men." He knew that Peter's protest was prompted by his desire to protect him. But Jesus' suffering at that moment was a growing pain, for he had to go beyond even the best judgment of his disciples. He had to show his followers that the heart of the gospel is the cross.

(b) Jesus asserts that we cannot be his disciples unless we deny ourselves at some points and take up our cross. To be manly enough to bear our burdens is good; to have fortitude to endure our thorns in the flesh is good; but these are not good enough to make us Christians. There must be some extra service, some self-denial which we do though we do not have to do it.

(c) Popular religion in our day tends to omit this principle of the cross, the heart of the gospel. Christ calls us to take up a cross. That does not mean we have to die as Jesus did; but it does mean we have to try to live as Christ did.—Ralph W. Sockman.

SUNDAY: SEPTEMBER SIXTEENTH

MORNING SERVICE

Topic: The Church Jesus Built

SCRIPTURE: Acts 2:1–4; 14–17; 22–24; 41–42.

The picture of the church is clearly drawn in the New Testament. The fundamental character of the church has never changed. As we read and study these verses from the book of Acts, the church book of the Bible, let us measure our church by this standard.

I. The first clear mark of the church which Jesus built is seen in Acts 2:1: they were bound together in a unity of Spirit.

(a) How different is the understanding of the church in so many places today. There are some congregations which are in almost perpetual civil war. When there is such dissension and such violation of the unity of the Spirit, a church cannot really be a New Testament church.

(b) Sometimes our churches are called democracies. But the literal meaning of the word *democracy* is the "rule of the people"—and that is exactly what the church is not. If we yield ourselves to the unity of his Spirit, God will lead the church in one accord.

(c) This vital characteristic of "togetherness" tells us something else about the church. Our *real* church membership is not just a record of our names on the church book. It is our actual presence in the fellowship of the church as it gathers in one accord. It is a living and vital relationship to the fellowship of the whole church, in worship, prayer, and service.

II. The power of the church comes from above.

(a) Christians may gather in a voluntary association of baptized believers, as many have described the church, but only the Holy Spirit of God can empower that association to be the church. The church is not simply a *human* institution—it is a *divine* institution.

(b) In this day when there is so much concern with spiritual gifts, it is important to remember one thing: the Holy Spirit of God never draws attention to himself—but, rather, bears witness to Jesus. When the true Spirit of God is at work, he will draw men to Jesus and exalt his matchless name!

III. What happened in this church when it was endued with power from on high? While all were witnessing to the saving power of Christ, Peter stood up in their midst, and lifted up his voice, and *preached* unto them!

(a) There have been many churches where preaching was reduced to a minor place. But there is no doubt that the apostolic church placed the preaching of the Word at the very center of its life.

(b) If someone should say, "Well, that was a missionary situation and they had to major on preaching," then we must reply: "It is still a missionary situation—there are more people who need the gospel today than there were in the world in the first century!"

What did Peter preach? In one word, he preached *Jesus*. He declared that the Old Testament had been fulfilled in him. He told of his life, his death, and his resurrection. And he concluded with an invitation —he called on his hearers to repent and be baptized in the name of Jesus Christ.

IV. In Acts 2:41, we read: "Then they that gladly received his word were baptized."

(a) Receiving this word about Jesus was the condition of their baptism; and the act of baptism was a picture of this word about the death, burial, and resurrection of Jesus. It is obvious that baptism was the sign by which they declared to the world that they were receiving Jesus.

(b) Then, "they continued steadfastly in the apostles' doctrine," the basic teaching by which they could grow in their Christian lives.

Each of these characteristics, so clearly portrayed in the Jerusalem church, can be traced again and again throughout the New Testament.—Wayne E. Ward.

Illustrations

MOMENTS OF GRACE. One day I was called to a home where a man had come under despair and great heaviness of spirit. As a young pastor I went to that home, not knowing what I should do, though wanting very much to bring the grace of God to a man who needed it. We soon found ourselves talking about the earlier experiences which he had had as a younger man, finding his life work and making the decisions that led him to maturity. As he recalled more and more of his life, there came to him without a word from me the awareness that the goodness of God had touched him. In the years past when need had come, the grace of God had been there. After a time, he took my hand and thanked me for coming, though actually I had done very little. But together we had remembered some things, and in the remembering, we had seen that the common experiences of his life had really been sacraments of the divine presence. Remembering these, he found God coming close again, and hope was restored.—Gene E. Bartlett, in *Pulpit Preaching*.

CHALLENGE OF HEROISM. One of the most stirring chapters in the history of man centers around the activities of Garibaldi, the great Italian leader. If you remember your history, you know that in 1848 the Italian Republic was set up in Rome in order that justice and liberty might be a reality. It was attacked by the old corrupt governments which surrounded it and which it had displaced. Rome was besieged, and while the Republic in Rome lasted much longer than anyone expected it to, it finally collapsed.

When the terms of capitulation were signed, a great multitude gathered in front of St. Peter's, and into the middle of that great crowd rode a man of courage and discipline by the name of Garibaldi. It had been he who had sustained them all the while. They cheered him. When at last the cheering had ceased, he said to them: "I am going out from Rome. I offer neither quarters, nor provisions, nor wages. I offer hunger, thirst, forced marches, battles, and death. Let him who loves his country with his heart, and not with his lips only, follow me." Historians record that the young men streamed after him into the hills, and because of Garibaldi's heroism and that of his followers, Italy is a fact in the world today.—J. Herbert Gilmore, Jr.

Sermon Suggestions

WHY GO TO CHURCH? Text: Heb. 12:22 –25. (1) It is a spiritual fellowship. (2) It is a universal fellowship. (3) It is an immortal fellowship. (4) It is a divine fellowship. (5) It is a redeeming fellowship.—James S. Stewart.

THE UNINTIMIDATED CHRIST. Scripture: Matt. 9:18–26. (1) Jesus was not intimidated by disease (vv. 20–22). (2) Jesus was not intimidated by death (vv. 23–26). (3) Jesus was not intimidated by disbelief (v. 24).—William E. McCumber.

Worship Aids

CALL TO WORSHIP. "We are laborers together with God: ye are God's husbandry, ye are God's building. According to the grace of God which is given unto me, as a wise masterbuilder, I have laid the foundation, and another buildest thereon. But let every man take heed how he buildeth thereupon. For other foundation can no man lay than that is laid, which is Jesus Christ" (1 Cor. 3:9–11).

INVOCATION. Today, O God, build us into a habitation fit for thy Spirit to indwell. We claim as the foundation of our works and worship, Jesus Christ, whom we praise and whose will and way we seek to follow, and in whose name we make our prayer.

OFFERTORY SENTENCE.   "As we have therefore opportunity, let us do good unto all men, especially unto them who are of the household of faith" (Gal. 6:10).

OFFERTORY PRAYER.   O thou who hast given us all that we have and hast made us thy own children, use our lives and material gifts for the spreading of the gospel to the ends of the earth as well as for the blessing of those already near and dear to us.

PRAYER.   Gracious Father, we humbly beseech thee for thy universal church. Fill it with all truth, in all truth with all peace. Where it is corrupt, purge it, and where it is in error, direct it; where it is superstitious, rectify it; where anything is amiss, reform it; where it is right, strengthen and confirm it; where it is in want, furnish it; where it is divided and rent asunder, make up the breaches thereof, O thou holy One of Israel; for the sake of Jesus Christ our Lord and Savior.—William Laud.

EVENING SERVICE

Topic: The Small Moment
SCRIPTURE: Isa. 54:7–10.

I. Our text speaks of a "small moment." It is the moment of wrath, when God has forsaken us and hidden His face from us. What is meant by a "small moment"? A "moment of wrath," the prophet calls it. He says that one scarcely dare say after him: "Because God is angry, because he has forsaken us, because he has hid his face from us." That is what is meant by this "moment."

II. Do we understand it better? We need much grace and truth before we really will accept the word of the Bible concerning the wrath of God. In Jesus Christ, we know what eternity is, that we are saved through God. But before we know this and since we constantly forget it, we simply cannot bear to hear of the wrath of God.

The honor of God may lie close to your heart and you gladly will grant that his thoughts are higher than our thoughts; but for the sake of the very honor of God, you will deny that his thoughts are so much higher than our thoughts as to compel us to concede that for "a small moment he has forsaken us."

III. You complain: "How disturbing, how intolerable, how unsatisfactory is the picture of our condition, if things are thus!" May we turn away from this truth because it is so disturbing and unsatisfying? You reply: "But God cannot always be angry, nor can he wholly have forsaken us!" Now you are really close to what the prophet says. For he says explictly: "A small moment have I forsaken thee! For a short time have I hid my face from thee!" Yes, God is angry with us, has hidden his face from us, has forsaken us, has let us follow our hearts' desires.

IV. Again, one may ask oneself whether one can and may seriously repeat after him what he has said here. True, the prophet says God will not always be angry, nor has he wholly forsaken us. No, God is not angry forever; he is angry so long as time lasts, but his grace is eternal.

Our acknowledging and our confessing are indeed true to that which we are at the moment; grace, that triumphs in our acknowledgment and confession, is eternal. And while it triumphs, the moment is to the "small moment" as an island in the endless ocean.

To wait for Him in hope and to be happy, because the Spirit confirms in our hearts what the Word says: "I will . . . saith the Lord!"—that is our portion. The answer to the second great word, that the prophet speaks, can only be faith. And faith that is not empty-handed is not faith.

V. But can we indeed believe? Is not everything only an artificial human comfort with which we deceive ourselves? What shall I say? The Christian church must learn again to proclaim the Word of God's grace and to listen to it as to God's Word.

Perhaps this is the greatest calamity of our time, that such preaching and hearing of the Word of grace, as the Word of God, has been taken from us and has not yet been restored to us.

God be praised, "who according to his great mercy, begat us again to a living hope by the resurrection of Jesus Christ from the dead!" He who will conquer us is the Spirit in whom we pray: "Our help and our beginning is in the name of the Lord who hath made heaven and earth."—Karl Barth.

SUNDAY: SEPTEMBER TWENTY-THIRD

MORNING SERVICE

Topic: From a Throne to a Cross

TEXT: Isa. 46:9–10.

The children of Israel had come to one of the great turning points in their history. They had been uprooted from the land of promise and set down in captivity by the waters of Babylon. Some unknown prophet stood up among them and wanted them to face that crisis with God. Life didn't make sense any longer. Unless—unless there was One whose purpose still held, who didn't have to accommodate himself to humanity's changing fashions, and who never would be made to look ridiculous!

"Remember, I am God!"

And this prophet is saying to the exiled people of God that, even with Babylon there in front of their eyes, there is One who is still on the throne. That's the answer he gives to the riddle of human life, with all of its ups and downs. There is a God over history!

I. These books from Genesis to Malachi gather all their things together, fill their lungs, and with a mighty shout proclaim that *he is*. Above this weird panorama of our little lives—and there's power in his hands.

(a) You can't just dismiss it with a curt and contemptuous gesture. These Jews have come in their day out of the East to dominate the heathen conscience of the West.

They knew what living was like! They had run up against the grim logic of its laws, as you have. They thought that somehow they were being confronted with a sovereign will. But they saw farther still. They saw the evil that seemed to grow out of the very nature of things. They knew it was rooted, oddly enough, in their own lives.

(b) They had bumped into life's rough walls and cut themselves on its sharp edges. And it didn't seem right. Maybe, when things went wrong, he was punishing them for their sins and, when all went well, rewarding them for their righteousness. And Job wouldn't let that stand either! There was more mystery at the bottom of it than ever he could compass!

Year after bitter year, these toiling generations strained and sweated with the puzzle. They had loved this land and fought for it—and were dragged away from it in the end. Everything taken but this thing that wouldn't die in their hearts. "Remember, I am God! There is none else. My counsel shall stand!"

(c) Their faith was what got them into trouble! It was a holy presence that more and more towered upon their lives. Nothing had happened to the facts of their tough existence. Something revolutionary had happened to the interpretation of the facts. The facts were still there and they were still unchanged, but they were facts under a stately rule that rested over human history and made sense of it. And from under that strong and tender rule, no living human soul could ever get clean away! They were there by the rivers of Babylon. We are here, because there's a will of God in this matter that has to be served!

(d) And that's where the Old Testament stops: looking down on all the pain and turmoil and shadow from that magnificent height! Just when his throne seems emptiest, "the Lord God omnipotent reigneth!"

II. But what's left to say is greater. To what's already said "is added this further astonishment." With the turning of a page, you are in the New Testament. "Now when Jesus was born in Bethlehem of Judea in the days of Herod the king. . . ." And suddenly it's clear to you that the God who is over history is in it, too!

(a) As far as the Bible goes, that's the second and final answer to the riddle of human life, "Remember, I am God." The Old Testament says this from a throne; the New Testament says it from a cross! And that's the whole terrific difference! Says it at the close of a radiant life that the world hated and hounded and struck in the face.

(b) People who began to guess, as they found themselves still confronted by this Christ, that the end had been God's from the very beginning; that all along he had been weaving a pattern with his fingers that they had never more than faintly glimpsed: as a man might stare at the knots on the underside of some huge tapestry, and only catch a hint here and there of the grandeur and the color of the master's work!

(c) To this riddle of life, there is no answer that's full and complete: no answer at all but that God is still making his way through the thick of it, with his own inscrutable love, and the glory of a dying Nazarene shining austerely out of every ill my flesh is heir to!

(d) That's the ground plan of our churches. You may not be able to see it so clearly, but it is! What if it were "the ground plan of the universe?" People tell me now and then, speaking of their lives, that they don't like the setup. What if the setup was a cross? What if it should be God's purpose to conform you and me to the image of his Son? And you know and I know where his Son died! What if he were coming to you here on Calvary out of eternity, through sin and defeat and suffering, all the very darkest things of life, to show you how deep they are, and how ready he is, and how unappalled? What if he were calling to you for nothing but your own eager willingness to be on his side against the world, to throw what weight you have into those great scales for justice and mercy and peace—and for the rest, to fix your sheer confidence where Christ's was fixed, to that ultimate goodness like a Father's care which is not only over history now but within it? For that ultimate goodness doesn't give up and grow tired or lose heart, but holds on and sees it through—until the very valley of trouble, as an old prophet has it, becomes a door of hope!

(e) The only answer to the riddle of life is the face of Jesus, which somehow refuses to fade from the picture that the ages keep throwing up against the sky! With that face there, the love of God doesn't seem to me to be a silly, unreasonable fancy, trying to look pretty no matter how ugly the things are that happen; it seems like creation's heart beating against my own.

(f) "Remember, I am God. There is none else. Declaring the end from the beginning. My counsel shall stand." When God said that from a cross, he said something that would hold. It held through that unutterable darkness on Calvary. I think it will not be shaken now!—Paul Scherer.

Illustrations

CHRISTIAN DETERMINISM. In one American city, a high school teacher of French, having placed on the blackboard in front of her students a full diagram of the zodiac with all of the major signs, asked each of the class members to say under what sign he or she had been born. All responded with the exception of one sixteen-year-old boy. Finally the teacher addressed the boy individually, asking, "Which of these is your sign, John?" "Not any of them," replied the boy. "I am under the sign of the cross." Not another word was said on the subject, and at the beginning of the next session, the board was clean.—Elton Trueblood.

THE NECESSARY CROSS. Too often, American evangelical Christianity presents the Good News of Christ as the solution to all human problems, the fulfillment of all wants, and a good way to make basically good people even better.

The cross suggests that this Good News is the beginning of problems we would gladly have avoided, the turning away from the quest for self-fulfillment, the ultimate mocking of our claims for goodness. The principalities and powers tremble only before the cross. Nothing less than death will do—painful, full-scale conversion, letting go, turning from ourselves and toward God.—William H. Willimon.

Sermon Suggestions.

NOW LIFE HAS MEANING. Scripture: Mark 14:3–9. Loss of meaning has become our pervasive malady. Christ puts meaning back. (1) He restores meaning in the face of all that defeats personhood. (2) He restores meaning in the face of lovelessness. (3) He restores meaning in the face of cynicism.—Merrill R. Abbey.

GOD'S AWESOME CHALLENGE. Scripture: Matt. 28:18–20. (1) His power. (2) His commission. (3) His world. (4) His teachings. (5) His presence.—Harold C. Bennett.

Worship Aids

CALL TO WORSHIP. "All we like sheep have gone astray; we have turned every one to his own way; and the Lord hath laid on him the iniquity of us all" (Isa. 53:6).

INVOCATION. Almighty God, our Father, who art holy, who lookest upon us, we come to thee because thou art holy and not because we are holy, but because we would be holy. Pity us, we beseech thee, with the influence of thy salvation. O God, restore unto us the joy of thine own holiness.—Frank W. Gunsaulus.

OFFERTORY PRAYER. "Let him who is taught the word share all good things with him who teaches" (Gal. 6:6 [RSV]).

OFFERTORY PRAYER. Our Father, we would honor thee in honoring those who serve in thy name. By our tithes and offerings we support and strengthen the work of our pastors, our missionaries, our denominational workers, our local church staff, and others worthily employed in thy Kingdom. Help us to support and strengthen them also by our prayers and goodwill, knowing that man does not live by bread alone, but first by every word that proceeds from thy mouth and then by the good words that proceed from our mouths.

PRAYER. O God, creator of the universe and our Father, thy greatness overwhelms us. We press to the outer limits of human knowledge, and at last we stand before thee alone. Before the mountains were brought forth, or ever thou hadst formed the earth and the world, even from everlasting to everlasting, thou art God. We profess to know nothing of thee but that which thou hast revealed. We trace thy works in the things thou hast made and stand amazed before thy wisdom and thy power. We see in the manifold acts of thy providence, especially in the gift of thy Son, our Lord and Savior, thy righteousness and thy loving kindness. Yet thou hast hidden so much from our sight and hast challenged our hearts with so many mysteries, that we must walk by faith and not by sight. When we cannot understand, help us to trust. When we cannot feel, help us to go on believing. And grant that our wilderness wanderings may at last be rewarded with new strength of character and greater ability to bless others with the very graces that we ourselves have received from thee.

EVENING SERVICE

Topic: When You Can't Understand Yourself

TEXTS: Rom. 7:15; Mark 7:15.

I. (a) Some scholars say that when Paul wrote that intensely personal passage, he was simply reminiscing. Other scholars think that he was describing an ongoing struggle in his heart. My opinion is that Paul is describing, from his own experience, a persisting problem for the Christian as he or she struggles through life. Paul is discussing not only past experience, but also experience potentially always present.

(b) This passage is an account of conflict that takes place deep within the person. You do at times find yourself not doing what you really want to do and doing things you loathe when you dare to think about them. You find that although you have the will to do the good, the decent, the compassionate, you sometimes haven't the inner power for it. We all know from our own experience something of the inner distress and confusion about which Paul writes.

(c) We sometimes talk a morality appreciably higher than the one we actually live by. We may espouse high standards of respect for the rights and needs of others, but that does not always keep us from indulging in malicious gossip about them or from trampling on another person's sensitivities with our hobnailed boots of selfish concern. We may acclaim principles of honesty and honor, but that does not always stop us from cutting ethical corners when it is to our advantage to do so.

II. What, then, can you and I do about our inner conflicts?

(a) We cannot resolve our inner conflicts by giving impulse a free gallop. Even the people who tell us that it is unnatural, even unhealthy, to suppress one's impulses recognize that the reins must be held quite tightly on most impulses if a tolerable sort of life is to be lived.

(b) The common belief seems to be that if we exercise a bit of willpower and show a little common sense we can somehow manage our inner conflicts.

(c) Most of us, as we mature, are able to work out moral compromises for ourselves. As we come into the middle years of life, we find that it is not too difficult to stumble along in a state of moral compromise—approaching at times the heights of goodness and honor, and always in danger of plumbing the depths of the dishonourable and the false.

(d) Despite our maturity, our worldly wisdom, our sense of self-sufficiency, we often find ourselves driven to cry with Paul, "I often find that I have the will to do good, but not the power. . . . My own behavior baffles me."

III. (a) But Paul doesn't stop here. He recognizes the futility of relying on his own resources. After sounding this note of despair, he quickly sounds a stronger note of hope: "I thank God there is a way out through Jesus Christ our Lord."

(b) In and through the practices of faith, we can be helped to escape the clutches of our own sinful nature and guided to peace and joy and fulfillment. This way of faith, this way in faith, is open to all of us. The grace of God—that is, the "energy" of God working in our hearts and minds—comes to us as we engage in the disciplines of faith: in worship and prayer and meditation, in embracing biblical insights, in service of witness and compassion. Faith will work for you if you work at faith, work hard at it, work regularly at it.—J. A. Davidson.

SUNDAY: SEPTEMBER THIRTIETH

MORNING SERVICE

Topic: Hired Hands

SCRIPTURE: Luke 10:1–9.

I. There are two essential aspects of the harvest that are related yet independent of one another. The first of these factors is that of ripeness, and the second is human activity. Both factors must be present at the same time for a successful harvest.

(a) Obviously, a harvest cannot occur until the crops have reached physical maturity. Any harvest before such maturity is futile. Physical maturity, however, requires that the crops receive the proper amount of sunlight, moisture, and warmth. In addition, the crops require the proper soil and cultivation in order to reach full physical maturity. In short, the ripeness of the crop is one of the necessary preconditions of the harvest.

(b) The second precondition for a successful harvest is that of human activity. Without the proper human activity, the precondition of the ripeness of the crop is useless. Human activity is the physical labor that is required to harvest the crop and prepare it for use. Without the necessary physical labor the ripened crops would rot in the fields and be of no value to anybody. The harvest, therefore, depends upon the successful interaction of the conditions of ripeness of the crop and human activity.

II. (a) Jesus of Nazareth understood the harvest in two interlocking ways. First, he understood the harvest as the culmination of God's redemptive work. Second, he understood the harvest as the mission of his disciples in the world. The harvest was thus the result of the combined efforts of God and man. God prepares humanity to receive the gift of his salvation and man carries the gift of salvation to his fellow men and women. The harvest is thus the beginning of the realizaton of the Kingdom of God through ministries of love and healing.

(b) Ripeness and human activity, the two elements of the harvest, constitute the essential relationship of gift and response that exists between God and humanity. Jesus understood ripeness to be a condition created primarily by the action of God in human life. This ripeness is the willingness and readiness of a person to turn to God in faith for a source of comfort, hope, love, and meaning for life. Jesus, during the course of his ministry, declared that the process of ripening that had continued across many years was nearly complete. The harvest was at hand. Men and women had reached sufficient maturity either to accept or reject their God.

III. The ripeness of humanity to accept or reject God presents to contemporary Christians, as well as to the first disciples of Jesus, a tremendous responsibility and opportunity. A "field" of "ripened humanity," much like a field of ripened grain, requires physical labor to harvest it and bring it into the fellowship of the Christian church. The physical labor and commitment to the harvesting of the many "fields" of "ripened humanity" must be our faithful response to the action of God in the lives of our fellow men and women. Our mission as a Christian people is to "harvest" those persons whom God has "prepared" for a meaningful relationship with him through the church of Jesus Christ. We must, therefore, seek those for whom life has lost meaning and value—persons dissatisfied with their present way of life, persons seeking new meanings and values, and persons apathetic and disillusioned. These are the persons God has most clearly "ripened" for the "harvest." These are the persons God has enjoined

us to seek and bring into our Christian fellowship.

IV. The harvest has two aspects: (1) that aspect over which God alone has charge—the "ripening" of human beings for a meaningful relationship with him; and (2) that aspect over which we have charge—the "reaping and gathering" of these persons into the body of Christ. Both of these elements together constitute the essence of the great harvest of Luke 10 into which Jesus sent his disciples. Such a participation in God's harvest is the essence of our mission as a Christian church. God has summoned us to be his disciples—his hired hands who will labor in the "fields" of humanity in order to make the harvest successful. He has chosen *us* for this most important work of his Kingdom. He challenges *us* to forget for a moment our own interests. He bids *us* enter into the "fields" of human life to pluck, from among the tares of pride and selfishness, hostility and doubt, the ripened souls and bodies of our fellow human beings. Through our unselfish efforts we thus nourish and sustain the body of Christ among men and more nearly realize the Kingdom of God upon the earth.—Rodney K. Miller

Illustration

LOVE IS PRACTICAL.   I once met a woman who had come out of a religious service all aglow. She said, "I love everybody." After a little conversation I discovered that there were some specific exceptions to her love. She made me think of those old-fashioned woolen mittens we used to wear. They kept the hands warm but you couldn't pick anything up when you had them on. Love for God may seem to warm our hearts, but it is not real unless it helps us to take hold of our neighbor's needs.—Ralph W. Sockman.

Sermon Suggestions

THIRSTING FOR GOD.   Text: Ps. 42:2. (1) There is in everyone an unconscious and unsatisfied longing after God, and that is the state of nature. (2) There is a conscious longing, imperfect, but answered; and that is the state of grace—the beginning of religion in a man's soul. (3) There is a perfect longing perfectly satisfied; and that is heaven.—Alexander Maclaren.

THE GOSPEL BEFORE THE GOSPEL.   Scripture: Isa. 40:31. (1) This is God's good news. (2) It is addressed immediately to a special need. (3) It is verified in human experience. (4) It is everlastingly true.—Adapted from J. Clifford.

Worship Aids

CALL TO WORSHIP.   "Worship the Lord in holy array; tremble before him, all the earth!" (Ps. 96:9 [RSV]).

INVOCATION.   O God, our loving Father, teach us today what to be thankful for, even if at the present moment our problems, our pain, or our need might lead us to believe that we have no cause for thanksgiving. Let thy Spirit open our eyes to thy unfailing goodness.

OFFERTORY SENTENCE.   "Upon the first day of the week let every one of you lay by him in store, as God hath prospered him" (1 Cor. 16:2).

OFFERTORY PRAYER.   Grant, O Lord, that not only what is taught in church, but also what is presented in the offering may flow out of a pure heart, a good conscience, and a sincere faith.

PRAYER.   Holy and merciful God! What are all our words, and what would our most fervent thanksgiving and praises mean compared with what you have done, are doing, and will still do for us and with us—compared with the new covenant, in which we all may already take our place?—compared with the grace by which you will put your law within us and write it upon our hearts? Enter our hearts! Clear away whatever might prevent you! And then speak further with us, lead us further along your path, the only good path: even when after this we once more separate, to return each to his own solitariness and tomorrow to his work!

So further your work outside this building also, and in the whole world as well! Have mercy on all who are sick, hungry, exiled, or oppressed! Have mercy on the powerlessness with which nations, governments, newspapers, and alas! even the Christian churches, with which all of us face the sea of guilt and trouble in the lives of present-day humanity! Have mercy on the lack of understanding because of which many of the most responsible and powerful of men see themselves driven to play with fire and conjure up new and greater dangers!

If your word were not at hand, what would be left for us to do but despair? But your word in all its truth is at hand and so we cannot despair, and we may and indeed we want to feel assured, so that even if the earth is moved under our feet, all things in their entire course are in your strong and loving hands and at the very last we shall be allowed to see that you have reconciled us and our dark world to you, that you have already brought its salvation and its peace despite all men's arrogance and despair: in Jesus Christ your son, our Lord and Savior, who died and rose again for us and all men.—Karl Barth.

EVENING SERVICE

Topic: The Transformed Life
TEXT: Romans 12:1–2.

"Learn to be different," a father would tell his children who argued for doing something by pointing out that other children were doing it. One of the children, now grown, commented, "Now we're all so different Daddy can't stand us."

Paul exhorts Christians to be different. This uniqueness is the very goal for which we were created and redeemed.

Paul calls on Christians to present to God their total person. This will be, on their part, an act of intelligent worship, grounded in their gratitude to God for his wondrous mercies. This will make them different.

Has your Christian experience made you different, or has it just made you odd?

We are involved in a great struggle. Will we reflect in our behavior the present age with its materialism, selfishness, and sin?

Or will we reflect the "age to come," with its spiritual power, its love, and its righteousness?

I. *There are strong pressures on us to conform.* Thus Paul exhorts, "Don't let the world around you squeeze you into its own mold" (Rom. 12:2 [Phillips trans.]).

(a) We have strong inner urges to belong to the group. This is not necessarily bad. It is a part of the emotional and psychological make-up that God gave us. On this motivation we base our appeals for good citizenship, honesty, purity, and patriotism.

(b) But the world around us does not always observe the highest standards. Its goals are often shortsighted. The world about us is not famous for putting human values above material concerns, though the world may use them as an inducement for legalizing its vices.

The standards of the world about us are not based on God's requirements, but on what can be expected of a person who has no regard for God and his will. But the world appeals to us, nonetheless. Its free and easy ways, its cavalier attitude toward responsibility, and its glitter and gold make the world exceedingly attractive.

(c) Let none of us assume, however, that we are left to choose freely about the world. A major campaign is being waged to capture our souls. The "engineers of consent" spend fantastic sums of money subtly to persuade us to buy their products or to vote for their candidate. Some of this propaganda, of course, is quite harmless. But much of it raises grave ethical questions. Obviously some of it is demonic. Therefore, let us be warned (see 1 Pet. 5:8 and 2 Cor. 11:14b–15a).

II. *Though we are strongly pressured to conform to the world around us, Christians have an experience that breaks the molds of worldly conformity.* "Be transformed by the renewal of your mind" (Rom. 12:2 [RSV]).

(a) We have a new identification. Our life is more involved with the "age to come" than with the present age. Thus earthly, human loyalties are superseded by our loyalty to the Kingdom of God. That is why Jesus said, "He who loves father or mother more than me is not worthy of me; and he who loves son or daughter more than me is not worthy of me; and he who does not take his cross and follow me is not worthy of me" (Matt. 10:37–38 [RSV]).

To the average man or woman, the Sermon on the Mount makes no sense. Why? The average person is identified with this world. The teachings of our Lord set forth the marks of one who belongs to the "age to come." There is a reversal of values. Though Nietzsche called Jesus' teachings "a slave revolt in morals" and tried to dismiss them as irrelevant, nothing else fits so well the deepest needs and desires of the Christian.

(b) Furthermore, we have a new standard. We do not gauge our conduct by what pleases us or by what will bring short-term pleasure to our family. We are inspired and constrained by the miracle of Christian love. Jesus held this up as the highest motivation when he said, "You shall love the Lord your God with all your heart, and with all your soul, and with all your mind. . . . You shall love your neighbor as yourself" (Matt. 22:37, 39 [RSV]). As John puts it, "We love, because he first loved us" (1 John 4:19 [RSV]).

(c) What shall we say, then, to these questions: Can a Christian do no better than to live for the present moment? Can a Christian do no better than to seek in everything the approval of the world? Quite plainly, the Christian is involved in powerful tensions in this world. However, he lives confidently today, because he is assured that the future is in God's hands. He can lay down his life even for those who persecute him and despitefully use him, because he is assured that God will use his sacrifice for the good and redemption of the ones for whom he suffers.

The true Christian's life is dedicated in every relationship and action by love. "Love is the fulfilling of the law" (Rom. 13:10). That, indeed, is the way that "you may prove what is the will of God, what is good and acceptable and perfect" (Rom. 12:2 [RSV]).—James W. Cox.

SUNDAY: OCTOBER SEVENTH

MORNING SERVICE

Topic: You Shall Be My People

TEXT: Lev. 26:12.

A great deal could be said about the meaning of this assurance for the people of Israel up to this day. There can be no doubt that the history of Israel reached its climax in Jesus Christ. The promise of our text was also fulfilled in him. It thereby became a trumpet sound that rings around the world. It rings for us also.

I. *I will walk among you.*

(a) To walk is to advance in a definite direction. We learn that God is not motionless. He is no inflexible being. He is not the prisoner of his own eternity. No, God is on his way; God comes and goes; God is the principal actor of a drama.

(b) I will walk *among you.* The roads where God walks and moves about as the living God are our roads, where we walk, drive our cars and board our streetcars, where we go our own ways. He lives in heaven, but he lives also on earth, even in our neighborhoods, among us and with us. He is the God who always and everywhere is *near.*

(c) "I will walk among you" is sometimes translated as "I will walk *in your midst.*" This is more precise. The living God is the center, the source, and the origin, but also the destination of our restless existence. The history of our lives unfolds because in their innermost center, God's own history unfolds. This binds us to him, this binds together the fragments of our lives, this binds us to one another.

Because he is the *living* God, who is near and who is one, he really walks among us, in our midst, whether we take notice or not, whether we like it or not. He will not grow bitter, nor will he be confounded in his love.

II. *And will be your God.*

(a) God says to us: "Since I am the living God who is near and who is one- almighty, holy, and merciful—I will be *your God. I* will care for you. I will carry you in my eternal thoughts. I will love you, but also call you to obedience in my service where I can make good use of you. With *you*, I am speaking this very moment."

God says furthermore: "As the creator of heaven and earth, as Lord of all men, I will belong to you."

God continues: "I will stand by you, I will take sides with you. I will declare my unconditional solidarity with you, against all odds—against the whole worldand all of mankind, if need be—and in particular, against your own self!"

(b) We might also say: God in his divine determination and his divine perfection will say yes to us. But God's yes is a holy and wholesome yes, comprising always a no. It is the no to everything in us and about us which he must reject for his sake and our own.

III. *And you shall be my people.*

(a) "*You*, really *you* shall be my people!" Such as you are now, not as future saints or angels. You with your transitory life and work, you with your restless thoughts, you with your inappropriate words, you with your big and small lies, with your subtle or sharp cruelties, with your slackness and sometimes with your shabby tricks, with your excitements and depressions. You are the dying who are utterly lost without me.

(b) "*My* people" implies that you shall be those who find in me their Lord and Judge, yet at the same time their merciful Father. You shall fear me, love me, call on me, turn to me every morning anew, seeking my face. Even better, you shall be my witnesses before the others who do not know me. *You* shall be the light of the world!

(c) "My *people*" is not to be overlooked either. You're not a sandpile of individuals. But called and gathered by me, you shall be a people of brothers and sisters. You shall support and help one another, perhaps timidly, perhaps boldly. You shall witness to one another, with or without words, that I live and walk among you.—Karl Barth.

Illustrations

SERVICE.   Senator Claude Pepper, the passionate and effective advocate for senior citizens, was asked by Morey Safer on "60 Minutes" what he would like to be remembered for. He replied that he had put in his will the request that these words be written on his tombstone: "He loved God and the people and he sought to serve both."

EXPERIENCE OF GOD.   Our experience of God as a present factor in our lives, inspiring us to fight evil while it is still preventable and transforming it into his messenger when it is inevitable, is the ground of our confidence that he will continue to reveal himself to us during our lives here, and that when our lives are over, he will provide opportunity for further fellowship in a life to come.—William Adams Brown.

Sermon Suggestions

THE COMPENSATIONS OF GOD.   Text: 2 Cor. 7:5, 6. What can enable us to ride out the storm? (1) We can turn to God's Word and be comforted. (2) We can enter into the needs and experiences of others and be enriched. (3) We can trust in God's presence, living and moving through everything, and go bravely on.—Adapted from James Moffatt.

OUR PENTECOST: FINDING THE SPIRIT. Scripture: Acts 2:1–21. Being a Christian is "a long falling in love with God." (1) The first stage: drawing near. (2) The second: mutual self-surrender. (3) The third stage: faith and trust. (4) The fourth stage: constant adjustment of the human to the divine.—E. Stanley Jones.

Worship Aids

CALL TO WORSHIP.   "Thanks be to God, which giveth us the victory through our Lord Jesus Christ" (1 Cor. 15:57).

INVOCATION.   Today we meet to worship in the assurance that in our Lord Jesus Christ, we are victorious both in this world and in the world to come. May the joy of this assurance radiate in our prayers, in our hymns, and in all our spoken and wordless acts.

OFFERTORY SENTENCE.   "Whatsoever ye do in word or deed, do all in the name of the Lord Jesus, giving thanks to God and the Father by him" (Col. 3:17).

OFFERTORY PRAYER.   Accept these our gifts, O Lord, as tokens of our mindfulness of thy presence in our lives. Grant us the will, the desire, and the love to be gracious and faithful stewards of the many blessings that thou hast bestowed upon us.—Rodney K. Miller.

PRAYER.   On the night when you were betrayed, Lord, you were giving thanks. Why weren't you bitter and anxious as we would be? We do not give thanks when someone turns against us. We vow revenge. It takes even less than betrayal to stir our ire: if the car breaks down, if the potatoes boil dry, if we hit our thumb with a hammer, if the store misbills us, then we act as though heaven's door had slammed in our face.

Yet, on the same night that a companion turned you in, and best friends deserted you, and prominent citizens tried you in a kangaroo court, and soldiers tortured you, on that very same night—you gave thanks.

O Christ, we acknowledge that we curse more than we praise, we damn more than we thank, we grumble more than we rejoice. Give us, Christ, the smallest portion of your grace so that whatever happens to us, we shall be glad simply to have lived and to have known your love.—Thomas T. Troeger.

EVENING SERVICE

Topic: Forgiveness as a Way of Life
SCRIPTURE: Matt. 18:21–35.

(a) There is no room for uncertainty about Jesus' meaning in our text. When he says "forgive seventy times seven" he means forgive without limit. The Christian ideal is to make forgiveness a way of life.

(b) But we cannot assume that people of the Church have actually been brought into this forgiveness style of life just because Jesus said it. Anyone who has tried to practice this high standard knows that it seems unnatural to keep exposing oneself, over and over, to the meanness and unfaithfulness of cruel and uncaring offenders.

(c) It is difficult to forgive as required of us, but how necessary it is in our time. The conflicts, rigid antagonisms, stored—up wrath, and seething resentments are like infections which run up our temperatures.

I. *The logic of not forgiving goes something like this:*

(a) People are basically selfish. They will use people, even abuse them, to gratify and fulfill their own desires. In addition, they act out of a certain inner necessity. They are compulsive. They are often incapable of amending their ways. They apologize, you relax, and they do it to you again.

(b) So why be stupid and leave yourself open to such behavior again under some broad policy of forgiveness?

(c) But a pattern of nonforgiveness requires so much energy that one almost feels the need to justify a big program of defense. We must magnify the evil of the offender and the threat of the anticipated offense. We can demonstrate how helpless we are. We can justify the protection of one's honor as the second law of the universe.

(d) But all this makes for a miserable existence, and we try to determine how life got to be such a rotten deal. Then we wonder if maybe God has abdicated his responsibility to make people act right. And if he can't handle it, we sure will, even if it kills us—and it probably will in the end.

II. *The wisdom of forgiving.*

(a) According to our text, to accept forgiveness as a way of life is to share God's spirit. The king in the parable was responsive to the creditor's plea. He did not give him more time to pay. He forgave him. He wiped the slate clean and sent him forth free of the obligation to pay what he did not have. Jesus taught that God deals with

us in just this way. There is no prospect that we will ever be able, on our own, to raise enough moral and spiritual capital to pay our debts. God stands ready to forgive so that we can face the future unencumbered. It is the policy of heaven and it applies throughout the universe, where the kingdom of God prevails.

(b) To forgive is to choose the more positive of two options. Unforgiveness tends toward decay, hate, fear, death. Forgiveness tends toward growth, love, openness, life. There is a certain kind of bitterness, heaviness, unhappiness, tenseness, closedmindedness, and spiritlessness which are almost always telltale marks of the infection of nonforgiveness. In marked contrast, forgiveness tends toward being fresh and clean inside. It lightens the load of life and brightens the human horizon. It enables one to risk singing and dancing and laughing and being free and friendly and helpful.

(c) To forgive is to invest in the creation of a more human and loving society. Yes, it does sometimes lead to suffering and pain and disappointment. But forgiveness is a powerful formative agent. The presence of a confirmed forgiveness makes a difference in any context.

(d) Even as we say Amen to the wisdom of Jesus, something within says, "Yes, but don't let anybody make a fool of you." In the midst of these contrary forces one needs a greater power to set us free to share God's spirit of forgiveness.

The power of which we speak is found when we stand under the shadow of the cross. The cross is God's clearest call to a forgiving life—style. At the cross we experience God's willingness to enter into the pain born of our sin and yet at the same time to love us in spite of our sin. But the death and suffering of Jesus was a class—action process. He suffered, bled, and died to win forgiveness for me as well as for those who will offend me.—James A. Forbes, Jr.

SUNDAY: OCTOBER FOURTEENTH

MORNING SERVICE

Topic: Better Than a Contract

TEXT: Matt. 20:15 (NEB).

I. *An earthly story.*

(a) No union today would dream of being without a work contract. That's how the workers protect themselves against exploitation by their employers. It would never occur to them that some generous employers don't want to exploit them and that they might, in fact, do better without a contract. The truth is that the unions don't want generosity, they want justice, they want their rights. As far as they are concerned, nothing is better than an iron-clad contract.

(b) One reason many stay away from church is that they think that the church will simply make demands on them and add to their burdens, and they don't wish to become involved. They need to be told that the church exists, first of all, not to ask them for something, but to give them what they cannot receive anywhere else. Christianity itself began not with a demand that God made on the world, but with the gift of his Son for the world's salvation. We do give to God as we learn to love and serve him, but first we receive from God, and we receive infinitely more than we give. That was the message of Jesus in his ministry, and nowhere does it come across with greater force than in his parable of the Laborers in the Vineyard. As a story of work and wages, it seems not only out of date, but out to touch with the realities of the work situation today. A modern grape grower would never have gotten away with such high-handed behavior.

II. *The heavenly meaning.*

(a) The story is a parable, and we have to remember what parables were on the lips of Jesus. Someone defined them as earthly stories with a heavenly meaning.

(b) This is one of the parables that Jesus told to explain the character of the Kingdom of God. The Kingdom was the constant theme of his teaching and it comes across with different meanings. Most often, Jesus speaks of the Kingdom as a personal and present reality which we can seek and enter and possess here and now, an order of obedience to God which he embodied and made visible in his own person. We grasp the meaning of it in this parable when we look closely at the characters and whom they represent.

(1) The laborers hired first thing in the morning represent the class known as "scribes and Pharisees." In the New Testament, they always seem to be giving Jesus a hard time, but the fact remains that they were the most religious, most respected, most morally upright members of Jewish society.

(2) The latecomers represented a class known as "publicans and sinners." They were the least religious, least respected, least morally upright members of Jewish society. They met Jesus and repented of their sins, and Jesus forgave them and admitted them to God's Kingdom.

(3) The employer in the story represents God. The owners of the vineyard knew very well that the latecomers who had worked only one hour did not deserve or expect a full day's wage, only a fraction of it. Yet he gave them a full day's wage, even though they had not earned it. He did so because he had a generous heart. Jesus told this parable to show that our God is like that—very generous and very kind.

III. *Good news.*

(a) That came as good news to life's latecomers, the publicans and sinners who were attracted to Jesus because he revealed to them the Father's generous heart. The most spectacular was the Penitent Thief whom the Romans crucified alongside Jesus.

(b) The apostle Paul was a latecomer. He never forgot that and never played it down. Paul lived our Lord's parable. He knew by experience that God does not pay wages. Sin pays wages, it give us exactly what we earn. God gives us what we do not earn.

IV. *Resentment.*

(a) We are still left with the resentment of the early morning laborers and are not entirely out of sympathy with it. Resentment is a very human feeling that spills over into religion, and that's not surprising, because people are still human even when they are being religious.

(b) What does God say to that? Surely what the employer in our Lord's parable said to the early morning laborers, "Why be jealous because I am kind?" The fact is that they ought not to have been jealous because of their employer's generosity toward the latecomers, but glad and grateful for it. On another day, the roles might be reversed and they might be the people hired at noon or three o'clock or one hour before sunset—then their employer's kindness would extend to them.

V. *Amazing grace.*

(a) Surely it is Good News that we don't get our rights before God, but something far better. Would it be Good News if we *did* get our rights? Suppose that when we reached the end of life's journey and stood before the great King upon his throne, we were accepted by God only in the measure that we have obeyed his laws and consciously served him here on earth? We should still get our rights, but it wouldn't leave much margin for error.

(b) The truth is that we cannot afford to be jealous because God is kind. We ourselves need his kindness. Thanks be to God that, in Jesus Christ, he gives us something better than a contract. He gives us his grace and love and generosity and forgiveness. The cross of Christ is God's eternal guarantee that we receive from him infinitely more than we give.—A. Leonard Griffith.

Illustrations

MEANING IN LIFE. You and I have seen the straitjacket of our "American way of life" fasten its grip upon our friends. We have seen them gradually kill spontaneity and imagination for the sake of forcing themselves into the narrow patterns of success. They become "well-adjusted" to the community: that means they occupy a certain income bracket, hold safe political opinions, and have no more than two children. They look back upon their earlier days, before the zippers on their straitjackets had begun to pin them down, as a time of foolish dreams. Actually those were days when they were still alive. They have "arrived" now; but in the process they have somehow lost themselves.—David E. Roberts.

ACRES OF OIL. There is an old story of a Pennsylvania farmer who sold his farm because an ugly, oily scum in the creek made the water unfit for the cattle to drink. Years later, he stood where an oil well had been dug down into the creek bed, leaned up against a fence, and sighed, "Ah, if I had only known."—J. Wallace Hamilton.

Sermon Suggestions

"EVEN IN SARDIS." Text: Rev. 3:4. (1) It is possible to be true and faithful under the most discouraging circumstances. (2) Even in the worst condition, there may be some redeeming features. (3) God never confounds the godly few with the ungodly many.—Joseph Parker.

NO CONDEMNATION. Text: Rom. 8:1–8. (1) We stand guilty before God and powerless to change that. (2) God loves us: through Christ and his Spirit he frees us from guilt and empowers us to obey him.

Worship Aids

CALL TO WORSHIP. "Blessed is the man that trusteth in the Lord, and whose hope the Lord is" (Jer. 17:7).

INVOCATION. O Lord, our God, you have called us to be your people, a people to bring honor and glory to your holy name. You have put us forth into the world as your witnesses. Strengthen us now by your Spirit in our inner selves that we may be and become that special people who call others also to praise and serve you.

OFFERTORY SENTENCE. "I will freely sacrifice unto thee: I will praise thy name, O Lord; for it is good" (Ps. 54:6).

OFFERTORY PRAYER. We wandered far, O Lord, but you came near. You delivered us in our time of trouble. You have given us good things to enjoy, which we do not deserve. Now we praise you, not only with our tongues, but also with our gifts. Bless and use these offerings that your presence may be brought near to others in their need.

PRAYER. O Lord, our God, we thank thee for all thy revelations which in times past have been sacraments to our souls. Once more, thou hast opened the gateway of another morning. Once more, the mountains and hills break forth into singing, and the trees of the field clap their hands. Lift up our hearts to praise thee. Let nature speak to us not of herself only, but of the eternal artist on whose palette all her colors have been mixed.

We thank thee for thy church, that fellowship of the sons and daughters of the Spirit who, across the generations, have kept the great tradition of goodness and truth. Many have been their names, various their beliefs, but at the center of their souls shone a great light, and by it thou hast made all the world more beautiful. Join us to their company. We rejoice in the music through which they have praised thee and the books in which they have revealed thee and lifted the earth nearer to the Kingdom of righteousness. We rejoice in the lives that, in their inner purity and truth, have stood for thee in scorn of consequence. Lift us up to be members of their company. Thus we would turn from the sordidness of life, from its din and passion, from its hectic busyness and its superficiality, and find once more our confident resource, our security, our tranquillity, our peace, and our power in thee.

Deepen our faith this day. Give us a new grasp upon things unseen and eternal. Save us from being slaves of our eyes and believing only what they see. Help us to understand that through the veil of the visible, the meanings of life just come, invisible, eternal, spiritual.

Quicken our hopes this day. Save us from the current cynicism of our generation, from its skepticism and its disbelief in the possibilities of human life. Lift us above its derogatory and condemning attitude that would kill all things that are right and make impossible anything that is lovely. Heighten our hopes, and send us out believing once more that in the heart of humankind are possibilities which thy touch, O living God, can quicken into reality.

Expand our love this day. O God, transcend our selfishness. Help us to rise above our hatefulness, our vindictiveness, our prejudice, and our provinciality. If any of us have brought hate into this house today, may we find it flowing from us because thy love has been shed abroad in our hearts.—Harry Emerson Fosdick.

EVENING SERVICE

Topic: God's Steward
SCRIPTURE: Luke 19:12ff.

"And Jesus said, 'Occupy till I come.' " The doctrine of the stewardship of the servants of God is a part of the very warp and woof of the Christian faith. It is far more interwoven in the fabric of the life of the church than we realize.

Whatever we possess of ability or talent, we owe it to God. It comes to us from the gracious hands of the Lord. And there is a holy purpose in the gift, the *oikonomia*, the stewardship that God has committed to us.

I. The committal is made to us for our own development. God commits the stewardship to us for our discipline, for our growth, for our development. God is not honored by persons of small spiritual stature, but God is honored in the giants of heart and in the giants of soul among his growing children.

If God does for us and does for us and does for us and does for us, and we do not do for ourselves, we become lazy and good for nothing. On the other hand, we are strengthened, we are developed by the *oikonomia*, the assignment the Lord has placed in our hands. We are to take it and work with it and develop it, pleasing unto God.

God speaks, and the church is the means by which God's people implement God's purposes on the earth. By what right does the pastor stand in the sacred pulpit and ask of his people their time and their energy and their property, their talents, yea, and their very lives? He does it because God has spoken and committed unto us a stewardship from heaven.

II. God has committed unto our hands the *oikonomia*, the dispensation of his grace, so that we might learn that all things are of his sovereign will in creation, in being, and in ultimate destiny. The foundation stone of all true religion is this: All things are of God, belong to God, and are to be used for God. This obviates the false distinction between secular and spiritual. No thing is beyond the pale of the interest of God. All things are in his hands. They belong to him.

As the church "belongs to the Lord," so ought all things pertaining to our lives to be no less equally dedicated and consecrated unto him. They belong to God. And they are to be used for him. We are stewards in the sense that we are partners in our own Father's house. God treats us as sons and daughters, and when I deal with what is God's, I deal with what is my very own.

III. God would, in this way, teach us how to use the substance of this world for our profit and His glory.

In an astonishing parable recorded in Luke 16:1–13, the Lord Jesus sought to impress upon his hearers the wisdom of using the materialities of this life to insure our future life. In this parable, our Lord is going to commend a rascal. But he did a smart thing, which Jesus said the children of light haven't got sense enough to do.

Our Lord is simply pointing out the obvious truth. That rascal, that dishonest steward, had sense enough to take the materialities of life and use them for his own future. God says that we can take the materialities of life and secure an inheritance in glory. Isn't that a marvelous thing, that we can take all the materialities of this life and make them to glorify God?

The steward of the parable had a day of reckoning. And Jesus commended him because in the day of reckoning he used what he had to secure himself for the future.

IV. Let me speak of our Christian giving, the use of our *oikonomia*, our stewardship, for the support of God's work in the earth. There are many reasons why people respond to a worthy use of what they possess. Sometimes they do it under coercion. Sometimes people give altruistically. Sometimes they give for the sake of enlightened self-interest. Sometimes they give for the sake of respectability. Every one of these reasons is irrelevant in Christian giving. The Christian reason for giving is gratitude to God, an overflowing, eternal thanksgiving.—W. A. Criswell.

SUNDAY: OCTOBER TWENTY-FIRST

MORNING SERVICE

Topic: A Tongue-tied Church

TEXT: 2 Kings 7:9 (Jerusalem Bible).

There is a shyness in speaking about the things of God. If the gospel is the Good News it claims to be, and if it has been entrusted to us, we stand condemned if we do not pass it on.

This is our day of opportunity, and we are tongue-tied. We not only do not speak; we seem to be incapable of doing so. Why?

I. We have no compelling incentive.

(a) Most of us are naturally talkative. In fact, some of us never stop. We talk about everything under the sun. But, let the conversation drift to religious matters and our flow of speech dries up.

(b) We must somehow distinguish between a diseased lust for numbers and a genuine concern for the glory of our King.

We've had it "put to us" about our lust for numbers and, without awareness of its chilling effect, we have lost our drive for souls. Nothing wrong with going after numbers, *if* we want to offer them to God for the glory of Christ!

II. We do not know what to say.

(a) Nothing hog-ties and tongue-ties the church like uncertainty concerning its message.

The church of our day is characterized by theological indecision as a result of the rapidity with which modern life is changing.

(b) Some now insist that what we need is a new gospel for a new age. What needs changing is the *presentation* of the gospel—*not* its content! We need to penetrate the social order not with a view to silence, but with a view to being heard! The final commission of our Lord, recorded at the end of the gospels, was neither to heal the sick nor to reform the social order, but to preach the gospel!

(c) The gospel never forgets man's dignity, but it offers not a shred of hope for his plight outside the death of Jesus Christ.

III. We are tongue-tied because we do not understand the role of the church in God's scheme of things.

We must never forget that God himself is the chief messenger. The gospel is God's gospel. He conceived it, gave it its content, and published it abroad.

He announced the gospel through his prophets, through his holy angels, through his Son, through his Spirit, and now through us also. It is through his Spirit that the witness is borne. We corroborate this. How? By the fellowship of the church, by the worship of the church, and by the evangelistic outreach of the church.

IV. We are tongue-tied because we have not relied upon the dynamics of the Holy Spirit.

(a) We must learn the difference between revival and evangelism. What is meant may best be understood by distinguishing between the ordinary and extraordinary work of the Spirit. Revival is a special moment of the Holy Spirit. In revival, God visits a district, and an entire area becomes aware of his presence. Such "revival" is the sovereign work of God. It is neither at the command nor control of men.

(b) Must evangelism wait on revival? No! As much as we may yearn for God to rend the heavens and come down and vindicate the holiness and might of his name, we must not in the meantime suspend the evangelistic task.—Carl E. Bates.

Illustrations

TOTAL DEDICATION. A leader of an important religious undertaking was honored by his friends not long ago, and in the course of the evening, many fine things were said about him and his work. In replying, he said he felt the eulogies were undeserved. He was deeply conscious of shortcomings, but he could claim to have done his best. "I can only say that I have given all I had—I have held nothing back."—Archer Wallace.

VASTNESS OF NEED. Too many men are like the Kentucky boy who had been reared behind a vast mountain. On his first trip to the city, he visited a hospital for the first time. Curiously and silently, he stared through every open door at sick people in room after room. "You know, mister," he commented. "I didn't know there were this many sick folks in all the world. I just didn't know." How like that little boy we are. Living behind mountains of indifference or preoccupation, we have failed to see the vastness of the earth and the needs of its people.—James L. Sullivan.

Sermon Suggestions

THE WAYS OF GOD'S GUIDANCE. Scripture: Ps. 25:9, 32:8, 73:24; Isa. 58:11. God will guide us in one or more or all of these ways: (1) He gives us general guidance through the person and character of Christ. (2) He guides us through the collective experience of the church. (3) He guides us through the counsel of good people. (4) He guides us through opening providences. (5) He guides us through natural law and its discoveries through science. (6) He guides us through a heightened moral intelligence and insight. (7) He guides us through the direct voice of the Spirit within us—he speaks to us in unmistakable terms in the depths of our being.—E. Stanley Jones.

THE PARADOX OF FAITH. Scripture: John 20:27, 17. (1) "Reach hither thy hand"— God's truth revealed. (2) "Touch me not" —God's mystery protected.—Adapted from Thomas K. Hearn, Jr.

Worship Aids

CALL TO WORSHIP. "They that wait upon the Lord shall renew their strength; they shall mount up with wings as eagles; they shall run, and not be weary; and they shall walk, and not faint" (Isa. 40:31).

INVOCATION. Help us, O Lord our God, to wait patiently before thee for the strength we need to win out in this world. Open our hearts to all that hymns and prayers, sermons and Christian fellowship can do to empower us to live victoriously for you.

OFFERTORY SENTENCE. "As ye abound in every thing, in faith, and utterance, and knowledge, and in all diligence, and in your love to us, see that ye abound in this grace also" (2 Cor. 8:7).

OFFERTORY PRAYER. We confess, O God, that sometimes our giving is the last important problem to solve in our Christian life. Help us to grow in this grace as we grow in all others.

PRAYER. God of our fathers and our God, give us the faith to believe in the ultimate triumph of righteousness, no matter how dark and uncertain are the skies of today.

We pray for the bifocals of faith—that see the despair and the need of the hour, but also see, further on, the patience of our God working out his plan in the world he has made.

So help thy servants to interpret for our time the meaning of the motto inscribed on our coins.

Make our faith honest by helping us this day to do one thing because thou hast said, "Do it," or to abstain because thou hast said, "Thou shalt not."

How can we say we believe in thee, or even want to believe in thee, when we do not anything thou dost tell us?

May our faith be seen in our works.— Peter Marshall.

EVENING SERVICE

Topic: On Walking with Jesus
SCRIPTURE: John 6:67–69.

How many church members would be left if all of us should be required suddenly to face the meaning of being a Christian?

The truth is, we are facing judgment every day. Little choices, as well as crucial decisions, tell the story of our inner life and loves.

There was a time when a crowd of five thousand had to confront openly and clearly the meaning of Christian discipleship. They would be Christians on their own terms. However, they would not be Christians on the terms of Christ himself. Only the twelve stayed with him.

I. We, too, are tempted to go away from Christ.

(a) We are tempted to go away from Christ because the majority go away from him. The crowd wields tremendous power. An uncommitted mind readily bows to majority opinion. But the voice of the people is not always the voice of God. There is no moral safety in taking refuge from God in a mountain of statistics.

(b) Also, we are tempted to go away from Christ because of the personal equation. Our own hopes may be shattered. The disciples shared the dreams and ideals of the crowd. They, too, looked for a Messiah who would fulfill their highest aspirations, and they were sure they had found him in Jesus. The twelve expected Jesus to give them status. They contemplated material security. They assured themselves of victory for the humiliated Jewish nation. But Jesus denied these things even to his intimates.

Many crushing events can tempt us to turn from Jesus with a toss of the head, as we mutter bitterly through clenched teeth. To be a fair-weather friend of Jesus is not hard, but to walk with him in stormy days is another matter.

II. In spite of powerful and persistent temptations to go away from Christ, some are persuaded to stay.

(a) With some, it is simply a matter of

stubborn refusal to be led by a sometimes brainless monster called "everybody." This moral obstinacy may be commendable. Sir Walter Scott produced novels in great number because he was determined to pay his debts before his died. Mark Twain went on strenuous speaking tours for the same reason. Dr. Norman Vincent Peale, overwhelmed by a storm of public criticism, was once tempted to quit the ministry. But his courage was restored by the words of an invalid father: "A Peale never quits."

(b) Others stay with Christ because they love enough to linger. They are those who know the meaning of loyalty and practice it. But loyal love is not ultimate truth. Jesus said, stretching his hand toward his discples, "Here are my mother and brothers! For whoever does the will of my Father in heaven is my brother, and sister, and mother" (Matt. 12:49–50 [RSV]).

(c) However, it appears that the minority stay with Christ because they are convinced that to stay is the only right thing to do. Such is the ultimate motive for Christian discipleship. But that motive may not quickly appear. Stubbornness and loyal love may have to hold the field for a while—until the truth becomes clear, until one is assured that to stay with Christ is the only right thing to do. This sometimes requires the surrender of a lesser loyalty. A young man brought up in a nominally religious home had a religious awakening and accepted Christ as a personal Savior.

He dedicated his life to the preaching of the gospel. His parents opposed his decision, but he went on with Christ and later had the joy of winning every member of his family.

(d) Involved in this stabilizing conviction are two elements:

1. *Faith*. Faith and conviction are not the same thing. Faith is first and leads to the conviction. A man is told something. He accepts what he has been told. He acts on what he has accepted because he considers his information reliable. Another man may be suspicious. He is not quite sure that what he hears is true. But he is willing to put it to the test. He plunges forward into the darkness of uncertainty because he believes that if he acts as if it were true, the experience will show him (see John 7:17).

2. *Knowledge*. We may assent to certain facts about Jesus before faith has really taken hold. But when faith operates, it leads us to an inner event and to outward changes that authenticate what we have accepted. Knowledge becomes an experience. Some men and women who believed in Christ had seen him in the flesh, had heard his voice, and had touched him. But others just as devout and willing to live and die for their Lord had not seen him, had not heard him, and had not touched him. They acted on faith, and faith flowered into knowledge. Peter said, "We have believed, and have come to know, that you are the Holy One of God" (John 6:69 [RSV]).—James W. Cox.

SUNDAY: OCTOBER TWENTY-EIGHTH

MORNING SERVICE

Topic: The Perfect Law
TEXT: James 1:25.

The author is really giving us here his definition of what *we* call the Sermon on the Mount. *He* calls it "the perfect law of liberty." We go to this sermon because the laws of life are written in it. We pulled it down from the shelves of heaven to wring from it the secrets of this workaday world.

I. There's something we've got to get and keep straight about this sermon Jesus preached. The very worst conclusion we

could arrive at would be to assume that he was throwing out here on the side of a hill a few bits of advice, reciting a list of statutes, or presenting us with half a dozen measuring rods by which we could gauge our righteousness or estimate our sin.

(a) That is one of the crucial mistakes we are forever making about the Christian religion. We are forever supposing that it consists chiefly in refraining from some vice and cleaving to some virtue. The most earnest among us keep frightfully busy, trying to steer a careful course through all the complicated moral problems of our generation. That's only Christian.

(b) No *sensible* person can possibly have any objection to such a program, but we can't afford to shut our eyes to the disastrous misconceptions which are involved in that whole approach. It's based, to begin with, on the assumption that behavior is the most important factor in the field. And it isn't. The most important factor is whatever it is that lies *behind* the behavior.

(c) We've really lost sight of God. Always it's *God* we've got to deal with in back of everything. The Bible keeps saying God. That's *all* it says! So does the Sermon on the Mount. It doesn't tell us how life works: it tells us how life works when God's in it. And that's different. Take *him* out of it and the whole *thing* is nothing but a fool's paradise!

II. By this time, we are in a position to get what it is specifically that James is driving at. He calls these things that Jesus said a *"perfect* law."

(a) Here is God's picture of what *he* wants: the only thing that's going to count in the world of tomorrow is whether or not these selves of ours have been put at God's disposal in the world of today—not for any deeds of our *own* that *we* do, but for *his* deeds that *he* can do. That's what Jesus was aiming at. He was trying terribly to help a man get rid of *himself*. Jesus was trying to undercut that battle by destroying the self in every one of us that gives this giant sin its vigor—the self that makes "the world hellish"—and is *our* hell.

(b) Take his sermon that way, and you'll *see* what sense it makes. There *is* something inside of us that can *die* as he keeps looking at us and talking: die and be buried and come alive again, a new creature! For ye are dead, writes Paul, and your life is hid with Christ in God. What's the use of asking if it *can* happen? It *does* happen! It may be that you and I can't really *do* anything more telling than this: "He that *loseth* his life for *my* sake shall *find* it."

(c) Freedom lies within the framework of this perfect law. And nowhere else. The Sermon on the Mount isn't a collection of lovely ideals. It isn't a code of behavior put out in a deluxe edition, intended for the use of people who want to be meticulously correct and "awfully nice." This whole thing is far deeper than action. God didn't have to come from heaven in Jesus of Nazareth to tell us what to do. He didn't have to go back home by way of a cross just for that. It's what you *are* that he's after. To take what Jesus says and ask if it's practical is beside the point. To wonder if it will actually work is an abysmal waste of wonder. What he says isn't about *doing* something. It's about *being* something!— Paul E. Scherer.

Illustrations

YOUR HEART'S DESIRE. There is a relevant story about a man who died and opened his eyes in the next world. As he looked around, his first thought was, "It could have been worse." He saw beauty, luxury beyond his dreams. An obliging attendant provided instant service for every whim. After a while, however, the man grew restless and impatient. He longed for the variety of simple refusal. One day he confronted his attendant with a demand, "I want something that I can't have without earning it." The attendant replied that he was sorry, but that particular wish could not be granted. Whereupon the man shouted out, "In that case, I will stay here no longer. I would much prefer to go to hell." Whereupon came the answer, "And where do you think you are, sir?"— Walter D. Wagoner.

LAW, LOVE, AND LIBERTY. Here is a daughter going abroad for a year. She and her mother are devoted to each other. From one point of view, it would be much easier for the girl, perhaps, if her mother gave her a list of twenty rules to keep if she was to be a dutiful daughter, pleasing her mother. That would leave the girl quite free to do anything she liked outside the ground covered by the twenty rules. But love is more binding than that. The mother gives her no rules, yet in the girl's mind and heart, there is a consciousness of what would please her mother and what would not. This knowledge is inconvenient, for it covers the whole of life, both the known and the unknown situations, both the present and the future. Because she loves her mother, she will always find the challenge and standard for her actions. She lives under love, and not under law.—Bryan Green.

Sermon Suggestions

SEEKING THE FACE OF GOD.   Text: Ps. 27:8–9. (1) There is here, first, God's voice to the heart: "Seek ye my face." (2) We have here the heart's echo to the voice of God: "My heart said unto thee, thy face, Lord, will I seek." (3) The third bend in the stream of thought here is the heart's cry to God, founded on both the divine voice and the human echo: "Hide not thy face far from me."—Alexander Maclaren.

DO YOU WANT TO BE HEALED.   Text: John 5:1–14. (1) We see ourselves here by the pool, crippled as we are. (2) The wonder is that Christ released us. (3) The forgiving love which released us sets us to following his command that we "sin no more" (v. 14).—Merrill R. Abbey.

Worship Aids

CALL TO WORSHIP.   "Stand fast therefore in the liberty wherewith Christ hath made us free" (Gal. 5:1).

INVOCATION.   Omnipotent God, stir us, open us, teach us, inform us, and shape us after the Christ we proclaim through the grace that claims us in eternal love.—E. Lee Phillips.

OFFERTORY SENTENCE.   "He that hath a bountiful eye shall be blessed; for he giveth of his bread to the poor" (Prov. 22:9).

OFFERTORY PRAYER.   Most gracious and benevolent heavenly Father, we offer unto thee these the fruits of our labor that we have come to possess. Accept and perfect our gifts unto thee, O Lord, that they may quicken in us a deeper love of thee and a greater desire to build thy Kingdom among men.—Rodney K. Miller.

PRAYER.   O Lord our God, our Father in Jesus Christ! We turn once more to you, as you have allowed us and commanded us to do. Be and remain from this day forward what you have been to us in your great might and mercy up to now, and still are today! If you enlighten us, we are enlightened; if you awaken us, then we are awakened. If you convert us, then we are converted.

And now we also earnestly ask you to be manifest and active, in your kindness and your severity, among all other men: among the young and the old, the sick and the healthy, the mighty and the weak, the Christians and the non-Christians, the responsible spokesmen and leaders of the people in East and West, and also among the countless thousands who listen to them and follow them and so share responsibility for what happens and what may still come about. All of them, all of us are in a time of trouble from which you alone can save us, and you are willing to save us. All of them, all of us are meant to praise you, to give you the honor. Let them, let all of us remember and realize that in the blood of your dear Son shed on the cross you have reconciled and united them and us and this whole poor world of ours with you and with one another: that our salvation is near us in him and that you have poured out your Holy Spirit over all mankind, so that he may make us alive too! —Karl Barth.

EVENING SERVICE

Topic: Protestantism Is Positive
TEXT: 2 Cor. 5:14.

A protestant is a protester. To protest is to object, and to object to something is negative—so the general notion is that Protestantism is negative. But our claim is that Protestantism is positive.

Protestantism is a protesting against something in order to proclaim something, and hence, Protestantism is positive.

I. Protestantism was a protesting against the wrong way of trying to get right with God and of getting other people right with God.

(a) Luther protested against the abuse of the doctrine of indulgences. Luther's protest against the abuse of the system led him ultimately to question the system itself.

(b) The doctrine of penance was the doctrine of what a person could do to make amends. Luther found that "do penance" was a mistranslation in the Latin Vulgate Bible for the Greek word which meant "repent." Luther discovered that what had been made a sacrament of the church rested in part on a mistranslation of a biblical text.

(c) You may ask, "What then, can you do to get right with God?" Nothing—in the way of doing things, either to make amends or to pile up merit. Luther discovered, by returning to the apostle Paul, that Paul set forth what God himself had done to get men right with him. It was through the life and death of Jesus Christ that God who makes the righteous demands, gave his own life and love to make men right with him. You can, by faith, respond to it, appropriate God's freely given grace, and thereby be set right in right relationship with God. Luther called that "justification by faith."

(d) The language of justification by faith was taken from the courtroom. But the heart of it was the same message as that of the Parable of the Prodigal Son. That's good news; it is the Good News—the gospel. The Reformation was the re-discovery of the gospel. That was, and is, positive Protestantism.

II. Protestantism was a protest against authority, as held and exercised in the church.

(a) Luther at first did not question the authority of the church as such, but only demanded that it be exercised in judging him according to the Scriptures and plain reason. When he was asked to recant, Luther replied, "Unless I am convicted by Scripture and plain reason, I cannot and will not recant anything. My conscience is captive to the Word of God."

But in that very statement of denial and defiance of authority, Luther made an affirmation of adherence to authority. That was positive Protestantism.

(b) In this matter of authority in religion, the question always is, "Do you want this authority for yourself, or do you want it to exercise over other people in coercion?" The Bible speaks of my condition, it makes available the grace of God to help my condition. That is all the authority or assurance you need for yourself.

(c) If authority over others is what you want, you have no right to that authority, save by the consent of others. Church government is for orderly procedure and to insure that the purpose of the fellowship will be accomplished. Our Lord himself is the only one to whom absolute authority is given in the matters of the Christian faith, practice, and government.

III. Protestantism was a protest against the denial of the freedom of the Christian.

(a) Luther declared, "The Christian man is the most free lord of all and subject to none." But that in itself is just a negative thing. Luther recognized this and had evidence of it.

There are many persons," he said, "who, when they hear of this liberty of faith, straightway turn it into an occasion of license."

(b) In order to keep Christian freedom from being merely negative, Luther laid down his second proposition: "A Christian man is the most dutiful servant of all, and subject to everyone."

IV. All of this means that to be a Protestant is not just to be anti-something. There are some who are just against anything that is Roman Catholic. There is another group that is just indifferent. There is also the idea that a Protestant is a person who does not have to do anything he does not want to do.

In a sense, that is true! The church has no exclusive hold on you. The hold on you must be Christ's hold on you. Paul, who threw off the yoke of Judaism and was thereby free, nonetheless said: "The love of Christ constrainth me."

If Christ does have his hold on you, then you will love the church and give yourself to it as Christ loved the church and gave himself for it. It will be not by what you protest against, but by what you freely, gladly, and lovingly do, that your Protestantism will be positive.—Charles L. Seasholes.

SUNDAY: NOVEMBER FOURTH

MORNING SERVICE

Topic: In the Beginning
SCRIPTURE: Genesis 1:1ff.
I. What sort of writing is this?
(a) First, let's be clear what it is not. It is not history—for history depends on contemporary documents and eyewitness accounts. Again, it is not science, as we know it. Behind the story there may lie the rudimentary science of Babylon, but the man who wrote this was certainly not speaking the language of the modern scientific textbook.
(b) What, then, is it? There are technical terms I could use, but the simplest thing to say is that this is art, the verbal vision of a consummate artist.
II. What I find in this passage as the answer to all these questions is the living, active, creating God. It doesn't really matter much that this thought chimes in with the "big bang" theory of the origin of the universe advanced by some modern scientists. What the Bible is concerned with is not just the mystery of ultimate origins, but the meaning, the creative purpose behind all that exists.
(a) Have you noticed that one of the most popular adjectives in modern speech and writing is *creative*? What the opening verses of the Bible are telling us is that there is meaning at the very center of all things and that through all there throbs the creative power of God. There is an exuberance about this passage that makes our cynical questioning, our literature of skepticism and despair, seem tired and flat. The key word in our universe is not *chance*, or *fate*, or *nothingness*, but *creativity* —the continuous action of a living God, the God who brings light out of darkness, and who finds it good.
(b) This is a totally different picture from the popular religious one of a God who set everything going long, long ago and then sat back to watch it tick until the day when it will inevitably run down. It is true that this story speaks of God finishing creation and resting on the seventh day,

but this is simply a picturesque way of indicating that creative energy, even God's energy, has its pause. Elsewhere we are left in no doubt about God's continuous creative power. For Jesus, the Father is continually at his creative work, and this is what he was reflecting in his own gift of new life, his own bringing of light out of darkness.
(c) This is how God speaks to us in this ancient Scripture. What more powerful and relevant word do we need today than this assurance that behind the void, within the chaos, of which we are so sensitive today, there is an ultimate creative Spirit, which not only pursues a purpose and imparts a meaning, but finds the whole process "very good"? The fact of creation, and the goodness of creation—these are biblical insights that can transform the whole outlook of modern man.
III. Then what about the central mystery of all—man himself? How can I understand this strange creature that I am?
(a) The answer of the Bible to this riddle is Adam, made in the image of God. This is Man, and this is his astonishing destiny —to reflect the Creative Spirit from whom all else derives, to share in the freedom of God himself. In this story, he is God's last creation—unique and alone. While all else is seen as proceeding from the creative power of God and then, as it were, automatically obeying his will, Adam is like a son—able to commune with God and to create on his own account. Here is the mystery and glory of mankind, exposed in a brief tale that says more than many volumes of philosophy.
(b) This is the story of Adam, the story of you and me. "So God created man in his *own* image, in the image of God created he him," and God gave him dominion. What does that mean? Surely that, as children of God, we are meant to explore and exploit the universe around us. This is why man's restless spirit is never content with the life of an animal, why we have roamed the earth and are now pushing toward the

stars, why we have tamed the resources of the earth and are now entering upon the secrets of the atom. The Creator has made little creators in his image. This is how the Bible speaks in this ancient tale. And what power is still behind these words! With such a vision of man, who could treat him as a mere cipher, a number on a card, a body to be used, a mind to be manipulated, computer fodder?

(c) And in the human family, God is still creating. He still calls us, one by one, to accept the destiny of sons and daughters. He still reveals his perfect Son, Jesus Christ, and offers to make us a new creation in him. He still brings light out of darkness, and still creates new fields for us to explore.—David H. C. Read.

Illustrations

LOVING GOD WITH THE MIND.　　In worshiping, seeking, and serving the invisible, our scientists have been worshiping, seeking, and serving God. It was this fact which was so wonderfully expressed by the devout heart of the immortal Kepler, discoverer of the laws of planetary motion, one of the greatest of all the searchers of the stars. Gazing in rapture upon the mystic spaces of the skies and seeing what no man had ever seen before, he fervently exclaimed, "O Lord, I am thinking thy thoughts after thee!"—John Haynes Holmes.

GOD STILL AT WORK.　　The Christian apprehends God's working preeminently in the life, death, and resurrection of Jesus Christ. . . . Here is Love that suffers, but here also is Love that triumphs. Tragedy itself, accepted, endured, transfigured, and redeemed, ministers to a new and richer life. Sin, suffering, and death are woven into the pattern of divine providence.—Peter Baelz.

Sermon Suggestions

MARKS OF VITAL CHRISTIANITY.　　Text: 1 Pet. 3:15. (1) The inner life of devotion. (2) The outer life of service. (3) The intellectual life of rationality.—Adapted from Elton Trueblood.

THE PORTRAIT OF A GOOD MAN.　　Scripture: Matt. 8:5–13. A man is good when: (1) He is interested in others. "Lord, my servant. . . ." (2) He has a proper view of himself. "I am not worthy." (3) He believes in the power of Christ. "Speak the word and my servant shall be healed." (4) He has an unusual faith. "I have not found so great faith."—V. L. Stanfield.

Worship Aids

CALL TO WORSHIP.　　"The Lord by wisdom hath founded the earth; by understanding hath he established the heavens. By his knowledge the depths are broken up, and the clouds drop down the dew" (Prov. 3:19, 20).

INVOCATION.　　O heavenly Father, who hast filled the world with beauty; open, we beseech thee, our eyes to behold thy gracious hand in all thy works; that rejoicing in thy whole creation, we may learn to serve thee with gladness; for the sake of him by whom all things were made, thy Son, Jesus Christ our Lord.—Book of Comon Prayer.

OFFERTORY SENTENCE.　　"I have shewed you all things, how that so laboring ye ought to support the weak, and to remember the words of the Lord Jesus, how he said, It is more blessed to give than to receive."—Acts 20:35.

OFFERTORY PRAYER.　　Blessed be thou, O Lord God, for ever and ever. Thine, O Lord, is the greatness and the power, and the victory, and the majesty; for all that is in the heaven and in the earth is thine. Thine is the Kingdom, O Lord, and thou art exalted as head above all. Both riches and honor come of thee, and of thine own do we now give thee, for the good of thy church and the glory of thy name.—Book of Common Order.

PRAYER.　　Eternal God, high above all yet in all, from whom to be turned away is to fall, to whom to be turned is to rise, and in whom to abide is to stand fast forever, we worship thee.

Like mountains whose summits are clad

in clouds, so is thy mystery to us. We thy children on this wandering island in the sky, a speck amid the vasts of space, look up to thee. O God, let us not be confounded by the empty spaces or afrighted by world beyond world unfathomable. As thou hast put us into a great universe, help us to see behind it and in it a great God and lift up our minds to say, like our fathers before us, "Before the mountains were brought forth, or ever thou hadst formed the earth and the world, even from everlasting to everlasting, thou art God."

Above all, we have come to thee that thou mightest make real to us the universe within. There lie our fortune and destiny, for there truth may walk in shining garments, and goodness grow glorious, and beauty be beautiful indeed. O thou who hast taught us through thy Son that the Kingdom of heaven is within us, make true, we beseech thee this day, that description of our lives.

Meet us in the secret places of our souls. Walk thou through the hidden rooms whence too often we have banished thee. Let all that is low and abominable, selfish, vindictive, and of a mean report be put from us. Cast it down, discard it, good Lord, and lift up whatever is excellent and beautiful, unselfish and of high repute.—Harry Emerson Fosdick.

EVENING SERVICE

Topic: At Home with God

Scripture: Luke 15:11–24 (rsv).

I. Let us be honest with ourselves and ask, How near and personal does God seem to us at this moment?

(a) That there is a God veiled in the mystery of things few, if any, of us, would deny.

But when I ponder the greatness of the Creator with a universe on his hands, I feel like the psalmist, as he said, "When I look at the heavens, the work of thy fingers, the moon and the stars which thou hast established, what is man that thou art mindful of him?" God seems so immeasurably great and man so infinitesimally small. It is pretty hard to feel close to God if we think of him only as Creator.

(b) We can advance, however, from a sense of God as impersonal Creative Power to an awareness of God as a Personality revealing himself through nature. Yet even this second step hardly makes God near enough for intimate personal communion. If all that we could know of God came through nature, we could scarcely find saving help in him.

If we are to have vital personal communion with God, we must advance beyond communing with him through nature to contact with him through persons.

II. Turn to the Bible. It opens with the story of creation. Then keep on turning the pages of the Old Testament and watch how the progressive understanding of the writers interprets God as drawing nearer and nearer.

And then came Jesus of Nazareth. The stories of his nativity made men feel that the Almighty God had stooped to our weakness and became incarnate in a babe born in a manger in a peasant land. The child grew, tempted in all points even as we are, and yet without sin. His matchless purity and power became the lasting miracle of the ages. He manifested such wisdom in his words and such power in his works that multitudes became convinced that he came from God.

Jesus revealed God as great enough to be adored and yet near enough to enter into personal communion with the lowliest.

Jesus epitomized the personal relationship of the individual to God in a matchless story which we call the Parable of the Prodigal Son.

III. This is the simple text of our message. And note how simple it is. Jesus would have us realize that the great God who made the heaven and the earth is as near and personal as a father to a son, that we can turn to God as directly as that boy went back to his father, that returning to God is like a homecoming, and that when we do come back to God, we are at home. That is the Good News which is at the heart of the Christian gospel.

(a) Note that he said, "I will arise and go." He did not ask his father to come and make him comfortable in his self-centered, indulgent living. If we are to have vital relationship with God, we must try to rise toward his greatness and not try to reduce him to our littleness.

One trouble with some of our thinking today is that in our effort to bring our religion down to earth, we forget the greatness of God. American churches need to recover and recultivate the element of *adoration*. We must take time to ponder God in his greatness and beauty and love. The trouble with too many of us is that we are trying to get God to work for us without taking the time really to worship him. Our Lord's Prayer teaches us to hallow the name of our Father in heaven before we ask him to give us our daily bread.

(b) Therefore, if we would feel close to God, let us, like the prodigal son in the parable, say, "I will arise and go to my father and I will say to him, Father, I have sinned against heaven and before you; I am no longer worthy to be called your son; treat me as one of your hired servants." And now go on. When we do turn to God in willingness to serve and obey him, then we discover what the prodigal boy found, namely that the father is coming toward us. The record of the gospel story is that "while he was yet at a distance, his father saw him and had compassion and ran and embraced him."

When we repent of our sins, humble our spirits, and surrender our wills to serve God, we do feel him drawing near to us. That is the testimony of multitudes who have tried it. I cannot prove it to you by any argument. It has to be discovered by experience. And it is this feeling of nearness to God that we crave.—Ralph W. Sockman.

SUNDAY: NOVEMBER ELEVENTH

MORNING SERVICE

Topic: Words That Hurt, Words That Heal

SCRIPTURE: Matt. 12:34b-37 (RSV).

Words have a power all of their own—literally, a power to hurt or a power to heal, a power to crush or a power to lift, a power to confuse or a power to inspire. Words give us access to virtually every dimension of life and words enable us to break out of isolation or anonymity; they establish our rapport, each with the other —and they also can drive us apart. They can build, create, strengthen, or they can wound, pierce, and crucify. Words are all these things. Let us focus attention upon a narrow range of vocabulary, specifically upon certain words which can hurt and some better ones that can heal. Behind these considerations is Jesus' teaching when he said, "Out of the abundance of the heart, the mouth speaks. The good man out of his good treasure brings forth good, and the evil man out of his evil treasure brings forth evil. I tell you, on the day of judgment, men will render account for every careless word they utter; for by your words, you will be justified, and by your words, you will be condemned."

I. What are some of those words which hurt? At once you may think of derogatory name-calling, of slanderous remarks; or even of gossip and backbiting. Certainly, words which assume these characteristics hurt, often deeply and irreparably. Gossip alone can be devastating. Probably all here have felt its effects; worse yet, a majority of us have participated in it, in all likelihood. The problem with gossip is the same as that of the torn pillow filled with feathers. The wind scatters those feathers, and try as one might, they are irretrievable.

II. There is a different category to hurtful speech, probably not immediately called to mind; it is these words about which we also should be greatly concerned, aware that our Lord himself was keenly sensitive to them. I think of words such as hunger, fear, hatred, injustice, oppression, and the whole range of humanly destructive experiences and attitudes which rob men and women of their dignity. Still permitted among us are many behaviors represented by the words just named. Yet what was Jesus' mission? At the synagogue in Nazareth, he stood to preach and said, "The Spirit of the Lord is upon me, because he has anointed me to preach Good News to the poor. He has sent me to proclaim release to the captives and recovering of sight to the blind, to set at liberty those who are oppressed, to proclaim the acceptable year of the Lord."

In effect, Jesus was countering the words which hurt. Not only with this speech, but with his entire life he advocated words and deeds that heal. He spoke of justice and hope, of power and love. Even as he spoke of forgiveness, he bestowed it. When he described the peace that passes understanding, he imparted it. From Jesus' lips came only words which heal—words which bind up the brokenhearted, which give meaning and purpose and resolve to life again.

III. The cynic might wonder, with all of these great words and themes available to humankind, why has not more come of them? In answer, it can be said that tremendous results are being sought when Jesus (or we ourselves) speak of mercy and goodness and forgiveness and love. These objects are not realized overnight. Of course, there is another answer—a humiliating one, really. It is that people have repeated these great words, the words with healing potential, but have not put their lives behind them. Every word which heals carries an independent power, but that power is realized in fullness when the lips which speak represent lives that care.

This is to say that when word and deed become one—as they did supremely in Jesus Christ—there is a force for good let loose in the word which has unlimited potential. We believe of Jesus, he was the living Word, the Word of God expressed in this world—and it is an apt designation. The incredible implication of his teachings is that those who are blessed by him in turn are to be his spokesmen, his word, in the world of today.

IV. All of that begins with the pronunciation of certain other words. It begins when each of us, freely and gladly, says to Jesus, "I will follow you." This declaration of intention opens us to everything that is true, honorable, just, pure, lovely, gracious, praiseworthy, and of good report. When we say to Jesus, "I will follow you," we agree to "speak the truth in love," to bear faithful witness to his name, and to fill our speech not with words that hurt, but with words that heal.—John T. Townsend.

Illustrations

THE PROBLEM OF LONELINESS. The most heartening experience of my own personal ministry has been to break through the isolation and loneliness that possesses many a veteran professional person, as well as rebellious young research men and scientists, and discover a spiritual wistfulness of stringent loneliness of being. They have gone beyond the point of no-return to the quaint and unsophisticated simplicity of the religious beliefs of their childhoods. Yet, they have not found in their vocation anything but competition, demands for almost ascetic discipline, and the few crumbs of gratitude given to them by the one out of ten persons they help who return to say thanks. They long for a "filial relation with the cosmos which has begotten them," as Gardner Murphy so aptly puts it. The Christian pastor and the community of faith that he represents have only dimly begun to become aware of the suffering involved in the spiritual homesickness of the average professionally and scientifically trained person.—Wayne E. Oates.

THE POWER OF ENTHUSIASM. Lord Macaulay did not give unqualified approval to all that the Puritans did, but he did pay tribute to their deep sincerity and their strength of conviction. He wrote: "The intensity of their feelings on one subject made them tranquil on every other. One overpowering sentiment had subjected to itself pity and hatred, ambition and fear. Death had lost all its terrors and pleasure its charms. Enthusiasm had cleansed their minds from every vulgar passion and had raised them above the influence of danger and corruption. They went through the world having neither part nor lot in human infirmities." Macaulay was writing of men who lived three centuries ago, yet a modern writer says substantially the same thing: "No heart is pure that is not passionate, no virtue is safe that is not enthusiastic."—Archer Wallace.

Sermon Suggestions

AUTHORITY OF THE WILL.   Text: John 5:
40. (1) The will is a basal fact of life. (2)
The will is the revelation of the life. (3)
The will can be submitted to Christ.—
Hugh Black.

THE NAME "CHRISTIAN."   Scripture:
Acts 11:26; 26:28; 1 Pet. 4:16. (1) A tribute
to the newness of the Christian faith. (2) A
tribute to the challenge of the new faith.
(3) A tribute to the nature of the new faith
as attachment to the person of Christ.—
Dwight E. Stevenson.

Worship Aids

CALL TO WORSHIP.   "If ye then be risen
with Christ, seek those things which are
above, where Christ sitteth on the right
hand of God" (Col. 3:1).

INVOCATION.   Almighty God, our Father, who brought again from the dead
our Lord Jesus Christ, help us to live the
lives of those who have been raised with
him to walk in newness of life. Give us high
aspirations in all things and lift our
thoughts above everything that would
keep us from fulfilling thy purpose for us.

OFFERTORY SENTENCE.   "Whatsoever ye
do, do it heartily, as to the Lord, and not
unto men; knowing that of the Lord ye
shall receive the reward of the inheritance;
for ye serve the Lord Christ" (Col. 3:23,
24).

OFFERTORY PRAYER.   O Lord our God,
who givest liberally and upbraidest not,
teach us to give cheerfully of our substance for thy cause and Kingdom. Let thy
blessing be upon our offerings, and grant
us to know the joy of those who give with
their whole heart, through Jesus Christ
our Lord.—*Book of Common Order*.

PRAYER.   O thou who art our maker and
our God, the giver and sustainer of life, we
would bless thy name at all times. Thy
praise would continually rise from our
grateful hearts.

We thank thee that thy power extends

beyond man's prowess and achievements,
that our towers never do quite touch the
sky, that always thou art more than we
have thought or preached thee to be.

We thank thee that a fall of snow can
hobble a mighty city, that strong head-
winds can slow our jets and make us late,
that heavy rains can force a cancellation of
public events, that high seas command the
respect of our sturdiest ocean-going ships.

In short, we thank thee, God, for everything and anything that humbles us before
the mystery of life and keeps us from the
folly of worshiping the works of our
hands. Thou alone art God and together
we would bless thy holy name.—Ernest T.
Campbell.

EVENING SERVICE

Topic: Communication: The Essence of the Family

SCRIPTURE: Prov. 15:1–5.

It can be said that the quality of your
marriage and the stability of your family
will be determined by the depth of your
communication. Communication is the essential ingredient in any healthy and
happy home.

How can we enhance the communication in our homes?

I. *The presuppositions*.

(a) You cannot not communicate. Some
people refuse to talk and by their silence
suppose that they are not communicating.
But they are communicating. By their silence, they are communicating apathy or
unconcern or hostility or disagreement.

(b) The key to good communication is
our willingness to listen. To enhance communication in the home, one of our most
urgent needs is to learn how to listen.

(c) Communication is hard work. Positive, productive communication does not
simply happen. We have to work at it. It
takes time and trust and tact.

II. *The pattern*. How then can we communicate with each other better? What kind
of words will lead to positive, productive
communication in the home, between husbands and wives, between parents and
children, between brothers and sisters?
We find a pattern in the Word of God. In
contrasting the upright with the wicked,

Solomon suggested four kinds of words that are conducive to proper communication.

(a) In verse 1, the writer of Proverbs mentions gentle words. The verse depicts an emotion that often occurs in the home: anger. The marriage relationship probably generates more anger than any other situation. The worst thing about anger in the home is that it blocks communication.

When anger comes into the home, how are we to respond? The writer of Proverbs says that we can respond with gentle words or with harsh words. If we respond with a harsh word, we will stir up the anger and further block communication. A gentle word, however, will put away the anger and open the communication lines again.

(b) In verse 2, the writer of Proverbs mentions true words. Wise words in the home are words that make truth attractive and appealing. They are true words. Dishonesty is another barrier to communication in the home because communication is based on truth and dishonesty undermines trust. Words that enhance communication in the home are words that refuse to wear the clothing of deceit.

(c) In verse 4, the writer of Proverbs mentions encouraging words. When a husband said to his counselor, "My wife makes me feel good about myself with a pat high on the ego," he was talking about encouraging words. When a writer suggested that we show our concern for our children with "the special vocabulary of affirmation," he was talking about encouraging words.

Nothing so enhances communication and inspires growth as a word of encouragement. Encouraging words instead of cruel words make communication flow, and they create an atmosphere for growth and development.

(d) In verse 5, the writer of Proverbs mentions corrective words. The fact that our words are to be gentle, truthful, and encouraging does not rule out the fact that our words in the home can be, and should be at times, corrective. Every person needs feedback. The best place to get that gentle, truthful, encouraging feedback is in the home from those who love us and have our best interests at heart. Learning how to give, and receive, constructive criticism is difficult to do, but it is a key to communication in the family.—Brian L. Harbour.

SUNDAY: NOVEMBER EIGHTEENTH

MORNING SERVICE

Topic: Thankfulness Makes the Difference

SCRIPTURE: 1 Thess. 5:12–18.

Life is a gift from God. To be a part of this world—even with all its troubles—is still a blessing, at least for those who don't have to struggle to have their basic needs met. Living can be what it ought to be when we maintain an attitude of thankfulness to God for his gift.

While most people would agree with this concept in principle, many of us lose our appreciation for the opportunity of living. That's sad. I'm not talking about the breathtaking-TV-thankfulness of those who own the latest consumer products. I am talking about a basic posture or attitude of thankfulness which informs all that we think, feel, and do. It isn't magic or hyper-spiritual, nor does it come easily, but it is possible and something we all need.

I. (a) King Saul awoke from an unusual afternoon nap one day soon to discover that he could just as easily not have awakened. Do you remember the story from 1 Samuel 24? David could have killed the intimidated ruler. Saul wept as David explained that he had no intention of killing him in order to take his throne. If he had wanted Saul dead, this conversation would never have taken place.

(b) Part of the tears which Saul shed that day, I think, indicated his thankfulness for living. His mad competition for sovereignty left him little time to be thankful about anything. In his way, Saul was committed to God, but he was preoccupied with snuffing out anyone who might do his divinely appointed job better than he. He was thankful for an instant here; let's give him credit for that. But his thanksgiving was only temporary. Before long, Saul would be caught up in his old way of life with no time for thankfulness.

(c) Most of us don't have to search ourselves a great deal before we find considerable identification with Saul. We're busy people. Studies, jobs, families, friends—they all take time. We're trying to do our divinely appointed thing, and sometimes we're not above some competition for beating out someone who might do some of our tasks better. In our really honest moments, we must admit that we rarely have time for thankfulness. Only when something drastic happens are we jolted into reality. We have to be reminded that we could not even have life before we appreciate it.

II. Others of us are thankful to God for our lives only when we feel that he has done something for us to make life more what *we* want it to be.

(a) One day Jesus passed by a group of ten leprous men standing on the outskirts of some unnamed village between Samaria and Galilee. They must have known him by what other people had told them or because of previous visits to their city. In utter desperation, they cried out at a distance, "Master, have mercy on us." Jesus healed them (see Luke 17).

(b) As you know, only one of the men took the time to thank Jesus verbally, though I think all of the men were thankful for life at the moment of healing, and at least inside they rejoiced for what God had done for them through Jesus. That's what they had wanted out of this encounter, and that's what they got. They believed; they had faith, or they couldn't have been healed. Yet only one took the time to give formal thanks, and he was likely the one who had the most profound and long-lasting spiritual experience. He might make thankfulness a way of life. The other nine would probably continue being thankful only when they felt God had added to their lives what they wanted.

Thankfulness makes the difference. Life is a gift from God. We ought to be thankful for that. Few people have learned and practiced the truth like Paul.

III. Paul made some suggestions to the church at Thessalonica (See 1 Thess. 5:12 –18).

"Give thanks in all circumstances," he wrote, and he did his best to live it, too. Near the end of his life, he wrote some revealing words from his cell in Rome. In thanking the church at Philippi for their gifts, he says, "I have learned, in whatever state I am, to be content" (Phil. 4:11). No doubt, this was something that Paul had to learn. This kind of attitude toward life doesn't come easily. In fact, it really is a matter of discipline coupled with an undying sense of life as God's gift.

I believe the same kind of attitude Paul had is within our grasp. I believe that our lives could be transformed if we really believed that thankfulness makes the difference, if in the midst of every experience we could internalize the truth: life is God's gift to me. I don't know what all might happen if we began living in this way, but if we could find the same kind of thankful contentment Paul found, wouldn't life be richer, fuller, more meaningful?—David Farmer.

Illustrations

INGRATITUDE.   Sir Winston Churchill once told ironically the story of the sailor who dived into the waters of Plymouth Harbor to save the life of a little boy. Three days afterwards, the sailor met the boy and his mother in the street. He saw the boy nudge his mother, and the mother stopped the sailor and asked, "Are you the man who pulled my little boy out of the water?" Expecting some kind of gratitude, the sailor smiled, saluted, and said, "Yes, madam." "Then," replied the mother, with increasing temper, "where's his cap?"—R. G. Crawford.

THE BIBLE'S PICTURE LANGUAGE.   I feel I must record here my sense of injustice that the Christian religion should be singled out as a target for criticism because it uses, and is bound to use, "picture language." We all do it every day of our lives, and we are none the worse for it. No one blames the accountant for talking of a "balance," the economist for speaking of "frozen assets," the electronics engineer for talking of a magnetic "field," the traffic controller for referring to a "peak" period, the electrical engineer for speaking of "load-shedding," or the town planner for talking of a "bottle neck." Not one of these words is literally true, but each conveys quickly, and pretty accurately, an idea which can be readily understood. I cannot see why we, who accept hundreds of such usages in everyday speaking and writing, should decide that an expression such as "seated at the right hand of the Father" is either literally true or totally false.—J. B. Phillips.

Sermon Suggestions

THE PILGRIM FAITH. Text: Heb. 11:8. Three aspects of the Christian life of obedience to which we are all called: (1) It is an experience in which we have to abandon our natural longing to plan ahead. (2) Obedience is absolutely and inextricably involved in faith. (3) Faith demands that we let go all false security and commit ourselves to an endless adventure.—John Huxtable.

HE DELIGHTS IN OUR GRATITUDE. Text: Matt. 15:36. To see the evidence of God's mercies, you have only to look. (1) Let us begin with the common blessings. (2) Let us give thanks to God for the special blessings. (3) Let us give thanks to God for the greatest blessing, his "unspeakable" gift, Jesus Christ.—W. E. Sangster.

Worship Aids

CALL TO WORSHIP. "Honor the Lord with thy substance, and with the first fruits of all thine increase: so shall thy barns be filled with plenty, and thy presses shall burst out with new wine" (Prov. 3:9, 10).

INVOCATION. We have been blessed, O God, beyond all that we could ask or think. Beyond all material things, we have been enriched in the more important matters of the spirit. We would pray for our daily bread, but realizing that we do not live by bread alone, we would pray that we might receive thine own self—known, loved, and obeyed—for what thou art: God of love and grace.

OFFERTORY SENTENCE. "Walk in love, as Christ also hath loved us, and hath given himself for us an offering and a sacrifice to God for a sweet-smelling savor" (Eph. 5:2).

OFFERTORY PRAYER. With this offering, Lord, we bring a harvest of gratitude for the health and wealth we enjoy, the wisdom and instruction we receive, the friendships and fellowship we experience. Allow these tokens of the fruit of our land to merge into the fruit of thy Spirit in proclaiming the gospel of salvation.

PRAYER. O God, we thank thee for life, and all the beauty and the wonder of it, for the people that we have known and loved, and for the rare opportunities that we have had to enter into the deeper things of life. Forgive, O God, our triviality, and overlook our foolish ways. Help us to deepen and cultivate our understanding of primary things, things that come first, and then give us the will and the grace to make this nation strong that it may endure and that it may not go the way of others into exile and oblivion.—Theodore Parker Ferris.

EVENING SERVICE

Topic: God of All Comfort

TEXT: 2 Cor. 1:3–4.

In Scripture, God is given many names and titles. The text declares him to be the "God of all mercies," or a merciful God.

Of all the names of God, none is dearer than this: he is "the God of all comfort." Let this be the Word of God to us.

I. *The nature of our comfort.*

(a) Authentic comfort is not the denial of reality. That is a natural early reaction to grief. In the initial shock of it, we say, "It doesn't seem real" or "I feel as though this is all a bad dream." But long-term denial does not contribute to our healing. Life must go on. We pick up the pieces and begin again. We do not try to run away from grief; we accept it and return to our duty.

(b) Some think comfort is a weak word. But that is not so. Comfort is a strong word. In the Greek, it has the same root as *paraclete*—a name for the Holy Spirit. It comes from two words which literally mean "to be called alongside."

II. *The source of our comfort.*

(a) We do not find comfort in trying to escape.

(b) We do not find ultimate comfort even in a brave philosophy. It is pollyanna to proclaim cheerily, "Every cloud has a silver lining." That attitude may be stoic, but there is no real gospel help in it. We need something more.

We certainly find consolation in the warm support of our friends and family. Yet while their words are consoling, they cannot bring lasting comfort.

(c) What we really need is divine comfort—"the God of all comfort." He is acquainted with grief. He saw his only Son die and was helpless to save him, if he was to save us. The truth is, we do not keep our faith—it keeps us.

III. *The scope of our comfort.*

(a) We find comfort even in physical suffering and limitations. Paul prayed about his "thorn in the flesh." It was not removed, but he learned that God's grace was sufficient for him to bear it.

(b) We are comforted in our anxiety and mental anguish. Never forget the ringing promise in Philippians 4:7.

(c) There is even the comfort of forgiveness for our guilt. We have the joy of sins forgiven, a new life in Christ, and the assurance of our salvation.

(d) We can find comfort in the face of death itself. That king of terrors, mankind's last enemy, was conquered on Easter morning. It lost its sting, its power to hurt us, at the resurrection.

IV. *The stewardship of our comfort.* Paul saw suffering not simply as misery, but as an opportunity for ministry.

You have suffered. And you have found comfort. You can comfort others in a way that someone else cannot. Remember that Jesus said when we do it for others we have done it for him.—Alton H. McEachern.

SUNDAY: NOVEMBER TWENTY-FIFTH

MORNING SERVICE

Topic: Facing the Future with Faith

Text: Jer. 32:15.

I. (a) Look at the background of this verse. It was a time of chaos and confusion in the ancient world. The army of Babylon flattened the nations as a bulldozer flattens a flower garden. Judah and Jerusalem lay directly in its path, their only hope being in a peaceful and honorable surrender. For the sake of their survival as a nation, the prophet Jeremiah counseled a policy of surrender to Babylon. Refusing to face reality, their leaders denounced Jeremiah as a traitor, and in order to silence his voice, they put him in prison.

(b) One day Jeremiah had a visitor—his cousin Hanameel who came not to comfort him, but to make an outlandish proposition. In the village of Anatoth, Hanameel owned a piece of property which had been in the family for four hundred years. This property he now proposed to sell. With the whole country about to fall into enemy hands, nothing was quite so worthless as real estate. Yet the absurd, brave humor of it all is that Jeremiah took him up on his ridiculous offer. He knew that the land would soon be conquered and the people carried away into exile, and he knew that even if he survived prison, he might be among the exiles and never see the property he had just purchased. At the same time, he foresaw something else. With his prophetic vision, he looked beyond the immediate calamity to a distant day when the political picture would change and the people of Israel would be released from exile in Babylon and allowed to return and rebuild their national life. He wanted to share that vision with his dispirited fellow countrymen, and that's why he purchased a piece of property about to be annexed by their enemies. It was an acted parable designed to put hope into their fainting hearts.

I. Jeremiah was a person who really faced the future with faith.

(a) We must have faith in the future simply because we have never been there before, and neither has anyone else. The future is unexplored territory. It may be a land flowing with milk and honey or it may be a barren wilderness. One thing is certain: we have to trust the future, we have to face it with faith, our only psychological equipment, or we shall not get there at all. Most people do trust the future. At least, they order their lives and the life of society as though they were going to be around and as though the world were going to be around for a long time. Despite any verbal pessimism caused by our worries about pollution, overpopulation and the atomic bomb, we still face the future with a healthy and courageous faith.

(b) What else can we do? We must regard the future as our friend, not our enemy, otherwise we shall not be able to cope with life. I don't know your circumstances, how unhappy your past or discouraging your present, but I do know that if you want to find any peace, any joy, any success in life at all, you must face the future with faith.

III. Such faith does not come easily.

(a) We see its depth and daring only when we see the total tragedy of Jeremiah's situation. It was not just the old story of military defeat. Behind it lay the apparent failure of God's experiment with his people Israel. It seemed such a colossal and catastrophic waste. That was the real tragedy of Jeremiah's day.

(b) And that is the real tragedy of our day. It comes into focus as we think of the church's wider work in the world and realize how many of the great spiritual achievements of the past have been ploughed under by the secular world culture. These are discouraging days for the church of Jesus Christ; and it takes more than a superficial optimism to serve the church with enthusiasm and confidence. Those who remain on board and continue to serve with loyalty and fidelity are the ones who believe in God and can therefore see beyond the storm of secularism and materialism to the clear sunlight of God's purpose.

IV. Such faith is always vindicated, as Jeremiah's faith was vindicated. (a) After seventy years of exile, the Jews were released from Babylon and allowed to return and rebuild their shattered country. The prophecy was fulfilled. Houses and fields and vineyards were again bought in the land. God works according to his own timetable. Under his providence, the picture may change in a single lifetime, as it is doing so marvellously in our day.

(b) The church may have been unwell for a time, but it is beginning to show signs of new life and to vindicate the faith of those who stayed with it and served it with loyalty and devotion.

(c) To that brave and stubborn faith, Jeremiah challenges our generation. In a world where man has been debased to the status of a fly on a windowpane, he dares us to believe in the dignity and worth of human personality. In a world which respects only the law of physical force, he dares us to have faith in the invincible power of the human spirit. In a world where years of goodwill have been wiped out in one moment of passionate evil or stupidity, he dares us to believe that it will all come back. In a world of greed, deception, violence and cruelty, he dares us to believe that no good thing is ever lost. In a world where so many people cannot see beyond the barren present, he dares us to hold a view of life that reaches to all eternity.—A. Leonard Griffith.

Illustrations

STRUGGLE.   Do you remember Goethe in his old age? "I will say nothing against the course of my existence. But at the bottom it has been nothing but pain and burden, and I can affirm that during the whole of my seventy-five years I have not had four weeks of genuine well-being. It is but the perpetual rolling down of a rock that must be raised up again forever."—C. F. Aked.

FAITH'S   EXPULSIVE   POWER.   Oscar Wilde says in the introduction to that fascinating little autobiography of his, *De Profundis*, that there were two great turning points in his life; the first, when his father sent him to college, and the second, when society sent him to prison. It was in the latter place that the gracious experience of faith's exclusive power took place within his soul. He was given only one thing in his lonely cell beside his cot, tin cup, and place for water and bread. This was his New Testament. It was in the original Greek, and Wilde, who was an excellent classical scholar, read it understandingly and explored its vast domain of spiritual experience with Christ. There for the first time he realized the beauty and power of a life of faith. Christ became to him more than merely a human name, and in this power of a newfound faith, he felt the old life of sordid evil and disgusting folly forever expelled.—William Lloyd Imes.

Sermon Suggestions

A WORLD GONE SANE. Text: Phil. 2:5. (1) A world gone sane would put human life and welfare at the center. (2) In a world gone sane, people would seek the things which bring lasting satisfaction. (3) A world gone sane would see that adjustment to the moral and spiritual order is the indispensable condition of human survival and welfare.—Adapted from Halford E. Luccock.

SPECIAL REASONS FOR PRAISING GOD. Scripture: Eph. 1:4–14. (1) We should praise God because he has elected us in Christ (vv. 4–6). (2) We should praise God because he has dealt with us according to the riches of his grace (vv. 7–12). (3) We should praise God because he has sealed us with the Holy Spirit until we acquire full possession of our inheritance (vv. 13–14). —Haddon W. Robinson.

Worship Aids

CALL TO WORSHIP. "Then the seventh angel blew his trumpet, and there were loud voices in heaven, saying, 'The power to rule over the world belongs now to our Lord and his Messiah, and he will rule forever and ever!' " (Rev. 11:15 [TEV]).

INVOCATION. Spare us not from the reality of thy presence, Holy God. Let us lay aside every encumbrance, so that in worship we may find God and be found of the God who brought us in love to this hour. —E. Lee Phillips.

OFFERTORY SENTENCE. "Offer unto God thanksgiving; and pay thy vows unto the most High" (Ps. 50:14).

OFFERTORY PRAYER. None of us, our Father, has failed to promise thee better than we do, or at least to yearn to do better. Now may we begin to pay off our promises in earnest and bring our good intentions to definite expression. Receive our tithes and offerings today as our sacrifices of thanksgiving and as payment of our vows.

PRAYER. Great is thy name, O God, and greatly to be praised. In thee all our discordant notes rise into perfect harmony. It is good for us to think of the wonder of thy being. Thou art most silent, yet most strong; unchangeable, yet ever changing; ever working, yet ever at rest, supporting, nourishing, maturing all things. O thou Eternal Spirit, who hast set our noisy years in the heart of thy eternity, lift us above the power and evils of the passing time, that under the shadow of thy wings we may take courage and be glad. So great art thou, beyond our utmost imagining, that we could not speak to thee didst thou not first draw near to us and say, "Seek ye my face." Unto thee our hearts would make reply, "Thy face, Lord, will we seek." And when we look up to thee, the words of our lips are words of humility and thanksgiving. Who or what are we that thou shouldst follow us with goodness and mercy all the days of life? We thank thee for our birth into a Christian community, for the church and the sacraments of thy grace, for the healing day of rest, when we enter with thy people into thy house and there make holyday; for the refreshment of soul, the joys of communion, the spiritual discipline, the inspiration of prayer and hymn and sermon. We thank thee for thy watchful care over body and soul alike. Thou hast kept our eyes from tears, or, if the tears came, thine own hand wiped them away. Thou hast kept our feet from falling, or if we fell, thou didst not forsake us, but guided us back to the holy paths of Christ. We praise thee for the myriad influences of good, conscious and unconscious, that have been about us, deeply penetrating our inner life, shaping and fitting us for thy Kingdom. Thou hast indeed forgiven all our iniquities, and healed all our diseases, and redeemed our life from destruction, and crowned us with lovingkindness. Therefore, would we call upon our souls, and all that is within us, to bless thy holy name.—Samuel McComb.

EVENING SERVICE

Topic: Foolishness or Power?
TEXT: 1 Cor. 2:1–2.

There was a day when the cross of our Lord and Savior, Jesus Christ, meant something to the church. They could not speak of it without a catch in the throat and a mist in their eyes.

I am persuaded, however, that for too many of us who name the name of Christ in this day, the cross is not "the power of God unto salvation" that once wrought conviction in the hearts of sinners. Instead, it has become mere foolishness to a vast segment of the world's people.

It had meaning once. It still has meaning for those with eyes to see. The message is so plain.

I. The cross is a vivid picture of sin.

(a) Sins come from that sinful disposition the Bible calls sin. God becomes suspect in our minds. That is what the old-time preachers meant when they preached on the cross and sought to convince their hearers that "their sin placed him there!" What they were attempting to say was this: there is that disposition in you which, given long enough to grow and develop in your life, ultimately will do to God what those who crucified him did to Jesus!

(b) This is what James spoke of when he said, "Lust when it conceives brings forth sin, and sin, when it is finished, brings forth death" (James 1:15). When is sin finished? Sin will not be finished until time shall be no more.

"Whose death?" My death, to be sure, but the death of God is also implied. "Sin, when it has finished its work, produces a disposition that could attempt to kill God!"

II. The cross is a picture of salvation.

(a) God created man with the power of contrary choice. God made the human race one, but, in the cross of his only begotten Son, you see him acting in justice upon rebellion and in love that pays the price for all sin. Now God can be "just, and the justifier" of those who believe. This is what the apostle Paul spoke of in 2 Corinthians 5:21.

(b) This opens a way not only for forgiveness, but for a new life to be granted to all who by faith receive it. No man need ever be separated from God because of an inherited disposition. Those who are seeking him may now find him. The barrier has been broken down. The curse has been removed. A way has been opened and whosoever will may freely come.

III. The cross is a picture of service.

(a) The cross says to each of us, "God may do with his sons what he did with his Son." This is the principle of the cross in the life of believers. Luke 9:23 might be freely translated to read, "If any man would come after me, *let him deny his right to himself*, and take up the cross resulting from this and follow me." This is the meaning of service. Some are seeking strange experiences these days. Others claim that none may come into true service unless they come by way of some ecstatic experience. Not so! There are no shortcuts, then or now, into Christian service. All must deny their rights to themselves and march under sealed orders to a destination not known to them.

(b) So many problems of the ministry would be solved by this commitment. Our dependence upon the rearrangements of circumstances would be laid aside if we had truly given up our rights to ourselves. Our "running away" from life's tough experiences and our lack of spiritual development as a result would somehow cease if we could "give up our rights to ourselves."—Carl E. Bates.

SUNDAY: DECEMBER SECOND

MORNING SERVICE

Topic: Getting Ready for Christmas
Text: Gal. 4:4.

Advent, in one of its aspects, is the period of preparation for the Feast of the Nativity, the birth of Jesus the Christ in Bethlehem. Advent is a time of getting ready. Let us ask, and answer, one question: "Who is getting ready for what?"

I. *The world's preparation for Christmas*.

(a) There will be many angry sermons preached this December, and next December, and for the Decembers to come, on how the world prepares for Christmas. This gaudy, merchandising approach, however, has a long and legitimate ancestry. It is the continuation of the ancient festival of the winter solstice, when people rejoiced that the sun had ceased to slide down the southern sky and had made the turn which would bring it back again to the northern hemisphere. Thus it was a time of rejoicing, of good fellowship, because of renewed hope in nature. It was marked by good eating and the giving and receiving of presents. Europe and America have adoped this Saturnalia with enthusiasm.

(b) Now this pagan festival was baptized by the church, around A.D. 325, when Christianity was imperially accepted as the official religion of the Roman Empire. We do not know exactly when Jesus was born, and December seemed as good a time as any, and the winter solstice a better period than most. So the ancient rites were "naturalized" into the Christian faith, with many of the old trappings accepted as valid. Thus the merchants' carnival is not wholly a secular fiesta. The world's advent hustle and bustle is not entirely pagan.

Yet this semisacred season of preparation is falling away from its baptism. Advent is observed by only a minority as the anticipation of the "Christ-mass."

II. *God's preparation for Christmas*.

(a) Let us swing to the opposite pole and ask: "How did God get ready for Christmas?" The moment we ask this question, we realize the difficulty in answering it, as the Bible constantly warns. Second Isaiah has written cautionary words in Isaiah 55:8–9. St. Paul adds his caveat in Romans 11:33–34. We cannot probe this mystery by the techniques of scientific research or historical analysis. We have to turn to men of competence in the realm of the spirit for an answer.

(b) St. Paul, in his Galatian letters, says this about the first Christmas: "But when the fullness of the time was come, God sent forth his Son, made of a woman" (4:4). That phrase "the fullness of the time" has fascinated the interpreters. It has been suggested that God chose this particular period for revealing his nature and purpose because, at the time of the birth of Jesus, Rome had given the world one government, Greece had supplied a common language, and Judaism had offered a worthy monotheistic faith. God did two surprising things at the nativity. First, he chose a most unlikely vehicle of revelation: the child of two very ordinary people in a third-rate part of the Mediterranean world. Second, God gave a surprising message: "Peace on earth to men of goodwill" (Luke 2:14), at a time when there was tension. God prepared for Christmas by deciding to give men hope. He would give them the hope which comes from renewed confidence that he cares for them. One can put this in abstract terms and say that "the eternal broke into time" once again in that manger cradle. Perhaps it is more easily grasped if we say that the first Christmas marks the beginning of God's new attempt to give men hope: a hope that was all wrapped up in a person.

III. *The Christian's preparation for Christmas*.

(a) How does the Christian get ready for Christmas? Remember that we are in the world. Therefore, we share in the culture, in the semi-Christian observance of the solar turn of the year, and we recognize it with joy and enthusiasm. Santa Claus, parades, stockings hung by the fireplace, decorated trees, and the exchange of gifts all have a valid place each December. On the other hand, we are also in the church. Therefore, we seek to understand what

God was trying to do about two thousand years ago, so that we may prepare ourselves properly for a proper Christmas observance.

(b) So we shall prepare ourselves to worship this Christmas. We shall send Christmas cards that really are cards for Christmas. We shall do unusual acts of service. We shall give gifts to those who can make no return except to say "thank you," rather than exchanging presents only with our families and friends. So we Christians enter, through Advent, into Christmas as men and women in the world and in the Church. For the Christian, there is a cultural and a religious observance of this season, with the secular and the sacred intertwined in the same occasion.

At this Advent season, we prepare for both the Yuletide and the Christ-mass, recognizing the place of each in our heritage, yet knowing which is the more important emphasis, if we are truly Christian. —James T. Cleland.

Illustrations

MISSIONARY SPIRIT. When fire had burned a church building, leaving the congregation sadly demoralized, the pastor asked Phillips Brooks what he would do under such circumstances. The reply was immediate. "The first thing I would do," said the great preacher, "would be to take up an offering for foreign missions." Many of us will not forget that when fire had destroyed the Highland Church in Shreveport some years ago, the members responded with incredible generosity in the amount of their Christmas offering for foreign missions. Is it any wonder that there arose from those ashes a church with a renewed spirit of missionary zeal and dedication?—E. Hermond Westmoreland.

GOD'S RIGHT TIME. When the time had fully come, God sent his Son. We cannot see that the time had fully come. But above time, God sits on his throne in his eternity and looks upon the world and its time, just as a doctor sits at the bed of a sick person who lies there in fever and knows nothing of the doctor. But the doctor listens carefully to the patient's breathing and takes his pulse, and then at a particular moment, stands up and calls the nurse and says, "Now is the time—now we shall operate." And then he performs the saving act. We do not know when it is time for God; we are the sick person, not the physician. But God knows the time, our time, which is his time. Time for him to act, to save. When the time had fully come, God sent his Son.—Emil Brunner.

Sermon Suggestions

FORERUNNERS OF RENEWAL. Scripture: Mal. 3:1–7b. (1) Renewal involves cleansing (vv. 2b-3). (2) Renewal involves judgment (v. 5). (3) Renewal involves return to covenant faithfulness (v. 7).—Merrill R. Abbey.

STRENGTHENED WITH MIGHT. Text: Eph. 3:16. (1) God means, and wishes, that all Christians should be strong by the possession of the spirit of might. (2) This divine Power has its seat in, and is intended to influence, the whole of the inner life. (3) It is limitless with the boundlessness of God himself.—Alexander Maclaren.

Worship Aids

CALL TO WORSHIP. "Repent ye: for the Kingdom of heaven is at hand" (Matt. 3: 2).

INVOCATION. O Lord, again with the turning of the year, we begin our pilgrimage toward Christmas. Our hearts as ever rejoice in the glad tidings of Christ, who is born in Bethlehem to be the Savior of all the world. If repentance can purify our hope, if for this season we may become pure-hearted, if now in this place we can welcome thee with all our souls and with all our strength, then grace us with thy most wondrous blessing through Christ who was born in the winter's dark to be the light of the world forever.—Samuel H. Miller.

OFFERTORY SENTENCE. "Greater love hath no man than this, that a man lay down his life for his friends" (John 15:13).

OFFERTORY PRAYER. Eternal and everlasting God, we offer this day our lives and means in grateful response to thy sustaining and forgiving love. Thy unchanging and purifying love is firm and sure, for thou first loved us and sought us from among thy whole creation. We thus most earnestly pray, O Lord, that thou wouldst empower us to use these fruits of our hands toward the task of reconciling all human flesh with thee.—Rodney K. Miller.

PRAYER. O merciful God, who didst come in Jesus Christ with saving power to a world that walked in darkness and in the shadow of death; we praise and bless thee for all those thy servants who helped prepare the way for his appearing, and for those who received him and gave to him the homage of their hearts and lives. For prophets who, in the face of tyranny, declared thy truth and thy righteousness; for psalmists who, in days of gloom, still believed in thy great goodness and sang praises unto thy name; and for innumerable simple folk who waited in patience and unfailing hope for the manifestation of thy glory; we raise to thee our grateful praise. Grant, we beseech thee, that we in this time may show forth thy salvation. Help us to put away all untruthfulness and all selfishness and greed, all malice and prejudice and cowardice. Let thy Holy Spirit cleanse us from all our sins, and teach us to love one another even as thou dost love us, that we may make manifest in our lives what thou canst do for thy faithful people. —Ernest Fremont Tittle.

EVENING SERVICE

Topic: Self-Denial
TEXT: Luke 9:23.

Jesus had a strange way of winning followers. He was not at all like us in that regard. To his would-be followers, Jesus of Nazareth said: "Deny yourself." Jesus did not call us to a way of softness, but to a way that is heroic. It's stunning when you think about it!

I. What is self-denial?

(a) Self-denial does not mean that somebody climbs into a mountain cave and becomes a hermit. Self-denial is not seeking martyrdom as a means of glory.

(b) Neither is self-denial doing without something. We ought to deny ourselves those things that are not good for us because they're not good for us—not as an act of some kind of religious self-sacrifice. Self-denial is not denying yourself something. It is denying yourself.

(c) Neither is self-denial to be equated with burden-bearing. A cross is something one takes voluntarily.

(d) Self-denial is the denial of one's own will. It's the abandoning of *my* will, *my* wishes, *my* desires, *my* security in order to come under voluntary obedience to the will of God. That's hard. Jesus was not tossing out something which we might consider on a sunny Sunday morning. He was talking about the taproot of our faith —our "followship." What is self-denial? Simply put, it's this: self-denial is saying no to self and yes to God.

II. Before you write off this matter of self-denial, let me remind you that you have two selves. We do have a natural self and a spiritual self. And when you talk about self-denial, you're really talking about the denial of one of those selves in order that the other might reach its highest potential.

We have a dual nature. But remember that if you refuse to deny one, then you are automatically denying the other. Either we discipline our lives, or they are spent in dissipation. Either we reach for the stars and dare to do what is right, or we remain earthbound and live a narrow, shallow plain. Either we give our lives to usefulness, to helping and lifting, encouraging and serving; or else they are spun out in a little selfish circle of uselessness.

III. Jesus is our example in this self-denial. He denied himself a great many things. He denied himself the acclaim of the crowds. On more than one occasion, they were ready to carry Jesus in triumphal procession. They were ready to declare him king! But he always turned away when those moments came. He denied himself human kingship in order that he might become the King of Kings. He denied himself glory for our redemption. Self-denial is submission, not to tyranny, but to love. This is what cross-bearing is about— denial of self and affirmation of God. The cross is above all. Christ is above all, given first place always.—Alton E. McEachern.

SUNDAY: DECEMBER NINTH

MORNING SERVICE

Topic: Powerful Living
TEXT: Matt. 11:11.

I drove into the service station and said, "Fill it up." The young man said, "Can't do it," to which I responded, "You don't have any gas?" He grinned. "We got plenty of gas. We just don't have any power."

There have been many times in my life when I have had that same problem. All the resources needed for an assignment were ready. The opportunity to minister or to serve had presented itself. The gas was there, but the power was off. Maybe the circuits were overloaded. Or maybe I had come unplugged. Whatever, the reason, I was trying to operate without contact with my source of power.

It need not be this way for the Christian. God in his infinite love has made it possible for the Christian to plug into his unlimited power.

John the Baptist is the outstanding example of a life lived in the power of God. Although his life ended in its prime, John powerfully accomplished his purpose. Jesus said of him, "Among those born of women, there has not arisen anyone greater than John the Baptist" (Matt. 11:11).

John the apostle introduces John the Baptist (see John 1:6–8). Matthew records his death at the hands of Herod, carrying out the tragic whim of the daughter of Herod's mistress (see Matt. 14:9–12).

John the Baptist lived with power. He died with power. His purpose in life was achieved through power. The cost was no less than everything he had.

What was the secret of John's power? Did he possess supernatural qualities? No, but he did live by three certainties that defined the course of his life.

I. *John was certain that he was sent from God.*

(a) In the prologue to his gospel, John the apostle introduces Jesus as the Light of the World, the Light that shines in darkness and cannot be put out. Anticipating the difficulty his readers will have in un-derstanding this, the writer at once brings John the Baptist into the story. He is a man, and he has come to explain the Light. Because he is a man, men will understand his message.

(b) Apparently, John the Baptist never strayed from his strong belief that God had sent him to be a witness. Among his followers were those who never accepted his witness. They accepted John, but not Jesus. To them, John constantly proclaimed that he was not the Christ, not even a prophet, but a mere voice crying in the wilderness, a voice sent from God.

(c) While he was a lonely herald without credentials, he was in touch with the God who sent him. He was a man obsessed by light when other men were content to live in darkness. He was a man willing to renounce the securities in which others thrived in order to depend entirely upon God to vindicate his message.

He was a man sent from God.

II. *He was certain that he had a singular purpose.*

(a) John was not sidetracked by the issues and events of his day. His only purpose was to point beyond himself in witness to Jesus. His only message was repeated over and over again, "The true Light that enlightens every person is coming into the world."

(b) Existing on locusts and honey, John might have been excused if he had delayed his preaching to have lunch in the best local restaurant. Called before the Jewish leaders to explain himself, his ambition might have been acceptable if he had assumed a major religious role. In light of the prominence of Herod and Herodias, surely no one would have condemned John if he had ignored the flagrant sins of the king. Perhaps he could even have become the court chaplain.

(c) Considering all else as insignificant, John gave himself wholeheartedly to his purpose. This is best seen in his encounter with the official delegation from the Jewish religious leadership in Jerusalem. Christians today who labor under opposition or even persecution can take courage from John's unflinching, powerful confession under pressure. Repeatedly, "he confessed, he did not deny" his faith. Also repeatedly, he negated himself, drawing attention away from himself and to the one person to whom he was a witness.

John's power was not dissipated. He brought it to focus on his singular, abiding purpose.

III. *John was certain of his commitment.*

(a) Toward the end of his ministry, John is confronted by his followers. With wounded pride, they tell John that all the people are going to Jesus. Why? John himself had baptized Jesus. John had begun his work first! How easy it is for our best efforts to become competitive spirits!

(b) Ever true to his purpose of bearing witness to the Christ, John lovingly witnesses to his own disciples (see John 3:28 –30).

(c) All that John had he brought into the service of the Lord. God who called him provided the power that made up the difference between what he had and what he needed. John was committed to receiving and using the power that was available.

Have you experienced that kind of power in your own life? Would you like to? It's possible. It comes from the same strong conviction that God himself has called and commissioned you. It is strengthened by a dedication to his purpose for you that supersedes any other opportunity that might come. It requires no less than wholehearted commitment.—Carolyn Weatherford.

Illustrations

THE WAY OF LIVING AND DYING.   Robert Penn Warren, in his novel *The Cave*, tells of an old man facing death by cancer. Recalling the vitality of his younger days and contrasting it with his approaching death, the old man says, "I reckon that living is just learning how to die and dying is just learning how to live."—Morris J. Niedenthal.

CLOGGED SOULS.   There is a spring near the city which was once a bubbling, gushing spring, over which the early settler built a stone spring-house. For years it had been neglected, until one of our citizens purchased the property and revived it. He dug down into the depths of the earth and rock and found it clogged with debris, which he cleaned away. The water was backed into the surrounding earth, but when its natural channel was opened up, it became a running spring. That is what happens to a mind that is gushing, bright, thought-giving, and producing when the debris of sense gratifications and senseless pleasures take possession. They clog up the normal flow of the mind and then it ceases to grow. That is what happens to the soul.—W. Stuart Cramer.

Sermon Suggestions

BIBLE SUNDAY.   Text: Rom. 15:5. In Christ of whom the Scriptures speak, we find: (1) the antidote to the poison of a foul memory; (2) the antidote to the drug of a fond memory; (3) the tonic of the expectant memory.—J. E. Fison.

INSECURITY.   Text: Ps. 121:1–2. Those who have loved this psalm were looking for something that could not be supplied by the hills or the material things of this world. What they needed could come only from God. How?

(1) Faith gives a man an understanding of what really matters. (2) Faith puts a man in touch with one who can see the future. —Alec Gilmore.

Worship Aids

CALL TO WORSHIP.   "The voice of him that crieth in the wilderness, Prepare ye the way of the Lord, make straight in the desert a highway for our God" (Isa. 40:3).

INVOCATION.   O God, prepare our hearts for the great things you would do within and among us today. Prepare our lives for the great things you would do for others through us. We await your help.

OFFERTORY SENTENCE.   "Every one of us shall give account of himself to God" (Rom. 14:12).

OFFERTORY PRAYER.   Merciful Father, you open springs in the desert and give good things to us when we least expect them. Grant us now one gift more: the grace of cheerful giving, even when personal circumstances make our stewardship difficult.

PRAYER. Lord, as we look back over the days just past, we marvel at your mercies. You have blessed us with your presence. You have heartened us with new opportunities. You have strengthened us with the gift of friends. You have helped us turn aside from many temptations. You have assured us of your forgiveness as we have confessed our sins to you and as we have made amends for wrongs done to others.

Show us how to be grateful and how to live out our gratitude. Help us to bring your presence near someone estranged from you, to open new doors for someone deeply discouraged, to share with someone the warmth of our Christian love, to bolster the moral courage of someone sorely tested, to assure someone that you truly will forgive all manner of sin. May we herald your coming with salvation.

EVENING SERVICE

Topic: Right or Wrong?

TEXT: 1 Cor. 6:12, 19–20; 8:9–12; 10: 23, 31.

(a) No problem in our world today is more difficult than the problem of distinguishing *right* from *wrong*. Most people simply follow the crowd and do just about what everyone else does.

(b) Jesus made one fact very clear: his followers cannot go with the crowd. It is a straight and narrow way which leads unto life . . . and few there be that find it!

(c) Jesus did not set down a list of legalistic requirements, like the Pharisees. Rather, he laid down some eternal principles . . . and called upon all Christians to make their decision about right and wrong in the light of these eternal principles and their love for Christ the Lord. In 1 Corinthians, we find some of these spiritual guidelines and see how Paul applied them to the Christians in his day.

I. The first principle of Christian conduct is plainly stated in 1 Corinthians 6:12:

"All things are lawful unto me, but all things are not expedient.

(a) When Paul says, "All things are lawful unto me, he means that everything which God has made is good—provided we use it in the right way. When God looked out upon his whole creation, he said that it was very good. The evil has come about by man's misuse of his own life and the things which God has made.

(b) When Paul says, "All things are not expedient," he means that all of the things in God's good creation can be used in ways that are wrong and destructive. Nothing is wrong with God's good creation, but something is terribly wrong with the hearts of those who misuse and corrupt this good creation.

(c) But Paul drives home this basic principle with the last words of the verse: "All things are lawful for me, but I will not be brought under the power of any." Anything which enslaves me, anything which gets a dominating control over my mind, my body, or my will—is wrong. My body belongs to God. It is the Temple of his Holy Spirit. Anything which defiles the Temple of the Spirit is a sin against God.

II. A second principle stands out in 1 Corinthians 8:9: "But take heed, lest by any means this liberty of yours become a stumbling block to them that are weak." The principle is clear: Christians must not do anything which causes those who are weaker to stumble over them. Paul is reminding us that we are also responsible for our brother, especially the younger one or the weaker one who is looking to us for an example. If we ignore his conscience and, by our example, cause him to stumble in his Christian journey, we are sinning against God and against him.

III. In chapter 10, verse 23, a third principle is underlined. Paul strips away the mask which covers so many of our moral decisions with these sharp words: "All things are lawful for me, but all things edify not," or "Not everything builds me up." There is a principle to live by.

Life is short, and time is precious. We simply do not have time to waste our minds and energies on things which tear us down. We ought to measure everything we read, everything we see, everything we do by this standard: "Does it build me up in body, mind, and spirit? Does it make my life purer and nobler? Or does it tear down and degrade my life?" Christians do not have the right to read or indulge in anything which does not build them up and make them stronger and better-informed servants of God.

IV. Paul places the capstone on these basic principles for Christian conduct in 1 Corinthians 10:31: "Whether therefore ye eat, or drink, or whatsoever you do, do all to the glory of God." This means that we should make known the very nature and purpose of God through the activities of our lives.—Wayne E. Ward.

SUNDAY: DECEMBER SIXTEENTH

MORNING SERVICE

Topic: Only a Word, But What a Word!
TEXT: Mark 14:36.

(a) The word *Abba* occurs just once in the gospels in Mark's record of Jesus' prayer in Gethsemane: "And He said, Abba, Father." *Abba* it is an Aramaic word, from the Semitic speech very like Hebrew, which was the mother tongue of Jesus. As Professor A. M. Hunter points out, beyond doubt it lies hidden behind all the passages where Jesus says, "Father," "my Father," "the Father."

(b) *Abba* was the word little Jewish children used at home to their human fathers. It was a colloquial, everyday, family word —"Dada." No pious Jew would have dared to speak in this fashion to the high and holy One who inhabits eternity. Yet Jesus did just this. He said "Abba, Father."

(c) It is a remarkable testimony to his sense of unshared Sonship, his unique relationship to God. And there is more to it than that. This word speaks about our own relationship to God. Jesus seems to say that only as we can repeat this childlike "Abba" can we enter God's Kingdom. Only a word, but what a word! Let us explore some of the implications of it.

I. Think of *sin* in the light of this word.

(a) The world may think lightly of sin, but not the children of God.

(b) To say "Abba" to God makes sin darker. For our sinning is not against an impersonal law, but a personal Love. If it is bad to break fixed moral laws, to defy the commands of a holy God, it is infinitely worse to strike a blow at a Loving Heart.

(c) To say "Abba" to God makes forgiveness brighter. If God is our Father, and such a Father, the question at once becomes, "Can God not forgive?" He so loved the world that he gave his only Son to redeem and save us. Only once in the Bible is God pictured as hurrying, running. Daringly Jesus pictured him doing this as the waiting father in his most famous parable: waiting for the prodigal son to return, seeing him on the way home, then running to meet him, forgive him, reinstate him with joy.

II. Think of *prayer* in the light of this word.

(a) Jesus gave us a God near and dear, a God as available as a good father to his children.

(b) Prayer to such a father may be offered in simple, natural language. Not self-conscious, stiff, formal, but spontaneous, direct, honest language. This doesn't mean that we can be irreverent in our approach to God or take liberties with him who is God over all and blessed for ever. It does mean that all barriers of formality and ceremony are swept away. It does mean that pious posing is out.

(c) This word *Abba* clarifies the purpose of our praying. Why does a child approach his father? To say thank you, to ask for things, perhaps to confess. So with us. Thanksgiving, petition, confession are essential parts of true prayer. But at the deepest level, prayer is simply being with the Father, seeking him for himself alone. That is prayer at its best. Relaxing in the Father's presence, resting in his peace, rejoicing in his reality, love, and care.

III. Think of *suffering* in the light of this word. How we think of God is vital to our attitude when the pains and troubles and setbacks of life hurl their challenges against us. Jesus, in his suffering, said: "Father!"

But how can we say "Father" with a sincere heart when we suffer? Doesn't our very suffering deny the fact of a caring God? No! Unless we interpret the word *Father* in sentimental terms. God has a much greater purpose in view than our immediate comfort, ease, happiness, success. His purpose is that we should grow in character, in holiness, in Christ-likeness. It is difficult indeed to see how this could happen without suffering. If there were no risk, or danger in life, where would we find fortitude and courage? If no discipline, where endurance and patience? If no suffering, where compassion?

IV. Think of *death* in the light of this word.

(a) People in general today try not to think of death. It remains the one certainty of this uncertain life.

(b) Now, if we can say from our hearts, "I believe in God the Father Almighty," we can go on to say, "I believe in the life everlasting." The one logically implies the other. If God is such a Father, if he loves us each one as though there were but one to love, if he sent his only Son to die for us and to rise again for our redemption—can he conceivably be content to lose his children at the end? Will all the travail of creation and redemption be lost—through old age, illness, a germ, a bomb? No! The risen Lord has gone before us. He will be there to receive us!—John N. Gladstone.

Illustrations

THE IMAGE OF GOD'S LOVE. If God had kept the whole heaven between us and him, if always he had been only ultimate Truth, like snow on some inaccessible mountain, how would we know him to be "good"? Or if he had come near as an angel, how could we have worshiped? What do angels know about human tears and laughter? If the name is "Jesus," we can account for the love in us, for our love might then be the broken image of his love.—George A. Buttrick.

SEEKING AND SOUGHT. Halevi, the mystic poet of the Middle Ages, exclaimed: "I have sought thy nearness, with my whole heart have I called upon thee, but when I went forth to find thee, I found that thou hadst been seeking me."—Abba Hillel Silver.

Sermon Suggestions

HOW TO REAR A MISSIONARY. Scripture: Acts 16:1–4. (1) Help him to love and stay close to the Book of Books. (2) Surround him with the best Christians you know. (3) Help him love God's work.—Bailey E. Smith

GOD'S GOVERNMENT OF THE WORLD. Text: Dan. 4:17, 25, or 32. (1) God rules the world (Ps. 9:7). (2) God rules the world with truth (Ps. 99:1). (3) God rules the world with grace (Ps. 97:1).—Simon Blocker.

Worship Aids

CALL TO WORSHIP. "I heard a great voice out of heaven saying, Behold, the tabernacle of God is with men, and he will dwell with them, and they shall be his people, and God himself shall be with them, and be their God" (Rev. 21:3).

INVOCATION. You are with us, O God, and we rejoice. You will be with us forever, and we shall rejoice forever. May thy wonderful promises, as well as our present experience, gird us with strength for every duty. Grant that no hindrance, however powerful, shall keep us from knowing thee and doing thy will.

OFFERTORY SENTENCE. "As every man hath received the gift, even so minister the same one to another, as good stewards of the manifold grace of God" (1 Pet. 4:10).

OFFERTORY PRAYER. Lord, you have given differing gifts to us all. There are many ways we can do each other good. Let none of us despise our own modest means of blessing. And help us to see that these fruits of our labors, which now we bring, are one important means by which we can serve you and minister to one another.

PRAYER. O God, who through faithful men didst prepare the way for thy coming in Jesus Christ to save us from our sins and bring us to everlasting life, grant that we also, in this time, may prepare thy way before thee, that thy Kingdom may come with power and in great glory. Suffer us not to be discouraged by the present conditions of the world, or by the afflictions and disappointments of life. And forbid that we should grow weary in well-doing. Make us to know that thy purpose of good is beyond defeat, and grant to us such a measure of thy patience that we may presevere in thy service and, by thy great love, bring healing and hope to others.—Ernest Fremont Tittle.

EVENING SERVICE

Topic: Power to Keep Your Standing Sure

TEXT: Romans 16:25 (NEB).

This verse points to what was most firmly believed by the first Christians.

God, expressing his Spirit in and through Jesus Christ, is the power that makes our standing sure, the power that guarantees our faith and sustains the church. As later generations of Christians experienced this power, the power of God in Jesus Christ, they tried to give intellectual expression to their experience, in order to clarify their thinking about it and to conserve their faith and make it communicable. This is the way in which Christian theology began and was developed, and out of this came doctrines to which labels were given.

Consider with me three of these labels that have expressed central realities of our faith for many centuries.

I. *Incarnation*.

(a) This is a term, coined by later Christian thinkers to designate God's coming into history in a special way in the person of Jesus. It is impossible to explain in propositions a reality that is presented in a person, and that is why all explanations of the incarnation, God's self-enfleshment, are inadequate.

(b) We should see the incarnation as a process of the life of Jesus. There was a maturing and a growing, with the Spirit of God commandingly present in his consciousness.

(c) The word *incarnation* does not so much point to the status of Jesus as to his purpose and function in God's scheme of things. We cannot adequately wrap our intellects around the incarnation, but at Christmas time we can express our awareness of its reality through the hymns we sing.

II. *Atonement*.

(a) This pertains to what has been called "the transaction at the cross." It has to do with the significance for us of the death of Jesus.

(b) Study of the New Testament causes one to think that atonement means reconciliation, not the paying of a penalty. One cannot think that on the cross Jesus was our substitute for punishment, but, rather, our representative, representing both our sin and our capacity for salvation.

(c) The basic Christian belief is that Christ's death on the cross somehow reconciles us to God and gives us fresh starts again and again. Christians may disagree on theories as to how it works, but the Christian consensus is that it does work.

III. *Resurrection*.

(a) Resurrection pertains to the Easter event, God's raising of Jesus Christ from death. The New Testament does not describe the actual event. We know only about its consequences.

(b) Its consequences begin when a small group of bewildered, frightened, despairing people are suddenly quickened into a tumult of enthusiasm as they become aware that Jesus is not dead but alive. That awareness, that resurrection experience, created the church—and all through the centuries, it has re-created the church as its people have encountered the living Jesus Christ in prayer and worship and, particularly, at the Lord's Supper.

(c) The resurrection event is a mystery beyond our comprehension, but awareness of the risen and living Lord Jesus Christ, the resurrection-experience, is the heart of our faith.—J. A. Davidson.

SUNDAY: DECEMBER TWENTY-THIRD

MORNING SERVICE

Topic: The Sermon from the Skies
TEXT: Luke 2:10–11.

Surely no message has ever been more significant than this Christmas proclamation of the heavenly visitor. What is the meaning of this message for our lives?

I. The promise of security—"Fear not."

(a) *This fearful age.* In the beginning, Adam confessed, "I am afraid," and all of his descendants have shared this common anxiety. We are afraid of war, of poverty, of the unknown future. Our fears multiply as we pin our hopes on various plans, only to see them disappointed. We are no longer secure in our own personal achievements.

(b) *The conquest of fear.* The angelic message proclaims the intervention of God to banish the fears of earth. In the coming of Christ, mankind was suddenly overwhelmed with the realization that we matter to God. Christmas promised the security that comes with the realization that God is determined to intervene in our behalf, even when he is not welcome! "Fear not!" Man's last word is God's first word. When we have nowhere to turn, God will break afresh from the heavens to visit and redeem his people.

II. The promise of satisfaction—"I bring you tidings of great joy."

(a) *The search for satisfaction.* We are determined to be a happy world. A flood of books promises happiness in life, even in the name of religion. And it is nearly killing us. Much of our laughter is hollow, for the world seems to pay off in counterfeit pleasures.

(b) *The Christian certainty of satisfaction.* Jesus came and preached "Good News." Everywhere he went, he left happiness behind. He described the Christian life as a wedding party, as the joy of unearthing a pearl of great price, as a wayward son restored to the delights of home. Thus he gave to every generation of his followers a new kind of gladness.

III. The promise of salvation—"For unto you is born this day a Savior."

(a) *Man's need of a savior.* Why is it, ultimately, that mankind feels insecure and unsatisfied in life? Some suggest heredity and inheritance; others propose some aspect of the environment. Jesus knew that it was sin. Dimly we begin to see his wisdom. Religion must deal with this hunger for redemption. This is the supreme promise of Christmas, that a personal Savior from sin is provided.

(b) Notice the full sweep of the salvation described by the Christmas sermons: he is a "Savior" who is "Christ" the "Lord." This means that he is a deliverer who will lead us out of bondage in obedience to his sovereign lordship. The miracle of Christmas is that God came to participate in our deepest dilemma. In the incarnation, Christ grappled decisively with sin at the level where we live, and forever offers men the strength of his conquest over it.—William E. Hull.

Illustrations

KNOWING GOD IN CHRISTMAS.   But how, then, are we to be sure that it *is* God in the Christmas story? Through surrender. He comes to us on his own terms, at his own time, and in his own way. Surrender is the only possible way we can know God. But actually this is the only way we can know anything or anyone. If I want to know a foreign language, I have to surrender myself to it until its structures and vocabulary and nuances of accent become a part of me. Indeed, if you would know your children, you have to surrender yourself to their world, their way of looking at things. Otherwise, even your children remain strangers.

This is what it is like to "let Christ be born in us today." This is why we cannot be spectators at Christmas, listening to the music, appreciating the symbolism of the pageantry, attending the Christmas services, and expect to find God there.—Edmund Steimle.

DIVINE PARTICIPATION.   It is the greatness and heart of the Christian message that God, as manifest in the Christ on the cross, totally participates in the dying of a child, in the condemnation of the criminal, in the disintegration of a mind, in starvation and famine, and even in the human rejection of Him. There is no human condition into which the divine presence does not penetrate.—Paul Tillich.

Sermon Suggestions

THE PURPOSE OF BETHLEHEM.   Text: Gal. 4:4–5. (1) The mystery of the love of the Father. (2) The miracle of the lowliness of the Son. (3) The marvel of the liberty of the Spirit of God.—Alan Redpath.

CHRIST HIMSELF IS CHRISTIANITY.   Text: Heb. 2:8–9 (Moffatt trans.). (1) The coming of Jesus was a prophetic fact. (2) The coming of Jesus was a momentously influential fact. (3) The coming of Jesus is a profoundly moving fact in personal experience. (4) The coming of Jesus is a very reassuring fact.—Harry Emerson Fosdick.

Worship Aids

CALL TO WORSHIP.   "The angel said unto them, Fear not: for, behold, I bring you good tidings of great joy, which shall be to all people. For unto you is born this day in the city of David a Savior, which is Christ the Lord" (Luke 2:10, 11).

INVOCATION.   Amid the world's darkness, O God, we seek a star which will give us hope and guide us on our way. Our days are troubled with the portents of despair, and the counsels of men have increased our anguish. Turn us from ourselves, lift our vision beyond our earthly empires, and let the dayspring from on high visit us. If the pilgrimage be long, sustain us by thy strength until we are made strong in the innocence of Bethlehem's Child.—Samuel H. Miller.

OFFERTORY SENTENCE.   "When they were come into the house, they saw the young child with Mary his mother, and fell down, and worshiped him: and when they had opened their treasures, they presented unto him gifts; gold, and frankincense, and myrrh" (Matt. 2:11).

OFFERTORY PRAYER.   Lord, Most Holy, accept our Christmas offering, as we who are recipients of the Bethlehem birth and a Calvary hope, come to thee through our faithful advocate, King Jesus.—E. Lee Phillips.

PRAYER.   Blessed Lord, who hast caused the dayspring from on high to visit us, to give light to them that are in darkness and in the shadow of death and to guide our feet into the way of peace, we pray that the Spirit of goodwill may so fill the hearts of all of us who call ourselves Christians that our love may reflect the Light of the World, drawing all men unto him. Especially do we pray for the homeless, and friendless, the forgotten by all men, those who spend this day in prison, those whose rejoicing is unhallowed by any true consecration to thee so that they know nothing of the great joy of possessing the Savior, those for whom the day recalls memories of happier times now gone by, those who are lonely for loved voices hushed in death, those who have lost an earlier faith, and all who wish they could believe the message of this day, but find themselves unable. Grant that we who have learned the truth of the good tidings and have found in Jesus our Savior deliverance from selfishness, distrust, and fear, may carry the gladness of this season throughout the year, rejoicing evermore because of thine unspeakable gift in him. —Henry Sloane Coffin.

EVENING SERVICE

Topic: God's Second Mile

SCRIPTURE: Matt. 5:39, 41; Phil. 2:1–11.

Let us look at what the coming of the Christ child should do for him, for her, who sees in Jesus the dramatic, even the unique, revelation of God.

I. The first passage, from the Sermon on the Mount, is one which makes us shake our heads in a puzzled, an angry, bewilderment (Matt. 4:39, 41).

(a) Going the first mile may refer to the Roman soldier's custom of obliging the people of a conquered nation to carry his impediments. Simon of Cyrene was compelled by the Roman soldiers to carry the cross of Jesus to the place called Golgotha (Matt. 27:32). So going the first mile symbolizes forced labor, enforced by law, custom, or might. But Jesus says that, when one has done the necessary stint, he should suggest that he will do another four laps. The first mile is required; the second mile is voluntary.

(b) Jesus illustrated this dictum in his parables. One thinks of the behavior of the Good Samaritan. Or, call to your remembrance the father of the Prodigal Son. Similarly, when Peter asked Jesus if he should forgive his brother seven times —a good mile—Jesus suggested seventy times seven, which must be one of the longest second miles on record (Matt. 18:21–22).

(c) Jesus exemplified this principle in his behavior. He chose a publicanus, a despised quisling of a tax-gatherer, as one of the innermost group of his disciples. He ignored justice for mercy in the case of the woman taken in adultery and in the incident of the woman with the alabaster box of Ointment. His outreach went beyond the Jews to a Samaritan woman at the well of Jacob, to a Roman army officer in a foreign army of occupation, to a Syro-Phoenician mother whose daughter was ill. And on the cross, instead of cursing or ignoring his executioners, he prayed: "Father, forgive them, for they don't know what they are doing." We may not have a high estimate of this second-mile ethic, but we have to recognize that the man who enunciated it lived and died expounding and exemplifying it.

(d) Now you have a valid question to put to me for me to put to Jesus: "Sir, why did you teach this, both in word and action?" Because that is how God behaves. And God is our norm, our standard, our example (see Matt. 5:45).

II. But why did enough people listen to Jesus, so that his words were recorded, and the church was formed, and his point of view is still a matter of hopeful and despairing concern to so many people? It wasn't merely because he was a great teacher, though he was.

(a) What made people accept and study and interpret and try to live his teaching was the fact of the resurrection, the Easter news that he was not holden of death. We would not celebrate the birth of the Christ child, if it had not been confidently believed that the man Jesus had been raised from the dead by the power of God. What the resurrection did was to place God's seal on the teaching of Jesus of Nazareth. More than that, it placed God's unique approval on Jesus himself. It showed Jesus and God cojoined in an unprecedented, an unparalleled relationship. And the New Testament makes use of all kinds of words and phrases to explain and interpret the affinity of God and Jesus: "Prophet," "Messiah," "Logos." We do not have to accept any of these terms to be Christians. What we need to accept in order to be Christians is a realization of the ultimate relation of Jesus and God which these terms try to express. Then, maybe, we can understand, appreciate, and accept what Jesus himself was trying to say when he said: "He that hath seen me hath seen the Father" (John 14:9). Christmas is God's second mile, though it took Easter to validate the fact.

(b) Isn't that what Paul is trying to say in the rhapsody which was the second part of our lesson (Phil. 2:1–11)? Don't read this as a piece of systematic theology, or you'll just bewilder yourself logically. Paul is speaking to the heart, not to the mind. This is poetry, not prose. It should be sung, not exegeted. Can you feel behind the words to the Good News of a God who so cares for us that, at Bethlehem, he tried, yet again, to let man know what He is really like—love, goodwill, mercy, a Father. And the glad response is *Gloria in excelsis, Deo!*—in gratitude that he, in Jesus, went the second mile, to our advantage. We have been talking about the Pauline rhapsody on Jesus in the Philippian letter. It is found in chapter 2, verses 5–11. Do you know what verses 1–4 are about? To paraphrase them, somewhat loosely, Paul says to his readers: "For goodness sake, behave yourselves." In verse 5, he ejaculates: "Have this mind among yourselves, which you have in Christ Jesus." They have both norm and example in Jesus, who was sent by God.

(c) There is a *noblesse oblige* about the life of a Christian: nobility obligates. Since we are God's people in Christ, we are obliged to an honorable and bountiful behavior, a royal generosity, a Godlike charity. It is an ethic of thoughtful extravagance, of motivated recklessness, of humorous excess. It kills its enemies by loving them, or it dies in the attempt. It renders to Caesar what is Caesar's. But that is just the first mile. It also renders to the God of the second mile what is rightly God's. And it happens most often at Christmas, which fact should tell us something.—James T. Cleland.

SUNDAY: DECEMBER THIRTIETH

MORNING SERVICE

Topic: Shepherds and Wise Men
Scripture: Matt. 2:1–11.

The story of our Savior's birth, as we have it in the New Testament, contains many striking contrasts and brings together some very obvious extremes. And there is no wonder that there are contrasts in this story. The writers who penned it were attempting to express, in common and understandable images, the meaning which their faith had come to see in the events taking place before their eyes. It was the story of the coming together of heaven and earth, of God and man. The symbolism of the contrasts included in the Christmas story expresses, indeed, a very central Christian truth.

I am thinking of the shepherds and the wise men. They were as different as one can imagine in almost every way. Yet, they had one thing in common: They came, both shepherds and wise men, to see the same little God-child and to worship him. And in coming and seeing and worshiping him, they were made one—in spite of all their contrasts and differences.

I. It seems obvious that the writers from whose pens these stories come wanted to proclaim that in this Christ-event heaven and earth had been joined together. But they also wanted to intimate that here, in response to this revelation of God, mankind, too, had been brought together and made one.

(a) In our time, the contrasts between men are threatening to overcome our unities. We find that culturally and socially, educationally and economically, politically and religously, there are walls built up between us. How can we ever come together and be one?

(b) In this God-child, God has proclaimed all men to be one, one in him, in spite of the many finite distinctions which separate us from each other.

II. But the story of the shepherds and the wise men tells us more. It speaks also of differences that are not reconciled. Let me try to bring this out by holding together the descriptions we have of the shepherds and the wise men.

(a) First, they each received their own specific call. The wise men saw a new star in the sky. The shepherds had a vision of angels.

The Christmas story tells of God calling each of these people in ways which are strikingly appropriate. They received their call, shepherds and wise men, each in a form which they had abilities to understand. There is a principle which seems to be emerging from this story: God does not communicate with us in one way only. God speaks in many ways, and whoever responds in faith and finds his way to Christ is called of God.

(b) There is a second contrast between the shepherds and the wise men. Each had their own specific motivation for coming. The wise men came to find the new king who had come to reign in Israel. The shepherds came to see the Savior whose birth had been announced to them. Again, a principle seems to emerge: God does not recognize only one motivation for coming to him. We are all acceptable to him, whoever we are, whatever our motivation for coming, when we come to his Christ.

(c) A third contrast is that the shepherds and the wise men had different ways to go.

The shepherds came from the fields near town. The wise men had a longer road to travel. Many ways, all ways may lead us to the Christ; and each one of us, whoever we are, shall have to find our own way.

(d) There is a final contrast which follows closely upon this: the shepherds and the wise men worshiped Christ in different ways. The shepherds came and saw him. The wise men fell down and worshiped him. And again, there emerges a principle from the story: all forms of worship are acceptable to God, as long as we worship in spirit and in truth. The Christmas story affirms that all worship is valid, when it is the expression of a heart's adoration for the Christ.—Thor Hall.

Illustrations

IMPERFECTION.   When you put a painting in candlelight to examine it, the imperfections do not appear; when you put it under the full glare of the sun, then you see how badly chosen are the colors and ill-defined the lines. So it is when we measure ourselves by God, we fall infinitely short; and when we compare ourselves with many who have given us inspiration, we feel a deep sense of unworthiness. But behind it all, and despite all of this, there is the tremendous consciousness of the mercy of God.—Fulton J. Sheen.

CHANGING THE PAST.   A pathetic struggle over their past is going on almost without interruption in many men and women in our time. No medical healing can solve *this* conflict, because no medical healing can change the past. Only a blessing that lies above the conflict of blessing and curse can heal. It is the blessing that changes what seems to be unchangeable— the past. It cannot change the facts; what has happened has happened and remains so in all eternity! But the *meaning* of the facts can be changed by the external, and the name of this change is the experience of "forgiveness."—Paul Tillich.

Sermon Suggestions

THREE LOOKS AT JESUS.   (1) A backward look (Isa. 45:22; John 3:15). (2) An up-ward look (Heb. 12:2). (3) A forward look (Tit. 2:13).—J. Clyde Turner.

LIFE'S MOST INDISPENSABLE POSSESSION. Text: Ps. 51:11. Let the light of the gospel fall upon this text and this experience. (1) Consider what it means to possess and to lose the Spirit. (2) Consider that thus to lose the Spirit is, of all deprivations, the most far-reaching and calamitous. (3) Consider the question: but is this risk real? (4) This is the most important to consider of all: the very fact that the psalmist could make this cry proved that the Spirit was still there.—James S. Stewart.

Worship Aids

CALL TO WORSHIP.   "The Spirit and the bride say, Come. And let him that heareth say, Come. And let him that is athirst come. And whosoever will, let him take the water of life freely" (Rev. 22:17).

INVOCATION.   O God, breathe upon us with thy Spirit and inspire us to worship thee with all our heart, so that we may be energized to serve thee with all our strength.

OFFERTORY SENTENCE.   "Verily, verily, I say unto you, He that believeth on me, the works that I do shall he do also; and greater works than these shall he do; because I go unto my Father. And whatsoever ye shall ask in my name, that will I do, that the Father may be glorified in the Son" (John 14:12, 13).

OFFERTORY PRAYER.   Our Father, how can we ever number the multitude of thy mercies? How can we begin to thank thee for all thy blessings? Yet we would try through these material gifts to say, We know that thou hast been good to us, and we are grateful.

PRAYER.   Turn us again to thee, O God, that as this year ends and time stands forth in the changes of our mortal life, in all its hopes and fears, we may be strengthened by thine eternal spirit to be steadfast, sustained in the midst of our troubled, tortured world and supported against every threat of despair and shame. Where we have failed, lift us by a new strength, consecrated in humility, to try again; where we have gone forward, steady our uncertain steps and guide us onward to higher ground. Everywhere be thou our companion and comfort, that we may not grow weary in well-doing, or vain in our self-satisfaction. Move us mightily by the grace that was in Christ Jesus our Lord, to make the small events of time the ample signs of thy Kingdom, blessing the sons of men with peace and joy.—Samuel H. Miller.

EVENING SERVICE

Topic: How to Be a Responsible Parent
TEXT: Eph. 6:4.

(a) What does it mean to be a parent? Certainly there is more to parenting than a biological function or a procreative event. The advent of test-tube fertilization testifies that parenting goes far beyond the physical aspects of childbirth. What does it mean to be a parent? It means just this—parenting is the acceptance of responsibility for a human life.

(b) Let us not look over this responsibility lightly, for it is a sacred trust. Surely it is not by accident that the biblical authors identify our relations to God and each other with family designations. In the family, we learn whether we are loved or unloved, accepted and important or isolated and insignificant. In the family, we learn whether we really matter or whether we simply exist. The family has more to do with the kind of person we will be than any other single factor. And within the family, the single most significant role in developing wholesome lives is that of the parent.

(c) Yet we need not feel overwhelmed by the task of parenthood or frightened to the point of exasperation. Parenting is an awesome responsibility, but we are not without help from the Scripture. Do we not want to be the best parents that we possibly may be? But how?—that is the question. The same question was being asked by Christian parents twenty centuries ago, and has surely been asked in every generation since then. Paul sheds light upon the question when he says, "Fathers, do not provoke your children to anger, but bring them up in the discipline and instruction of the Lord." How may we be responsible parents?

I. Responsibility begins as we realize the worth of our children.

(a) Such worth is rooted in the understanding that every person is of limitless value, worthy of dignity and respect, that all human life is sacred. As with any precious gift God has entrusted to our care, we are bound to be more conscientious when we realize its limitless value. And so it is with our children.

(b) Too often we see our little ones only as miniature adults, and we are disappointed or even angry when they act like the children they are. Or we may regard the worth of children only as a potential to be developed. But the greatest worth of children is simply that they are children. The joy and brightness of life is no where evidenced more beautifully than in the bright smiles and happy faces of giggling children.

(c) It would do all of us good if we would emulate the characteristics of children. There is little wonder that Jesus called the little children unto him, for of such is the Kingdom of God. There is within the willingness to trust, the desire to please, the excitement of accomplishment, and the questioning yet loving spirit of the child something that resonates with the spirit of Christ.

(d) If we take Paul's advice, we are to take our children seriously. "Provoke not your children to anger, but bring them up in the discipline and the instruction of the Lord." This means that your child has such inherent value that only the best is good enough for him or her. And that which is best is a home where love reigns supreme, where the name of God is spoken often, where Jesus Christ has a central part in all that goes on there.

II. In seeking to be responsible parents, we need also to appreciate the power of our influence. Many people will affect the lives of our children, some in a positive way, others negatively. But no other people will so touch their lives as will mother and father.

(a) One man has said that Christianity either stands or falls with the propagation of the gospel from one generation to the next. As such, Christianity is always only one generation from extinction. That is, if one generation fails to convey adequately the gospel message to the succeeding generation, the message will be lost. When we see that most Christians have come from homes where God was honored through Christ-serving parents, we begin to see how much influence we have on our children.

(b) The church plays its part in "bringing them up in the discipline and instruction of the Lord," but its influence is only partial. Teachers, friends, heroes—they will all have their due impact, but the most consistent and influential impact will be from you, the parents, those who have accepted the responsibility of parenting.

III. Responsible parenthood recognizes the limits of parental authority.

(a) Such authority is bound on the one hand by God. God has never sanctioned any authority simply for the sake of authority. The child is commanded: "Obey your father and mother." But notice that there is a qualifier: "Obey your father and mother in the Lord." And that is quite a difference. It is this singularity of purpose that ultimately limits the parent's authority. The final authority in all matters is the Father.

(b) On the other hand, there is another limiting factor to the parent's authority—time. The sooner we recognize this, the better it will be. We will not always be able to exercise authority in our children's lives. They do grow up—and become responsible for themselves. And what a painful thing it is!

(c) Along with limited parental authority and increased freedom as the child grows and matures, the burden of responsibility begins to shift. As long as the child was totally dependent on you, you were totally responsible for him. But when he began to grow and mature and each year became a little more independent, you had to give up a little more of your responsibility. And because time refuses to hold still, at some time we are forced to allow our children their total freedom. And how it may hurt!

(d) We must not look upon our children's growing up, and maybe away, as losing them. If we have done our best in parenting that we can do, then we have to allow our children the freedom to pursue life on their own terms. It takes a lot of faith and trust, in God and in the child. That, I am convinced, is the best way. Mistakes will be made. Pain may follow. But it is God's way—the way of allowing human freedom. It must be our way, too.—Lee McGlone.

SECTION XII. Ideas and Suggestions for Pulpit and Parish

PREACHING THROUGH DIALOGUE. Pastor Thomas Conley of Atlanta has found an effective and interesting way of presenting theological truth. He works his message into a narrative that comprises the sermon. In the dialogue of the fictional pastor with one or more other characters, all essential aspects of the issue are covered.

ETHNIC DINNER. As a prelude to hearing a message by a long-time missionary in the South Pacific, the First United Methodist Church of Kalamazoo, Michigan, served a Polynesian dinner for the congregation.

STUDENT ADOPTION. What is called the Student Adoption Ministry is a means by which the First Baptist Church, Clemson, South Carolina, has helped students during their college years. Singles, couples, and families are asked to serve as "parents" for two or more university students during the school year.

ROOM AT THE INN. As the Christmas season approached, members of Trinity Episcopal Church in San Francisco became concerned about homeless people who were spending nights on streets or in parks of the city. With help from a city agency that provided cots, the church opened its fellowship hall each night to seventy-five homeless persons. Church members donated blankets and provided a simple breakfast in the morning for several months, until the homeless could find more permanent quarters.

HELP FOR SERMONS. Three or four times a year, Gene Bartlett, pastor of First Baptist Church, Newton Center, Massachusetts, asked four people to help him for one month in the preparation of his sermons. They met on Sunday afternoon for an hour and a half and discussed the text for the next Sunday, responding to the pastor's questions and raising their own, as well as sharing experiences related to the theme. Later in the week, the pastor took final responsibility and wrote the sermon himself.

DISCIPLE-MAKING. Win Arn and Charles Arn have described an effective method of evangelism through a church's "potential congregation." While not neglecting its own church families in ministry and nurture, the church reaches out to the church members' extended families—that is, to relatives and friends. This is done by planning the church's programs with both groups always in mind. Members of the potential congregation should be identified by name, information gathered on each, needs identified, and programs developed. If one program does not appeal to an individual, another will. These relatives and friends are the church's best prospects.—*Church Growth: America*.

MAKING LOVE TANGIBLE. Pastor James Sorrell and his congregation in Johnson City, Tennessee, followed a fourteen-week program called "One Hundred Days of Christian Love," in which suggestions were offered for practical ways to show Christian love. Each week, a different area of emphasis extended opportunities to show this love—to enemies, real or imagined, to neighbors, to those who serve you, to fellow-believers, to a stranger, etc.

WORSHIP ON THE BEACH.   Pastor Charles M. Moody of Deltaville, Virginia, extended the ministry of his church by conducting services of worship at 8:30 each Sunday morning during the summer months at a beach near Deltaville. The half-hour services were attended mostly by vacationers who liked the natural setting, the simplicity of the service, the lack of formality, the casualness of dress, and the early hour of the service. Some one-fifth of persons attending indicated that they were inactive church members. In nine summers and 135 Sundays, the services were rained out only three times.—*The Theological Educator*.

LIFE-LONG LEARNING.   Pastor Ernest White and the Wyatt Park Baptist Church, St. Joseph, Missouri, inaugurated continuing education programs for senior adults. For eight weeks each fall and spring, classes in a wide variety of subjects have been taught by qualified teachers. From twelve to twenty classes meeting simultaneously have explored such subjects as the Bible, English literature, travel, bridge, finance, and exercise.

CHRISTIAN SYMBOLS.   A layman in the Northside Drive Baptist Church of Atlanta personally covered with needlepoint the kneeling pads at the communion rail and the bottom of the offering plates as well. The needlepoint presents the symbols of the Christian faith.

A LITTLE SEMINARY.   One church definitely fulfilled Elton Trueblood's recommendation that every church become "a little seminary." The church training program was moved from Sunday night to Wednesday night and revamped. A complete curriculum with a semester by semester set of courses was instituted, with three courses being offered each semester. The composition of the classes is determined not by age, but by interest. Eventually the participant can get a broad theological education.

FAMILY EVANGELISTIC PLAN.   A friendship dinner, to which the entire family of every prospect for church membership is invited, has become an effective means of evangelism for the Wyatt Park Baptist Church, St. Joseph, Missouri. A host family invites the prospect and his family for a dinner at a neutral place, not at the church! The people invited are assured that there will be no preaching and no obligation. Two or three laymen give simple testimonies on "What the Church Means to Me." There is follow-up to guide and encourage those who wish to unite with the church.

NEW FORMS OF WORSHIP.   David James Randolph, minister of Christ Church (Methodist), in New York City, believes that "the process of change in worship may be more important than the product of change." He suggests these eight steps to more meaningful worship: (1) worship, (2) study in a small group, (3) gather data, (4) review and create resources, (5) design the service, (6) worship, evaluate, (7) evaluate, (8) worship.—*God's Party*.

RETHINKING THE ORDER OF WORSHIP. Horton Davies proposed the option using the several movements of the traditional pastoral prayer as the framework of the order of worship. A psalm or anthem could express adoration; a congregational hymn, confession; a psalm or anthem, thanksgiving; a prayer, supplication and intercession; the sermon, dedication. The service so conceived of makes a long pastoral prayer unnecessary.

REASONS FOR JOINING.   Twelve reasons for joining the church should suggest what pastors and laity can do to help prospective members. Edward A. Rauff asked 180 people to respond to the question, "Why did you join the church?" The answers given, from the most frequent to the least, are: (1) family relationships and responsibilities, (2) the influence of Christian people, (3) a church visit, program, special event, sacred act, (4) a search for community, (5) personal crisis, (6) the end of rebellion, (7) the influence of pastors, (8) God's intervention, (9) the journey toward truth, (10) a feeling of emptiness, (11) the response to evangelism, and (12) the reaction to guilt and fear.—*Church Growth: America*.

GOD'S GIFT OF ENERGY. At a youth center on the Isle of Iona, in Scotland, a church group built a large solar water heater, which provided 70 percent of the water for the center's kitchens. The purpose was to make a prophetic point on the Christian stewardship of resources.

INCARNATIONAL SERVICE. A Christmas Eve service of worship, featuring the significant events in the life of Christ, has been an impressive experience in the life of the Wyatt Park Baptist Church, St. Joseph, Missouri. Old Testament prophecy prefaces these events, which are portrayed in hymn, anthems, Scripture reading, other reading of prose or poetry, the Lord's Supper, and, climactically, baptism, in which the note of resurrection with Christ is sounded.

GATHERING PLACE. As part of their outreach to young adults, the members of First Covenant Church in Oakland, California, have transformed one of their Adult Center classrooms into a coffee house, complete with round tables, candles, and an appealing menu. Called the Mars Hill Coffee House, the place provides an informal and relaxed atmosphere where young people from the congregation and the community can gather. As an added attraction, speakers from the church and the community are invited on a regular basis to speak on issues of contemporary concern.

PARK-A-TOT. A church in Henderson, Kentucky, has a "Park-A-Tot" program two days a week for thirty-three weeks a year when public schools are in session. The purpose: to give mothers an opportunity for "a day out."

PRAYER LETTERS. As an associate pastor for many years, A. Donald Anthony wrote prayer letters to members of the churches he served. Taking the names of a few of the members at a time, he would write a personal letter to each individual, telling them that for a certain period of time, at a particular hour, he would remember them in prayer. He asked them to join him, if possible, at the same time in prayer. He found that this deepened their fellowship and comradeship in the work of the church.

LOVE IN ACTION. St. Columba's Episcopal Church in rural Inverness, California, was an oasis of shelter and protection for numerous families made homeless one January by winter floods and mudslides. Now central to the natural disaster plan for the surrounding communities, the church has installed a generator on the property and has built a storage structure for food and first-aid supplies. In the event of a major storm or flood, the church is prepared to be a virtual Noah's Ark for the people in the area.

MEET YOUR DEACON MONTH. During one month early in the year, each church family will receive a visit from the deacon who has been assigned the oversight of the particular family. The church bulletin announces that deacons will be visiting each family. Assistance by other deacons is given where needed to ensure that every home has been reached.

CONGREGATIONAL COOPERATION. A United Methodist and a Presbyterian congregation in Norfolk, Virginia, found fellowship-enriching experiences and cut costs by pooling resources and working together on specific church activities. Evangelistic services, vacation church school, youth groups, and entertainment programs are some of the areas administered by a joint committee of the two churches.—*Your Church*.

BROADCASTING GOOD NEWS. Shirley Pollock visited a church where the sermon concluded in the church parking lot. The Junior Church children were waiting outside. As the listeners left the church, they were each handed a colorful, gas-filled balloon with a Bible verse and the name of the church tucked inside. The minister gave the cue as the last parishioner left the sanctuary, and five hundred balloons ascended, carrying God's Word and the church's concern to others.—*Leadership/82*.

ENERGY CONSERVATION.   Fifty percent of the energy loss through the single thickness of a stained glass window can be saved, according to Donald Samick of Spring Valley, New York. Using a protective covering will reduce energy loss and noise from the outside, resist vandalism and accidental damage, and protect leading and glass from environmental corrosion.—*Your Church*.

AN HOUR IN PRAYER.   Dick Eastman of World Literature Crusade has suggested a way of praying for an entire hour by structuring the hour with twelve scripturally based aspects. Each hour is divided into twelve five-minute points of focus, using appropriate Scripture verses for inspiration and direction. The focal words are: praise, waiting, confession, the Word, intercession, petition, the Word (praying it), thanksgiving, singing, meditation, listening, and praise (ending as you began).

WEDNESDAY WORSHIP.   The First Baptist Church, Henderson, Kentucky, inaugurated a mid-week service of worship, designed on the order of Sunday morning worship, the purpose being to accommodate members on vacation or away on weekends during the summer months.

CHURCH WORK SCHOLARSHIPS.   Each summer a church gives two college scholarships to young people in their membership, basing the awards on their leading a summer recreation ministry in a lower income neighborhood.

FISH AND BREAD.   On the Sunday after Easter, members of Christ Church Cathedral in Louisville had a commemorative biblical breakfast at the Riverfront Plaza/Belvedere. This Episcopal congregation gathers each year for "Breakfast by the Shore," commemorating Jesus' appearance to his disciples by the Sea of Tiberias following the resurrection. Prayer, singing, Scripture reading, and Christian fellowship, as well as the breakfast of fish, bread, juice, and fruit, mark the occasion.

The Rev. Spencer Simrill said, "It is a chance for young and old and different people to get together outside of a church setting."—*The Louisville Times*.

THANKSGIVING DINNER.   A church mission near Times Square provides Thanksgiving dinner each year for poor New Yorkers. Lambs's Manhattan Church of the Nazarene enlists the service of many denominations in its work. Volunteers for waiting tables include actors and actresses accustomed to such work between acting jobs. The Rev. B. J. Weber, associate pastor, told one group of mission guests, "Instead of taking from one another, we need to serve one another in love. That's the message of God."—*The New York Times*.

HOSPITAL VISITATION.   Pastor Ernest White organized a visitation program in his church to ensure that every hospitalized church member would be visited each day. The senior minister would do the visitation one day per week and be available for all emergencies and special requests.

CRAFTS FOR YOUTH.   Pastor Richard Tweeney of the Church of Christ (Disciples) at Carrollton, Ohio, developed a youth group of more than twenty enthusiastic fifth and sixth graders in less than three months. It grew from a craft project in Vacation Bible School and was called "The King's Kids." Though games, refreshments, and a story with a Christian application were important parts, the main attraction was crafts and the gaining of useful skills and knowledge. Prizes help to motivate the kids in their crafts and in their attendance at worship, Sunday school, and youth meetings.—*Your Church*.

THE CHILDREN'S CORNER.   Pastor Barry Bence of the Lutheran Church of the Cross in Manitoba and his congregation have found that "children's corners" are a vital part of their ministry of the Word. During each Sunday service, the children spontaneously act out a parable or Old Testament story as it is read by the pastor, or they act out a little biblical drama they have planned in advance. Pastor Bence says, "Children's corners not only reach the children, but allow the children to help serve the Word to our whole community." —*The Christian Ministry*.

YEAR-END GIVING.   In addition to emphasis on weekly giving, the Trinity Baptist Church of San Antonio emphasizes year-end giving. Eleven-month stewardship reports are given to each member, newsletter articles remind members of their pledges, and during the last week in the year, the newsletter publishes the year-end hours of the business office. Also, the announcement time in the service of worship is used in this promotion. J. W. Fortner, business administrator of the church, says, "It can become a part of the stewardship program of a church and it should be handled as a joint approach of the pastor and the lay leadership."— *Church Administrator*.

OPERATION BACKYARD.   On four Saturdays in April, church members bring rakes, shovels, pickups, and baskets, and go through the streets and alleys gathering trash in an area of from forty to fifty square blocks. They offer to help people with special problems to put their yards in shape. A pastor said that this had had the positive effect of more solidly identifying the church with the neighborhood.

CHRISTIAN CLOWNING.   The First Baptist Church, Alexandria, Virginia, sponsored a course in the art of clowning as a means of ministry, witness, teaching, and outreach.

INFANT DEDICATION.   One church has added a wider dimension to the public dedication of infants. Besides involving the church family and the parents in the commitment to bring up the child in the nurture and admonition of the Lord, there is an attempt to include as much of the extended family of the child as possible (such as grandparents).

OF SPARROWS AND PEOPLE.   A group of Quaker youth, the Junior High Young Friends of the Long Lake Meeting, Traverse City, Michigan, raised an acre of sunflowers to help feed the hungry. They had as a theme: "Help feed the starving people of the world while you feed your birds." They exchanged sunflower seeds for donations and sent the money received to CARE, Inc., which had promised to multiply their contributions eight times.— *Quaker Life*.

PASTOR TO THE JOBLESS.   In order to give moral support, suggestions, and information to "professional, managerial, white-collar types" who had lost their jobs, Pastor Robert Thompson began meeting with groups. This was not an employment agency, but it resulted in a number of them finding jobs. Practical discussions about resumes and interviews, as well as the strengthening of self-esteem, have contributed to the value of the program.—*Christian Herald*.

DEVOTIONAL GUIDE.   The Crescent Hill Baptist Church, Louisville, Kentucky, provided a day-by-day devotional guide, with Scripture readings, meditations, and prayers, for use by church members throughout the Advent season. Bible texts are assigned, but each writer develops them as he or she chooses.

THEOLOGICAL EXTENSION SCHOOL.   An associate minister on a church staff, who was working on a project for his Doctor of Ministry degree in seminary, opened a theological extension school. He offered courses of interest to pastors who had not completed their formal education and to lay people, for which an accredited denominational college gave college credit.

COMMUNITY THANKSGIVING.   In St. Joseph, Missouri, the churches come together for a community thanksgiving service on the Wednesday evening before Thanksgiving Day, rotating from church to church each year. The preacher is always from another church, not the host church. This has had the effect of actually binding the churches more closely together, as well as symbolizing their caring, says a participating pastor.

SECTION XIII. *A Little Treasury of Illustrations*

PERSISTENCE.   The story of Elizabeth Barrett Browning will be dear to all gentle souls as long as we read books and delight in them. Elizabeth Barrett Browning was, in our common phrase, "a martyr to ill health." But when was ever a martyr of finer spirit than hers? In early life, she was hurt by a fall from a horse. Her spine was injured. Her lungs were affected. She suffered from hemorrhage. Until she married, she was kept prisoner by an insane father, and until she died, she was an invalid. Her father positively gloated over invalidism and all its morbid surroundings. She breathed an atmosphere of night and death. But the fiery brain burned on—and its flames still leap from her ashes. She had her Greek authors bound to look like novels for fear her physician would forbid continuous study; and, propped up on her couch by cushions, she wrote with a pencil on slips of paper—all her white, feeble hands could hold—works that the world will never let die.—C. F. Aked.

THE GREATEST LESSON.   The greatest lesson of life has been learned when one has accepted the fact that, whatever his other activities, he can best aid the coming of the Kingdom of God by loyalty to the near duties which once seemed small, but which somehow loom large with advancing years—the maintenance of a fearless soul in the maze of common life, the steady cultivation of a living faith in a loving God who holds and controls the destiny of man, and the jealous safeguarding of inner peace, which is the just heritage of a quiet conscience.—Charles Henry Brent.

DISCIPLINE OF TROUBLE.   Sometimes earth-shaking experiences seem about to destroy us. A farmer said that a fruit tree could become rootbound and unproductive. However, he said, someone who knows what he is doing can place a charge of dynamite under the tree, explode it, loosen the soil, and make the tree grow and produce again. Trouble may do the same for a Christian.

RENEWAL.   A very wise woman of my acquaintance, not given to emotionalism in religion, suggests that "most of us need to be reconverted about once in three years." God's gifts come to us bit by bit, but they come afresh unendingly.—Henry P. Van Dusen.

SOMEONE TO TALK TO.   There was a three-year-old grandchild of a woman in my congregation. He was incarcerated with her all day, every day while the parents were in the fields and working at school. He invented an imaginary playmate. I don't blame him. His grandmother blamed him. And she said, "If you speak of Herman one more time, I'm going to bat you. Now come in here and let's have lunch." She was a good and pious woman. She bowed her head to pray, and when she got through, he asked, "Grandma, who are you talking to?"—William L. Hendricks.

THE POWER OF A DARE.   As a small boy, before the time of drainage ditches, I lived in the country surrounded by swamp lands. Those were days of chills and fever and malaria. When I came to the city to school, I was sallow-cheeked and hollow-chested. One of my teachers, George Warren Krall, was what we then called a health crank. One day he seemed to single me out personally. He said, "I dare you to be the healthiest boy in the class." I chased the poisons out of my system. I built the body that has equaled the strongest boys in that class, and has outlived and outlasted most of them.—Adapted from William H. Danforth (1870–1955), *I Dare You!*

HAPPINESS OR JOY? "Happiness," in the usual sense, is not what the Bible means when it talks about "joy" and "rejoicing." The sculptor Rodin has made this very clear in two small statues which he called "The Hand of the Devil" and "The Hand of God." One of these is of smoothly polished marble and shows a cupped hand cradling a human figure. Everything is peaceful, and the figure lies there limp, inert, untroubled. It is something of a shock to see that the sculptor has carved on *this* statue, "The Hand of the Devil." His meaning is clear, though, when we turn to his symbol for "The Hand of God." Here much of the stone is quarry-rough, but thrusting upward from its center is a powerful hand which seems to cleave the marble with its motion. In its grip, this hand also has a human figure, carrying it upward out of unconsciousness.—H. George Anderson.

MEANING OF DEATH. In everyday life, man is inclined to misunderstand the meaning of death. When the alarm goes off in the morning and frightens us from our dreams, we experience this awakening as if something terrible were breaking into the world of our dreams. And, still caught in our dreams, we often do not (at least not immediately) realize that the alarm wakes us up to our real existence, our existence in the real world. But do we mortals not act similarly when we approach death? Do we not equally forget that death awakens us to the true reality of our selves?

Even if a lovingly caressing hand is waking us up—its motion may be ever so gentle, but we do not realize its gentleness. Again, we only experience an intrusion upon the world of our dreams, an attempt to finish them off. Likewise, more often than not, death appears to be something dreadful, and we hardly suspect how well it is meant.—Viktor E. Frankl.

A WORD FROM FATHER. On the first day of January, 1797, Horatio Nelson, then a captain on a ship in the Mediterranean, wrote his father: "My dear Father, on this day I am certain you will send me a letter." It is a touching indication of the often-forgotten family affection which lies behind and helps to account for a brilliant career. Nelson, no boy but a man of thirty-nine, knew that his father would not forget him, and on New Year's Day would send him a message. Sons and daughters of a far more devoted and faithful Father can surely look up, as we stand at the outset of another stretch of life's untried way, and tell him: "On this day I am certain thou hast a word for me."—Henry Sloane Coffin.

FALSE PROPHETS. William Hull said that a church that hires a preacher to tell them what they want to hear may discover that they have bought Judas Iscariot.

COMMITMENT. An issue of *Leadership* carried an item by Fred Smith, who related this incident from a remembrance of Maxey Jarman, a close friend: One of Jarman's favorite stories was of Jeb Stuart, who signed his letters to General Robert E. Lee, "Yours to count on."—C. Neil Strait.

FAITH. One of Peter DeVries' characters stated as his "basic principle": "It takes a lot more faith to live this life without faith than with it."

MIND OVER ENVIRONMENT. Sam Levenson, author and humorist, said, "I was raised a virtually free American in East Harlem, a section of New York that was called a slum by sightseeing guides and a depressed area by sociologists. Both were right. . . . Yet, paradoxically, I never felt depressed or deprived. My environment was miserable; I was not."

OBSTACLES.   Actress Marie Dressler said to author Adela Rogers St. Johns: "Life is always knocking me to my knees, but after all that's the best position in which to pray."

OUR DEBTS.   Many years ago, a wealthy student at Williams College was accused of defacing college property and was sent to see President Mark Hopkins. He came in arrogantly, took out his purse, and asked how much were the damages. This was too much for President Hopkins, who commanded the young man to sit down. "No man," said the president, "can pay for what he receives here. Can you pay for the sacrifice of Colonel Williams who founded the college? Can you pay for the half-paid professors who have remained here to teach when they could have gone elsewhere? Every student here is a charity case."—Gerald Kennedy.

THE   HUMBLE   EXALTED.   Albert Schweitzer was a brilliant young man. He achieved distinction in theology and in music and went on to earn a doctorate in medicine. While he was a student, he served as assistant minister in a busy parish. He was a skilled interpreter of the organ music of Bach. He had attained fame even as a young man and could have had a successful career in any of several fields. He gave up public acclaim, however, and buried himself in French Equatorial Africa to bring medical care to people to whom he felt he owed an immense debt. Some observers thought, no doubt, that what he did was professional suicide. Yet the verdict of the years brought this humble man fame beyond anything that could have been his if he had clung to a weathly clientele in antiseptic examining rooms or to applauding crowds at organ concerts.—James W. Cox.

GOD'S   CHOICEST   HELPERS.   Kenneth Scott Latourette, a noted church historian, spoke to a small group of seminary students. He said that the real history of the church had never been written. It was the people whose names we do not know who have really carried forward the work of God—more so than anyone else. He said that we write the stories of popes, bishops, and noted preachers and theologians. But the deacon who arrived early on a wintry Sunday morning to build fires at the little country church, and the talented young woman who sang consoling songs at all the local funerals—these are the people who make church history.

INNER CHANGE.   When Ernest F. Tittle was minister of the First Methodist Church in Evanston, he took strong positions on social and political issues. He encountered opposition both outside and within his church. A businessman who had once been among those alarmed by his message said, after many years had gone by, "I remarked the other day, 'How Dr. Tittle has changed.' Then I caught myself and said, after thinking about it for a minute, 'No, *I* have changed!'"

WORSHIPING GOD.   A man can no more diminish God's glory by refusing to worship him than a lunatic can put out the sun by scribbling the word *darkness* on the walls of his cell. But God wills our good, and our good is to love him (with that responsive love proper to creatures). And to love him, we must know him: and if we know him, we shall in fact fall on our faces. —C. S. Lewis.

DEEP LIVING.   "Captain, I suppose you know every sandbank in the river," said a passenger on a Mississippi steamboat in the old days. "No, I don't," said the captain, who had learned a lot of wisdom from Old Man River. "It would be a waste of time," he added. "What! A waste of time?" exclaimed the passenger. "If you don't know where the sandbanks are, how can you pilot the boat?" "Yes, a waste of time," the captain repeated. "Why should I go kicking about among the sandbanks? I know where the deep waters are."—Joseph Fort Newton.

POWER OF COURAGE.   Samuel Shoemaker told the story of a college girl's remarkable influence. She sat down at a cafeteria table with five other girls, and began by saying grace silently with her head down. The others laughed. When she raised her head, she said to them in a nice but firm way, "What were you laughing at?" They said, "You know," and went on snickering. "Aren't you grateful?" she asked. "For what? We paid for the food," they said. "Where did you get the money?" she queried. "Family," they said. "Where did they get it?" she asked. "Worked for it," they said. "Where did they get the strength—where does it all come from?" she asked. That evening at supper, two more of them said grace. The next day all six of them said it with her. After that, she had the whole lot in a prayer group!—Adapted from Shoemaker in *Pulpit Digest*.

A MISSION FIELD.   Kay Jordan, who lives in Batavia, Illinois, told me a beautiful story about the final illness of her father. He was Dewey Lee Trotter, a country preacher in Alabama.

"Daddy died in 1963 in the Memorial Hospital in Anniston, Alabama," Kay said. "He was hospitalized about four weeks before he died, and I remember one of the maids, a black woman. She insisted on coming back to work on her day off, long enough to clean Daddy's room."

When Kay suggested that it wasn't necessary for her to do this, the maid explained, "Well, you see, it's this way: somebody else might get in a hurry and bump Reverend Trotter's bed, and I don't want that to happen."

By now, Kay's curiosity was really aroused, so she asked why this woman was so concerned about a patient she barely knew.

"Mrs. Jordan," the maid explained, "there was a time when I wanted to go overseas as a missionary. But I've only got a third-grade education, and I've been so disappointed that all I could do was work as a maid. Then one day your Daddy showed me that this hospital could be my mission field.

"You see, Mrs. Jordan, your Daddy gave me a purpose for living, so that's why I want to clean his room every day that he's still living. And I don't want anyone to bump his bed."—Robert J. Hastings.

PROVIDENCE.   Dr. Dennis Kinlaw tells of a nineteen-year-old who began reading the New Testament with no prior background, no one to instruct or encourage him. The second time through, he came to a relationship with Jesus Christ. He read about Christ's concern for the whole world. He bought an atlas and began praying over a page of that atlas each day. Gradually, one page seemed to draw his interest. It was the page on which Colombia and Venezuela were listed.

One day he liquidated his assets and purchased a one-way ticket to Caracas. As he tried to get through customs, he was asked a number of questions: "How long do you plan to stay?" "Who's sponsoring you?" When he answered "God," they wanted an address!

He was told he would have to return to America. As he was waiting for a flight back to the United States, he went into the airport coffee shop and took the only empty table. Soon a gentleman asked to join him, as all other tables were filled.

They began talking and the Latin American gentleman inquired of the young man's business in Venezuela. When he learned that the young man was interested in the Indians, he asked if he could help. The young man inquired who he was and found that he was the personal secretary to the president of Venezuela.

In a few hours, the young man had a signature that would allow him to stay in Venezuela.

The young man worked among the Indians and took the gospel to many of them. And, at the same time, he did his college work at the University of Caracus.

When asked why he went, this was his reply: "I had found an intimacy with Jesus that I was afraid I'd lose if I didn't stick my neck out!"—C. Neil Strait.

GOD'S ELECTING LOVE.   As this freely electing love, the love of God for us is unconditional, strong, and victorious. It is a burning fire which cannot be quenched. It is wholly trustworthy. It is a rock to which we can cling without fear of its crumbling. It is a refuge to which we can flee without doubting whether it will stand. It is nourishment which is always prepared for those who hunger and thirst for love, and is never withheld from them. We have only to see that we are not worthy of it, that we have forfeited it, that we cannot secure it of and for ourselves, that we can only receive and accept it. We can only long and trust that God is the freely electing God for us, and that we ourselves are freely elected by him.—Karl Barth.

FORGIVENESS.   In an Indian tribe in Mexico, the sentence, "I forgive you" is translated, "My face heals toward you!"—C. Neil Strait.

GOD AND OUR PRAYERS.   In *The Power of Prayer Today*, George Buttrick tells of the picture drawn by one of his granddaughters of their lake cottage: "a strange crisscross of lines smudged with many a small fingerprint." Noting that it was not possible to recognize the cottage from the picture, Dr. Buttrick reminds us that he did not need the picture, but he did wish it. Our prayers to God are like that: God does not need our prayers, smudged and stained though they are, but God does want them.—Robert U. Ferguson.

IMPORTANCE OF SHARING.   When a humble Chinese woman's grandson became ill, she took him to Canton to be treated in a missionary hospital. While there, she heard the gospel and believed and prayed for her grandson's healing.

After that prayer was answered, she returned to her village. Sometime later, a friend's grandson was dying and this woman shared Christ with her and prayed for the sick child. This baby's health was also restored and the family became Christians—one son even became a Baptist minister. The baby who was healed grew up to be a medical doctor and served in a Baptist hospital. This boy's son grew up to be a president of the Baptist World Alliance. He was David Y. K. Wong.—*The Baptist Program*.

FREE GIFTS.   Wanting to do something nice for people, our youth decided to hold a free car wash.

They contacted a service station in a convenient location, but the baffled owner gave several reasons why he couldn't oblige. So, they decided that the church grounds would be an ideal place for the free wash.

The tacked up "Free Car Wash" signs, stationed themselves in front of the church to motion cars in, and waited. Some people, curious about the sign, drove by the church slowly, staring, shaking their heads, and driving on.

Some smiled, waved to the youth, and kept going. Some stopped and asked the youth, "What's the catch?" Some had no time.

Thirteen drivers came in, some skeptical, some confident, but all accepting the free gift.

I was astounded at the similarities of the youths' experience with that of the Good News of God's free gift of salvation through faith in Jesus Christ our Lord.—Lin Hartung, in *The Lutheran Witness*.

ONE PERSON'S POWER.   When I was an undergraduate in college, William Newton Clarke was a professor in the graduate department in the university. I was having a perplexing time with my religion then. I had thrown almost all of it overboard. During my sophomore year, wild horses could hardly have dragged me inside a church. I started out for my junior year telling my family that I was going to clear God out of the universe and begin all over to see what I could find. But there, walking across the campus, was William Newton Clarke. He knew more about modern thinking than I began to know; yet there he was, a Christian, an intelligent, forward-looking, intellectually honest Christian. His very presence seemed to say, "Essential Christianity is not irreconcilable with modern knowledge. He who is afraid to face facts does not really believe in God. Come, the truth shall make you free." I have had a grand time in the ministry these forty years and more, but I am sure it was not geography or climate, economic determinism or technological industry that put me there. It was a person —William Newton Clarke—who opened the door.—Harry Emerson Fosdick.

TREASURES OF THE PAST.   Imagine a woman who has lost her husband after only one year of marriage. She is desperate and sees no meaning in her future life. It would mean much to such a person if she now could realize that her one year of marital bliss can never be taken from her. She has rescued it, as it were, into her past. From there, nothing and nobody can ever remove this treasure. Even if she should remain childless, her life can never become meaningless once her peak experiences of love have been stored in the storehouse of the past.—Viktor E. Frankl.

ROAD TO GOD. My argument against God was that the universe seemed so cruel and unjust. But how had I got this idea of *just* and *unjust*? In the very act of trying to prove that God didn't exist—in other words, that the whole of reality was senseless—I found I was forced to assume that one part of reality—namely, my idea of justice—was full of sense. Consequently, atheism turns out to be too simple. If the whole universe has no meaning, we should never have found out that it has no meaning; just as if there were no light in the universe and therefore no creatures with eyes, we should never know it was dark.—C. S. Lewis.

CONFORMING TO THE WORLD. A young lady once seriously assured Thomas Carlyle that she accepted the universe, and the sage of Chelsea caustically assured her: "Egad, ma'am, you'd better." And in one sense, we all have to conform to this world—its physical laws, its primal ordinances. It is indeed good to conform to the world in that sense.—W. D. Davies.

REPRESSED ANGER. A man who cannot express his hostility toward the man for whom he works, because he might lose his job, may be motivated to express his hostility toward his automobile when it won't start. Or he may take out his feeling upon his son who makes a lot of noise, or upon his daughter, or upon his wife. They are close, they are available, they are vulnerable. When these escape, the individual takes it out on himself. Hostility may take the form of migraine headaches, or a lame foot, or a weak eye.—Howard Thurman.

MODERN SAINTS. Reinhold Niebuhr once wrote of his Detroit congregation: "The people are a little discouraged. Some of them seem to doubt whether the church will survive. But there are a few who are the salt of the earth, and if I make a go of this, they will be more responsible than they will ever know." And again, of a faithful elderly woman within that congregation: "She thanks me for praying with her and imagines that I am doing her a favor to come to see her. But I really come for selfish reasons—because I leave that home with a more radiant faith of my own. My confidence in both man and God is strengthened."—Elizabeth Achtemeier.

A THIEF IN RETURN. It took nerve for the thief to return. He still could have been prosecuted for his crime committed three years earlier. But he couldn't help coming back.

"I just had to come and apologize to you and ask your forgiveness and tell you of Jesus Christ who is my Savior," the thief told the Brazilian family he had robbed. "Christ has changed my life."

Then he shared the message of Jesus Christ with this family in Niteroi, and one by one, the entire family came to know Jesus Christ. They saw the difference Christ had made in a thief and wanted to know him personally.—*The Baptist Program*.

FAITH AND HEALING. When I asked Dr. Schweitzer how he accounted for the fact that anyone could possibly expect to become well after having been treated by a witch doctor, he said that I was asking him to divulge a secret that doctors have carried around inside them ever since Hippocrates. "But I'll tell you anyway," he said, his face still illuminated by that half-smile. "The witch doctor succeeds for the same reason all the rest of us succeed. Each patient carries his own doctor inside him. They come to us not knowing that truth. We are at our best when we give the doctor who resides within each patient a chance to go to work." The placebo is the doctor who resides within.—Norman Cousins, *The Anatomy of an Illness*.

FEAR. Howard Thurman writes of a particularly rough time in his life—months after his wife's death: "I was aware that God was not yet done with me, that I need never fear the darkness, nor delude myself that the contradictions of life are final."—C. Neil Strait.

RESOLUTIONS.   Jesus did not spend his life in trying not to do wrong. He was too full of the earnest love and longing to do right—to do his Father's will. And so we see, by contrast, how many of our attempts at purity fail by their negativeness. . . . I do think that we break almost all our resolutions not to do wrong, while we keep a large proportion of our resolutions that we will do what is right. Habit, which is the power by which evil rules us, is only strong in a vacant life. It is the empty, swept, and garnished house to which the devils come back to hold still higher revel.—Phillips Brooks.

ATHEISM.   We know the type of student (or maybe a teacher) who declares in and out of season, in a very self-satisfied way, that he is an "atheist." The sureness with which he speaks, and the reasons he gives, do not persuade us of the atheistic position nearly so well as they persuade us that he has reached only a certain garrulous level of immaturity.—Gordon W. Allport.

HOW TO.   A young woman, who is a member of the church I serve, once told me that she missed something in my week-by-week preaching. I had asked for her comments, and so I welcomed her willingness to speak without qualms or hesitation. "You preachers are forever telling us what to do," she said, "but you seldom tell us how to do the things you preach about. *Please tell me how*."—Theodore F. Adams.

DECIDING AHEAD.   Take a case: here are a boy and girl, feeling affectionate because they have been holding hands, eating pizza, and listening to the Beatles! She's wearing *Chanel No. 5*, which he gave her; and he's wearing *Hai Karate*, which she gave him (only she's clever—she removed the instruction book on self-defense before she gave him the cologne!). Now shall we say to them in this condition of amorous intoxication brought on by pizza, holding hands, the Beatles, *Chanel No.*

5, *Hai Karate*, and now the moon, that they should decide right then and there what love would have them to do? Of course not! They need principles which will guide them to make decisions about their behavior on a date before the evening begins. The Christian Good News is that this help is available in the Scriptures and in the wisdom of the church community (Exod. 20:14; Matt. 5:27; Mark 10:6 9).—Harry N. Hollis, Jr.

WHAT IS SEX?   A tough word to define, that's what it is! No dictionary is really big enough to define sex, because sex is as large as life itself. Sex is more than having an hourglass figure or a Tarzan physique. Sex is more than tingling with cold chills of excitement while holding hands in a movie. Sex is more than the physical act of intercourse. Sex (or a better word is *sexuality*) is not just our genital organs, but is a part of our total personality which affects all our relationships from the time we are born. Sex is our maleness or femaleness, which is a part of our whole being.—Harry N. Hollis, Jr.

PERSONAL TESTIMONY.   Some religiously enthusiastic people spend much time saying, "Come and see what the Lord has done for my soul," and although there is nothing unnatural or hypocritical about this, they frequently fail to allow for comments from their hearers, usually unexpressed, which would surprise and sadden them. Don't insist on taking people to heaven in your own personal Cadillac.—Erik Routley.

THEFT OF TIME.   The minister who embezzles money to support poor members of his congregation is at once dismissed and sent to prison; but the minister who embezzles time which belongs to his family in order to concern himself with the care of his congregation seems to the rest of us exceptionally pious and estimable.—Theodore Bovet.

OPTIMISM VERSUS RESIGNATION.   In his *Anatomy of an Illness*, publisher Norman Cousins relates that because of a wrong diagnosis, he was sent to a tuberculosis sanitarium at the age of ten. During his six months there, he learned that the patients divided themselves into two groups: "those who were confident they would beat back the disease and be able to resume normal lives, and those who resigned themselves to a prolonged and even fatal illness." He joined the optimistic group, who involved themselves in creative activities, and had little to do with those who had resigned themselves to the worst. He said, "I couldn't help being impressed with the fact that the boys in my group had a far higher percentage of 'discharged as cured' outcomes than the kids in the other group."

GOD AND NATURAL LAW.   Insofar as we are loyal to Christ, we are convinced that, with God, all things are possible (Mark 10:27). Natural law, far from being sovereign, is subservient to God's purpose. A strict naturalism, which denies the objective power of prayer to produce events, is simply a repudiation of the gospel of Christ. The Christian operates in a world of greater magnitude than does the dogmatist who claims, in his arrogance, that there are things that God cannot do. Natural laws, we believe, are God's vehicles rather than his controllers.—Elton Trueblood.

NEEDY STRANGERS.   A startling story in the newspapers may help open our eyes. A Puerto Rican woman in New York City had just learned that her husband had been arrested. She didn't know where or when or why. So she ran to the nearest pay phone in the corner tavern to see if she could find out more about it. She was frightened, of course. And the pay phone did not work. Frustrated and excited, she tried to explain her problem to others in the tavern. They could not understand her Spanish nor she their English. In her fear and growing frustration, she became frantic and so they called the police. The police only served to make her more frightened and frantic. She wept and screamed. So they took her to the mental ward in a general hospital. There her behavior became even more frantic and bizarre. Finally, after a couple of days, a social worker who could speak Spanish visited her and the story came out—along with the fact that she left two tiny children in her apartment. When they rushed to the apartment, they found the two babies had starved to death while she had been in the hospital.—Edmund Steimle.

CHRISTIAN LIVING.   A note from a Christian mother to her son shared the death of her husband: "Dad died in his sleep last night—ready!"—C. Neil Strait.

INDEX OF CONTRIBUTORS

SERMON TITLE INDEX

(Children's stories and sermons are identified cs; sermon suggestions, ss)

313

SCRIPTURAL INDEX

INDEX OF PRAYERS

INDEX OF MATERIALS USEFUL AS CHILDREN'S STORIES AND SERMONS NOT INCLUDED IN SECTION X

INDEX OF MATERIALS USEFUL FOR SMALL GROUPS

INDEX OF SPECIAL DAYS AND SEASONS

TOPICAL INDEX

ACKNOWLEDGMENTS

Acknowledgment and gratitude are hereby expressed to the following, for kind permission to reprint copyrighted material from the books and periodicals listed below:

ABINGDON PRESS: An excerpt from *There Are Sermons in Stories* by William L. Stidger. Copyright renewal © by John W. Highland, William S. Hyland, and Heather Hyland Mote; digest of a sermon, "Love Your Enemies," from *The Hard Commands of Jesus,* by Roy Pearson. Copyright © 1957 by Abingdon Press; extracts from a devotional from *Everyday Religion* by J. F. Newton. Copyright renewal © 1977 by Josephine Newton Morris; excerpts from *The Temple in the Heart* and *Making Friends with Life,* by James Reid.

BAKER BOOK HOUSE: Excerpts from a sermon by Carl E. Bates in *Effective Evangelistic Preaching,* ed. by Vernon L. Stanfield. Copyright © 1965 by Baker Book House; a children's sermon, "God's Flashlight," from *40 Object Sermons for Children,* by Joe E. Trull. Copyright © 1975 by Baker Book House.

CHOSEN BOOKS: Excerpt from *Super Natural Living;* copyright © 1982 by Betty Malz. Published by Chosen Books, Lincoln, VA 22078.

THE CHRISTIAN CENTURY FOUNDATION: Digest of sermon, "Triumph and Tears," by James T. Cleland. Copyright © 1968, Christian Century Foundation. Reprinted by permission from the April 1968 issue of *The Pulpit,* now *The Christian Ministry;* excerpt from "Children's Sermons" Symposium, by Barry Bence. Copyright © 1982 Christian Century Foundation. Reprinted by permission from the January 1982 issue of *The Christian Ministry;* excerpt from Lenten Meditation, "The Freedom of Necessity," by Ronald Goetz, © 1982 Christian Century Foundation. Reprinted by permission from the March 3, 1982, issue of *The Christian Century;* excerpt from article, "Notes on Sacred Space," by E. A. Sövik, © 1982 Christian Century Foundation. Reprinted by permission from the March 31, 1982, issue of *The Christian Century;* excerpt from Lenten Meditation, "The Cup of Death," by William H. Willimon, © 1982 Christian Century Foundation. Reprinted by permission from the March 31, 1982, issue of *The Christian Century;* excerpt from article, "The Limits of Kindness," by William H. Willimon, © 1982 Christian Century Foundation. Reprinted by permission from the April 14, 1982, issue of *The Christian Century;* excerpt from "M.E.M.O.: A Hero's Patience," by Martin E. Marty, © 1982 Christian Century Foundation. Reprinted by permission from the April 14, 1982, issue of *The Christian Century.*

CHRISTIAN LIFE COMMISSION of the Southern Baptist Convention: Excerpts from pamphlets on sex and sex education by Harry Hollis.

CHURCH ADMINISTRATION, a publication of the Baptist Sunday School Board: Excerpts from an article by J. W. Fortner, "Promotion of Year-End Giving," June 1982.

THE CHURCH OF SCOTLAND: Two prayers from *The Book of Common Order* of the Church of Scotland, by permission of the Committee on Public Worship and Aids to Devotion.

CONSULTATION ON CHURCH UNION: The Lectionary for the Christian Year, from *A Lectionary,* copyright © 1974.

J. M. DENT & SONS LTD.: Digest of chapter, "The Light of Life," from *Parables from Nature,* by Margaret Scott Gatty ("Mrs. Gatty"), London: J. M. Dent & Sons, Ltd.; New York: E. P. Dutton & Co. 1907. Everyman's Library Series; three extracts from *The Temple,* by W. E. Orchard.

DODD, MEAD AND COMPANY, INC.: Several prayers in *A Book of Prayers,* by Samuel McComb.

EDUCATIONAL MINISTRIES, ABC: A communion meditation from Robert E. Keighton, *The Minister's Communion Service Book*, published by Judson Press, 1940. Used by permission of Judson Press.

WM. B. EERDMANS PUBLISHING CO.: Digest of a sermon from Karl Barth, *Come Holy Spirit.*

EXPOSITORY TIMES: Excerpts from sermons by R. Leonard Small, J. E. Fison, Owen E. Evans, Norman C. Parsons, and Cecil Northcott; excerpts from "Charlie the Chemist," by Rita F. Snowden, "Salary" and "Prayers God Doesn't Answer," by John R. Gray, "Revolution," by J. Ithel Jones, and "The Right Kind of Operation," by James Wright.

FLEMING H. REVELL COMPANY: Several excerpts from *Prayers of Frank W. Gunsaulus.*

FORTRESS PRESS: Excerpts by Gene Bartlett and Walter J. Burghardt from *Preaching About Death*, edited by Alton M. Motter; excerpt by H. George Anderson from *Renewal in the Pulpit*, edited by Edmund A. Steimle.

FOUNDATIONS: Digest of a sermon, "Christ Will Come Again," by Markus Barth. Published by the American Baptist Historical Society in *Foundations*, January 1963.

GENERAL MOTORS CORPORATION: Excerpt from Paul Garber printed in *The Changing Challenge.*

GUIDEPOSTS ASSOCIATES, INC.: Two stories and three excerpts from *Guideposts.* "The Red Badge of Mercy," by Dina Donohue, reprinted by permission from *Guideposts Magazine.* Copyright © 1959 by Guideposts Associates, Inc, Carmel, New York 10512. All rights reserved. "The Doll Lady," by Dina Donohue, reprinted by permission from *Guideposts Magazine.* Copyright © 1957 by Guideposts Associates, Inc., Carmel, New York 10512. All rights reserved. "The Courage to Be Different," by Arthur Gordon, reprinted by permission from *Guideposts Magazine.* Copyright © 1957 by Guideposts Associates, Inc., Carmel, New York 10512. All rights reserved. "The Cigar and the Circus," by Norman Vincent Peale, reprinted by permission from *Guideposts Magazine.* Copyright © 1958 by Guideposts Associates, Inc., Carmel, New York 10512. All rights reserved. "On Flag Day," by Elizabeth Sherrill, reprinted by permission from *Guideposts Magazine.* Copyright © 1958 by Guideposts Associates, Inc., Carmel, New York 10512. All rights reserved.

HARCOURT BRACE JOVANOVICH, INC.: Excerpts from *Best Sermons* 1925, 1926 and 1927, edited by Joseph Fort Newton.

HARPER & ROW, PUBLISHERS, INC.: Excerpts from *The Gift of God* by W. A. Cameron. Copyright 1925 by Harper & Row, Publishers, Inc; *Robertson's Sermons* by Frederick W. Robertson; *These Twelve*, by Charles R. Brown, copyright 1926 by Charles R. Brown; *The Hope of the World*, by Harry Emerson Fosdick, copyright 1933 by Harper & Row, Publishers, Inc., renewed 1961 by Harry Emerson Fosdick; *A Book of Public Prayers*, by Harry Emerson Fosdick, copyright © 1959 by Harry Emerson Fosdick; *Deliverance to the Captives*, by Karl Barth, copyright © 1961 by SCM Press; *Fresh Every Morning*, by Gerald Kennedy, copyright © 1966 by Gerald Kennedy; *Profiles in Courage*, by John F. Kennedy, copyright © 1955, 1956, 1961 by John F. Kennedy; *Prayers for Daily Use*, by Samuel H. Miller, copyright © 1957 by Samuel H. Miller.

HOME MISSION BOARD of the Southern Baptist Convention: A children's sermon, "Angel of the Grass," by Robert W. Bailey.

THE LOUISVILLE TIMES: Material from an article appearing April 19, 1982, by Clarence Matthews, "Church Relives Bible Story with Fish and Bread." © 1982 by *The Louisville Times.*

LUTTERWORTH PRESS: Digest of a sermon, "The Living Lord," by Emil Brunner.

THE NEW YORK TIMES: Copyrighted material from an article appearing November 25, 1982, by Glenn Fowler, "At Lambs Mission, Musical Dinner for the Poor." © 1982 by The New York Times Company.

PILGRIM PRESS: Walter Rauschenbusch, *Prayers of the Social Awakening.* Boston: The Pilgrim Press, 1909.

PULPIT PUBLISHING COMPANY: For excerpts from *Pulpit Digest, Pulpit Preaching*, and *The New Pulpit Digest.*

RANDOM HOUSE, INC.; ALFRED A. KNOPF, INC.: Permission to paraphrase a portion of "The Boy Who Talked with Animals" from *The Wonderful Story of Henry Sugar and Six More*.

SAINT ANDREW PRESS: Digest of "To Whom Shall We Go?" from *To Whom Shall We Go?* by Donald M. Baillie, published by The Saint Andrew Press in 1955.

SCM PRESS LTD: A prayer by Karl Barth, *Call for God*, SCM Press 1967.

CHARLES SCRIBNER'S SONS: A Christmas Prayer by Henry Sloane Coffin, from *Joy in Believing*. Copyright © 1956 Dorothy Prentice Coffin.

SEABURY PRESS: A prayer from *Prayers* by Theodore Parker Ferris. Copyright © 1981 by The Seabury Press; digest of a sermon from *The New Life* by Theodore Parker Ferris. © 1961 by The Seabury Press. Used by permission of The Vestry of Trinity Church, Copley Square, Boston, Massachusetts.

SOUTHERN BAPTIST CONVENTION EXECUTIVE COMMITTEE: Excerpts from *The Baptist Program*, copyright 1982.

SOUTHERN BAPTIST THEOLOGICAL SEMINARY LIBRARY: Excerpts from a sermon by Jesse B. Weatherspoon in the seminary archives.

SUNDAY SCHOOL BOARD of the Southern Baptist Convention: Excerpts from a Sunday School Lesson from *Sunday School Adults*, Jan.–March 1961. Copyright © 1960 The Sunday School Board of the Southern Baptist Convention. All rights reserved; excerpt from the devotional, "The Hand of God," by Charles Treadway; and from *Open Windows*, July–Sept. 1963. Copyright © 1963 The Sunday School Board of the Southern Baptist Convention. All rights reserved.

THE UPPER ROOM: Excerpts by Paul L. A. Granadosin, "Helpful Strangers"; William Nicholl, "God's Goodness"; Olive I. Clark, "Honeysuckle"; Grady Roe, "The Best Part of Church"; Astrid Sirles, "Look for the Blessing." Reprinted from *The Upper Room*, copyright © 1982 by The Upper Room, 1908 Grand Avenue, P.O. Box 189, Nashville, TN 37202; excerpts from *Pockets*, two from the October 1982 issue and one from the September 1982 issue. Copyright © 1982 by The Upper Room, 1908 Grand Ave., P.O. Box 189, Nashville, TN 37202.

WESTMINSTER PRESS: An excerpt digested from "The Living Lord," from *I Believe in the Living Lord: Sermons on the Apostles' Creed*, by Emil Brunner, translated and edited by John Holden. Copyright © MCMLXI W. L. Jenkins; an excerpt digested from "The Science of True Prayer," from *The Practice and Power of Prayer*, by John Sutherland Bonnell. Copyright © MCMLIV, by W. L. Jenkins. Digested and used by permission of The Westminster Press, Philadelphia, PA; an excerpt from *The Preaching of the Gospel*, by Karl Barth, translated by B. E. Hooke. English Translation © S.C.M. Press Ltd. 1963. Published in the U.S. by The Westminster Press, Philadelphia, PA.

YOUTH MAGAZINE and the Reverend Leslie Merlin: An excerpt from the January 1982 issue of *Youth Magazine*, United Church Press.

Special appreciation is due the following authors or their representatives for permission to include portions of their work: ERNEST T. CAMPBELL for permission to quote his prayer; ALICE MEAD CLELAND for excerpts from sermons by her late husband, James T. Cleland; MRS. CHALMERS COE for excerpts from sermons preached by her father, Paul E. Scherer, on Sunday Vespers; BISHOP NORBERT GAUGHAN for an idea on which a children's sermon, "The Importance of Numbers," was based. His article appeared in *Catholic Digest*, May 1982, and this idea as developed is used with Bishop Gaughan's permission; JAMES REID for a sermon, "God and the Individual," from *Making Friends with Life*, published by Cokesbury Press; and for "God's Tools or His Partners?" from *The Temple in the Heart*, also published by Cokesbury Press; DONALD SAMICK, P.O. Box 291, Philmont, N. Y. 12565, for material from an article on Energy Conservation, published in *Your Church*, March/April 1982; AHLEIDA SEEVER for excerpts from a sermon by her late husband, Harold W. Seever; JOHN M. TITTLE for two prayers by his father, Ernest Fremont Tittle; MRS. STIRLING TOMKINS, JR. for excerpts from sermons preached on National Radio Pulpit by her father, Ralph W. Sockman.